SEVENTH EDITION

The Policy-Based Profession

An Introduction to Social Welfare Policy Analysis for Social Workers

SEVENTH EDITION

The Policy-Based Profession

An Introduction to Social Welfare Policy Analysis for Social Workers

Philip R. Popple
University of Texas at Arlington

Leslie Leighninger
Arizona State University

with

Robert D. Leighninger
University of California, Berkeley

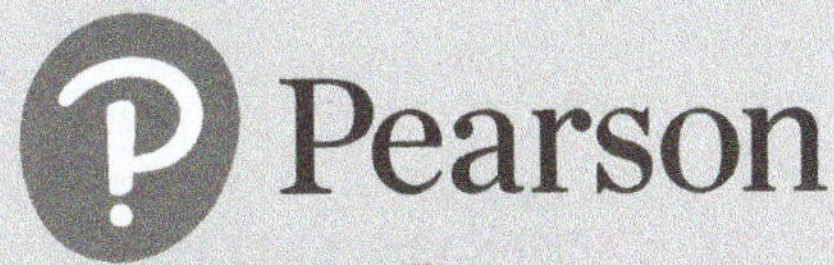

330 Hudson Street, NY, NY 10013

Director and Publisher: Kevin M. Davis
Portfolio Manager: Rebecca Fox-Gieg
Content Producer: Pamela D. Bennett
Portfolio Management Assistant: Casey Coriell
Executive Field Marketing Manager: Krista Clark
Executive Product Marketing Manager: Christopher Barry
Media Project Manager: Lauren Carlson
Procurement Specialist: Deidra Smith
Cover Designer: Melissa Welch, Studio Montage
Cover Photo: Ohad Ben-Yoseph/Moment Open/Getty Images
Full-Service Project Management: Thistle Hill Publishing Services
Composition: Cenveo® Publisher Services
Printer/Binder: LSC Communications
Cover Printer: LSC Communications
Text Font: Dante MT Pro Regular, 10.5/13

Library of Congress Cataloging-in-Publication Data
Names: Popple, Philip R., author. | Leighninger, Leslie, author. | Leighninger, Robert D., author.
Title: The policy-based profession : an introduction to social welfare policy analysis for social workers / Philip R. Popple, University of Texas at Arlington, Leslie Leighninger, Arizona State University with Robert D. Leighninger, University of California, Berkeley.
Description: Seventh Edition. | New York, NY : Pearson, [2019] | Revised edition of The policy-based profession, [2015] | Includes bibliographical references and index.
Identifiers: LCCN 2017055895 | ISBN 9780134794297 (pbk.) | ISBN 013479429X (pbk.)
Subjects: LCSH: Social workers—United States. | Public welfare—United States. | Social service—United States. | United States—Social policy.
Classification: LCC HV91 .P677 2019 | DDC 361.3/2—dc23
LC record available at https://lccn.loc.gov/2017055895

ISBN 10: 0-13-479429-X
ISBN 13: 978-0-13-479429-7

Preface

For the seventh edition of *The Policy-Based Profession: An Introduction to Social Welfare Policy Analysis for Social Workers,* Dr. Robert Leighninger, editor of the *Journal of Sociology and Social Welfare,* has been added as a named author. Bob has, in fact, been a shadow author since the very first edition of this book, but as his contribution has slowly grown, it has become obvious that he deserves formal recognition. Thanks to Bob for everything he has contributed to this book.

This book is written for students at both the baccalaureate and master's level of social work education. It is organized into four sections. The first outlines a policy-based model of the social work profession that explicitly recognizes the social welfare policy system as a major factor in social work practice, and in fact as a defining criterion of the social work profession. The second section presents a model of policy analysis that divides the task into three major facets of the policy context: historical, economic, and social. The third section of the book applies the policy analysis framework to representative policies and policy issues in the fields of public welfare, aging, mental health, substance abuse, health, child welfare, and immigration. The final section, "Taking Action" expands the book's treatment of the increasingly important area of politics and social welfare policy, and the social work profession's continually increasing emphasis on policy practice as an area of interest.

The previous edition of this book included, for the first time, a chapter on health policy. This was done, of course, in recognition of the Affordable Care Act (Obamacare) as an important addition to our country's safety net. Because we now have Donald Trump as president and the Republicans control both houses of Congress, the ACA is under serious attack, although all indications are that the act will prove much more resilient that its attackers ever imagined. Because health care is one of the major social welfare policy areas currently in play, we have made significant revisions, updates, and expansions to the health policy chapter.

For the seventh edition we have added, also for the first time, a chapter on immigration policy. We have done this for two major reasons. One is that immigration is now front and center as a major social justice issue with the current president's attempts to restrict immigration by proposing to build a wall on the border with Mexico and by placing what amounts to a ban on immigrants from majority Muslim countries. The second reason, of course, is that many social work clients are immigrants, and many of them are undocumented, so immigration policy is critical to their well-being; the social workers who assist them must be familiar with this policy area. On a more personal note, all of the authors either currently or recently have been affiliated with universities that are Hispanic-serving institutions. We have watched the struggle of students brought to this country as small children, who have done everything right, who are now earning professional degrees and facing the huge barrier to beginning their careers of being (through no fault of their own) undocumented. We were heartened by President Obama's executive order establishing the Deferred Action for Childhood Arrivals

(DACA) program and are hopeful that Congress will turn it into black letter law. By the time this book is published, the DACA issue will likely have been resolved. Parts of the immigration chapter will undoubtedly remain permanently relevant. This chapter explains that our country has periodically gone through periods of intense anxiety about immigration and has often responded in ways that are not constructive, but it has always emerged from the crisis ever more diverse and ever stronger. We are confident that this will happen once again.

Every chapter in this new edition has been updated to cover the most recent research, theories, and political developments related to each field of practice presented. Significant new material includes the problem of drug dependence among military veterans, the opioid epidemic, and the problem (and often tragic results) of social media bullying. In each area covered, we have purposefully avoided presenting a comprehensive (and soon outdated) overview of all current policies. Rather, our intent has been to choose a current example of a major social welfare issue within each policy area. Using these examples, we have sought to acquaint students with a process and skills for understanding policies that they can continue to apply in their professional practice. We hope that by teaching students to use a policy analysis technique, which we have termed *practitioner policy analysis,* we will equip them with a skill that will be useful throughout their careers and from which they can develop additional policy practice skills.

New to This Edition

The seventh edition of *The Policy-Based Profession: An Introduction to Social Welfare Policy Analysis for Social Workers* has been thoroughly updated to reflect current issues that affect social work policy:

- Content regarding the relevance of historical analysis in social welfare policy analysis has been strengthened (chapter 4).
- In keeping with the increasing emphasis in social work education on teaching policy practice skills, the relationship of policy analysis to practice with individuals, families, and small groups has been strengthened throughout.
- The health chapter (chapter 9), while acknowledging that it cannot keep up with the ongoing struggle to repeal and replace the Affordable Care Act, does discuss some of the favorite policies of those who favor repeal, specifically individual health savings accounts and separate high-risk insurance pools. There is also an example of a little discussed health care reform approach—concierge medicine.
- This edition includes a new chapter on immigration (chapter 11). The chapter discusses the epic drama of our glorious and not-so-glorious history of wave after wave of new arrivals and how each welcomed (or didn't) the next wave. Readers are challenged to decide whether current immigration stimulates or weakens our economy, whether it threatens the jobs of high-tech engineers and construction workers or creates new jobs in both areas, whether keeping the right people out of the country is worse than letting the wrong people in, whether immigrants commit more or fewer crimes than native-born citizens, whether refugees are carefully vetted before being allowed into the country or they just walk in, and other perplexing and debatable issues.
- Additional attention is directed to program evaluation as a policy analysis technique (chapters 10 and 13).

- Additional case vignettes illustrating the importance of understanding social welfare policy for direct practice social workers have been added throughout.
- Chapter 8 combines and updates the material formerly presented in the separate mental health and substance abuse chapters. The new chapter includes material on the opioid epidemic, problems faced by returning veterans, and recent responses to suicides caused by cyberbullying.
- The seventh edition includes updates on research and theory references, as well as references to the most current material (all chapters).

Pearson Enhanced eText

The seventh edition of *The Policy-Based Profession: An Introduction to Social Welfare Policy Analysis for Social Workers* includes the following Enhanced eText features:

Check Your Understanding: Embedded assessment questions appear as a link at the end of each major chapter section in the Pearson eText. Using multiple-choice questions, the self-checks allow readers to assess how well they have mastered the content.

Chapter Review: At the end of each chapter, short-answer questions encourage readers to reflect on chapter concepts. We have provided feedback to support the development of thoughtful responses.

Acknowledgments

We are grateful to the following people for assistance in researching and writing this text: Laura Dase, Barry Daste, Joseph Delatte, Wendy Franklin, Kenneth Miller, Matt Leighninger, Judith Kolb Morris, Shannon Robshaw, Todd Akins, J. Dennis Tyler, Catherine Lemieus, Anita Evans, Tanya Blom, Kim Chapman, Natisha Nason, David Austin, Ronald B. Dear, Nelson Reid, Paul H. Stuart, James L. Wolk, Nancy Kropf, Marie-Antoinette Sossou, and Carole Cox. We are also grateful to the members of the first Ph.D. class of the School of Social Work at Louisiana State University, and to the students in the spring 2013 sections of Social Work 3303 (BSW), Social Welfare Policy and Services, and the spring 2017 sections of Social Work 5303 (MSW) Foundations of Social Welfare in the School of Social Work at the University of Texas at Arlington.

Many thanks to the reviewers of this new edition: Sheri Boyle, California University of Pennsylvania; Reneé Daniel, Daemen College; Patience Togo Malm, St. Cloud State University; and Daniel B. Rosen, Metropolitan College of New York.

Brief Contents

Contents

Part One

Social Welfare Policy and the Social Work Profession

For me the realization of the importance of policy to social work practice came in a blinding flash, or an epiphany, as my theologically inclined friends would say. As a social work master's student, I had had little interest in policy, preferring to spend my time learning psychopathology, therapeutic techniques, group process, and all of the other sexy stuff taught in a typical social work graduate program. When I graduated, I became a training specialist for a large state department of social services; my primary assignment was to train the child welfare staff. In my new position, I developed and provided training programs on behavior modification techniques, risk assessment, and transactional analysis. I even included a session on an early version of the *Diagnostic and Statistical Manual*. The only time I ever thought about policy was during the session for new employees in which I would discuss office hours, dress code, sick leave, vacation, and retirement.

I'm not sure whether it was because state office staff thought I was especially good or because they thought I was especially obnoxious, but I became the person of choice to supply mandated training in regions lacking training specialists. So I was sent to the largest office in the state—which had a staff so hostile that they had run out three training specialists in less than a year—to provide a series of three-day training sessions on how to fill out a new form.

This was a guaranteed loser for me. The staff hated state office; hated training; and, most of all, hated forms. I asked the director of training why she didn't just issue the staff guns and then dress me in a shirt with a target on it. The director told me not to worry; this was going to be great. This was not merely a simple bureaucratic form we were asking the staff to use but really a system to train them in principles and techniques of task-oriented social services (which the state office had begun to call TOSS). The staff would fill out a simple form for each of their cases, a form that would require them to select and prioritize from a standard list of codes, one or more goals for each case and then to list objectives required to reach each goal. The form would be updated each month with progress monitored by a computerized information system. The director showed me all the professionally developed curriculum material I would be supplied with to teach the staff this new problem-solving approach to social work practice.

When I began my first training session, it was as big a nightmare as I had imagined. The staff argued every step of the way. They said that task-oriented social services and the problem-solving method were fine, but they were already using this approach without the use of any long and complicated form. They argued that the reporting system would just get in the way of their work. They presented case after case that none of the preselected goals would fit. One guy, wearing the uniform of the professional radical of the era (beard, semilong hair, denim workshirt, American flag tie), selected a chair at the back of the room, leaned it against the wall, and promptly fell asleep. I figured that as long as he didn't start snoring I would consider the day a success. He did, and I didn't.

The training was held on the campus of a college with a school of social work. By the end of the first day, I was thoroughly depressed and wandered over to the school in hopes of finding someone who could help me salvage this disaster. I ran into an acquaintance who was a professor of social policy. As she liked to keep tabs on activities of the Department of Social Services, she was happy to talk to me. She patiently listened to a lengthy tirade about my day, looked at the training material, and said, "Of course this is going badly. This form has nothing to do with social work practice and the staff knows it. This form has to do with social policy, but your state office staff doesn't think the field staff can understand and appreciate policy. They think the staff will only respond to issues if they are presented in terms of direct practice." Over takeout Chinese food, she spent much of the evening explaining social service funding to me, pointing out that the state could receive reimbursement from the federal government for 90 percent of the cost of services related to family planning, 75 percent for social services to welfare-eligible children, but less than 50 percent for services to children not eligible for welfare. She said, "Obviously, the state wants to report services in the categories where they will receive the highest match. The higher the rate of reimbursement, the greater the amount of services the state will be able to provide. Staff can understand and appreciate this; why don't you just tell them?"

Following the professor's advice, and with an armload of books and photocopied journal articles she lent me, I returned to my hotel and stayed up most of the night revising my curriculum. The next morning, I faced my now more-hostile-than-ever class and explained that we were going to approach the TOSS form from a slightly different angle. I spent about an hour discussing social service funding streams and how the state could maximize services by accurately reporting services to the federal government. I then deconstructed the form to show how, although it might have some slight relation to task-oriented social services, its actual purpose was to get the best reimbursement rate we could for services provided. To my surprise, the staff had become quiet and attentive; they were even showing some glimmer of interest. At the end of my presentation, the guy at the back of the room, who had resumed leaning against the wall but had not fallen asleep, leaned forward so the front legs of his chair hit the floor with a crash, and almost yelled, "Oh, I get it. This form's to screw the feds. I can do that!" I responded that I preferred to view it as a system to maximize the federal reimbursement the state could legitimately claim under existing laws, but if he wished to view it as screwing the feds, that was all right with me.

Once I made the purpose of the form clear, teaching the staff how to use it was relatively simple. In fact, we finished the training session a whole day early. I surveyed the class to see how they would like to spend the time left. They decided that they would like to discuss new techniques of social work practice, as long as the techniques did not involve any state office forms.

—Philip Popple

1

The Policy-Based Profession

VLADGRIN. Shutterstock

The state office administrators in the example given in Part One assumed that the social workers to be trained would not be receptive to a social policy explanation because of what Bruce Jansson refers to as the mythology of autonomous practice. By this Jansson means that social workers tend to approach practice under the assumption that they and their clients are relatively insulated from external policies. This mythology has led the profession to develop practice theories that focus heavily on the individual dimension of problems, causing a general disinterest in their *policy* context. Jansson (1990) states, "This notion of autonomous practice has had a curious and persistent strength in the social work profession" (p. 2). This perception of social policy also appears internationally, as illustrated by a study of the social policy curriculum in Australia. The author, Philip Mendes (2003), states that "in practice social policy seems to be peripheral to most social work courses in Australia" and that "social work students [have] the impression that social policy is simply about theoretical knowledge, without any need for practical application" (p. 220). In this chapter, we argue that the mythology of autonomous practice has been directly related to social work's efforts to achieve professional status. These efforts have been based on a flawed theory of what professionalization means, a theory that equated autonomy with private practice and that assigned primary importance to the development of practice techniques.

LEARNING OUTCOMES

- Explain the function of social work in society, including a definition of the social welfare institution, and relate this to the two targets of social work.
- Describe how micropractice, including Porter R. Lee's conceptualization of social work as cause and function, came to dominate professional social work.
- Discuss social work's pursuit of professional status, how the market-based model was adopted and thus led to the embrace of micropractice, and how the policy-based model changes the definition of social work practice.
- Analyze the wisdom of social work adopting medicine as its professional model, including whether social work has become more like medicine or if medicine has become more like social work.
- Discuss the relation of policy to social work practice, differentiating between social work policy specialists and generalist direct-practice social workers.
- Explain why understanding social welfare policy is important for direct-practice social workers.

CHAPTER OUTLINE

We will argue that looking at social work within a more up-to-date and accurate theory of professions leads to the conclusion that policy is not only relevant to the day-to-day activities of social workers but is also central to the definition and mission of the profession. We will also argue that the profession's recent emphasis on competencies demands that social workers' mastery of policy must go beyond simply understanding it as the context of practice to the development of demonstrable skills (Council on Social Work Education, 2015; Petracchi & Zastrow, 2010). Before we can get to these topics, however, we must first look at the function of social work in society and how policy became relegated to secondary status in the profession, a victim of social work's professional aspirations.

THE TARGET OF SOCIAL WORK—THE INDIVIDUAL AND SOCIETY

Stuart (1999) observes that "social work's unique and distinctive contribution to American life, often expressed as a dual focus on the person and his or her environment, resulted from a specific frame of reference that linked clients and social policy" (p. 335). By this Stuart means that we do not limit our concern to a person's intrapsychic functioning; we also seek to understand and manipulate factors in the environment that contribute to his or her problems. Some of these environmental factors are close to the person—for example, family, job, and neighborhood. However, people are also affected by factors in the larger environment—affirmative action laws, public welfare programs, United Way fund-raising campaigns, church positions on social issues, and the like. The social work profession is distinctive for its interest in all these factors and issues.

Thoughts for Social Work Practice

The practice perspective that differentiates social work from other helping professions is referred to as person-in-environment. The environment part of this equation includes a client's family, job, finances, and so forth. It also includes the policies providing the client with critical resources and services. Think about the benefits to a client of his or her social worker understanding these policies, that is, not being prey to the myth of autonomous practice.

The Social Function of Social Work

Social work's concern with person-in-environment stems from the profession's social function. Social work is the core technology in the social welfare institution, the institution in society that deals with the problem of dependency. Dependency occurs when an individual is not adequately fulfilling a role (e.g., providing physical care for his children) and social institutions are not providing adequate supports to enable the individual to fulfill a role (e.g., good quality, affordable child care is not available), and these situations cause problems for the community that require a response. By this we mean that every person in society occupies a number of social positions or statuses (mother, teacher, consumer, citizen, etc.), and attached to each of these positions are a number of social roles (nurturing children, communicating information, shopping, voting, etc.). These positions and roles are located within social institutions that support people in their efforts to meet role expectations successfully. For example, the role of employees occurs within the economic institution, which

Thoughts for Social Work Practice

Do you agree or disagree with the concern of some social workers that defining the focus of social work as moving people from dependence to interdependence makes it a social control profession? Could this also make it a social change profession?

must be functioning well enough to provide jobs for most people. When an individual is doing everything necessary to fulfill a role and the appropriate social institutions are functioning well enough to support the person's role performance, we have a situation we refer to as interdependence (Popple & Leighninger, 2011).

When most people and institutions are functioning interdependently, society operates smoothly. However, when people fail to perform roles adequately or social institutions fail to support people sufficiently in their role performance, social stability is threatened. Common examples of individual role failure are as follows:

- A woman is unemployed because she has difficulty controlling her temper.
- A single father leaves his two-year-old son at home alone for an extended time while he goes fishing.
- A fifteen-year-old does not attend school because he prefers to sleep late and play video games.

Examples of failure of social institutions to support individual role performance are as follows:

- A woman is unemployed because Wall Street financiers have bought the company for which she worked, sold off its assets, and laid off most of its workforce (Alexander, 2017).
- A single father leaves his two-year-old son at home alone while he works because there is no affordable day care available.
- A fifteen-year-old with a learning disability does not attend school because the school does not offer a program that meets his special needs.

The Dual Targets of Social Work

Because of the dual focus of the social welfare institution, the social work profession also has two targets. One target is to help individuals having difficulty meeting individual role expectations. This is the type of social work generally referred to as social work practice with individuals, families, and small groups, also referred to as *micropractice* or clinical social work. The other goal of social work is to deal with those aspects of social institutions that fail to support individuals in fulfilling role expectations (Atherton, 1969). This type of social work, sometimes referred to as *macropractice* or social work administration, policy, and planning, is what we are concerned with in the study of social welfare policy.

The Dominance of Micropractice

Social workers have long recognized that micro- and macropractice are complementary, but they have generally emphasized the micro, individual treatment aspect of the profession. The early social work leader and theoretician Mary Richmond referred to the dual nature of social work as *retail* and *wholesale,* saying, "The healthy and well-rounded reform movement usually begins in the retail method and returns to it again, forming in the two curves of its upward push and downward pull a complete circle" (Richmond, 1930, pp. 111–112). By this she meant, according to Richmond scholar Peggy Pittman-Munke (1999), that social work policy should be designed

> to utilize the rich material gathered through painstaking casework in a way which causes the problem to wear flesh and bones and breathe, to aggregate the data

> to present statistics which will convince policy makers of the need for reform, to organize and mount a successful campaign to see the legislation become a reality, and then to use case work as a way to evaluate the outcome of the legislation.

Another early leader, Porter R. Lee, referred to these aspects of social work as *cause* (working to effect social change) and *function* (treatment of individual role difficulties). He felt that function was the proper professional concern of social work. Lee (1937) argued that a cause, once successful, naturally tended to "transfer its interest and its responsibility to an administrative unit" that justified its existence by the test of efficiency, not zeal—by its "demonstrated possibilities of achievement" rather than by the "faith and purpose of its adherents" (pp. 4–9). The emphasis of the function was on "organization, technique, standards, and efficiency." Fervor inspired the cause, whereas intelligence directed the function. Lee felt that, once the cause had been won, it was necessary that it be institutionalized as a function to make the gains permanent. He saw this as the primary task of professional social work.

The opinions of Richmond and Lee have continued to represent the position of the vast majority of social work professionals. Practice with individuals, families, and small groups to treat problems of individual role performance continues to be the focus of most social work. Even though social workers will admit that problems with social institutions are at the root of most client problems, we have tended to persist in dealing primarily with the individual client. There are three main reasons for this tendency: (1) The individual is the most immediate target for change, (2) U.S. society is generally conservative, and (3) social work has chosen to follow a particular model of professionalism throughout most of the twentieth century.

The Individual Is the Most Immediate Target for Change

An individual with a problem cannot wait for a social policy change to come along and solve the problem. For example, the main reason a Temporary Assistance for Needy Families (TANF) mother runs out of money before the end of the month is, no doubt, the extremely small amount of money she receives, an *institutional* problem. If the size of the mother's grant were to increase, her problem might well disappear. However, this is not going to happen in the near future, so the social worker must concentrate on aspects of the mother's behavior that can be changed to stretch out her small budget and to help her develop skills in manipulating the system to ensure that she receives the maximum benefits to which she is entitled.

The Conservative Nature of U.S. Society

Another reason for the social work profession's strong emphasis on individual role performance is that U.S. society is rather conservative and firmly believes in the notion of individualism. We strongly believe that people deserve the majority of credit for any success they experience and, conversely, deserve most of the blame for any failures. We resent, and often make fun of, explanations of people's personal situations that attribute anything to factors external to the individual (Wilensky & Lebeaux, 1965). Explanations that attribute poverty, for example, to factors such as the job market, neighborhood disintegration, racism, and so forth, will often be dismissed as "bleeding-heart liberal" explanations. In a society characterized by such attitudes, a model of social work that concentrates on problems of individual role performance is obviously much more readily accepted and supported than one that seeks environmental change.

Professionalization

The final explanation of social work's emphasis on treating individual causes of dependency and de-emphasizing institutional causes is little recognized but of key importance. This is the model of professionalism that social work subscribed to early in the twentieth century, and social work's subsequent efforts to achieve professional status have been based on this model. It is to this model that we now turn.

Check Your Understanding 1.1
Check your understanding of The Target of Social Work–The Individual and Society by taking this brief quiz.

SOCIAL WORK'S PURSUIT OF PROFESSIONAL STATUS

Social work as a paid occupation has existed for only a little over 100 years. From the very beginning, those engaged in the provision of social services have been concerned, some would say preoccupied, with the status of their activities in the world of work, specifically with gaining recognition as a profession rather than simply as an occupation.

When social workers began to organize to improve their status, there was a conflict between those who thought the new profession should concentrate on institutional causes of dependency (social welfare policy) and those who were more interested in developing techniques and knowledge useful for helping individuals experiencing role failure (social work practice). Social work leaders such as Samuel McCune Lindsey at the New York School of Social Work, Edith Abbott at the Chicago School of Civics and Philanthropy, and George Mangold at the Missouri School of Social Economy argued for a profession based on social and economic theory and with a social reform orientation. Mangold (1914) stated:

> The leaders of social work . . . can subordinate technique to an understanding of the social problems that are involved. . . . Fundamental principles, both in economics and in sociology, are necessary for the development of their plans of community welfare. . . . Courses in problems of poverty and in the method and technique of charity organizations are fundamental to our work. But the study of economics of labor is quite as important, and lies at the basis of our living and social condition. . . . The gain is but slight if our philanthropy means nothing more than relieving distress here and helping a family there; the permanent gain comes only as we are able to work out policies that mean the permanent improvement of social conditions. (pp. 86–90)

On the other hand, a number of social work leaders believed that the new profession should concentrate on the development of practical knowledge related to addressing problems of individual role performance. The Charity Organization Society leader Mary Richmond advocated using case records and the experiences of senior social workers to train new workers in practical techniques of work with individuals. Frank Bruno (1928) argued that social work should be concerned with "processes . . . with all technical methods from the activities of boards of directors to the means used by a probation officer to rectify the conduct of a delinquent child" (p. 4).

The debate regarding the focus of the new social work profession came to a head at the 1915 meeting of the National Conference of Charities and Correction. Abraham Flexner, famed critic of the medical profession, had been asked to prepare a paper for the conference analyzing social work as a profession. Flexner (1915) began his analysis with the first clear statement of traits that differentiate professions from "lesser occupations." He asserted that

> professions involve essentially intellectual operations with large individual responsibility; they derive their raw material from science and learning; this material they work up to a practical and definite end; they possess an educationally communicable technique; they tend to self-organization; they are becoming increasingly altruistic in motivations. (pp. 285–288, 581, 585)

Following his definition of profession as a concept, Flexner measured social work against this definition. He found that social work strongly exhibited some professional traits—it was intellectual, derived its knowledge from science and learning, possessed a "professional self-consciousness," and was altruistic. However, in several important criteria, mainly those of educationally communicable technique and individual responsibility, Flexner found social work lacking.

Regarding social work's lack of an educationally communicable technique, Flexner felt the source of the deficiency was the broadness of its boundaries. He believed that professions should have definite and specific ends. However, "the high degree of specialized competency required for action and conditioned on limitation of area cannot possibly go with the width and scope characteristic of social work." Flexner (1915) believed that this lack of specificity seriously affected the possibility of professional training. "The occupations of social workers are so numerous and diverse that no compact, purposefully organized educational discipline is possible" (pp. 285–288).

In the area of individual responsibility, Flexner (1915) felt that social workers were mediators rather than responsible parties.

> The social worker takes hold of a case, that of a disintegrating family, a wrecked individual, or an unsocialized industry. Having localized his problem, having decided on its particular nature, is he not usually driven to invoke the specialized agency, professional or other, best equipped to handle it? . . . To the extent that the social worker mediates the intervention of the particular agent or agency best fitted to deal with the specific emergency which he has encountered, is the social worker himself a professional or is he the intelligence that brings this or that profession or other activity into action? (p. 585)

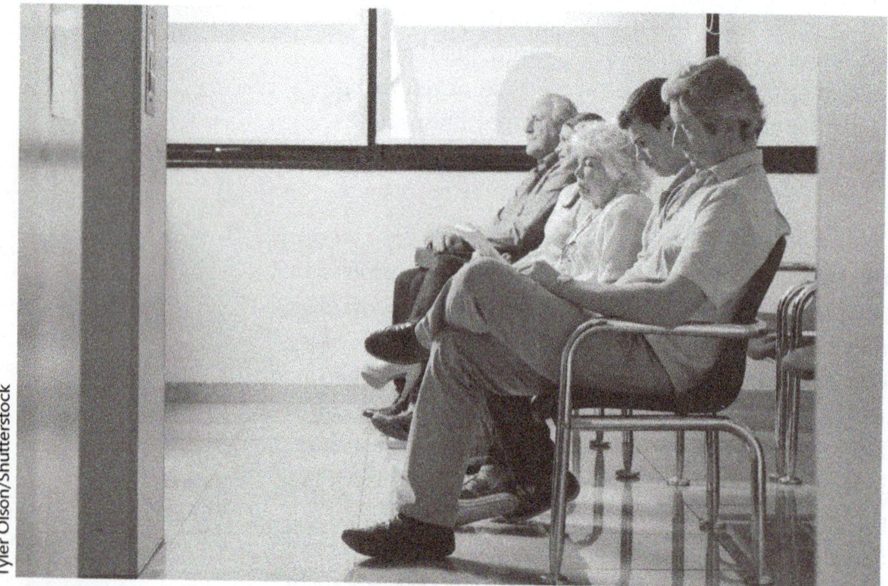
Tyler Olson/Shutterstock

The conditions under which clients receive services are a direct result of social welfare policy.

Social workers took Flexner's message to heart such that "Is Social Work a

Profession?" is probably the most frequently cited paper in the social work literature. David Austin (1983) asserts that Flexner's "model of an established profession became the most important organizing concept in the conceptual development of social work and, in particular, social work education." Following the presentation of the paper, social workers consciously set out to remedy the deficiencies identified by Flexner, mainly the development of an educationally communicable technique and the assumption of "large individual responsibility."

In the area of technique, the profession chose to emphasize practice with individuals, families, and small groups, or *social casework* as it was then called. The committee charged with responding to Flexner's paper stated, "This committee . . . respectfully suggests that the chief problem facing social work is the development of training methods which will give it [a] technical basis" (Lee, 1915, pp. 576–590). The committee felt that the social work profession had the beginning of an educationally communicable technique in the area of social casework and that the profession should narrow its focus to emphasize this. This view was institutionalized in 1919 when the American Association of Professional Schools of Social Work was founded, dominated by educators who subscribed to the Flexner model for the profession. At an early meeting, it was voted that students receive training in casework, statistics, and community service. F. Stuart Chapin, director of the Smith College Training School for Social Work, proposed that social legislation be included as a fundamental curriculum area. This was voted down, based on the argument that social legislation lacked clarity and technique and was not suitable for fieldwork. Likewise, settlement house work was considered to be unsuitable for professional education. Settlements emphasized "mere neighborliness" and were opposed to the idea that their residents were more expert than their neighbors (Lubove, 1965). Thus, within a relatively few years following Flexner's paper, social work had all but eliminated knowledge and skills related to social policy from the profession's domain, substituting a nearly exclusive focus on techniques demonstrated as useful in helping individuals solve problems of role functioning.

The second area in which Flexner considered social work deficient in meeting the criteria of professionalization is that of "assuming large individual responsibility." Flexner was referring to what is now generally termed *professional authority* or *autonomy.* According to Greenwood (1957), "In a professional relationship . . . the professional dictates what is good or evil for the client, who has no choice but to accede to professional judgement." Professional autonomy is closely related to professional expertise because it is on expertise that authority or autonomy is based.

Although neither Flexner nor any other theorist said it directly, social workers have come to equate professional autonomy with a private practice model of service delivery. Two reasons for this interpretation come to mind. The first is that Flexner's model of a profession was based on medicine, which he viewed as the prototypical "true" profession. Because the predominant model of medicine during most of the twentieth century was private practice, social workers naturally assumed that private practice was the key to autonomy. The second reason is that a person with no boss—as is the case in private practice—is obviously autonomous. But whatever the reason, the result of this interpretation has been to push social work further away from policy toward an individual treatment model of practice. As Austin (1983) has observed,

> the emphasis on distinctive method also reinforced a focus on the casework counseling interview as the core professional technique in social work. This was

> a technique that could most readily be adapted to a private-practice model—a model that has been viewed by many practitioners as a close approximation to the medical model of professionalism that Flexner had in mind. (p. 369)

In summary, for better or for worse, the adoption of a model of professionalization based on Flexner's criteria caused, or perhaps simply accelerated, the trend in social work to define the profession as being focused on role difficulties of individuals (casework) and to de-emphasize concern with the institutional causes of role failure (social welfare policy). Social workers were concerned with identifying and demonstrating an educationally communicable technique. Casework with individuals and families appeared to be more promising than a concern with social welfare policy, which was—and still is—amorphous and hard to conceptualize. Social workers were also concerned with being able to practice autonomously, which they came to associate with private practice. The types of professional roles associated with social policy almost always occur in large organizations, which have traditionally been viewed as threats to autonomy. The definition of professional autonomy as ideally occurring in private practice has furthered the perception of social welfare policy as tangential to the social work profession.

Thus, social workers' concern with professionalization has been an important reason for the relatively low interest in social welfare policy in the profession. It appears, however, that this model of professionalism contains some major errors. Flexner's model of professionalism was based on medicine; it assumed that medicine was a prototypical profession and that, as other occupations began to achieve professional status, they would increasingly resemble medicine. It is now apparent that medicine, rather than being a prototypical profession, was in fact an anomaly (Ritzer, 1975). For various social and political reasons, medicine was able to escape both the corporation and the bureaucracy, and thus was able to control its domain completely and determine most of its own working conditions (Starr, 1982). However, rather than social work developing and becoming more like medicine, things have moved in quite the opposite direction. Medicine is now coming under the control of the corporation and the bureaucracy and, in terms of occupational organization, is coming more and more to resemble social work. These developments indicate errors in the Flexner model of professions and call for a reexamination of the concept. This reexamination should develop the concept so that professionalism can be understood without assuming that professionals should be private practitioners and high-level technicians. In the following section, we attempt such a reexamination.

Check Your Understanding 1.2

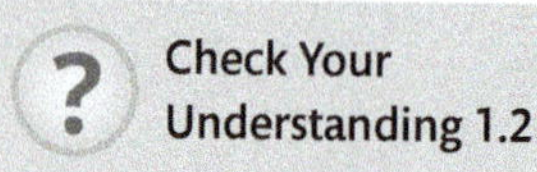

Check your understanding of Social Work's Pursuit of Professional Status by taking this brief quiz.

THE POLICY-BASED PROFESSION

The model developed by Flexner might well be termed the *market-based profession*. This model, based on the medical profession in the early part of the twentieth century, assumes that the professional is essentially a small-business person. The product that the professional is selling is his or her expertise. The basic relationship, illustrated in Figure 1.1, is dyadic. The consumer comes to the professional stating a problem, the professional diagnoses the problem and prescribes a solution, the consumer requests the solution that the professional provides, and the consumer pays the bill. The demonstration of specific techniques is key in the market-based model because these represent the "products" that the professional is selling. Autonomy is assumed in this model to result from the fact that the professional is his or her own boss.

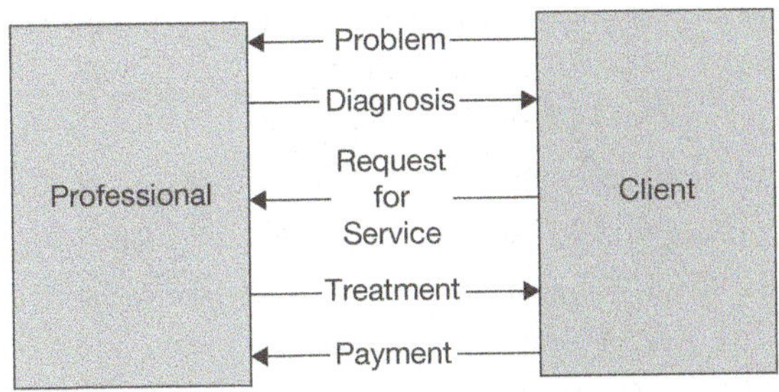

Figure 1.1
The Market-Based Profession

Two general developments accelerated over the course of the twentieth century and indicate that the market-based model of professions no longer reflects reality accurately, if it ever did. The first is that the trend in all professions has been for professionals to become employees in organizations rather than private practitioners. Even medicine, long viewed as the ideal independent profession, shows signs of an eroding independent practice base. Paul Starr (1982) observes:

> The AMA [American Medical Association] is no longer as devoted to solo practice either. "We are not opposed to the corporate practice of medicine," says Dr. Sammons of the AMA. "There is no way that we could be," he adds, pointing out that a high proportion of the AMA's members are now involved in corporate practice. According to AMA data, some 26 percent of physicians have contractual relationships with hospitals; three out of five of these doctors are on salary. . . . Many physicians in private practice receive part of their income through independent practice associations, HMOs [health maintenance organizations], and for-profit hospitals and other health care companies. The growth of corporate medicine has simply gone too far for the AMA to oppose it outright. (p. 446)

Although the number of social workers in private practice has steadily increased in recent years—and, as social workers succeed in their efforts to be eligible for third-party reimbursement (insurance), this number will increase even more—it is certain that a high proportion of social workers will continue to earn their living within organizational settings. Thus, a common work setting for professionals in many fields has become a public or private bureaucracy rather than a private practice.

The second development that indicates the market-based model of professions is outdated is that professional practice, even in private settings, is increasingly subject to the dictates of external bodies. The psychiatry profession developed the *Diagnostic and Statistical Manual* in response to pressure from insurance companies to classify various treatments for insurance reimbursement. This manual is now the bible guiding the practice of mental health professionals, regardless of what they may feel about the evil of labeling. The practice of lawyers is subject to the dictates of banks, title companies, and state and federal justice departments, as well as the entire court system. Before a physician can hospitalize a patient, an insurance company generally has to approve the proposed treatment for payment; once the patient is in the hospital, the length of stay is usually determined not by the patient's physician but by the insurance company, managed care organization, or governmental agency that will eventually pay most of the bill.

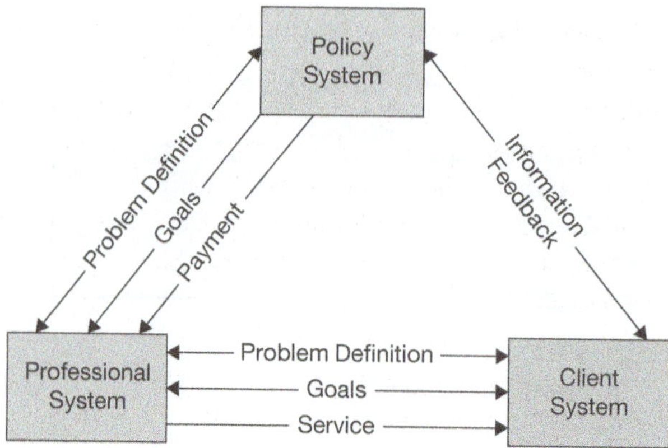

Figure 1.2
The Policy-Based Profession

Social workers in "private practice" receive most of their income through membership in managed-care panels, where they are paid by large insurance companies or HMOs. The list of examples could go on and on to illustrate our point that even professionals who are in so-called independent practice are now subject to all sorts of influences and controls by external organizations.

The model of professionalism reflecting occupational reality in the twenty-first century is called the *policy-based profession*. This model, illustrated in Figure 1.2, is based on a triadic relationship. The triad is composed of three systems—the professional system, the client system, and the policy system. The policy-based model recognizes that, although a professional provides services on behalf of a client, it is often not the client who requests the services, defines the problem, or pays the professional.

Recognizing that professions are now predominantly policy-based rather than market-based leads to two major revisions of the traditional way of looking at professions, each contributing to the argument that social welfare policy must be a central concern of the social work profession. The first regards the matter of expert technique and the second regards practice within an organizational setting.

Expert Technique

According to Flexner and all the social theorists following him who subscribe to the market-based model, an occupation becomes recognized as a profession by developing techniques in the same way a business develops a product: by marketing the technique and, if successful, "accomplishing profession," to use Robert Dingwall's (1976) term. This process, however, does not follow from what we know of the history of professions. All professions were recognized as professions *before* they had any particularly effective techniques. This includes medicine, which was not particularly effective until the twentieth century. Many professions—the clergy, for example—do not now and probably never will have such techniques. By pursuing this trait (developing marketable techniques), social workers have defined a number of areas as outside the scope of the profession, generally areas related to social welfare policy, because they were not seen as amenable to the development of specific, educationally communicable techniques.

Rather than expert technique, *social assignment* appears to be crucial for an occupation to be recognized as a profession. Professions exist for the purpose of managing problems critical to society; the successful profession is recognized by society as being primarily responsible for a given social problem area. Medicine is charged with dealing with physical health, law with management of deviance and civil relations, engineering with the practical applications of technology, education with the communication of socially critical knowledge and skills, and social work with the management of dependency. All professions have wide and complex bodies of knowledge, and all have a theory base. However, the degree to which this knowledge and theory is translated into educationally communicable techniques varies widely. Medicine and engineering have rather precise, educationally communicable techniques; law and the clergy have techniques that are somewhat less precise. Rather than specific techniques, these professions base their authority on mastery of complex cultural traditions. The important point is that the possession of technique is not what is crucial for the development of a profession; rather, what *is* crucial is the identification of one occupation over others to be given primary responsibility for the management of a social problem (Popple, 1985).

Professional Practice within an Organizational Context

Traditional theory, based on Flexner's work, equates professional autonomy with the autonomy of the independent practitioner who is his or her own boss. Over the course of the twentieth century, more and more professionals came to work in traditional bureaucratic organizations, and the question arose whether this development erodes the very basis of professional autonomy. The theoretical position that argues this most forcefully is called *proletarianization*. This thesis emphasizes the loss of control that professionals supposedly experience when they work in large organizations. According to Eliot Freidson (1984),

> this thesis stems from Marx's theory of history, in which he asserts that over time the intrinsic characteristics of capitalism will reduce virtually all workers to the status of the proletariat, i.e., dependent on selling their labor in order to survive and stripped of all control over the substance and process of their work. (p. 3)

Supposedly, in organizations, the authority of the office is substituted for the authority of professional expertise. In other words, a person working in a bureaucracy is required to take direction from any person who occupies a superior position in the organization, regardless of whether the person has equal or greater expertise in the professional task being performed. Thus, when employed in an organization, a professional does not have autonomy.

Sociologists who have studied professionals working in organizations have found that the fears of losing professional autonomy in such settings have been greatly exaggerated. Instead, the organizations in which professionals typically work—hospitals, schools, law firms, social agencies, and so forth—have developed as hybrid forms that deviate from the ideal type of bureaucracy in order to accommodate professionals. Freidson (1984) states

> studies [of professionals in organizations], as well as more recent developments in organizational theory, call into question the validity of the assumption that large organizations employing professionals are sufficiently bureaucratic to allow one to assume that professional work within them is ordered and controlled by strictly bureaucratic means. (pp. 10–11)

A number of developments have enabled professionals to work in organizations while maintaining sufficient autonomy to perform their professional roles. First, professionals have come to be recognized as a special group under U.S. labor law because they are expected to exercise judgment and discretion on a routine, daily basis in the course of performing their work. In other words, discretion is a recognized and legitimate part of their work role. Second, professionals are subject to a different type of supervision than are ordinary rank-and-file workers. Ordinary workers are generally supervised by someone who has been trained as a manager, not as a worker in the area being supervised. Professionals, however, generally are entitled to expect supervision only from a member of their own profession. In social agencies, supervisors, managers, and often even executive positions are reserved for persons trained and licensed as social workers (Freidson, 1984, pp. 10–12).

Check Your Understanding 1.3
Check your understanding of The Policy-Based Profession by taking this brief quiz.

SOCIAL WORK AS A POLICY-BASED PROFESSION: PRACTICE IMPLICATIONS

Recognizing that social work is a policy-based rather than a market-based profession clarifies and legitimizes the place of social welfare policy as a central concern. First, the policy-based model, while recognizing that the development of technique is important for any profession, also recognizes that functions do not need to be excluded from a profession's concern simply because they are not amenable to the development of narrow, specific procedures. This recognition legitimizes the inclusion of policy content such as policy analysis, administration, negotiation, planning, and so forth. Such inclusion has often been questioned because it was viewed as not being amenable to the development of "educationally communicable techniques." Second, the policy-based model recognizes that the social work profession will probably always exist in an organizational context and that social work's long experience in providing services within this context should be viewed as a strength rather than a weakness of the profession. Finally, the policy-based model explicitly recognizes the policy system as a major factor in social work practice and emphasizes that understanding this system is every bit as important for social work practitioners as understanding basic concepts of human behavior.

A number of roles within social work are described as policy practice roles, including roles mentioned previously—planner, administrator, policy analyst, program evaluator, and so on. In the years following the Flexner report, there was a good deal of debate whether these were really social work practice roles or something else, perhaps public administration. Tortured rationales were often developed that defined these roles as casework techniques applied to different settings and populations. The 1959 Council on Social Work Education (CSWE) curriculum study, for example, concluded, "As the administration project progressed, it became more and more clear that what we were discussing in the preparation of social work students for executive level positions was social work [practice] in an administrative setting and not administration in a social work setting" (Spencer, 1959, p. 9). Over the years, however, these roles have come to be defined as legitimate areas of social work practice without resorting to defining them as social casework applied to a different setting. Many graduate schools of social work now offer a concentration in administration, policy, and planning, often called macro social work practice.

Social Welfare Policy and Social Work Competencies

Largely driven by changes in standards set by the educational accrediting body, the CSWE, the social work profession in recent years has become increasingly concerned with specifying and measuring competencies, that is, what graduate social workers can demonstrate that they can actually do. It is interesting to note that the definition of competencies and discussions around this topic almost exactly tracks what Flexner called "educationally communicable techniques" almost a century ago. The difference is that we now recognize that social work responded to Flexner's critique by developing a far too narrow conceptualization of what social work competencies are. If you will recall from our previous discussion, following Flexner, social work moved to define the social work technique as almost exclusively practice with individuals, families, and small groups, at the time called social casework. It is interesting to understand that historians recognized the folly of this approach far earlier than social workers. Roy Lubove, for example, wrote in 1965, "If social work could claim any distinctive function in an atomized urban society with serious problems of group communication and mass deprivation, it was not individual therapy but liaison between groups and the stimulation of social legislation and institutional change" (pp. 147, 106–107, 220–221). Over the past fifty years, administration and policy, which has become known as macropractice, has assumed a major role in the definition of professional social work. However, it has only been since the 2008 revision of social work school accreditation standards, which were carried forward into the 2015 standards and emphasized the demonstration of competencies, that is, techniques that have been educationally communicated, that the profession has turned to the difficult issue of demonstrating the skills that macrolevel social workers can actually demonstrate.

The 2015 Educational Policy and Accreditation Standards (EPAS), the document that the CSWE uses to accredit undergraduate and master's level social work programs (doctoral level programs are not accredited by the CSWE), identifies "engage in policy practice" as one of nine competencies that schools must demonstrate they are teaching students. Four areas of knowledge, values, and skill are identified as contributing to this competency:

- Social workers understand the history and current structures of social policies and services, the role of policy in service delivery, and the role of practice in policy development.
- Social workers understand their role in policy development and implementation within their practice settings at the micro, mezzo, and macro levels and they actively engage in policy practice to effect change within these settings.
- Social workers recognize and understand the historical, social, cultural, economic, organizational, environmental, and global influences that affect social policy.
- They are also knowledgeable about policy formulation, analysis, implementation, and evaluation. (CSWE, 2015)

In the following chapters, we address each of these areas of the competency. For the historical knowledge area, we not only include information on the history and development of each of the major areas of social welfare services, we also include information aimed at developing skills in historical research methods, including the importance and use of primary source material, so social workers reading this text will be competent to update this knowledge on their own. For the second area, policy practice, we have included chapters on politics and on how social workers can take action to improve policy. For the third area, understanding influences that affect social policy, we include seven chapters looking at how these influences affect policies in the areas of poverty, aging, mental health, health, child welfare, and immigration. The final competency area, policy analysis, formulation, implementation, and evaluation, is the main focus of this book. For this we provide a detailed policy analysis outline in the introduction to Part Two, three chapters expanding and elucidating the outline, and the seven chapters mentioned above illustrating the use of the outline to analyze major social welfare policies.

Policy Practice as a Social Worker Role

Social welfare policy has always been part of the education of social workers. For most of the twentieth century, it was taught as part of the foundation curriculum for reasons similar to American history being taught to high school students. American history is taught based on the belief that this content, while of little applied value, is necessary information for students to understand their role as citizens. Likewise, social welfare policy content used to be considered to be of little practice value but was necessary for social workers to understand and value their function as professionals. This view began to change in the 1980s when scholars such as Bruce Jansson (1984) began to argue that policy should not be simply a foundation area but also a specialization that has come to be called policy practice. More recently, Jansson (2008) has begun to differentiate what social workers do as *policy advocacy*, which he sees as a specialized part of policy practice. *Policy practice* is seen as a function of anyone or any entity (General Motors, for example) who wants to establish new policies, improve existing ones, or defeat the policy initiatives of others. Policy advocacy, according to Jansson (2008), is policy practice that aims to help relatively powerless groups improve their resources and opportunities.

For the purposes of this text, we define policy practice as that aspect of social work macropractice that is concerned with policy advocacy, development, and analysis within the framework of social work values, particularly the value of social justice. The other two major aspects of social work macropractice, community development and organizing, and organizational management and leadership, are outside the scope of policy practice. The major methods of policy practice are identified as legislative advocacy, reform through litigation, social action, and social welfare policy analysis (Figueira-McDonough, 1993). The latter method is the major focus of this text.

One final question about policy practice: Is it a role reserved for specialists or is it part of the role set of all practicing social workers? Our answer to this is that it is both. A number of social workers, trained at the MSW level with specializations in macropractice, spend their careers as policy practitioners. Examples of such positions in other careers are legislative aide to a Congress member, policy analyst for state agencies such as departments of mental health, and lobbyists for social welfare organizations such as the Child Welfare League of America. In this text, however, we are most concerned with the policy knowledge and skills needed by direct-practice social work practitioners whose major role is not policy. Although policy may not be the major concern of a frontline social worker (a child protective services worker, for example), this worker's professional responsibilities still involve policy concerns. As Rocha (2007) has noted ". . . if a social worker has a client who experiences a problem maneuvering through the maze of social programs and we assist her or him in gaining resources, then we are performing case advocacy. But if we see client after client having the same problem, then it becomes a waste of valuable time and resources to individually advocate for each client. That is when policy practice comes into play."

The Importance of Understanding Social Welfare Policy for the Direct-Practice Social Worker

This text, as previously mentioned, is not aimed mainly at social workers preparing for specialized policy practice roles. It is also aimed at people interested in more traditional direct-practice roles with individuals, families, and small groups. In this chapter, we have argued that the study of policy is relevant, in fact a *necessity,* for this group because policy is built into the very fabric of social work practice just as much as the study of human behavior. Social work's concern with policy is a logical extension of our person-in-environment perspective. Up to this point, this discussion has been rather abstract and theoretical. The reader is justified at this point in looking for specific examples of the ways policy affects direct practice. The following, although not a complete classification of ways that policy directly relates to practice, offers a few of many possible examples.

Policy Determines the Major Goals of Service

A basic component of social work practice is the setting of case goals. As illustrated by the vignette at the beginning of the chapter, the range of possible goals is not entirely up to the judgment of the individual social work practitioner but rather is greatly restricted, and sometimes actually prescribed, by agency policy. A good example of this is shown in child protective services. For a number of years, protective service policy was based on goals that have come to be referred to as "child rescue." The idea was that when the level of child care in a home had sunk to the level of neglect or abuse, the family was probably irredeemable and the appropriate strategy was to get the child out of the home to a better setting. Based to a certain degree on case experience and research results, but probably more on the outcomes of a number of lawsuits, policy is now shifting to the goal of family preservation. This means that, before a child is removed from the home, the social worker must demonstrate that a reasonable effort has been made to help the family while the child is still in the home. The point is that family preservation now figures prominently among the goals of child protection social workers, not because thousands of social workers have individually come to the conclusion that this is the most appropriate goal, but because policy now specifies that this be the goal of choice.

Policy Determines Characteristics of Clientele

Policy analyst Alvin Schorr has pointed out how agency policy, often in subtle ways, determines the type of clients that social agency staff will deal with. If the agency wishes to serve a middle-class clientele, they can attract this type of client and discourage poorer clients by means of several policy decisions. First, by locating in the suburbs, the agency services become more accessible to the middle class and less so to poorer segments of the population. Second, what Schorr (1985) terms *agency culture* can be designed to appeal to the middle class—whether the waiting room is plush or bare and functional, whether appointments are insisted on or drop-in visits are permitted, whether the agency gives priority to clients who can pay for services, whether the agency has evening and weekend hours or is open only during the day, and so forth.

Policy Determines Who Will Get Services

Ira Colby (1989) relates a situation in which an anonymous caller contacted a state department of social services to report that a fourteen-year-old girl had been at home alone for several days with nothing to eat, and the caller wanted the department to "do something." The supervisor who was working intake that day

> was torn about what action to take. On the one hand, [she] wanted to send a worker out to verify the referral and provide any and all available services; yet, the department's policy clearly classified this case as a priority three—a letter would be sent to the caretakers outlining parental responsibilities. . . . In [this state], each child protective services' referral is classified as a priority one, two, or three. A priority one requires that a worker begin work within twenty-four hours after the agency receives a referral; a priority two mandates that contact be made within ten days; a priority three requires no more action than a letter or phone call. Cases are prioritized based on a number of variables, including the alleged victim's age and the type and extent of the alleged abuse. (Colby, 1989, p. v)

Most social workers are employed in agencies with policies specifying who can and who cannot receive services and some method of prioritizing services.

Policy Specifies, or Restricts, Certain Options for Clients

Policy often requires that a social worker either offer or not offer certain options. For example, social workers who are employed by Catholic Social Services are generally forbidden to discuss abortion as an option for an unplanned pregnancy. Social workers at a Planned Parenthood center are required to explore this option. When one of the authors began work for a state welfare department, during the first six months of his employment, he was explicitly prohibited by agency policy from discussing birth control with welfare recipients. During the last six months of his employment there, policy was changed to explicitly *require* him to discuss birth control with all welfare recipients.

Policy Determines the Theoretical Focus of Services

Although less common than the other examples, in certain instances agencies have policies that require social workers to adopt a certain theoretical orientation toward their practice. For a number of years there was a schism in social work between the diagnostic school (followers of Sigmund Freud) and the functional school (followers of Otto Rank). Social agencies sometimes defined themselves as belonging to one school or the other and would not employ social workers who practiced according to the other perspective. Currently, some agencies define themselves as behavioral, ecosystems, feminist, and so on, and frown on other approaches being applied by their staff. One of the authors once prepared a training curriculum for child protective services workers on behavioral principles; it was rejected by the state office training division because "this is not the way we wish our staff to practice."

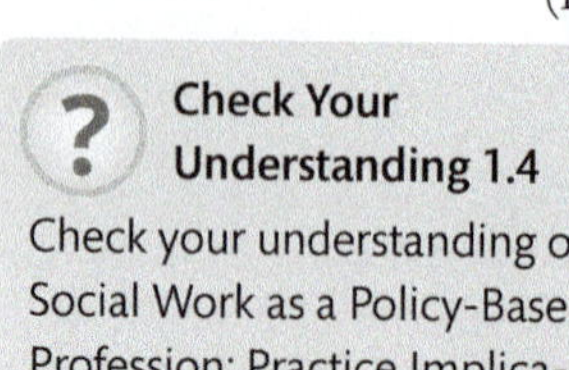

?
Check Your Understanding 1.4
Check your understanding of Social Work as a Policy-Based Profession: Practice Implications by taking this brief quiz.

CONCLUSION

Although few social workers enter the profession because of an interest in social welfare policy, every social work practitioner is in fact involved in policy on a daily basis. Social work agencies are created by policies, their goals are specified by policies, social workers are hired to carry out policy-specific tasks, and the whole environment in which social workers and clients exist is policy-determined. We often think of policy in terms of social legislation, but it is much broader than that. As Schorr (1985) has noted,

> [P]ower in terms of policy is not applied on a grand scale only; the term "practitioner" implies consideration of policy in terms of clinical relationships and relatively small groups. These may be as consequential as or more consequential for the quality of everyday life than the large-scale government and private hierarchical actions that are more commonly regarded as policy. As practitioners practice policy, they may choose any of a variety of instruments. They may simply decide differently about matters that lie within their own control, they may attempt to influence their agencies or they may take on more deep-seated and, chances are, conflict-ridden change. These are also choices that practitioners make.

The problem with which we began this chapter shows why social work students who desire to be direct practitioners need to study social welfare policy. The answer should be clear by now. Because social work is a policy-based profession, practitioners need to be sensitive to, and knowledgeable about, the dynamics of three systems—the client system, the practitioner system, and the policy system. Human behavior in the social environment curriculum concentrates on the dynamics of the client system, the social work practice curriculum concentrates on the practitioner system, and the social welfare policy and services curriculum focuses on the policy system. All three are equally important to the preparation of a direct-practice social worker.

Recall what you learned from this chapter by completing the Chapter Review.

2

Defining Social Welfare Policy

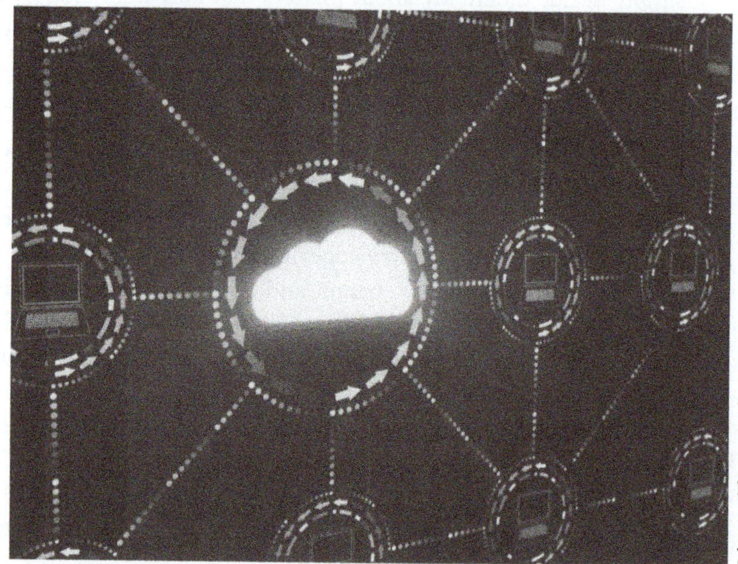

3dreams/Shutterstock

LEARNING OUTCOMES

- Explain why some social workers and social scientists would like to use the term *social well-being* instead of *social welfare*.
- Discuss the reasons that social welfare policy is a complicated concept to define.
- Explain why social welfare policy, as an area of social work, involves more than merely the actions of government.
- Identify and define the three levels of social welfare policy.
- Relate the importance of social work practitioners understanding social welfare policy to the identification of social workers as street-level bureaucrats.

CHAPTER OUTLINE

The last time Bud hit her, something deep inside Sarah snapped. She yelled; screamed; hit him with a sixteen-ounce can of pork and beans; and finally, after regaining some control, called the police. By the time the officers arrived, Bud had agreed to move to his brother's, at least for a while. After four years of physical and emotional abuse, Sarah just wanted to take her four-year-old daughter Megan, get out of the situation, and begin putting her life back together. However, it seemed that at every step there was some policy or other to contend with.

First, there was the problem of getting untangled from the criminal justice system. Sarah really did not want Bud to go to jail; she just wanted him out of the house. She explained this to the police officers when they arrived and requested that the complaint be dropped. They said they would like to do that, but department policy stated that an arrest had to be made any time there was a domestic violence complaint. After Bud spent the night in jail, Sarah explained the same thing to the judge. The judge said that it was his policy in domestic violence cases to send the perpetrator to prison unless the couple agreed to attend marital counseling. Sarah and Bud agreed to do this, even though Sarah was not optimistic about it.

The next problem was in complying with the judge's order. Sarah first called their medical insurance company, who explained that their benefits policy paid for marital counseling only if alcohol or drug abuse was the cause of the problem. Simple relationship difficulties were not covered. Sarah then called the mental health unit at the Methodist hospital; they told her that their policy excluded clients who were seeking counseling due to a court order. The hospital board felt that involuntary clients were not motivated and therefore would not benefit from treatment. Finally, Sarah was able to get an appointment with a social worker at the local YWCA women's center.

Bud lasted in counseling exactly one session. He said that the social worker, Julie Draughn, was a "feminazi" and he wasn't about to listen to her. Sarah was not surprised at Bud's reaction, but she thought what Julie had to say was kind of nice and was certainly food for thought. Julie believed that social policy in the United States was evolving from a traditionally patriarchal, hierarchical system, one that forced women into dependent roles, into a more egalitarian system that freed women from subservience, at the same time placing greater demands on them for independent contributions. She tried to explain to Bud that this policy evolution would also eventually free men from burdens that had often crushed them in the past, but he wasn't having any of it. His last words to Sarah were that if she was so damn liberated she had better not count on him for any support at all, financial support included.

After Bud made good on his threat and refused to contribute anything to Sarah and Megan's expenses, Julie Draughn referred Sarah to the state Department of Human Resources (DHR) office to apply for assistance. The eligibility worker at DHR told Sarah that state policy required that a child support order be obtained before she would be eligible for any help. When she did obtain an order, the amount, $400 per month, when combined with the small income she received from a part-time job, exceeded the maximum that eligibility policy allowed for receipt of financial assistance. Eligibility policy for the Supplemental Nutrition Assistance Program (SNAP, also known as food stamps) is somewhat less stringent (income less than 125 percent of the poverty level), so Sarah and Megan at least got some food assistance. In a similar fashion, Sarah found she was eligible for rental assistance under a policy referred to simply as Section VIII, which would enable her to get a decent apartment for a very affordable rent. However, when she visited the housing authority office, the worker explained that Section VIII is a capped program, not an entitlement program, meaning that eligible applicants such as Sarah can be helped only until the program's revenue-sharing grant runs out. She was told that they were currently out of money and that she would be placed on a waiting list with an average wait time of two-and-a-half years. After two of the court-ordered support payments, Bud disappeared, never to be seen again, so Sarah and Megan were able to qualify for public assistance.

Two years after her separation and subsequent divorce, Sarah has become somewhat of an expert on social welfare policy. After her living situation became stabilized, Sarah researched the educational assistance policy and was able to develop a strategy to obtain assistance with tuition, books, and day care while she attended a local university to obtain a degree and a teaching certificate. However, halfway through the program, public assistance policy changed; it no longer permitted recipients to attend a four-year program. Sarah was forced to drop out of the teacher education curriculum and reevaluate her options, finally deciding to enroll in the local two-year technical college in a dental assistant training program. She is still working part-time but carefully monitors her income to be sure that it does not exceed the maximum allowable for the various benefits she receives. She occasionally feels guilty about not contributing as much as she possibly can to her own support, but she realizes that the purpose of all these policies is to encourage her to become a self-supporting, tax-paying citizen, and that is exactly her own goal.

Sarah's story illustrates the vast impact of policy on social welfare clients, but more important for our purposes in this chapter, it illustrates the multiple meanings of the term *social welfare policy* and hence some of the difficulties in discussing and studying the subject. The term *social welfare policy* sometimes refers to broad social philosophy, sometimes to the narrowest administrative rule. When people use the term *policy*, they are usually referring to the actions of government, but social welfare policy often involves activities of the voluntary sector of the economy, of religious groups, and (more and more) of profit-making businesses. The purpose of this chapter is to look at the many meanings of the term *social welfare policy* and to clarify the way it is used in this text.

SOCIAL WELFARE POLICY—BASIC DEFINITION

To define the concept of social welfare policy, we must break the concept into its two constituent parts—*social welfare* and *policy.* We dealt briefly with the term *social welfare* in Chapter 1, where it was defined as the institution in society that deals with the problem of dependency. Recall that by *dependency,* we mean situations in which individuals are not fulfilling critical social roles (a parent is not adequately caring for a child, a person is unable to support him- or herself financially, a child consistently breaks the law, etc.) or in which social institutions are not functioning well enough to support people in their role performance (the unemployment level is so high that a person cannot get a job despite being qualified, for example). The social welfare institution deals with these situations in order to help maintain social equilibrium.

Policy is a rather loose and imprecise term for which there is no generally accepted definition in the academic literature (Pal, 2009). Some frequently cited definitions are as follows:

- A purposive course of action followed by an actor or set of actors in dealing with a problem or matter of concern.
- Policy implies choice, that is, decision-making possibilities within a range of feasible alternatives.
- A "standing decision" characterized by behavioral consistency and repetitiveness on the part of both those who make it and those who abide by it.
- In its most general sense, the pattern of action that resolves conflicting claims or provides incentives for cooperation (Anderson, 2011; Eulau & Prewitt, 1973; Frohock, 1979; Pal, 2006).

? Check Your Understanding 2.1
Check your understanding of Social Welfare Policy—Basic Definition by taking this brief quiz.

As the term is generally used, *policy* means principles, guidelines, or procedures that serve the purpose of maximizing uniformity in decision making.

Thus, the very simple beginning definition we will use for the term *social welfare policy* is: principles, guidelines, or procedures that serve the purpose of maximizing uniformity in decision making regarding the problem of dependency in our society. This seems simple enough but, as you will see in the remainder of this chapter, *social welfare policy* is a slippery and elusive term.

FACTORS COMPLICATING THE DEFINITION OF SOCIAL WELFARE POLICY

Complicating any attempt to reach a clear and simple definition of *social welfare policy* is the fact that the term is used in many different ways by many different people and to refer to many different things by any one individual. The following sections discuss some aspects of the term that can lead to a lack of clarity and precision in its use.

Social Welfare or Social Well-Being?

A recent development, one that may or may not turn out to be a long-term definitional problem, is the advocacy by some in the policy sciences to eschew the term *welfare* and substitute it with the term *well-being*. The reasons given for advocating this change are etymological, arguing that the term *welfare* actually means having a good trip or journey and that, to quote Dean (2012), "In using the term well-being, however, I am focusing *not* on how people 'fare' (on their goings or doings), but on their 'being' (on the essence of their lives)" (pp. 1–2).

Thoughts for Social Work Practice

Social workers and other social welfare advocates are constantly trying to lessen the stigma of benefit programs for the poor by changing their names from, for example, charity to welfare to human services. The latest welfare reform effort changed "aid" to "temporary assistance." In what ways, if any, do you think the population served by social workers benefits from these name changes?

It is interesting that the rationale for changing the term *welfare* to *well-being* is stated as a matter of definitional clarity when it is doubtful that this is the real motivation. A much more likely reason for this change is the fact that the term *welfare* carries with it a high negative stigma in western society. The term *stigma,* as used by sociologists, refers to an aspect of a person's life that ruins his or her identity. The stigmatized individual is a person whose social identity calls into question his or her full humanity—the person is devalued, spoiled, or flawed in the eyes of others and, as a consequence, is denied full social acceptance. There is no doubt that in U.S. society considerable stigma is attached to the term *social welfare* and consequently to the receipt of social welfare services. By attempting to change the term *welfare* to *well-being,* policy analysts are doing the same thing that virtually every state in the union has done by changing the name of the Department of Public Welfare to another, supposedly more positive name like the Department of Family and Children's Services, in a public relations attempt to make the whole enterprise more appealing to society as a whole (Popple & Leighninger, 2011).

In this text, we will continue to use the older and more widely accepted term *welfare.* While we sympathize with attempts to reduce the stigma attached to the provision and the receipt of social services, we think that the arbitrary change of terms only leads to conceptual ambiguity.

Social Welfare Policy and Social Policy

The provision of parks for relaxation and recreation is an example of social policy, but not of social welfare policy.

As you become familiar with the literature of social work and social welfare, you will find that the terms *social welfare policy* and *social policy* are often used interchangeably. This practice can be misleading because the terms do not have exactly the same meaning. Social welfare policy is a subcategory of social policy, which has a broader and more general meaning. David Gil (1992), for example, uses the term *social welfare policy* to refer to societal responses to specific needs or problems such as poverty, child maltreatment, substandard housing, and so forth, and uses *social policy* to refer to efforts to "shape the overall quality of life in a society, the living conditions of its members, and their relations to one another and to society as a whole" (p. 3). In a similar fashion, Hartley Dean (2012) defines social policy as

> . . . the things you need to make life worth living: essential services, such as healthcare and education; a means of livelihood, such as a job and money; vital but intangible things, such as love and security. Now think about the ways in which these can be organized: by government and official bodies; through businesses, social groups, charities, local associations and churches; through neighbors, families and loved ones. Understanding these things is the stuff of social policy.

Martin Rein says that social policy is "not the social services alone, but the social purposes and consequences of agricultural, economic, manpower, fiscal, physical development, and social welfare policies that form the subject matter of social policy" (Dear, 1995; Gil, 1992; Rein, 1970).

The term *social policy* is frequently used in a philosophic sense. As Gil (1992) observes, when used in this sense, the term refers to the collective struggle to seek enduring social solutions to social problems and conveys a meaning almost the opposite of the term *rugged individualism.* When used in this sense, social policy is equated with the struggle for equality in social and economic life. The term *social policy,* as used by many theorists, "goes far beyond conventional social welfare policies and programs. . . . Core functions of social policies [are viewed as] the reduction of social inequalities through redistribution of claims, and access to resources, rights, and social opportunities" (Gil, 1992, p. 3). Much of British writing on social policy, notably that of Titmuss and Marshall, reflects the social policy as the social philosophy approach. These writers view social policy as synonymous with increasing government involvement in social life and the pursuit of greater equality, equity, and social justice (Blakemore, 1998).

Thus, *social policy* is a term that includes some elements that we exclude from our definition of *social welfare policy.* Items such as libraries, parks and recreation, and various aspects of the tax codes and of family law are included in the domain of social policy because they deal with the integrative system and the overall quality of life. The continuing struggle of humanity for equality is also a central feature of social policy discussions. Although these things are clearly related to *social welfare policy,* they are not central to the way we use the term in this text. We do not include these ideas in our definition of the domain of social welfare policy because they are not related to the problem of dependency or to specific categorical programs.

Social Welfare Policy as an Academic Discipline and a Social Work Curriculum Area

There is an additional complication for the social worker seeking to understand the term *social welfare policy:* The term has somewhat different meanings when used to refer to an area of academic inquiry as opposed to an area of the social work curriculum. As an area of academic inquiry, social welfare policy is a subfield of sociology, political science, history, economics, and—of course—social work. In addition, over the past decade or so, a number of academic schools and departments have emerged specifically for the study of policy; social welfare policy is a basic area of study in these schools. As the term *social welfare policy* is used in these disciplines, it refers nearly exclusively to the activities of government. In addition to the definitions cited earlier, scholars in these disciplines generally add something similar to the following:

- Public policy covers all areas in which governments make decisions: the economy, immigration, transportation, international relations, the military, the environment, health care, education, and social services. (Anderson, 2011, p. 3)
- Public policy is the combination of basic decisions, commitments, and actions made by those who hold or affect government positions of authority. (DiNitto, 2016, p. 2)
- Public policy is what governments do, why they do it, and the difference that it makes. (Dye, 2006, p. 11)
- Social welfare policy is anything the government chooses to do, or not to do, that affects the quality of life of its people (Gerston, 2004, p. 32). Although many social workers in the area of social welfare policy share the traditional academic definition, the term is often used by social workers in a broader fashion. As will be discussed in the next section, many social welfare services are provided by private nonprofit, many times religious, agencies. These agencies have policies that affect social workers and their clients and must be understood if social workers are to comprehend their working environments fully. Also, an increasing number of services are being provided by the profit-making sector. Day care for children, disabled adults, and the elderly; residential and foster care for children; home health services; behavioral health care; retirement and nursing homes; and low-income housing are only a few examples of rapidly growing social welfare services provided by the profit-making sector (Ryan, 1999). Scholars in traditional policy areas would be quick to point out that services provided by private nonprofit agencies and by private businesses often receive a portion of their funding from government programs and so should probably come under the heading of actions of government. This is true, but it is also true that the social workers employed by these organizations are not government employees, and the programs come under a wide range of policies that are entirely nongovernmental in nature.

The term *social welfare policy* also refers to a specific area of the professional social work curriculum. The accrediting body of social work programs is the Council on Social Work Education (CSWE). The Educational Policy and Accreditation Standards of CSWE, under the heading "Engage in Policy Practice," specifies that social workers

- are knowledgeable about policy formulation, analysis, implementation, and evaluation
- identify social policy at the local, state, and federal level that impacts well-being, service delivery, and access to social services
- assess how social welfare and economic policies impact the delivery of and access to social services
- apply critical thinking to analyze, formulate, and advocate for policies that advance human rights and social, economic, and environmental justice (CSWE, 2015, p. 8)

This definition encompasses the term *social welfare policy* as used in traditional academic disciplines but also contains tangential areas. Thus, in social work programs, it is not uncommon to find courses with titles such as The Social Work Profession or Social Welfare History included as part of the social welfare policy curriculum.

Also, in the social work curriculum, *social welfare policy* often refers to a practice method, *policy practice,* as defined in Chapter 1. Policy analysis, as taught in the traditional academic disciplines, is central to the method but additional, generally *interpersonal,* skills are also included that are usually not central to these other fields. Jansson (1994) identifies four basic policy practice skills needed by social workers:

> They need analytic skills to evaluate social problems and develop policy proposals, analyze the severity of specific problems, identify barriers to policy implementation, and develop strategies for assessing programs. They need political skills to gain and use power and to develop and implement political strategy. They need interactional skills to participate in task groups, such as committees and coalitions, and persuade other people to support specific policies. They need value-clarifying skills to identify and rank relevant principles when engaging in policy practice. (p. 25)

Thoughts for Social Work Practice

In what ways do you think policy practice skills are similar to, and in what ways different from, micro skills taught in social work practice classes?

These are skills familiar to anyone educated as a generalist social work practitioner, but they are applied in a different context. In a later work Jansson (2008) added negotiation as a specific skill needed by macro social work policy practitioners saying: "Macro policy advocates have to be effective negotiators. They need to make concessions that appear reasonable, yet they cannot be perceived as 'pushovers' who will always back down" (p. 158). This skill will be addressed in some detail in Chapter 13.

Social Workers Are Interested in Social Welfare Policy in All Sectors of the Economy

Although social welfare is generally thought of as the responsibility of government, keep in mind that the social welfare system in the United States grew out of activities of the private sector; the government assumed responsibility very reluctantly. It would not be an overstatement to say that the social work profession itself is a result of policies of private, voluntary, social welfare agencies. In the nineteenth century, private agencies joined to form Charity Organization Societies specifically for the purpose of developing policies and procedures that would rationalize dealing with the growing problem of dependency in large cities. Shortly thereafter, the agencies realized that a major barrier to the rationalization of philanthropy was the lack of qualified staff. The agencies then began to formulate policies for training and hiring personnel; this eventually resulted in the emergence of social work as a profession (Popple, 2018).

During the course of the last century, the government assumed a larger and larger role in the provision of social welfare services. However, the private sector still provides a significant proportion of services. The Organization for Economic Cooperation and Development (2011) reports that in 2011, the United States spent 19.6 percent of gross domestic product (GDP) on public social service programs and 9.2 percent of GDP for private social programs. Thus, the private sector of the economy still provides approximately 32 percent of all social welfare services and benefits, a very significant proportion (Kirkegaard, 2015, p. 3).

Private social service agencies have policies that affect their employees and clients in much the same manner as governmental policies. For example, the United Way organization has policies in every area that, to use our earlier definition of policy, set down principles, guidelines, and procedures that maximize uniformity in decision making for member agencies. Examples are policies that set criteria and procedures for an agency to become affiliated with the United Way, establish priorities for funding, establish financial accounting and reporting standards and procedures, and suggest personnel procedures and guidelines.

It is apparent that the private, for-profit sector is becoming increasingly important in the social welfare enterprise. Ryan (1999) observes that

> the real revolution is that the social service market is now accepting providers that have a decided for-profit bent. In marked contrast with earlier years, when for-profits were excluded from the social services—frowned upon as unfit partners for government—the public sector now sees business not as a pariah but as a role model. This radical transformation in public-sector attitudes has spurred—even dared—for-profits to move into the social services delivery system. (pp. 129–130)

For-profit nursing homes, adult and child day care, home health services, alcohol and drug treatment centers, managed-care mental health systems, phobic and eating disorder clinics—all have appeared on the scene in recent years. Like public and voluntary agencies, all these for-profit organizations have policies that affect clients and staff. As we will discuss in the chapters on physical and mental health, policies of profit-making agencies present a special concern to the social work profession because of the high potential for conflict between providing services that are in the best interest of the client and services that are most profitable for the organization.

There is a tendency to define policy as only public policy. To understand fully the context in which they practice, social workers need to understand the policies of all three sectors of the social welfare system and the interaction among them.

Eric Crama/Shutterstock

Social action activities are generally aimed at macrolevel policies.

The Multiple Levels of Social Welfare Policy

An additional point that needs to be dealt with before we can fully define social welfare policy is that policy exists on several levels. The policies at the various levels are referred to as macro-, mezzo-, and microlevel policies.

Macrolevel Policy

Macrolevel social welfare policy involves the broad laws, regulations, or guidelines that provide the basic framework for the provision of services and benefits. Most macrolevel policy is generated by the public and the private nonprofit sectors. The macrolevel policy arena we most commonly think of is the public sector, in which macrolevel policies take the form of laws and regulations. Examples are Title XX of the Social Security Act, the Americans with Disabilities Act, and the Older Americans Act. After passage, all of these acts were translated into detailed federal regulations that specify issues of implementation, evaluation, and so forth. The private nonprofit sector also generates macrolevel policies to guide its efforts to deal with problems of dependency. For example, the 200th General Assembly (1988) of the Presbyterian Church (U.S.A.) developed an eighty-three-page policy statement on health care that dealt with health care benefits for church employees and with the church's stand on the general problems of the health care system. The private for-profit sector responds to, and attempts to influence, macrolevel policies more than it generates such policies on its own.

Mezzolevel Policy

Mezzolevel (midlevel) policy is administrative policy that organizations generate to direct and regularize their operations. Every social worker who has ever worked for a state social services department is familiar with the ritual followed with new employees: A supervisor will help a new employee pull up three or four lengthy manuals on the organization's website with instructions to spend the day reviewing them. There will generally be a personnel policy manual, which sets out all the rules and regulations regarding pay, benefits, insurance, office hours, holidays, evaluations, grievances, retirement, and the like. Then there will be a financial policy manual, which outlines procedures and forms for budgeting, purchasing, travel, supplies, financial reporting, and so on. Finally, there will be one or more manuals outlining the policies governing the particular program area in which the social worker is employed. For example, the Supplemental Nutrition Assistance Program (SNAP), or food stamp, program will have manuals describing intake, eligibility, recordkeeping, what is and is not appropriate to discuss with an applicant, referrals, and so forth.

Much of mezzolevel policy is, of course, in direct response to macrolevel policy. For example, SNAP (food stamps), as set out in federal regulations, requires that state welfare departments respond to an application within thirty days, except in cases in which the family is expected to have an income for the month of less than $150 and less than $100 in cash and savings, in which case the department must respond within seven days. The macrolevel federal regulations containing this policy are sent to the state agencies, which must translate it into mezzolevel policy by setting out specific procedures so the department can comply with the policy of the federal Food and Nutrition Service.

Microlevel Policy

Microlevel policy is what happens when individuals such as social workers translate macro- and mezzolevel policy into actual service to clients. As we discussed in Chapter 1, social work is a profession with a good deal of autonomy, which means individual social workers have great latitude for interpreting and implementing a given policy. The political scientist Michael Lipsky (2010) refers to social workers as "street-level bureaucrats" who, he says, "make policy in two related respects. They exercise wide discretion in decisions about citizens with whom they interact. Then, when taken in concert, their individual actions add up to agency behavior" (p. 17). Recognizing the importance of microlevel policymaking rests on the following question: If Congress passes a law stating that individuals are entitled to a certain benefit (macrolevel policy) and state and local agencies develop regulations and procedures for delivering the benefit (mezzolevel policy), but the social workers charged with delivering the benefit do not support the policy and obstruct the process to an extent that few people actually receive the benefit, what actually is the policy? The policy is that people do not get the benefit.

The following example illustrates the importance of microlevel policy far better than any theoretical discussion. One of the authors was at one time the training director for a large region of a state social services department. He would periodically get requests from the state office to conduct training for the food stamps program staff on eligibility policy. The request would be the result of complaints from college students who had applied for food stamps and whose applications had dragged on and on over one technicality after another, in spite of the fact that the macro- and mezzolevel policies clearly stated that college students who met other eligibility requirements were eligible to receive food stamps. The problem, however, had nothing to do with the staff not *understanding* eligibility policy. Rather, the eligibility determination workers tended to be women who, due to one life situation or another (marriage, pregnancy, husband becoming unemployed, etc.), had dropped out of college after two years (the amount of college required for a food stamps eligibility worker position) and taken a job with the department of social services in order to support their families. The attitude of the workers in this particular office was "When I needed money, I dropped out of school and got a job; I didn't expect the government to support me." They collectively felt that the policy of making college students eligible for food stamps was wrong. As a result, they had developed techniques to discourage applications from this group, and if a student persisted in applying, the workers would do everything possible to slow the process further. The result? The actual policy in this particular office was that college students were not eligible for food stamps.

Many people would say that the existence of microlevel policy significantly different from macro- and mezzolevel policy is an indication of bad management. Effective management should be able to bring individual practice into line with organization policy. Due to the nature of their work, however, this is not possible with social workers. As Lipsky (2010) observes, because problems resulting from microlevel policy

> would theoretically disappear if workers' discretion were eliminated, one may wonder why discretion remains characteristic of their jobs. The answer is that certain characteristics of the jobs of street-level bureaucrats make it difficult, if not impossible, to severely reduce discretion. They involve complex tasks for which elaboration of rules, guidelines, or instructions cannot circumscribe the alternatives. (p. 32)

This situation is the result of two factors: "First, street-level bureaucrats often work in situations too complicated to reduce to programmatic formats . . . [and] second, street-level bureaucrats work in situations that often require responses to the human dimensions of situations" that are too varied and complex to reduce to routinized procedures (Lipsky, 2010, p. 24).

Recognition of the existence of microlevel policy provides one of the strongest arguments for the promotion of policy-driven professions such as social work. If the performance of workers cannot be controlled by standardized work rules, as is the natural practice in bureaucracies, then controls must be internal to the workers. The most effective means of developing these internal controls is through professional training and socialization in certain values and a code of ethics. The food stamps eligibility workers described here, incidentally, were not professional social workers. At one time they would have been, but in the late 1960s, in what was known as separation of services, eligibility functions in welfare departments were redesignated from professional social work positions to high-level clerical jobs. One of the rationales for this change was that social workers exercised too much individual discretion and that clerical-level staff would be more amenable to organizational control. The result appears to have been the creation of a workforce that is effectively under the control of neither organizational rules nor professional ethics and standards of behavior.

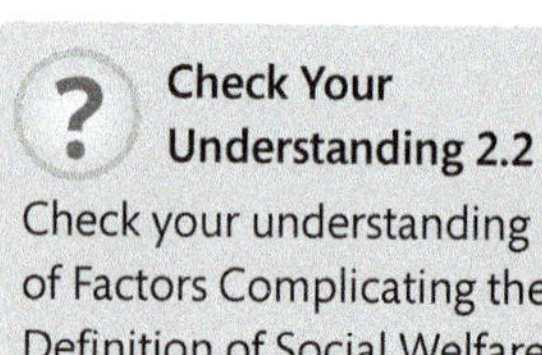

Check Your Understanding 2.2

Check your understanding of Factors Complicating the Definition of Social Welfare Policy by taking this brief quiz.

SOCIAL WELFARE POLICY—A WORKING DEFINITION

By now it should be apparent that there is no one correct (or incorrect, for that matter) definition of *social welfare policy.* The term is broad and general, and its definition is similar to the story of the blind people describing an elephant—how you define it depends on which part you are in contact with. The upshot is that it is crucial for people addressing the subject of social welfare policy to be clear on how they are using the term. For our purposes in this text, we will use the following definition:

> Social welfare policy concerns those interrelated, but not necessarily logically consistent, principles, guidelines, and procedures designed to deal with the problem of dependency in our society. Policies may be laws, public or private regulations, formal procedures, or simply normatively sanctioned patterns of behavior. Social welfare policy is a subset of social policy. Social welfare policy as an academic discipline is less concerned with specific policies than it is with the process by which those policies came into being, the societal base and effects of those policies, and the relationship between policies. Those studying social welfare policy as an area of the professional social work curriculum share the concerns of the traditional academic disciplines but have as primary concerns the relationship of policy to social work practice and the ways that social workers, both as individuals and as members of an organized profession, can influence the policy process.

Check Your Understanding 2.3

Check your understanding of Social Welfare Policy—A Working Definition by taking this brief quiz.

CONCLUSION

This text is aimed mainly at people training to be direct-service social work practitioners. Therefore, our major goal is to help develop skills of policy analysis that will enable practitioners to understand and, when possible, affect the policy context of their practice. We will pay a great deal of attention to macrolevel policy in the public sector because this is the area having the greatest effect on social work practice. However, we will also devote significant attention to mezzo- and microlevel policy, in recognition of their great impact on social work practice, and to the influence of the voluntary sector and for-profit sector policy.

Recall what you learned from this chapter by completing the Chapter Review.

Part Two

Social Welfare Policy Analysis

In Part One, we sought to identify policy as central to the social work profession and to define the term. It logically follows that if policy is as important as we assert, then it is important to develop systematic means of studying and understanding policy in all its dimensions. This is the goal of Part Two. We begin by discussing what policy analysis is (a very slippery subject in its own right), and then move on to discuss the analysis of various dimensions of social welfare policy. We will basically follow the outline presented below. Before you become overwhelmed with the level of detail presented, note that we are presenting this as a way of simplifying the immensely complex subject of policy analysis, not as a model to be actually applied in all its detail by a social work practitioner. This outline can be applied at any level of detail, from one very specific policy (i.e., the Older Americans Act) to a general policy area (i.e., social welfare policies enacted to deal with the problems of elderly citizens). It is not always necessary to apply the whole framework in every policy analysis; policy analysts in the real world selectively apply various parts of the outline, guided by the specific policy they are concerned with and the purpose of the analysis. In Part Three of this book, we will demonstrate how practitioner policy analyses are done, using examples from poverty, aging, health, mental health, substance abuse, and child welfare.

POLICY ANALYSIS OUTLINE

I. Delineation and Overview of the Policy under Analysis
- A. What is the specific policy or general policy area to be analyzed?
- B. What is the nature of the problem targeted by the policy?
  1. How is the problem defined?
  2. For whom is it a problem?
- C. What is the context of the policy being analyzed (i.e., how does this specific policy fit with other policies seeking to manage a social problem)?
- D. Choice analysis (i.e., what is the design of programs created by a policy and what are the alternatives to this design?)
  1. What are the bases of social allocation?
  2. What are the types of social provisions?
  3. What are the strategies for delivery of benefits?
  4. What are the methods of financing these provisions?

II. Historical Analysis
- A. What policies and programs were previously developed to deal with the problem? In other words, how has this problem been dealt with in the past?
- B. How has the specific policy/program under analysis developed over time?
  1. What people, or groups of people, initiated and/or promoted the policy?
  2. What people, or groups of people, opposed the policy?

C. What does history tell us about effective/ineffective approaches to the problem being addressed?

D. To what extent does the current policy/program incorporate the lessons of history?

III. Social Analysis

A. Problem description

1. How complete is our knowledge of the problem?
2. Are our efforts to deal with the problem in accord with research findings?
3. What population is affected by the problem?
   a. Size
   b. Defining characteristics
   c. Distribution
4. What theory or theories of human behavior are explicit or, more likely, implicit in the policy?
5. What are the major social values related to the problem, and what value conflicts exist?
6. What are the goals of the policy under analysis?
   a. Manifest (stated) goals
   b. Latent (unstated) goals
   c. Degree of consensus regarding goals
7. What are the hypotheses implicit or explicit in the statement of the problem and goals?

IV. Economic Analysis

A. What are the effects and/or potential effects of the policy on the functioning of the economy as a whole—output, income, inflation, unemployment, and so forth (macroeconomic analysis)?

B. What are the effects and/or potential effects of the policy on the behavior of individuals, firms, and markets—motivation to work, cost of rent, supply of commodities, and so forth (microeconomic analysis)?

C. Opportunity cost; cost/benefit analysis

V. Political Analysis

A. Who are the major stakeholders regarding this particular policy/program?

1. What is the power base of the policy/program's supporters?
2. What is the power base of the policy/program's opponents?
3. How well are the policy's/program's intended beneficiaries represented in the ongoing development and implementation of the policy/program?

B. How has the policy/program been legitimized? Is this basis for legitimation still current?

C. To what extent is the policy/program an example of rational decision making, incremental change, or change brought about by conflict?

D. What are the political aspects of the implementation of the policy/program?

VI. Policy/Program Evaluation

A. What are the outcomes of the policy/program in relation to the stated goals?

B. What are the unintended consequences of the policy/program?

C. Is the policy/program cost-effective?

VII. Current Proposals for Policy Reform

3

Social Welfare Policy Analysis

Monkey Business Images/Shutterstock

Marian Mochozuki has been awarded a contract by her state Department of Mental Health to evaluate an experimental program to provide supported employment for people with developmental disabilities. Instead of working with high-functioning clients in sheltered workshops, the program will attempt to place the lowest-functioning clients in real jobs, for real pay in real community businesses. There will be job coaches at the work sites. Pay will be adjusted according to the efficiency of the worker using Department of Labor standards so that the employer will not be subsidizing the workers. Otherwise this will be real work in the community, not "work activities."

Marian believes in full participation of program staff in the design, execution, and interpretation of the evaluation. The first step will be a discussion with program staff to find out their perceptions of what they are trying to accomplish and their criteria for success. This may sound unnecessary because the project has a mission statement in writing, but Marian knows that sometimes there is a discrepancy between what staff members think they are doing and what the mission statement says they are

LEARNING OUTCOMES

- Distinguish between "universal" and "selective" provision in the allocation of benefits provided by a social policy.
- Differentiate among the seven approaches to policy analysis.
- List four examples of "in-kind" benefits.
- Discuss the advantages and perils of "contracting out" public services.
- Differentiate between "process" and "outcome" in the conduct of a program evaluation.

CHAPTER OUTLINE

supposed to be doing. Staff members are unlikely to buy into the evaluation unless they know that the evaluators understand their work.

The evaluation will involve both quantitative and qualitative methods. The quantitative data will be collected by questionnaires to be filled out monthly. This is extra work for staff workers, so it is important that they believe it is worthwhile. Marion has worked with evaluators who regard program staff as cattle to be herded into the barn and milked. Under those circumstances, the data produced can be sloppy, incomplete, or even false. Therefore, when she pilot-tests the instrument with a sample of the staff, Marian adds after every question another question: "Is this information useful to you?" She tries as much as possible to trim the items to those generally regarded as useful.

To supply qualitative data, open-ended interviews will be conducted on-site with a sample of program participants, their parents, job coaches, the job recruiter, and employers. Marian will also try to find an employer who was asked to participate and declined. This will provide insight into the obstacles faced by the program in the community. Interviewing participants whose IQ is unmeasurable in many cases and who may or may not talk is a challenge, but an attempt will be made. Interviewing parents may seem less problematic, but there are challenges there as well. Marian knows that parents are going to be reluctant to criticize the program. They have a major stake in the program's continued operation. If it is closed down, their son or daughter will have lost an important opportunity. And this is not a market situation: There is no other place to go. So criticisms will be elicited carefully.

After the evaluators have done a preliminary analysis of the data, a conference will be held to report their findings to program staff. This must be built into the evaluation budget, not organized on the fly. Staff members may well have different interpretations, and these will be discussed at the conference. Evaluators will take them into consideration when they submit their final report.

Thoughts for Social Work Practice

Why is it important that those being evaluated fully support the evaluation? Beyond what was done in Marian's evaluation, can you think of other ways to gain a buy-in from program staff being evaluated? How might managers, staff members, clients, and community members have different interpretations of the data? What do you think the maximum length of a questionnaire should be?

Sometimes a policy study appears that is so interesting and well written that people read it for relaxation and enjoyment. Joseph Stiglitz's (2012) *The Price of Inequality* is one example. This, unfortunately, is a rare occurrence. Generally, people read policy literature for practical reasons, namely, to gain an understanding of the dynamics of our collective response to various social problems. Policy analyses are read to answer questions such as: How do we deal with poverty? What do we do about health care for people who are sick but have no insurance and no money? What is being done to help children who are being mistreated? Is our response to drug abuse the best one and, if not, what other options are available?

When you seek the answers to questions such as these, you will first consult the policy analysis literature. Two aspects of this literature will puzzle you, at least initially. First, you will notice that the policy analysis literature is spread all over the library. Some are shelved, as you would expect, with the social work literature. You probably won't be too surprised to find some policy material with sociology, political science, history, and economics. A small amount, less predictably, will be with business, and a rather substantial amount will be with religion and philosophy.

Second, once you have ferreted out sources on a policy issue (for example, on antipoverty policy), you will find that, though different sources deal with the same topic, the approaches look very different. Some policy analyses look like literature, being composed mostly of stories. Some look like mathematics texts, with lengthy and complex formulas, tables, and graphs. Some look like stories in a newspaper or magazine (in fact, may *be* stories in newspapers and magazines). To help prevent the confusion you may experience in simply identifying and locating sources of policy analysis, we must discuss the policy analysis field.

THE MANY MEANINGS OF POLICY ANALYSIS

Like most terms and concepts in the study of social welfare policy, the term *policy analysis* tends to be used in vague and inconsistent ways. David Bobrow and John Dryzek (1987) refer to the policy analysis field as "home to a babel of tongues." The late Aaron Wildavsky, a leading figure in the policy analysis field, argued that it is unwise to even try to define the term, saying, "At the Graduate School of Public Policy in Berkeley, I discouraged discussions on the meaning of policy analysis. Hundreds of conversations on this slippery subject had proven futile, even exasperating, possibly dangerous" (Wildavsky 1979, pp. 2, 3, 16). He referred to policy analysis as that which "could be learned but not explained, that all of us could sometimes do but that none of us could ever define." Although we sympathize with Wildavsky's frustration, we believe that, at least for social workers whose primary interest is not policy, it is necessary to deal with the term before any progress can be made in learning policy analysis skills. The definition we like is based on the one offered by the Canadian political scientist Leslie Pal (2006): "Policy analysis is the disciplined application of intellect to the study of collective responses to public problems." This definition is sufficiently broad to include the wide range of policy analysis approaches we describe but is still precise enough to exclude many other types of social work knowledge-building activities.

A key to defining and dealing with the term *policy analysis* is the recognition that it is broad and general. In many ways, it is analogous to the term *research,* which we all realize means many different things depending on how it is used by different people in different contexts. We all recognize the difference between a husband saying to his wife, "We need to do some research on state parks before we plan our summer vacation," and a social worker saying, "I have received a $250,000 grant to do research on the relationship between drug usage and marital instability." In a similar fashion, the term *policy analysis* is used to refer to everything from the processes citizens use to familiarize themselves with issues prior to voting, to a multiyear, multimillion-dollar project to set up and evaluate programs using different approaches to financial assistance.

Table 3.1 presents a typology for categorizing different approaches to policy analysis. The table identifies four major dimensions on which policy analysis approaches vary. The first is the sophistication required of the person conducting the analysis. From the top of the table downward, the sophistication required diminishes. For the top two types, academic social science research and applied policy research, the analyst is generally educated at the doctoral level in policy analysis or in a related social science or applied social profession such as public administration or social work. These analysts generally spend a large proportion of their time conducting policy studies that are read and critiqued by other policy researchers and/or by actual policymakers. Because their purpose is to create new knowledge, the results are generally published in fairly accessible sources. These may range from books and articles available in a good library to proceedings of professional conferences that may be widely circulated; to monographs and reports available in microform and on the Internet; to photocopied in-house reports, which are less widely distributed. Because of the rigorous nature of the methods and the wide availability of results of these types of analyses, they often form the database for other approaches to policy analysis.

The next two approaches, social planning and agency planning/policy management, are generally conducted by professionals educated at the master's or doctoral level in applied social professions, often social work. They generally have specialized in

Table 3.1 Approaches to Policy Analysis

Policy Analysis Approach	Purpose	Consumer	Method
Academic social science research	Constructing theories for understanding society	Academic community	Rigorous empirical methodology, often quantitative
Applied policy research	Predicting or evaluating impacts of changes in variables that can be altered by public and/or private programs	Decision makers in the policy area	Formal research methodology applied to policy-relevant questions
Social planning	Defining and specifying ways to ameliorate social problems and to achieve a desirable future state	The "public interest" as professionally defined	Survey research, public forums, expert and/or citizen panels
Agency planning/ policy management	Defining and clarifying agency goals; explicating alternatives for achieving those goals; evaluating outcomes of attempts to achieve those goals	Boards of directors, funding agencies, interested citizens	Databases, management techniques (Program Evaluation Research Technique, flow charting, decision analysis), survey research, public forums, expert and/or citizen panels
Journalistic	Focusing public attention on social welfare problems	General public	Existing documents, expert sources (professionals, scholars, people affected by the problem)
Practitioner policy analysis	Understanding the policy context within which an individual social worker functions	The social worker doing the analysis	Existing literature, government and other documents available on the Internet, expert sources
Citizen policy analysis	Clarifying issues for participation as an involved citizen in a democracy	The citizen involved in the analysis of elected officials that citizen wishes to influence	Existing literature, elected and appointed officials

Source: Adapted from D. L. Weiner and A. R. Vining, *Policy Analysis: Concepts and Practice*, 4th ed. (Upper Saddle River, NJ: Pearson/Prentice Hall, 2004), p. 26.

policy/planning/administration in graduate school. Policy analysis usually constitutes only a small proportion of their jobs, with most of their time being devoted to running an agency, coordinating a community social service program, monitoring program compliance, or any of a number of other macropractice roles. The results of these analyses are generally published in-house and are distributed to members of the organization employing the analyst as well as interested community persons.

The next two types are journalistic and practitioner policy analysis. The people who do these analyses generally are not educated specifically in policy analysis, and policy research is only tangential to their primary professional role. However, they need to develop a fairly sophisticated understanding of complex policy issues. The journalist needs to communicate with the general public, and the social work practitioner needs to understand relevant policy in order to function effectively on a daily basis. Journalistic policy analysis is generally presented in either written or electronic form in the public media and is generally based entirely on the work of academic social science researchers or applied policy researchers, usually supplemented by original reporting on the effects (both intended and unintended) of policies on beneficiaries. It is important to note that, although journalistic policy analysis is not based on original research, this in no way detracts from its importance. The inspiration for the massive social programs of the Kennedy and Johnson administrations in the 1960s is generally credited to an essay review of several policy studies, notably Michael Harrington's *The Other America* (1962), written by journalist Dwight McDonald (1963) and published in *New Yorker Magazine*. Randy Shilts's *And the Band Played On: Politics, People, and the AIDS Epidemic* (1987) has had a significant impact on AIDS policy. Practitioner policy analysis is the focus of the remainder of this text, so it won't be described further here.

The lowest level of sophistication is that of the citizen analyst. The purpose of this type of analysis is for a person to obtain the information required to carry out the responsibilities of an informed citizen. Although we classify this as the least sophisticated approach to policy analysis, we should note that many citizens become quite skilled in studying policy. This type of analysis is the major focus of voluntary citizen groups such as the League of Women Voters.

The next three dimensions of the approaches to policy analysis (purpose, consumer, and method) are sufficiently explained in the table. The main point is that, when you read policy analysis literature, you need to identify which approach to analysis the author is using. Most of the literature concerns the top two levels of sophistication and is generally read by people who identify themselves as policy analysis professionals. This literature can be frustrating for the social work practitioner who has neither the time nor the inclination to become skilled in the application of highly sophisticated, often mathematical, techniques such as difference equations, queuing models, simulations, Markov chains, and the like. Fortunately, in recent years a literature has been developing that addresses the needs of practitioners (Chambers & Wedel, 2013; Irwin, 2003; Hudson, Lowe, & Horsfall, 2016).

Check Your Understanding 3.1

Check your understanding of The Many Meanings of Policy Analysis by taking this brief quiz.

METHODS OF POLICY ANALYSIS

In addition to different approaches to policy analysis, different methods may be employed within any of the approaches. A number of different schemes have been developed for differentiating among methods of policy analysis. Our discussion categorizes policy analysis as descriptive analysis, process analysis, or evaluation (Gilbert & Terrell, 2013; Pal, 1987).

Descriptive Analysis

Descriptive policy analysis can be further subdivided into four types: content, choice, comparative, and historical analysis.

Content Analysis

Content analysis is the most straightforward type of policy analysis. This is not the type of content analysis where qualitative data in texts are subjected to quantitative analysis. It is simply a description of an existing policy in terms of its intentions, problem definition, goals, and means employed for achieving the goals. Content analysis is most often employed by agencies charged with administering a policy and is generally published in manuals, brochures, and annual reports of the agency. Occasionally, special interest groups such as the National Association of Retired Persons will publish content analyses of policies under which members may receive benefits.

Content analysis is generally not widely circulated to the general public and rarely is published in standard academic outlets. One of the most accessible, and certainly the most useful, sources of content analysis is the *Green Book* (House Committee on Ways and Means, 2016), which is available on the House of Representatives Committee on Ways and Means website. It provides descriptive information about federal assistance programs under the jurisdiction of the Ways and Means Committee, such as Social Security, Medicare, Supplemental Security Income, Unemployment Insurance, Railroad Benefits, Trade Adjustment Assistance, Temporary Assistance for Needy Families, Child Support Enforcement, Child Care, Social Services Block Grant, Child Welfare, and the Pension Benefit Guaranty Corporation. In addition, the *Green Book* has appendices covering Federal Benefits and Services for People with Low Income, Social Welfare Programs in the Territories, Federal Benefits for Noncitizens, and Poverty.

Choice Analysis

Largely developed by social workers Neil Gilbert, Paul Terrell, and the late Harry Specht, choice analysis is a systematic process of looking at the options available to planners for dealing with a social welfare problem. Gilbert and Terrell (2013) describe this type of analysis as dealing with choices that "may be framed in program proposals, laws and statutes, or standing plans which eventually are transformed into programs. The elements of this framework, of course, are not physical structures of the sort a microscope might reveal. Rather, they are social constructs that are used in the intellectual process of making choices" (pp. 42–43). The four primary dimensions of choice are described in some detail below.

Bases of allocations The first dimension of choice involves the following question: *What are the bases of social allocations?* Gilbert and Terrell use the phrase "social allocations" to describe decisions about who will benefit from a policy. They draw two major distinctions in allocation: universal and selective provision. In the first case, "benefits [are] made available to an entire population as a social right" (Gilbert & Terrell, 2013, p. 710). Universalism assumes that all citizens are "at risk," at some point, for common problems. The classic exam of universal benefits is Social Security for the elderly and those with disability. Unemployment insurance is another example of a benefit made available to an entire group of people—those who have worked a specified length of time and are now unemployed. Since the 1930s, provision for these groups of people has been considered a basic right and therefore a responsibility of the government. Eligibility depends solely on characteristics such as age and prior attachment to the workforce. Factors such as present income or geographic location are irrelevant.

The alternative to universal allocation is selectivity. In the language of social welfare policy, *selectivity* has a specialized meaning: the allocation of benefits based on individual economic need. This is generally determined through an income test (called a "means test"); those below a certain income level are eligible to receive benefits. Students often get confused about this concept because *selectivity* suggests a variety of ways to distinguish who will be provided for (such as all mothers of young children, all nearsighted people, or all intelligent high school students seeking college scholarships). The best way to understand selectivity in social welfare is to remember its tie to income level and the fact that there is no national consensus that the benefits are a fundamental right of the recipient.

Social welfare policymakers also speak of "universal versus categorical" distinctions. In this context, the word *categorical* refers to particular groups of poor people, for example, low-income women and children, elderly individuals, or those with handicaps. Public welfare benefits and Supplemental Security Income (SSI) are examples of categorical public assistance programs. Because these programs are based on need, they are also considered a selective approach to allocating benefits.

There are many arguments for and against each type of approach. The universal basis of allocation carries relatively little stigma and fits with democratic notions of equal treatment for all. It also provides political support; everybody benefits. Recipients can be seen as citizens or consumers. Programs for particular subsections of the population are more vulnerable. Groups who vote regularly and have their own advocacy organizations can protect their programs. Groups who participate less in the political process and who have fewer resources, for example, low-income people, are more likely to see their programs sacrificed when budget cuts are proposed.

Proponents of selectivity herald its cost-effectiveness; instead of resources being spread over a vast population, money or services can be used where they are most needed. This can help fill in the gaps between needy and non-needy groups. Debates over the future shape of Social Security in our society involve these issues, with some observers suggesting that we should stop paying Social Security to those who don't need it and instead target more money to the less-well-off elderly.

Critics of selectivity argue, however, that it may be more cost-effective to provide social welfare benefits across the board rather than to spend time and money sorting out those who are "truly disadvantaged." These critics add that selectivity leads to a two-track system; benefits for low-income groups don't seem as important to society as benefits for the majority and are thus allowed to be of lesser quality. This was one argument in the recent health care reform debate; the system people can afford to pay for (on their own or through insurance) is often superior to publicly financed health care for everyone (see Chapter 9).

The broad universal–selective distinction is perhaps most helpful in discussing government income maintenance programs such as Social Security and Temporary Assistance to Needy Families. Within the wide variety of social welfare programs, however, there are additional ways of allocating benefits. For example, benefits can be provided to groups of people with specific common needs that are not met in the economic market. Such groups might include high school dropouts or the residents of a deteriorated urban neighborhood. Another principle of allocation is compensation; this is based on membership in a group, such as war veterans, that has made a specific contribution to society. Veterans' benefits are generally made available to individuals without regard to economic need. Finally, people may qualify for assistance through technical diagnosis of a condition such as a physical handicap or mental illness. Table 3.2, developed by Gilbert and Terrell, gives a good example of various bases for allocations of benefits.

Types of benefits The second dimension of choice is concerned with the following question: *What are the types of social benefits to be provided?* A traditional way of categorizing types of provision is to distinguish between "in-cash" or "in-kind" benefits. Monthly unemployment checks are a good example of the former. Indirect forms of cash benefits, although not often viewed as such, include tax credits and exemptions such as the homeowner's deduction for mortgage interest (Huttman, 1981). Benefits-in-kind are actual goods or services. They include items such as used clothing from the Salvation Army, free inoculations for schoolchildren, and subsidized housing. Social

Table 3.2 Alternative Bases for Allocation of Day Care Services

Conditions of Eligibility	Alternative Criteria for Allocations
Attributed need	All families Single-parent families Families with student parents
Compensation	Minority families Military families Families of workers in specified occupational groups
Diagnostic differentiation	Families with special needs children Families in short-term crises situations
Means-tested need	Families whose earnings and resources fall beneath a low income standard

Source: Neil Gilbert and Paul Terrell, *Dimensions of Social Welfare Policy*, 8th ed. (Boston, MA: Pearson, 2013), p. 117. Reprinted/Adapted by permission.

services (for example, counseling, job training, or referrals) are a special type of in-kind benefit.

As in the case of universal and selective bases of allocation, policymakers debate the merits of cash versus in-kind benefits. Cash benefits are credited with allowing the recipient to maintain some sense of choice and control, a feature held to be important both in a democracy and a market economy. In-kind benefits, especially concrete goods, can be seen as undermining an individual's dignity and sense of responsibility. A familiar example is the Christmas basket for the poor, which may be perceived by recipients as a demeaning and patronizing type of assistance.

An advantage attributed to benefits-in-kind is the ability to ensure that the provisions will be used exactly as intended. Parents won't be tempted to "drink the welfare money"; a box of surplus foodstuffs will feed the family, whereas a food allowance might be absorbed into the general household income. These arguments imply that recipients, for whatever reasons, make unwise choices. A different, less judgmental, justification for in-kind benefits stresses efficiency and economy of scale, as in the publicly funded school lunch program.

Vouchers constitute a compromise between the two types of benefits. These are used like cash but are targeted for particular purchases. The Section 8 program, for example, uses housing vouchers that guarantee that the government will pay the landlord a part of a family's rent. Vouchers are touted both for providing freedom of choice in a particular commodity or service area and for ensuring that the benefit is used as intended. However, the notion of freedom of choice may be illusory, as when housing discrimination prevents minority families from using their vouchers in certain neighborhoods, or when there just isn't enough housing, which is increasingly the case. Some voucher systems, such as food stamps (now called the Supplemental Nutritional Assistance Program [SNAP]), are more successful, although even here individuals can encounter stigma as they proceed through the grocery checkout line.

Experiments in vouchers for private schools have attracted a good deal of attention. President George W. Bush was a champion of the use of vouchers, although Congress did not support his 2002 proposal to provide federal vouchers for poor students in "failing" schools. Some states and cities have established their own voucher programs.

Polls indicate that many Americans like the idea of vouchers, although support weakens if funding for them would decrease money for public schools (Schlomo, 2001). So far, research on the use of vouchers for children attending substandard public schools has failed to yield "conclusive evidence that these programs consistently improve student achievement" (Zernike, 2002).

Critics of publicly funded vouchers include not only those worried about funding of public schools but also African American parents who are skeptical about the acceptance of their children in white suburban schools. The fact that vouchers are often used for attendance at religious schools is another concern. In 2002, a close decision of the U.S. Supreme Court upheld the state of Ohio's publicly financed voucher program, even though nearly all the vouchers were used for religious schools. Decisive as the ruling seemed, policy analysts noted at the time that it might not translate into widespread use of vouchers because opposition to them in other states would continue and because private and parochial schools lacked the space to accommodate all applicants. In fact, in 2006 the Florida Supreme Court struck down a voucher program for students attending failing schools. The court based its ruling on the fact that the state constitution barred Florida from using taxpayer money to finance a private alternative to the public system. The lawyer speaking against the voucher system represented the NAACP; the American Civil Liberties Union (ACLU); and the Florida Education System, the state's largest teachers' union. He argued that the state was paying for the "religious indoctrination of young children." The ruling ordered the end of a program that Governor Jeb Bush had considered one of his chief accomplishments.

As in housing vouchers, discrimination against minorities and the poor will probably persist. In Ohio, for example, suburban schools had to agree to accept voucher students, yet none of them did. In Colorado, the state supreme court upheld vouchers, although the American Civil Liberties Union is currently challenging that state's school voucher program, arguing that it violates the state constitution because it provides public money to religious schools ("Colorado School Voucher Ruling Appealed," 2013; Dillon, 2002; Follick, 2005; Pierre, 2002; Steinberg, 2002).

Indiana has one of the nation's largest and fastest-growing school voucher programs in the country. It was supposed to allow students to escape underperforming schools. Yet in 2016, five years after it started, 52 percent of voucher recipients were never in public schools. Thus, state taxpayers are covering tuition expenses previously borne by families to the tune of $53 million. Only 3 percent of recipients came from failing schools. This may be because private schools can set their own admissions requirements. Instead of promoting diversity, vouchers seem to be increasing segregation. The first Trump budget allocated $20 billion to school choice, and President Trump has appointed a secretary of education, Betsy DeVos, whose primary commitment is to private and religious schools (Brown & McLaren, 2016; Bendix, 2017).

One further distinction in benefits occurs most frequently in, but is not limited to, the area of services. Receipt of services such as counseling or medical care can be voluntary or mandatory. Court-ordered therapy for people who abuse children may have a different success rate than that chosen more or less freely by a client (we say "more or less" because the decision to seek counseling may well be influenced by family, peers, or others). Social workers struggle these days with decisions over voluntary versus mandatory services in a number of areas. For example, should we force people living on the street to enter shelters or insist that emotionally withdrawn nursing home residents join in the daily crafts class?

Delivery structure The third dimension of choice is concerned with *the structure of the delivery system*. After the "who" and "what" questions have been resolved, this set of policy choices is about how services or benefits will be delivered. There are a variety of administrative or organizational structures for doing this. A key distinction is the degree of centralization and/or coordination within the system. Will benefits be provided by a variety of agencies with little coordination, or will they be brought together, either under one roof or through an interorganizational network? Children's services are an example of a decentralized system in many states: Foster care and protective services are handled through a public child welfare department; adoption programs are carried out through both public and private agencies; and children's health care is provided in public health departments, school clinics, and private doctors' offices. These separate organizations may have little interaction with one another. Even within a single agency, the various programs and departments may operate relatively autonomously. Gilbert and Terrell (2013) note that with the funding reductions in recent years, many of these choices are now directed toward strategies for rationing services and for contracting publicly funded services to private agencies.

One way to centralize services is to link them within one organization. For example, a shelter for homeless families might provide job counseling, health care, day care for children, recreation programs, and a public welfare office branch all within one facility, stressing careful coordination between units. Another approach linking the programs of various agencies is utilized in the field of gerontology. Publicly funded local area agencies on aging are responsible for area-wide planning of social services for the elderly, for monitoring local programs affecting the elderly, and for coordination of specific federal programs.

Centralized or coordinated systems are often more convenient for clients to use, can allow for comprehensive planning of benefits, and tend to lessen duplication of services. On the other hand, centralization (in particular) usually involves a more complex bureaucracy, increasing the distance between clients and administrators (Chambers & Wedel, 2005). Decentralized or less-coordinated systems generally increase autonomy and diversity in mission and approach, and may lead to a competition among programs that may increase quality. In implementing policy, planners have to decide which type of structure is best in meeting policy goals.

There are many other features of delivery system structure that policymakers must consider. These include the degree of citizen participation in program decisions, the types of employees used to provide benefits (professionals, nonprofessionals, or consumers), and ways of relating to racial and ethnic needs (Gilbert & Terrell, 2013). A particularly important distinction among the organizations providing benefits exists between public and private agencies. We turn to that distinction in the following discussion of modes of finance.

Financing benefits The final dimension of choice analysis relates to decisions on *how benefits are financed*. This can be done in a variety of ways: through taxation, voluntary contributions, or fees. Federal, state, and local taxation is, of course, a public levy on citizens; it supports public social welfare programs such as public assistance, Social Security (through a special payroll tax), public health programs, and services to veterans. Voluntary contributions are charitable donations to private agencies or programs. Local giving is often coordinated by United Way or Community Fund organizations. Fees for services are charged by both private nonprofit and for-profit agencies and occasionally by public agencies.

Social welfare benefits are provided by public governmental organizations on federal, state, and local levels; by private nonprofit or voluntary agencies; and by private for-profit groups. The last two decades have seen rapid growth in entrepreneurial social welfare services run on a corporate model. Important examples of these human services corporations include for-profit psychiatric and medical hospitals, home health care systems for the elderly, child care programs, foster care provision, and job training and job placement programs for welfare recipients (Jimenez, 1993).

The social policy picture would be much simpler if each category of organization depended on a single type of funding, but one of the most important characteristics of the U.S. social welfare system today is its complicated mixture of funding sources for all three types of agencies. This mixture has a long tradition in the United States, though it has become more complex in recent years. Before discussing the overlapping nature of funding, however, we will look at the goals, advantages, and disadvantages of each type of agency in its purest form.

A system of public social welfare programs can be described as representing the general public will. It is financed by U.S. citizens and thus publicly sanctioned to do certain things. Theoretically, at least, public agencies will be openly accountable for their actions. Public social services are presumed to be available on an equitable and nondiscriminatory basis. Public financing means command of greater resources than are generally available in the private sector. Finally, the public services can reap the advantages of economies of scale as they provide their benefits.

Private agencies have certain general characteristics, although the nonprofit and for-profit versions each have their own particular attributes. Private social service agencies are often thought to be more innovative in services and more likely to experiment with alternative organizational models. Many of the crisis phone lines of the 1970s and 1980s, for example, were developed by small private organizations. Proponents of private agencies also describe them as more responsive to the needs of specific groups in the community (as in the case of religious social service agencies) and better able than large government organizations to personalize services.

Voluntary agencies, which receive a great deal of support from the public, have been characterized as performing social welfare tasks that neither the government nor the for-profit sector is willing to carry out. Because they are generally directed by community boards, it is assumed that they respond to community needs and goals. The for-profit sector is touted particularly for its cost-effectiveness and ability to produce better services through competition. Because consumers pay for services, it is argued, the for-profit agency will be responsive to their choices (Hill & Bramley, 1986; Independent Sector, 1988).

The truth lies somewhere among all of these claims. Although the possibility for accountability is probably greater in the public sector, the public may have only limited influence on government agency policy. By the same token, voluntary agencies do not always represent their total communities; boards may consist of businesspeople and professionals who do not necessarily respond to the needs or desires of disadvantaged groups. Consumers of services in for-profit agencies may not have sufficient information to make informed choices about which service is best, as in the cases of mental and physical health care. In addition, the goal of maximizing profits may take precedence over a commitment to meeting clients' needs (Hill & Bramley, 1986; Sosin, 1986).

In addition, cost-effectiveness may or may not occur in any of the three types of agencies; for example, in the health arena, it can be argued that duplication of expensive equipment by private hospitals has contributed to the rise in health care costs. Although for-profit and voluntary agencies can indeed experiment in new kinds of service delivery, some public agencies have been able to do this as well. Sometimes private agencies avoid what they consider to be unpopular innovations for fear of discouraging contributors. Often an important variable is the size of the organization; large bureaucracies in both public and private agencies may hamper innovation and lead to impersonal treatment (the big private hospital may be just as daunting to patients as the large public welfare office is to its clients). In sum, though certain broad distinctions can be made about the differences in mission and operation among the three agency types, it is clear that these distinctions are sometimes blurred.

Rather than relying on any one approach to social welfare, the United States has opted for a mixed public/voluntary/for-profit system. What is known as "contracting out" for services—a process in which a state public welfare department, for example, pays a private organization to provide child welfare services—has been with us in some form for a long time. By the mid-1830s, for example, many states subsidized private institutions, such as orphanages run by religious groups, for the care of dependent children. Since the 1960s, government subsidies have increased dramatically. Until recently, the bulk of government social welfare contracts have gone to voluntary agencies; however, in the 1990s, an increasing number of contracts were going to for-profit groups, with the promise of saving money (Crenson, 1998; Trattner, 1999). Those promises have not been fulfilled. Cost savings were minimal and usually obtained by paying lower salaries and cutting benefits. This had a negative effect on local economies and increased inequality. Services also suffered. A study of the voucher program in the District of Columbia concluded that it had not improved student achievement and may even have worsened it. It also noted that students felt safer in their new schools. An advisor to the study believed that parents were willing to accept inferior instruction as an acceptable trade-off for safety, which is a sad commentary (Petr & Johnson, 1999; Greenwood, 2014; Surgey & Lorenzo, 2013; Green, 2017).

The U.S. government has also been taking another look at federal funding for social services provided by religious groups, including churches. Such funding has occurred on a small scale for some time, and in 1996 Congress passed legislation allowing religious groups to compete for contracts from the U.S. Department of Health and Human Services. Building on a campaign promise, former President George W. Bush began work on his "faith-based initiative" shortly after taking office. Arguing that faith can accomplish what secular programs cannot, Bush proposed that religious groups have the right to contract with other federal agencies and to use federal dollars for a wide variety of services for people in need. Whereas earlier recipients of federal money were generally large agencies such as Catholic Charities, Bush was particularly interested in bringing federal money to individual religious congregations. It appeared that this focus might be especially appealing to African American congregations, which have had a long tradition of providing charitable aid in their communities (Bruni & Goodstein, 2001; Silk, 2001).

Not surprisingly, Bush's proposals unleashed a vigorous debate, both in Congress and among the public at large, over the boundaries between church and state. According to one survey, most Americans were ambivalent about the president's plan. Although they supported giving federal grants to religious social service providers, they believed the proposal placed too little emphasis on holding religious groups accountable. The plan raised fears that religious agencies and congregations would attempt to proselytize, forcing their beliefs on recipients of aid. Opponents also pointed out that some religious agencies do not hire people of different religious backgrounds and discriminate against gays and lesbians. Religious groups themselves were divided; some welcoming the prospect of government resources, others worrying about red tape and federal regulations (Ettenborough & West, 2001; Keister, 2001; Woodward, 2001).

Failing to get legislation passed to sanction expansion of federal funding for religious social services, Bush turned to a series of executive orders. One such order makes it easier for religious groups to be funded by allowing those receiving federal contracts to maintain the practice of taking religious affiliation into account when hiring staff. Such changes in federal regulations have served to relax laws that previously made some groups ineligible to receive government funds. In the meantime, the debate over federal support for religious social services continues ("Faith-Based by Fiat," 2003; Meckler, 2003).

The growth in government contracts for social welfare services, whether secular or religious, is one factor in the increasingly close relationship between the public and private sectors. The private sector also depends to a great extent on government funding sources such as Medicaid and Medicare. The striking rise in the number of for-profit hospitals and home health care facilities, for example, is due in large part to an increase in government expenditures on health care. To make things even more complex, the line between for-profit and nonprofit social welfare activities has blurred. As voluntary agencies have witnessed a decline in contributions as a portion of their resources, they have turned more and more to what has been called the "commercialization" of their financial base, charging more fees for services and even selling products. In addition, for-profit companies have begun to compete successfully with nonprofit groups for government funding, leading some charitable organizations to seek to work collaboratively with the for-profits. For example, when Lockheed Martin received a contract for welfare-to-work services in Dade County, Florida, it subcontracted with a number of nonprofit agencies to deliver those services (Ryan, 1999).

By now, you may be thoroughly confused and wondering what all of this has to do with social work. The bottom line is effective and equitable service to clients. Social workers must continue to gauge what these developments mean to people who need assistance and whether they ameliorate such problems as poverty and poor health. Evaluation research is needed to determine the advantages and disadvantages of specific public and private approaches, and social work practitioners must observe and evaluate the results of different programs for their individual clients.

Comparative Analysis

This type of policy analysis involves systematically comparing policies across two or more settings. The most common form is cross-national analysis: The policy in one nation (in these examples, the United States) is compared with policies of other nations regarding the same problem. More limited comparisons, between states or communities or between public and private service provisions, for example, are also possible and useful. This is a rich approach because it provides policy analysts with "natural experiments" of alternative approaches to social welfare problems.

The recognized masters of this type of analysis in social work are Sheila Kamerman and Alfred Kahn (1981, p. xi), who have produced a number of comparative studies of social welfare policies. An example of a cross-national analysis is their study of child care, family benefits, and working parents in which they compared policies in the United States with those of five European countries. They introduce this study as follows:

> This report . . . deals with one of the major family policy questions facing industrial urban societies, or perhaps the major question: . . . what are the optimum response alternatives . . . to a situation in which parents are in the paid labor force, want to have children, and want to rear them successfully? Modern societies have a stake in both childbearing and successful child rearing, but the consequences of different policy responses have not been given detailed, systematic examination. After surveying fourteen country patterns, we selected six countries which have adopted different approaches. The options represent a continuum, with those in the middle involving different mixes. . . . We have placed all this in societal context, given an overview of where children under three actually are during the day, and assessed the debate and interest group positions in each country. There is a secondary review of research on costs, effects, prices, and who pays.

An example of comparative analysis of policies within the United States is Kamerman and Kahn's study of child care policy: In this study, they compare local child care initiatives, state child care actions, private approaches, public school systems as child care providers, employers and child care, and family day care (Kahn & Kamerman, 1987). Comparative analysis may use any or all of the methods of policy analysis discussed in this chapter.

Historical Analysis

It is difficult, if not impossible, to analyze any current policy without at least a brief review of preceding events. Historical analysis, as a policy analysis type, goes well beyond this and is based on the assumption that current policies can be fully understood only if we have a thorough understanding of their evolution. Content analysis defines *policy* as what currently exists, but the historical orientation views policy as patterns of behavior by the state and private groups extending over a long period of time. If a policy is the continuation of a long trend, as in the case of the Affordable Care Act legislation, historical analysis seeks to explicate that trend and to understand why it has continued. On the other hand, if a policy is significantly different from earlier policies in the same area, such as the old-age insurance portion of the Social Security Act of 1935, for example, the purpose of historical analysis is to explain the reasons for the departure from standard practice. Historical policy analysis methods will be discussed in greater detail in Chapter 4.

Process Analysis

Process analysis is less concerned with policy content than with how a policy comes into being. The focus of this analytic approach is on the interactions of the many political actors, which include public officials, bureaucrats, media, professional associations, and special interest groups representing those likely to be affected either positively or negatively by a policy. An understanding of the process is necessary to fully comprehend the content of a policy.

One of the better examples of a process analysis is Steiner's study of family policy in the United States. As part of this study, Steiner (1981) looks at foster care policy, specifically at the process that eventually resulted in the Adoption Assistance and Child Welfare Act of 1980. Steiner found a number of dynamics to be important in shaping the bill that was eventually passed, including the following:

- The Catholic church, which in the 1930s opposed inclusion in the Social Security Act of federally funded foster care for urban areas. This was to protect already existing agreements between the church and several large cities for the funding of Catholic children's homes.
- Academicians, who failed to develop a useful theory on which to base public policy for children in foster homes.
- Child welfare social workers, who often did not actively seek to involve biological parents in case planning because "deemphasizing the biological parent is the safest approach for the child welfare worker, who carries in his or her head two injunctions: do the child no harm and do not embarrass the agency."
- Foster parents, who were too diverse a group to be able to get together to support a specific program.
- The Department of Health, Education, and Welfare (now Health and Human Services), which had no new data or new plans to bring to Congress in support of any expansion of services.
- The Child Welfare League of America, whose main concern was opposing any attempt to put a cap on spending for foster care and related services.

The result of all these forces was a piece of legislation that did not break significant new ground in dealing with the problem of children who need substitute care.

Evaluation

If there is a theme that describes social welfare policy in recent years, it is increasing skepticism. Voters, elected representatives, bureaucrats, and academics have all ceased to assume that social welfare programs are good simply because they have good intentions. One result is a demand for evaluation of all aspects of social welfare policy. Rather than simply describing or explaining social welfare policy, evaluation is intended to judge it. The evaluation process may judge a policy's logical consistency, empirically evaluate its effectiveness and efficiency, or analyze its ethical character.

Logical Evaluation

Logical evaluation is similar to content analysis in looking at the content of a social welfare policy in detail. It goes beyond content analysis, however, by assessing a policy's internal rigor and consistency. Logical evaluation generally evaluates a policy in terms of three possible dimensions—singly or in combination. Because social welfare policies generally have more than one goal, the first dimension of logical evaluation entails assessing the internal consistency of a policy's multiple goals. Financial assistance policy, for example, has a goal of getting people to go to work and also has a goal of enabling mothers to take good care of their children. Because taking good care of children may well involve staying home with them rather than working, these goals are often in conflict.

There may also be a logical inconsistency between the goals of the project and the outcomes that are presumed to measure the success of the program. A job training program is supposed to put people to work. Therefore, you would expect the measure of success to be how many graduates of the program get jobs. Instead, some programs measured success in whether participants completed training or whether they reported liking the program. That's easier to measure but not logically consistent with program goals.

The second dimension of logical evaluation involves assessing the consistency between a policy's goals and the means for achieving these goals. Many programs focus on symptoms rather than causes and on remediation rather than prevention. Enormous amounts of money can be spent on keeping low-birthweight babies in neonatal emergency care units, while it would be much less expensive to ensure that mothers get proper prenatal care and nutrition. Prisons cost much more than jobs programs for inner-city teens. The effects of child abuse are severe and long-lasting. Parental education and a stable family income might prevent a lot of misery at a cost lower than foster care.

The third dimension of logical evaluation involves assessing the difference between intended and unintended consequences. As Pal (1987) has observed, "Even when goals are consistent and there is a clear logical relationship between ends and means, public policies may have unintended consequences that can be worse than the original problem" (pp. 27–38). A well-known example of this type of evaluation is the 1984 critique of the welfare system conducted by conservative analyst Charles Murray. Murray (1994) argues that, although the goals of social welfare policy between 1950 and 1980 were to help people become self-sufficient, the effect was exactly the opposite. The reason he gives for this is that, in his opinion, the system became so generous in its attempts to help people that it became more attractive to go on welfare, and once on, to stay on welfare rather than to "tough it out" by getting a job, getting married, and working to rise through the system. J. D. Vance makes a similar indictment of the people he grew up with in Appalachia and Rust Belt Ohio. But unlike Murray, he takes full account of how structural unemployment and poverty contributes to this (Vance, 2016).

Quantitative Evaluation

Social welfare policies are created to solve pressing social problems, and in so doing they expend large sums of money. Thus, it is natural to demand a rigorous, data-based evaluation of whether policies achieve their intended goals and at what cost. There are generally two parts to quantitative evaluations: effectiveness (sometimes called *outcome*) evaluations and efficiency (sometimes called *cost-effectiveness*) evaluations. These evaluations encompass a wide range of research methods, and a huge literature has developed related to both the methods and the politics of evaluation (Chen, 2005; Schalock, 2001; Royse, Thyer, & Padgett, 2010; Grinnell, Gabor, & Unrau, 2015).

The most common type of evaluations are ex post facto evaluations of programs that are set up and operating at the time researchers are brought in to assess their effectiveness and efficiency. One of the best-known examples of this is the evaluation of the Head Start Program conducted by Learning Corporation and Ohio University in 1968. The Head Start Program was begun in 1964 as one of the main efforts of the Office of Economic Opportunity. The premise of the program (heavily influenced by culture-of-poverty theory) was that poor children performed at a lower level in school than nonpoor children because they came from homes in which adequate cognitive preparation for school was absent. The program originally provided eight weeks of intensive educational preparation and, in many areas, this was soon increased to one year. The intent was that poor children would be brought up to the same level of educational readiness as nonpoor children and hence would be able to compete successfully in school.

The evaluators randomly selected 104 Head Start programs from across the country; about two-thirds were eight-week and one-third were full-year programs. Children who had completed the program and were, at the time of the study, in first, second, or third grade and were matched in socioeconomic background with children who had not gone through the program. The children were all given batteries of tests of educational achievement and cognitive development. In addition, parents were interviewed and teachers of both groups were asked to rate the children on achievement and motivation. The results of the evaluation were disappointing because the researchers found little evidence of effectiveness, although the parents of the children in the program voiced great satisfaction with it (Westinghouse Learning Corporation and Ohio University, 1969). In spite of the evidence of low effectiveness, Head Start remained, and still remains, a very popular program. This fact relates to the political nature of policy in general, as discussed in Chapter 6.

In addition to outcome evaluations, there are also *process* evaluations. Here, instead of reporting their conclusions at the end of the study, the evaluators report findings to the program managers and staff as they go along. This allows adjustments in the program immediately.

A less common type of evaluation is the policy experiment. In this type of evaluation, research questions and hypotheses are developed and a program to test them is designed following generally accepted social science criteria. A recent example of a well-done policy experiment concerns the disappointing results of early Head Start evaluations. Reviewing the weak Head Start results, policymakers theorized that perhaps Head Start intervention needed to begin before age three. The Secretary of the Department of Health and Human Services appointed an Advisory Committee on Services for Families with Infants and Toddlers, and this committee recommended a comprehensive, two-generation program to provide intensive services that begin before the child is born and follows the child's development through the critical first three years of the child's life. The program, called Early Head Start, began in 1995/96 with programs funded at 143 sites.

Mathematica Policy Research was hired to conduct an experimental evaluation of the results of this program. The evaluation was conducted by selecting seventeen sites and then randomly assigning program applicants to the Early Head Start Program or to a comparison group not assigned to the program. The children and families in both groups were then monitored and measured on a number of variables, including cognitive development, language development, social–emotional development, parenting outcomes, parent's progress toward self-sufficiency, subsequent births to parents, and father–child interaction. The results of this study, completed in 2005, were summarized as "a consistent pattern of statistically significant, modest, favorable impacts across a range of outcomes when children were two and three years old, with larger impacts in several subgroups. Although little is known about how important this pattern of impacts sustained through toddlerhood will be in the long run, reductions in risk factors and improvements in protective factors may support improved later outcomes" (Love, Kisker, Ross, & Schochet, 2005).

Ethical Evaluation

All types of policy analysis discussed thus far are, at least theoretically, value-free. To demonstrate this, Pal (1987) uses the following example of an analyst asked to evaluate the Nazi regime's policy of concentration camps:

> It would be possible to provide a description of the "final solution," an analysis of the processes that caused it, and a logical and empirical evaluation. Auschwitz could be described, its background and establishment detailed, determining political forces as well as its organizational processes outlined, logical consistency of policy probed and even an analysis of efficiency conducted. The analyst's ethical judgement could be withheld while these technical analyses were undertaken. But the concentration camps were and are an affront to civilized ethics, and it is entirely appropriate to judge them in these terms.

One of the major points we make throughout this text is that social welfare policy is heavily value laden. The issues that social welfare policy deals with are, at their core, issues of good and bad, right and wrong, should and shouldn't. Therefore, ethical evaluation is a common and important type of social welfare policy analysis. Because there are sharp differences between value systems, ethical policy evaluations are often controversial.

One of the best examples is the pastoral letter of the American Catholic bishops, "Economic Justice for All: Catholic Social Teaching and the U.S. Economy" (National Conference of Catholic Bishops, 1986). The bishops begin the letter by clearly stating six moral principles that provide an overview for the vision they wish to share:

1. Every economic decision and institution must be judged in light of whether it protects or undermines the dignity of the human person.
2. Human dignity can be realized and protected only in community.
3. All people have a right to participate in the economic life of society.
4. All members of society have a special obligation to the poor and vulnerable.
5. Human rights are the minimum conditions for life in community.
6. Society as a whole, acting through public and private institutions, has the moral responsibility to enhance human dignity and protect human rights.

Based on these moral principles, the bishops then analyzed a number of policy issues. They found the U.S. social welfare system deficient in a number of areas and recommended changes, such as providing financial assistance recipients with an adequate level of support (they deplored the finding that "only 4 percent of poor families with children receive enough cash welfare benefits to lift them out of poverty"), establishing national eligibility standards and a national minimum welfare benefit level, and making two-parent families eligible for welfare assistance in all states. It is interesting to note that, although the bishops were almost certainly aware of the discouraging final report of the Seattle and Denver Income Maintenance Experiments (SIME/DIME—see Chapter 6), which found more generous approaches to income maintenance such as a negative income tax actually reduced work participation by recipients, one of their concluding recommendations was that the negative income tax "is another major policy proposal that deserves continued discussion." Apparently, based on the moral principles the bishops were using as the framework for their analysis, the fact that a quantitative evaluation had indicated that the negative income tax resulted in lowered labor force participation did not detract from the attractiveness of this approach.

Myvector

Policies with selective benefits may gain less political support than ones with universal benefits.

Policy Analysis Methods as Ideal Types

While reading the preceding discussion of policy analysis methods, you may have asked yourself questions such as: How can you do a historical analysis without it also being descriptive? Aren't empirical evaluations based on some ethical principles (for example, SIME/DIME obviously embraces the work ethic)? Don't ethical evaluations use data as the basis for some of their arguments? These questions point out that none of the methods we have described actually exists in pure form in the real world. Rather, they are what sociologists refer to as *ideal types*. That is, we have artificially separated them and described what they would look like in pure form if such a form existed. In reality, there is much overlap among the methods, and most policy analyses contain elements from several of them. Good policy analysis almost always begins with solid description and historical analysis; always is based on the best empirical data available; and then proceeds to focus on logic, efficiency, effectiveness, or ethics. In addition, good policy analysis is often comparative.

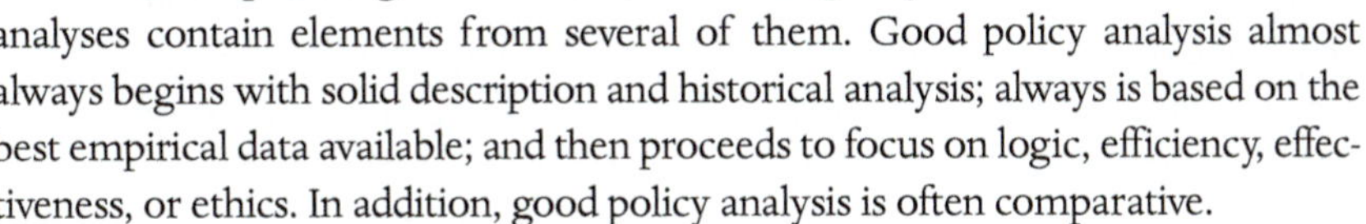

Check Your Understanding 3.2

Check your understanding of Methods of Policy Analysis by taking this brief quiz.

POLICY ANALYSIS AS SCIENCE, ART, AND POLITICS

As a rule, policy analysts consider themselves to be social scientists and what they do to be science. Policy analysts generally employ conventional methods of social science, beginning with formulating the problem and proceeding to stating the hypotheses, developing data collection procedures, collecting and analyzing data, drawing conclusions, and generalizing from the results. When attempting to read a policy analysis textbook, the lay reader can easily be overwhelmed by the complexity of the technical methods employed.

Although there is no doubt that policy analysis seeks to be a science, and there is little doubt as to the appropriateness of this quest, it is important to understand that there are limits to the degree that conclusive knowledge can be obtained regarding policy questions. Charles Lindblom (1980) gives four reasons why analysis cannot provide conclusive answers to policy questions:

1. Policy problems are simply beyond the analytic capacities of human beings. Lindblom explains that "the basic difficulty stems from a discrepancy between the limited cognitive capacities of the human animal and the complexities of policy problems. Even when extended by a range of devices from written language to electronic computers, the mind at its best simply cannot grasp the complexity of reality."
2. Policy issues are based on values and interests that are often in conflict. A policy that may be optimal based on the values and interests of one group may be in

conflict with those of another group. For example, what is the correct abortion policy? For one group, the right of a woman to choose is the paramount value, and for another, the right of a fetus to live is most important. It is impossible to quantify these values and reach an absolute conclusion.

3. The more a policy analysis approaches complete understanding of an issue, the more time and money will be required to conduct it. Most policy decisions cannot wait until "all the data are in" and therefore are made based on less than complete information. For example, the SIME/DIME studies referred to previously took nine years and many millions of dollars to conduct yet provided only partial answers to a few rather limited questions regarding the optimal approach to income maintenance.
4. A purely analytic formulation of the question that a policy addresses is impossible. What is the problem for antipoverty policy? Is it lack of motivation among the poor? Lack of equal opportunity? Inadequate economic growth? These questions contain moral components and, as such, must be settled by politics rather than analysis.

If policy analysis cannot be purely scientific in the sense that single, definitive answers are rarely found, what does this mean? First, it means that we must recognize that policy analysis is as much an art as it is a science. Wildavsky (1979) asserts that policy analysis is synonymous with creativity. "Analysis is imagination. Making believe the future has happened in the past, analysts try to imagine events as if those actions already had occurred." One of the means for doing this is what is known as the thought experiment. This means simply taking a program, either real or imaginary, and—as systematically as possible, based only on logical thought—analyzing the likely effects.

The conservative analyst Charles Murray (1994) does this to great effect in *Losing Ground*. He describes a young couple, Harold and Phyllis, who are not married but are seriously involved; they have learned that Phyllis is pregnant. Murray proceeds to imagine what their behavior would have been in 1960, when there were few social programs to assist them, and in 1970, when there were generous AFDC benefits (he places them in Pennsylvania, a state with benefits among the highest in the nation), public housing, Medicaid, food stamps, as well as other programs. His conclusion from the thought experiment is that in 1960 they would have chosen to get married and to take jobs, even unattractive ones, because there were no other options available. This choice, he argues, would have put them on the first rung of the ladder of success, or at least to participation in mainstream U.S. society. In 1970, Murray imagines, they again would have taken the rational course of action—which now would be to *not* get married so Phyllis could avail herself of all the "generous" social program benefits. This would result in Harold's eventually drifting off because his role had become extraneous to the lives of Phyllis and the baby, who would be doomed (his view) to a life as a single-parent welfare family. From this, Murray concludes that present social welfare policies result in more harm than good and probably should be discontinued. As this example illustrates, thought experiments, perhaps even more than other forms of policy analysis, are heavily influenced by the political perspective of the analyst.

Whatever the technique employed, the impact of those policy analyses is due more to their art than to their science. Analyses such as Murray's conservative *Losing Ground*, or Harrington's liberal *The Other America*, or even television documentaries such as Public Broadcasting's *Eyes on the Prize* or Edward R. Murrow's famous *Harvest of Shame* have been well written and well organized and because of this have had a great impact.

This leads us to introduce an important point that will be noted again in Chapter 6: Policy analysis—whether conducted using rigorous, scientific methodology or more as an art—is, in the final analysis, political. Lindblom (1980) argues that analysis, regardless of its form, becomes part of the play of power, a tool of persuasion. He uses the term *partisan policy analysis*. By this he means that effective policy analysts realize that their analysis will be used in the play of power. They therefore target it to people or groups of people they wish to influence. This is done by taking the values of the group or person to be influenced and analyzing the policy to show how those values can be furthered. For example, imagine that an advocate for increased economic assistance to the poor was attempting to get support for increased welfare benefits from a member of Congress known for supporting defense spending. The advocate for the poor would attempt to demonstrate that increased welfare benefits would in some way serve the interests of national defense, perhaps by improving the health, education, or social adjustment of the young people who make up the pool of potential soldiers. Although this example may be a little farfetched, the point is not. Policy analysis, be it art or science, is used as one of a number of tools of persuasion in the political process.

Check Your Understanding 3.3

Check your understanding of Policy Analysis as Science, Art, and Politics by taking this brief quiz.

CONCLUSION

In this chapter, we have knowingly strayed a bit from the major focus of this text; we have addressed policy analysis more from the perspective of professional academic policy analysts and less from the viewpoint of practicing social workers who need to understand the context of their practice. There is a reason for this: When you begin to conduct your own practitioner policy analysis using the methods described in the following chapters, you will be relying heavily on the work of professional academic analysts. Their work can be confusing unless you understand a few simple points, described in this chapter. Now, with this basic understanding of the policy analysis field, we proceed to address methods you can use in your own practice.

Recall what you learned from this chapter by completing the Chapter Review.

LEARNING OUTCOMES

- Explain why understanding the history of a social policy is critical for a complete policy analysis.
- Discuss examples from colonial poor relief, orphan asylums, and disabilities policy to illustrate historical policy analysis.
- Explain why understanding the history of an agency is important for social workers employed by that agency.
- Distinguish between primary and secondary sources of data for historical research, and describe the advantages and disadvantages of each.
- Identify at least five sources of data useful for a historical analysis of a social welfare policy.
- Critique Charles Murray's *Losing Ground* and Francis Fox Piven and Richard Cloward's *Regulating the Poor a Historical Analyses of the American Welfare System*.

CHAPTER OUTLINE

4

Policy Analysis from a Historical Perspective

NEIL ROY JOHNSON/Shutterstock

In a recent article in *The Atlantic*, historians Graham Allison and Niall Ferguson (2016) argue that, regarding history, most Americans live in "the United States of Amnesia" and, what's more, many American policymakers live there too. They believe that the problem is so great and so significant that there should be developed a White House Council of Historical Advisors with a structure and role similar to the Council of Economic Advisors. They advocate for the development of applied history, writing "For too long, history has been disparaged as a 'soft' subject by social scientists offering spurious certainty. We believe it is time for a new and rigorous 'applied history'—an attempt to illuminate current challenge and choices by analyzing precedents and historical analogues . . . Applied historians would take a current predicament and try to identify analogues in the past. Their ultimate goal would be to find clues about what is likely to happen, then suggest possible policy interventions and assess probable consequences" (p. 28).

Allison and Ferguson are mainly concerned with how an understanding of history can be helpful in the analysis and practice of foreign policy. Their argument can very easily be extended to other areas of policy, including social welfare. In previous chapters we have described a several ideas that are useful to know about social welfare policies, including their political implications, their economic contexts, and their social consequences. Historical analysis of policies helps us understand how and why all these things came together to create a particular policy. Policy history addresses such questions as: Why did the federal government (or the state government, or the Greenacres Children's Treatment Centre) pick that particular problem to address, and why did it proceed to deal with it the way it did? It gives us some idea of what worked in the past and what didn't, and points the way to possible changes. It also allows us to engage in contemporary policy debates provoked, for example, when a politician announces that orphanages should be brought back, that child labor laws are "truly stupid," or that health care costs can be reduced without limiting care by substituting high-risk insurance pools for a requirement that insurance policies cover preexisting conditions.

This chapter discusses the historical analysis of policies. We describe the role and usefulness of a historical approach in understanding and dealing with the policies you will encounter on the job, whether they originate in the agency or from the legislative environment outside it. We give examples of policy history and show how you may conduct your own historical analysis. When done well, historical studies are an indispensable tool for policy analysis.

Thoughts for Social Work Practice

Some social workers who ignore policy as much as possible do so not because they are victims of the myth of autonomous practice but because they believe policymakers are ignorant of the difficulties many of these policies create for social work practitioners and therefore create policies that are entirely unhelpful. How might a Council of Historical Advisors, one that included experts on social history, help remedy this problem?

HISTORICAL CONTEXT OF SOCIAL WELFARE POLICIES

The Role of History in Understanding Policy

The policy of isolating people with mental illness in institutions has a long and complicated history. Like many social problems, it has been through pendulum swings of initiative, reaction, and overreaction. This particular pendulum is still swinging.

In the colonial era, "crazy" people were locked in attics or cellars or turned out to wander the countryside. In the 1840s, Dorothea Dix persuaded legislators that crazy behavior was actually the result of an illness and people exhibiting it should be given shelter in an "asylum" where they could be properly cared for and treated, a new approach called *moral treatment*. Over time asylums, now called state mental hospitals, became warehouses where treatment was minimal and quality of life was deplorable. By the 1950s, new psychotropic drugs that controlled symptoms allowed patients to return to their families or live independently. Community mental health centers would provide outpatient support. Deinstitutionalization began in the 1960s and proceeded quite rapidly. States saved money by closing hospitals, but the funding was not passed on to the community mental health centers. Treatment devolved to dispensing drugs. Those who were not compliant with their drug regime disrupted their families and communities, often becoming homeless and, once in a great while, violent. Anguished families and overstretched police officers pled for involuntary commitment of the noncompliant mentally ill, which might allow the manic and psychotic behavior to stabilize, but civil rights issues and sheer lack of inpatient facilities make this extremely difficult. Without understanding the history of institutionalization, it is difficult to grasp the complexity of the current situation.

An understanding of the outcome of previous policies helps us evaluate present proposals and claims for success. For example, many people regarded the changes in public welfare instituted in the mid-1990s as an abrupt shift in the way we deal with families with dependent children, not realizing that the new program follows a long history of welfare-to-work initiatives, which have met with only limited success. The current welfare program, Temporary Assistance to Needy Families (TANF), is almost universally considered to be a success because welfare rolls have significantly declined, even though all evidence concludes that the suffering of the poor has increased (Institute for Research on Poverty, 2017). It is now clear from studying the history of welfare reform that the goal has always been to reduce the welfare rolls; reducing poverty has always been a secondary (at best) goal.

History, then, helps us understand and deal with current policies. It gives us some sense of how and why particular programs and approaches developed and how well they achieved what they set out to do. Of course, what they "set out to do" is a matter of interpretation. As we will see in Chapter 5, the *manifest* (openly acknowledged) goals of a program are often different from the *latent* (indirect) functions of that same program. For example, the manifest function of a particular day center for homeless people was to provide a place for them to rest, shower, and participate in social activities. However, the latent function of this center was to keep homeless people from using the downtown branch of the public library as a day center. Some latent functions are unintentional, such as the increase in homelessness brought on in part by deinstitutionalization. Because historical analysis includes the examination of a policy or program's goals and effects, such analysis is an important tool in recognizing and evaluating both latent and manifest functions.

Despite these arguments in support of the contribution history makes to policy analysis, some researchers criticize the historical approach as lacking the "scientific precision" of other methods (Heineman, 1981; Hudson, 1982; Reid, 1974; Tyson, 1992). In fact, most social work Ph.D. programs will no longer permit a student to write a historical dissertation (Fisher, 1999). These critics are often quantitative methodologists who stress careful construction of hypotheses and the use of statistical data. What they fail to recognize is that much historical research relies on elements familiar to social scientists: the development of hypotheses or guiding questions, systematic gathering and analysis of evidence to understand the relationships between factors being studied, and the discovery of patterns or the creation of principles to explain these relationships (Barzun & Graff, 1985; Shafer, 1980). Although historical study can make use of statistical data, it draws also on a rich variety of other sources: interviews, memoirs, government documents, minutes of meetings in which policies are debated, and so forth. Overall, as Michael Reisch (1988) has persuasively argued, the study of history helps one develop "essential skills of analysis and critical judgement" (p. 3)—elements central to any research endeavor.

Examples of Policy History

What does policy history actually look like? The following examples include both national and regional social welfare policies and policies developed within social work agencies. Each example includes discussion of the questions asked by the researcher, the sources used, and the conclusions drawn.

Colonial Poor Relief

The problem of dealing with the continued existence of poverty in the United States dominates much current social policy debate. What is the best way to help individuals off the welfare rolls? What is the most effective way to provide for those who remain on welfare? How can we structure our economy to provide employment opportunities for all? These are questions that policy analysts struggle with almost every day. Geoffrey Guest's (1989) study of colonial poor relief documents suggests that these same questions have been asked for several hundred years. As Guest notes, boarding paupers in private homes was the principal method of poor relief in colonial America. Local governments paid families to house dependent individuals such as widows and the destitute aged. Despite the prevalence of this approach, Guest could find no detailed historical accounts of how the system worked in practice. Most of the surviving county, town, and parish records gave only the names of the householders who kept the poor and the amounts paid to them. Guest argues that lack of detailed evidence to the contrary has allowed historians to assume that people's willingness to take dependent individuals into their own homes was a sign of widespread generosity to the poor during the colonial period. Historians have posited that a decline in this humanitarian spirit helped lead to a shift in policy during the mid-1800s, in which the boarding system was phased out "in favor of committing the destitute to poorhouses" (Guest, 1989, p. 93).

The discovery of a remarkable collection of court records from Somerset County, Maryland, for the period 1725–1759 enabled Guest to examine the boarding-out program more carefully and to come to conclusions that conflict with earlier interpretations of the motives behind colonial poor relief. The new data consisted of the "actual petitions for poor relief by householders who were keeping the poor and by individuals seeking relief for themselves or their dependents" (Guest, 1989, p. 95). Using these petitions, Guest could ask: How did the boarding-out policy actually work? Why did private householders agree to care for the poor? Did the demise of this system and the development of institutions for the poor signify a decline in the charitable impulse?

Guest found that most householders (usually wealthy planters) who took in paupers did so reluctantly. Many of the boarders were incapacitated and needed constant care. Once individuals had kept a pauper, they almost never volunteered to take in another. Officials rarely considered the wishes of the poor in making placements. To maintain the cooperation of householders, the court paid much more to those who boarded paupers than it did to those recipients of relief who were allowed to remain in their own homes. In other words, care of the dependent poor in Somerset County during the colonial period was not the sympathetic and generous response envisioned by most historians. Guest concludes that colonial communities used the boarding-out approach primarily because the number of dependent individuals was small and because it was more cost-effective to board them than to institutionalize them. The later use of poorhouses did not signify a change in attitude so much as a reaction to the higher costs of boarding an increasing number of poor people.

What Guest has presented is a careful study of the reasons behind the choice of a boarding system that kept poor people in a family setting as opposed to the use of institutions such as poorhouses. Much of social welfare history documents the shift back and forth between community-based and institutional responses to dependency. Case histories such as this one examine the implementation and effects of these responses in the past. They also give us important insights into the motives behind such policy choices. Guest's conclusion that economic considerations played a larger role than humanitarian impulses in the maintenance of a boarding system for the poor is food for thought when we analyze current social welfare programs.

The Use of Orphan Asylums

Eve Smith (1990, 1995) analyzed the use of orphan asylums from the latter part of the nineteenth century through the 1930s. She was drawn to this topic in part because problems in the present foster care system have caused some social workers, and even some politicians, to suggest a return to institutions for the care of dependent and neglected children. In what ways, Smith asked, did institutions such as orphanages function in the past? How well did they work? Are they appropriate models for today's needs?

To answer these questions, Smith used annual reports of orphanages from the time along with magazine articles, government reports, and social welfare conference speeches describing the treatment of children in institutions. In addition, like Guest, she turned to a less-used source of data: the actual case records of children from two different orphan asylums. These records included not only the comments of orphanage workers about children and their families but also letters back and forth between parents, children, and staff. Such sources provide an intriguing insight into daily life in the orphan asylum and the purposes that these asylums served.

You may have noted with surprise the references to parents and families in the preceding paragraph. Smith (2001) found, as have other researchers, that orphanages dealt more often with children who had parents than with actual orphans. "From the beginning," she explains, "most institutionalized children were 'half-orphaned' children of single or deserted parents and most would eventually return to their families." Smith's contribution to our understanding of the functions of orphanages is her stress on the way single parents were served by such institutions and on the way they themselves used the orphanages to cope with the problems of single parenthood. As the case records show, many parents, usually single mothers, voluntarily placed their children in institutions when they could no longer afford to care for them on their own. Often they contributed a small sum of money toward the children's support. Generally, they maintained contact with their children and orphanage staff and were involved in decisions about their children's upbringing. If family finances improved, sometimes due to the return of a deserting father, the children left the institution to rejoin the family. (See Box 4.1.) The orphanage thus served as an important resource for poor single parents and as a way for society to deal with children in poverty.

BOX 4.1 Cooperation between Parents and "Orphanages"

Beginning in the mid-1920s . . . the [New York] Society for the Relief of Destitute Children of Seamen offered supplementary pensions to a number of parents in order to keep families together. While some parents accepted the assistance and the social work supervision that went with the money, others did not.

An example of a deserted mother who refused the agency's offer, saying she "preferred work to charity," was Mrs. E. When her husband left, she asked for care for her three children, went to work as a domestic (caring for her employer's child), and paid the society approximately half of her wages. Thereupon began an eight-year partnership—agency and parent—in raising the children.

Mrs. E. bought the children's clothes, and visited regularly. She took them to the doctor and dentist when she could get time away from her job, and had much to say about the course of their lives. The society supervised the children and their schooling (they were "A" students), eventually placing them in foster homes found by Mrs. E.; arranged for medical and dental services; and supplemented Mrs. E.'s financial contribution. They discontinued assistance in 1933, when Mrs. E.'s salary had increased and the society was pressed for funds.

Source: Eve Smith, "The Care of Children of Single Parents: The Use of 'Orphan Asylums' through the 1930's," presented at the Annual Program Meeting of the Council on Social Work Education, March 1990.

Smith's study contains several important policy implications. First, she argues there is little evidence that past children's institutions would be appropriate programs for today's foster children. The orphanages served a population of dependent children with parents who generally remained involved in their care and who, by paying part of the bill and advocating for their children, were able to retain some power over their youngsters' lives. Most children in orphanages were "normal"; their institutionalization was due largely to poverty. Today's foster children, Smith (2001) maintains, "are much less likely to have a parent or parents who can or will ever assume their care" (p. 1). In addition, they appear to have higher levels of emotional and physical problems. The two groups of children thus have different needs that will not be served by the same types of programs.

Smith's study also reminds us that the people served by social welfare programs should not be viewed simply as passive recipients of care. Her documentation of parents' use of the orphanage system as a way to provide for their children when their own resources had failed is evidence of the way in which clients can influence the shape of social policies and programs.

In 1999, Speaker of the House Newt Gingrich proposed that welfare payments to single mothers be withdrawn and the money used to build orphanages. This brought protests against "tearing away babies from their mothers," but also showed that both Gingrich and his critics were unaware that, as Smith discovered, earlier "orphanages" were not just homes for children without parents but also functioned as a support for single mothers and operated with their participation. The debate produced at least one defense of bringing back orphanages, a book by Richard McKenzie (1999), an economist with ties to the libertarian Cato Institute, called *Rethinking Orphanages for the Twenty-First Century*. McKenzie grew up in an orphanage and argued that they were nothing like our picture of them from Charles Dickens's *Oliver Twist*.

In 2011, as a presidential candidate, Gingrich returned to his concerns for the children of single mothers, arguing that they were not learning "work habits" at home and should be put to work as janitors in their schools. He stated that child labor laws were "truly stupid." Critics replied that the census showed that most of these kids had mothers who were working very hard at low-paying jobs and not lacking for examples of work habits. But perhaps restrictions on jobs for those under 14 should be revisited. One must remember that the laws resulted from the health-endangering and life-threatening jobs in mines and factories that children as young as eight were forced into early in the twentieth century. Current laws allow work in some nondangerous jobs and family businesses. Should their opportunities be widened?

Smith's emphasis on clients—their problems and strengths—represents a relatively new kind of history, sometimes called "history from the bottom up." In chronicling social welfare developments, this approach focuses not on presidents, lawmakers, and heads of national organizations but rather on more anonymous policymakers and on the "recipients" of social welfare programs. It looks at "ordinary people," working class and poor; immigrants, minorities, and women; members of self-help groups; and laypeople involved in creating policies. It uses sources such as social work agency case histories, the records of mutual aid associations, and the minutes of local chapters of national reform organizations. This type of history is particularly fruitful for social workers due to its emphasis on the stresses and strengths of ordinary individuals and on how social movements and institutions affect them and are affected by them. Some further examples of the approach are Anne Firor Scott's (1993) study of women's associations and their gradual shift from self-help to social reform activities, and Susan L. Smith's (1995) *Sick and Tired of Being Sick and Tired,* a record of the health activism of African American midwives, nurses, and women's club members.

Policies for Those with Handicaps

Smith and Guest are both social workers with research competence in social welfare policy history. Historians have also become interested in the examination of social policy, and in fact policy history or "public history" is a newly emerging area of the discipline. Its practitioners seek "to sort out the relationships among policymakers' intentions, the evolution of governmental policy, and the short-range and long-term impact of specific measures" (Achenbaum, 1983, pp. 21–23). Edward D. Berkowitz (1989) presents a good example of public history in his work on the development of state and national policies to deal with disability. Berkowitz, like other public historians, uses his historical analysis to understand current policy problems and to make recommendations for reform.

In his exploration of disability policy in the United States, Berkowitz asks two major questions: (1) How does U.S. public policy respond to the situation of physical disability, and (2) How have these responses developed? The study is based on the hypothesis that the United States has no single disability policy but rather a set of disparate programs working at cross-purposes (Berkowitz, 1989). In order to understand the nature of these programs, Berkowitz relied primarily on the records of the U.S. Social Security Administration and of state offices for the handicapped as well as on interviews with past and present policymakers.

Berkowitz studied five major disability programs in the United States, including workers' compensation, national disability insurance, and the state-run vocational rehabilitation system. He found that each program had developed problems, sometimes unanticipated by the policymakers, sometimes emerging despite policymakers' attempts to avoid them. In proposing disability insurance, for example, the Social Security Administration had intended to establish a uniform national program administered by the federal government. Determination of applicants' eligibility was to be carried out by federal examining teams, thus avoiding the inconsistencies created by multiple disability boards and the overinvolvement of lawyers in the system. However, private insurance companies, physicians, and state governments lobbied against the plan. The American Medical Association, for example, feared federal disability insurance as an entering wedge for the creation of national health insurance. Political opposition led to a compromise program, Social Security Disability Insurance, in which states play an administrative role. Although the federal government establishes a basic definition of permanent disability, states have the authority to determine who fits the definition and is eligible for benefits. The strictness of the federal definition and the complexity of state eligibility systems have led to increased use of the courts to contest unfavorable rulings. Despite the original intentions of its creators, disability insurance has become a complicated and inconsistent program that frequently relies on attorneys and the courts (Berkowitz, 1989).

In reviewing the other disability programs, Berkowitz found similar problems within programs and a lack of coordination between them. The history of disability policy suggests that these problems have arisen because of the lack of a broad political following for disability programs; differences of philosophy between policymakers; conflicting political pressures from state governments, doctors, and other groups; and the difficulties in defining disability.

Berkowitz argues that the system needs reform and that historians can help in that reform. History is important, he argues, because it brings order to a complicated and confusing picture. Historical analysis shows the development of each disability program and the interactions between programs over time. Based on this overview, Berkowitz makes a variety of recommendations to policymakers. He notes, for example, the ongoing failure of disability policy to blend income maintenance and rehabilitation approaches. As a partial remedy, he suggests that the disability insurance program distinguishes between individuals, often older, who should be helped to retire on a disability pension, and workers who are capable of returning to the workforce and would like to do so. Disability insurance, he suggests, could provide "independence initiatives" to the latter group in the form of vouchers for attendant care, modification of transportation and architectural barriers, and so forth. Using his historical training to develop a broad view of disability policy, Berkowitz (1989) thus makes an important contribution to the review and potential reform of current approaches.

Historical Analysis and Policy Practice

Unlike the previous examples, the history of agency policy is often informal and unwritten. Yet awareness of an agency's development is an important tool for understanding current agency programs and policy. This awareness can help workers and administrators appreciate agency strengths and analyze and deal with agency shortcomings. Knowing something about the development of the policy and the key actors in that development can be an essential ingredient in getting it changed.

The junior staff members of a small outpatient mental health center were concerned about a center policy regarding information gathered from clients. When an individual came to the center seeking help voluntarily or under the direction of a court or other agency, he or she went through a lengthy intake process. As part of this process, the social worker interviewing the client prepared an intake form that included personal items such as name, age, marital status, and employment; a short description of the client's perception of his or her current difficulties; a psychiatric diagnosis; and details on any past psychiatric hospitalization. Because the center received the bulk of its funding through the state, a copy of the form was sent to the state Department of Mental Health. The state department used these records in research on such factors as the numbers of persons with a particular diagnosis served in a given year.

The staff members' concern stemmed from the fact that, although clients were not identified by name, their Social Security numbers were to be provided at the top of the form. Fresh out of graduate training that stressed client rights and the importance of maintaining confidentiality, several social workers worried that client names and details of their emotional difficulties could be linked through use of their Social Security numbers. What was to prevent this information from being shared with other departments in the state bureaucracy? The fact that the State Department of Motor Vehicles had a policy of denying drivers' licenses to people who had been hospitalized for psychiatric problems was especially worrisome. What if, the staff members speculated, the Department of Motor Vehicles could gain access to the mental health department records and use them when clients applied for drivers' license renewals? One social worker who had served in the U.S. Army likened this to the past use of military discharge codes to discriminate against job applicants.

These new employees had been taught that evaluating the effects of agency policies on clients was a legitimate part of their job and that changing policies was sometimes necessary. They reasoned that in order to try to change the intake form policy, they would have to discover its origin. At first, they assumed that the state Department of Mental Health mandated the use of Social Security numbers. This, in fact, is what they were told by several mental health aides and one of the clinic's secretaries. ("Oh, that's a state policy" is a common response when one is looking into an unpopular or cumbersome regulation.) Yet when they examined the state mental health handbook, they could not find the policy. They consulted a reference librarian at the local university; he was unable to find any such rule in the published regulations related to state legislation on mental health. The social work supervisor at the mental health center, who had worked there for four years, couldn't supply an answer.

Finally, they approached the senior psychologist, who had been with the clinic since its founding twelve years earlier. "Oh, that rule," he said, "actually, as far as the state's concerned, the information on Social Security numbers is optional. But you know how our director is—Dr. Molson is really a very traditional psychiatrist who believes in detailed recordkeeping and crossing all the *t*'s. I don't think it would occur to him to worry about protecting clients from possible information leaks within the bureaucracy. He's pretty strong-minded, you know—you don't want to suggest changes to him unless it's really serious."

Having discovered the source of the policy, the new staff members worked hard to convince the senior psychologist that the practice was unnecessary and potentially harmful to clients. They elicited his help in initiating a discussion of the use of Social Security numbers at the next staff meeting. With the legitimacy that a senior staff member lent to their issue, they were able to convince the clinic director that client identities were not really necessary for mental health research and that leaks of information could jeopardize the trust that the clinic attempted to develop with its clients. As a result of this intervention, the space for Social Security numbers was deleted from the intake form.

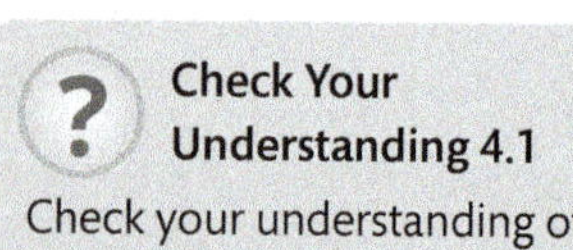

Check your understanding of Historical Context of Social Welfare Policies by taking this brief quiz.

This incident illustrates the use of historical analysis in understanding and changing a policy. In this case, the staff discovered where the policy came from, who initially promoted it, and why. They used this information in their successful effort to eliminate the policy. Note that blaming the policy on a higher level of administration is not unusual. Sometimes this is genuine ignorance; sometimes it is a way of avoiding the issue. Without such information, the staff members might have wasted time advocating for change with the wrong people and might have lost credibility by showing ignorance of the policy's origin.

METHODS OF POLICY HISTORY

How is policy history carried out? The preceding examples give some sense of the process of historical analysis. In this section, we provide more specific guidelines for carrying out that process.

One of the most important tasks in historical analysis is the formulation of hypotheses or guiding questions related to the issue or program to be studied. Historians differ somewhat on how structured this formulation should be. Those with a social science orientation tend to stress the development of formal hypotheses regarding what the historical data will reveal. Those with a humanities orientation find it more appropriate to draw up a number of questions, adding perhaps some hunches, to bring to the study of the evidence. In either case, the researcher needs to have a guiding framework for approaching a mass of detail. Without this framework, the study might be no more than a descriptive exercise, with little sense of pattern or meaning. The researcher would not know exactly what to look for in the data or how to organize the final document. As Barzun and Graff (1980) note, the historian is like a traveler, who pieces together "the 'scenery' of the past from fragments that lie scattered in many places" (p. 198). To do this, the researcher soon develops "a guiding idea to propel [him or her] along the route, a hypothesis ahead of the facts, which steadily reminds [the traveler] of what to look for" (Leashore & Cates, 1984, pp. 24–25).

In a study of the development of sexual harassment policies in social work agencies, for example, the researchers approached the data (interviews with agency administrators and staff members as well as agency policy documents) with the following questions in mind: (1) How did the policies on sexual harassment in these agencies come about? (2) Why were these policies developed at the time they were? Were they the result of lobbying on the part of female administrators and staff? and (3) What is the past and present nature of these policies? Not only did these questions provide guidance for conducting the study—for example, helping the researchers decide what to ask in their interviews—but they also aided in the structuring and recommendations of the final report (Leighninger et al., 1987). Another way to approach this study would have been to develop a specific hypothesis, such as: "Sexual harassment policies are most likely to develop in agencies with women administrators at the top level," and to examine the histories of a number of agencies to see if that hypothesis made sense.

The next step in developing the history of a social welfare policy, practice, or organization is to gather evidence related to the major questions or hypotheses. Primary sources include letters, diaries, oral histories, board and committee minutes, testimony at congressional hearings, administrative records, newspaper articles about an event written at the time the event was taking place, and similar sources of direct data regarding events.

The best history relies on a variety of kinds of data. Secondary sources summarize and synthesize the historical material, giving you a good place to start. These sources reflect the biases of the writer, however, both in terms of the selection of material to present and in its interpretation. Such biases are not always made clear to the reader. Although primary sources can also include bias (for example, firsthand reporters of political rallies are real people with their own ideological perspectives), by examining a number of different primary sources, you can strive to develop a balanced picture of what actually occurred. The description of the development of a policy on confidentiality in the agency where you work would be incomplete, for example, if it relied only on the minutes of the committee drawing up the policy. You might also want to consult the written requirements on confidentiality put out by the state organization that funds the agency and to interview agency staff members and administrators who were present when the policy was constructed and implemented.

Historians distinguish between primary and secondary sources of data. Primary material consists of records made at the time an event occurred by participants or direct observers of the event. Secondary sources are reconstructions of an event by persons without firsthand knowledge of the event. A letter from Jane Addams to a colleague regarding strategy for passing child labor legislation is a primary source; a chapter in a textbook on labor law describing Addams's involvement would be a secondary source.

Secondary sources often do an important job of orienting you to the area you want to study. They can provide an overview and a context for your policy history. However, they generally present conclusions drawn by the author, based on his or her interpretation of the evidence existing at the time the material was written. If you want to draw your own conclusions based on the evidence, and particularly to use new data that have come to light or new theories about the development and nature of social welfare policies, you will need to examine the original sources yourself.

This is not to say that primary sources are bias-free. They, too, represent the values, judgments, and preconceptions of the observer or participant recording an event. However, historians attempt to control for bias by using a variety of primary sources—and, indeed, of secondary sources. If you were investigating the history of an agency decision regarding which sorts of client problems to deal with and which to refer, for example, you would want to interview staff members at various levels and not just the agency director.

In the past, the first stop for anyone undertaking research of any kind was the library. These days, enormous amounts of information are available on the Internet. Just remember that it's easy to get lost in this ocean of data. You will probably need help navigating, and librarians are still valuable resources. And there are times when being physically in the library stacks will expose you to things you might not find online.

You can browse the catalogues of your university and many other libraries around the country. You'll be looking for topics or key words like "sexual harassment." Here is the first case where being in the stacks may be a useful supplement to online searches. Sometimes you notice on the shelf a book that is relevant to your search but would not have been found by your key word. Perhaps it is on a related topic, but you had not thought of the relationship while sitting at your computer.

Abstracts of historical articles can be found electronically, as well as in hard copy, in sources such as *American History and Life* and *Historical Abstracts*. Other tools for finding books and articles on social welfare history include a new heading (Social Welfare and Public Health) in the Recent Scholarship Section of the *Journal of American History*; a category on Social Work Profession—History in *Social Work Abstracts*; Trattner and Achenbaum's (1983) *Social Welfare in America: An Annotated Bibliography*; Stuart and Herrick's (2005) *Encyclopedia of Social Welfare History in North America*; Paul Stuart's (2015) *Oxford Bibliography of Social Welfare History in the United States*; and many other indices and abstracts with subject matter specializations like gender, gerontology, crime, or addiction. It may take time to sort through them online; the advice of a librarian may save you a lot of sweat.

Be aware that abstracting services are only as good as their abstracters. They can't and don't cover the universe, and they may have their own biases. The National Association of Social Workers covers all the journals they publish in *Social Work Abstracts* but is less comprehensive in its coverage of journals they don't publish.

Among social work journals, *The Social Service Review* and *The Journal of Sociology and Social Welfare* are particularly likely to publish historical articles. Review articles in *Reviews in American History* offer excellent orientations to current trends and debates in social welfare history. In any book or article that you find useful, look carefully at its bibliography and footnotes for further sources. Take advantage of the work already done by others.

The Encyclopedia of Social Work, now available online, covers historical topics and biographies of social welfare leaders; Walter Trattner's (1996) *Biographical Dictionary of*

Social Welfare in America is also a good source of information about important figures in social welfare (Holden, Baker, Covert-Vail, Rosenberg, & Cohen, 2009). *The Dictionary of American Biography, Dictionary of American Negro Biography*, and *Notable Women: The Modern Period* are other helpful sources of biographical data.

These are some of the "official" sources one can find online. There are also hundreds of organizations, advocacy groups, professional associations, and blogs with websites that dispense information. Some are reliable; some are nutcases. *Wikipedia* covers a vast range of topics and can be very useful as a starting point. Its entries usually have bibliographies. But anyone can contribute to it, and its monitors can't verify everything that is added. People and organizations are constantly trying to place information favorable to them in the entries and wipe out unfavorable bits.

So who do you trust? It's good to be skeptical of everyone. Having multiple sources is the best defense. Everyone has biases, but you can usually tell what they are and decide how far you want to go with them. Past performance is another guideline. If the source has been reliable in the past, it deserves more trust than one that is usually wide of the mark. Some people throw up their hands and say: "You can't trust anybody." But if that were the case, we would be unable to go anywhere or do much of anything. We all develop a sense of who and what to trust in our daily lives. That same sense can be developed over time as you work your way through your sources. Total cynicism is unhelpful.

Once you have an overview of a policy history area, you will want to turn to the original sources. Using original sources may seem daunting at first. The range of evidence is vast: memoirs, correspondence, minutes of committees, agency manuals containing rules and policies, client case histories, court testimony, government reports, and census reports. You may be further intimidated to learn that the historical evidence is not always written and can include interviews with key policymakers and staff of social work agencies, oral histories, photographs, films, and even songs. Our policy history of the Benton Park Crisis Center, for example, drew in part from a large scrapbook that included news clippings, photographs, and other material documenting major events in the life of the agency. As you pursue a historical analysis, you may sometimes find yourself caught up in the fun of this "sleuthing" game, in which you use your imagination to determine what has gone on in the past. Occasionally, one stumbles across an exciting "find," such as a mouldering box of case records dating back to the early 1900s in an agency basement. More usually, a painstaking search is involved, in state and local libraries, archival collections, organization headquarters, individual agencies, and collections of oral histories, in order to locate pertinent sources. Fortunately, guides are available for a number of these holdings and collections.

Archives are places where unpublished records are collected, cataloged, and made available to researchers. They may be housed in libraries, organizations, universities, and museums. Tracking where the records of particular individuals or organizations are stored can be a tricky task. One help is the *National Union Catalogue of Manuscripts*, available in libraries. There are several important archival collections in social work and social welfare, including the Social Welfare Archives at the University of Minnesota; the Social Work Archives at the Smith College School for Social Work; and the records collection at the Center on Philanthropy, Indiana University, Indianapolis. Individual archives have their own directories, for example, the directory of the University of Minnesota's Social Welfare History Archives Center (1970) and supplements to it (Trattner, 1986).

The articles "Archives of Social Welfare" by Clarke Chambers in the eighteenth edition of the *Encyclopedia of Social Work* and "Social Welfare History Archives" by David Klaassen in the nineteenth edition are excellent starting points for locating primary sources. The nineteenth edition also contains Leslie Leighninger's entry "Historiography," which gives an overview of the use of historical sources. The directory of the University of Minnesota's Social Welfare History Archives can be found in many university libraries. Other useful archives include the U.S. National Archives, the Archives of Labor and Urban Affairs at Wayne State University; Temple University's Urban Archives Center; and the Rockefeller Archive Center in North Tarrytown, New York. The social work and other libraries at Columbia University in New York have an extensive collection of materials on social welfare history, including a large collection of annual reports, publications, and conference proceedings from leading social agencies and organizations. Many states maintain archives that include material on public social welfare programs and policies, and some agencies also store their administrative and client records. In addition, authors of books on social work and social welfare history generally describe the archival sources they have used in their notes and bibliographies.

Libraries of major universities, especially those with schools of social work, can also be sources of primary material on social welfare history topics. The social work collection will often include issues of social work journals dating back to the early 1900s, as well as the complete *Proceedings* of the National Conference of Social Work (formerly National Conference of Charities and Correction), dating from the 1980s back to 1874, as well as the *Encyclopedia of Social Work,* ranging from the first edition published in 1929 to the twentieth published in 2008 and now available, with periodic updates, online. You will also find the annual published reports of various social welfare organizations, such as your state's public welfare or mental health departments and selected private agencies and institutions. A search in the Louisiana State University library, for example, produced a fascinating set of reports regarding the patient census, types of treatment, and size and condition of the physical plant in large state hospitals in the 1930s and 1940s.

Newspapers and newsmagazines provide firsthand reports of social welfare developments and interviews with both policymakers and the recipients of social services. Many of these, such as the *New York Times* and the *Washington Post,* have their own indexes. The *Times* index goes back to 1851. There are also an incredible number of U.S. government reports and statistical publications, almost all easily accessible online. Just a few examples of these are the *U.S. Statutes at Large,* which is organized chronologically; federal statutory laws, organized by subject, found in *The United States Code*; criminal justice statistics found in *The Uniform Crime Report*; just about any statistic you can think of related to the population of the country in *The U.S. Census Bureau, Current Population Reports*; and statistics related to the poor and to antipoverty programs in the *P-60 Series on Poverty. The Statistical Abstract of the United States,* published every year by the Government Printing Office, is a very handy tool and can be found at www.census.gov/statab/www. The Census itself is available at www.census.gov. In addition, a keyword search will yield U.S. government data on nearly any social welfare topic you may be researching.

A special kind of individual record is the oral history, which is a recorded interview with a person about his or her past and often about that person's participation in particular historical events. These interviews are transcribed and then made available through special oral history collections, often housed in university libraries. Historians may use oral histories conducted by others or carry out their own (Leighninger, 1995). The Smith College Social Work Archives and the Social Security Project at the Oral History Collection of Columbia University are important repositories of oral histories related to social work and social welfare.

Related to oral history is a research technique known as interviews with key informants. This technique, more familiar to journalists than to social scientists, consists of interviewing people who, by virtue of job and/or training, are recognized as experts. People commonly used as key informants are academic researchers, agency executives, legislators and their aides, and social activists. Often forgotten, but possessing an important perspective, are the clients of programs created by social welfare policies and the social workers staffing these programs. Gaining the firsthand perspective of people actually involved in the policy you are analyzing can be extremely useful, whether their perspective is from the top down or the bottom up.

Social welfare organizations, agencies, and schools of social work also create their own unpublished records. These include annual reports, minutes of committee meetings, agency manuals and regulation books, memos, client surveys, and case records (such as those used by Eve Smith in her study of orphanages). Sometimes these are still locked in some dusty file cabinet in a school or agency office. Sometimes they have been donated to local or state libraries, archives such as the Social Welfare History Archives, or state history collections. In figuring out whether these records still exist and where they are located, one place to start is the organization itself. The records of many national social welfare organizations can be found at the Social Welfare History Archives, as can the committee minutes, yearly conference proceedings, and other memorabilia of professional associations such as the National Association of Social Workers.

The case records of social agencies are particularly helpful to social welfare historians when they try to understand the lives of ordinary citizens (Allen & Montrell, 1981). If you are planning to use an agency's client records, you must be sure to receive permission from the agency administration and to follow your university's Human Subjects Review Board policies for protecting subject rights.

The addition of a client perspective helps make policy histories more complete, as does attention to the issues of women and minorities, who constitute a large proportion of the clientele of social welfare programs and who have also played significant roles in the development of the social work profession. In addition, women and minorities have been a driving force behind informal self-help organizations. There is a growing body of historical literature on the roles and position of women and minorities in the social welfare system. These include studies of women and public welfare by Abramovitz and Gordon; biographies of African American social welfare leaders by Carlton-LaNey, Peebles-Wilkins, and Rouse; and histories of the women's clubs and self-help movement by Lerner and Scott (Gordon, 1988; Stadum, 1992). The works of these authors include a number of references to archival and other sources related to race and gender in social welfare. There are, for example, specialized oral history collections such as the Black Women Oral History Project at the Schlesinger Library, Radcliffe College; archival collections at Howard University and other institutions; and programs such as the Center for Research on Women, Memphis State University, which provide computerized searches of databases in its particular topic area.

As historical evidence is gathered, it must be evaluated and interpreted. The end product, or conclusions, will relate to the guiding questions or hypotheses with which you began your quest. A number of questions can be asked about the evidence, including:

- Is it authentic? If you are dealing with historical documents, it is unlikely they are fake, but it does happen. If there are multiple copies in existence, falsification is unlikely. It would be difficult to make up something after the fact and then insert it into multiple archives, for example, newspaper notices of Barack Obama's birth. If there is only one copy, the authenticity of the content must be determined. This may come down to the reputation of the person producing the document. Is there a way of determining the date of the document? Things can be added to files after the fact of a legal challenge. A clinician's diary may include entries added months or years later.
- Were the accounts of witnesses to an event or participants in a meeting believable? Was this person actually present when the committee debated the matter? Did the individual have strong prejudices regarding the issue? How long after the event did the witness make his or her report?
- What was the intent of the document in question? Was it simply to report or to persuade? Who was the intended audience?

The use of multiple sources of evidence helps in weeding out inaccuracies and inconsistencies and in recognizing biases. In addition, all historical sources should be read with an understanding of the time and context in which they were written. One should be careful not to evaluate material from the past from a present-oriented point of view, sometimes called "presentism." For example, flowery, openly affectionate language between women was common in the late 1800s and was not an indication of a physical/sexual relationship; Jane Addams's correspondence with women friends and colleagues should therefore be read with that in 1971 mind. Similarly, social workers writing about African Americans in the 1920s rarely questioned the injustices of segregated social agencies. Although this is overtly racist by today's standards, it reflected the very limited consciousness of racial injustices characteristic of many whites at the time (Abramovitz, 1988; Burwell, 1994; Carlton-LaNey, 1994; Chandler, 1994; Diner, 1970; Gordon, 1991, 1994; Lerner, 1974; Muncy, 1991; Peebles-Wilkins, 1989; Rouse, 1989; Scott, 1992). That does not make their actions or attitudes any less racist; it just raises the question of what we might reasonably expect of them. It also makes the achievements of those who rose above the limited awareness of their times all the more praiseworthy.

The final stage of the analysis is deciding what the evidence has to say in relation to the hypotheses or questions of the study. In history, as in any other research topic, interpretation of the data must be careful and systematic. As Barzun and Graff (1985) explain, the historian uses the evidence with "informed common sense" to demonstrate the probability that a certain event occurred for particular reasons and with particular results.

Another common mistake that can lead to misinterpretation of historical evidence is the cross-cultural error, or the lack of understanding of values and customs of another culture. White social welfare historians, for example, have tended until recently to ignore the importance of self-help groups in the African American community as a form of social welfare organization. Similarly, one can make the mistake of assuming that the ideas and lifestyle of a particular group represent all of society. Those who have studied the domestic lives of middle- and upper-class women in the Victorian era have sometimes falsely concluded that it was typical for women of this period to stay at home providing a nurturing environment for husbands and children. In that same period, however, many poor and working-class women were employed outside the home, took in boarders, or did paid work in the home to help support their families. Other types of misinterpretation can be demonstrated by looking at two important books on social welfare, Charles Murray's (1984) *Losing Ground* and Frances Fox Piven and Richard Cloward's (1971) *Regulating the Poor*. These works are not strictly histories; they might best be called sociological studies of past policies and events. They constitute policy analyses that use historical methods to attempt to make sense of current social issues. It is therefore useful to analyze them based on some of the same criteria one would use in assessing the accuracy and usefulness of a historical study.

As we discussed in Chapter 3, Murray's book was published during the Reagan era and gained immediate popularity among conservatives as a justification for reductions in government social programs. Murray is a former journalist and political scientist formerly associated with the Manhattan Institute, a conservative think tank. His study focuses on this question: Why, after twelve years of greatly increasing expenditures on government social welfare programs, was the percentage of Americans in poverty in 1980 (13 percent) the same as it had been in 1968? Murray seeks to answer this question through a wealth of statistics, discussion of policy experiments, and reconstructions of the possible motives behind the actions of the poor. He concludes that government social programs did worse than fail to alleviate poverty; they were in fact responsible for creating poverty in the United States in the 1960s and 1970s (Jencks, 1985; Murray, 1994).

Murray argues that, according to a variety of indicators, including the rate of poverty, poor people were becoming worse off in the late 1960s, just as the War on Poverty social programs were beginning to take effect. He describes the growth in federal spending on social welfare, the development of new programs such as job training and community action projects, and the loosening of regulations regarding who could receive benefits. He then details increases in crime, unemployment, divorce, and the number of households headed by single women, as well as the end to a previous decline in the poverty rate. He attributes these disturbing phenomena to increased spending, changes in programs, and ultimately to the fact that the "new rules" of welfare made it "profitable for the poor to behave in the short term in ways that were destructive in the long term." Using a fictitious low-income couple named Harold and Phyllis, who were unmarried and expecting a child, Murray (1984) describes a scenario in which the only reasonable choice for such individuals was to live together on what was then Aid to Families with Dependent Children (AFDC) rather than to marry and seek employment and financial independence.

At first reading, Murray's analysis seems convincing, especially to those who suspect a connection between welfare and dependency. Yet as numerous scholars have pointed out, he makes a number of errors in presenting and interpreting his data. The first of these is what Barzun and Graff (1985) call "generalizing beyond the facts." In other words, the writer produces a broad generalization based on limited facts and fails to test the generalization with negative examples. This occurs, for example, when Murray argues that welfare programs encourage marital breakup and the rise in female single-parent households. To make this generalization, he relies on the results of a social policy experiment: the implementation of a negative income tax program in several U.S. localities during the late 1960s and 1970s (the SIME/DIME experiments discussed in Chapter 3). Using a financial supplement, the program brought the income of selected groups of low-income individuals up to the poverty line for a three-year period; control groups received no supplement. In some areas, the divorce rate of the experimental group was much higher than that of the control group. From this finding, Murray generalizes that "welfare undermines the family." He thus equates the negative income tax with all welfare programs. He does not look for other examples (e.g., the rate of marriage dissolution among AFDC recipients in similar or other time periods) against which to test his findings. In fact, the bulk of research examining the relationship between welfare benefits and marital breakup has been inconclusive, with some studies showing no relation between the two and others reporting only a small impact of AFDC benefits on divorce. Interestingly, some studies show that women's participation in the labor force *also* increases marital dissolution (Barzun & Graff, 1985; Wilson & Neckerman, 1987).

Murray comes to other misinterpretations through errors in his analysis of the data. Much of his argument regarding the negative results of War on Poverty programs rests on the observation that government welfare spending increased dramatically during the late 1960s and the 1970s. Yet the bulk of these expenditures was in programs for the elderly. Help to the nonelderly poor through means-tested programs showed only modest growth, much of which was in benefits to the disabled. Expenditures for AFDC expanded little in the 1970s; between 1972 and 1980, real benefit levels for AFDC recipients fell by about 30 percent. Thus, Murray's linkage between rise in government expenditures for the nonelderly, nondisabled poor and the increase in poverty for this group makes little sense (Ellwood & Summers, 1987; Jencks, 1990; Schwarz, 1983, pp. 1–36).

Finally, Murray falls into the trap described by Barzun and Graff (1985) as reducing all the diversity of history to "one thing," such as characterizing the French Revolution as resulting solely from a conspiracy. "A true researcher," they observe, "shows the parts that make up the complexity." Yet Murray too often fails to examine this complexity or to explore the context within which trends like a rise in poverty or in marital dissolution rates occur. As historian Michael Katz (1986) notes, Murray tells us the story of federal social policy in a "contextual vacuum." He ignores factors such as changing occupational structures, rising unemployment, and transformations in U.S. cities during the 1960s and 1970s. To illustrate, if we look again at Murray's use of the negative income tax experiment, we note that he is content to present the evidence that divorces increased among some of the experimental groups. He does not question why this happened or what it was about the particular policy that encouraged divorce or made it possible. Did increased financial resources, for example, allow women to escape from abusive relationships? Asking such questions might help us to understand more fully why divorces occur (rather than to pin them to the single cause of welfare policy) and perhaps even guide us in developing policies that would strengthen marriages (Barzun & Graff, 1985).

The idea of reducing a historical event to one thing is part of a discussion of the notion of causation and how it might be approached historically. Frances Fox Piven and Richard Cloward's (1971) study *Regulating the Poor* is similar to Murray's work in its attempt to trace the causes of a particular phenomenon, in this case fluctuations in welfare benefits, over time. Although Piven and Cloward make comparisons of several historical periods rather than rely on data from only one or two decades and although they provide more of the context of the situation they are studying, they nevertheless can be criticized for presenting an overly simplistic picture of the reasons behind government expansion in welfare programs.

Regulating the Poor was published in 1971; its authors had participated in welfare reform movements during the 1960s. Cloward was a sociologist and social worker; Piven is a political scientist and urban planner. As scholar–activists, the two combined social science theory and historical analysis in a study of the rise and fall in the numbers on welfare rolls over time. The central thesis of the book is that public welfare exists primarily to control the poor. Piven and Cloward argue that "relief arrangements are initiated or expanded during the occasional outbreaks of civil disorder produced by mass unemployment, and are then abolished or contracted when political stability is restored. . . . Expansive relief policies are designed to mute civil disorder, and restrictive ones to reinforce work norms" (p. xxiii). In other words, public relief programs are based on the need to control dissension among the unemployed (by increasing welfare payments) and to regulate the labor market (by forcing people into low-income work when relief is cut back). This is a social control argument that attributes the development of social policies and programs to the desire of those in power to maintain order for their own advantage (Achenbaum, 1983; Piven & Cloward, 1993).

To arrive at their conclusions, Piven and Cloward trace relief practices in Europe from their beginnings in the sixteenth century through the rise of capitalism. They then look at data on the relief rolls in the United States from 1930 through the 1960s. This approach is called historical trend analysis, the examination of data over time in order to ascertain certain patterns. By comparing the patterns of welfare contraction and expansion to social and political events such as race riots and other unrest, Piven and Cloward (1993) conclude that changes in welfare policy were designed primarily by elites to regulate the poor (Rochefort, 1981).

Piven and Cloward (1971) make a meaningful contribution to our thinking about social welfare policy by alerting us to the fact that the desire to keep low-income people from "causing trouble" can indeed influence the type and amount of welfare that society provides. This understanding prevents us from viewing the development of social policy simply as the story of an ongoing humanitarian march toward progress. Piven and Cloward also help us to appreciate the connections between the purposes of welfare, the political process, the occupational structure, and the market economy. Yet despite providing at least some of the context that Murray lacks, their analysis is problematic because, in the end, it sees the social control motive as the primary factor in the shaping of public welfare (Alexander, 1983; Patterson, 2000).

Their conclusion is troublesome on two counts: Like Murray's work, it stresses a mechanistic, single-factor explanation of a complex phenomenon, and it encourages simple assumptions about cause and effect. A number of writers have criticized *Regulating the Poor* for reducing the growth and decline of public welfare to one element, social control, rather than seeing this factor as one among many. They have questioned whether the model developed can be accurately applied to other historical periods (similar to the argument that Murray neglected to find other examples against which to test his conclusions). If relief rolls do not exhibit the same pattern during the Revolutionary period in American history, for example, this may cast doubts on Piven and Cloward's findings (Achenbaum, 1983; Mohl, 1963).

In addition, Piven and Cloward's thesis raises questions about the search for causation in history. Have the two authors shown that the need for social control "causes" change in the welfare rolls? Here Piven and Cloward may have fallen into a dangerous trap, the prediction backward from results to motives. True, policymakers and public officials may often seek to maintain order and the status quo. But we can't base our conviction that this is so solely on the outcomes of social programs. In addition, much can happen between the creation of a policy and its implementation. Budget committees, rules and regulations, and the actions and personalities of public welfare administration and staff intervene to affect the policy outcome. Given this complexity, the relationship between motives and results becomes unclear in either direction. Finally, we might ask whether it is reasonable to look to history for causes at all. Barzun and Graff (1985) have commented that what history shows about the past is not the "cause," but the conditions accompanying an event's emergence. Causation is really the picture of a long chain of events rather than the notion of a single element, such as the motives of a group of policymakers (Achenbaum, 1983; Rochefort, 1981).

Clarke Chambers (1990), a major social welfare historian, believes "the past is the most practical thing we can study" (p. 12). This is a wise statement yet not in the way that many think. Too often we expect history to provide us with neat formulas for avoiding past mistakes and with clear descriptions of what caused certain events. As our critique of Murray and of Piven and Cloward suggests, good history gives us context and a view of complex, interacting forces rather than single-factor explanations of the past. What can we do with this history? We can analyze the failures and successes of past social programs for suggestions—but only suggestions—of what might work today. We can learn about the relationships between policymakers' intentions, the evolution of policies, and the impact of those policies in the past to try to understand such relationships in the present. We can be alerted to the importance of social, political, and economic factors in policy and program development. Finally, we can try to fathom where we've been in order to understand where we are.

To give you a real-world sense of all this, we end this chapter with a policy history of a social agency in a midsized, Midwest community. This is the sort of history you might develop yourself as you begin to work at an agency. It is guided by the questions of how an organization developed its policies and programs and how that earlier development affects its operations today. The history is based on interviews with the agency's administration, staff, and board members; local newspaper articles about the organization over the past thirty years; and agency records, including a large scrapbook documenting staff training, retreats, and other activities.

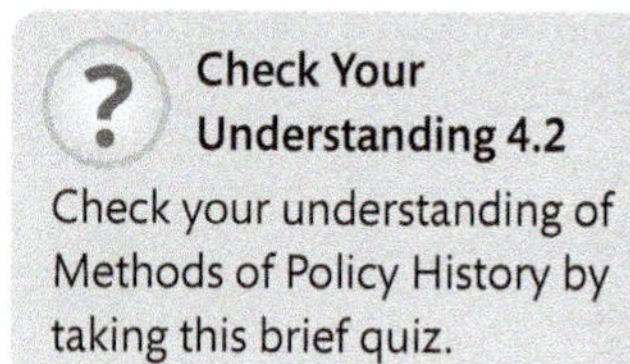

Check Your Understanding 4.2

Check your understanding of Methods of Policy History by taking this brief quiz.

THE BENTON PARK CRISIS CENTER

The Benton Park Crisis Center is located in a residential area of a Midwest city. It currently functions as a crisis and referral agency with a telephone hot line, outreach mental health services, and educational programs for public school students on substance abuse and suicide prevention. It has a paid professional staff of six and a large body of volunteers. It is in some ways similar to, and in other ways quite different from, the center that was established more than thirty years ago.

The crisis center opened in the summer of 1970. At the time, the main city high school was located a block away. Because of overcrowding in the high school, the lack of after-school recreational facilities, and the general proclivities of teenagers, many young people hung around in the neighborhood before and after classroom hours. This was also a time of anxiety about drugs, rebellion, delinquency, and a "hippie element" among the young, and, though many adult fears were exaggerated, real problems—bad trips, attempted suicides—did exist.

Responding to the concerns of local residents and of businesspeople in the neighborhood, a handful of volunteers opened a recreational and drop-in center whose goal was to prevent drug abuse and provide alternative activities for teens. The initial group that backed the center included a juvenile court judge, a probation officer, and several local businesspeople and homeowners. The center was located in a building owned by the city and made available at a low rent; it had almost no funding other than some voluntary donations.

The drop-in center offered some discussion and counseling groups and various recreational activities and was open to all on a twenty-four-hour basis. Perhaps not surprisingly, the facility was forced to close down almost immediately. The open-door policy and the small volunteer staff meant a lack of control; overnight "crashing," drinking in closets, and similar events were embarrassing signs that the center was perhaps encouraging rather than preventing problem behavior. However, the agency reopened shortly, this time with more structure and a federally funded worker from a program similar to today's Americorps to offer services and help coordinate the volunteers. Slowly, the center became a place to go and do particular things rather than a building in which to hang out.

Within the next two years, the center hired an executive director (paid but on a minimal level), a substance abuse counselor with a professional degree, and a part-time workshop coordinator. Staff and programs were still funded by donations, and the reliance on community volunteers remained. Being close to the drug abuse problem and other crisis situations promoted a spirit of mutual interdependence among volunteers, paid staff members, and the young people who frequented the center. A sense of support was established that has lasted throughout the program's history.

Following the hiring of paid staff members, the center received some state funding for substance abuse services through the local community mental health board. Staff members had not vigorously sought this funding; rather, the mental health board, not too sure about what to do with these state funds, decided to give them to the one agency that had developed a reputation for working on the problem of drug abuse. Increases in funding helped encourage more structure in the organization. There was less reliance on volunteers and a larger program of counseling by professionals. A drug educator was hired to do preventive work in the schools. Still, an art workshop and other recreational programs remained, as well as a body of volunteers, although these now began to receive formalized training for their activities.

A major focus of volunteer activity was staffing a telephone hot line to answer crisis calls from the community. Initially, this had simply been a business phone for the center, but as the organization became recognized as "the place that knows about drugs and is willing to help," people facing drug problems themselves, or families and professionals involved at a secondary level, began to call the center for assistance. Gradually, the center again expanded its use of volunteers and developed the extensive system of volunteer screening and training that is one of its hallmarks today. The hot line developed into a twenty-four-hour crisis counseling and referral telephone service, handling not only drug-related problems but also the full range of human difficulties, from suicide calls to mental health problems to requests for information on welfare services and emergency housing. Calls now came from people of all ages.

By the mid-1970s, the recreational and art workshop programs were in decline, spurred by the relocation of the high school to the outskirts of the city. In response to occasional nighttime use of the center's building by individuals with mental illness looking for shelter, the staff reluctantly decided to lock the facility at night. In the meantime, state funding increased, including some funding specifically for mental health services, and with the increase came more outside control over programming. Drug and mental health programs were emphasized by funding requirements; no special financial aid existed for activities such as the art workshop. In addition, state licensing had been developed for substance abuse services. Complying with the licensing brought new restrictions for the center, such as regulations about the sorts of staff needed and detailed rules about the format and content of notes on client contacts. New and innovative programs were harder to launch. Still, volunteers continued to work on the phone line, and an informality and sense of mutual support among staff members remained.

Mental health funding led to the hiring of professionally trained "mental health screeners" who could respond to psychiatric emergencies. The fact that their outreach assessment work sometimes led to commitments of individuals to mental hospitals brought a value dilemma to the agency. Was the center, which prided itself on allegiance to the client and to the principle of self-determination, about to become identified with "the system" and with social control? Gradually, however, as emergency calls increased and taxed the skills and energies of volunteers, mental health screeners came to be seen as important backups for the work of the center. The fact that screeners tended to be individuals who were former volunteers with additional training helped in making this transition.

In the past ten years of its history, the Benton Park Crisis Center has added more staff, received additional funding from the local United Way, and shifted program priorities from substance abuse to mental illness, in part due to a change in the types of clientele seeking help. The consolidation of the county substance abuse and mental health planning agencies under a single human services umbrella has actually made adaptation of programs to client needs somewhat easier, as funds now come from a common source. For some time, the center had been part of an alcohol and substance abuse council; it recently became incorporated under a separate board of directors. This new autonomy helped formalize the move from a drug abuse services mission to a goal of dealing with a broad range of crisis problems in the community. There has been a resurgence of innovative activity in the organization. The phone line remains a strong asset, still staffed primarily by volunteers, including interns from a nearby university's undergraduate social work program. The visitor to the center today is impressed not only by the array of professional services but also by the cheerful camaraderie of the "phone room" and the comfortable informality of staff offices.

The crisis center thus combines innovation and standardization; volunteer and professional help; and casualness and regulations concerning paperwork, staff screening, and the like. As a new worker, you might find these combinations confusing. To make sense of this milieu, you might seek out the sort of historical information we have presented. The history of the Benton Park Crisis Center would help you see how a variety of elements—the needs of the community and the clientele, the requirements of funding and licensing agencies, the social and economic conditions of the surrounding community, and the traditions embraced by the staff—have all shaped the direction and spirit of the agency.

Check Your Understanding 4.3

Check your understanding of The Benton Park Crisis Center by taking this brief quiz.

CONCLUSION

To some, history may seem like a dry collection of facts and figures from the past. We hope, however, that you will see its importance in your work with individuals, groups, organizations, and communities. The history of an individual, family, or neighborhood will enable you to put current situations and issues into perspective. In addition, as in our example of the Benton Park Crisis Center, knowing what has happened in the past will help you respond in a knowledgeable way to current issues and increase your ability to carry out organizational change.

Recall what you learned from this chapter by completing the Chapter Review.

5

Social/Economic Analysis

LEARNING OUTCOMES

- Explain why defining the policy is a critical first step in policy analysis.
- Explore the topic of problem definition and explain why objective conditions are not, by themselves, sufficient explanations of how we define social problems.
- Discuss the relationship between theories of human behavior and social welfare policy formulation and analysis.
- Discuss major American values and identify those that you consider to be most important for understanding our social welfare policies.
- Discuss and give examples of stated and unstated goals and explain why identifying both is important for understanding social welfare policies.
- Explore why every social welfare policy is, in a sense, an experiment.
- Explain the purpose of the economic analysis section of a practitioner policy analysis.

CHAPTER OUTLINE

ASDF_MEDIA/Shutterstock

The Personal Responsibility and Work Opportunity Reconciliation Act of 1996, reauthorized in 2006, was scheduled for another reauthorization in 2010. This did not happen until 2016, although programs supported by the bill, mainly the Temporary Assistance for Needy Families (TANF) block grant, have continued to operate under continuing resolutions until the reauthorization finally passed in 2016. During the seven years of reauthorization debates, we had conversations with a number of people who were familiar with the bill. Here is what a few had to say:

> *A member of a governor's office staff:* We have been very supportive of the TANF program ever since its inception in 1996. We like that the states are given more leeway in designing programs that will reflect the economic and political realities in their own states. We are particularly supportive of the provision of the reauthorization bill that allows the states to apply for demonstration grants called "social impact partnership projects." We do, however, have some concerns about some of the provisions of the reauthorization bills. We are particularly concerned with the increase in the work participation rate from 50 percent to 70 percent, with penalties to states that fall below the new level. With the current economy, we are having trouble meeting the 50 percent rate, and the new level will be nearly impossible to meet. We are also very concerned with the House bill that increases day

care funding by only $1 billion, an amount that won't even make up for inflation. If this version passes, we will need to cut down on the amount of day care we can fund, and that will make the 70 percent work participation rate even more difficult to satisfy.

A community organizer: Both the House and Senate versions stink, as does the original bill. The only thing that protects poor people and promotes social justice is national-level control of programs. You move control to the local level and the same bunch of good old boys who have run things for years will exert their power and do everything possible to save money. What we will see between the states is a race to the bottom to see who can develop the cheapest, most punitive welfare system possible.

A minister in a conservative Christian church: This bill places the emphasis of the welfare system on work, exactly where it should be. The former system rewarded people for staying home and doing nothing. After a few years, nothing becomes all you are able to do. Also, there was no "stick" to make people get off their duffs and become self-supporting and self-respecting. The new system helps people but tells them in no uncertain terms that they have only two years to get their lives together and they better get to it. I think this is great.

A city manager: I know everyone is putting their arms out of joint patting their own backs over the TANF program but, as for myself, I see problems. It's OK to encourage, even to force people to get jobs, but I'd like to see some concern about what type of jobs. It does little good to place a mother of three into a minimum-wage job with no benefits and no opportunity for advancement. She won't be able to afford day care, she won't be able to afford medical care, and so on, so when these benefits expire she will be out on the street. The reauthorization bill, particularly the House version, is even stingier with benefits to support people transitioning to employment. What will we do when people without adequate jobs begin to be thrown off the rolls? These people are not elderly Eskimos who will go out on the ice to die. They'll set up housekeeping on the streets of our cities and then the same group of business owners who are now so enthusiastic about this bill will be in my office demanding that I get the street people away from the fronts of their stores.

These people are all talking about the same policy, and they are all knowledgeable about its details and mechanics, yet they have very different interpretations about whether it is good or bad; what values it reflects; what its goals are; and whether its effects are likely to be positive, negative, or nothing at all. Answering these and similar questions is the task of the social/economic section of a social welfare policy analysis.

In this chapter, we look at those sections of the outline presented on page 32 under the headings of Social Analysis and Economic Analysis. The basic task of social/economic analysis is fairly straightforward—to gain an in-depth understanding of what our society considers to be social welfare problems, how we seek to deal with these problems, why we deal with them in the ways we do, and what will be the probable consequences of dealing with them in one way versus another or, perhaps, of not dealing with them at all.

DELINEATION OF THE POLICY UNDER ANALYSIS

Before the policy analysis process can begin, a critical first step is to specify carefully the boundaries of the policy you intend to analyze. Policies have vague and overlapping boundaries that can easily shift over the course of an analysis unless the analyst has carefully specified them and is constantly aware of the need to maintain focus. For example, imagine that you have been hired as a social worker with a state child protective services agency and you wish to research the policy context of your new job. Before you begin, you must decide: Do I wish to analyze the overall topic of child welfare policy? Only policy that concerns child abuse and neglect? Only child abuse and neglect policy in my state? Foster care policy in my agency? Or one specific law such as the 2010 reauthorization of the Child Abuse Prevention and Treatment Act? If your concern is protective services policy in your agency, are you going to limit your analysis to child protective services, or do you want to include adult protective services? You can, of course, look at several of these or all of them if you are willing to do the work. However, once you define the topic, you must stick with that definition.

Once you have defined your policy topic, the next step is to identify the policy *realm* you are concerned with. Staying with the example of child welfare, you need to decide whether you are interested in only government-sector activities, such as state-financed foster care; enterprise-sector activities, such as for-profit therapeutic day care; or voluntary-sector activities, such as church-sponsored children's homes. Because of the interaction between the realms of policy, in most cases you will need to look at all three, although you will probably concentrate on only one.

The major problem we find with the work of student policy analysts is that they fail to specify the boundaries of their analysis clearly and therefore tend to change focus, often more than once, during the course of the analysis. In the case of one student's analysis we recently read, for example, when the social analysis was conducted, the focus was on public-sector child welfare in general, concentrating on the Adoption Assistance and Child Welfare Act of 1980. When the political analysis was done, the focus changed to adoptions policy of the voluntary sector, looking at changes in private adoption agencies since 1970. The economic analysis concentrated on the development of for-profit day care providers. The focus kept changing until the historical analysis, which dealt with church-sponsored child care institutions. Rather than doing one coherent policy analysis, the student had done one section of each of five separate analyses. The first rule of policy analysis is: Specify the policy you wish to analyze as carefully as possible and keep that specification before you throughout the entire analysis. The purpose of this is similar to that of a scientist who states a research question and hypothesis or of a historian who draws up a list of questions in order to keep the research on one path throughout its course.

> **? Check Your Understanding 5.1**
> Check your understanding of Delineation of the Policy Under Analysis by taking this brief quiz.

SOCIAL PROBLEM ANALYSIS

The next step in social/economic analysis is to clearly and completely identify and define the problem the policy addresses. Social welfare policies are hypothetical solutions to perceived social problems. For this reason, the definition of the problem is the heart of the policy, the key to understanding its logic. Gerry Brewer and Peter deLeon (1983) state that the policy process "begins when a potential problem . . . is first sensed, i.e., problem recognition or identification. Once a problem is recognized, many possible means to alleviate, mitigate, or resolve it may be explored quickly and tentatively" (p. 18). Thus, the first step in practitioner policy analysis is to decipher what problem the formulators of the policy under analysis had in mind when they designed the policy. The definition of the problem addressed by a social welfare policy may be vague and obscure, sometimes even misleading. The problem definition phase of a policy analysis is a critical step, the complexity of which should not be underestimated. Leslie Pal (2014) states, "There is universal agreement that the key factor [in policy analysis] is the problem or at least the definition of a situation considered problematic. . . . The reason problem structuring is so important is that policy analysts seem to fail more often because they solve the wrong problem than because they get the wrong solution to the right problem" (p. 101).

Our initial inclination when faced with the task of defining social problems is to view them as objective conditions that a large number of people think we need to do something about. When problems are defined this way, the definitions seem obvious—a policy regarding homelessness deals with the problem of people who have no homes; an antipoverty policy deals with the problem of people without enough money. However, sociologists point out that objective conditions are not, by themselves, sufficient explanations of how we define social problems—the process of problem definition has other important dimensions. In a work that has come to be considered a classic in the social problem literature, Malcolm Spector and John Kutsuse (1987) define social problems as "the activities of individuals or groups making assertions of grievances and claims with respect to some putative conditions" (p. 75). In other words, social problems are labeled, constructed, and defined by individuals and groups, and these labels are accepted or rejected by society based more on the power and skill of the individual or group than on any objective manifestation of the condition being defined. An extreme example of this perspective on social problems is a statement by sociologist Pierre van den Berghe (1975), who argues that "there is no such thing as a social problem until someone thinks there is. Social problems have no more objective validity than ghosts. They exist only in the minds of those who believe in them. . . . It seems axiomatic to me that the solution to a 'social problem' is for people to stop defining it as such." A number of influential people have proposed exactly this as the solution to the problems of the abuse of marijuana, and prostitution—simply stop defining these behaviors as problems and they will cease to be problems.

The social construction of social problems is of critical import for understanding social welfare policies. Let's look, for example, at the problem of homelessness. The problem could be defined in terms of the large number of people who are suffering because they have no permanent and decent shelter. From this definition, the obvious policy response would be programs to provide an increased supply of low-cost housing and supportive services to enable people to take advantage of the housing. Using this definition, we can understand the policies of an organization such as Habitat for Humanity. But what of the policy of the city of Phoenix, where the city council dealt with the homeless by removing their support system, including closing shelters, alcohol treatment programs, and residential hotels; closing public parks at sundown; and ordering the public works department to spray kerosene on trash so as to render any leftover food inedible (Higgins, 1983)? Obviously, the problem for the city of Phoenix was not that people were suffering due to lack of shelter and needed to be housed but that homeless people were cluttering up the streets and needed to move elsewhere.

Thoughts for Social Work Practice

Social workers deal with many clients who engage in behaviors defined by our society as social problems, such as substance abuse or sex work. Do you think it is necessary for the social worker to accept society's definition of social problems? Why or why not?

When attempting to define the problem being dealt with by a particular social welfare policy, it is helpful to ask, "For whom is this a problem?" and, "Who will benefit as a result of the policy?" In the case of Phoenix, the problem being dealt with by the policy is clearly not experienced by the people without any shelter. The intended beneficiaries of the policy appear to be businesspeople and property owners in the areas with large homeless populations, not the homeless people themselves.

It is also helpful to break problems down into primary problems and derivative problems. In the case of mental health policy, the primary problem is that there are a number of people who are suffering because of psychological illness of one sort or another. Derived from this are problems of employers who have employees who are not very productive, children in single-parent homes, people living on the streets of Phoenix, and the list goes on. Most social welfare policies deal with the derivative problems.

Finally, it should be noted that a policy is often a response to more than one problem, and this often creates tensions and inconsistencies in the policy. Financial assistance policy seeks to deal with a number of problems simultaneously, prominent among which are the facts that many people are unable to earn a living, that many poor children are not receiving adequate care, and that the level of family breakup is increasing. Some policy analysts argue that it also deals with the problem of regulating the labor market (Blakemore, 1998; Piven & Cloward, 1971). Aspects of the policy that address one of these problems may be in direct contradiction with those addressing others. For example, TANF policy requires that welfare recipients take jobs that may well result in deterioration in the quality of care provided to the recipients' children. The reason for this is that the employed parent will not be home with the children, but the job provided for the person most likely will not pay enough to purchase adequate child care.

? Check Your Understanding 5.2

Check your understanding of Social Problem Analysis by taking this brief quiz.

FACTS RELATED TO THE PROBLEM

In this section of the policy analysis, we assess the information we actually "know" about a social welfare problem. Two major areas must be explored in this phase of a policy analysis. The first is an assessment of the completeness of the knowledge regarding the problem—how many facts do we know about it, and what is the state of knowledge regarding cause-effect relationships. The second area is the one in which we generally have quite a lot of knowledge regarding any social welfare problem—what do we know about the population affected by the problem?

Completeness of Knowledge Related to the Problem

One of the most important factors in understanding social welfare policy analysis, and in understanding any social welfare policy area, is the realization that there is a tremendous amount we really don't know about most social welfare problems. We have any number of theories, and we have a seemingly infinite number of discrete facts about any one problem, but when it comes to actually knowing why certain people are poor, why the rate of violent crime is increasing, how we can improve the school performance of inner-city kids, our knowledge often is incomplete.

In some areas, the knowledge base is much more complete than in others. We know quite a lot, for example, about health care. We know that by increasing the availability of prenatal care, we can reduce the number of birth defects. We can even calculate how much money we need to spend to eliminate a certain number of birth defects and compare that to the cost of repairing or managing the defects that result from the lack of care. In mental health policy, by comparison, the degree of completeness of knowledge is fairly low. For years we have developed policies that provide psychotherapy to persons suffering from psychological disorders without much evidence that the provision of these services does any good (Tavris, 2003).

Recently, in response to advances in knowledge of the biochemical basis of mental illness, we are establishing policies that provide pharmaceutical treatment to patients, but we are learning that the lack of supportive counseling greatly diminishes the effectiveness of prescribed medications.

Thus, it must be recognized that most social welfare policies are actually experiments. Based on the completeness of the knowledge, we can state that some are more experimental than others. The primary questions in health policy revolve around what services we want to provide and how we want to deliver them. We have a pretty good idea regarding the results. In mental health, public assistance, and family policy, the primary questions are: What services should we provide? and Will they work? In many cases, we really don't know.

Population Affected by the Problem

The one area about which we know quite a lot regarding most social welfare problems is the characteristics of the population affected by the problem. How large is the population? What are the population trends? We obviously tend to worry more about a problem that affects a large population than we do about a small one, but what probably worries us most is a problem that is rapidly growing. AIDS, for example, does not affect as large a population as cancer, but we were initially terrified because it was growing and the rate of growth appeared to be increasing. Now that the level of AIDS in the United States is stabilizing, the panic has subsided, although concerns about its growth worldwide have increased.

After we have established the population size and the growth trends of the problem under analysis, we then look at the defining characteristics of the population affected—the statistics on age, sex, race, family structure, geographic distribution, and so forth. These characteristics often lead to some interesting hypotheses about how we deal with the problem. Continuing with the example of AIDS, it is interesting that the level of concern, as indicated by the amount of money spent on AIDS research and treatment, began to increase dramatically when significant numbers of heterosexual, nondrug users began to show up in the statistics.

Check Your Understanding 5.3

Check your understanding of Facts Related to the Problem by taking this brief quiz.

THEORY OF HUMAN BEHAVIOR UNDERGIRDING THE POLICY

It is curious that we as social workers frequently overlook the obvious fact that the objective of many, if not most, social welfare policies is to effect some form of behavioral change. Public assistance policy seeks to increase recipients' labor-force participation, child welfare policy seeks to improve people's quality of parenting, criminal justice and juvenile justice policy seek to decrease law-violating behavior, and so on. Thus, every policy is based on some, rarely explicitly stated, theory of human behavior. To understand a policy, and to understand why many policies are ineffective, we need to determine what theory of human behavior the policy is based on and whether the theory is valid and applicable.

Most social welfare policies are based on some version of the rational choice perspective on human behavior. This perspective views people as rational beings who make choices based on self-interest. Rational choice theory assumes that people are purposive and goal oriented; that humans have sets of hierarchically ordered preferences (generally called *utilities* in this theory); and that, in choosing lines of behavior, human beings make rational calculations with respect to the costs and benefits of various alternative behaviors (Turner, 1998).

The version of rational choice theory perhaps most familiar to social workers is social exchange theory. This theory is based on the minimax principle, which simply states that people will make choices based on an assessment of which course of action will minimize costs and maximize rewards. Behavior is explained using the simple calculus of rewards minus costs equals outcome. It is assumed that if the result of this calculation is positive, the person will choose the behavior; if it is negative, the person will avoid the behavior (Hutchison, 2008; Thibaut & Kelley, 1959).

Probably the clearest example of rational choice theory in social policy is in the area of criminal justice. We continue to increase the penalties for crimes based on the belief that people make rational choices regarding the commission of crimes. We envision a person saying to himself, "If I rob this store and get caught, the maximum penalty I'll get will be one year in prison. That's not so bad and I really need the money, so I guess I'll do it." We then enact legislation to increase the penalty and assume that the person's conversation with himself will change to "If I rob this store and get caught, I'm sure to get at least five years in prison. That's really a lot so I guess I'd better not do it."

Social workers know that, although rational choice certainly plays a major part in people's behavior, many other factors also enter into the equation. Many policies fail, or are much less successful than they could be, simply because they are based on an inadequate understanding of the behavioral dimensions of the problem being addressed. One of the major contributions that social workers can make to policy analysis is bringing a much more sophisticated, nuanced, and multidimensional understanding of human behavior to the table than is usually known among policy professionals.

Check Your Understanding 5.4

Check your understanding of Theory of Human Behavior Undergirding the Policy by taking this brief quiz.

SOCIAL VALUES RELATED TO THE PROBLEM

We have observed that the definition of social welfare problems is largely socially constructed and that the level of knowledge regarding most problems is incomplete. Based on these observations, it should come as no surprise that values constitute what is probably the most important dimension for understanding social welfare policy. David Easton's (1956–1957) classic definition of politics as "the authoritative allocation of values for society" could just as well apply to social welfare policy. To understand our society's response to social welfare problems, you must inquire as to what values support a policy and what values a policy offends.

What major U.S. values lead people to support or oppose various responses to social welfare problems? Probably the best analysis, although now a bit dated, is that developed by sociologist Robin Williams (1970). Williams identifies fifteen major value orientations in U.S. society (Tropman, 1989; Williams, 1979). These are discussed in the following paragraphs.

Achievement and Success

U.S. society is marked by a great emphasis on achievement, particularly occupational achievement. Ours is a competitive society, and people who don't measure up in the competition are looked down on. Social welfare policies deal with problems closely related to lack of success. Poor people have not achieved occupationally, people experiencing marital discord have not succeeded in their relationship, people with psychologically disturbed children are viewed as having failed as parents, and so forth. Thus, almost any social welfare policy faces an uphill struggle for public support in that it generally deals with a problem that violates this basic value. A frequent response to this value by social welfare policymakers is to couch policies in terms that indicate that the policy will attempt to instill this value in its clients. A program started by the state of Alabama in response to the Welfare Reform Act of 1988, for example, is entitled Project Success.

Activity and Work

Numerous observers, from Tocqueville in 1841 up to the most recent, have noted that Americans place a high value on being busy. Even in our leisure activities, we emphasize some form of purposeful, action-oriented behavior. However, the primary manifestation of this value is in relation to work. Williams (1979) observes, "Directed and disciplined activity in a regular occupation is a particular form of this basic orientation" (p. 459). Work has become almost an end in itself, valued even when it is not necessary for economic survival. Observe, for example, that the first thing most winners of large sums of money in lotteries are quoted as saying is some variant of the statement, "I'm not going to quit my job." Because many social welfare programs provide people with means of existence that are not tied to work, they are immediately suspect in the eyes of many Americans. The TANF program, passed as part of the 1996 Personal Responsibility and Work Opportunity Reconciliation Act, enjoys great popularity precisely because it forces people to go to work.

Moral Orientation

Americans generally view the world in moral terms—right and wrong, good and bad, ethical and unethical. The recipients of social welfare benefits are often suspected of having engaged in behavior that is morally bad or of having not engaged in behavior that is morally good. Some welfare mothers, for example, have had children without benefit of marriage, have dropped out of school, and are not working, all behaviors we are likely to condemn as bad, perhaps even sinful. This moral orientation has often led to differentiation between recipients of services and benefits as "worthy" or "unworthy."

Humanitarian Mores

Caring for one another, particularly those who are perceived as less fortunate and suffering through no fault of their own, is a key value in U.S. society. Williams (1979) points out that one manifestation of this value is the fact that fully one-third of the adult population participates in some form of voluntary service. This value serves, to a certain extent, to counter punitive social welfare policies that occasionally emerge out of our moral orientation.

Efficiency and Practicality

Our society places a high value on good stewardship of time and material resources. We feel a compulsion to continually seek the best means possible for achieving a certain end. This value has several important consequences for the social work profession. The first is a historic interest in developing better technical means to deal with social welfare problems. For years, social workers have sought to develop a "science of social work." Another way this value manifests itself is in our continual concern with accountability, that is, in demonstrating that social welfare programs are being run efficiently and are having the intended effects. It is ironic that the end result of this value is often antithetical to the value itself. For example, it has been estimated that as much as 40 percent of a social worker's time in public agencies is spent doing paperwork, mostly for the purpose of documenting that the agency is doing its job efficiently and effectively. During training sessions on procedures for completing time documentation forms, a frequent—and legitimate—question is "Where on this form do I put down all the time I spend filling out this form?"

Progress

Americans hold charter membership in what Williams (1979) has called the "cult of progress," believing that things can, and should, continually be getting better. The historian Henry Steele Commager (1947) has observed that "throughout their history Americans have insisted that the best was yet to be. . . . The American knew that nothing was impossible in his brave new world. . . . Progress was not, to him, a mere philosophical ideal but a commonplace of experience" (pp. xi, xiv). Because of this belief, U.S. society has never accepted the position of many other societies, both past and present, that social problems are simply a part of the natural order of things and that attempts to change social conditions are as useless as trying to change the ocean's tides. We are continually attempting to do something about conditions such as poverty, ill health, crime, violence, and so forth. An unfortunate side effect of this value is that, if a policy or program does not demonstrate immediate results, we tend to grow impatient with it quickly and abandon it in order to try something else. Poverty, for example, has been around for thousands of years; when the War on Poverty didn't eliminate it in three years, Congress became disillusioned and began to dismantle the policy.

Material Comfort

The United States is an acquisitive and materialistic culture. This statement really requires no more justification than to look at the lifestyles of friends and acquaintances and at what is emphasized in TV commercials and online ads. We equate material possessions with happiness and success. The relevance of this value for understanding social welfare policy resides in the fact that people needing social welfare services generally, though not always, are people who are experiencing a low level of material comfort. This raises difficult questions concerning what level of material comfort they have a right to and what the rest of society has an obligation to provide. We also believe that a lack of material comfort can be a good thing because it will tend to spur people to solve their own problems to gain the material comforts they desire. (The comedian Red Skelton once said, "I've got a solution to poverty—tax the poor; give them an incentive to get rich.") One of the major principles of financial assistance policy ever since the 1601 Elizabethan Poor Laws has been that of less eligibility. This is the notion that the level of material comfort of people receiving the highest level of welfare benefits should always be lower than the level of the least comfortable working person.

Equality

The value of equality constitutes a steady theme throughout U.S. history. Yet, as Williams (1979) notes, "few other value complexes are more subject to strain in modern times" (p. 472). We express strong support for the idea of equality as a philosophical principle, but our society is characterized by a high degree of inequality, and most Americans believe this is as it should be. The explanation for this apparent discrepancy is that when most Americans speak of equality, they mean equality of opportunity, not of outcome. We believe people should have an equal chance in life and find elements such as ascribed social status, old boy networks, and the like to be deeply offensive. Social welfare policies that help achieve equality of opportunity, such as Head Start, are warmly supported by most people in the United States. Policies that smack of equality of outcome, whether this is the intent or not, such as guaranteed annual income, race and gender hiring quotas, and the like, always face strong opposition.

Freedom

As anyone who has taken a high school civics class is aware, the concept of freedom is complex and multidimensional. Obviously, freedom does not mean freedom from all external control. In the United States, *freedom* generally refers to a preference for control by diffuse social processes rather than by any definite social organization. For example, the practice of neighborhood segregation by race or religion has been made illegal because it violates the value of freedom by forcefully excluding people from certain residences by law. However, few people are totally free to live wherever they wish simply because they can afford only certain neighborhoods. Thus, in the United States, freedom generally means freedom from excessive and arbitrary external restraint. This way of looking at freedom has resulted in "a tendency to think of rights rather than duties, a suspicion of established (especially personal) authority, a distrust of central government, a deep aversion to acceptance of obviously coercive restraint through visible social organization" (Williams, 1979, p. 480). The value of freedom has important consequences for understanding almost any social welfare policy. Social welfare policies are often viewed as increasing the rights of one group and decreasing the freedom of another. Child protection laws increase the rights of children to a minimal standard of care, but they reduce the freedom of parents to rear children in any way they see fit without interference by government; financial assistance policies increase the rights of individuals to live with a certain degree of dignity, but they decrease the freedom of taxpayers to enjoy the fruits of their own labor; health care policy increases the rights of people to receive medical care, but it decreases the freedom of physicians to practice medicine as they wish; and so on.

External Conformity

Even though the U.S. self-image celebrates individualism, it has been frequently noted that we have a rather low tolerance for those who do not conform to accepted standards. Williams (1979) observes that "American 'individualism,' taken in broadest terms, has consisted mainly of a rejection of the state and impatience with restraints upon economic activity; it has not tended to set the autonomous individual up in rebellion against his social group" (p. 485). By and large, we do not approve of those who vary too far from the norm in dress, behavior, manners, lifestyle, or whatever. Social welfare policies are often directed at people who do not conform to some important standard; they may be unmarried mothers, teenagers who don't go to school, people who use drugs, or adolescents who refuse to comply with adult authority figures. Social welfare policies directed at these groups are generally aimed at helping them but often have an underlying purpose of attempting to control, and sometimes eliminate, the nonconforming behavior.

Science and Secular Rationality

Americans have great faith that the methods of science will eventually solve all, or nearly all, problems of living in our physical and social world. We believe that even the seemingly intractable social problems addressed by social welfare policies will eventually succumb to the onslaught of scientific method. At the present time, however, we are still some way from good, useful knowledge applicable to most social welfare problems, and this causes much frustration among policymakers.

Nationalism-Patriotism

Every society is characterized by some degree of ethnocentrism—that is, the belief that membership in that group is preferable to membership in any other group. In the United States, this feeling is quite strong, although probably no stronger than in many other areas of the world. (In some traditional cultures, people outside the culture are not even considered to be human.) In the United States, nationalism-patriotism has one unique dimension: a sense of missionary zeal to spread U.S. economic and governmental institutions throughout the world, generally by nonmilitary means. Many nations have, in the past, sought to conquer other nations in order to dominate them and thereby gain wealth and advantage. The United States wishes for other nations to adopt its way of doing things not directly for its own advantage but because its citizens feel they, and consequently the rest of the world, will benefit if they do so. Nationalism-patriotism is a value complex that does not have a great relevance for understanding social welfare policy, but it does have some. In Chapter 3, we discussed cross-cultural comparison as one approach to policy analysis. Cross-cultural comparisons often result in findings that are embarrassing to the United States because they show that we, who like to think of ourselves as world leaders, often rank below some developing nations on social indicators such as infant mortality. Appeals to the value of nationalism-patriotism can often be more effective in engendering sympathy for social welfare proposals than appeals to more obvious values such as humanitarianism.

Democracy

It goes almost without saying that one of the star positions in the U.S. constellation of values is a belief in the democratic process, that is, decision making with every person's preferences being weighed. Democracy is sometimes problematic, however, in social welfare policy. The reason for this is related to what Tocqueville (1845) referred to as the "tyranny of the majority." This means that if everything is done by majority rule, people, or groups of people, who are not part of the majority can suffer some harsh consequences as a result of never getting their way. African Americans, Hispanics, lesbians and gays, same-sex couples, and migrant workers have all suffered because the majority has not been sensitive to their problems. Social welfare policies often face strong opposition based on the argument that they are undemocratic because they benefit a minority group against the will of the majority. Employment-related benefits for same-sex spouses is probably the clearest current example of this.

Individual Personality

In the United States, we place an extremely high value on the worth and dignity of the individual. We also place a heavy load of responsibility on the individual in the form of credit for success and blame for failure. In many areas of the world—Japan is probably the most frequently cited example—the well-being of the group is the central value, and individuals are expected to defer their own wishes to the collective welfare of the group. This is not the case in the United States. Groups are viewed as collections of individuals formed for the purpose of facilitating the goals and promoting the welfare of individual members. The value of individual personality is critical for understanding social welfare policy in this country. By their very definition, social welfare policies involve collective provisions for the assistance of individuals. Thus, they generally involve sacrifice by individuals for the good of the group. For example, public social welfare policies require individuals, sometimes against their will, to sacrifice part of their income, in the form of taxes, to finance provisions for people without enough money to live on. This is deeply offensive to many Americans and guarantees opposition to any proposed expansion of social welfare programs.

Racism, Sexism, and Related Group Superiority Themes

Although the United States is characterized by strong values of democracy, individualism, humanitarianism, and so forth, we have to recognize that there also are what Williams (1979) refers to as "deviant themes, contrary to the main thrust of American society," namely, racism, sexism, and related prejudices. Because these themes run counter to so many of our other value clusters, we have attempted to resolve them through numerous pieces of legislation. However, we must recognize that they are still present to a much greater degree than we care to admit. Ugly as the value cluster of racism, sexism, and so forth, may be, we must recognize its existence if we are to understand social welfare policies fully. The common perception is that the majority of beneficiaries of most social welfare policies are minorities and women, and thus these policies are often equated with these groups. On the one hand, social welfare policies often receive support from individuals and groups who support attempts to redress the effects of discrimination against minorities and women. In fact, many policies, such as affirmative action and minority scholarships, are often proposed specifically for this purpose. On the other hand, individuals and groups often oppose social welfare policies and, although they generally don't admit this, the reason for the opposition is often directly a result of racism and sexism.

Thoughts for Social Work Practice

Social work clients are often caught between conflicting American values. For example, a poor single mother often must choose between the value of work (she should be gainfully employed to support herself and her child) and the value of being a good parent (she should have time to nurture, supervise, and maximize the development of her child). A woman working enough hours at near-minimum wage to support her family does not have the time to maximize her child's development; a woman maximizing her child's development does not have enough time to support her family fully by working. How can a social worker help a person deal with these contradictory values?

Contradictions in the U.S. Value System

As you may well have figured out from thinking about the values discussed previously, they do not result in a uniform pattern but rather are shot through with conflicts and contradictions. We are motivated to help the poor by our value of humanitarianism, but this is mitigated by other values: *moralism,* which leads us to believe that poverty is somehow related to improper behavior; *individualism,* which places responsibility for problems and for their solutions at the feet of the individuals affected; and the value of activity and work, which causes us to suspect that welfare programs encourage nonwork behavior. Policies to assist groups who are victims of oppression, such as women, African Americans, and lesbians and gays, are encouraged by our belief in equality but are retarded by values of *democracy* and *freedom,* which lead us to suspect that by promoting the rights of one group we will be discriminating against another, and, below the surface, by *racism, sexism,* and *group superiority* themes. Thus, our social welfare policies often appear to be illogical because they are attempting to balance numerous conflicting values.

Check Your Understanding 5.5
Check your understanding of Social Values Related to the Problem by taking this brief quiz.

GOALS OF THE POLICY UNDER ANALYSIS

In *Alice in Wonderland,* Alice has the following exchange with the Cheshire Cat:

> "Would you tell me, please, which way I ought to go from here?"
> "That depends a good deal on where you want to get to," said the cat.
> "I don't much care where—" said Alice.
> "Then it doesn't matter which way you go," said the cat. (Carroll, 1971, p. 51)

Unlike Alice, the designers of social welfare policies have fairly specific destinations, or goals, in mind. To understand a policy, it is necessary to understand just what these goals are. This task constitutes the next stage of the social analysis.

A policy goal is the desired state of affairs that is hoped to be achieved by the policy. As with many areas of policy analysis, the task of determining goals appears simple at the outset, but once you are into it, you discover that it can be extremely complex and often misleading. There is a rich sociological literature on the subject of goals that deals with the topic in much greater depth than we need to here (Etzioni, 1964; Georgiou, 1973; Perrow, 1961).

Policies generally are directed toward more than one goal, and these multiple goals are often in conflict with one another (Gupta, 2001). This is a result of the conflicts in the value structure of U.S. society discussed previously, in combination with the political nature of policymaking. Child welfare policy, for example, pursues two often incompatible goals. On the one hand, we seek to ensure that all children grow up in a safe home. On the other hand, we seek to ensure that a child can grow up in his or her own family. Ensuring the safety of children can involve removing them from their families; keeping families intact can involve putting children at risk. In a similar fashion, mental health policy has a goal of preventing mentally ill people from harming themselves and/or others but also has a goal of putting people in the "least restrictive environment." Obviously, the less restrictive an environment becomes, the greater the risk of disturbed persons harming themselves or others. Financial assistance policy seeks to support people at an adequate level but also has a goal of motivating people to work. If the level of assistance ever becomes such that it truly could be defined as adequate, this presumably would lower the recipient's motivation to work.

In almost all cases, policies are directed toward different levels of goals, often distinguished as *goals* and *objectives*. The goal of a policy is a general and abstract statement of the state of affairs the policymakers seek to accomplish. A goal is generally difficult to measure and often is not even intended to be accomplished. It is rather a benchmark, a statement that provides general direction to the activities of the programs set up under the policy. For example, the goal of a state policy regarding child welfare staffing was stated as: "To assure that all dependent and neglected children in the state receive the highest possible quality services from experienced, professionally trained social workers and allied personnel." Objectives are derived from goals and are specific, concrete, measurable statements. The objectives derived from the state child welfare personnel goals were:

1. Increase the number of competent, practice-ready BSW and MSW candidates applying for employment in child welfare in the Department of Human Resources (DHR).
2. Improve the retention of child welfare staff in DHR.
3. Increase the responsiveness and effectiveness of the State and Departmental Personnel systems in certifying qualified applicants for employment in DHR child welfare positions. (Alabama Department of Human Resources, 1991)

The final, and probably the most important, aspect of goals we must understand in order to do a social analysis is that policies contain unstated, as well as stated, goals. Stated goals are sometimes referred to in the literature as official or manifest goals, and unstated goals are often called operative or latent goals. This is the single most important item in understanding why there are so many policies that seem to make no sense yet are never effectively reformed. High school teachers, for example, often express their frustration that they have difficulty teaching because so many of their students "have no business in school"; in other words, the students are not interested in learning and are not benefiting from being in the classroom. The teachers ask why the school system does not adopt a policy encouraging these young people to leave school, get jobs, and not return to school until they are ready to benefit from it. The reason school systems do not adopt this seemingly rational policy is that, although the stated (official, *manifest*) goal of school systems is to educate young people and prepare them for adult life, an unstated (operative, *latent*) goal of every public school system is to keep young people off the street and out of the full-time job market until they are eighteen years old. Therefore, dropout prevention is always a goal of schools, even though any teacher realizes that many prevented dropouts do not benefit in any way from their additional years in school and in fact often interfere with the education of other young people.

Another example of the difference, and often conflict, between stated and unstated goals, and one of more relevance to social workers, is public assistance policy. The public welfare system has been reformed again and again, but none of the reforms has ever had much of an impact on our country's dependent population. For example,

> Temporary Assistance for Needy Families (TANF) is a block grant created by the Personal Responsibility and Work Opportunity Reconciliation Act of

> 1996, as part of a federal effort to "end welfare as we know it." The TANF block grant replaced the Aid to Families with Dependent Children (AFDC) program, which had provided cash welfare to poor families with children since 1935. Under the TANF structure, the federal government provides a block grant to the states, which use these funds to operate their own programs. States can use TANF dollars in ways designed to meet any of the four purposes set out in federal law, which are to: (1) provide assistance to needy families so that children may be cared for in their own homes or in the homes of relatives; (2) end the dependence of needy parents on government benefits by promoting job preparation, work, and marriage; (3) prevent and reduce the incidence of out-of-wedlock pregnancies and establish annual numerical goals for preventing and reducing the incidence of these pregnancies; and (4) encourage the formation and maintenance of two-parent families. (Coven, 2003)

As will be discussed further in the chapter on antipoverty policy (Chapter 6), the authors are skeptical about this policy's potential to permanently reduce economic dependency. The reason for our skepticism has to do with our analysis of the unstated goals of the public welfare system. We argue that the primary operative goal of the public welfare system is to manage economic dependency as efficiently as possible while preserving the social and economic status quo in the society. Thus, policies that significantly redistribute power and resources will not be considered. Without significant redistribution of power and resources, there is really no solution to the problem of economic dependency. In other words, the operative goal of the welfare system is not to eliminate dependency but rather to manage dependency while preserving the wealth and power of the rest of society.

Check Your Understanding 5.6
Check your understanding of Goals of the Policy Under Analysis by taking this brief quiz.

HYPOTHESES UNDERLYING THE POLICY

The next step in the analysis of a social welfare policy is to identify the hypotheses or theories on which the policy is based. In most areas of social welfare, the state of knowledge is incomplete; little is known about cause-effect relationships. Thus, every social policy is in effect an experiment and, like all experiments, contains one or more hypotheses. The hypotheses and theories undergirding a policy are rarely explicitly stated and generally must be inferred from other statements.

A hypothesis is an if-then statement: If we do *X*, then *Y* will happen. A careful reading of a policy statement will reveal the hypotheses on which the policy is based. The TANF program, for example, hypothesizes that *if* we require welfare recipients to work in return for their grants, *then* they will learn work skills necessary for regular employment; *if* we provide basic education and job training, *then* recipients will find jobs and leave the welfare rolls; *if* we place a time limit on receipt of assistance, *then* people will be motivated to become self-supporting.

Behind every hypothesis is a theory that may be partially or totally incorrect. The theory behind TANF is that welfare dependency is a result of individual shortcomings in the recipients and that if we address these shortcomings, we can reduce the welfare rolls. Social workers, sociologists, and economists have recognized for years that many of the problems behind the "welfare mess" reside mainly in the social and economic structure of society, not exclusively in the individual recipient. These are problems involving the number of jobs available, the amount these jobs pay, and the support infrastructure necessary for people to be able to take advantage of the jobs that are available. Social policies will continue to fail unless financial assistance policy begins to address hypotheses such as *if* enough decent-paying jobs are made available, and *if* adequate support services such as day care and transportation networks are put in place, *then* people will become self-supporting.

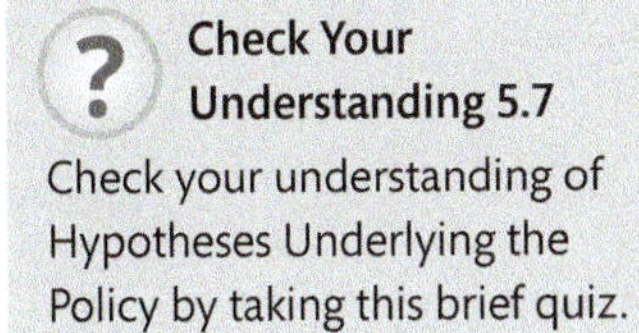
?
Check Your Understanding 5.7
Check your understanding of Hypotheses Underlying the Policy by taking this brief quiz.

ECONOMIC ANALYSIS

A central concept in the study of economics is that of scarcity. That is, economics is based on the assumption that there is not now, nor will there ever be, enough resources to satisfy all of our needs and wants. Thus, economics is concerned with the matter of choice: How do we choose to distribute scarce resources? Questions of choice in resource allocation revolve around questions of *effectiveness* (Do the measures we support work?), *efficiency* (How much benefit do we get for a given expenditure of resources?), and *equity* (Are resources divided fairly?).

Social welfare policies involve the expenditure of large quantities of money—money that could be spent for alternative social welfare policies or even for other things altogether. Probably the most volatile policy issue is that social welfare benefits are largely financed by tax money, which many people feel would be spent more effectively, efficiently, and equitably if it were left in taxpayers' pockets to spend as they wish. Thus, the economic ramifications of social welfare policies are of critical interest.

As discussed in Chapter 3,economic analysis of social welfare policies can be extremely technical and complex, generally requiring a competence in higher-level mathematics. The economic analysis section of a practitioner policy analysis need not be so complex. What this section of an analysis should do is employ the general perspective of an economist to ask questions related to what the effect of a given policy, or policy proposal, might be on the distribution and consumption of scarce resources. In addition, economists have a certain perspective on individual behavior, one that is somewhat different from that of most social workers (Levitt & Dubner, 2005). In the economic analysis section, we look at the macroeconomic ramifications of a policy, analyze the opportunity cost, and assess the implications of the policy for the behavior of individuals, using an economic style of interpretation.

Macroeconomic Analysis

Macroeconomic analysis is concerned with aggregate economic performance. It looks at questions of output, income, inflation, and unemployment. These are the main items of economic interest you view on cable news—what is happening to the gross national product, the gross national income, the inflation rate, and the unemployment rate. Taken together, these broad measures give us some idea of our collective economic health.

The macroeconomic analysis section of a social welfare policy analysis asks what the effect of an existing or a proposed policy is, or is likely to be, on aggregate economic performance. Will the policy increase or decrease productivity and, consequently, profits? What will the effects be on the rate of employment? Will the policy contribute to an increasing rate of inflation? Minimum wage/living wage legislation probably provides the clearest illustration of macroeconomic concerns with a social policy. Every time the minimum wage is increased, critics voice the concern that it will result in higher unemployment due to employers laying off employees they can no longer afford; business failures resulting from marginal enterprises failing under the burden of increased payroll costs; and inflation due to merchants increasing prices to cover the higher cost of doing business, which, of course, results in the value of the increased wage eventually being no more than the wage it replaced. A typical concern is voiced in an article in *City Journal:* "The living wage poses a big threat to [cities'] economic health, because the costs and restrictions it imposes on the private sector will destroy jobs—especially low wage jobs—and send businesses fleeing to other locales" (Malanga, 2017, p. 1).

Macroeconomic analysis also asks what the effects of the larger economy are on the social problems that the policies seek to redress. Loic Wacquant and William Julius Wilson, for example, assert that welfare reform initiatives have always been failures because they insist on incorrectly identifying the cause of welfare dependency as individual inadequacy. Welfare reform proposals "have paid too little attention to the broader economic and social-structural factors that are responsible for the crystallization of a large underclass and persistent welfare dependency" (Wacquant & Wilson, 1989). They argue that an effective welfare policy will need to deal with macroeconomic issues, mainly full employment at an increased minimum wage (Wacquant & Wilson, 1989).

Opportunity Cost

Because social welfare policies involve the expenditure of scarce resources, policy analysis inevitably involves some study of the costs. Cost accounting and auditing are, of course, important administrative functions, but they are not what we are concerned with here. Rather, we are concerned with how the cost of a certain policy, or proposed policy, compares to policy alternatives. This is referred to by economists as *opportunity cost.*

The opportunity cost of a policy consists of all the outcomes or benefits that must be sacrificed if that particular policy is adopted rather than an alternative policy. In other words, given finite resources, if we spend our money to implement one proposed solution to a social problem, we are not able to implement alternative solutions. Although advocates of prevention rarely use the term, opportunity cost is what they are talking about when they criticize social welfare policy in a number of areas. They point out that we spend so much money keeping people in jail that we can't afford community programs that might prevent a number of people from ever getting in trouble with the law; we allocate so many resources to foster care that we are not able to provide adequate family preservation services to prevent foster care being needed in the first place; we spend too much on law enforcement and drug treatment programs and too little on drug prevention education and counseling. Opportunity cost is used to assess alternative social welfare policies, but it is also used by critics of the welfare system to argue that the money spent on welfare benefits could be better spent on something altogether different and that the poor would benefit most from this alternative allocation. Conservatives such as George Gilder, Martin Anderson, and Charles Murray argue forcefully that spending money on welfare benefits depresses the economy (a macroeconomic analysis) and that if the money were available for investment instead, it would result in economic growth, which would make jobs and opportunities for advancement available for the poorest Americans

(Anderson, 1978; Gilder, 1981; Mead, 1986). In other words, the opportunity cost of welfare programs is that businesses cannot expand and provide jobs that would be preferable to welfare.

Effects on Individual Consumer Behavior

The economist looks at behavior in a way that is somewhat different from other social scientists. The economic explanation of behavior is based on an assumption that Gordon Tullock (1972) refers to as the "90 percent selfish" hypothesis. This means that, although people may occasionally act in generous and selfless ways, in the overwhelming proportion of instances they will seek their own best interest. The economist will add the following disclaimer: Economic analysis of behavior makes no claims that it can explain the behavior of any one individual, only behavior in the aggregate. Thus, the economist cannot explain the behavior of the individual physician who could make $150 per office visit treating private patients yet chooses instead to serve Medicaid patients at a reimbursement rate that is only a fraction of this amount. However, economists will predict with a high degree of confidence that, under the conditions just described, most physicians will treat as many private patients as possible and treat Medicaid patients only when they have no private patients available.

Historically, the economic analysis of effects of policy on individual behavior has been one of the driving forces behind financial assistance policy. This policy has been guided by what is known as the doctrine of less eligibility. This refers to the policy principle that a person living on welfare should always be worse off than the lowest paid working person. Guided by the 90 percent selfish hypothesis, this assumes that if people can do as well or better on welfare than they can by working, most people will choose to live on welfare. This was the foundation of critiques of welfare programs, leading up to the 1996 welfare reform, that the welfare system had become too generous and the result was that it had sapped people's motivation to work and improve their lives. One author, for example, says,

> expanded welfare programs [since the 1960s] made it economically rational for women to have children out of wedlock, for fathers to desert wives and children. By 1970, the package of welfare, food stamps, Medicaid and housing subsidies provided a gross income higher than many working people earned. Small wonder that a sizable number chose the world of welfare. (Methvin, 1985)

The TANF program enacted in 1996 is specifically designed to make life on welfare less secure so as to motivate people to work hard to get off the rolls.

A rather extreme example of an economic explanation of behavior regards the problem of homelessness. Lawrence Schiff (1990) says:

> in plain English, the welfare state is in essence providing, for a large percentage of the homeless, a lifestyle that would cost roughly $10,000 to $12,000 were it to be purchased in the open market, possibly a little less at some of the worst (read: city-run as opposed to private-contract) shelters. And the greater the monetary value of the benefits in kind—i.e., housing, food, clothing, medical care, etc.—the larger the number of people willing to consider homelessness as a viable option. For the question is not whether the homeless would really prefer to have

permanent residences. Of course they would. They are simply subsidized to not obtain the skills and make the sacrifices necessary to obtain such housing, when substandard accommodation is available free.

Check Your Understanding 5.8
Check your understanding of Economic Analysis by taking this brief quiz.

As will be discussed in Chapter 6, analyses of the actual behavior of welfare recipients cast doubt on this purely economic explanation of behavior.

Using the economist's perspective on behavior, the policy analyst asks what the effects of a policy are likely to be on individual behavior. The assumption is that people will be utility maximizers. That is, they will behave in the way that will result in the greatest benefit and the lowest cost to them.

CONCLUSION

In this chapter, we have looked in more detail at the social and economic analysis section of our policy analysis model. As should be obvious from the discussion, conducting a social welfare policy analysis is not a simple, straightforward project. Many areas are vague and poorly defined. Because the actual goals of many policies are not the same as the stated goals, and because policies often reflect values that we as a society do not care to admit we possess, the real goals and values of a policy will often be hidden and sometimes will not even be recognized by the people actually involved in formulating and implementing the policy. Also, policies seek to solve problems about which there is little agreement as to the definition of the problem or the desirable solution. Uncovering these vague and often highly emotionally charged aspects of a policy is the task of the social/economic analysis. It more often resembles an art than a science.

Recall what you learned from this chapter by completing the Chapter Review.

Part Three

The Framework Applied

Regardless of how focused on individual practice a social worker is, he or she is often sharply brought back to the realization that practice occurs within a policy context and that practitioners will experience problems and provide inadequate services if they do not understand this context. We have devoted the last four chapters to a detailed description of various approaches to, and techniques for, policy analysis. In the following four chapters, we provide examples of how this information can be applied to some social work practice settings.

Why is skill in policy analysis helpful for a direct practice social worker? Consider the following conversations the authors had with former students at an alumni gathering several years ago (names have been changed).

Samantha Bowen received her B.S.W. degree four years ago and works as a financial and employment planner in the Temporary Assistance for Needy Families (TANF) program in a large northern state. Sam told one of the authors:

> I've been working since graduation as a financial and employment planner. I feel very confident of my social work skills in helping my clients problem-solve. However, now that I'm considered a senior staff member in the office, I'm being called upon more and more often to do things like address civic groups about the Temporary Assistance to Needy Families (TANF) program, to serve on community committees and boards related to services to poor people, and I've just been assigned as the practice representative to the state committee charged with the responsibility of monitoring the welfare reform plan in our state. My knowledge and expertise in social work practice is of little use to me in fulfilling these tasks. These tasks all require knowledge of laws, regulations, economics, program effectiveness, and stuff like that. After four years I'm beginning to realize that there is a lot about my job that I simply don't understand. Also, I'm really tired of people buttonholing me at a party, asking my opinion about this or that welfare program, and then looking at me like I'm some sort of a fool because I don't know much, if anything, about it.

Beth Stapleton reported on her job as a social worker with a large hospital:

> I really love my job, particularly dealing with families in crisis. It is so exciting and so satisfying helping them sort out issues, come to grips with the reality of their situations, and make plans for managing in the future. I really feel good when I receive cards or visits from former clients who tell me that they didn't even know what a social worker was before their hospital experience, but that the presence of me and my colleagues was the thing that enabled them to survive the crisis. But it's so depressing that I may not be able to do this much longer. With all the health care policy changes, cutbacks, and uncertainty in the face of proposals for reform of the Affordable Care Act, it looks like social

> workers may be relegated to doing discharge planning with no clinical work at all. I wish I had a better grip on where health care reform is going and how social workers will fit into it.

Janice Kozinski stood out from her colleagues at the reunion largely due to the fact that she arrived driving a Lexus GS 430 and was wearing a $600 suit. She told a group of classmates from the MSW program:

> Being a social worker doesn't mean you can't prosper. After working in community mental health for three years, I got together with two of my colleagues and we went into private practice. After we became familiar with government and insurance company policy, we opened an outpatient phobic disorders clinic and an inpatient substance abuse clinic. Within four years we had clinics in twelve locations. Last year we were bought out by a national health care corporation. As part of the deal I received a large block of stock in the parent company and the job of vice president of clinical operations. I find that the efficiency inherent in the profit-making sector results in far more good for clients than the bureaucratic nonsense I had to put up with in community mental health.

Following the reunion, Janice offered one of her classmates, Raphael Ramirez, a job as director of social services at one of her clinics. He called one of the authors and said:

> I'm really conflicted about the offer. It's a great job by all of the standard criteria, but I really worry about profit goals interfering with treatment goals. The reputation of Janice's outfit is that every client referred to their clinics is assessed as needing twenty-one days of inpatient treatment, no more and no less. The reason for this is, of course, that twenty-one days is generally the maximum that most insurance plans will cover for this type of thing. It also concerns me that when I told Janice I'm a family therapist and have little expertise in either phobic disorders or substance abuse, it didn't really concern her. Her response to my concern was to say, "You're fully licensed, aren't you? Then what's the problem?"

Bill Bouchet had been working for a state child protective services program as a child welfare worker for three years since earning his BSW. He told a group of classmates about a discussion he had with a state senator at a political rally:

> When I told the senator about my job, the senator said, "Tell me, Bill, do you believe in the philosophy that seems to be dominant now in your department that it is nearly always best to leave a child with the natural parents? This seems unconscionable to me and many of my fellow legislators. Parents who do some of these things to their kids should lose their right to be parents. Surely we can do better by this state's kids than to leave them in unwholesome and often dangerous home environments. All this stuff about family preservation seems to me to be so much liberal pap designed to mask the unpleasant fact that evil does exist, is irreparable, and is present in many of these parents." Fortunately, we were interrupted before I could reply because I was stunned. I work in the Families First unit and believe in it. But I feel I should write the senator a letter explaining the approach and correcting his misrepresentations. However, I'm really not sure where to start.

Mustafa Alleem works as a social worker in a large senior citizens center. He told a group of his classmates:

> The elderly people who are members of various groups I lead at the center are all feeling really uneasy. It seems like every week one of them comes in with some new rumor about what is going to happen to their entitlements. One week it was the matter of privatizing social security benefits, another it was increasing the co-pay for Medicare services, another time it was lowering the income for eligibility for Medicaid. They were really panicked a while ago when a group of them went to the community center to hear a congressional candidate who advocates the total elimination of entitlement programs and replacing them with means-tested programs, which he estimated would reduce the number of beneficiaries by 40 percent. I spend a lot of time processing these folks' feelings, but I really wish I could give them more concrete information on how real these threats to their security are. I suspect that some of the rumors are just that—rumors. However, some may be real and I feel a responsibility to separate facts from rumors so we could begin to develop strategies to deal with the true threats.

The situations described here are all very different in terms of the people involved, the fields represented, the levels of sophistication, as well as a number of other differences. They have one thing in common, however—they all involve social work practitioners who find themselves in the position, whether they would describe it this way or not, of needing to conduct a policy analysis.

The first thing most social workers who find themselves in this situation will do is go online to look up policy analyses in the area they are concerned with. What they will find are studies conducted by professional policy analysts of various types. These are fine, but they have two major shortcomings. The first is that—given the time it takes to do a policy study, and then write, edit, and finally distribute the findings—much of the material will be dated before it reaches the consumer.

The second shortcoming of analyses by policy professionals from the perspective of the social work practitioner is that they almost always deal only with what we identified in Chapter 2 as macrolevel policy. In addition, they almost always deal exclusively with public policy. Mezzo- or agency-level policy and private-sector policy are rarely dealt with, even though this may be the most important information for the social work practitioner to have.

The solution to the problem of gaining access to current information regarding policies that affect social work practitioners is to become skilled in what we refer to in Chapter 3 as practitioner policy analysis. There is nothing esoteric or complex about conducting a practitioner policy analysis. It is really nothing more than taking a basic framework for analysis, such as the one presented at the beginning of Part Two, and filling in the information regarding a specific policy or policy area mainly using library and Internet research skills. Sources of information for practitioner policy analysis and skills for accessing these sources are discussed in the appendixes.

In the following chapters, we demonstrate how our policy analysis framework might be applied by the social workers described in the preceding vignettes. Each chapter involves either the major program or the hottest current issue in five broad social welfare policy arenas. In the economic assistance arena, we look at TANF and current welfare reform efforts; in the area of aging, we discuss entitlement programs, mainly

Social Security; in mental health, we look at the rapid expansion and increasing influence of managed care and the profit-making sector; in child welfare, we direct our attention to family preservation; and, for this edition, because of the current intense political concern with immigration, we have added a chapter on this topic.

As you read the following chapters, you will notice that our policy analysis framework provides a guide but not a rigid template for our analyses. Some of the outline sections are important for some of the areas but not for others. For example, economic analysis is central to any discussion of the TANF program but of only minor importance for understanding family preservation. We do believe, however, that historical analysis is central to any policy analysis. There are several reasons for this. The first is our belief that it is virtually impossible to understand any current situation without studying its antecedents. The problem with many current social welfare policy proposals is that the people instigating them have no knowledge or understanding of history. President George W. Bush's proposals to privatize social security and Reagan's attempts to return much of the responsibility for social welfare to private charity are good examples. The assumption seems to be that the public sector assumed responsibility for social welfare out of some misguided liberal desire to extend the scope of government. In reality, the public sector assumed responsibility for social welfare only when the Great Depression bankrupted private charitable agencies and thus demonstrated the inability of a private system to deal with the massive social and economic disruptions characteristic of a modern urban industrial state. The government assumed responsibility not because it wanted to, but because it had to. Thus, historical policy analysis reveals that proposals to privatize large portions of the welfare system are not only wrongheaded but also just plain foolish.

The second reason we emphasize the historical dimension in practitioner policy analysis is that historical research is manageable for most social work practitioners. Elements of policy analysis such as economic analysis and evaluation are so complex that a complete job generally cannot be done unless one has extensive specialized training and adequate resources. Historical analysis can be successfully done by anyone with a good general education; training in some basic principles, as laid out in Chapter 4; and a willingness to do some careful detective work to uncover the best sources. This is not to say that historical analysis can be done sloppily or that most historical analysis is well done. It cannot, and it is not. It constantly amazes us how many people who attempt historical analyses are ignorant of the basic principles discussed in Chapter 4 or are too lazy to apply them.

We conclude each chapter with a look at current proposals for policy reform. We include this section even though we realize that by the time this book is off the press, this section will have become part of the history section—the proposals we describe will have been acted on and been killed, adopted, modified, or simply abandoned. This brings us back to the reason we are spending so much time discussing how to analyze policy rather than simply providing analyses and leaving it at that. Social welfare policy changes so fast that even the very first person to read this book will have to read our Current Proposals section as the last part of the history section and will have to go out and do his or her own analysis to find out, as the folksy commentator Paul Harvey used to say, "the rest of the story."

6

Fighting Poverty: Temporary Assistance for Needy Families

NinaMalyna/Shutterstock

When Monica was in kindergarten, she loved the paper clock that her teacher pinned to the bulletin board to teach the class to tell time. Every third week it was Monica's turn to be in charge of the clock, moving the big and little hands to show 8:30 when school began, 10:00 for morning recess, 11:30 for lunch, 1:30 for afternoon recess, and finally 3:00 for time to go home. Now that Monica is an adult with three kids by a father who is charming and lovable but rarely able to offer any concrete support, living off low-wage jobs interspersed with welfare benefits, Monica hates the paper clock. The paper clock is now on the wall of the cubicle of her Temporary Assistance to Needy Families (welfare) case manager, Ms. Springer. On Monica's first visit to the office to apply for TANF, Ms. Springer explained to her that she would have lifetime eligibility for TANF of only 60 months. If she used up all 60 months, she would never again be able to receive benefits and would be completely on her own. To drive home this point

LEARNING OUTCOMES

- Explain the shift is welfare philosophy represented by the replacement of the Aid to Families with Dependent Children (AFDC) program with the Temporary Assistance to Needy Families (TANF) program.
- Discuss the relationship between the increasing population in orphanages in the early twentieth century and the development of public welfare in America.
- Explore the changing value system in the United States that contributed to the replacement of AFDC with TANF.
- Explain welfare reform strategies aimed at limiting the number of people eligible for welfare and strategies aimed at moving people off welfare and onto self-sufficiency.
- Explain the onion metaphor for the poverty population and relate this to the TANF concept of number of barriers to self-support.
- Differentiate between Labor Force Attachment and Human Capital Development work program approaches and explain the TANF work-first approach in relation to these.
- Discuss ways in which TANF is succeeding and ways in which it is failing.

CHAPTER OUTLINE

Ms. Springer had tacked a paper clock, just like the one Monica remembered from kindergarten, to her bulletin board with the label "TANF Clock" and she explained that each minute represented one month of TANF eligibility and when one hour was up on the clock Monica would no longer be eligible for any benefits.

Monica was introduced to Ms. Springer and her clock when Randy, the father of the two children she had at the time, suddenly disappeared, leaving her with no money, overdue rent, and a car that was about to be repossessed. Monica was working as a clerk at a convenience store but a month after Randy's disappearance, she was laid off. The manager claimed he had to lay her off because business was slow, but Monica was sure the real reason was dental abscesses she had developed that not only were very painful but gave her disgustingly bad breath. She suspected that her co-workers and customers had complained to the manager. With her chronic pain and her breath smelling like a sewage pit, she realized her chances of finding a job were slim, so on the advice of a friend she applied for TANF.

When Monica went in for her two-hour eligibility interview with Ms. Springer, she was required to take out a child support order against Randy, even though she had no idea where he was and, even if he could be found, he would be totally incapable of providing any support. Ms. Springer told her that you never know what someone is capable of until you ask. After processing Monica's application Ms. Springer told her that she has good news and bad news. The good news was that she qualified for a TANF grant of $465 per month and that in her state, eligibility for TANF automatically qualified her for SNAP (food stamps) and Medicaid. She was required to sign an Agreement of Personal Responsibility committing her to working toward self-sufficiency, that is, getting a job and getting off welfare. Ms. Springer told Monica that she needed to go immediately to a dentist who would accept Medicaid, get her teeth fixed so she would be employable, and then meet with a financial and employment planner (FEP), who would give her a literacy test, document her work history, and assess employment-related skills. After this was done, an "independence plan" would be developed that would chart Monica's path from welfare dependency to employment and independence. The bad news Ms. Springer gave Monica was that even though she could not begin work until her dental problems were fixed, the problems were not severe enough to qualify her for disability, so her TANF clock would begin running immediately.

It took ten months for Monica to complete her dental treatment and find a job. Ms. Springer congratulated her on finding a job but pointed out that her TANF clock was now ten minutes after the hour. The job Monica had found was making hamburgers at a fast-food restaurant and paid a little more than minimum wage but provided no insurance, vacation, retirement, or sick leave. The job did not go well. The manager thought Monica was too slow and kept nagging her to "pick up the pace." When she did speed up, she made mistakes, and he then criticized her for sloppy work. Monica finally lost her temper and told the manager that he could either have the sandwiches fast or he could have them right. He told her that if she couldn't do both she couldn't work for him and fired her on the spot.

Following the ill-fated fast-food job, it took Monica eleven months to find another job. This time she was hired to stock shelves in a big-box store. She really liked the job and felt that perhaps it had a future. Ms. Springer was, of course, there to point to the hands on the TANF clock that showed twenty-one after the hour, meaning that only 39 months of eligibility remained. This job lasted fourteen months, at which time Monica resigned. She quit the job because her older daughter Tracy began to have serious behavioral problems in school, and the school counselor told her she had to find a way to spend more time with Tracy making her feel loved and secure and also helping with her school work with which she was struggling. When Monica went to see Ms. Springer to reapply for benefits, she was told that under TANF policy she had quit her job without "good cause" and so would receive a sanction, meaning she would be punished for quitting. The sanction would be that she would be denied benefits for one month. Ms. Springer, of course, reminded her that the TANF clock was running and warned her that a second sanction would result in a three-month suspension of benefits, a third sanction would carry a six-month penalty, and the fourth would mean permanent ineligibility for benefits no matter how many minutes were left on her TANF clock.

Monica spent eighteen months at home with her daughter, who had been diagnosed by the community mental health center as depressed and a suicide risk. She was required by the TANF office to be actively seeking work or else in job training to maintain her eligibility during this time. To prove she was seeking work, Monica was required to provide proof that she had applied for jobs each month. She had no intention of returning to work until she felt her daughter was doing better, so each month she would apply for jobs she knew she had no chance of getting and dutifully provide the TANF office with copies of the applications. Monica was acutely aware that people considered her to be a loafer and a leech because she was being supported by the government and not working. She was also aware that there were people who abused the system and were not working because they were lazy, but she felt she was not a member of this group. As she explained to a friend from church, "If you're taking care of yourself and your kids, then you're doing what you're supposed to do. I'm taking care of my kids, especially Tracy who has special needs. That is work. That is my job."

During Tracy's crisis, Monica spent a lot of time at the school and became friends with a counselor in the special education department. She told her friend that now that Tracy was doing better, she would be returning to work. The counselor told her of a federally funded program that would be starting at the school in the fall and encouraged her to apply for a job as a teacher's aide in the program. Monica followed this advice and was given the best job she had ever had. As a teacher's aide, she was paid $14.00 an hour and given health insurance and personal and sick days, and she felt the pride that came with being able to tell people she met, "I'm a teacher." When she told Ms. Springer about the new job, Ms. Springer congratulated her and, as usual, pointed to the TANF clock and reminded Monica that only 31 minutes remained on it.

The teacher's aide job lasted only nine months (one academic year), at which time Monica was laid off because the federal funding for the program was not renewed. After experiencing a good job, Monica was reluctant to go back to flipping burgers or stocking shelves for minimum wage. She met with her FEP and presented a plan to attend the local community college to get an associate's degree in child development that would qualify her for permanently funded teacher's aide positions. Mr. Farnsworth, her FEP, told her he was sympathetic to this plan but that the TANF program was based on what was called a work-first philosophy, which meant she was required to take any job at all that was available rather than build up skills that might lead to better jobs. Monica stuck to her idea of finding another "good job," one that paid a living wage and included benefits for 15 months, during which time Mr. Farnsworth kept encouraging her to apply for what he called "realistic jobs," which meant jobs that paid poorly; had no benefits; and, as Monica told her friends, "a monkey could do." She finally relented to the pressure of the TANF clock, which Ms. Springer pointed out had only 16 months remaining and took a job for minimum wage as night clerk at a gas station. This job lasted five months, at which time she quit after being robbed at gunpoint.

When Monica went to see Ms. Springer to reapply for benefits, she was told that once again she had quit her job without "good cause" and was given a three-month sanction. Fortunately, Randy had reappeared, although Monica did not report this to anyone, and he moved in with her. Because he was going through one of the rare periods when he had a job, he was able to support her and the kids. When her three-month sanction was over, Randy once again lost his job and disappeared, leaving Monica pregnant. She had found a job at a grocery store and worked until the baby was born, at which time she once again began to receive TANF. Under TANF policy, she was not required to begin to seek work until the baby was three months old. Monica was so overwhelmed with the new baby and with Tracy's problems, which had intensified when she became a teenager, that it was a year before she found a job, this time as a clerk at a dry-cleaning store. Once again, she was earning a little more than minimum wage with no job security or benefits of any kind.

Monica is now facing life with three minutes left on her TANF clock. Even if she once again becomes unemployed, she doubts that she will reapply for TANF because it will not be worth the hassle for only three months of benefits. She has no clue at all where Randy is and what he is doing. She suspects he is out of her life forever because he knows he owes her nearly $20,000 in child support that he has no way of paying. Her job pays her about three-quarters of the federal poverty line, which means that she is eligible for food stamps, Medicaid, and subsidized child care. She began the process of applying for subsidized housing five years ago. After two years she was able to get her name on the waiting list and she has finally gotten a voucher, which will enable her to get a decent place to live with rent of only one-quarter of her income. However, if she loses her job, without a welfare safety net, she will not be able to pay even this and will become homeless. She often thinks of the year that she was a teacher's aide: "If only they had let me go back to school instead of obsessing on that damn TANF clock, maybe that could be my permanent life."

Welfare reform, always a hot-button issue, assumed center stage in the political arena when Bill Clinton, as a candidate, promised to "end welfare as we know it." When the Republicans seized control of the 104th Congress, they made the reform of welfare a key plank in their Contract with America. After a protracted fight that included one presidential veto of a welfare reform bill, President Clinton, on August 22, 1996, signed H.R. 3734, the Personal Responsibility and Work Opportunity Reconciliation Act (PRWORA) of 1996. This act changed the basic architecture of the public assistance system, which had been in place since the 1935 signing of the Social Security Act, by replacing the Aid to Families with Dependent Children (AFDC) program with a new program called Temporary Assistance for Needy Families (TANF). This new act leaves us facing an uncharted landscape in public assistance. As President Clinton noted when he signed the act, "This is not the end of welfare reform; this is the beginning. We have to fill in the blanks" ("Clinton Signs Controversial Welfare Bill," 1996).

As we have noted elsewhere, the term *welfare* conceptually refers to a wide range of programs (Popple & Leighninger, 2011). Included in the category are programs such as Social Security, Worker's Compensation, Supplemental Security Income, and a number of others. However, it is clear that when speaking of welfare, or welfare reform, only one program is being referred to—public assistance, which used to be the AFDC program and is now TANF. Public assistance is the public program designed to aid the very poorest members of our society. Although it is true that men and married couples could technically qualify for AFDC and are eligible for TANF, in reality, beneficiaries of public assistance have always been, and will continue to be, almost entirely women and their children.

Although the trend throughout the twentieth century was to move welfare programs to the federal level, programs for women and their children have remained under tight state control. AFDC was run through a joint federal–state partnership, with the federal government providing a set of regulations governing the operation of the program and approximately 75 percent of the funding. The individual states provided the additional 25 percent of funding and set their own eligibility and benefit levels. Under the TANF program, the states have even more control of the program, with the federal government providing only the most general guidelines. States are allowed to use TANF funding in any manner "reasonably calculated to accomplish the purposes of TANF." This situation has resulted in wide variations in the program, with 2016 maximum monthly benefits for a family of three ranging from a low of $170 in Mississippi to a high of $923 in Alaska. This lack of uniformity between states was considered a weakness of the AFDC program. Under TANF it is defined as a strength because the theory is that each state will experiment with different approaches, increasing the likelihood that some effective innovations will be found.

Thoughts for Social Work Practice

A social worker helping a TANF-supported client must be constantly aware of the policy implementing a 60-month time limit. Are there any ways that this time limit can be used in a constructive fashion to help a client improve his or her life?

To qualify for public assistance, a person must be very poor. Under AFDC, total liquid assets for a family could not exceed $1,000; if the family owned a car, its market value was limited to $4,000. Under TANF, these figures vary from state to state, with most allowing $1,000 to $2,000 in cash and some limiting the value of a car an applicant can own. If a family's assets exceed state guidelines, they are required to spend their assets before qualifying for aid. Generally, benefits come in a package that includes Supplemental Nutrition Assistance Program (SNAP; also known as food stamps) and Medicaid. These additional benefits theoretically provide a family with sufficient resources to survive. Benefits under TANF are even stingier than those under AFDC because the federal regulations require only that states spend an amount equal to at least 75 percent of their historic spending level (called maintenance of effort [MOE]) and provide options for the additional 25 percent to be spent for purposes other than direct assistance.

A number of scholars have observed that a major thrust of welfare reform during the latter half of the twentieth century was an effort to separate programs believed to be for the "deserving poor" out of the welfare category and to define them as social insurance, a nonstigmatizing category. Donald Norris and Luke Thompson (1995) note:

> First many elderly were covered under Social Security. Later the number of elderly who were covered was expanded. Subsequently, many people with disabilities were given aid through the vocational rehabilitation acts, and later, through Supplementary Security Income. Many of the unemployed were covered under systems of unemployment compensation, either through companies or through state governments. Gradually, these groups of "deserving poor" recipients became isolated from AFDC recipients. (p. 4)

Feminist scholars such as Linda Gordon and Theresa Funiciello have argued that we have systematically separated programs used by men and whites from programs used largely by women and minorities and defined the former as social insurance, a category with little stigma, and the latter as welfare, a highly stigmatized category and one always considered in need of reform (Gordon, 1995). The TANF program reinforces this stigmatization process through its institutionalization of the idea that remaining home to rear children is not a legitimate social role for poor women.

With the passage of the Personal Responsibility and Work Opportunity Reconciliation Act of 1996, we began a new era in public assistance policy. For the prior sixty years, the receipt of financial assistance by the needy was considered a right of citizenship, the federal government cast itself in the role of leading the states toward more progressive and humane social policies, staying home and parenting children was defined as a legitimate social role for the mothers of small children, and the reality that work was not available for all people was at least implicitly accepted. All these have now changed. Financial assistance is now to be granted only on a temporary basis, the federal government has abdicated its leadership role and now seeks only to get out of the way of the states, women are expected to be in the labor market, and it is assumed that jobs are available for all people if they will just look hard enough and accept whatever comes along. In the following sections, we look at the factors that have led to the current situation, attempt to make some sense of the situation, and make some projections about where the nation will go from here.

Much of the study of public assistance relies on historical data. The most important questions involve trends in numbers of recipients, the length of time on assistance, the number of recipients who become employed, the number who leave the welfare rolls and stay off, and the number who leave but then return. The PRWORA passed in 1996 and implemented in 1997 makes this analysis difficult for two reasons. First, the federal government has changed the data-collecting procedures, which makes comparisons to data prior to 1997 difficult. Second, because the law has been in effect for, historically speaking, a relatively brief time, trends within the program are harder to discern, although we are reaching a point where some clear trends are emerging (Institute for Research on Poverty, 2017). The fact that the first ten years after passage of the law were ones of extraordinary economic growth makes assessment of the effects of the new program even harder to calculate. Now that the economy has had a recession and is experiencing a very slow recovery, perhaps we are beginning to get a better idea of the true impact of the TANF program. As a result of these factors, some of the data in this chapter refer to the now-defunct AFDC program. Although we may not be comparing apples and oranges, we realize that we are comparing tangerines and oranges—similar things, but not really an exact comparison. This is not the most desirable policy analysis situation, but it is, unfortunately, unavoidable.

HISTORICAL ANALYSIS

The idea of public assistance, defined as the obligation of the government to provide an economic safety net for people, and of people's right to expect such a safety net based simply on citizenship, has a very short history in the United States. As recently as the end of the nineteenth century, this idea was considered absurd and offensive by most people. The great philanthropic leader of the nineteenth century, Josephine Shaw Lowell, stated the opinion of many people involved in the early development of social work in this country when, at the 1890 National Conference of Charities and Correction, she said:

> Every dollar raised by taxation comes out of the pocket of some individual, usually a poor individual, and makes him so much the poorer, and therefore the question is between the man who earned the dollar by hard work, and the man who, however worthy and suffering, did not earn it, but wants it to be given to him to buy himself and his family a day's food. If the man who earned it wishes to divide it with the other man, it is usually a desirable thing that he should do so, and at any rate it is more or less his own business, but that the law, by the hand of a public officer, should take it from him and hand it over

> to the other man, seems to be an act of gross tyranny and injustice. . . . The less that is given [of public assistance] the better for everyone, the giver and the receiver. (Lowell, 1890)

Based on this belief that government had no right to levy taxes in order to provide financial assistance to people, there was really no such thing as a large public assistance system until the twentieth century. Throughout the nineteenth and the early years of the twentieth century, poverty and related social problems were dealt with primarily through local voluntary organizations, with gifts from wealthy donors (such as Lowell) providing most of the financial support. The little public support provided was mostly through a means known as *indoor relief*. This meant that assistance was provided to people only through institutions such as poorhouses, orphanages, mental hospitals, schools for the deaf and blind, and so forth. The provision of direct cash benefits to people, a practice known as *outdoor relief*, was frowned on because it was believed to encourage indolence and dependency. If direct cash relief was provided, it was thought that it should not come from tax revenues and that only a voluntary organization was capable of the level of scrutiny and supervision of recipients that prudence required.

As the twentieth century dawned, the rapid growth of urbanization, industrialization, and immigration resulted in a level of poverty and related social problems that threatened to swamp private charities. Many people were becoming concerned with the number of children who were residing in orphanages not due to parental desertion or death but because of parental poverty. These were generally the children of widows who could not earn enough money to support their children and so placed them in orphanages because it was the mother's only option. In response to this problem, developments early in the century began to reestablish financial assistance as a public responsibility. The first development was the establishment in a number of cities, Kansas City being the first in 1908, of boards of public welfare to carry out "duties of the city toward all the poor, the delinquent, the unemployed, and the deserted and unfortunate classes in the community, and to supervise the private agencies which solicited money from the public for these purposes" (Halbert, 1918). The second development was the 1909 White House Conference on Children convened by President Theodore Roosevelt. A major recommendation of this conference was that children should not be separated from their parents simply for reasons of poverty. A system of outdoor relief was strongly endorsed as being preferable to institutional placement.

Following the White House Conference on Children, advocates for the poor began to lobby successfully for state welfare laws that became known as "mothers' pensions." This rather strange term was borrowed from the powerful and popular industrial insurance movement, which was successfully lobbying for worker's compensation, unemployment insurance, and retirement programs as measures to insure workers against the risks of industrial employment. The perspective implied in the name "mothers' pension" was that women with children were productive workers of a sort and had a right to insurance against widowhood, the primary threat to their livelihood, just as men had a right to insurance against industrial accident. The first mothers' pension laws were passed in Missouri and Illinois in 1911. Within two years, similar laws were passed in seventeen additional states, and by 1919 thirty-nine states had mothers' pensions programs.

There are two aspects of the mothers' pension movement that are particularly important for understanding the history of public assistance. The first is that these programs were aimed, to quote President Theodore Roosevelt, at "children of parents of worthy character" (Lubove, 1968), which meant women who were widowed or who had disabled husbands. A small percentage of recipients were divorced mothers, but these were considered worthy only if it could be demonstrated that the divorce was no fault of the women, primarily instances in which the husband had deserted the family. The programs were never intended for the children of unwed mothers, and very few such children received aid. The second important aspect of these laws is that they were based on a traditional model of the family in which the mother was expected to stay home and care for her children. The very name "mothers' pensions" implied that being a wife and mother was analogous to a career and that widows were entitled to support when this career was disrupted. There were no work provisions, or even expectations, contained in these laws.

Although mothers' pension programs established an important precedent in the development of public assistance, it was not until the Great Depression of the 1930s that state and federal government actually began to play a major role. Mothers' pensions programs were always quite small; in 1930, for example, fewer than 3 percent of female-headed households received benefits under these programs (Handler & Hasenfeld, 1991). Private agencies, with substantial local government support, continued to provide the bulk of financial relief. The central role of private agencies was strongly endorsed by social workers and leaders in philanthropy, who questioned the morality of government providing assistance and doubted the ability of government to provide efficient and effective professional social services. This situation began to change rapidly with the onset of the Depression in 1929 and its increasing severity into the 1930s.

The Depression shocked the nation in general, and social workers in particular, into the realization that local programs supplemented by private relief agencies were not adequate for dealing with the massive economic problems of an urban industrial society. When the Depression hit, private agencies almost immediately ran out of money and began to rely to a much greater extent than previously on state and local governments for assistance. The state and local governments in turn got into financial peril and turned to the federal government for assistance. The realization that private agencies and state and local governments could not cope with the economic crisis, along with the fear that if something dramatic was not done radical political change might well occur, resulted in the passage of the Social Security Act in 1935. This act was the first national framework for a social welfare system. The Social Security Act, as it finally emerged after many compromises, was designed to alleviate financial dependency through two lines of defense: contributory social insurance and public assistance. One of the public assistance programs was Aid to Dependent Children (ADC), a program established to serve single mothers with small children, basically the same group targeted by state mothers' pension laws. This is the program that later was called Aid to Families with Dependent Children (AFDC) in recognition of the fact that mothers as well as their children were receiving assistance.

It is not surprising that AFDC became more and more controversial over the years because evidence indicates that its designers did not really understand what they were passing and certainly could not predict what the program would eventually become. Scholars often romanticize New Deal programs and characterize their designers as humanists and liberals with a far-reaching vision of a just society and a realistic plan for achieving it (Mizrahi, 1996). However, the evidence indicates that the designers of the AFDC program supported it only because they believed that the program was temporary and would wither away as social insurance came into effect. Further, the designers of AFDC never imagined that the program would support the children of unwed mothers. Franklin Roosevelt characterized welfare as "a narcotic, a subtle destroyer of the human spirit" and argued that federal job creation was far preferable to welfare (Levitan & Gallo, 1993). Edith Abbott, a social worker and prominent social reformer, advocated for AFDC with the assurance that it would support only "nice" families (Gordon, 1994). Social worker and Secretary of Labor Frances Perkins supported the program under the misunderstanding that the term *dependent mother* referred only to women who were widows, married to disabled workers, or divorced due to no fault of their own. It never occurred to her that unwed mothers would be included in the definition of *dependent* (Reilly, 1983). Historian Linda Gordon (1994) states that

> the authors of the New Deal welfare programs, often thought of as spiritual allies of contemporary liberals, would severely disapprove of what the New Deal programs have subsequently become with liberal encouragement: a source of more-or-less permanent support for single mothers who, in many instances, are not white and "not nice." (p. 299)

By the 1950s, policymakers began to realize that the AFDC program was not going to wither away and was in fact providing benefits to a number of people considered "undesirable." The fact that the program did not wither but instead grew, often at an alarming rate, led to calls for welfare reform.

Reform strategies can be lumped into two large categories. The first category is attempts to limit the number of people eligible for the program. These policies have taken the form of "suitable home" and "man in the house" rules and residency requirements. The suitable home and man in the house rules stated that aid would not be given to children who were living in immoral environments, generally defined as home situations in which it appeared that the mother was having a sexual relationship with a man to whom she was not married. These rules were struck down by the Supreme Court in 1968 in *King v. Smith*. Residency requirements denied assistance to any person who had not resided in a locale for a certain period of time, sometimes as long as five years. These requirements were declared unconstitutional by the Supreme Court in the case of *Shapiro v. Thompson* in 1969.

The second group of reform strategies has included efforts to move people off welfare and onto self-sufficiency through rehabilitating the recipient or else removing environmental barriers. There has been a series of these efforts, beginning in the mid-1950s and continuing to current reform efforts. The one element that unites all these efforts is their uniform lack of effectiveness. Major strategies have been:

Thoughts for Social Work Practice

Very few social workers are currently employed by the TANF program, and those who are generally do not provide direct services to recipients. Some argue that this is good because TANF policy does not allow for ethical professional social work practice. Others argue that this is bad because TANF recipients are sorely in need of expert services and that social workers working within TANF agencies could humanize the program. What do you think?

Social Service Strategies

Amendments to the Social Security Act in 1956 and again in 1962 facilitated the provision of social services to welfare recipients. The idea was that social workers would help recipients solve the problems that were preventing them from being self-supporting. This approach lost credibility when welfare rolls did not decline but actually increased at a rapid rate following full implementation of the strategy in the 1960s.

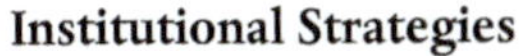

Institutional Strategies

First tried in the 1960s as part of Lyndon Johnson's War on Poverty, these attempted to empower individuals and neighborhoods. These programs were based on a "blocked opportunity" thesis that attributed poverty to environmental variables. These programs rapidly ran into political problems, welfare rolls did not decline, and they were discontinued after a very short life. In the 1980s, a few institutional strategies were implemented, namely, enterprise zones and public housing "ownership" initiatives, but these have also met with little success.

Human Capital Strategies

In the 1960s, as the social service and institutional strategies were losing popularity, the argument was advanced that a more direct approach to poverty was called for. This approach simply said that people were poor because they could not get good jobs, and they could not get good jobs because they did not possess valuable skills. Economists refer to a person's saleable skills and attributes as human capital. To address this problem, a series of job training programs has been attempted, beginning in the early 1960s with the Manpower Development and Training Act (for the disadvantaged in general) and the Community Work and Training Programs (specifically for welfare recipients). In 1967 the Work Incentive (WIN) program was implemented, which was a joint effort of state welfare departments and employment service offices. This program required all AFDC recipients without preschool-age children to participate. As will be discussed in the next section, the human capital approach continues to be popular, its latest manifestations being the 1988 Job Opportunity and Basic Skills (JOBS) program, basically an extension and expansion of WIN, and the work and training requirements that are central to the TANF program that replaced AFDC in 1996.

Job Creation and Subsidization Strategies

One of the major criticisms of the human capital approach is that no jobs are available for most of the participants. Various attempts have been made to counter this criticism by creating public service, or publicly subsidized private-sector jobs. The Works Progress Administration and the Civilian Conservation Corps of the Depression era serve as models for this approach. In recent years, the most popular version of this approach has been providing subsidies to employers to offset the costs of creating new jobs for low-skill workers. The Targeted Tax Credit and the WIN Tax Credit are two examples. A popular, if somewhat perverse, twist on this approach is the TANF requirement that recipients who do not obtain paid employment within a time limit perform unpaid community service in return for their grant.

Child Support Strategies

This approach was developed in response to the changing composition of AFDC caseloads, where the majority of cases were children with living fathers who did not provide support. In the mid-1970s, the federal Office of Child Support Enforcement was created to assist states in efforts to gain and enforce child support from absent fathers. Federal legislation in 1984 and 1988 strengthened child support provisions. When a woman applied for AFDC, she was required to identify the father of her children and file for a child support order if she hadn't already done so; if she had and the father was delinquent, she was required to swear out a warrant for collection (Corbett, 1993). This policy has continued under TANF, even though research has demonstrated that the cost of collection efforts greatly exceeds the amount of child support recovered (Hays, 2003, p. 77).

The Effort to Reform Welfare

In the 1980s, with the election of Ronald Reagan to the presidency and the beginning of a long conservative trend in society, pressure for substantial welfare reform began to mount. The first major effort climaxed in 1988 with passage of the Family Support Act, viewed by many as a major reform of welfare and one that would quiet the calls for reform for many years. This was not to be. Almost before the ink was dry on the Family Support Act, critics began to complain that it had not gone far enough and to demand even more drastic reforms. These efforts resulted in the passage, and subsequent veto by President Clinton, of the Personal Responsibility Act of 1995. Following the veto of this act, the 104th Congress modified the bill slightly and passed the Personal Responsibility and Work Opportunity Reconciliation Act of 1996. In what many viewed as a crass example of political opportunism, President Clinton signed the bill into law on August 22, 1996. These welfare reform efforts have been examples of what Thomas Corbett (1993) labels the "make work pay" and the "make 'em suffer" strategies. The "make work pay" strategy is based on the idea that people make rational choices and, thus, if we want people to choose work over welfare, we need to provide work opportunities that will enable them to be substantially better off than they are while receiving assistance. The "make 'em suffer" strategy is based on the same basic idea but comes at it from the opposite direction. Rather than attempting to provide options more attractive than welfare, these strategies impose penalties on a range of behaviors that are seen as counterproductive to becoming self-sufficient. Welfare recipients are required to attend school, participate in work training, immunize their children, and similar things. If recipients do not accept these responsibilities, they are penalized by reductions in their welfare grants.

The 1988 Family Support Act, primarily a "make work pay" effort, had as its centerpiece an employment and training program called Job Opportunities and Basic Skills (JOBS). The purpose of this program, commonly called "workfare," was to provide the necessary resources (education, training, and child care) to enable welfare recipients who were capable of working to do so, and it included provisions requiring them to take advantage of these resources.

This attempt at welfare reform was not a success. The AFDC rolls continued to rise, and by 1996 no state had come anywhere close to meeting the federally mandated goal of having 20 percent of recipients in jobs or job training.

Due to the apparent failure of the 1988 Family Support Act to meet its initial goals and to conservative concern that the bill was too soft on recipients, welfare reform was attempted again in the 104th Congress. In 1996, H.R. 3734, the Personal Responsibility and Work Opportunity Reconciliation Act of 1996, was passed and signed into law by President Clinton. The major provisions of H.R. 3734 are as follows:

- The Aid to Families with Dependent Children (AFDC) program was replaced by the Temporary Assistance for Needy Families (TANF) program.
- Under TANF, states receive a block grant in an amount calculated to be the highest of (1) the average payment they received under AFDC in fiscal years 1992 through 1994; (2) the amount they received in fiscal year 1994; or (3) the amount they received in fiscal year 1995. (AFDC was an uncapped entitlement program. The states had a right to reimbursement from the federal government for 75 percent of the cost of AFDC grants up to an unlimited amount, as long as they followed regulations.) States have much more freedom regarding how to spend TANF money than they had under AFDC, but when it is spent they have no right to additional funds from the federal government. A contingency fund has been established to

help states that exceed their block grant amounts, but this is available only under specific and limited conditions (i.e., an exceptional increase in unemployment).

- Adults receiving cash benefits are required to work or participate in a state-designed program after two years or their payments will be ended. This work requirement is defined as one individual in a household working at least thirty hours per week.
- States must have at least 50 percent of their total single-parent welfare caseloads in jobs by 2002. States that fail to meet this requirement will have their block grant reduced by 5 percent or more in the following year. States are allowed various exemptions and disregards in this calculation with the result that, as of 2017, no sanctions have been levied.
- States are allowed to sanction, through a reduction or termination of cash benefits, people who fail to fulfill the work requirement.
- Payments to recipients using federal funds must end after a maximum of five years for all spells (times receiving assistance) combined, thereby requiring that families become self-supporting at that point.
- Persons immigrating to the United States after the passage of H.R. 3734 will be ineligible for most means-tested programs, including TANF, food stamps, and Medicaid, for their first five years of residence.
- Illegal aliens will be barred from all means-tested programs. (U.S. House of Representatives, 1996)

President Clinton expressed reluctance to sign this bill, saying, "You can put wings on a pig, but that still does not make it an eagle." He also expressed the belief that the 105th Congress would repeal or soften significant portions of the legislation. However, the late Senator Daniel Patrick Moynihan, probably the leading expert on social welfare policy in the Senate at the time, strongly asserted his belief that the votes simply would not be there to modify this law. As predicted by Senator Moynihan, there have not been as yet any major modifications to soften this law.

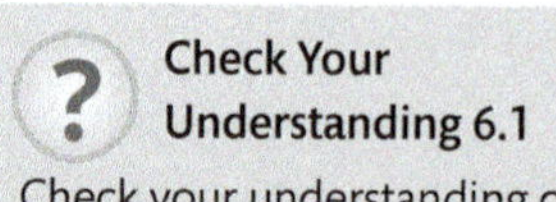

Check Your Understanding 6.1
Check your understanding of Historical Analysis by taking this brief quiz.

SOCIAL ANALYSIS

From the previous section, it is apparent that public assistance in this country has always been controversial, generating many strong feelings about what the problem is and about the character of those benefiting from the program. In this section, we attempt to provide an accurate description of the problem, the population affected, the state of our knowledge regarding these, and the social values that shape our public assistance programs. Because the TANF program did not go into effect until July 1997, some of the data available relate to the AFDC program (Administration for Children and Families, Office of Family Assistance, 2016).

Problem Description

At the heart of our chronic dissatisfaction with our welfare programs is the fact that public assistance addresses two different problems, and the solutions to these problems are inherently contradictory. On the one hand, public welfare deals with the problem of child poverty. The solution to child poverty is fairly simple and straightforward—the provision of cash and other benefits to poor children in levels sufficient to lift them out of poverty.

On the other hand, public assistance is concerned with the problem of adult dependency, people who are perceived as not doing the things necessary to be fully functioning, contributing members of society. The solution to this problem is also fairly straightforward—reduce or completely eliminate benefits in order to force people to support themselves. The difficulty is, of course, that it is not possible to pursue these two goals simultaneously. If we raise benefits in order to reduce child poverty, we risk encouraging adult dependency. If we become harsh and stingy in order to reduce adult dependency, children will inevitably suffer. Because it is not possible to maximize two divergent goals at the same time, we address them serially, first paying attention to one and then to the other (Cyert & Marsh, 1963). Thus, a round of welfare reform that reduces child poverty by increasing benefits will be perceived as increasing adult dependency and will lead to a reform effort to counteract this. The reform effort will attempt to reduce dependency by cutting benefits, which will increase child poverty and lead to calls for reform because of this. The process will go round and round ad infinitum. This partially explains why the TANF first reauthorization bill, which scheduled for 2001, was not passed until 2006, and the second, scheduled for 2010 is yet to be passed. The program survives on continuing resolutions, the most recent being the Consolidated Appropriations Act of 2017.

Population

A large part of the unpopularity of public assistance has to do with the public's perception of characteristics of the recipients and of the program. The stereotype of the typical recipient is a never-married minority-group woman living in the inner city of a large urban area, having her first child at a very young age, having a large number of children, and receiving assistance on a more or less permanent basis. In addition, the public perceives the size of the population and cost of the program as being huge and growing at an ever-increasing rate. Like most stereotypes, this one contains a seed of truth but is highly oversimplified. The following is a description of the TANF population based on the most accurate and recent data available.

Size

In 2015, an average of 1,333,707 families, averaging 2.3 members, received TANF, for a total of 3,067,526 recipients (Table 6.1). This sounds like a large number, and indeed it is, but it is less than 1 percent of the U.S. population. As shown in Table 6.2, the size of the AFDC caseload rose at a truly alarming rate between 1960 and 1975, but the rate of growth slowed considerably until 1990, when it once again began to grow at a rapid rate. In 1994, two years before the passage of TANF, the welfare population began to decline. Following the passage of TANF, the welfare population continued to decline. The decline accelerated until 2002, when the caseload was at the lowest level since 1960. The caseload reached a low of 1,802,567 in 2006, at which point the economy entered a recession and the rolls once again began to increase. In 2010, with the recession easing, the caseload began to decline again until the current record low level.

Cost

Although the welfare rolls were growing until 1994, the expenditure, adjusted for inflation, has declined since 1976. In 1976, total payments (in 1990 dollars) came to approximately $22 billion. By 1990, this amount had shrunk to about $18.5 billion. The cap for total federal cost of the TANF program is set at $16.5 billion, which was the actual 1994 federal

Table 6.1 Characteristics of the TANF Population, 2015

Monthly average number of TANF families	1,333,707
Average number of persons in TANF families	2.3
Average number of children	1.8
Average monthly grant	$398.00
Distribution of number of children in TANF families	
Zero	1.8
One	50.1
Two	27.5
Three	13.0
Four or more	7.4
Distribution of cases by ethnicity	
White	27.5
African American	29.7
Hispanic	36.9
Asian	2.0
Multiracial	1.9
American Indian or Alaskan Native	1.1
Marital status of TANF parents	
Single	72.3
Widowed	0.4
Married	13.0
Separated/divorced	14.3
Education (Age 20 or older)	
Less than 10 years	13.9
10–11 years	24.7
12 years	53.9
More than 12 years	7.5
Unknown	0.4
Work Participation	
Male recipients	27.8
Female recipients	26.5

Source: Adapted from data in U.S. Department of Health and Human Services, Office of Family Assistance, *Characteristics and Financial Circumstances of TANF Recipients Fiscal Year 2015.*

government expenditure on the AFDC program. The reason for this decline in expenditures is that, although the number of AFDC families expanded until 1994, the average size of these families declined and the size of the average AFDC grant also declined at a rapid rate (Table 6.3). Adjusted for inflation, the average AFDC payment dropped from $676 in 1970 to $434 in 1990 and to $381 by 1993 (Committee on Ways and Means, U.S. House of Representatives, 1995; Jost, 1992; U.S. Department of Health and Human Services, 1995). The average TANF payment in 2015 for a family with two children was only $398 per month. The Center on Budget and Policy Priorities estimates that cash assistance

Table 6.2 AFDC/TANF Caseload Size, 1960 to 2003

	Recipients	Families	U.S. Population	Percentage of Year Population
1960	3,005,000	787,000	180,671,000	1.7
1965	4,329,000	1,039,000	194,303,000	2.2
1970	8,466,000	2,208,000	205,052,000	4.1
1975	11,165,185	3,498,000	215,973,000	5.2
1980	10,597,445	3,642,380	227,726,000	4.7
1985	10,812,625	3,691,610	238,466,000	4.5
1990	11,460,382	3,974,322	249,913,000	4.6
1995	13,652,232	4,876,240	263,034,000	5.2
2000	5,964,000	2,269,000	281,400,000	2.1
2005	4,593,686	1,914,036	296,410,404	1.5
2010	4,364,981	1,847,155	308,745,538	1.4
2015	3,067,526	1,333,707	320,090,857	.96

Source: U.S. Department of Health and Human Services–Administration for Children and Families. *Fact Sheet–Welfare*, www.acf.dhhs.gov/programs/opa/facts/tanf.htm; U.S. Department of Health and Human Services, *TANF Eleventh Annual Report to Congress*, December 2015; U.S. Department of Health and Human Services, Office of Family Assistance, *Characteristics and Financial Circumstances of TANF Recipients, Fiscal Year 2015*, http://www.acf.hhs.gov.

Table 6.3 Average AFDC/TANF Family Size and Monthly Benefit

Year	Average Family Size	Average Monthly Benefit (in Constant Dollars)
1970	4.0	676
1975	3.2	576
1980	3.0	483
1985	3.0	443
1990	2.9	434
1995	2.9	373
2000	2.6	349
2005	2.3	354
2010	1.8	336
2015	2.3	398

Source: Committee on Ways and Means, U.S. House of Representatives, *Overview of Entitlement Programs: 1995 Greenbook* (Washington, DC: U.S. Government Printing Office, 1995), p. 325; U.S. Department of Health and Human Services, Office of Family Assistance, *TANF Eleventh Annual Report to Congress, 2016*, various tables; U.S. Department of Health and Human Services, Office of Family Assistance, *Characteristics and Financial Circumstances of TANF Recipients, Fiscal Year 2015*, various tables, www.acf.hhs.gov.

for families with children are now at least 20 percent below their 1996 levels when adjusted for inflation (Floyd & Schott, 2013, p. 1). More detail regarding the cost of the AFDC and TANF programs is provided in the section on economic analysis.

Race

As was the case with the AFDC program, the majority of TANF recipients are minority group members, and that majority is increasing. In 2003, 63.5 percent of TANF recipients were minorities, and by 2015 this had increased to 70.6 percent. The composition of this minority/majority has also dramatically changed in a short time. Between 2003 and 2015 the percentage of TANF recipients who were African American has declined from 36.6 percent to 29.7 percent, while the Hispanic percentage has increased from 20.7 percent to 36.9 percent. The increase in Hispanics is mostly a reflection of the increasing size of this group, going from 12.3 percent of the population in the 2000 census to nearly 18 percent in 2015. The decline in the percentage of recipients who are black, however, cannot be explained by demographic trends because the percentage of the overall population made up by this group has only increased slightly.

The real significance of the racial and ethnic differences in the TANF population becomes apparent when these numbers are looked at in relation to the composition of the overall U.S. population. Approximately 72 percent of the total population is white, whereas whites constitute only about 27.5 percent of the TANF population. Less than 1 percent of white households receive assistance. African Americans make up about 13 percent of the U.S. population but account for 29.7 percent of TANF recipients. Approximately 4 percent of African American families receive assistance. Hispanics make up about 18 percent of the population and account for 36.9 percent of TANF families. Approximately 3 percent of Hispanic families receive TANF benefits. These factors account for the popular stereotype of TANF being almost exclusively a minority program even though almost a third of recipients are white.

Family Size

Another popular stereotype of the TANF program is that welfare recipients have very large families. Actually, welfare families are not particularly large. Data from 1995 indicate that mothers on AFDC gave birth to an average of 2.5 children, compared to an average of 2.1 children for mothers not on AFDC (Figure 6.1), and that fertility rates for welfare recipients were declining and, in fact, have continued to decline. In 2015, the average number of children in a TANF household was 1.8. The average number of children born to all women in the United States was also 1.8, indicating that the fertility rate of TANF mothers is exactly the same as that of the general population.

Mothers' Marital Status

In fiscal year 2015, 85.2 percent of TANF mothers were either not married or were separated/divorced. Births to single mothers for the overall population of women were 40.3 percent. These figures reflect the rapidly changing social norms regarding marriage and parenthood. In 1960, only 5.2 percent of children were born to unmarried mothers (U.S. Department of Health and Human Services, Administration for Children and Families, 2012).

Age of Mothers

TANF mothers are younger than those who do not receive TANF, averaging thirty years of age, compared to thirty-four years for mothers not receiving TANF. Eight percent of TANF parents are teenagers, and 17 percent are thirty-nine years or older.

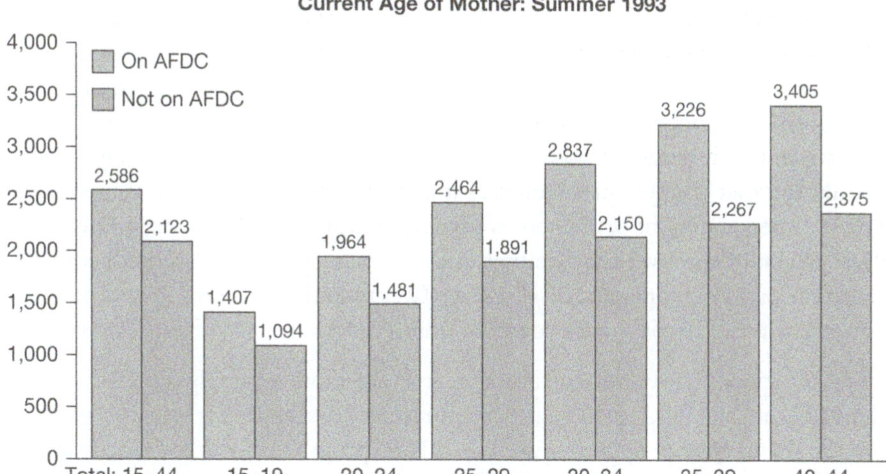

Figure 6.1
Fertility Rate of AFDC and Non-AFDC Mothers

Source: Bureau of the Census Statistical Brief, *Mothers Who Receive AFDC Payments—Fertility and Socioeconomic Characteristics* (Washington, DC: U.S. Government Printing Office, March 1995).

Education

The number of years of schooling is significantly less for TANF recipients than for the general population. More than one-third (38.6 percent) of TANF recipients never completed high school, compared to only 12 percent of nonrecipients. It is interesting that the educational level of TANF recipients is lower than it was for AFDC recipients. This is probably a result of the large number of recipients who have recently left the rolls. It is reasonable to guess that those with the highest educational levels are those finding employment and exiting the program.

Length of Time on Welfare (Spells)

Policy analysts refer to the length of time a person is on assistance as a *spell*. The major concern of policymakers, as well as of the general public, about public assistance programs is their belief that recipients get on the rolls and never leave. It is precisely this concern that is behind the TANF time limit of two years for any one spell and five years for the total of all spells. This is a somewhat troublesome area to discuss because the terms can be confusing and the same data can be presented in ways that create different impressions. For example, critics of AFDC asserted that 65 percent of recipients of AFDC received assistance for eight or more years, while defenders of the program said that nearly 60 percent of people were on AFDC for less than two years. Both are, in fact, using the same data, and what both say is equally true. How can this be?

The answer is that statistics regarding welfare spells look quite different depending on whether, by "time on welfare," you are referring to everyone who has ever had a welfare spell or to the length of the spell of people currently on the rolls. Let us explain by way of the following example:

> Imagine you are asked to compile statistics on average length of room rental in a small apartment motel in your town. The motel has ten units, and you find

> that eight of the units have been occupied by the same people for the entire previous year. The other two units have been rented by different people each month. Thus, the motel has had a total of thirty-two tenants (the eight year-long tenants and twenty-four who each rented one of the other two rooms for a month). If someone were to ask you, based on your analysis, what the typical tenant in the apartment/motel is, you could answer in one of two ways. You could say that the typical tenant was a long-term renter, because at any one time 80 percent (eight of the ten) were long-term renters. However, you could just as honestly answer that the typical tenant was a short-term renter because over the past year 75 percent of all guests (twenty-four short-term renters out of a total of thirty-two) rented a room for only a month.

The situation with welfare spells is similar to the motel example. Of all the persons who ever began an AFDC spell, 59.25 percent received assistance for less than two years. So, for the majority of people who used the AFDC program, it worked exactly as it was intended. Almost 60 percent of people who received assistance used it to help them over a temporary life crisis (death in the family, divorce, illness, job layoff, etc.), and then they got back on their feet and continued life as productive, tax-paying citizens. Few people in our society begrudge the program as it worked for these people.

However, of the people on the AFDC program at any one time, the current spell for 49 percent of them was longer than eight years. If all the spells of the people on the program at any one time were added, 65 percent of the recipients had spells totaling eight or more years. Thus, 65 percent of the people on AFDC at any one time were clearly stuck in the program. They became dependent on it, and, for some reason, be it personal limitation or lack of opportunity, they were unable to escape. Nearly everyone agreed that something different was needed for this segment of the population. This is the challenge for the TANF program.

The TANF rolls have been falling rapidly, but most likely many, probably most, of those leaving are those who would have been short-term recipients under the AFDC program. Government data indicates that a majority of TANF recipients remain only for a short time and that a small minority are in the program for a long duration. In 2015, 35.9 percent of adults on TANF had been in the program for less than a year, another 21.7 percent less than two years, and only 15.1 percent more than four years. A little more than 6 percent of the TANF cases have been receiving benefits for more than five years. They are being supported by various federal and state extension policies that allow them to exceed the 60-month time limit.

We do not want to leave the impression, easily gotten from the above figures, that people leaving TANF are always doing this for happy reasons. The positive case closures are for reasons of employment (16.9%), marriage (0.7%), and somehow obtaining resources exceeding TANF eligibility levels (2.7%). This works out to about one-fifth of TANF leavers doing so for positive reasons. The other four-fifths leave the rolls because they reach federal or state time limits (2.7%); are dismissed from the rolls for some rule violation, referred to as being sanctioned or failure to comply (28.9%); or other reasons such as children reaching the program time limit (38.7%). The remaining 9.4% of case closures are classified as "voluntary," which usually means that the recipient has tired of fulfilling all the requirements involved in staying on the TANF rolls.

The onion metaphor As should be apparent from the preceding information, the welfare population is much more diverse than the popular stereotype. Corbett (1993) developed a useful metaphor relating the various parts of the welfare population to layers of an onion. The outer layer consists of recipients who receive assistance for two or fewer years. These people generally enter welfare due to a discrete and easily observable event in their lives—illness, job loss, divorce, or the like. They generally have comparatively high education, recent work experience, ability, and motivation and, with a few supports, will reenter the labor market in a short time. The only thing this group needs is short-term financial help and some assistance in regaining entry into the labor market.

The middle layer of the onion is composed of people who receive assistance for two to eight years (under TANF definitions two to five) and are often on-and-off-again recipients. These people have limited options. They generally have some basic skills and education, but the employment opportunities do not exist to elevate them out of poverty on a permanent basis. Their fortunes are highly related to the functioning of the economy. When the economy is doing well, members of the middle layer will have opportunities available to them that allow them to escape welfare, if perhaps not poverty. When the economy is doing poorly, because of their relatively low level of education and skills (human capital), people in this layer will be the first to be laid off. Appropriate interventions for members of this layer are educational/vocational preparation to help them be more competitive and measures to strengthen the economy.

The core of the onion is composed of recipients who remain on assistance for eight or more years, sometimes referred to as being *systems dependent*. This is the group we usually picture when discussing public welfare. In addition to low earning capacity brought on by lack of education, training, and job experience, this group also faces barriers to self-sufficiency such as drug abuse, psychological problems, health problems, abusive personal relationships, and so on. This group is also often suspected of lacking basic motivation and of possessing values that are not conducive to work. This group requires far more extensive interventions to achieve self-sufficiency than do members of the two outer layers.

Finally, there is the very inner core. These people are permanently functionally limited due to severe physical or emotional impairment. For these people, self-sufficiency is simply not a realistic objective. The response to this group, according to Corbett (1993), should be to recognize that they will never be totally self-sufficient and to develop nonstigmatizing ways of providing income support. Corbett (1993) believes, "An expanded disability program (e.g., a liberalization of Supplemental Security Income) seems an appropriate vehicle through which to assist this group" (pp. 4–5, 9–12). All of this has clear implications for the reform of TANF.

TANF time limits One of the centerpieces of the TANF program is the sixty-month lifetime limit on receipt of assistance. According to Corbett's typology, there are two groups, those he calls the core and the inner core, who most likely will not be able to achieve self-sufficiency. What will happen to these people? From the beginning, this has been one of the big questions of the TANF program. As it turns out, the sixty-month time limit is not inflexible. A family can continue to receive benefits for longer than sixty months in one of three ways. The first is referred to as an *extension*, whereby states can continue to provide benefits in situations of hardship or domestic violence. The second is referred to as *exemptions*, whereby the TANF clock does not run under certain circumstances, such as child-only cases (the child is receiving benefits but the caretaker is not) or cases living on an Indian reservation or in an Alaskan Native village. Extensions and exemptions, referred to as maintenance of effort (MOE), cannot total more than

20 percent of a state's total caseload. The third means of extending benefits beyond sixty months is that states may elect to continue recipients on benefits by paying for them with out-of-state funds, under what is referred to as separate state programs (SSPs). As of 2015, 175,319 families were receiving benefits under an extension, 890,124 under MOE or SSPs.

Relevant Research

A vast amount of research relevant to welfare reform is available, most of which is systematically ignored by policymakers. In Chapter 3, we briefly mentioned the New Jersey, Seattle, and Denver income maintenance experiments, the largest and most ambitious attempts to test an alternative approach to public assistance. We will only tangentially mention these studies here, even though they are considered landmarks, because the approach they tested, known as a guaranteed annual income or negative income tax, is a liberal welfare reform approach no longer in the public assistance policy arena. The largest body of research relevant to welfare reform consists of numerous studies being conducted for the purpose of evaluating current reform efforts. These will be discussed in some detail in the section on evaluation. There is also a good deal of research on the economics of welfare, some of which will be reviewed in the economic analysis section. In this section, we review research that studies one of the greatest concerns of welfare policymakers—whether the receipt of welfare promotes undesirable behavior among recipients.

A constant feature of welfare policy is the fear that, by giving people assistance, we will somehow damage their moral character by, in the terminology of economics, exposing them to moral hazard. Major concerns are that receipt of public assistance will promote family instability by enabling women to leave their husbands or to have children without ever being married; that receipt of welfare will damage the recipient's spirit of independence (i.e., will make the person permanently dependent); and, finally, that children who grow up in welfare households will think being on welfare is a normal state of affairs and will hence be more likely to turn to welfare for their own support when they become adults.

David Ellwood and Mary Jo Bane (1984) have studied the relation of welfare receipt to family formation. They looked at a list of family structure variables and, using several databases, analyzed the effects of welfare receipt on these variables. The data indicated no effect of welfare receipt on births to unmarried mothers and only a small effect on divorce, separation, or the establishment of female-headed households. Interestingly, the one really significant effect of welfare they found was that, in states with low benefit levels, welfare mothers were more likely to live with their parents than they were in high-benefit states. Their conclusion was that there is little evidence that receipt of welfare was a primary cause of variation in family structure.

The effect of more generous welfare payments on family stability was also one of the major questions in the income maintenance experiments. Findings from the experiments in Gary, New Jersey, and the rural studies were inconclusive. However, the findings from Seattle and Denver indicated that the more generous negative income tax benefit was strongly related to increased marital dissolution rates for both blacks and whites. Rates for Hispanics also increased, but increases were smaller and not statistically significant. These data were reanalyzed in the late 1980s, using more sophisticated statistical techniques, and the positive relation between the program and increased rates of marital dissolution was found to be spurious. However, by the time the reanalysis was released, the damage to the idea of a negative income tax as a welfare approach had been done, and the topic was no longer in the policy arena (Greenberg, Linksz, & Mandell, 2003).

Lerman (2002) reviewed the first five years of TANF data looking for effects on family structure. Consistent with the findings of Ellwood and Bane, he found that the policy changes had no effect. In fact, the proportion of married recipients has continued to decline, as has the rate of married parenthood generally.

A popular stereotype of public assistance is that children who grow up in welfare households will be much more likely than nonwelfare children to become welfare-dependent adults themselves. This is related to the "culture of poverty" idea referred to earlier—that children who grow up on welfare will be taught values that are positive toward welfare receipt and therefore will not have the aversion to welfare that people who did not grow up in welfare households generally have. Consequently, the argument goes, when times get tough, these people will be more likely to turn to welfare for support than will people who grew up in nonwelfare households. Using fourteen years of data from the University of Michigan's Panel Study of Income Dynamics, Martha Hill and Michael Ponza (1984) looked at the intergenerational transmission of welfare dependency. They found that welfare children typically did not become welfare-dependent adults. Only 19 percent of the children from African American welfare families and 26 percent of children from white welfare families were heavily welfare dependent in their own homes. In terms of intergenerational transmission of welfare dependency, there were no statistically significant differences between African Americans who grew up in welfare-dependent homes and those who did not. For whites, the only significant difference was for people who grew up in homes with the very highest level of parental welfare dependence, and even these differences were not consistent across all of the models tested (Duncan & Hoffman, 1988; Hill & Ponza, 1984; "Poverty across Generations," 1983).

It should be noted that questions concerning the relationship between welfare receipt and the behavior/character of recipients are extremely complex and the research results are not clear to the point of being unassailable. However, as Greg Duncan and Saul Hoffman (1988) state,

> The fact that several million individuals are persistently dependent on welfare raises questions of whether welfare itself promotes divorce or out-of-wedlock births, discourages marriages, or instills counterproductive attitudes and values in recipients. Sparse evidence on the effects of welfare on the attitudes of recipients fails to show any such links.

Has welfare policymaking been affected by relevant research? The evidence does not indicate that it has. Why is this so? The answer is that the research evidence is in direct conflict with some very deeply held U.S. values.

Values and Welfare Reform

As is the case in most areas of social welfare policy, in public assistance, deeply held values supersede empirical knowledge. Public assistance exists at the intersection of two conflicting sets of values, one supportive of welfare and one deeply antagonistic to it. The values that are antagonistic to welfare are the following:

The United States as the Land of Opportunity

Most of us sincerely believe that in this country there is opportunity for everyone, if only a person looks for it. Anyone with a good heart and a willing spirit can find work and get ahead. The idea that in our postindustrial, international economy there is no place for many workers offends this belief. Public welfare is seen as an accusation that the economy does not work well and, as such, is seen as almost un-American.

Individualism

Americans believe that individuals are autonomous and have control over their own destinies. We believe that people should get full credit for their successes and take full blame for their problems. We are still fascinated by, uplifted by, and—more important—believe in the rags-to-riches American success story. We reject the notion of collective responsibility for individual problems. As public welfare is, by definition, collective responsibility, we think it is a bad thing. Individuals should support themselves and not rely on their neighbors.

Work

Work is considered important because it provides the means for survival. However, we also think of work as a moral virtue, valuable for its own sake, not just for its contribution to our material well-being. Laziness and idleness are viewed as evidence of weak moral character. Because welfare allows people to survive without working, we tend to suspect that it is a contributor to immorality. As such, public welfare is viewed as more of a moral problem than an economic one.

The Traditional Nuclear Family

The nuclear family—husband, wife, and children—is viewed as the main pillar of a stable, moral society. This type of family is considered a moral virtue, and the more a family deviates from this ideal, the greater the degree of social disapproval. As the welfare population is primarily composed of female-headed families with a high proportion never married, the morality of these families, and by extension the whole program, is suspect.

In support of public welfare are the following values:

mantisdesign/Shutterstock

One of the jewels in the crown of American values is the expectation that everyone will work hard. People receiving TANF are viewed as violating this value and thus the program's emphasis on getting recipients to work is a very popular feature.

Humanitarianism

Although some of our values may be rather harsh, at the core the American people believe that it is wrong, even sinful, to allow other people, especially children, to suffer when we have it in our power to help.

Sense of Community

David Ellwood (1988) has stated, "The autonomy of the individual and primacy of the family tend to push people in individualistic and often isolating directions. But the desire for community remains strong in everything from religion to neighborhood. Compassion and sympathy for others can be seen as flowing from a sense of connection with and empathy for others" (pp. 16, 18).

Thus, our values regarding public welfare amount to what Lloyd Free and Hadley Cantril (1967) have referred to as a "schizoid combination of operational liberalism with ideological conservatism." On the one hand, strongly held values lead us to conclude that providing financial assistance to people is a bad thing. Assistance leads, in the public mind, to people giving up individual responsibility for their lives; it allows people to live without working, which encourages the development of sloth and laziness, major character flaws; it allows women to have children and to raise them without husbands, which is seen as contributing to family breakdown. On the other hand, we feel driven out of a sense of compassion and desire for community to help people who are suffering. This value conflict over public assistance is really not hard to understand. The different values relate to the different objectives of the TANF program discussed earlier. The objective of doing something about the problem of child poverty is addressed by our values of humanitarianism and desire for community. The objective of discouraging adult dependency is addressed by the values of individualism, work, and family. Ellwood (1988) asks, "Can we design social policies that are consistent with all these values or that at least minimize the conflicts between them?" He concludes, and we agree, that "the conflict is inevitable."

Check Your Understanding 6.2

Check your understanding of Social Analysis by taking this brief quiz.

ECONOMIC ANALYSIS

Although we generally classify public assistance as social welfare policy, we must recognize that, at its core, it is *economic* policy. The need for public assistance results from a failure in our economy to provide a place for everyone. Thus, probably the most important questions about public assistance are economic questions. The major macroeconomic questions are: How much does welfare cost? Is the cost growing? What are the employment prospects of welfare recipients in the market economy? The major microeconomic concern is whether welfare receipt serves as a work disincentive: Is the total package of benefits so great that a person is better off on assistance than he or she would be working, thus leading to a rational economic decision to favor welfare over work? A second microeconomic concern has to do with the economic effects of welfare receipt on family formation. A final microeconomic concern, one that has not been given much attention but deserves more, is: What are the behaviors that welfare recipients actually engage in to survive on the minimal grants they receive?

Macroeconomic Issues

Listening to politicians and to the popular media leads to the conclusion that public assistance is tremendously expensive and is driving our economy into ruin. It is also frequently alleged that the cost of public assistance has been increasing at a rapid rate and has been a major contributor to past federal budget deficits, although this concern has lessened after the implementation of TANF (Sutch, 1996).

How Much Does Public Assistance Actually Cost?

The surprising answer is that in terms of the total government budget, not very much. In 2013, combined federal and state TANF expenditures totaled $31.6 billion. States spent about 28 percent of this for cash grants to families and the remaining 72 percent for supplementary services such as child care and work-related programs and administrative costs. In absolute terms, of course, this is a lot of money, and, presented with nothing to compare it to, it does seem like a reason for major concern. However, when viewed in context, the amount seems small. The 2013 federal budget alone amounts to more than $3.5 trillion. The federal share of TANF was far less than 1 percent of this figure. Between 1997 and 2011, the amount spent on TANF grants (in constant dollars) actually declined by $4.3 billion. By way of comparison, in 2011 the Department of Defense received $712 billion, and $11 billion was allocated to the Troubled Assets Relief Program (TARP). Thus, it can be seen that public assistance is not a major contributor to either federal or state deficits, and cutting costs for the program by replacing AFDC with TANF has not resulted in a great savings, although states are somewhat better off.

Is the Cost of Public Assistance Growing?

The other common macroeconomic concern regarding public assistance is that its cost is growing at a rapid rate and is, in fact, out of control. This is also not true. The reason for this perception of the growth of public assistance probably has to do with the fact that data on the cost of AFDC, and now TANF, have generally been lumped in with general social spending, which has increased by 49 percent since 2002. However, the lion's share of the increase is accounted for by programs other than TANF, notably health-related programs, nutrition programs, and the Earned Income Tax Credit. Even when looking at total social spending, many accountants and economists argue that the rate of growth has been very moderate. The Office of Management and the Budget, in its 2016 analysis of historic federal spending, concludes that means-tested (welfare) spending has actually declined, constituting 3.1 percent of the budget in 1975, 1.7 percent each year from 1989 to 2008, further declining to only 1.1 percent in 2015 (Office of Management and the Budget, 2017, p. 11).

Prospects for Employment of Welfare Recipients

One of the major provisions of the TANF program is a limit of two years for any one welfare spell and a lifetime limit of five years for the total of all spells. This has been referred to as a "shock-therapy" approach, basically telling recipients that they have only a limited amount of time to get their lives together and then they, and their children, will be on their own. Central to this provision is the assumption that there is work for everyone if they will just do what is necessary to obtain it. Thus, a key research question for public assistance policy is whether this assumption is true.

An interesting opportunity for a natural experiment on this shock-therapy approach occurred in Michigan when the state terminated its general assistance (GA) program in 1991. General assistance was a state-financed welfare program intended to benefit people who look very much like the TANF population but who are not eligible for TANF

Ranta Images/Shutterstock

Since the earliest social welfare legislation one of the main goals has been to eliminate begging from public spaces. With the TANF program we have, if anything, lost ground toward achieving this goal.

for one reason or another, generally because they do not have children at home. Sandra Danziger and Sherrie Kossoudji looked at former GA recipients in Michigan two years after their termination from the program to see how they had fared. They found that about one-half of former recipients with a high school diploma or GED were working, but fewer than one-quarter of those lacking these credentials were employed. Among those who were working, very few were earning enough money to elevate themselves over the poverty line. This study "suggests that welfare recipients who reach the time limit, but are not offered work opportunities, will have difficulty obtaining and holding jobs" (Testimony of Sheldon Danziger, 1996).

Prior to the implementation of TANF, a number of scholars predicted that the labor market would not be able to absorb the inflow of former welfare recipients (Danziger, 1996). Their gloomy predictions, at least initially, turned out to be incorrect. Early data indicated that people exiting welfare were generally working and were enjoying incomes much greater than they had as recipients (Coe, Acs, Lerman, & Watson, 1998). A study of labor markets in twenty large metropolitan areas concluded that the markets had been able to absorb the new workers without increasing the unemployment rate (Lerman, Loprest, & Ratcliffe, 1999). However, it should be noted that the implementation of TANF occurred in what Brauner and Loprest (1999) refer to as "stellar labor market conditions." Now that the economy has slowed and TANF caseloads are beginning to rise in many states, the employment picture for people leaving welfare, as well as for those who have recently left, may be quite different (Loprest & Zedlewski, 2002). A 2015 report by the Center on Budget and Policy Priorities found that, after the economic downturn that began in 2007, nearly all of the employment gains attributed to TANF have disappeared. The report concludes that, although "the sharp improvement in employment among single mothers in the 1990s is often attributed to welfare reform, research has shown that other factors—especially a very strong labor market (with unemployment as low as 4 percent) and the Earned Income Tax Credit (EITC)—were far more important" (Center for Budget and Policy Priorities, 2011).

The conclusion from an analysis of the macroeconomic aspects of TANF is that the cost is so small in relation to other parts of the economy that its effects on the economy are minimal. Neither substantial reductions nor increases in welfare benefits will have any great effect on aggregate measures of the performance of the economy.

Microeconomic Analysis

Is Public Assistance a Work Disincentive?

The major microeconomic concern with public assistance is that it serves as a work disincentive. The argument goes that people given a choice between living on welfare or working for a living will choose to work only if they will be significantly better off as a result of doing so. As Sar Levitan and Frank Gallo note, the total package to which a welfare recipient is entitled (cash grant; food stamps; Medicaid; and, in some cases, subsidized housing) often exceeds the compensation available from low-wage work. They note that in 1991 the average nonworking mother with two children received almost $7,500 in combined AFDC/food stamp benefits, compared with $8,900 earned income from a minimum-wage job (Levitan & Gallo, 1993). If the person received subsidized housing, or if the job did not include free medical insurance, the total welfare package would exceed the minimum-wage job by a good margin.

The evidence regarding the degree to which welfare acts as a work disincentive is mixed and generally finds less of an effect than logic would predict. Frank Levy and Richard Michel (1986) conducted a longitudinal comparison of welfare benefits as a proportion of the average wage of workers in the retail trade industry. Their hypothesis was that the higher the ratio of welfare to wages, the more likely it would be that people would choose welfare over work. Thus, if welfare benefits were increasing relative to wages, the size of the welfare rolls should show an increase; if welfare benefits were declining relative to wages, the welfare rolls should shrink. Analyzing twenty-five years of data, they found that this relationship did not hold. Although the ratio of welfare to wages declined during this period, the welfare rolls expanded (Levy & Michel, 1986). After conducting a thorough review of the literature, economist Robert Moffitt came to a different conclusion. He found that "the available research unequivocally indicates that the AFDC program generates nontrivial work disincentives" (Moffitt, 1990). The researchers whose work Moffitt (1990) reviewed found that the amount of work reduction was small, however, ranging between 1 hour to 9.8 hours per week. The income maintenance experiments that tested the more generous negative income tax approach to welfare assistance also hypothesized that the approach would result in a reduction in the hours of work by members of the experimental groups. Like the researchers reviewed by Moffitt, they found that this was indeed the case, but that the reductions were small. Husbands in the experimental group worked 119 hours per year (7 percent) less than control group husbands, wives worked 93 hours (17 percent) less, and female family heads worked 113 hours (17 percent) less.

In any case, with the implementation of TANF, this concern becomes moot. In passing TANF, policymakers accepted the assumption that public assistance is a work disincentive and structured the program to enforce labor market participation.

Economic Survival Strategies of Welfare Recipients

States determine the level of welfare benefits based on a concept called "level of need." Level of need is what the state determines as the minimum amount families of various sizes need to survive. The state then sets a percentage of this amount, usually around 50 percent, as the public assistance grant level. Now, the question the authors have often pondered is this: How in the world do we expect people to survive when, by our own calculations, we provide them with one-half of the minimum amount necessary for survival? Sociologist Kathryn Edin and anthropologist Laura Lein (1997) have researched this question and have come up with an answer: People cannot, and do not, survive on welfare benefits alone.

To study the question of how welfare mothers survive economically, Edin interviewed a sample of fifty women in Chicago in 1989, and she and Lein interviewed several hundred more in Massachusetts, South Carolina, and Texas between 1990 and 1994 (Edin, 1991; Edin & Lein, 1997; Jencks, 1974). They invested considerable time developing relationships of trust with the women in their sample; based on these relationships, the women were willing to reveal candid details of their economic lives. Edin and Lein collected detailed data on the women's household budgets and on their sources of income. What they found is that the women were not able to come anywhere close to making ends meet on the amount they received from the combination of welfare and food stamps. In the Chicago sample, for example, the women had average monthly expenses of $864 and average income from welfare and food stamps of $521. Thus, their average monthly shortfall was $343.

With an average monthly shortfall of $343, how did these mothers survive? The answer found by Edin and Lein is that virtually all of the women had additional sources of income they did not report to the welfare department (reported income would result in a reduction of the welfare grant, although generally not dollar for dollar). The women's sources of income varied. Some income was obtained from family and friends, some from the absent fathers of the children, some was earned in the regular economy and hidden from authorities by means of false Social Security numbers, and some (a very small amount, averaging only $38) was earned in the underground economy through activities such as drug dealing and prostitution. The average family income from the Chicago sample was $897, $521 obtained from welfare and food stamps, and $376 obtained from unreported sources. Through these means, the women were able to cover their basic monthly expenses with an average of $33 of discretionary income left over.

The Effects of Public Assistance on Family Structure

It has long been a major concern of public assistance policy that by allowing women to have children without being married, welfare assistance encourages single parenthood. This concern intensified as the proportion of AFDC children who were born out of wedlock grew from 38 to 60.4 percent between 1979 and 1994 (Administration for Children and Families, 2005). One explanation for this increase is that it simply reflected changes in U.S. mores, which now define unwed parenthood as acceptable when only a few decades ago it clearly was not. Another explanation, however, is that the increase in the proportion of welfare recipients who are unwed mothers is, at least partially, due to perverse economic incentives not to marry, created by welfare programs. The argument, nicely summarized by economists Levy and Michel, is based on one long advanced by black writers, first W. E. B. Du Bois in 1899, later by E. Franklin Frazier in 1939, and most recently revived by Harvard University sociologist William Julius Wilson. The idea is that if a man does not have an adequate job and has few prospects for finding one, he will not be viewed as an acceptable prospect for marriage. In inner-city areas, the number of men who have jobs that pay more than a woman can get on combined public assistance benefits (TANF, SNAP, Medicaid, housing) is decreasing. "Thus if welfare benefits are higher than the incomes of a significant portion of men, it may provide an incentive to create more female-headed families" (Levy & Michel, 1986).

Levy and Michel (1986) analyzed this theory using data from the *Current Population Survey* conducted on an ongoing basis by the Census Bureau. They found that in 1960, 69 percent of black males aged twenty to twenty-four and 83 percent aged twenty-five to thirty-four had incomes above the average AFDC grant of $1,269. By 1983, only 38 percent of black males aged twenty to twenty-four and 71 percent aged twenty-five to thirty-four had incomes greater than the average AFDC grant, which was $4,741. They conclude that this data confirms Wilson's (1987) findings that the increase in female-headed families in black inner-city areas is due to the decrease in the number of men who are able to provide an income large enough to support a family at above-welfare levels. It is important to note that Levy and Michel do not conclude that rising welfare benefits are responsible for the decline in two-parent families. Indeed, as noted previously, in constant dollars the actual amount of welfare benefits has been declining. Rather, the culprit appears to be the lack of employment opportunities available to people with low education, little experience, and few job skills.

The concern that public assistance may be a contributor to the formation of single-parent families was central to the 1996 welfare reform legislation that replaced AFDC with TANF. Three out of four legislated purposes of TANF specifically address family formation objectives: (1) end the dependence of needy parents on government benefits by promoting job preparation, work, and marriage; (2) prevent and reduce the incidence of out-of-wedlock pregnancies and establish annual numerical goals for preventing and reducing the incidence of these pregnancies; and (3) encourage the formation and maintenance of two-parent families (Administration for Children and Families, 2016). These objectives have been pursued through two primary means. The first is the Healthy Marriage and Responsible Fatherhood Initiative, which provides grants to support "a range of activities to increase access to marriage strengthening services and awareness about the values and benefits of healthy marriage for children, adults, and communities." The most prominent of these activities has been a widely distributed compendium providing basic facts and information from research studies on marriage and its benefits, as well as examples of existing programs, curricula, and promising practices. Other frequent activities include grants to support the development and implementation of an array of marriage and relationship skills classes and related marriage-strengthening services. In 2015, the initiative provided grants to 91 organizations in 27 states and one territory to promote healthy marriage and relationship education, responsible fatherhood, and reentry services for current and formerly incarcerated fathers. Under the Deficit Reduction Act of 2005 and reauthorized under the Claims Resolution Act of 2010, the Healthy Marriage Initiative is funded at $150 million each year to support healthy-marriage and fatherhood programs. Research on programs funded under this initiative indicates that they either had no impact or a negative impact on the relationships of the couples who took part (Mencimer, 2012). Concern has been expressed that the programs funded by the Healthy Marriage Initiative do not adequately recognize the degree to which people, and a disproportionate number of TANF recipients, enter romantic relationships with personal experiences of abuse and partner violence. Research has found that, counter to the basic assumptions of the Healthy Marriage Initiative, TANF mothers have the same values regarding marriage and parenthood as the rest of the population but are wary of entering long-term romantic commitments due to their very negative experiences with such relationships in the past (Taylor & Vogel-Ferguson, 2011).

The second means of addressing out-of-wedlock births specifically concerns the belief that teenagers were having children as a means of setting up their own households and thus escaping parental control. Rebecca Blank (1997) has named this the "independence effect" of welfare and has found some evidence supporting its existence. TANF requires that mothers younger than 18 years of age must live with a parent or guardian and must be enrolled in high school in order to receive welfare benefits, thereby eliminating this supposed benefit of pregnancy for young teenagers. There is some early evidence that this policy may be contributing to a reduction of the fertility rate of 15- to 17-year-old girls (Lopoo & DeLeire, 2006).

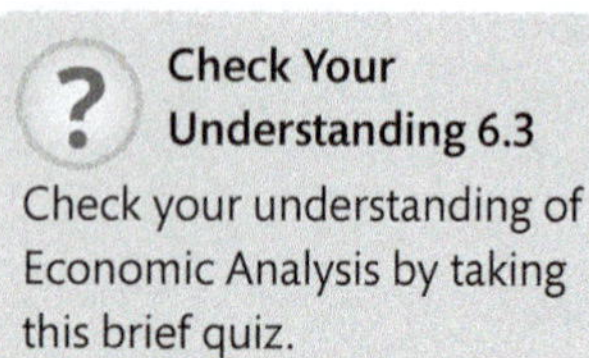
Check Your Understanding 6.3
Check your understanding of Economic Analysis by taking this brief quiz.

EVALUATION

For the thirty years prior to its end, the primary goal of the AFDC program was to get recipients into jobs and thereby off the rolls. Before 1967, it was generally accepted that AFDC was intended to allow deserving mothers to remain home with their children. Work was, undoubtedly unintentionally, discouraged through a policy that reduced the amount of a recipient's grant dollar for dollar when that person had earned income. In 1967, the policy of AFDC officially changed to encourage work through the passage of the Work Incentive (WIN) program. The WIN program employed a carrot-and-stick approach, the carrot being a formula that decreased a recipient's grant at a rate equal to only a portion of earnings so she would always be better off working than not. The stick was a provision that allowed states to drop people from the rolls who declined to participate in employment or training "without good cause." Various iterations of the WIN program remained in effect until the program was replaced in 1988 with the Job Opportunity and Basic Skills (JOBS) program, the centerpiece of the Family Support Act (Patterson, 1994). The TANF program emphasizes employment even more heavily, with the new twist of time limits. Recipients are now eligible to receive assistance for only two years for any single welfare spell and for a lifetime total of five years for all spells combined. The TANF program adopted a new philosophy of welfare known as "work first." This philosophy holds that training is preferable to idleness, but work, regardless of the type, is preferable to training. Under the AFDC program, a recipient could enroll in a registered nurse training program even if nurse's aide jobs were available. Under TANF and work first, the recipient is required to take the job as a nurse's aide, even if at minimum wage and results in the recipient not finishing the RN program.

Thus, the most important evaluation questions currently facing public assistance policymakers relate to the effectiveness of employment training and placement programs for TANF recipients. The most critical questions are: Do recipients who are provided with these services actually get jobs? Do those who get jobs earn enough to get them off the welfare rolls and out of poverty? What is the relationship between the jobs obtained and the quality of life of former recipients? Do job programs result in cost savings for the programs? Fortunately, there has been significant effort expended to evaluate employment programs for welfare recipients.

Most evaluations of welfare-to-work programs have found positive results for the programs, but in all cases the results have been slight. The WIN program had very poor results. Historian James Patterson (1994) reviewed evaluations of WIN and found that out of 2.8 million eligible welfare recipients, only 400,000 actually enrolled in WIN, and only 52,000 found paid employment at only slightly more than the minimum wage.

Ronald Reagan's work-oriented welfare reform program in California, passed in 1971 when he was that state's governor, has often been cited as a model for national welfare reform efforts. However, an evaluation of that program found that, although the stated goal of the program was to place 30,000 welfare recipients in jobs, at its peak it managed only 1,000 placements (Kirp, 1986).

The poster child for welfare-to-work programs is the GAIN program in Riverside, California. This program, started under the JOBS program, has demonstrated the largest measured impacts to date. Judith Gueron (1994) summarizes the evaluation results as "double-digit increases in the share of AFDC recipients working, a 50 percent increase in average earnings, a one-sixth reduction in welfare payments, impressive effects on long-term recipients." However, she notes that this is an exceptional program, and the difference between it and more typical programs is wide. She concludes, "The more typical program, while achieving positive results, remains severely strapped for funds, does not reach most of the people who could theoretically be subject to its mandates, and has not dramatically changed the message of welfare" (Gueron, 1994). Moreover, Teresa Amott (1992) reports that, although the California program has achieved significant results, the actual earnings of the average participant were only $785 greater over a two-year period than the earnings of members of a control group who did not participate in the program.

Levitan and Gallo (1993) reviewed thirteen experimental studies (evaluations that included a treatment/experimental group and a control group) that were conducted on employment programs between 1978 and 1993. They found that the employment rate of the treatment group subjects was statistically higher in five studies, the same or lower in six studies, and unknown in the remaining two. In eleven of the thirteen studies, the experimental group members had statistically higher earnings than the control group. However, once again, although earnings increased significantly, the amount was small—ranging for one year from a low of $12 to a high of $1,607.

The appeal of the work-first approach adopted by the TANF program is a result of a number of experimental evaluations of two types of work program approaches conducted in the 1980s and 1990s. These approaches are known as labor force attachment (LFA) and human capital development (HCD). The LFA programs emphasized low-cost, short-term services, in turn emphasizing job search skills and labor market experience. This strategy posits that the nonworking poor can best build work habits and skills, advance their positions in the labor market, and eventually escape welfare dependence by gaining work experience at any job regardless of how unstable or low paying it is. The HCD approach is based on the belief that, for the poor to escape welfare, they need first to improve their education and skills, that is, increase their human capital. These experimental evaluations concluded that the LFA programs produced more favorable results than the HCD approach and hence the welfare-to-work emphasis of the TANF program (Kim, 2010).

A review of welfare-to-work evaluations reveals that the basic assumption of these programs may be false. This assumption, particularly strong in the LFA approach, is that welfare recipients do not want to work and that to get them to work requires two things. The first is a stern motivator, such as a time limit on welfare, to scare them into seeking self-sufficiency. The second is the provision of a few resources such as brief education, training, and job counseling programs to help them capitalize on their motivation to become self-sufficient. But virtually every evaluation prior to the passage of the Personal Responsibility and Work Opportunity Reconciliation Act found no real problem in recipient willingness to work. The problems that have been found all are related to the fact that the programs seriously underestimate the barriers to employment for most long-term welfare recipients. On the one hand, the level of problems that recipients have with health, drug abuse, low ability level, low intelligence, lack of job experience, child care, transportation, and so forth, contribute to very low employability of many recipients. On the other hand, the number of jobs available that require few skills and a generally low ability level is inadequate in all but the best economic times. To mount a really successful welfare-to-work program would require two changes. First, many more services and resources would need to be put at the service of clients than is currently the case. Second, the government would need to intervene in the job market and create jobs of last resort to prevent former recipients from having to return to the welfare rolls during periods of economic downturn. Levitan and Gallo (1993) argue: "Society's work is never done. There is no shortage of useful work that could be performed to fulfill needs unmet by the market economy. The limited skills of AFDC recipients would dovetail well with child care, long-term care, and other services that already rely heavily on unskilled low-wage labor."

Is TANF Succeeding?

To answer the question of whether welfare reform is succeeding, we first must ask what is meant by success. Public policymakers, and much of the public in general, seem to define the success of welfare programs by the single criterion of reduction in the number of recipients, and this was indeed the original criterion for judging the program's effectiveness. However, as the TANF program has matured, and clearly demonstrated effectiveness as judged by this original measure, evaluation criteria have expanded. Evaluations now, in addition to caseload reductions, are looking at the degree to which TANF provides a safety net for people facing hard times, the success of TANF in lifting children out of deep poverty, and how successful the program is in increasing sustained labor force participation. The October 2012 Congressional Research Service Report for Congress on TANF concludes, "Policymakers also face questions about whether the sole focus of the assessment of TANF's success ought to be welfare-to-work. TANF has evolved into a program where cash assistance represents less than 30% of its funds. Policymakers thus face questions of whether consideration might be given to developing measures and assessment of how well TANF does in meeting other goals related to improving the circumstances of families with children" (Bopp & Falk, 2012).

TANF and the Welfare Rolls

In 1996, Congress passed the Personal Responsibility and Work Opportunity Reconciliation Act, the legislation that set up the TANF program, in spite of the negative results of evaluations of prior programs that mandated work for welfare recipients. The opinion of much of the country at that time was that the growth of the welfare rolls was out of control and some hard-nosed measures were needed in order to stop the alarming increase. Little noted by policymakers or the general public was that the rolls had actually been declining for two years, dropping from 5 million to 4.5 million between 1994 and 1996, the year the Personal Responsibility and Work Opportunity Reconciliation Act became law.

The general perception of TANF, based exclusively on the criterion of reduction in the number of recipients, is that the program has been an unqualified success. As can be seen from inspection of Figure 6.2, the number of cases has declined from 4,876,240 just before the beginning of the program in 1996 to 1,333,707 in 2015. This represents a decrease of nearly 73 percent, a truly remarkable number. This figure would indeed be cause for celebration if all the people leaving the welfare rolls had achieved self-sufficiency and a better life, but this is not the case. Studies of families that have left the TANF rolls show that, at any point in time, about 60 percent are employed and 40 percent are not (Kim & Joo, 2009). Several factors account for the number of people who have left TANF without being employed. One is that a number of applicants have been placed in diversion programs rather than being certified for TANF benefits. There are two types of diversion programs. In the first, the state agency administering TANF offers an applicant a one-time cash payment, in return for which the person gives up her eligibility for assistance for a specified period of time. The idea is that the one-time payment will solve the immediate problem, or problems, that are preventing the person from working and being self-sufficient (car repair, work wardrobe, back rent, and the like). If the person spends the money and still is not in a position to work, she is out of luck until the period for which she has agreed expires. In the second type of diversion program, a number of states require applicants to look for work for a specified period of time before their application

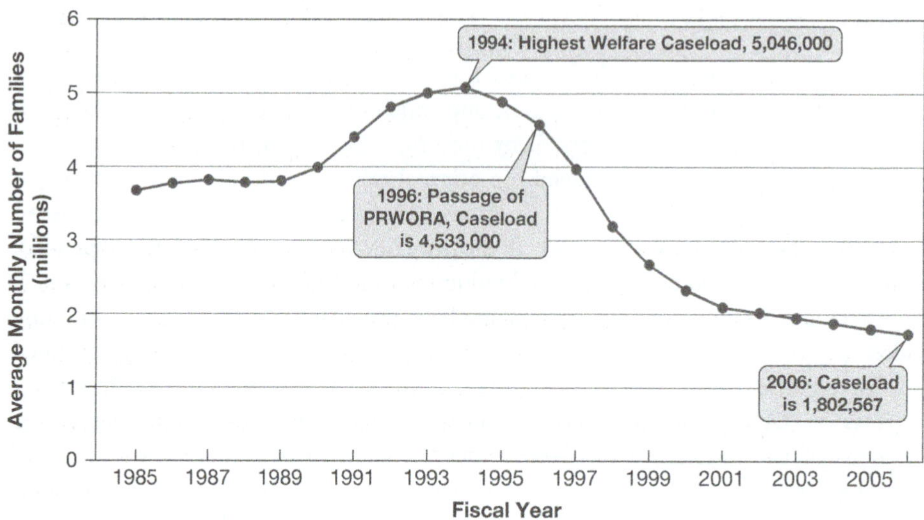

Figure 6.2

Total Welfare Cases, 1985–2006

Source: Adapted from Alan Weil and Kenneth Finegold, *Welfare Reform: The Next Act* (Washington DC: Urban Institute Press, 2002), p. 38. Original source note: Administration for Children and Families (1988–1997); Office of Planning, Research, and Evaluation (2000), and Administration for Children and Families (2000a, 2000b, 2001a, 2001b); 2002 data from TANF Sixth Annual Report to Congress; 2003–2006 data from TANF Seventh Annual Report to Congress, December 2006. Reprinted by permission.

for TANF will be accepted. Many do not find work but become so discouraged by the bureaucratic hassle that they never return to complete the application process.

The second factor that explains why so many people have left TANF without being employed is that they have been sanctioned (read "kicked out of the program") for failing to comply with program rules (Coven, 2002). A recipient can be sanctioned for something as minor as failing to respond to a letter directing her to attend a meeting. Inspecting various government reports, Lens (2002) concludes that sanctions have increased by 30 percent nationally since 1994 and that in any given month, approximately 5 percent of a state's total welfare caseload is under sanction. In addition, records indicate that sanctions are often applied incorrectly. In Wisconsin, for example, it was found that 44 percent of the penalties imposed on recipients in a five-month period were later found to have been erroneous (Lens, 2002).

So, if the welfare rolls have declined by 2,503,249 cases since 1996, and if 40 percent of these have left for reasons other than getting a job, this means that approximately 1,001,300 poor families have been abandoned to fend for themselves without any government assistance. We do not know exactly what is becoming of these families, but a reasonable guess is that they are turning to family and friends, people who probably have few extra resources themselves, or they are living on the streets or in shelters. Lens (2002) concludes, "In sum, disentitling otherwise eligible people by diverting them from the rolls or by terminating assistance cannot be equated with the individuals achieving self-sufficiency."

TANF and the Quality of Life of the Poor

The second criterion that must be assessed in judging whether TANF is successful is the effect of the program on the lives of those it is intended to help. This is the question asked by those concerned with an ethical evaluation of TANF, and the results give ample reason for concern. Obviously, for the 40 percent of people who have left the

TANF rolls but are not employed, the effect of TANF has been negative. But what of the 60 percent who have managed to enter the labor market? Are they, as frequently stated by conservative politicians, on the first step of the American ladder of success, or are they just squeaking by? Although we are sure that there are a number of former TANF recipients whose lives are steadily improving, the evidence coming in suggests that, for many, the program has not led to a better life.

Wages of former recipients The first problem for former TANF recipients is that most are making very low wages. Using data from the National Survey of American Families, Loprest (2001) found that the median wage (50th percentile) of former welfare recipients in 1999 was $7.15 per hour; those at the 25th percentile were earning $6.05, and those at the 75th were earning $9.00 per hour. A Mathematica study of a cohort of 2000 New Jersey TANF recipients found that, at the end of the 60-month period studied (2003), the average monthly earning of TANF leavers was $1,646, a little less than $20,000 annually (Wood, Moore, & Rangarajan, 2008). This is about 30 percent more than the 2003 federal poverty threshold for a family of three. In addition to low wages, few of the jobs held by former recipients provide good benefits. The Mathematica researchers found that many of the TANF leavers continued to rely on government supports such as food stamps (40 percent), housing subsidies (32 percent), and government health coverage (57 percent). Even these low wages result in incomes considerably in excess of welfare grants for those who are working full-time. However, a large number of former welfare recipients have jobs that are only part-time. As a result of these factors, about 52 percent of those who left the welfare rolls for jobs in 1999 still had incomes below the poverty level (Nightingale, 2002). A 2016 conference sponsored by the University of Wisconsin Institute for Research on Poverty reviewed the research on the results of TANF and found a "lack of significant positive effects of TANF on average family income . . . Single mother family poverty rates have declined under TANF, but there is evidence that deep poverty has increased" (Institute for Research on Poverty, 2017).

Does TANF increase labor force participation? The theory behind welfare reform is that, once people enter the labor market, they will begin to get raises and promotions. Thus, the fact that many former recipients are in very low-paying, scant-benefit jobs is not seen as a major problem. Backers of TANF believe that this is a problem every working person faces; we all start off in the mail room, so to speak. Does it appear that their current employment will be the first step on the road to success for most former TANF recipients? There is not yet good data on this question. Analysts have expressed concern, however, over the prospects for former recipients. This concern is based on analyses of the twenty-first-century job market that conclude that skills and education are essential for upward mobility. The work-first philosophy of TANF requires that a person choose work over education and training, regardless of the situation. Lens has reviewed the research literature on the relation of level of education to income and to the likelihood that a person will exit and stay off welfare. The data revealed a clear relationship between education and income level and a link between high school graduation and not returning to welfare. The link between earning a college degree and permanently exiting welfare was even stronger. Lens (2002) concludes that

> far from ensuring self-sufficiency, . . . an approach [such as work first] relegates welfare mothers to the low end of the labor market, a vulnerable place in good and bad economic times. It also ensures that the gap in wages based

> on educational level will persist and endure as poor women, forced to choose between losing their benefits or feeding their families, are trapped in low-paying jobs.

Revisiting this question in 2012, sociologist Sheila Katz reviewed the research on labor force participation during the first fifteen years of the TANF program and found evidence that it increased rapidly during the first five years of the TANF program, slowed in 2001, and completely stalled before the recession even began in 2007. She concludes, "Welfare reform's 'work first' approach did not create lasting upward economic mobility for low-income families." Katz (2012) argues that a resumption of the HCD approach, specifically providing higher education for welfare mothers ". . . will create opportunities for lasting upward mobility, even in times of recession."

Are adequate support services available? As anyone in the labor market knows, holding down a job can be expensive. Good-quality child care can cost well over $100 a week. In an urban area that lacks a good public transportation system, a reliable car is essential to steady employment. A car involves not only the expense of purchase, but also substantial operating expenses for gas, repairs, and insurance. Do the math. A person earning the federal minimum wage of $7.25 per hour cannot afford expenses such as these. The designers and administrators of the TANF program are aware of this problem, and in response states are now spending 65 percent of their TANF budget on non-assistance defined as "child care, transportation assistance and other supports for those who are employed, [as well as] non-recurrent short-term benefits, Individual Development Accounts, refundable earned income tax credits, work subsidies to employers, and services such as education and training, case management, job search, and counseling" (Administration for Children and Families, 2016). There is concern that even this may not be enough. There are time limits on child care subsidies for women who leave TANF. As this benefit runs out, a number of former recipients may be forced to return to the program because they cannot afford to purchase child care at full cost. The transportation problem is also serious, and solutions appear to be far off. After an analysis of the transportation problem for former TANF recipients, Lens (2002) concludes, "none of [current transportation reform] attempts really address the root of the problem, and transportation problems persist. To get welfare recipients to work, no less than a radical restructuring of public transportation systems may ultimately be needed." A former recipient who has been placed in a job far from her home, without reliable transportation resources or involving a bus trip requiring three transfers and two hours, is soon going to be back on the welfare rolls.

Welfare reform and the well-being of children Because TANF requires parents to work rather than stay home with their children, possible adverse effects of the program on children have been a major concern. To address this concern, the Administration on Children and Families contracted with Abt Associates, Child Trends, Manpower Demonstration Research Corporation, and Mathematica Policy Research to assess the impact of welfare reform on the lives of children. The research was called the Project on State-Level Child Outcomes, and data was collected in Connecticut, Florida, Indiana, Iowa, and Minnesota. The primary data source for each state study was a survey that focused mainly on children who were between the ages of five and twelve at the time of the survey. The children were surveyed, and then a follow-up survey was conducted at intervals varying from 2.5 to 6.5 years, depending on the state. The main findings from the five states were summarized in the *TANF Seventh Annual Report to Congress* as follows:

- There is little evidence that these programs resulted in widespread harm or benefit to young school-age children.
- In two states, positive impacts on children's functioning appear to be related to increases in family income. In a third state, increased family income had a neutral effect.
- In two states, the programs had the most favorable impacts on children in the most disadvantaged families, such as those with a longer history of welfare receipt or less work experience. In the three other states, there was little difference in the pattern of impacts on young school-age children by the level of family disadvantage.
- The programs increased children's participation in child care.
- Although the studies mainly focused on young children, data on a limited number of measures on outcomes for adolescents were collected. This data indicated that the programs sometimes had negative effects on adolescents' school performance.

Basically, the studies did not find strong evidence that TANF (*TANF Seventh Annual Report to Congress*, 2006) is having strong effects on children's lives in either a positive or a negative direction.

Recently, concern about TANF has focused on its failure to lift children out of deep poverty. Deep poverty is defined as income less than 50 percent of the official poverty line. A recent analysis of TANF by the Center on Budget and Policy Priorities found that TANF lifted 21 percent of children who otherwise would have been in deep poverty, as compared to the AFDC program in 1995 (its last year of operation), when AFDC lifted 62 percent of children who otherwise would have been in deep poverty. The report concludes, "TANF benefits are too low to bring many families out of poverty. Unfortunately, TANF has proven far less effective at lifting families out of deep poverty—that is, incomes below half the poverty line—than AFDC, mostly because fewer families receive TANF benefits than received AFDC benefits (The erosion in the value of TANF benefits has also contributed)" (Center on Budget and Policy Priorities, 2012).

Problems facing the TANF program There is evidence that the early, spectacular, reductions in the welfare rolls have now slowed and perhaps ended. There are a couple of reasons why the caseload decline is coming to an end.

TANF caseloads are not reaching the "inner core of the onion" Earlier in the chapter, we discussed Corbett's onion metaphor that illustrated different types of poverty. Burt (2002) has presented a similar idea specifically related to problems of TANF recipients. She observes that recipients can be classified into three different groups based on their barriers to self-sufficiency. The first group, similar to Corbett's outer layer of the onion, comprises recipients with barriers that resources can overcome quickly. These are people who in most cases need simple resources such as child care, transportation, or job search assistance. Removing these barriers and getting the recipient to work is a simple matter of providing services or resources, and the services and resources needed are obvious. The second group, similar to Corbett's middle layer and core, are recipients with barriers that are treatable, controllable, or reversible with adequate and appropriate resources.

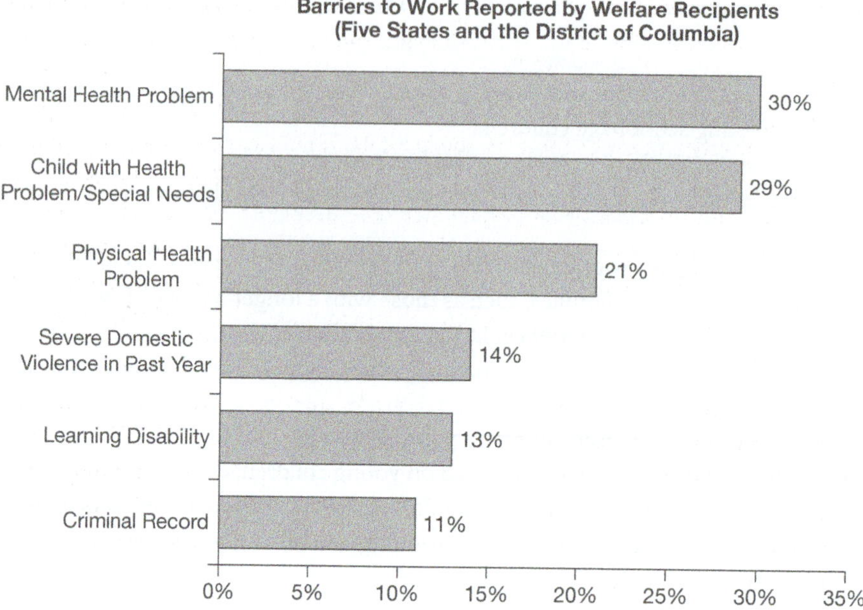

Figure 6.3

Barriers to Work Reported by Welfare Recipients (Five States and the District of Columbia)

Source: Congressional Research Service (CRS) based on data in Hauan, Susan and Sarah Douglas. Potential Employment Liabilities Among TANF Recipients: A Synthesis of Data from Six State TANF Caseload Studies. U.S. Department of Health and Human Services (HHS), Office of the Assistant Secretary for Planning and Evaluation. October 2004.

The barriers for this group include physical and mental illnesses or disabilities, addictions, illiteracy, lack of basic work-related skills, inability to speak or understand English, lack of work experience, or recent release from a correctional institution. To get this group to work, the TANF agency must provide support during a period of treatment that may last for a number of months and then must be prepared to provide intensive and lengthy postemployment support. The final group, analogous to Corbett's inner core, faces permanent conditions. These are people with permanent and severe physical disabilities, chronic mental illness, or learning or developmental disabilities (Burt, 2002). A 2004 study by Hauan and Douglas (2004) found that almost one-third of TANF recipients reported at least one serious barrier to employment (see Figure 6.3).

Data on recipients who have left TANF and on those who have not reveal that the majority of the leavers are those with less serious barriers to self-sufficiency. Data from the National Survey of American Families have been used by Zedlewski and Alderson (2001) to look at six potential barriers to work faced by welfare recipients: (1) poor physical or mental health, (2) less than high school education, (3) having a child under the age of one, (4) having a child on Supplemental Security Income (SSI), (5) low proficiency in English, and (6) lack of work experience. They found that 56 percent of recipients with no barriers were working, but only 20 percent of those with two or more barriers were working. Some of these recipients with serious barriers may be eligible for Supplemental Security Income on the basis of their disabilities, but many are not because of the extremely restrictive eligibility requirements that exclude all but the most seriously disabled. Increasing the work participation rates is going to become more and more difficult for states in the coming years as a greater percentage of the pool of recipients consists of those with a serious barrier or several barriers.

Welfare reform has been in a virtuous cycle This is a term coined by Weil and Finegold (2012) to describe the first eight years following the passage of PRWORA in 1996. The first decade following the passage of PRWORA were years ideal for the implementation of work-oriented welfare policies because they were characterized by an exceptionally strong economy, healthy state budgets, the federal requirement that states maintain their AFDC spending levels, and the block grant structure that has required the federal contribution to the states to stay constant even when the number of recipients has been falling. These last two factors have resulted in state social service departments having extensive resources to provide support services for recipients seeking employment and for those who have recently left the welfare rolls to help them make the transition to work. Weil and Finegold (2002) say:

> Yet this virtuous cycle could just as easily become vicious. Low unemployment and sustained economic growth have contributed to the recent decline in welfare caseloads. A recession will reverse these trends while straining state budgets. . . . The new structure of welfare may make the highs and lows of policy more extreme than they were in the past. The United States has been living through the highs; it has yet to experience the lows.

The U.S. economy has slowed beginning with the 2007 recession, and indications are that it may be a long time before it completely recovers. It appears that the virtuous cycle is over, and the TANF rolls are reflecting the changed economy.

Check Your Understanding 6.4
Check your understanding of Evaluation by taking this brief quiz.

CONCLUSION

We have presented a large amount of data in a fairly brief space regarding the public welfare system in the United States. Much of this information may seem contradictory and confusing. However, based on the data presented, we think it is possible to come to several conclusions. These are outlined in the following sections.

American Values Related to Welfare Have Permanently Changed

When Aid to Families with Dependent Children, the first national welfare program in the United States, was passed in 1935, the value on which it was based was clear. What's more, there was a national consensus regarding this value. This value was that women with children, especially small children, should be able to stay at home with them. Over the next sixty years, this value slowly and steadily eroded. This change was due to several factors, the first being a general change in the role of women in society, resulting in many women working rather than caring for children full-time. The second is the growth of the AFDC program until its cost became a great concern for many people, who began questioning whether we could afford to have poor women stay at home rearing children. The third factor is that the composition of the AFDC recipient population changed. When the program was enacted, it was thought that the recipients would be widowed white women. By the 1960s, the typical recipient was an unmarried minority-group mother. Racist though it may be, this factor resulted in a major loss of support for the idea that welfare mothers should be able to stay at home rather than work.

The TANF program that replaced AFDC is based on a different core value. This value is that work and self-support is a person's primary obligation to society, hence the term *personal responsibility* in the legislation that created TANF. The key result of this value change is that the research reviewed above showing that employed former recipients have undesirable jobs, receive low pay, have few benefits, and often remain below the poverty line is pretty much beside the point. There is a near national consensus that it is *always* better for a person to be working than to be supported by public welfare.

The conclusion we draw from this is that if we as social workers want to improve the lives of the poor, we will be far more effective if we seek to improve work and supporting services than if we agitate to loosen the work requirements for recipients.

Welfare Is Not the Problem; Poverty Is the Problem

It is an obvious but too often ignored truism that welfare is a response to poverty. The welfare reform debates in recent years have almost ignored the evidence that poverty in our country is increasing. The distribution of income has become rapidly more unequal in recent decades. Summarizing a report by the "painstakingly nonpartisan, ultra-respectable Congressional Budget Office," economist Paul Krugman (2012) reports on the rise in inequality between 1979 and 2007. The report "found that Americans in the 80th to 99th percentiles . . . had seen an income rise of 65 percent over that period . . . families near the middle did only about half that well, and the bottom 20 percent saw only an 18 percent gain. But the top 1 percent saw its income rise 277.5 percent and . . . the top 0.1 percent saw even bigger gains . . . According to the CBO [Congressional Budget Office], the share of after-tax income going to the top 1 percent rose from 7.7 percent to 17.1 percent of total income; that is, other things being equal, a roughly 10 percent reduction in the amount of income left over for everyone else" (Krugman, 2012). Both the number and the percentage of people below the poverty line decreased at a steady rate between 1959 (when we first started counting) and 1978. This population then increased, rising from 24.5 million people, 11.4 percent of the population in 1978, to 36.9 million people, 14.5 percent of the population in 1992. In 1994, the poverty population began to decline until 2001, when the poverty rate was 11.7 percent, or 32.9 million people. As the economy has begun to slow, the poverty rate is again increasing, rising to 12.7 percent, or 37 million people, in 2004, and to 15.1 percent, or 46.3 million people in 2011 (Walt, Proctor, & Smith, 2012). The reasons for these fluctuations are numerous, complex, and not fully understood. We will not go into them here. Suffice it to say that solving the welfare problem is not the answer to solving the problem of poverty, as policymakers often imply. Rather, solving—or at least dealing with—the poverty problem is the answer to solving the welfare problem. It is apparent, however, that TANF is directed much more at the welfare problem than at the poverty problem.

Public Assistance Is a Social Condition, Not a Social Problem

In the classic book *The Unheavenly City,* Edward Banfield (1970) made a useful distinction between urban problems and urban conditions. He defined an urban problem as something that could be fixed, such as potholes and broken water mains. Urban conditions are things that are permanent, or very nearly so, and simply must be managed as well as possible. Banfield (1970) identified poverty as an urban condition.

We think Banfield's observation is a useful conclusion to the discussion of welfare reform. Many things about the welfare system can be improved. However, we need to recognize that in a large, rapidly changing, urban, postindustrial society, we will always need a large welfare system. In other words, welfare is simply a condition with which we should make peace. Leo Perlis (1962), a union organizer, hit the nail on the head when responding to an earlier welfare reform initiative:

> The current somewhat apologetic emphasis on rehabilitation [of welfare recipients] seems almost obscene—as if rehabilitation would not cost more (at first at least), as if rehabilitation is always possible (in the face of more than 4,000,000 jobless among other things), as if rehabilitation is a substitute for relief for everybody and at all times. I think we all need to make a forthright declaration that direct public assistance in our competitive society is unavoidable, necessary, and even socially useful.

Recall what you learned from this chapter by completing the Chapter Review.

7

Aging: Social Security as an Entitlement

LEARNING OUTCOMES

- Compare the advantages of maintaining Social Security as a "universal" program versus making it based on need.
- Discuss the current ability of both public and private pensions to provide security to workers in old age.
- Assess the extent to which the survival of Social Security is an economic problem or a political problem.
- Justify prolonging the life of someone who has a terminal illness and wishes to die.
- Contrast the advantages of privatizing Social Security with the advantages of keeping it as a public program.

CHAPTER OUTLINE

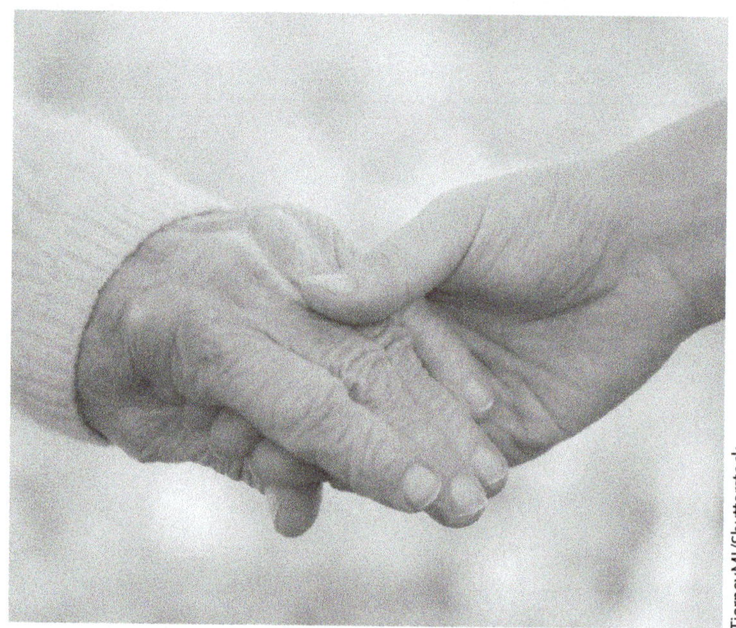

TierneyMJ/Shutterstock

Maggie, a thirty-four-year-old working on her income tax return, comments to her mother, "You know, a lot of money from my paycheck goes for Social Security—but I figure Social Security probably won't be around when I'm older." Her mother, who teaches social work and social policy, is horrified. How could her daughter be so convinced by the scare tactics of people who want to dismantle the Social Security system?

> Agnes and Jesse Moorhead have a small apartment and two cats. Mr. Moorhead retired from his custodial job ten years ago. The couple lives modestly, but they go out to dinner and a movie with friends every few weeks and take a short vacation at a nearby lake each summer. Mr. Moorhead has only a small pension, so they rely chiefly on Social Security for their income. "It's not a huge amount," Mrs. Moorhead says, "but it's enough to keep us going. And it certainly gives me peace of mind to know that check will come every month."

Most Americans today, with little or no memory of the Great Depression, cannot recall the extraordinary social and economic conditions that led to the creation of Social Security. Although we are far wealthier a society than we were then, we still face the inequities and abrupt dislocations that led to the creation of Social Security. Will this protective system—which some have called the bedrock of the U.S. welfare state—still be there when those now in their early thirties begin to retire? If it does exist in the 2060s, will it be in the same form? Will people be able to choose between participating in Social Security and investing their own money toward retirement? Will methods of financing benefits be different, and will they be available only to certain groups of people, such as the needy? Will we still think of it as the major entitlement program in our country's social welfare system? Some talk about the need to fix Social Security before the retiring baby boomers "bust the federal budget." Others, based on their belief in the basic strength of the U.S. economy, are confident that universal social programs such as Social Security can be shored up by federal surpluses and will continue to be entitlements that we can depend on (Sloan, 2012).

Thoughts for Social Work Practice

If clients are upset about the predictions of the demise of Social Security, how do you help them sort through the various conflicting claims? Why do you think these predictions keep resurfacing?

Thoughts for Social Work Practice

Couples often worry about money. It's a common cause of divorce. Would a public or a private retirement plan provide more reassurance for people when they reach retirement age?

The term *entitlement* has been talked about a good deal in the past few years. It has been applied not only to the old-age insurance part of the Social Security Act but also to the many other programs making up the U.S. safety net. In the late 1990s, ideological conflicts between a Democratic president and Republican majorities in Congress led to close scrutiny of our social welfare system and its costs and benefits and to a national debate over "who's entitled" and to what. Welfare clients have not fared well in this debate; their "entitlement" to ongoing public aid was dashed by the federal welfare reform legislation of 1996.

Some of the participants in the discussion of entitlements have taken the issue to extremes. Robert J. Samuelson (1996), for example, calls our belief in a network of entitlements a fantasy. In his book *The Good Life and Its Discontents: The American Dream in the Age of Entitlement*, Samuelson pictures postwar America as a time when we expected all social problems to be solved; poverty, racism, and crime to recede; and a "compassionate government" to protect the poor, the old, and the unfortunate. "We not only expected these things," Samuelson notes, "after a while, we thought we were entitled to them" (Samuelson, 1996; King & Greenberg, 2011). Thus, Samuelson recasts the notion of a mutual obligation in our society to achieve security for all into the image of a childish "wish list" in which all of us want gifts and candy that we don't truly "deserve."

Since the arrival of the Tea Party in 2008 we have added a new layer of complexity to the debate, with many of the loudest voices for smaller government also chanting: "Hands off our Social Security." A *Wall Street Journal*/NBC News poll in March 2011 found that "tea party supporters, by a nearly 2-to-1 margin, declared significant cuts to Social Security 'unacceptable.'" The Tea Party's successor, the House Freedom Caucus, has taken a radically different position. They would cut benefits for all but the poorest recipients, raise the retirement age to 69, reduce cost-of-living adjustments (COLAs), and cut taxes for the highest earners. President Donald Trump campaigned on preserving Social Security and Medicare, and has kept that promise in his first budget proposal. But a fight is looming (Editorial, 2016; Peterson & Timiraos, 2016; DeSilver, 2015). Defenders of entitlements view them as the expression of society's obligation to the poor, the elderly, and the unemployed. Some argue that all citizens have a right to economic security, whereas others stress that certain entitlements, such as Social Security, are in fact earned benefits. Discussions of Social Security thus become inextricably tied up in contemporary debates about the purpose and desirability of entitlements.

THE PROBLEM THAT SOCIAL SECURITY WAS DEVELOPED TO SOLVE

In any society in which the vast majority of people depend on wages for their income, old age will present an economic problem. Once people have stopped working, they must find another source of revenue to pay the rent or mortgage, the grocery bill, and the doctor's bill. Wealthier members of society will have built up savings and acquired other assets for this occasion. They may have inherited money and property from their parents. Some workers will receive good pensions from the companies where they worked. But many will enter retirement and old age with only small savings and pension funds and perhaps a paid-off mortgage—or no assets at all.

Today, almost all people age sixty-five and over have another source of income: their monthly Social Security benefits. Before the Social Security Act was passed in 1935, the only public old-age pensions that existed were limited to certain groups of people—veterans, federal civil service employees, and employees of some state and local governments. Some workers received help through the private pension program of their unions or places of employment. Most elderly people depended on savings; help from their families; assistance from public and private charity (which was generally quite limited); and, as a last resort, the local poorhouse. Not surprisingly, a large proportion of the elderly worked as long as possible to forestall the poverty of old age. In 1930, almost 60 percent of men over sixty-five were still employed (Achenbaum, 1986; Orloff, 1993).

The Great Depression devastated most of these sources of income. Bank closures wiped out lifetime savings, unemployed children could not help elderly parents, older people lost their jobs at even higher rates than younger workers, failing companies closed down their pension plans, and the coffers of both private charities and local public assistance programs quickly dried up. Describing the crisis, economist (and later Senator) Paul Douglas declared that the Depression "increasingly convinced the majority of the American people that individuals could not themselves provide adequately for their old age and that some sort of greater security should be provided by society" (Achenbaum, 1986, p. 16).

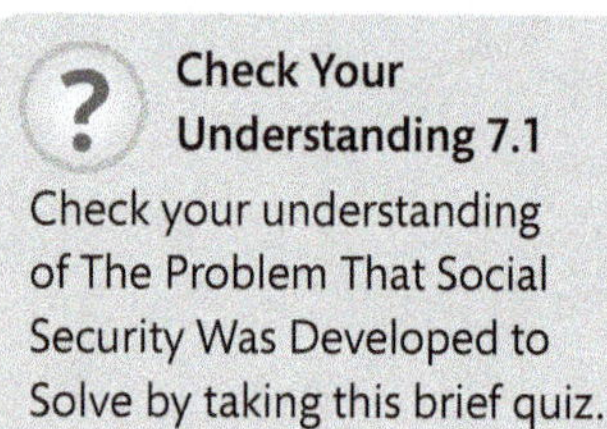

?
Check Your Understanding 7.1
Check your understanding of The Problem That Social Security Was Developed to Solve by taking this brief quiz.

THE SOCIAL SECURITY ACT OF 1935

The economic crisis of the Great Depression brought about a recognition of fundamental economic insecurities in U.S. society. In response, President Franklin D. Roosevelt and his advisors crafted and won passage of the 1935 Social Security Act. This legislation, perhaps more than any other major social policy, has been subject to continued change and expansion.

Social Security is a social insurance program. An insurance program, whether public or private, is a way for people to protect themselves and their families against the risk of an adverse event like an automobile accident, a serious illness, or death. It invites people to pay a small amount of money, called a "premium," on a regular basis into a fund out of which they will receive a payment or "benefit" should an adverse event occur. Some people may never have an accident or illness and never need benefits. Others may get benefits that are far greater than the premiums they paid. Overall the system should balance out, but is most likely to do so if the pool of participants is large and diverse. An automobile accident company that insures only very bad drivers will soon go bankrupt. Similarly, a health insurance program cannot survive if it has too many old and sick members and not enough of the young and healthy. We will see how this works in the area of health insurance in Chapter 9.

A public insurance program just has to maintain that balance. A private program has to maintain the balance plus make a profit for investors in the company. An important point to remember is that those who buy private insurance don't expect to get their premiums back if they don't have an accident or illness. This is not understood by many Social Security participants, who often think of their contribution as "their" money. In fact, their contributions are going to support people retiring now; when they retire, they will be supported by other people. A lot of those people will be immigrants, as we'll see in Chapter 11.

The Social Security Act of 1935 is a broad piece of legislation that includes two social insurance programs and three "welfare," or public assistance, programs, along with several smaller programs, such as vocational rehabilitation and child welfare services. Although social insurance benefits were to be made available to people of all income levels, public assistance payments would be made only to those determined by states to be financially needy. The two programs of direct relevance to the elderly are described in Titles I, II, and VIII. Under Title I, "Grants to States of Old-Age Assistance" (OAA), the federal government would reimburse states for 50 percent of the amount they spent on public (cash) assistance to poor people over the age of sixty-five. Each state was required to have a statewide plan for old-age assistance, and its system of administering the grants would have to be approved by the federal government.

Title II, "Federal Old-Age Benefits," contains what most consider is the program synonymous with the term *social security*—a federal system of old-age insurance. The program created a federal trust fund, the Old-Age Reserve Account, to which funds would be appropriated each year to provide monthly payments to retired people sixty-five and over. Excluded from the program were farm laborers and domestic servants (many of whom were African American), U.S. government employees, state and local government employees, and workers in nonprofit agencies. Old-Age Benefit payments would begin in 1942. For workers whose total wages between the start of the program and the time they reached sixty-five were $3,000 or less, monthly benefits would amount to one-half of 1 percent of these wages. This would amount to the munificent sum of $15 a month. As a mild measure of income redistribution, workers making higher salaries would receive a much lower percentage of their salary for all wages in excess of $3,000. No retired worker could receive more than $85 a month (Burns, 1936).

Title VIII detailed the source of funding for the old-age insurance program: federal taxes to be paid by both employers and employees. For the first few years of the program, workers and employers would each pay the federal government 1 percent of the first $3,000 of the worker's annual wage. The percentage paid would rise every three years thereafter, to a final level of 3 percent in 1949. Then, as now, workers with lower wages paid proportionately more of their income into Social Security than did people with higher wages (Burns, 1936, pp. 246–247; Samuelson, 2011).

The other social insurance program of the Social Security Act is a joint federal–state unemployment compensation system detailed in Titles III and IX. Under these titles, the federal government was authorized to appropriate funds to help states administer benefits to unemployed workers. States would collect a payroll tax from employers of eight or more individuals and would give these revenues to the federal government. The federal government would keep the revenues in a central fund for each state; that fund would be used to pay unemployment benefits to workers. Employers would be given federal tax credits to offset most of their payroll taxes. Each state would enact its own unemployment insurance law, which would determine levels and duration of benefits. These laws would have to be approved by the federal government, but the criteria for approval related to administrative matters rather than to the amount or length of payments.

The Social Security Act also brought into existence joint federal–state programs of public assistance for dependent children and the blind. Title IV, "Grants to States of Aid to Dependent Children" (ADC), established a system in which the federal government covered one-third of a state's expenditures for the support of needy children in families with one caretaker (usually a widowed or divorced mother). As in unemployment compensation, state plans were to be approved by the federal government, but approval was again limited to administrative procedures and did not include minimum levels of benefits. A similar program for public assistance payments to needy blind persons was included in Title X, with funds provided half by the federal government and half by the state. In both the ADC and Aid to the Blind programs, the percentage paid by the federal government was calculated on benefits up to a certain amount; if states paid more than that amount to beneficiaries, they would have to cover the excess.

This is the part of the act that we generally think of as the "welfare system" and is not usually thought of as an entitlement. Robert Samuelson, who we saw earlier arguing against the whole idea of entitlements, later turned the argument around by arguing that Social Security, generally seen as an entitlement, was actually a welfare program. Perhaps we can at least agree that they are all government programs to protect citizens against poverty.

? Check Your Understanding 7.2
Check your understanding of The Social Security Act of 1935 by taking this brief quiz.

Finally, the act established a new federal entity, the Social Security Board, to administer the old-age insurance system and the federal portions of the other programs. The board was also responsible for approval of state programs for unemployment compensation, old-age assistance, and aid to children.

HISTORICAL DEVELOPMENT OF SOCIAL SECURITY PROGRAMS IN THE UNITED STATES

Although the 1935 Social Security Act may have seemed a bold policy innovation on the part of the Roosevelt administration, each program established by the act drew on precedents dating back at least to the early 1900s. A complex set of social, political, and economic factors influenced the development of the social insurance and public assistance provisions elaborated in 1935. A thorough history of this development, and of the subsequent implementation and amendments of the act, would run to hundreds of pages. We present a brief analysis here, concentrating primarily on programs related to the elderly.

Precedents of the Social Security Act

The creation of federal old-age insurance is often viewed as a watershed in U.S. social welfare history. Historian Mark Leff (1987) describes the program as "both the pearl and the pillar of the American welfare state, a political marvel that has beaten the ideological odds and has allowed Americans to receive government checks without stigma." In developing this "political marvel," the architects of the Social Security Act built on a patchwork of existing programs. The idea of old-age pension plans was not new in the 1930s. The public sector had taken the lead in establishing such programs. The federal government established public pensions for U.S. veterans of the Civil War. Although at first these applied only to financially needy and disabled veterans, by 1912 old age alone could qualify former soldiers to receive benefits. Veterans' pensions had become a broad and generous system of social provision, including payments to many widows and dependents. In addition, at the turn of the century most major U.S. cities provided pensions for firefighters and police officers. The majority of states had retirement plans for schoolteachers by 1916, and in the early 1930s a number of states established mandatory pension laws for their residents. In 1920, a federal Civil Service Retirement System was established (Achenbaum, 1986; Orloff, 1993; Skocpol, 1995).

Businesses and corporations had also developed pension plans as one part of a private social welfare system that emerged in the United States in the 1880s. Based both on moral arguments and the desire for a more efficient and docile workforce, employers created a variety of social welfare amenities, including retirement programs. At the same time, some trade unions established pension plans. However, union and corporate programs together covered only about 14 percent of U.S. workers in 1932 (Berkowitz & McQuaid, 1992; Orloff, 1993).

Nor was the idea of social insurance new in the 1930s. Beginning in the Progressive era, reformers such as Isaac Rubinow, Abraham Epstein, and Jane Addams promoted programs based on those developed in Germany and England, in which the government used tax money to protect people against the inevitable hazards of an industrial state: industrial accidents, disability, ill health, and unemployment. To the reformers, social insurance represented a source of public funds that could spread the cost of dealing with such risks across a large number of people. It also allowed for some redistribution of income from the wealthy to the less well-off. To further these goals, Rubinow helped form the American Association for Labor Legislation. The association provided research and model bills to states experimenting with various programs to aid unemployed and retired workers (Berkowitz & McQuaid, 1992; Stoesz, 1996).

Despite such activity, the idea of a national public system of old-age insurance was slow to catch on. Americans held fast to ingrained beliefs in self-help and private responses to need. Even the developing labor movement did not initially back public old-age benefits, preferring to trust the union's ability to improve wages and provide security.

Creation of the Social Security Act

Forces let loose during the Depression changed all this. The 1929 stock market crash led to unprecedented levels of unemployment and was particularly devastating for the elderly. A relatively small and scattered array of private, state, and local social welfare programs quickly proved inadequate to deal with rising levels of need. Traditional beliefs in independence and self-reliance were badly shaken.

When Roosevelt took office in 1933, he faced the challenge of coping with the country's deepening crisis. Although at first pursuing temporary relief measures such as those provided by the Federal Emergency Relief Administration (FERA), the president was loath to simply replace the traditional poor law system with federal funds. His belief that more permanent relief should stress jobs over handouts led to the creation of vast public works programs; his commitment to "rebuilding many of the structures of our economic life and reorganizing it in order to prevent a recurrence of collapse" led to a program of social insurance (Berkowitz, 1991).

Political forces helped shape this move toward social insurance, particularly where it pertained to the problems of old age. The desperation of the elderly was portrayed in numerous letters to the White House. One citizen noted,

> I am about 75 or 76 years old and Have Labored Hard all My Days until depression Came on and I Had No Job in three years. . . . Please Sir do what you Can for me I am to old to be turned out of doors. (Achenbaum, 1986)

Older people like these formed a major support for increasingly popular flat-rate pension plans, such as that proposed by Dr. Francis Townsend, a retired California physician. Starting in his home state, Townsend built a national movement for a program that promised to end the Depression by giving everyone over age sixty a pension of $200 a month. Financed through federal taxation, the plan would bolster the economy by requiring recipients to spend the entire $200 within thirty days. By 1934, Townsend claimed 5 million supporters. Other utopian schemes included Louisiana Senator Huey Long's proposal to give $30 a month to every poor person over age sixty and to finance this "Share Our Wealth" program through income, inheritance, and other taxes. Long, who had originally supported Roosevelt, was beginning to emerge as a potential political rival. In addition, the Lundeen bill, one supported by the Communist party and a number of social workers, other professionals, and unemployed workers, was introduced into Congress in 1935 and received wide support. The Lundeen bill would have guaranteed to all persons willing to work but unable to find a job an income equal to the average wages in their district and would have provided a social insurance scheme for the elderly. Calls for action, especially to deal with unemployment, came also from social work organizations and increasingly powerful unions representing unskilled workers (Achenbaum, 1986; Altmeyer, 1968; Burns, 1936; Cates, 1983).

Clearly, Roosevelt needed to maintain his political support and to keep control of the reform agenda. In June 1934, he responded to political pressures and to the country's continued economic distress by announcing to Congress his intent to find a sound means for providing "security against several of the great disturbing factors in life—especially those which relate to unemployment and old age." He proceeded to create the Committee on Economic Security (CES) to make recommendations for a broad program of legislation to ensure that security (Achenbaum, 1986).

The committee was chaired by Secretary of Labor Frances Perkins. She was the first woman to hold a cabinet position. She had worked as a social worker at Hull House and had a long, illustrious career as a policymaker and administrator. The Department of Labor Building is named for her. The committee included other cabinet members and FERA administrator Harry Hopkins. Hopkins was also a social worker. Two University of Wisconsin labor economists played important roles in the legislative drafting process. One, Edwin E. Witte, served as executive director of the CES, while the other, Arthur J. Altmeyer, chaired an accompanying technical board. Experts (government officials and academics) on the technical board and on the CES staff did much of the actual work in formulating the legislation and presenting major policy issues to CES members for their review (Downey, 2009; Perkins, 1946; Altmeyer, 1968).

Thus, a large group of people with different skills and perspectives came together to develop a social insurance program. In their decision making, CES members brought to bear not only their own points of view, but also their sense of the general thinking of the president. In addition, they were sensitive to issues of constitutionality, as previous Supreme Court decisions had cast doubt on how far the federal government would be allowed to go in enacting social legislation. Administrative feasibility, public and congressional reactions, and technical problems in financing and implementation were further factors to be considered. The committee's expert advisors, while tuned in to technical issues, were less concerned about constitutionality and congressional acceptance. Perkins referred to working with them as similar to "driving a team of high-strung unbroken horses." In a good example of the messy world of policymaking, academics, politicians, and top officials in the Roosevelt administration all plunged together into uncharted waters to develop a politically, economically, and administratively feasible national economic security program (Altmeyer, 1968; Berkowitz, 1991; Perkins, 1963).

To complicate matters, as historian Andrew Achenbaum has noted, there was not a clear consensus about the major thrust of an economic security plan. Although some New Deal scholars have portrayed the development and implementation of the Social Security Act as following a set ideology, it seems more accurate to view the process as reflecting a fundamental ambivalence and lack of clarity about goals. Achenbaum describes two potentially conflicting social policy objectives related to Social Security: social adequacy and equity. *Adequacy* referred to assisting people based on their actual need, *equity* to giving assistance based on what people had put into the system. The former was sometimes called welfare and included a redistribution of income; the latter emphasized principles of self-reliance and fairness: Recipients would receive benefits based on what they had contributed (Achenbaum, 1983; Coll, 1988). Is this then an entitlement?

Roosevelt himself seemed to have had both approaches in mind when delivering his economic security message to Congress. The president spoke of "the security of home, and the security of livelihood" as constituting "a *right* which belongs to every individual and every family *willing to work* [italics added]" (Achenbaum, 1983, p. 19). This ambivalence between a program that based benefits on citizens' rights and one that rewarded people for contributions based on work was ingrained in the U.S. Social Security system from the beginning (Achenbaum, 1983).

The work of the CES and its staff led to a broad program that combined the two approaches. The bill that emerged contained old-age insurance and unemployment compensation tied to wage contributions (the equity approach) as well as more traditional public assistance measures (the social adequacy approach). The social adequacy/income redistribution goal even played some part in the old-age insurance program because low-income workers got a larger percentage of their wages back in benefits than did higher-income workers.

The bill also drew on existing U.S. values and systems. Wage-based old-age insurance and unemployment compensation programs supported the work ethic. A neighborly sense of compassion for deprived children helped justify the ADC proposal, which at the time was considered a rather minor part of the Social Security Act. The same sense of compassion undergirded extra assistance for the poor elderly; in addition, this aid was seen as a justifiable benefit for folks who "deserved help" in their later years. Most parts of the new system fit the U.S. brand of federalism, with its stress on states' rights. Whereas old-age insurance broke new ground as a large, nationally administered program, unemployment compensation was shaped by the individual plans of each state, and the federal government was given relatively minimal control over the assistance programs for children and the elderly. For example, states had complete say in determining the level of benefits in the ADC program, leading to a wide range in benefits that still exists in public welfare today.

Two important issues raised during the bill's development concerned the scope of coverage and financing. For a number of reasons, two groups were excluded from participation in the old-age insurance plan: domestic servants and farm workers. CES staff visualized the plan as particularly important for industrial workers who had relatively low salaries. Because these workers tended to have a stable relationship with a single employer, it would be easy to administer a payroll tax on them and their employers. Farm workers and servants might receive in-kind benefits in addition to their wages, such as room and board, and because they were seen as having many employers, collection of a payroll tax might be difficult. An argument could thus be made to exclude these groups, at least for the time being. Yet the fact that many of these workers were African American farm laborers and female domestic servants adds another, more sinister dimension to their exclusion—the influence of Southern legislators anxious to control their workforce and the apathy of many of the policymakers regarding the plight of African Americans in the United States. As a result, half of the African American workforce was excluded from benefits (Berkowitz, 1991; Gordon, 1994; Quadagno, 1988).

Financing the old-age insurance portion of the Social Security Act through payroll deductions drew fire from progressives and radicals in the 1930s and, as we will see later, that criticism still surfaces today, although from other types of groups and for other reasons. Detractors asserted that tying benefits to income levels maintained a system of economic inequality and failed to produce the resources needed to give a meaningful amount of aid to all the elderly. The usual interpretation for this financing decision by the bill's creators is that Roosevelt and his policymakers needed to cast social insurance as an earned benefit rather than a handout in order to get it passed. Although this was an important factor, other considerations played a part as well. The social insurance systems of European countries were financed out of general tax funds. Roosevelt and the other architects of old-age insurance rejected this approach in part because federal tax revenues at the time were quite low—less than 5 percent of the population paid federal income taxes in the 1930s. In addition, both the president and the expert staffers of the CES were leery of future attempts by Congress to change appropriation levels for social insurance.

Although we tend to think of old-age insurance as the linchpin of the Social Security Act, the program actually had little support in Congress and was almost dropped when the bill went through committee. To safeguard the program from politicians in the future, it seemed necessary to create a separate, more easily protected trust fund. Thus, for ideological, political, and economic reasons, the opportunity to use general taxes to create substantial income redistribution and a more reasonable level of aid to the elderly was lost (Altmeyer, 1968; Berkowitz, 1991).

The bill drew both praise and criticism as it went through Congress. Those supporting the plan included national women's organizations, the American Association of Social Workers, organized labor, liberal politicians, and even the U.S. Chamber of Commerce. However, many businesspeople and Republican politicians opposed it, focusing most of their disapproval on the provisions for old-age insurance. Detractors called this "the worst title in the bill . . . a burdensome tax on industry" that would establish "a bureaucracy in the field of insurance in competition with private business." Fears of the oppressive hand of "big government" were added to this strenuous defense of the private market system. From the other end of the political spectrum, radical critics argued that the plan did little to change the negative effects of the market system. Despite these criticisms, Roosevelt and the CES succeeded. Through compromise, careful management in the legislative system, and popular demand for change, the bill passed by wide margins in both the House and Senate (Altmeyer, 1968; Witte, 1963).

The Social Security Act, for all its flaws, was a milestone in the history of U.S. social welfare programs. It cleverly joined welfare and insurance programs, state and federal levels of financing and implementation, and the often conflicting U.S. values of mutual responsibility and self-reliance. Although the old-age insurance portion did not attack income inequalities the way some had hoped, it nevertheless included a slightly redistributive measure that paid the poorest workers a higher percentage of their income (note that because this percentage was figured on a lower income, they still got less money than better-off workers). Moreover, as the following section shows, the act created a program capable of slow and steady expansion and reform.

Changes in Social Security

The Social Security system has proved a remarkable example of incremental policy change. Before the first old-age insurance benefits were even distributed, a set of amendments had begun to alter the act's balance between equity and social adequacy. Through the years, subsequent changes have broadened the bill's scope and liberalized its benefits.

The first changes, made in 1939, were largely a response to political pressures. Because the first old-age benefits were not due to be paid until 1942, there was a long period before the advantages of the new system would be felt. In the meantime, workers' deductions were piling up in a reserve fund, which was, at least in theory, not to be used for anything else. (In reality, the government bought U.S. treasury bonds with the funds, thus loaning itself money with which to finance current operations.) Workers experiencing their first payroll deductions wondered where their money was going. They also lost some spending power, which hurt the economy. Those who were already elderly had to wait five years to receive aid; this put pressure on the Social Security Act's state-administered old-age assistance (OAA) program. The Social Security Board worried that expanding the assistance program would make politicians less likely to support future growth in social insurance. At the same time, older people's groups pressed for programs with broader coverage, and politicians criticized the social insurance financing arrangements (Berkowitz, 1991).

Roosevelt and the Social Security Board responded with rhetoric that expressed one thing and a set of amendments that did another. To keep old-age insurance from being overshadowed by OAA, defenders sharpened the distinction between social insurance and welfare and promoted insurance as an effective alternative to welfare. But to mollify critics of the program, they proposed a liberalization of social insurance benefits that in fact diminished the work-related aspects of the insurance program and moved it more toward the social adequacy, or "welfare," approach (Achenbaum, 1983; Berkowitz, 1991).

A major change was the addition of family benefits. Monthly benefits were established for the survivors of both active and retired workers and for the dependent children of retired workers. By emphasizing care of widows and children who were likely to be needy, the amendments suggested a more paternal role for the government as provider of family support. Encouraging a continued fuzziness regarding the program's actual goals, the new benefits were still couched in the language of work-related insurance. This was not *entirely* misleading because the new beneficiaries qualified through their relationship to a wage earner who had contributed to the system.

In addition, the 1939 amendments allowed benefit payments to begin in 1940 and lowered the combined worker–employer taxes from 3 to 2 percent. These changes, all voted into law, at the same time liberalized benefits and lowered taxes, not necessarily a winning formula for long-term financing of the program. After 1939, the Social Security program continued to grow incrementally. Extensions in benefits were approved relatively easily in the periods of economic expansion up through the early 1970s. A part of the motivation continued to be the goal of expanding social insurance at the expense of public assistance programs. In 1950, benefits were raised substantially, bringing old-age insurance to a parity with OAA. Four years later, regularly employed farm workers and domestic workers were finally brought into the system, along with people who were self-employed (Altmeyer, 1968, p. 283).

Financing was still not satisfactorily addressed, however. Although the Social Security Administration recommended that increased benefits be funded by general revenues, Congress chose a plan of gradually rising payroll tax rates, even though it had failed to implement such mandated tax rises in previous years (Berkowitz, 1991). The continued reliance on payroll deductions to finance the Social Security program reinforced the notion that workers were setting up their own "private savings accounts" for help in old age. Many people did not understand that their deductions were being used to support current retirees.

In 1956, social insurance was extended to workers with permanent disability aged fifty and older; once they reached sixty-five, recipients could receive regular old-age insurance benefits. The initial Social Security Act did not include a basic disability insurance program. It did provide for those who were blind, but only through a federal–state program of means-tested assistance. The changes in 1956 were made acceptable by linking disability with retirement (reflecting the equity, or work-related, approach to social insurance). Benefits were promoted as payments "to unfortunate individuals who had to 'retire early, because of mental or physical impairment.'" In 1960 the "social adequacy" goal undergirded an amendment to extend benefits to disabled workers of all ages and their dependents. (Today over 8 million nonelderly disabled workers and their dependents receive Social Security benefits.) What was now Old Age, Survivors', and Disability Insurance (OASDI) also received further boosts in benefits. By 1961, all workers were allowed to retire, with reduced benefits, at age sixty-two. Congress also allowed increases in payroll taxes, to 3 percent, in 1960 (Achenbaum, 1983; Social Security Administration, 1998).

The rediscovery of poverty during the Kennedy and Johnson years brought dramatic changes in Social Security programs for the elderly, changes that an expanding economy seemed well able to support. Three OASDI benefit increases were authorized in five years. In addition, an elusive quest for a federal health care program, which had been proposed intermittently since the 1920s but always rejected as politically insupportable, was finally partially realized through the creation of Medicare and Medicaid in 1965. Medicare provided acute-care health benefits to all old-age insurance recipients over age sixty-five. Medicaid gave health care coverage to those in the Social Security assistance programs, including old-age assistance. By now, social insurance had become one of the country's most popular social programs, with a large number of stakeholders.

In 1968, Republicans bent on recapturing the presidency found it politically advantageous to include expansion of the Social Security system in the party platform. Once Nixon was elected, competition between a Republican president and a Democratic Congress to retain the "elderly vote" led to significant reforms and expansion in OASDI. In the presidential election year of 1972, a plan was adopted to tie benefits received after 1975 to increases in the cost of living. This automatic, annual cost-of-living adjustment (COLA) was based on the assumption that wages, and concomitant payroll taxes, would continue to rise. The COLA thus seemed feasible and affordable. Other changes included extending Medicare coverage to the disabled and transforming the jointly funded federal–state OAA into a federally funded Supplemental Security Insurance (SSI) program. And, most spectacular of all, Congress passed a 20 percent increase in OASDI benefits. But Nixon did not raise the level of the payroll tax. This, along with the stagnation of wages in the mid-1970s, encouraged a crisis mentality regarding the Social Security insurance programs that persists today (Achenbaum, 1983; Jansson, 1997; "Social Security," 2005).

The first crisis came in the 1980s, when benefit payments threatened to exceed incoming tax revenues—due in part to the serious inflation of the preceding decade. Congress and the Reagan administration responded to the depletion of the reserve fund with a series of mostly incremental adjustments to the Social Security program. These included advancing the age at which people became eligible for benefits, increasing the payroll tax paid by workers, and initiating taxation of the benefits received by people with incomes above certain levels (something that current admirers of Reagan tend to forget). These changes created large surpluses in the reserve fund, which, it was hoped, would prepare the country to handle the retirement of the baby boomers in the twenty-first century (Achenbaum, 1983; Cohen, 1983). It was not just the population bulge of the boomers that would challenge the system. People were now living longer. When Social Security was created, not many people lived beyond 65.

Check Your Understanding 7.3

Check your understanding of Historical Development of Social Security Programs in the United States by taking this brief quiz.

CONTEMPORARY ANALYSIS OF SOCIAL SECURITY

Thanks to the continued expansion of Social Security (as the old-age/disability insurance program is now popularly called), the economic position of older citizens has vastly improved. Much of the change occurred in the 1960s. At the beginning of the decade, 35 percent of the elderly were poor despite Social Security benefits; at its end, only 25 percent lived below the poverty line. The figure dropped to 15 percent by 1979. This demonstrates the great success of the Social Security program. Yet the consensus supporting the program is beginning to unravel. Issues regarding Social Security's goals, coverage, and financing are raised by politicians, beneficiaries, and the public.

Social Analysis

Social Security coverage is now almost universal for U.S. workers. In February 2017, approximately 66.3 million people (retirees and their dependents, underage survivors of deceased workers, and the disabled) receive a Social Security check each month.

The average stipend was $1,129.55 a month, or $14,994.60 a year. For individuals over age 65 living alone or with nonrelatives, Social Security is 43.2 percent of their income. For those below the poverty line, it is 62.3 percent. The poverty rates for Americans age 65 or older is 8.8 percent overall, but there are wide differences within this group. For whites, it is 6.6 percent; blacks, 18.4; Hispanics, 17.5; and Asians, 11.8 percent. Social Security plays a big role in alleviating elder poverty. In 1959, 35.2 percent of elders were poor; only 10 percent were poor in 2014 (Bethell, 2005; U.S. Social Security Administration, 2015, 2017; Administration on Aging, 2015).

Social Security's inequities and its inability to provide a firm safety net for lower-wage workers reflect competing social values. As shown in the discussion of the program's history, both the larger Social Security system and the social insurance plan drew on ideas of equity and social adequacy. Recall that *equity* refers to a sense of fairness in the distribution of benefits based on contributions that workers made into the system. The U.S. work ethic undergirds this approach. *Social adequacy,* in contrast, stresses provision of a "basic floor of protection," or level of income to all who need it, unrelated to contributions. Social Security can be considered an intergenerational commitment or a collective responsibility "to provide at least a subsistence income to the most vulnerable of citizens." Thus, an additional outcome of social adequacy measures is redistribution of income from the better-off to those with fewer resources (Tropman, 1987; Stevenson, 1998).

The conflict between equity and social adequacy boils down to the simple question: Do you deserve help because you are poor or because you worked hard and contributed to the system? Of course, even this question isn't really simple—poor people may work hard and still get low salaries; others, such as homemakers, may do unpaid labor and not get the chance to pay anything into the system. And we also need to remember that Social Security isn't like an individual savings account; the contributions of current workers support the older generation.

In the United States, people generally rank self-reliance over interdependence, thus finding equity a more "legitimate" basis for providing aid. When Social Security began, then, policymakers prudently portrayed the old-age insurance plan in the language of work and contributions. However, the notion of helping the less fortunate, particularly those, such as the elderly, whose poverty seems no fault of their own, still has a place in the U.S. value system. Thus, the Social Security Act combined assistance and insurance programs, and both the act and subsequent changes brought an element of social adequacy into the old-age insurance program. Our ambivalence over the relationship between those two goals continues to complicate the debate over how to reform Social Security.

The question of who "deserves" help is closely connected to current discussions of entitlement. Attacks on the growth of entitlements bring up the same issues of who should be given government assistance and why. Although it is becoming popular to portray almost all public assistance and social insurance programs as entitlements, that concept had a more limited meaning when our modern social welfare system began in the 1930s. The architects of the Social Security Act did not even include the term in the act, stressing instead the right of wage earners to benefits. As Roosevelt explained, "We put the payroll contributions there so as to give contributors a legal, moral and political right to collect their pensions." While social insurance was justified as an "earned right," developers of the Social Security Act based the public assistance titles on a different conception of right: a poor person's "statutory right" to assistance, "even though that assistance was conditioned on need." The official rhetoric supporting the act and its later modifications suggests that this was a two-tier model of rights, with earned rights constituting the more legitimate ones (Altmeyer, 1968; Witte, 1963).

The use of the term *entitlement* probably originated in legal discussions of welfare in the 1960s. In a 1965 *Yale Law Journal* article, Charles B. Reich (1978) used *entitlement* to describe the idea that "when individuals have insufficient resources to live under conditions of health and decency, society has obligations to provide support, and the individual is entitled to that support as of right." Legal scholars fleshed out this idea further as they argued that entitlements could be construed as property rights, which could not be denied or cut off without notice and a fair hearing. They contended that ownership could be seen in terms of two different sets of property rights, involving either control over something tangible that one owns or control rights over income or other resources, such as welfare and social insurance benefits, needed for personal autonomy. This new interpretation of property as something intangible as well as tangible means, for example, that professionals have a constitutionally protected property right regarding licenses that affect their ability to practice. Such licenses cannot be denied, just as tangible property cannot be taken away or confiscated without due process. Using similar reasoning, the Supreme Court ruled in 1970 that welfare recipients had certain constitutional rights to their entitlements and that the government could not cut these off without due process. The Court argued that it had become realistic "to regard welfare entitlements as more like 'property' than a 'gratuity,'" or charity (Brigham, 1990; Christman, 1994; Moynihan, 1994; Reich, 1978).

Such sophisticated legal arguments are not in most people's minds when they discuss entitlements today. Neither, probably, are such definitions as "services, goods, or money due to an individual by virtue of a specific status" (*Social Work Dictionary*) or "the state of meeting the applicable requirements for receipt of benefits" (U.S. Social Security Administration, 1995). Instead, people tend to think of a two-tiered system that includes "earned entitlements," such as Social Security, and "income-based entitlements," such as AFDC, and often tend to perceive the former as much more legitimate than the latter (*Annual Statistical Supplement to Social Security Bulletin 1995*, 1995, p. 374; Baker, 1987; Cates, 2005).

Critics on the left argue that both kinds of entitlement are perfectly legitimate. However, there is a growing movement on the right to lump all types of entitlement together and to characterize the whole notion of entitlement as a false one, which has subtly "subverted personal and institutional responsibility." Under titles such as "Escaping the Entitlement Straitjacket," conservatives label entitlements "a problem" and question whether "popularly accepted 'rights'" should be "allowed to destroy the economy." The denigration of entitlements and the claims that they are no longer affordable can be seen as a means of diverting attention from other ways to manage the budget. These ways include increasing taxes, especially for corporations and people with high incomes, and/or decreasing tax breaks, such as the waiver of local property taxes for some businesses and the use of home mortgage interest as a tax deduction. Just as in the equity versus social adequacy debate, confusion and ambivalence over the meaning and role of entitlements cloud public discussion of potential changes and improvements in Social Security (Ornstein, 1994; Samuelson, 1996).

Political Analysis

As we have seen, the notion of entitlements is politically charged. Now, as at the beginning of Social Security, a number of stakeholders are concerned about the system and its possible reform. These include current retirees, disabled workers, and their dependents; low-income workers; the children of aging parents; organized groups representing the elderly; current wage earners; employers; labor unions; the public at large; members of Congress; members of the executive branch of the federal government; politicians running for office; think tanks of all ideological persuasions; program administrators; private pension companies; and human services professionals such as social workers.

As Social Security has expanded, both the numbers and categories of beneficiaries have increased. One of the program's greatest protections is the sheer number and potential voting power of those assisted by it. The elderly in particular represent a large percentage of the electorate, and they vote in greater numbers than any other age group. However, there are subsets within this group with different agendas and needs. For example, those retirees who experienced the Depression often have different views of the role of government in social provision than do the baby boomers, now retiring, who lived through several decades of cutbacks in social spending. Then, too, people receiving Social Security because of disabilities may have another set of concerns.

Although elderly beneficiaries cast a good proportion of the votes on election day, a more concentrated type of power is exercised through the various citizen and professional organizations that make up the "Gray Lobby." By far the strongest of these is the American Association of Retired Persons (AARP), with a membership of 37.8 million people. The association is one of the biggest and most politically powerful organizations in the country. It has opposed most attempts to make cuts or other changes in Social Security that it believes would disadvantage older Americans. They did, however, support President George W. Bush's prescription drug program, which was passed with no provision for paying for it other than borrowing and is now a major contributor to the budget deficits, which have become a major if belated concern for Republicans.

Conservative politicians have wielded a good deal of power in questioning the stability of Social Security funding, discussed in the next section, and in casting doubt on the desirability and legitimacy of entitlements. From the other side of the floor, liberal Democrats have generally defended the system. Think tanks, such as the conservative American Enterprise Institute and the Cato Institute, and the liberal Urban Institute, help provide the support for politicians' positions.

The general public has been somewhat ambivalent about support for Social Security and other entitlements, particularly when the federal government plays the dominant role in their financing and administration. Older voters, however, have generally steered away from Republican reform plans to shrink the federal government and have put more trust in the Democrats' traditional commitment "to protect the Social Security system." They are also leery of changes that might negatively affect their benefits. Younger workers may fear the demise of Social Security before they can benefit from it. Some may long for the chance to put at least part of their Social Security payroll taxes into the stock market, where they might get a greater return than if the money remained under government control. Younger workers may also resent the fact that their payroll deductions support current retirees, although a number of workers, especially middle-aged ones, are cognizant of the fact that Social Security helps to support their aging parents.

What most stakeholders are concerned about today is how to maintain a viable Social Security system, with good benefits, in the face of the current wave of baby boomer retirements. We turn now to the debates over how best to do this.

Economic Analysis and Proposals for Reform

When we wrote the first edition of this text in 1997, we noted that "the major issue regarding Social Security . . . is the solvency of the reserve fund." By the mid-1990s, projections had indicated that the system's income from payroll taxes would be greater than payments to beneficiaries up until the year 2013. At about that time, analysts predicted, the retirement of the baby boomers would cause an increase in beneficiaries that might engulf the system. This could lead to complete depletion of the trust fund in 2029. Pronouncements of a "Social Security crisis" received a great deal of publicity, causing politicians and policy analysts to rush to develop solutions ("The Growing Need for Social Security," 2005).

During the Clinton administration, worries about the future solvency of the system seemed less pressing. In 1998, the annual forecast by the trustees of the Social Security program extended the deadline for the depletion of the fund to 2032, an effect connected to a continuing economic boom. A still-cautious Clinton put "saving Social Security for the twenty-first century" at the top of his agenda in his 1999 State of the Union Address and pledged to use budget surpluses to shore up the program before taking any other actions or cutting taxes. However, in his address a year later, Clinton spent far less time on the issue, concluding, as one reporter put it, that "times were good enough to call for [modest] tax cuts and more social spending" (Passell, 1996).

Five years later, claims that the Social Security system was in crisis suddenly reappeared. In his State of the Union address in February 2005, President George W. Bush warned the nation that without changes, the country's largest and costliest social program was headed for bankruptcy. Government actuaries had recently projected that the system's trust fund would have exhausted its reserves by the year 2042. To "strengthen and save" the program, Bush proposed adding individual, private investment accounts to the traditional system. These changes would not affect people fifty-five and older, reflecting the president's promises not to change Social Security for current or near retirees. But beginning in 2009, according to the proposal, those under fifty-five could enroll in private accounts. The president did not say how the plan would cover the "transition costs" during the shift, which were estimated at $2.2 trillion over the first 10 years (Goldstein, 1998; Hunt, 2005; Lacey, 2000).

After the State of the Union address, Bush embarked on a tour through five states to promote his shift from the New Deal to the "ownership society." These tours had mixed results. By the end of March 2005, support for individual accounts was lower than when he had proposed them a month earlier, and his own approval rating was in the mid-40 percent range (Crenshaw, 2005; Raum, 2005; Rosenbaum, 2005; Stevenson, 2005; Wiles, 2005).

Polls conducted by *USA Today* and the AARP found most older people who responded opposed the change. Support for the plan weakened further when people learned the details. For example, almost half of those supporting private accounts changed their minds upon learning how much the transition would cost them. A *Washington Post* survey reported that almost half the respondents felt the government should be mainly responsible for ensuring at least a minimum standard of living for retired elderly people, and 35 percent felt individuals themselves should be responsible (Basler, 2005; Fineman, 2005; Kornblut, 2005; Morin & Russakof, 2005).

By June, public support for the president's approach was falling rapidly. Sixty-three percent of respondents to a national poll felt his proposals would not improve the long-term financial stability of the Social Security system. Eighty percent said it was the government's responsibility to provide "a decent standard of living for the elderly." Basically, the public was not rallying around the vision of a new Social Security system ("Survey Detects Pessimism on Social Security Payouts," 2005; Toner & Connelly, 2005a, 2005b; "War Clouds: Bush's Poll Numbers," 2005).

Groups representing the elderly, professional organizations, and unions also weighed in on the president's proposals. Members of the National Association of Social Workers participated in rallies across the country to express their concern about the privatization of Social Security and held a rally of several thousand people near the Capitol in Washington (Greenhouse, 2005; "Privatization Fought," 2005; "Social Security: Where We Stand," 2004).

Interestingly, many polls showed that seniors' real worries were the rising cost of health care rather than the state of Social Security. An AARP survey found that three of four respondents aged fifty and over were "'very concerned' about the availability and costs of health care" (Stranahan, 2005).

Clearly, most of the Bush's proposals to "save the system" did not resonate with various constituencies or make sense to economists and other experts. The idea of private accounts is a good example. As Robert Greenstein, executive director of the Center on Budget and Policy Priorities, explains, although some Americans could reap windfalls, "you'd likely also have a significant number of losers" due to the ups and downs of the stock market. Another analyst presents this scenario: Suppose you set aside $1,000 a year for forty-three years and earned 4.6 percent annually on your investment. Your account would grow to $221, 552 in today's dollars. This money would be yours on retirement, and would probably be paid out to you in increments of about $16,000 a year. But since Social Security's *guaranteed* benefits would be reduced by about $151,900 (the amount you could have contributed to Social Security but instead contributed to your personal account, plus 3 percent interest), your annual gain would only be about $5,000. And, due to the normal risks of the stock market, if you earned less on your investments, you might not have any gain at all (Rosenbaum, 2005; Stranahan, 2005; Weisman, 2005).

In the end, Bush's proposal failed to make it through Congress. The president's drive for changes in the system ran into a solid wall of public opposition and quickly collapsed. Had Bush succeeded in placing the retirement funds of many Americans in the stock market, they would have been vaporized in the 2008 financial meltdown, the current budget problem would be a lot worse, and many people would be facing retirement in poverty (Brooks, 2005; Krugman, 2006).

During the 2008 presidential campaign, both Barack Obama and John McCain made proposals for dramatic changes to the Social Security system. McCain said he was open to "an array of ideas, such as raising the retirement age, reducing scheduled increases in benefits and allowing younger workers to put money they currently pay for Social Security taxes into personal savings accounts" (Bacon, 2008).

Once elected, Obama put Social Security on the back burner and devoted most of his attention to health care reform. But in April 2011, the administration reported that the Social Security Trust Fund would be depleted in 2024, three years earlier than previously estimated. In past years the fund ran a surplus because more workers were paying into it than retired workers drawing on it. Retiring baby boomers have now reversed this ratio. Also contributing to the shortfall is the simple fact that people are living longer and drawing more benefits. After 2024, Social Security would be able to cover only 75 percent of the promised benefits. This is hardly the total collapse of the system envisioned by some younger citizens. Social Security would still exist, new money would be coming in, and retirees would continue to be paid. But a 25 percent cut in benefits would be a severe blow to those for whom Social Security is their primary income. Therefore, the system needs to be fixed.

So, how do we fix it? A variety of modifications are more like tweaks than radical overhauls. Earnings above $106,600 are currently not subject to the payroll tax. That cap could be raised. The tax itself could be raised gradually over 20 years at a rate of 1/20 of a percent. Coverage could be extended to state and local government workers, thus bringing in more revenue. Instead of allowing recipients to start collecting earlier or later than the designated Full Retirement Age (FRA), collecting at the FRA could be required. This would greatly simplify the system, cut down on bureaucracy, and save money. A further variation would be a means test. The rich and the superrich don't need Social Security but are entitled to it anyway. If benefits were tied to need, some money would be saved. However, the big trouble with two-tiered programs is that they soon lose political support. Finally, benefits could be cut, but less for low-income recipients. This is less radical than a means test and could retain political support. Some believe that benefit cuts are inevitable anyway. But the system is certainly fixable.

To put this in a larger economic and political context, extending the life of the system's trust fund into the twenty-second century, with *no* change in benefits, "would require additional revenues equal to only 0.54 percent of GDP. That's less than 3 percent of federal spending." In fact, that is less than we spent on the war in Iraq. Also, the Bush tax cuts were three times larger than the Social Security shortfall. If not for those two events, we might not be having a Social Security crisis (Dionne, 2005; Krugman, 2004; Meckler & King, 2009; Obama, 2009; Quinn, 2004; Shear, 2009).

The move to privatize Social Security did not die with the collapse of the Bush initiative in 2009. It was part of Paul Ryan's 2010 "Roadmap for America's Future." It was dropped when Republicans won the House, but it is obviously central to his philosophy of government and will no doubt stay alive as long as he has a political career.

The Older Americans Act

Making sure that elders have sufficient income to live comfortably in their later years is the centerpiece of social policy for aging Americans. But there are further concerns. Their limited income will go further, their lives will be happier and more dignified, and other public resources will be conserved if seniors can continue to live independently. Institutional services are expensive and restrictive. Most of us would prefer to live (and die) in our own homes. To keep us living independently, a number of services are helpful. Housekeeping help, home-delivered or congregate meals, transportation, job retraining, and protection from abuse can make a big contribution to aging in place. Family caregivers can also receive support, including respite care.

For these purposes, the Older Americans Act was enacted in 1965 as a part of President Lyndon Johnson's Great Society Program. Individuals age 60 and above, particularly those with low incomes, members of minority groups, and/or those living in rural areas are the targets of this legislation. In 2014, $1.88 billion was used to keep 11 million people living independently.

The Administration on Aging was established within the Department of Health and Human Services. Funding is channeled through 56 state agencies, two tribal organizations, two Native Hawaiian organizations, and 600 area agencies on aging. The Older Americans Reauthorization Act was passed in 2016 during the Obama administration. It had bipartisan support, something we can no longer take for granted for even the worthiest causes.

Federal appropriations have changed little over the last decade, though inflation and costs of living have. And the number of people over 60 has continued to grow. Therefore, the program and its many services are squeezed further and further. Its future is unclear (Fox-Grage & Ujvari, 2014; Government Relations and Policy, 2016).

President Trump's first budget proposal does not look good at all for seniors. It proposes to cut Low-Income Home Energy Assistance, which helps poor elders keep the heat on in the winter; the Energy Department's weatherization assistance, which helps them retain what heat they have; the Senior Community Service Employment Program, which offers job training for those not ready to retire; the Legal Services Corporation, which provides legal aid to low-income seniors; and Meals-on-Wheels. Budget Director Mick Mulvaney said: "You can't spend money on programs just because they sound good." He did not say specifically, but it was implied that it was "just not showing any results." There are many studies of the program that document the results (Singletary, 2017; Carroll, 2017; Rubenstein, 2017).

Pensions

Uncertainty among some Americans about the future shape of Social Security has now been joined by an awareness of the growing erosion in the U.S. system of public and private pensions. Until recently, you could be confident that if you worked long enough, you could count on a predetermined stream of income upon retirement from your employer. Currently, about 35 million working people in the United States are counting on a fixed pension, funded by their employers and paying a monthly benefit for life. Now they're wondering if that benefit will be there when they retire (Quinn, 2005; Toner & Rosenbaum, 2005; Walsh, 2005).

The traditional pension was widely available to U.S. workers up until the 1980s, but since then it has been vanishing from the U.S. workplace. In 1983, more than two-thirds of households headed by people age forty-seven to sixty-four had someone earning a pension. By 2001, less than half did. Some companies, like Sears, simply stopped providing pensions. Starbucks, Home Depot, and Dell never provided them at all. Other companies have eliminated pensions for new workers. Due to bankruptcies, companies such as Bethlehem Steel canceled or reduced the pensions of many or all of their retirees. IBM froze its pension plan as of 2008, meaning that no new money would be added to employee's pension accounts after 2007. Janet Krueger, who retired from IBM after twenty-three years, was told that she would no longer be eligible for the monthly checks of one-third of her salary, and "would instead receive a one-time lump sum equal to about two-thirds of my yearly salary—and nothing more than that" (Pension Benefits Guarantee Corporation, 2012; Wild, 2005).

The financial meltdown of 2008 prompted more large corporations like Verizon and Chrysler to cut their pension plans. Some of America's largest pension funds lost ground that spring ("Blueprints for Recovery of Big 3," 2008; Walsh, 2008). More pension changes followed. The Pension Rights Center has three lists of companies who have moved to

401(k) plans, lump-sum payouts, or frozen pensions. The lists are long enough to extend to the end of this chapter. Included are L.L.Bean, DuPont, U.S. Steel, the Boston Red Sox, the Washington Post, Kodak, Boeing, Major League Baseball, Herman Miller, Honda, Chrysler, Macy's, General Motors, Clorox, Xerox, Walt Disney, General Electric, Kraft, Sunoco, Anheuser Busch, 3M, Coca-Cola, and Hewlett-Packard. That's just the beginning. Some companies are on more than one list (Pension Rights Center, n.d.).

Many companies have been replacing their traditional pension, or "defined-benefit," plans (which guarantee a predetermined monthly income after retirement, usually based on the numbers of years worked and the employee's salary over the years) with "defined-contribution" investment plans, such as 401(k) plans. In the latter, employees put aside a portion of their pay for retirement tax-deferred, and the company contributes a partial match. Whatever is in the investment account when employees retire is what they get; thus, this type of retirement money is tied to the ups and downs of the stock market. Furthermore, there is no restriction against companies reducing or ending contributions to their employees' 401(k) plans if times get tough. In 2003, 45 percent of workers covered by a company retirement plan had a traditional defined-benefit pension. In 2005, it was only 20 percent. In 2010, it was under 5 percent, with another 10 percent having a combined defined-benefit/defined-contribution plan. Although defined-contribution plans have the advantage of allowing employees to take their retirement investments with them when they change employers, these plans are generally not worth as much money as the employee would have accrued in a traditional pension. They also must be managed by the individual workers, who can easily make investment mistakes. And should the markets take a downward turn or collapse just when the worker plan to retire, the result can be disastrous (Crenshaw, 2004; Dugas, 2004; Fetterman, 2006; McSherry, 2006; Porter, 2005; Quinn, 2005; Walsh, 2004; Wiles, 2005).

The recent bankruptcies of large companies, particularly in the airline industry, have made the situation worse. United Airlines is the best example. When the company went into bankruptcy in 2003, due to declining passenger travel, increasing jet fuel costs after 9/11, and rising pension and health benefits costs, it won the right in bankruptcy court to terminate its four employee pension plans. This move released the corporation from $3.2 billion in pension obligations for the following four years, shifting the payments to the federal agency in charge of guaranteeing pensions, the Pension Benefit Guaranty Corporation (PBGC), created by the Employees Retirement Income Security Act (ERISA) in 1974 (Beck, 2004; Maynard, 2005; "United's Pension Debacle," 2005).

The PBGC is the U.S. government's "pension insurer." It collects premiums from corporations and uses this money to help workers when companies cannot fulfill their pension obligations. It is interesting that in an era that idealizes individualism and privatization, what we see here is an opposite force, collectivization of corporations' risks and responsibilities. A corporation that cannot meet its contracted obligations does not have to go it alone but can turn to a cooperative association, a federal agency created by public policy, to keep it afloat. Indeed, eliminating a pension plan considerably lightens the company's balance sheet and immediately makes it more valuable. This is very convenient economically, less so morally (Bailey, 2006; Beck, 2004; Crawley, 2012; Marsh, 2012; Weber, 2006).

In 2012, American Airlines approached the biggest pension default in U.S. history. It was $8 billion short of meeting its pension obligations. The PBGC argued that default was not necessary; the company compromised by simply freezing pension benefits. A subsequent merger with U.S. Airlines averted the crisis.

The status of pension funds for public sector employees has also become precarious. Generally, teachers, police officers, and other public employees have been guaranteed retirement benefits far richer than private pensions, but elected officials have often failed to set aside enough money to cover promised benefits. Facing a $2.6 billion bill for state workers' pensions, Arnold Schwarzenegger, then-governor of California, tried in 2005 to control costs by switching workers from traditional pension plans to 401(k)-style plans. The state governments of Michigan and Virginia had been successful in making such a change, but Schwarzenegger was forced to withdraw his plan after loud protests from public employees' unions (Cauchon, 2006; Dao, 2005; "The Terminator Takes Aim at State Pensions," 2005).

Cities are now declaring bankruptcy. Detroit, Michigan; Central Falls, Rhode Island; and Pritchard, Alabama, led the way. The bankruptcies of San Bernadino, Stockton, Vallejo, and Loyalton, California, have put such a strain on the California Public Employees Retirement System that it is now $170 billion in debt (Reed, 2016; Walsh, 2016).

Some unions have their own pension systems for workers who are employed by nonrelated companies in the same field. They are financed by union dues. As union membership declines and retirements increase, payouts become a problem. In 2014, the Kline-Miller Multi-Employer Pension Act allowed unions to appeal to the Labor Department to cut benefits. Ironworkers Local 17 was recently allowed to cut benefits by 50 percent. There are 67 such appeals covering 1 million workers in the system and others are expected (Savage, 2017).

When the economy was performing well, public employers thought they could count on a good return on their investments and could afford to put less into pension funds. They were essentially borrowing from the funds so that they could maintain or even increase their budgets without raising taxes. Some states even invested in the credit-default swaps, mortgage-backed securities based on subprime mortgages, and other schemes dreamed up by Wall Street bankers. Of course, their investments evaporated in the 2008 financial collapse, and massive debts resulted.

Some argue that the main culprits in the crisis are the unions themselves, who have bargained such high benefits for their members. And it is generally the case that over the years public employees have traded the lower salaries that government jobs offer for better benefits and long-range job security. Others point out that the benefits alone would not have caused the crisis had the employers funded them at scheduled rates and not plundered them to engage in risky investments. Underfunding of pensions was also a tactic used by corporations to make companies appear more profitable. An important component to the crisis was, of course, the crash of the stock market in 2007–2009. The market recovered considerably and by late 2013 was at record highs. Current analysis suggests that public pensions are manageable as long the recovery continues and public employers resume funding of pensions at scheduled rates.

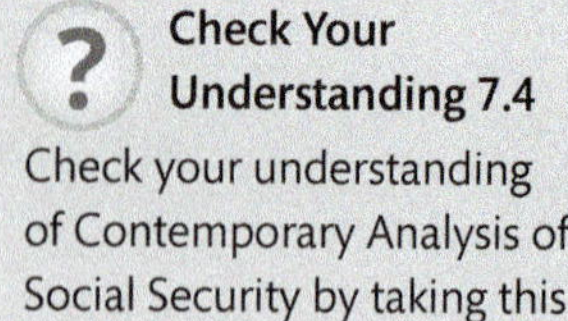
?
Check Your Understanding 7.4
Check your understanding of Contemporary Analysis of Social Security by taking this brief quiz.

END OF LIFE

Dying is not usually thought of as a focus of social policy. We all have to do it and don't see why the government should be involved. But if enormous public and private resources have to go into prolonging life past an individual's capacity to enjoy it, if hospice and other end-of-life services are benefits or entitlements, and if health care should have to be rationed, then dying may have policies attached to it. And if some regard end-of-life services and decisions as constituting the creation of "death panels," then dying becomes politicized.

"My mother wanted to die, but the doctors wouldn't let her." Journalist Evan Thomas's mother firmly refused all the tests and procedures her doctors wanted to perform to keep her alive (Thomas, 2009). Joe Klein, also a journalist, faced both similar and opposite problems. His mother said: "Just pull the plug; let me die." She had signed a do-not-resuscitate order. She had stopped eating, but he decided to authorize the insertion of a feeding tube. His father took the opposite stance. Suffering from renal failure and dementia, he raged against dying (Klein, 2011).

The Hippocratic Oath teaches physicians to "first, do no harm." They also respond to their patients and their family members who usually want to cling to life as long as possible. Increasingly, they have at their disposal miraculous new drugs, instruments, and procedures that will allow them to do this. Though increasingly expensive, these things are often paid for by private insurance and/or Medicaid. Physicians get personal and professional satisfaction from being lifesavers. If they are financially compensated by the fee-for-service system, they will also be economically rewarded. If that were not enough incentive, they know that if they fail to do their utmost to extend a patient's life, they might suffer a lawsuit that could ruin them financially. Thus, we have a situation where it will be very difficult for Thomas's and Klein's mothers to have their wishes honored.

Medicaid is now experiencing considerable financial stress (which will be discussed in a later chapter). About one-third of its money goes to the last two years of its recipients' lives. This creates a situation where serious consideration of the best use of resources is essential. There may be better ways of allocation. Klein discovered the Geisinger Health System, where staff are on salary, care is case-managed so that various health professionals are not operating independently, medical information is shared so that medications are monitored for possible conflicts, and staff talk plainly to patients and family members about their conditions and their options. The much-better-known Mayo Clinic operates in a similar manner. In one study, the system produces an 18 percent reduction in initial hospital visits, a 36 percent reduction in return visits, and a cost savings of 7 percent (Klein, 2011).

The infamous death panels, which were simply incentives for patients to have a chance to talk with their doctors about how they wanted to deal with death, were found not only to improve the quality of life for patients but also decrease health care costs by 35 percent. At least one wife of a cancer patient wished they had been able to have such a conversation to "work through their choices." She thought that "knowing the price tag on the care he was getting might have helped him make choices that were consistent with the life he had lived. The seven-year bill for his care was $618,616. I believe he would have liked a chance to play a more active role in how we spent enough money to vaccinate 600,000 children in the developing world. That's how he would have seen it" (Bennett, 2012).

Though we may all be equal in death, we may not all be equal in dying. Like all aspects of social work, hospice care requires culturally competent practice. African Americans may not understand hospice and hospice may not understand African Americans. Some African Americans have a cultural preference according to which a patient should not die at home. They may not understand palliative care and want curative care to be continued even if it is no longer effective. They may also fear that palliative drugs like morphine may cause death rather than relieve pain. Outreach efforts and culturally sensitive social workers are clearly called for (Jackson, 2005; PBS Newshour, 2015).

Check Your Understanding 7.5

Check your understanding of End of Life by taking this brief quiz.

CONCLUSION

Is it fair to tax higher-income people at a greater rate than middle- and lower-income earners to redistribute resources? Is it reasonable to privatize the Social Security system in a way that would jeopardize poorer people's chance at a reasonable retirement income? Issues of equity and adequacy undergird the debates about Social Security reform. The various factors of choice analysis—how and to whom benefits are allocated, what benefits are provided, how benefits are delivered, and the method of financing—all relate to the desired balance between fairness and adequate provision, independence and mutual responsibility, and government and private market approaches. Values and ideology play a crucial role in Social Security policy choices.

Pensions present other dilemmas. How much should employers be concerned with their workers after retirement? Should they move to defined contribution plans, which place retirement management in the hands of individual workers? Would this increase poverty for elders who made poor investment decisions? Perhaps employers should simply stop offering retirement benefits. They could leave it all to Social Security. Since Social Security is currently not adequate for a comfortable retirement for most workers, employers could increase their contribution to the system. This would free them from negotiating and administering their own pension program and free them from the premiums of the PBGC. Businesses could then concentrate on what they are supposed to do best: business. For those concerned with the size of government, this would increase one government program but entirely eliminate another; in the larger context of the historic shift of economic risk from public and private insurance programs, the risk would be borne by individual families (Hacker, 2006).

End-of-life decisions are perhaps the most morally conflicting of all. Most of us regard life as sacred and want to preserve it at all costs. But what if "all costs" involve extreme pain and suffering? Should we have the right to end our own lives in such circumstances? What should our loved ones do if we are beyond consciousness and have no hope of regaining it? Is it moral to expend great financial resources on prolonging life when they could be used for the care and cure of nonterminal patients? Does anyone have the right to sit on a "death panel"?

The U.S. system of old-age security combines public and private provisions for older Americans through Social Security and employment-based pensions. However, both Social Security and private pensions are often inadequate in providing an economically secure future for all citizens. It is important to recognize that Social Security has demonstrated significant progress in reducing poverty among the elderly. It also has a broad base of political support because the vast majority of Americans are eligible for benefits. The challenges to the program are basically small compared to the good the system accomplishes or could be expected to accomplish.

Recall what you learned from this chapter by completing the Chapter Review.

8

Mental Health and Substance Abuse

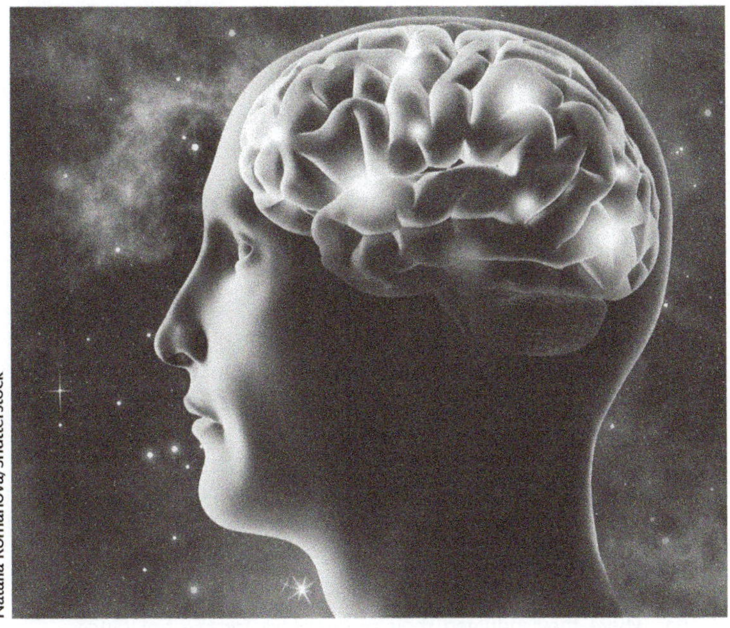

Natalia Romanova/Shutterstock

Seung Cho had a social anxiety disorder called selective mutism that made it painfully difficult for him to speak in public. Students taunted him in high school, and teachers were angry at his refusal to respond. In eighth grade, he wrote an essay saying he "wanted to repeat Columbine." Fairfax County school officials took notice and crafted a special education plan for him that included being excused from class participation and getting him private therapy. With such help, he was able to graduate and enroll in Virginia Polytechnic Institute. The university was not told of his difficulties, and he soon encountered similar problems. Students and teachers were aware of his discomfort, isolation, and anger. He was hospitalized briefly in his junior year, but his parents were not told, and the university took no further action. In the spring of his senior year, Seung Cho bought two handguns and entered two campus buildings, killing 32 students and faculty before killing himself (Schulte & Craig, 2007).

Jeff Cabot pulled into the high school parking lot just before 8:00 Saturday morning. The SAT lay ahead; if he was going to get into Princeton, he'd have to nail it. He unscrewed a capsule of orange powder, formed a neat line on the car armrest,

LEARNING OUTCOMES

- Assess the utility of mandatory drug tests.
- Identify the main obstacles to reintegrating veterans into the community.
- Compare the demographic groups affected by the opioid epidemic with those addicted to crack or cocaine.
- Discuss the effectiveness of the supply versus the demand approaches to mitigating drug addiction.
- Judge the extent to which better mental health services could curb gun violence.

CHAPTER OUTLINE

and snorted it through one nostril. Elsewhere in the parking lot, eight of his friends were doing the same. He knew it would keep his memory sharp and his focus tight. Two years later, he explained to his drug counselor that this was what got him addicted to Percocet and eventually heroin (Schwarz, 2012).

Manny Bojorquez sat on his bed with his pistol and what was left of a bottle of Jim Beam. He has just learned that his fellow Marine Joshua Markel, with whom he had served in Afghanistan, had committed suicide. Markel was the sixth member of his unit to do so since returning home eighteen months ago. He had performed his duties as a machine-gunner with grim humor and had seemed to have made a stable adjustment to civilian life. "If he couldn't make it, what chance do I have," thought Manny. He pulled the trigger. Somewhat later, he was surprised to find himself alive. The gun had jammed and he had passed out.

After the eighth suicide, Manny asked the VA for help. It didn't go well. His therapist, he concluded, had not read his file. She told him he would just have to get over the deaths of his friends. "It's like a bad breakup with a girl," she said. He threw a chair across the room and stormed out. He tried again a year later. Since some of his friends had had bad reactions to the drugs they were told to take and one had actually used them to commit suicide, he told them: "No drugs." "We understand," they said. As he left, he was handed a bag of pills. He tried them. They didn't help. He flushed them down the toilet.

But he stayed in touch with his unit. One night he got a text from Noel Gerrero saying goodbye. He called immediately, but Noel hung up. Manny called 911. The police arrived just as Noel was swallowing pills.

They got together a few weeks later and had lunch at a taqueria, where they indulged their mutual love for the hot sauces that their families had sent to them in Afghanistan. They talked a long time, even reliving the experiences they had tried to forget. The next day they went running. They felt better, at least for a while (Phillips, 2015).

Thoughts for Social Work Practice

If you are counseling someone who is potentially violent, how much information should you share and with whom? What is your responsibility in relation to a client's privacy versus to those in the community he or she might hurt? How do you design a policy that protects both?

Thoughts on Social Work Practice

Marijuana has for some time been assumed to be a gateway drug: one puff and it's only a matter of time until you're shooting heroine. This does not seem to be the case. What about other drugs? What about this orange powder that Jeff is snorting? What about prescription pain pills like Oxycontin? How do you know if they are gateway drugs? If they are, how do you convince the user of the dangers of escalation? How do you intervene?

Thoughts on Social Work Practice

Some argue that the best substance abuse counselors are former addicts. Many social workers disagree. But could the same argument be made for those counseling veterans? The suicide rate among veterans is very high even for those who have not experienced combat. Why do you think that is? Some believe that returning veterans miss the intense sense of purpose and group solidarity they experienced in the military. What could be done to improve the reintegration of returning veterans into their communities?

THE PROBLEM OF MENTAL ILLNESS

One of the difficulties in planning for and funding mental health services is that, in the eyes of many insurers and employers (among others), mental illness is characterized by the four "uns"—it is "undefinable, untreatable, unpredictable, and unmanageable." In addition to such factors as lack of precision in diagnosis, it is much harder to calculate the number of people with mental illness than of those with physical ailments. Nevertheless, broad generalizations can be made about prevalence rates. The National Alliance for the Mentally Ill (NAMI) estimates that 18.5 percent of American adults—about one in five adults—suffer from a diagnosable mental disorder in a given year. The incidence of the most serious mental illnesses is smaller: major depression, 6.9 percent; bipolar disorder, 2.6 percent; and schizophrenia, 1.1 percent (NAMI, 2015). The Center for Disease Control estimates that 13 to 20 percent of children had a mental disorder in any given year and that $247 billion is spent on treating childhood mental disorders (2017).

The costs of mental problems to individuals, families, and employers are high. The annual cost of untreated mental illness in lost earnings alone is estimated to be $201 billion. It has surpassed heart conditions, the former number one in cost, which was $147 billion in 2013. In 1996, heart condition costs were $105 billion, while mental illness was only $79 billion (Roehrig, 2016). The effects in terms of emergency health care, crime, domestic violence, and property damage would further increase the cost to society of not treating mental disorders. Compared with heart disease, diabetes, and back pain, depression generally leads to the longest average length of disability time. Although our discussion so far has focused largely on serious mental illness, it is important to remember that most of us have or will encounter at some point in our lives the kinds of problems—mild depression, anxiety, or stress in our marriages or relationships with parents—that make it difficult to function in our jobs or other areas of daily life (Kessler et al., 2008).

Despite the aura of unreliability and unchangeability, mental illness *can* be dealt with. On the one hand, the rehospitalization rate among persons with severe mental illness is quite high, and treatments for mental difficulties may take longer than those for other health problems. On the other hand, the National Institute for Mental Health reports that 60 percent of those medicated for schizophrenia improve. Studies have shown that psychiatric rehabilitation services for adults can reduce time spent in a psychiatric hospital, raise earning power, and increase the individual's level of independent living. Relatively low-cost outpatient treatment is often effective in helping people with phobias and other anxiety disorders.

Check Your Understanding 8.1

Check your understanding of The Problem of Mental Illness by taking this brief quiz.

THE PROBLEM OF SUBSTANCE ABUSE

Substance abuse, like mental illness, affects many people in our society and has led to a variety of policy responses. Individuals' use of alcohol or illegal drugs has ramifications for parents, siblings, friends, human services professionals, and their communities. Incarceration, drug testing, and agency treatment policies are just three of the myriad of policies relating to substance abuse, including laws prohibiting the possession, use, and distribution of drugs; state and local ordinances regulating the sale of alcoholic beverages; "no use" and even stricter "zero-tolerance" policies in elementary and high schools; and federal appropriations of funds to states with the requirement that these be spent on treatment and prevention of alcoholism and drug addiction.

According to the 2015 National Survey on Drug Abuse and Health, an estimated 27.1 million Americans age twelve and over, or 10.1 percent of the population, were current users of illicit drugs. Another 138.3 million Americans aged twelve and over reported current use of alcohol, with 24.9 percent reporting binge drinking and 6.5 percent qualifying as heavy drinkers. The costs of substance abuse in terms of lost productivity, health care expenditures, and crime run into billions of dollars each year. Yet only a small percent (10.8) of those with drug- or alcohol-related problems get treatment at a specialized facility (defined as a rehabilitation or community mental health center, inpatient hospital; self-help groups are not counted in this calculation) (Substance Abuse and Mental Health Services Administration [SAMHSA], 2016). Clearly, substance abuse is an issue affecting many of the client groups, organizations, and communities that social workers work with.

The designation of substance abuse as a "problem" has less consensus than does mental illness. The line between substance use and abuse can be unclear. Alcohol, for example, is a legal substance throughout most of the United States; many people use it in moderation in their everyday lives. Marijuana, until recently classified as an illegal substance, is now available in some states for medical use in relieving the symptoms of illnesses such as AIDS, cancer, and glaucoma. In some states, it is now legal as recreational drug. Definitions of substance dependence and abuse do not always clarify the notion of harmful consequences. SAMHSA has now combined substance abuse and dependence into "substance use disorder" and defines it as ". . . recurrent use of alcohol and/or drugs [which] causes clinically and functionally significant impairment such as health problems, disability, and failure to meet major responsibilities at work, school, or home." Diagnosis is based on "evidence of impaired control, social impairment, risky use, and pharmacological criteria" (SAMHSA, 2015). But failure to fulfill major responsibilities may be due to a variety of factors, and the role of drug or alcohol use may be difficult to tease out (SAMHSA, 2015).

Although "abuse" is thus a somewhat slippery concept, we can at least define the "substances" involved in most substance abuse policies in the United States. These include illegal drugs, or those substances on a "controlled list" whose manufacture, sale, possession, or use is prohibited by law. These substances include cocaine, certain inhalants, hallucinogens, methamphetamine, and heroin. Some substances on the controlled list, such as morphine, can also be used legally by prescription. In addition to illicit drugs, *substance abuse* also refers to legal drugs, such as alcohol and tobacco. These are more loosely regulated. Although the dangers of tobacco use have been receiving more and more public attention, this chapter focuses on the use of drugs and alcohol. Substance abuse constitutes a problem on the national, state, community, organizational, family, and individual levels. Alcohol abuse kills 88,000 people a year. It costs an estimated $249 billion a year. A large portion of these costs result from the negative effects of alcohol consumption on health, but lost productivity is another important component. The picture is similar for drug abuse, although illegal use of drugs adds additional high crime costs. These include reduced earnings due to incarceration and national and state expenditures on the criminal justice system and drug interdiction. Both alcohol and drug abuse also lead to spending on various kinds of treatment (National Institute on Alcohol and Alcoholism, 2017).

Individual businesses and other organizations suffer from reduced employee productivity and from job accidents caused by inebriated or incapacitated workers. All of us, for example, have read headlines about school bus crashes that were attributed to alcohol or drug abuse by the driver. Communities, too, feel the effects of substance abuse; again, a common newspaper story is that of the neighborhood group that has finally been able to close down the crack houses in its area or to take back the local park from drug dealers. Many of the local ordinances regarding retail liquor establishments stem from community concerns about public drunkenness or the use of alcohol on Sunday.

Social workers are well aware, of course, that individuals and their families can be adversely affected by substance abuse. One concern is the effects of drugs and alcohol on the development of the fetus. Research into the impact of maternal drug use is complicated and, as yet, not entirely conclusive. On the one hand, illicit drug use during pregnancy has been associated with very low infant birth weights. It also appears that a woman's use of cocaine, particularly during the last month of pregnancy, can have some effect on the fetus. Researchers have found, for example, that "at one month of age, cocaine-exposed infants were about three times more likely to be jittery, irritable, and difficult to console than nonexposed babies." On the other hand, the 1980s myth of the inconsolable and permanently damaged "crack baby" has now largely been debunked. As researchers have examined prenatal cocaine exposure more carefully, they have found that the effects on fetuses are subtle and that poverty, poor maternal health, and the use of multiple substances by pregnant women are also important factors (Azar, 1997; Lewis, 1998; Okie, 2009; Martin, 2010). The effects of alcohol and other substances on the fetus have been more clearly demonstrated. Alcohol abuse by women who are pregnant can lead to *fetal alcohol syndrome,* which can cause mental retardation and physical defects. Women who smoke cigarettes also risk adverse effects on their infants (Crosson-Tower, 1998; MedlinePlus, 2017).

Social workers working with the families of those with substance abuse problems find that such abuse can seriously affect family functioning. For example, the children of alcoholic parents are often seen in social agencies for a variety of problems. Homelessness, domestic violence, and high-risk behavior by adolescents are among the many problems attributed in part to substance abuse within the family.

Finally, some population groups may encounter more problems related to substance abuse than others. Among people age twelve and older, rates of current illicit drug use varied greatly by major racial/ethnic groups in 2015. The national average was 10.2. The rate was highest among American Indian and Alaska Native youths (14.9 percent). The rates were 8.9 percent for Hispanics, 12.4 for African Americans, and 4.1 percent for Asians. Alcohol abuse is one of the five leading causes of death for American Indians, although this varies by tribe or community. Researchers have postulated that certain minority groups, including American Indians, may possess genetic traits that predispose them to alcoholism. However, few of these genes have yet been discovered. Whites drink more than other ethnic groups at 60.9 percent, Blacks are next at 48.3 percent, then Hispanics at 47.5 percent, Asians at 42.9 percent, and Native Americans at 41.2. In earlier surveys, Native American lead ethnic minorities (SAMHSA, 2016).

Binge drinking (five or more drinks within a few hours once a month) is more evenly distributed. Whites again lead at 26 percent, followed closely by Hispanics at 25.7 percent, Native Americans at 24.1 percent, and blacks at 23.4 percent. Asians (14 percent) are least likely to binge. Underage drinking is also a problem. Of children twelve to seventeen years old, 9.6 percent are using alcohol; 5.8 percent are bingers (SAMHSA, 2016).

Drug-related law enforcement has more serious effects for African Americans than for whites. Although African Americans constitute only 12 percent of the population, they account for 38.7 percent of all prisoners and 44.6 percent of all drug offenders. Analysts have noted the tendency in our country to exaggerate the use of drugs among minorities and to single them out for special attention. For example, when fears of a crack cocaine "epidemic" spread in the late 1980s, new laws established mandatory five-year sentences for possession of 5 grams of crack (used mostly by minorities). To receive the same penalty for powdered cocaine (used mainly by whites) required possession of 500 grams. As reporter Jonathan Alter (1999) notes, "Crack and coke are pharmacologically identical; only the delivery system (smoking versus sniffing) varies." This spiked the incarceration rate and increased racial disparities. But recently the prison population is declining with similar racial disparity; the crack generation is getting out (Alter, 1999, 2011; Goode, 2013; Grossman, Chaloupka, & Shin, 2002).

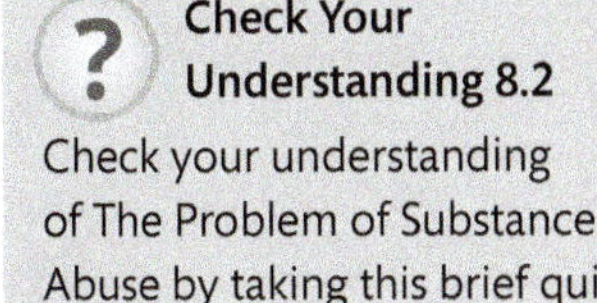
?
Check Your Understanding 8.2
Check your understanding of The Problem of Substance Abuse by taking this brief quiz.

THE HISTORY OF SUBSTANCE ABUSE POLICIES

Using the criminal justice system to deal with people who abuse drugs has a long-standing tradition in the United States, but it is just one of many responses to substance abuse in U.S. history. Interestingly, in the mid-1800s the notion of drug abuse was almost unheard of. Codeine, heroin, morphine, and similar substances appeared in such seemingly innocent concoctions as Gadway's Elixir for Infants, Dr. James's Soothing Syrup Cordial, and Victor Infant Relief. Opium was as common as aspirin is today. All were sold in nonprescription forms and advertised in family magazines. Small doses of cocaine were part of the formula of Coca-Cola until 1905. Morphine was used freely in the treatment of wounded soldiers during the Civil War. After the war, its use spread widely among civilians for pain relief and treatment of stomach ailments. Although physicians began to recognize the problem of morphine's addictive quality, there remained only minimal restrictions on its use. Warnings about the dangers of opium were similarly ignored. As long as the use of these substances was seen as medically based and confined largely to the middle and upper classes, little public concern was aroused (Davis & Stasz, 1990).

Alcohol use was also initially a common and accepted part of normal life. Drinking was a ritual in social, political, and religious occasions during the colonial period. The colonists were serious drinkers, with the average male over fifteen years old drinking about six gallons of alcohol each year. Average consumption in the 1980s, in contrast, was less than three gallons. Attitudes began to change, however, during the early years of the republic. Leaders such as Thomas Jefferson and John Adams wanted new citizens to be people of "virtue," temperate in their habits. These ideas were supported by physicians such as Dr. Benjamin Rush, who had begun to see the alcohol addiction process as "a series of moral and physically degenerative stages" (Davis & Stasz, 1990).

By 1855, the prohibition movement had become an important factor in U.S. life, and thirteen states had passed temperance laws. About a decade or so later, drug addiction also became a public concern. One of the major reasons for these shifts in attitude in the later 1800s seems to have been the changing context of alcohol and drug use. This use now appeared to many to be connected with race, class, and religion. White traders' introduction of whiskey to Native Americans, who were unaccustomed to this new substance, soon led to stereotypes of the "drunken Indian." Irish Catholics, Italians, other immigrants, and the urban poor in general were similarly criticized for heavy drinking. Middle-class Anglo-Saxon citizens used the slur of drunkenness to separate themselves from these "outside groups." Many charity workers of the times blamed "drink" as an important factor in a family's dependency on outside help (Davis & Stasz, 1990).

In the case of drugs, Chinese immigrants played a similar scapegoat role. Chinese laborers who came to the United States after the Civil War established the practice of smoking opium in the West Coast cities where they settled. First San Francisco, and then the California state legislature, passed laws against "opium dens" and imposed heavy fines or imprisonment for the smoking of opium. While medical use of opium and other drugs continued, the street use of such substances led to widespread concern similar to public reactions toward drug use today (Davis & Stasz, 1990).

The campaign against drugs, and particularly against alcohol, began to take on the form of a moral crusade. The temperance movement developed alliances with other reform groups, such as antislavery and populist organizations. Many in the first wave of feminists joined the ranks of the prohibitionists, forming the powerful Women's

Christian Temperance Union. The business community also tended to support prohibition because it had an interest in maintaining the sobriety, and hence efficiency, of workers. By 1919, the movement had achieved its goal—the outlawing by the Volstead Act of the sale, manufacture, and transportation of all alcoholic beverages. This became the Eighteenth Amendment to the Constitution.

With somewhat less fanfare, opponents of addictive drugs helped pass the Pure Food and Drug Act in 1906, which required the labeling of all medicines and other preparations containing habit-forming drugs. Eight years later, a much stronger bill was passed. The Harrison Narcotics Act mandated the registration and taxation of production and distribution of heroin, morphine, and cocaine. Although the act was meant to regulate, not prohibit, the use of these drugs, eager U.S. Treasury agents turned it into a mandate for the prohibition of all such substances. Physicians were jailed for prescribing heroin and morphine to addicts and for using these drugs to alleviate the pain of the terminally ill. Both drug and alcohol control had come under the jurisdiction of the police rather than the physician or the moral reformer (Cohen & Levy, 1992).

Prohibition, of course, was extremely difficult to enforce and brought with it the unintended consequences of increased criminal activity, gang warfare, and police corruption. The career of Chicago gangster Al Capone was greatly enhanced by selling illegal alcohol. If you want an example of unintended consequences of well-meaning social policy, think of Al. The Volstead Act was repealed in 1933. Its repeal was helped by ideological arguments regarding individualism and free choice in the drinking of alcohol, posed particularly by a new coalition of urban dwellers, ethnic Americans, and a growing middle class. Making alcohol legal would also restore huge tax revenues to the government and provide jobs for the unemployed in the midst of the Depression. With the repeal of Prohibition, breweries and distillers began their transformation into today's powerful multimillion-dollar industry. By the end of the 1930s, one historian notes, "Prohibition was seen by most as a ridiculous and costly mistake, and an unacceptable intrusion by the government into personal behavior" (Davis & Stasz, 1990; Woodiwiss, 1998).

However, support still remained for laws against drugs. The Harrison Act of 1914 had established a coercive national policy against habit-forming drugs. In 1930, the Federal Bureau of Narcotics was formed to fight the perceived "drug menace." Drug addiction began increasingly to be seen as intrinsically criminal. It also continued to carry racist overtones, as shown in attacks on marijuana use by Hispanics and African Americans (despite the fact that marijuana was also being used by whites). Between the formation of the Narcotics Bureau and the early 1960s, thousands of drug users and dealers served lengthy prison sentences. The majority of those convicted were minorities of color who were often unable to pay for lawyers who could raise constitutional rights issues such as entrapment by undercover agents and illegal search and seizure practices. Ironically, the bureau had to be replaced by a new agency in the early 1970s, as it was found to be full of agents who had taken bribes, sold confiscated drugs, and engaged in other acts of corruption (Cohen & Levy, 1992; Woodiwiss, 1998).

By the 1960s, the U.S. government had established two different policy approaches to the control of drugs: the reduction of the supply of drugs through law enforcement and the reduction of the demand for drugs through prevention and treatment. The "demand approach" was represented by the Narcotic Addict Rehabilitation Act of 1966, which allowed for the nonpunitive incarceration of addicts for purposes of treatment. But the "supply approach" was clearly paramount and remains the government's dominant drug policy today. The foundation of this approach is a network of federal and state statutes and laws that define *controlled substances* and prohibit their possession, use, manufacture, and distribution. An important example of such legislation is the federal Comprehensive Drug Abuse Prevention and Control Act of 1970, which separates drugs into five classes according to their potential for abuse, their effects, and their medical usefulness. Among drugs included in the most serious and next most serious classes (based on greatest potential for abuse and so on) are heroin, marijuana, and cocaine (Cohen & Levy, 1992; Husak, 1992).

The act also created a commission to assess patterns of marijuana use and to study its impact on public health and safety. This was in part a reaction to the fact that marijuana use was growing among young people in the 1960s and was entering the mainstream. Users were now as likely to be white as African American and to come from both middle-income and poorer families. Reacting against heavy sentences for college students charged with possession of marijuana, older adults helped create a more permissive attitude toward the use of the drug. The commission created by the 1970 act concluded that only sale, and not possession, of marijuana should be prohibited (Harrell, 1995).

The commission's recommendation met with strong resistance from President Nixon, who was elected in 1968 as a "law and order" president. During his term in office, Nixon launched a strong attack on drugs that included attempts to cut off supply by putting pressure on the major foreign producers of the U.S. supply, particularly Turkey and Mexico. The federal antidrug budget was doubled between 1970 and 1971 and doubled again in 1972. A new agency was created, the Drug Enforcement Agency, to control supply. However, Nixon also promoted drug treatment as a way of diminishing the demand for drugs. As part of this effort, in 1973 he established the National Institute on Drug Abuse (NIDA) to help fund state and local antidrug treatment and prevention programs and to carry out research on drug use. During most of the years of Nixon's presidency, more stress was put on prevention and treatment than on controlling supply, with the former approach receiving two-thirds of the federal antidrug budget. The same treatment approach characterized Nixon's establishment, in 1970, of the National Institute on Alcohol Abuse and Alcoholism (NIAAA), which was the first major federal agency established to deal with alcoholism since the repeal of Prohibition (Burke, 1992; Harrell, 1995).

Ronald Reagan reversed this emphasis. He tried to wage an all-out war on drugs in the 1980s, paradoxically at a time when drug use was actually declining in the United States. Marijuana use had fallen and cocaine use had leveled off. This war was based chiefly on law enforcement, and the proportion of the federal antidrug budget spent on prevention and treatment plummeted. It was the largest increase in drug law enforcement funding and manpower in the nation's history. Addiction as a moral failure reemerged, encapsulated in the mantra of the campaign led by Nancy Reagan: "Just say no" (Burke, 1992; Harrell, 1995).

In this war, drugs and crime were seen as intertwined enemies, with the 1984 Crime Control Act expanding the asset forfeiture laws that penalized drug traffickers, establishing mandatory sentencing guidelines for drug offenses, and increasing criminal penalties. The Defense Department and the FBI were given broad powers in the fight against drugs, and money and personnel were poured into border patrol efforts to stop drugs from crossing into the United States (Burke, 1992; Harrell, 1995).

The rise of the crack cocaine "epidemic" in the mid-1980s added further fuel to the Reagan administration's antidrug efforts. While the drop in drug use among the general population continued, crack, a cheap and highly addictive substance, recruited many new users from low-income and minority populations. This reinforced the notion that drug use was essentially a problem for lower-class, inner-city African Americans. The traditional components of the war on drugs continued also, with two more antidrug laws being enacted that added more mandatory sentence categories, expanded international drug control efforts, and created a "drug czar" in the form of a cabinet-level official in charge of national efforts to control the supply of and demand for drugs (Burke, 1992; Harrell, 1995).

Responses to the abuse of alcohol were much less dramatic in the 1980s, but important legislation was passed. In part due to lobbying by an advocacy group, Mothers Against Drunk Driving (MADD), a 1984 act required states to raise the minimum legal drinking age to twenty-one in order to qualify for federal highway transportation funds. The Reagan administration transferred much of the responsibility for drug and alcohol treatment and prevention programs to the states via block grants and decreased federal funding for these services (Burke, 1992). The amount of private insurance coverage for the treatment of addiction dropped at the same time.

President George H. W. Bush continued the Reagan approach of using law enforcement to wage the battle against drugs and of pouring billions of dollars into this effort. Yet, by the end of the 1980s, many experts had concluded that attempts to cut off supply had failed as an antidrug policy. By the early 1990s, the number of inmates in U.S. prisons reached 1 million, with drug-related convictions playing a major role in this growth. The proportion of incarcerated drug offenders who were African American grew. Efforts had been made to help drug-producing countries apprehend suppliers. Bush ordered the invasion of Panama and had its President Manuel Noriega arrested on drug charges. Bush's drug czar, William Bennett, railed against "whole cadres of social scientists, abetted by whole armies of social workers, who [feel] that the problem facing us isn't drugs at all, it's poverty, or racism." He reasserted the need for strict criminal penalties (Harrell, 1995; Human Rights Watch, 2000; Stoesz, 1996).

Approaches to combating drug abuse began to shift somewhat during the Clinton administration. Policy debate focused less on illegal drugs and more on the related problem of violent crime among juveniles. Federal drug control staff members were reduced. Stress was put on police–citizen cooperation in the areas of drug enforcement and prevention. This latter, demand-focused approach was strengthened by federal grants for the creation of drug courts under the 1994 Violent Crime Control and Law Enforcement Act. Such courts combine intensive probation, mandatory drug testing, and treatment as alternative punishment for nonviolent and first-time drug offenders. However, federal spending on drug abuse prevention and research remained less than that on antidrug law enforcement measures (Harrell, 1995; Inciardi, McBride, & Rivers, 1996; McCloy, 2001).

One of the most intriguing developments in recent years, however, may have little to do with Clinton administration policies, state drug laws, police activity, or treatment programs. This is the rather sudden drop in the number of people using crack cocaine. Although the New York City police commissioner attributed the change to the city's policy of "zero tolerance" for anyone openly using or selling drugs, almost every major U.S. city with drug problems, no matter what its policing policy, has witnessed the same decline in crack use. The decline was in the fifteen-to-twenty age group. It appears that a generational revulsion against the drug may have occurred, with crack dealers being seen by the young as "the biggest losers on the street."

But the decline in use of one type of drug does not rule out the possibility that a different drug or drugs will rise in popularity. Young people are increasingly experimenting with new "club drugs" or "designer drugs" such as Ecstasy. In addition, college students are taking prescription stimulants like Adderall and Vyvanse to help them study. These are powerful drugs (Class 2 on the Controlled Substance scale, comparable to cocaine,

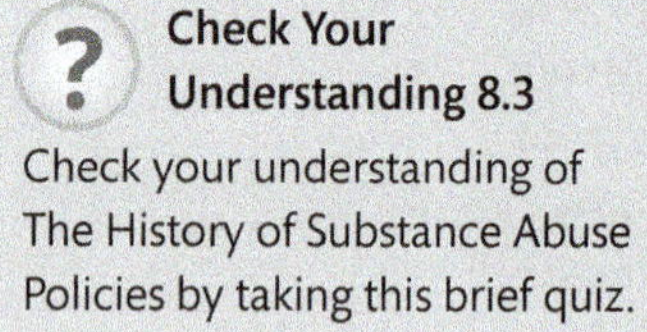
Check Your Understanding 8.3
Check your understanding of The History of Substance Abuse Policies by taking this brief quiz.

and compared with Valium, which is only Class 4). They can serve as a gateway to abuse of painkillers and sleep aids. Among teens, marijuana use has gone down. It was 11.6 percent in 2002, declined to 9.3 percent in 2008 but went back up to 10.1 percent in 2009 and has leveled off there (Egan, 1999; National Institute on Drug Abuse, 1999; Schwarz, 2012; U.S. Department of Health and Human Services, 2011).

HISTORY OF MENTAL HEALTH POLICY

Even more than with substance abuse, the driving forces of mental health policy have seesawed back and forth between individual and collective explanations and solutions. In colonial times, mental illness was both an individual responsibility and a community problem. In small communities, the person acting strangely was someone you knew, maybe even a relative. Uncle Ezra's peculiarities were less threatening because you'd lived with them all your life. "Colonial records are filled with examples of people who behaved in bizarre and disruptive ways but were allowed to move about freely and even to retain important positions of responsibility." Those whose families could not afford to care for an afflicted relative were sometimes boarded out at community expense. There were sometimes alms houses for the poor that could accommodate deviant behavior. Unfortunately, there were also jails, which might be the shelter of last resort. Residence was the key to the system. Following the Elizabethan Poor Laws, responsibility ended at the town limits; outsiders were not welcome (Gamwell & Tomes, 1995, p. 20; Rothman, 1971).

Bizarre behavior sometimes had a less benign interpretation in colonial times. If it wasn't someone you knew, and if the cause could be blamed on someone else, it might lead you to hunt for witches. Demonic possession was a theory espoused by many, including the famous Puritan minister Cotton Mather. The Salem Witch Trials of 1691 escalated from three young women presumed to be possessed to over 100 people being accused of being in league with the devil. Nineteen were executed. When those accused began to include upper-class individuals and even Mather himself, Mather decided things had gone too far (Gamwell & Tomes, 1995).

As the population grew, cities expanded, and factories were introduced, community responsibility became inadequate. States took a role, building asylums for those who could not stay with their families. They were usually outside town because it was assumed that calm, quiet surroundings would lead to a cure. By 1860, twenty-eight of the existing thirty-three states had public institutions for those with mental illnesses. However, simple isolation from the stresses of the city did not prove to be a cure, so reformers like Dorothea Dix lobbied for more scientific treatment under medical supervision (Levine, 1981; Lieby, 1978).

But cures were not found. Residency became long-term. Conditions in the institutions deteriorated as did public concern for the inhabitants. Social Darwinism was the prevailing social philosophy, which assured people that their success was due to their hard work, intelligence, and virtue. The less fortunate were lazy and less intelligent. You had no responsibility to worry about them. In this atmosphere, mental illness once again became an individual, perhaps hereditary, defect (Hofstadter, 1944).

In the first decade of the twentieth century, a new concern for those with mental illness developed. New hope for cures through psychiatry was nurtured by reformers and new appreciation for the importance of the community was discovered. The Mental Hygiene

Movement argued for outpatient treatment and aftercare programs. Social workers reinforced an environmental approach to treatment. Short-term therapy, family care, and renewed attention to "problems of living" were pushed. But they were soon overwhelmed by the inertia of the state institutions, whose populations were growing and who were sucking up the majority of the funding. They increasingly became warehouses, where treatment was rare and living conditions often unspeakable (Dain, 1980).

World War II jolted the system with the dual revelations that 12 percent of enlistees had to be rejected for psychiatric reasons and 40 percent of those who were discharged had some kind of psychiatric disability. Veterans of combat returned with what was then called "shell shock" or "battle fatigue." The National Mental Health Act of 1946 gave grants to states for treatment programs outside state hospitals and created the National Institute of Mental Health to conduct research into mental illness and to train service providers (Levine, 1981).

In the mid-1950s, psychotropic drugs became available for treating serious mental illnesses. At last, there was a solution to warehousing those with chronic diagnoses. They could be returned to the community with medication that would keep them stable and allow them, it was hoped, to get jobs and lead normal lives. A new system of community mental health centers would be created. Congress created the Joint Commission on Mental Health and Illness in 1955 that called for such a program, but implementation lagged. In 1963, President John F. Kennedy was challenged to provide matching funds to the states to provide a full range of services, including prevention (*Action for Mental Health,* 1961; Levine, 1964).

Deinstitutionalization was in full swing by the 1970s. States welcomed the opportunity to reduce their budgets and closed one hospital after another. The bright new community mental health system, however, was unprepared for the numbers that swept over them. State funding from the hospitals went to other needs and rarely followed hospital residents into the community. Some coped well and proved that those who charged that institutionalization itself promoted crazy behavior were right. Others coped less well, could not hold jobs for long, and were soon homeless. Many stopped taking their medication (Castellani, 2005; Torrey, 1997).

President Ronald Reagan's Omnibus Budget Act of 1981 ended federal funding for community mental health and gave states block grants to do what they wanted with social services and mental health programs. Since this carried less money than states had been receiving, further cuts were inevitable (Braddock, 1987; Tessler & Goldman, 1982).

The Americans with Disabilities Act was passed in 1990 under President George H. W. Bush. It outlawed job discrimination based on physical or mental disabilities. Employers are required to provide "reasonable accommodations" so that a worker can get to the worksite and do the job, assuming that the worker is otherwise capable of performing the essential functions of the job and that the disabilities are marginal to this. In the case of mental illness, this is most likely to apply to simply denial of a job application based on admission of a history of illness. It cannot be automatically assumed that someone can't do the job. The person has to have a chance to demonstrate that she or he can. What a reasonable accommodation might be is easier to see with physical disabilities than with mental disabilities. It might be a flexible work schedule that allows time to meet medical appointments or having regular feedback on job performance (Pardeck, 1998; U.S. Equal Employment Opportunities Commission, 2002).

Mental illness was confirmed as appropriate in the ADA by the Supreme Court in 1999, and specific diagnoses are listed in the ADA's *Questions and Answers*. Under George W. Bush, the act was amended in 2008 (*American with Disabilities Act: Questions and Answers*).

Parity, the equal insurance coverage of mental and physical conditions, has been sought by mental health advocates since 1950. In 1996, Congress finally passed a parity law, sponsored by Republican Senator Pete Domenici (New Mexico) and Independent Senator Paul Wellstone (Minnesota). Increased receptivity for such legislation stemmed partly from revelations by Domenici, Senator Phil Gramm (Texas), and other public figures about the impact of mental illness on their own families. Opposition to the bill from insurers and employers led to its limited scope; the measure applies only to equality of lifetime and annual dollar limits for mental and physical health insurance coverage. It does not require parity in co-payments and deductibles and does not prohibit limits on the number of mental health treatment sessions or psychiatric hospital days. Smaller companies are exempted, and the provision does not apply if employers choose not to offer any mental health coverage at all (Frank, Koyanagi, & McGuire, 1997).

In 2008, a new bill, named after Domenici and Wellstone, who died in a 2002 plane crash, was passed. It closed some of the loopholes in the 1996 law by requiring parity in deductibles, co-payments, and out-of-pocket expenses and in setting treatment limits. It was sponsored in the House of Representatives by Republican Jim Ramsted (Minnesota), a recovering alcoholic, and Democrat Patrick Kennedy (Rhode Island), who has been treated for depression and drug dependence. Kennedy called it "one more step in a long civil rights struggle to ensure that all Americans have the opportunity to reach their potential" (Editorial, 2008; Pace, 2009; Pear, 2008).

The 2008 act had its problems. It applied only to employers with 50 or more workers. And it did not mandate universal psychiatric benefits, so there were still disparities between psychiatric and nonpsychiatric treatments. The Patient Protection and Affordable Care Act of 2010 is finally filling the gaps. Outlawing denial of coverage for preexisting conditions is vitally important because most mental illnesses are of long duration. Half of the major diagnoses start by age 14 and three-fourths are present by age 25. The provision that children can stay on their parents' policies until age 26 is also a help. The Affordable Care Act treats psychiatric illness like any other; fair and rational treatment is now possible. These features remain popular even among those who want to repeal the ACA (Friedman, 2012).

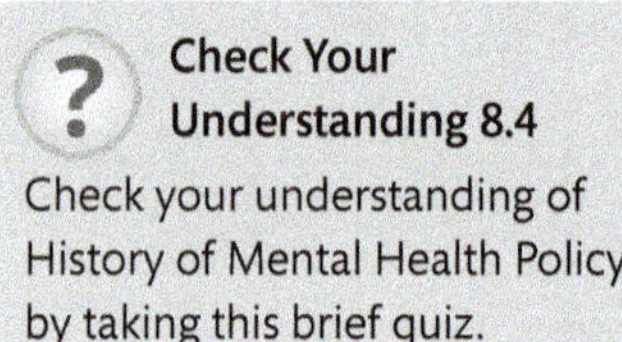

Check Your Understanding 8.4
Check your understanding of History of Mental Health Policy by taking this brief quiz.

SOCIAL ANALYSIS

Mental Health

Various values and assumptions support efforts to offer treatment to individuals with emotional problems. Humanistic motives compel us to want to help those in difficulty, especially when the problem does not seem to be their fault. Whereas mental illness was once seen as the result of immorality or possession by demons, we have come to view it either as a disease or as a set of reactions to "problems in living." The disease, or medical, model of mental illness is the more prevalent one in our society. It carries with it the assumption that psychological problems are a type of illness amenable to treatment by a psychiatrist or other highly trained mental health professional. Treatment can be on an outpatient basis or in a hospital. Medication is often part of the therapist's armament. Recently, those following a disease model have focused on genetic factors and the functioning of biological mechanisms in the brain.

The "problems in living" approach is part of what fuels a community mental health model of psychological problems. This model sees psychological difficulties in their broader social and economic context. It stresses interventions in people's environment in order to prevent or at least alleviate mental illness. This approach owes much to the 1961 book published by psychiatrist Thomas Szasz titled *The Myth of Mental Illness*. Szasz argued that the behaviors that brought psychiatric diagnoses were not a product of disease but were caused by the inability to understand or handle the pain caused by such things as grief; job loss; political oppression; poverty; or toxic relationships with marital partners, friends, or family. A psychiatric diagnosis deprived a person of power and freedom, and also of personal responsibility (Szasz, 1974). This helped spawn a patient advocacy movement in the 1960s. It also called attention to the tendency of psychiatry to categorize all sorts of normal behaviors as diseases. For example, shyness could be seen as a disease called "social anxiety disorder."

Private service providers tend to emphasize the medical model, perhaps because the image of the highly trained therapist dealing out specialized treatments is a more credible and concrete one to sell to customers. Public agencies that work with people who have more apparent economic and social stresses are gaining an appreciation of the importance of community-based and preventative services, even though this approach necessitates changes in the ways they have traditionally operated. Both areas have encouraged greater reliance on outpatient treatment than on hospitalization, in part for therapeutic reasons, in part because outpatient treatment is less expensive.

Another set of values and assumptions in play here is the belief in the ability of market forces to solve both economic and social problems and the concomitant suspicion of government's ability to do so. Large-scale health reform proposals, which will be discussed in the next chapter, usually combine elements of government and private intervention, but are often seen by many as relying too heavily on "big government." This creates a highly favorable environment for entrepreneurial agencies that offer to prove the ability of private enterprise to grapple with the enormous problem of health costs in the United States.

Substance Abuse

A particularly important factor in studying alcohol and drug abuse policy is an understanding of the conflicting values surrounding the use of these substances. One basic differentiation is between a view of the use (and particularly "misuse") of drugs and alcohol as criminal behavior and/or as a moral failing, and a view of it as some type of illness or the outcome of certain environmental circumstances. Responses based on the first view include moral campaigns against substance abuse and the imprisonment of those who use or deal drugs. Responses consistent with the second view lead to therapeutic interventions and community development programs.

Another polarity in thinking about substance abuse is the contrast between the libertarian view that such behavior is a matter of individual right and the opposing view that it is the responsibility of the government to protect citizens from the threats to health and safety posed by drug and alcohol use. Libertarian policies might include free drug markets and the acceptance of recreational use of substances as long as such use does not harm others. Those who believe in government responsibility to prevent the misuse of drugs and alcohol would support controls ranging from incarceration of offenders to deterrence through law enforcement and rehabilitation (Harrell, 1995).

Substance abuse brings in a third set of assumptions. Abuse may be a disease, or the result of problems in living. It can also be seen as a moral failing or personal weakness.

As such, it is the responsibility of the individual to decide to take control of his or her life. This might involve enrolling in a self-help group like Alcoholics Anonymous for social support, but if abuse is a moral failing, public policy can have limited effect.

There are important gaps in our understanding of the causes and patterns of drug and alcohol use. Some scientists link drug addiction to effects on brain processes. Some researchers who study alcoholism have systematically investigated whether there is a genetic component to the phenomenon. Yet both these approaches are still in fairly early stages, with hypotheses not fully confirmed. Similarly, research into the effects of treatment and prevention programs has had uneven success. Many evaluations of specific programs or interventions have not used good experimental designs or representative samples. Costs of these programs and possible unintended consequences have not always been examined and reported. Prevention programs are particularly difficult to assess because it is hard to isolate the specific factors at work (Bride & Nackerud, 2002; Harrell, 1995; National Institute on Alcohol Abuse and Alcoholism, 1995; Young, 1994).

However, progress is being made in some areas of treatment, prevention, and policy evaluation. Interdiction and crop eradication do not reduce the availability of drugs substantially. On the other hand, random drug testing has reduced drug use in the armed forces. Drug prevention programs that utilize community involvement, a focus on the family, comprehensive services, and appealing activities as an alternative to drugs have been found to be more effective than prevention programs that focus on only one of these factors. Most studies examining the effects of state legislation raising the minimum legal driving age have concluded that these laws lead to declines in teenage night fatal crashes, which are those most likely to involve alcohol (Harrell, 1995).

One thing that the standard study of abuse—the U.S. government's National Survey on Drug Abuse and Health—fails to show is the extent of substance abuse among homeless, institutionalized, and other populations who are not included in their sample. Estimating substance abuse among homeless people is difficult because they are hard to survey. Surveys in shelters miss those who live on the streets, and the groups may differ. NAMI estimates that 20 percent of homeless people living in shelters have serious mental illness, and if you add substance abuse, the number comes to 46 percent (NAMI, 2015).

As we noted earlier in this chapter, large numbers of people have difficulties with drugs and alcohol. Although the media and law enforcement activities often focus on minorities, substance abuse is found among people of all ethnic and racial backgrounds. Sociologists noticed long ago that culture had an effect on abuse. It was not a problem for Italian Americans because drinking took place in homes as part of normal family life. For Irish Americans, drinking was a male activity, usually took place outside the home, and was seen as a way to escape or sublimate sexual and emotional problems. This led more easily to abuse.

This ethnic contrast is revealing, but we need a larger context for understanding drug use. More recently sociologists see it as a combination of individual choices and social pressures. This intersection helps explain who decides to use drugs and who doesn't. Contrary to popular perceptions, social factors can help control use and allow users to continue to function in normal ways and "take care of business." A drug subculture that provides norms, attitudes, and behaviors for control can guide this evolution. It can become a stable "life structure." But if the life structure is uprooted, the user can lose control, and use can escalate to the point of destruction. Some users, however, actually quit on their own, a "natural recovery." This also goes against conventional understanding. Hence, we must discover and reinforce the social structures that make this possible (Bennett & Golub, 2012; Golub, Bennett, & Eliott, 2015).

Golub et al. (2015) believe we are in the midst of a "pharmacological revolution" where we are confronted by an increasing variety of drugs with an increasing variety of appeals. They identify five reasons for taking drugs: (1) recreation, (2) finding meaning, (3) medication/self-medication, (4) cosmetic alteration, and (5) performance enhancement. Some are more integrated into the mainstream culture than others, but all have potential for abuse. Most important, all may be controlled if we know how to construct social structures or subcultures that can do it.

Check Your Understanding 8.5

Check your understanding of Social Analysis by taking this brief quiz.

POLITICAL ANALYSIS

Mental Health

The list of stakeholders in mental health policy is lengthy, including clients, employers, state health officials, providers, federal and state legislators and other government leaders, advocacy groups, and the broader public. This section provides a brief overview of the major players and their points of view.

Clients and their families are at the receiving end of mental health care. They want effective and accessible help, and most would like some control over the type of assistance they get and the way it is delivered. Some are the people who provide the horror stories to newspapers and magazines: "After my allotted sessions were over, I could only see a psychiatrist fifteen minutes every three months to have my depression medication checked." Some may be concerned about confidentiality issues that arise when details of their problems are discussed between their therapist and an unknown gatekeeper. Others are largely satisfied with their care.

Most mental health consumers are not organized with other clients or families to advocate for good treatment, although some have joined the ranks of client groups or organizations for family members, such as the National Association for the Mentally Ill. Many clients have access to at least a rudimentary grievance procedure in the agency that provides care, and others have gone further and pursued lawsuits.

Employers and state health administrators are at the center of the system. The current rise in insurance premiums is a problem for businesses, which will pass along a proportion of the increase to their employees. State Medicaid and mental health officials, who are more publicly accountable and whose health care planning decisions are more visible, are particularly likely to address concerns about quality of care, in addition to cost issues.

"Mental health providers" sounds like a unified group but actually encompasses a number of professions. Although the public often thinks of psychiatry as the major source of mental health practitioners, social workers actually dominate the field numerically: 60 percent of mental health professionals are clinically trained social workers. (This number comes from a 2017 press report, though the data may be from much earlier.) The University of Southern California states that mental health is one of the top five most popular careers, and jobs may increase 20 percent through 2018. Other professionals include psychiatrists, psychologists, psychiatric nurses, and counselors (Whitaker & Arrington, 2008; NASW, 2017; MSW@USC Staff, 2016).

Physicians in general have been powerful stakeholders in health issues, with their major organization, the American Medical Association (AMA), often exerting enormous influence over health policy through lobbying activities. Managed care organizations (MCOs), followed by accountable care organizations (ACOs), both of which are discussed in the next chapter, have emerged as a counterbalance to this power, subjecting managed care doctors' decisions to external review by gatekeepers and becoming a force in determining their incomes (often reducing them) (Hagland, 1999; Hilzenrath, 1997; Steinhauer, 1999).

Legislators, governors, presidents, and presidential candidates also have a large investment in the development of health care policies such as managed care. They must respond to the conflicting demands of powerful, well-organized stakeholders, such as employers and physicians. They are sensitive to the voters' call to keep down taxes and to make health care affordable. Legislators, public officials, insurance companies, and hospital administrators must also respond to the pressures of health care advocacy groups. Many such groups have taken an interest in mental health managed care. They include the National Association of Mental Health, a large and well-established organization that lobbies for increased funding for mental health programs and effective treatment for those with mental illness; the National Alliance for the Mentally Ill, a group composed of the families and friends of the mentally ill; the Bazelon Center for Mental Health Law, the leading national legal advocate for people with emotional problems; children's advocacy organizations such as the Federation of Families for Children's Mental Health; and client support and advocacy groups such as the National Mental Health Consumers' Self-Help Clearinghouse. Many national advocacy organizations have state branches that lobby for effective public-managed mental health programs. In addition, professional associations, such as nurses' groups and the National Association of Social Workers, advocate regarding both client and provider issues (Campbell, 1998).

Mental health advocacy reflects the strong commitment that clients should receive adequate services from an accountable managed care entity. Advocates urge a number of improvements, changes, and protections, including effective grievance and appeal procedures; coverage of a full array of treatments and interventions, including community-based services such as housing programs and vocational training; greater use of outcome measures; parity or equality of insurance benefits for those with physical and for those with mental illness; and adequate attention to the needs of those with severe and chronic mental illness.

Substance Abuse

As in other policy areas, there is a long list of stakeholders involved in substance abuse issues. These include self-help groups such as Alcoholics Anonymous (AA), with its related groups for teens and for the families of those with drinking problems, and Narcotics Anonymous (NA). AA was founded in 1935 by two former alcoholics; currently the organization has approximately 2 million members in 150 countries. The only requirement for membership is a desire to stop drinking. Members meet regularly to share their experiences with alcoholism and to learn to follow AA's famous Twelve Step Program, which includes admitting their powerlessness over alcohol and the need to turn to a Higher Power for help in overcoming alcoholism (Alcoholics Anonymous, 1999). There are also citizens' organizations, such as Mothers Against Drunk Driving (MADD), which may constitute powerful lobbying bodies.

People who abuse alcohol and drugs, and the families of these individuals, are obvious stakeholders in substance abuse policies. Minority groups, as we have observed, are particularly vulnerable because they often have specific alcohol and drug concerns related to stigma and to interactions with the law enforcement and legal systems. Generally, however, neither those who abuse substances nor their families are organized into groups that could affect the development of legislative, legal, or treatment responses.

Professionals and direct-care staff members are another group of stakeholders. Although a relatively small percentage of social workers currently work directly in the substance abuse area (4 percent in 2007), social workers do play important roles in the field. They function as case managers, counselors, administrators of substance abuse treatment programs, and policymakers. In addition, problems with drug and alcohol affect many clients and families with whom social workers work. A survey of members of the National Association of Social Workers (NASW) found that 71 percent of those sampled had been involved with clients who had substances abuse problems in the previous year. These problems must often be addressed directly. In recognition of the growing importance of the field, and in response to membership interest, the NASW is now offering a specialist credential in substance abuse (O'Neill, 2001; "Specialist Credentials Are Readied," 1999; Whitaker & Arrington, 2008).

The impetus for the new credential stemmed also from the profession's desire to enhance acceptance of social workers' competence in a multidisciplinary field that includes medical doctors, psychiatrists, psychologists (who have developed their own substance abuse certification), and drug or alcohol counselors, a number of whom are former substance abusers. These counselors have their own credentialing process, and there can be tension between them and psychiatrists, social workers, and others in the field. Those counselors with personal experience with abuse often argue that they alone can truly understand the situation of the addict or alcoholic, whereas the traditional professionals stress the importance of their advanced training and their greater ability to be objective about the client's problems. Because of the pervasive stigma against substance abuse in our society, some of these professionals may have difficulty working with counselors who have had substance abuse problems (Cohen & Levy, 1992; Narcotics Anonymous, 2000).

Many groups within the legal and law enforcement systems are also stakeholders. These include city and state police, county sheriffs, federal narcotics agents, lawyers, judges, and the U.S. Surgeon General. The U.S. Defense Department and the Bureau of Alcohol, Tobacco, and Firearms both play a role in dealing with drug traffickers. These are just two of the over forty federal agencies, offices, and programs involved directly in substance abuse work (Harrell, 1995). Public officials and politicians on the city, state, and national levels also weigh in with their own approaches to substance abuse policy.

Groups with a strong financial interest in the consumption of drugs and alcohol don't necessarily come to mind immediately as major stakeholders, but they are indeed. Lobbyists for the multibillion-dollar alcoholic beverage industry seek to protect it from government regulation and higher taxes on its products. The industry actively promotes its products in stores, on billboards, and in the print and broadcast media. This use of advertising helps make the advertising industry another player in our field of interest groups. Public health advocates are a counter-interest group, pointing out the dangers of alcohol and criticizing the advertising business for its tendency to glamorize drinking, encourage the heavy consumption of alcohol, and target vulnerable groups.

Companies and farms that produce drugs, and the traffickers and dealers who deliver and sell them, are in a somewhat different position as stakeholders. Their activities are defined as illegal, and thus they cannot openly lobby politicians and officials.

Yet they can sometimes exert a strong force under the table through bribery and extortion, and they can also fight back against those waging the war on drugs with physical force.

Finally, average citizens and taxpayers often play a major role in substance abuse policy. When public concern about abuse has been aroused, votes increase for "tough on crime and drugs" politicians, including presidential candidates. Public opinion polls regarding alcohol and drugs can influence policymakers at all levels.

It is important to recall the larger context in which all these stakeholder negotiations take place. When the use of alcohol and drugs can be seen as widespread across the various sectors of society, prohibition and government regulation become far less serious concerns. However, once drug and alcohol use is consistently identified with groups "outside the mainstream"—minority groups, "wild youth," or the homeless—the public becomes aroused to "do something about the problem" and to wage war on substance use and abuse through legal and other actions.

Drug Testing

We consider this a political issue because it stems from the belief that undeserving people take advantage of the welfare system. Those who are hostile to public assistance in general are likely to suspect that welfare recipients are often drug users. They don't want public money wasted on them. Getting tough on drug addicts and/or welfare cheaters is a common campaign platform. Also, it has little to do with evidence of actual drug use.

Of particular concern to us is the phenomenon of drug testing among groups that are essentially "captive audiences," such as people receiving welfare. St. John's County, Florida, was one of the first local governments to require such testing. In 1996, local officials ordered that anyone applying for county assistance for certain types of medical care must first submit to a urine test for illegal drug use. Those failing the test would be denied medical services. The new policy was in part an attempt to control costs, in part an effort to promote "personal responsibility" on the part of people receiving public aid. A federal court ruled in April 2012 that Florida governor Rick Scott's law requiring random testing of state employees was unconstitutional. Florida's testing of welfare recipients has been halted pending similar judicial review. Critics noted that Scott had a multimillion-dollar stake in a company selling drug tests (Booth, 1996; Sulzburger, 2010).

Maryland was the first state to propose mandatory drug tests for all Aid to Families with Dependent Children (AFDC) applicants, a policy option approved in the Clinton administration's welfare reform act of 1996. In December of that year, a legislative committee of the Maryland General Assembly endorsed a drug testing policy in which an applicant who refused to take the test would be denied all cash benefits. Those for whom the test showed evidence of drug use would have to complete a state-paid treatment program; failure to enter or complete the program would lead to a reduction in the family's payments. Supporters of the proposal argued that it would strengthen families "by ensuring that cash benefits are spent on needy children, not on their parents' drug habits" (Jeter, 1996).

Other states have initiated similar policies. The Louisiana legislature passed a law in 1997 requiring drug screening, testing, education, and rehabilitation for all welfare recipients. Interestingly, this law was part of a larger package that required drug testing of state employees, elected officials, and college students on state scholarships. This initiative was described as part of "a drive to root out drug abuse by people who benefit from taxpayer money" (Anderson, 1998; Associated Press, 2003; Booth, 1996; Meyers & Redmond, 1998).

Clearly, one assumption behind such policies is that a good number of welfare applicants and recipients abuse drugs. Yet, as our policy analysis framework asks, what do we actually know about this phenomenon? Maryland budget analysts estimated that 10 percent of welfare clients abused drugs and would need treatment; the chair of the legislative committee proposing testing put the figure at 16 percent. South Carolina welfare officials weighed in with a 12 to 15 percent estimate for recipients in their state. However, in the first year of the mandated drug screening program for welfare clients in Louisiana, only 2 percent were identified as drug users. A Chicago program that tested applicants for child welfare jobs in 2008 also had only a 2 percent positive rate. A Michigan program, adopted in 1999 and in force for five weeks before it was halted by a court challenge, found 8 percent testing positive, however, all but three were for marijuana. Quest Diagnostics, a company that performed 9 million workplace drug tests in 2006, found 3.8 percent positive results. It should be remembered at this point that drug tests, being one-time events, indicate only drug use, not abuse or addiction. This suggests that the assumption that drug addiction, or even drug use, is common among welfare recipients is based more on prejudice than research (Coates, 1999; Cox, 2007). Interestingly, the actual economics of drug testing may be the most potent factor in limiting its use. Simply put, drug testing on a large scale is expensive. Michigan's program costs $7 million. Chicago stopped its testing, which costs $23.50 per person, for budget reasons. The more accurate and complete the test, the more it costs. In the case of Maryland's policy, state budget analysts predicted it would cost $1.2 million annually to test all welfare applicants. Outside experts calculated an even higher sum, adding that because the tests related to a public benefit, extra precautions would have to be taken to confirm their validity and protect against legal challenges. In addition, money would have to be put into increased treatment services, which one state senator estimated at $10 million a year. Less than two months after the proposal was made, the Maryland legislature dropped the testing plan, opting instead for in-depth interviews, conducted by professionals, to detect chronic drug addiction (Jeter, 1996, 1997; Singer, 2011).

Lack of evidence of significant drug use among welfare recipients has not bothered advocates of these laws. Arizona, Kansas, Mississippi, Missouri, Oklahoma, Tennessee, and Utah found, at a cost of $1 million, lower rates among welfare recipients than in the general population. Yet Montana, Wyoming, and Texas proposed new bills in 2015. Wisconsin governor Scott Walker also wanted to test applicants for food stamps and unemployment. He succeeded. He is now proposing the testing of Medicaid recipients as part of the Republican replacement of the ACA. In 2017 congressional Republicans proposed drug testing for applicants for unemployment. This prompted congressional representative Gwen Moore (D-WI) to reintroduce her "Top 1 Percent Accountability Act" (Covert & Israel, 2015; Nelson, 2017), which calls for drug testing of people who claimed more than $150,000 in itemized tax deductions.

Check Your Understanding 8.6
Check your understanding of Political Analysis by taking this brief quiz.

ECONOMIC ANALYSIS

Mental Health

The economic aspects of mental health and illness are hard to separate from the larger issues of health policy. Therefore, we will put off this discussion until the next chapter.

Substance Abuse

As we noted earlier, there is a definite economic aspect to substance abuse. In addition to calculating the financial costs of abuse to individuals, families, businesses, and the country as a whole, any analysis of economic issues related to abuse must also examine the economic role of large liquor producers and distributors; advertising companies; and, on the drug side, distributors and individual dealers. Although the profits of producers and dealers in the drug market may be hard to estimate, those of the alcohol industry are a matter of public record. The sale of alcoholic beverages is big business in the United States, bringing in $219.8 billion in 2016 ("Facts on the Alcoholic Beverage Industry," 2016). Moreover, this is a fairly concentrated industry, with three producers dominating the beer market (InBev/Anheuser-Busch, Miller Brewing, and Molson Coors) and five companies commanding most of the hard liquor market.

A growing national movement toward moderation in the use of alcohol has led to slower growth in company profits; to counteract this, alcohol producers have sought new consumers through expansion into international markets and the development of new products. New and old products need advertising, itself a lucrative business. Critics have assailed the use, as well as the specific placement, of advertisements for beer, wine, and liquor. Their targets have included billboards promoting cheap liquor in low-income minority neighborhoods and television beer commercials aired when young children might be watching. One study found that children who were more aware of such advertisements "held more favorable beliefs about drinking and intended to drink more frequently as adults" ("Alcoholic Beverages and Tobacco," 2008; Grube & Wallack, 1994; Saunders, 1995).

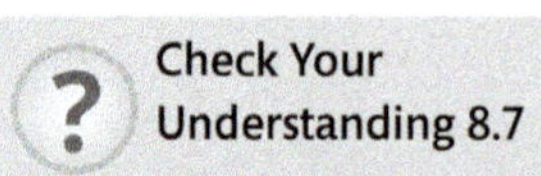

Check your understanding of Economic Analysis by taking this brief quiz.

SEPARATION OF TREATMENT FOR THOSE WITH MENTAL HEALTH AND SUBSTANCE ABUSE

So far, we have been following mental illness and substance abuse on parallel tracks. Here is a place where they come together, or should. The combination of substance abuse and mental illness is not at all unusual, and a number of clinicians argue that the most effective way to deal with the situation is to tackle both issues at once in a program specifically tailored for what is often called "dual diagnosis." Yet only recently have the barriers against coordinated treatment of the dually diagnosed begun to fall.

Concurrence of substance abuse and mental health problems (sometimes called *comorbidity*) is far more prevalent than most people, including many health and human services professionals, realize. According to the 2011 National Survey on Drug Use and Health, people with a mental illness were more than twice as likely to use illicit drugs as those without: 25.2 percent versus 11.8 percent. And they are more likely to abuse drugs: 17.5 percent versus 5.8. Of those with a serious mental illness, 31.5 percent are illicit drug users. In the 18 to 25 age group, 36.8 are drug abusers. Alcohol abuse is also found in 17.5 percent of those with a serious mental illness. Conversely, of drug abusers, 42.3 had a mental illness.

Within the phenomenon of dual diagnosis, certain combinations of disorders are particularly strong. The co-occurrence of bipolar (manic-depressive) disorders and addictive disorders is especially high; schizophrenia is also high in co-occurrence. About 30 to 60 percent of those with alcoholism also suffer from clinical depression.

Conduct disorders, such as aggressive behavior, frequently accompany alcoholism in men (Leukefeld & Walker, 1998; Zimberg, 1993).

As you read these figures, you may be wondering what coexistence actually means and how it comes about. For example, is depression a cause of alcoholism, which occurs when depressed people drink to make themselves feel better? (Researchers give this a fancy name: *self-medication.*) Or can drug or alcohol abuse produce the kinds of delusions that characterize schizophrenia? Sorting out issues of "which came first" and whether one condition can mimic the symptoms of another has indeed been a problem in defining the phenomenon of dual diagnosis. Many of those who study this condition have come to the conclusion that while reactions to drugs or alcohol can produce symptoms similar to those of mental illness, the presence of two distinct disorders at the same time can also occur. This might simply take place simultaneously with no interdependence between the two conditions, or substance abuse and mental disorders might stem from common biological vulnerabilities, or one condition might be accentuated or aggravated by the other. Finally, some practitioners and program planners argue that regardless of the debates about the causes of the dual-diagnosis phenomenon, real-life clients are suffering from the condition and need to be helped (Ciolino, 1991; Leukefeld & Walker, 1998; Zimberg, 1993).

Although treating dually diagnosed clients in programs specifically designed to deal with their problems sounds sensible, it has been met with great resistance from professionals and policymakers in both the mental health and substance abuse arenas. One problem on the mental health side has been the negative attitudes of some clinicians toward people who abuse substances, and their pessimistic assessments of the effectiveness of treatment for addiction. In the 1940s and 1950s, psychiatrists treated alcoholism with psychoanalysis; when this failed, they often concluded that alcoholism was not treatable with psychodynamic approaches. At the same time, AA members and others in the substance abuse field developed a critical attitude toward psychiatrists and psychotherapy (Zimberg, 1993).

Negative feelings between these two sets of stakeholders have contributed to and been reinforced by organizational and economic arrangements in the fields of mental health, drug addiction, and alcohol abuse at the federal level. When the National Institute on Alcohol Abuse and Alcoholism was created, it was housed in the National Institute for Mental Health. However, in 1973, the two federal agencies were separated, and the National Institute on Drug Abuse was developed as a third distinct entity. Each had its own funding stream and particular set of missions. The federal divisions have generally been mirrored in state-level agencies.

Fortunately, the policy of using separate treatment facilities or of ignoring one condition entirely has begun to change. An apparent increase in the number of people with dual disorders has helped, along with research indicating both the high prevalence of dual diagnoses and the lack of expertise in managing these situations. In addition, the psychiatric profession has begun to accept the role that it can play in addictive disorders, as shown, for example, in the recent creation of a subspeciality of addiction psychiatry. On the federal level, substance abuse and mental health services have been combined under the Substance Abuse and Mental Health Services Administration (SAMHSA). Finally, treatment programs that focus on those with mental health and substance abuse disorders have begun to develop. The availability of appropriate services for dually diagnosed adolescents, for example, has increased significantly (Pagliaro & Pagliaro, 1996; Zimberg, 1993).

Check Your Understanding 8.8

Check your understanding of Separation of Treatment for Those with Mental Health and Substance Abuse by taking this brief quiz.

The new treatment programs generally begin with detoxification in order for clinicians to get a clearer picture of what is occurring. Yet this is seen as part of a more comprehensive therapeutic approach, generally coordinated by a multidisciplinary team experienced in both mental health and substance abuse treatment. Although the methods of dealing with one disorder may conflict with those used in the other (for example, schizophrenic individuals often have great difficulty interacting with people in group settings, such as AA meetings), the new treatment teams are developing appropriate adaptations for work with the dually diagnosed population (Gold & Slaby, 1991; Kirk & Kutchins, 1997).

EMERGING POLICY ISSUES

Diagnostic and Statistical Manual of Mental Disorders-5 (DSM5)

The *DSM,* published by the American Psychiatric Association, has been around since 1952. The fifth edition came out in March 2013. Its purpose is to help psychiatrists diagnose psychological problems. It has become a policy tool because a recognized diagnosis is necessary for getting approval for third-party payments, like those from insurance companies or Medicaid. The assumption is that psychiatric conditions are defined by a group of symptoms. The problem is that so far there is not much scientific explanation for what causes the symptom. Even worse, symptoms may not lead to reliable diagnoses. Two doctors may come to different diagnostic conclusions observing the same symptoms. This was demonstrated in the APA's field trials in 2011. Even Major Depressive Disorder and Generalized Anxiety Disorder, which one critic calls the "Dodge Dart and Ford Falcon of the *DSM*" came out with low reliability scores (Tavris, 2013).

Another problem is that the manual makes a lot of everyday behaviors into possible diseases. Grieving for a lost loved one longer than two weeks can be diagnosed as clinical depression. There is also "disruptive mood dysregulation disorder" to apply to teenagers who are a persistent pain in the neck. Some of you might be suffering right now from "caffeine intoxication" as you struggle to stay awake while reading this text. (We hope not!) You can imagine what a boon this is to the pharmaceutical companies. Look at all the television and magazine ads (Friedman, 2013).

The National Institute of Mental Health is responding to the challenge of basing diagnoses on biology and neuroscience. They hope to find the genetic markers, brain circuits, chemical imbalances, and neurotransmitters behind the symptoms. Their goal is to produce this by 2020. In the meantime, defenders of the *DSM* say that it continues to give a common language to clinicians. You don't have to know the neurobiology behind mental illness in order to treat it (McHugh, 2013).

Autism and Vaccination

Having a child with autism is agonizing and often exhausting for parents. The range of functioning is amazingly broad; some autistic kids go on to college, others barely speak. A clue to this variability is in the diagnostic label itself, which is not "autism," but rather "autism spectrum disorder." Treatments and therapies also vary widely; some may be effective with some children, but not others, and are usually very expensive. Theories of causation are equally diverse. In the 1950s, "refrigerator moms"—cold and uncaring parents—were blamed. More recent research is investigating potential genetic influences.

A whole social movement has coalesced around the theory that vaccinations are the cause of autism. Some researchers suggest that the higher autism rate in the Pacific Northwest might indicate that wet weather is to blame (Kalb, 2008; Waldman, Nicholson, Adilov, & Williams, 2008).

One important policy issue is the extent to which public schools are obligated to deal with autism. The Individuals with Disabilities Education Act of 1997 requires free and "appropriate" education for students with disabilities up to age twenty-two. But schools that are closing sports and arts programs to meet draconian budget cuts are not likely to be able to offer anything nearing appropriateness, assuming that they know what "appropriate" is. Private tuition and therapy can cost $60,000 per student per year. Some parents are suing for reimbursement of such fees. Even students who make it to college, some of whom are exceptionally bright, find they need some special supports. A private program called College Living Experience offers tutoring, financial counseling, social events, and even help with shopping and cooking. It costs $35,000 a year. County school systems in Maryland are now providing such transition services for their students going to college. As more parents press legal demands for these services or reimbursement for their costs, and as public budgets continue to evaporate, there may be a special education train wreck in our future (Minaya, 2007; Schemo & Medina, 2007).

Perhaps the most interesting policy debate on autism is its relationship to vaccinations. Despite many studies showing that there is no link between autism and vaccinations, some parents remain convinced that vaccinations cause autism. Hollywood celebrities like Jim Carrey and Jenny McCarthy have entered the debate. The case of 9-year-old Hannah Poling energized the crusade, after the federal government conceded that a vaccination may have caused Hannah's autism. Tests, performed by her own father, showed that she had a preexisting mitochondrial disorder, which could have been aggravated by the shots and then developed into autism. The condition is extremely rare, and the Center for Disease Control and Prevention stated that the case "made absolutely no case that vaccines are a cause of autism." One theory is that a preservative used in vaccines, thimerosal, is the agent responsible. But thimerosal was removed from childhood vaccines in 2001, and the incidence of autism has not declined. The American Academy of Pediatrics issued a 21-page report of studies on the relationship of vaccines to autism up to 2013 showing no association (American Academy of Pediatrics, 2016). None of this has calmed the anti-vaccine activists.

The controversy was dramatically inflamed in 1998 when Andrew Wakefield, a British physician, published an article in a prestigious journal, *The Lancet,* claiming to have found in a study of twelve children that they had contracted autism as a result of vaccination. Subsequent investigation uncovered that he manipulated the data and had taken a large amount of money from interests who had an alternative vaccine to market if the standard one could be discredited. *Lancet* retracted the article, *The British Medical Journal (BMJ)* declared it fraudulent, and the UK General Medical Council withdrew Wakefield's license to practice medicine. But by this time, considerable damage had been done. Enough parents stopped vaccinating their children that rates of disease rose and children died. Not only are infants who have not been vaccinated at risk, but adults with weakened immune systems may also be infected. An author in the *Annals of Pharmacology* called it the "most damaging medical hoax of the last hundred years" (Allday, 2013; Flaherty, 2011; Poland & Jacobson, 2011; Mnookin, 2011; Winsten & Serazin, 2013).

The debate is not always civil. A pediatrician and vaccine researcher who has written a book summarizing the scientific evidence for vaccines and questioning purported cures for autism has received death threats. Autism affects approximately one in every 150 eight-year-olds, which is not an insignificant number. Yet a ban or curtailment of childhood vaccines would place all of these children at risk of death from a return of epidemics of childhood diseases that once killed thousands (Begley, 2009; Harris, 2008; Johnson, 2009; McNeil, 2009; Offit, 2008).

And the return is underway. In 2014, in the area of Columbus, Ohio, surrounding Ohio State University, 483 cases of mumps were discovered. In 2015, 59 people, many of whom had visited Disneyland, came down with measles. Measles has been a problem elsewhere in California, specifically Orange County. New York City had its own outbreak. Whooping cough and meningitis are also making a comeback; the former killed 9-month-old Brady Alciade in Chicopee, Massachusetts, and the latter left 6-year-old Jeremiah Mitchell living with prosthetic arms. In response, many school boards, medical practices, and legislatures are tightening requirements for vaccination. Three out of five bills introduced between 2009 and 2012 have passed; all 31 bills calling for looser exemption standards failed (Kluger, 2014; Nagourney, 2015; Alcindor, 2014; Hotez, 2017). In California, a state law requiring all students be vaccinated before kindergarten produced a dramatic increase in vaccination rates with little public resistance (Allday, 2017).

What supports the continuation of this delusional thinking? In some cases, it is simply anecdotes from parents who had things happen to their children in conjunction with a vaccination. Also, there are so far no other definitive explanations of what causes autism. Peter Hotez, a pediatrician at Baylor College of Medicine, says, "There is strong evidence that genetics pays a role. . . ." And that is something parents don't want to hear. Any other explanation is preferable (Hotez, 2017).

Mental Health in Cyberspace

The communication and information devices that are seemingly indispensable parts of our lives—cell phones, smartphones, iPads, Facebook, Twitter, and the Internet—have mental health dimensions that may soon be matters of social policy. In one study, people diagnosed with borderline personality disorder (BPD) were asked to record their moods on electronic diaries several times a day. This gave therapists new insight into the extreme variability of their positive and negative mood swings. The lead author of the study predicted that Palm Pilots could be programmed to serve as proxy therapists, offering coping skills to their users, as needed. More recently, robots as therapists are being discussed. The costs and benefits of such proxy therapy may soon be factored into public and private insurance coverage (Trull et.al., 2008; Weir, 2015; Jolly, 2016).

Internet chat rooms are a potential source of social support for people with a variety of problems and aliments. They can share their experiences and learn how others cope without leaving their homes. This could be comforting and therapeutic. It might also magnify fears and anxieties. Those who believe aliens or government conspirators are controlling their minds will find others to confirm their worst nightmares. In the 1970s and 1980s, a number of people reported being abducted and experimented upon in alien spaceships. A more recent fear is "gang stalking," the belief that some people are under 24-hour surveillance by organized groups, often riding in red and white cars. When those who think they are victims of gang stalking express their fears to others, they are told they are insane. So it is a source of great comfort to find websites of like-minded victims. Under professional direction, such groups might be directed to assess their experiences and determine to what extent they may be delusional. On their own, these groups will more likely reinforce and magnify their terrors. Will this result in some attempt to control Internet chat rooms? Might therapeutic interventions via the Internet become part of professional practice (Kershaw, 2008)?

Internet communication may also be a vehicle for serious harm. When 13-year-old Megan Meier committed suicide, it appeared to be a reaction to rejection by an Internet "boyfriend." The "boyfriend" was actually the creation of the mother of one of her school friends who was trying to punish Megan for comments she had made about her daughter. The mother was convicted of three misdemeanor charges of computer fraud, and the crime of cyberbullying entered public awareness. Many think that the prosecution was an extreme reaction to this sad situation, but computer fraud is already a well-established crime, and jail time is common even for first offenders (Steinhauer, 2008).

Audrie Pott, a 15-year-old skier, soccer player, and violist, was raped by 16-year-olds at a party. One of them sent pictures to all her classmates. A week later she killed herself. In the same month, similar crimes took place in Ohio and Nova Scotia. The latter also led to suicide. The Pott family worked to get new legislation that would stiffen penalties on cyberbullying and try adolescents accused of sexual assault as adults, "Audrie's Law" was signed by Governor Gerry Brown on September 3, 2014. Audrie's parents also obtained a settlement with the parents of the assailants, which included their being interviewed for a documentary. The movie, called *Audrie and Daisey*, was directed by Bonni Cohen and Jon Schenk, and can be streamed through Netflix (Mather, 2013; Abele, 2016).

The Mental Health of Veterans

The wars in Iraq and Afghanistan have been going on for over sixteen years and may finally be coming to an end. There are mental as well as physical costs to subjecting people, even those who have been trained for it, to long and repeated periods of violence. Returning soldiers usually have difficulty adjusting to peacetime and resuming family relationships. This is to be expected, and problems are usually of short duration, but some are not. Since the wars in Afghanistan and Iraq began, veteran suicides have steadily increased to the point that they are higher than domestic rates. The rate has doubled since the wars began. More veterans have now killed themselves than died in combat in Afghanistan.

Burlingham/Shutterstock

Veterans often have difficulty adjusting back to peacetime and resuming family relationships.

Some of this can be attributed to posttraumatic stress disorder (PTSD). Of veterans treated by the Veterans' Administration, 30 percent have been diagnosed with PTSD. There are undoubtedly many more who suffer from this condition and refuse to report it. But surprisingly, nearly a third of those who committed suicide from 2005 to 2010 were never deployed. It is also interesting that the number of suicides does not increase with multiple deployments. Something beyond combat must be at the root of this problem.

PTSD, however, does increase with multiple deployments. A 2008 RAND Institute study estimated that 300,000 veterans, approximately 20 percent of returning veterans, suffered posttraumatic stress disorder or major depression. After a third tour, the number increased to 30 percent. Among noncommissioned officers (i.e., sergeants, those with more training and experience than the average recruit), 12 percent suffered from depression, anxiety, or acute distress. The number went up to 19 percent after a second tour and to 27 percent after a third. The cost of PTSD in terms of medical care, lost productivity, and lost lives could be as much as $6 billion (Shanker, 2008; Tyson, 2008).

Soldiers routinely avoid seeking treatment because they believe it will jeopardize their standing in the eyes of their comrades and superiors, endanger promotions, or even end their military careers. They are often right. The soldier's ethos is to tough it out. This attitude persists even after discharge. Thus, even if help were available, something that cannot be taken for granted, veterans will not ask for it, which of course only guarantees that the problems and their consequences will get worse. Some Army physicians are advocating mandatory screening. This, they argue, is the only way to defeat the stigma. Another means of counteracting stigma would be to consider mental wounds equal to physical ones and award the Purple Heart medal to those with PTSD. The idea was immediately rejected by the Pentagon, but the fact that such a radical assault on military tradition could even be considered is testimony to the seriousness of the problem. Recent research looking for biomarkers of traumatic brain injury (a frequent result of roadside bombs) and PTSD may make it easier to make a case that mental wounds are as real as physical ones (Alvarez & Eckholm, 2008; Dao, 2013; Klein, 2013; Ruelas, 2008; Spiegel, 2008; Zoroya, 2008; Lee, 2015).

Despite a major scandal at Walter Reed Hospital in 2007 and the resignation of the Secretary of the Army, the VA is still slow to respond to requests for help. Many of those who committed suicide had requested treatment but were unable to get it. In 2016, another scandal broke when it was revealed that VA hospital administrators had falsified records of waiting lists. This cost John Shinseki, the Secretary of Veterans Affairs, his job and sentenced administrators to two years' probation. The history of the Second Battalion, Seventh Marine Regiment's tour in Helmand Province, Afghanistan, in 2008 illustrates many of these problems. The soldiers in this battalion experienced eight months of almost constant combat, suffering the highest casualty rate—20 dead, 140 wounded—of any Marine battalion that year. After their return, from April 2009 to February 2015, thirteen members of the unit had committed suicide and several others had tried. Six of the thirteen had tried to use VA services. They had difficulty getting appointments, had bad responses to the medications offered, and felt that the therapists had little understanding of their problems. They tried to stick together through social media, putting each other's numbers in their cell phones and even creating a spreadsheet listing their locations, so that when a call for help went out, someone could respond with a physical presence (Phillips, 2015).

The unit produced other creative responses. Jake Woods founded Team Rubicon, discussed below. The family and friends of Clay Hunt, who shot himself in March 2011, drafted the Clay Hunt Suicide Prevention for Veterans Act, with the support of various veterans groups. Despite being temporarily blocked by Senator Tom Coburn (R-OK), who wanted it to be funded by budget cuts, it was signed by President Obama on February 12, 2015. It requires third-party evaluations of VA programs; the creation of a central website for information on available services; extending time for posttraumatic stress disorder services; cooperating with nonprofit mental health organizations; and, perhaps most important to the men of the Second Battalion, Seventh Marine Regiment, starting an official peer support program (Phillips, 2015; Lamothe, 2015).

The reason that the men of the Second Battalion, Seventh Marine Regiment had such trouble coming home was not just because of the horrors they had experienced and caused, says Sebastian Junkers, a journalist and documentary filmmaker, but that the communal, egalitarian, and interdependent society that had sustained them in war just did not exist at home. They are not given useful work to do, they have no community comparable to the one they served and sacrificed for, and they have no one but each other to understand what they have been through. The only role they are given is "victim," which will allow them to reintegrate as long as they take their pills and submit to therapy. Junker was embedded with the 173rd Airborne Brigade Combat Team in the Korengal Valley, an area not unlike Helmond. His unit experienced the same kind of constant combat as did the Second Battalion, Seventh Marine Regiment. His co-director and cinematographer, Tim Hetherington, was killed there. He does not blame PTSD for the veterans' reintegration problem. He makes his argument in his book *Tribes: On Homecoming and Belonging*. One of his reviewers, Matthew B. Crawford, summarizes the argument this way: PTSD "may be a medical term for a cultural problem" (Junker, 2016; Senior, 2016; Crawford, 2016).

Veterans are organizing themselves to provide help to their comrades looking for a sense of purpose in civilian life comparable to their military service. Team Rubicon mobilizes veterans to perform emergency services in disaster areas all over the world (Team Rubicon, 2017). Team Red, White & Blue conducts group exercise-therapy classes. Mission Continues, based in St. Louis, repairs community buildings. Such nonprofit organizations could use federal policy support as well as professional social work services. And wouldn't it be nice if the service careers that social workers have chosen for their life's work turn out to be models for repairing the lives of wounded warriors (Dokoupil, 2012)?

Gun Violence and Mental Health

Sad to say, every day in the United States hundreds of people kill each other with guns. Most of them, as far as we know, have no problems with mental illness. Also, the vast majority of people with mental illness pose no danger to others. Of the small minority who might be violent, most only commit battery, for example, punching. Only 2 percent of the potentially violent use weapons, and guns are only one fragment of that category. So statistically, the intersection of guns and mental illness is extremely small. Nonetheless, some of the most spectacular mass shootings of recent years have been committed by people who showed signs of serious mental disturbance. And quite of few of them were students.

The incident at Virginia Tech in 2007 was notable for its very high casualty rate, but it is only one of several horrific mass shootings. In January 2011, Jared Loughner, a 22-year-old student at Pima Community College in Tucson, Arizona, went to a community meeting organized by congressional representative Gabrielle Giffords with a handgun and several high-capacity magazines. He opened fire on the crowd, killing six people, including a 9-year-old girl, and wounding thirteen others. Giffords miraculously survived. A middle-aged woman ended the slaughter by tackling Loughner while he was reloading.

James Holmes, a University of Colorado graduate, walked into a suburban theater in July 2012 with multiple weapons including an assault rifle with a 100-round drum magazine. He killed 12 people, most were in their twenties but one was a 6-year-old girl, and injured 58 others, including a 3-month-old infant. In December 2012, Adam Lanza, a Western Connecticut State University dropout, shot his way into Sandy Hook Elementary School in Newtown, Connecticut, killing the principal, the school psychologist, four other adult staff members, and 20 first-graders. He had several guns but used mostly an assault rifle with high-capacity magazines. In June 2013, after killing two family members, 23-year-old John Zawahri hijacked a car and drove to Santa Monica College where he had been a student, killed two others and wounded five. He had been prevented from buying guns because a background check turned up a previous psychiatric hospitalization. However, he was able to assemble an assault rifle from parts bought separately. He also was able to acquire high-capacity magazines even though they cannot be legally bought or sold in California.

On May 24, 2014, Elliot Roger, a student at Santa Barbara City College, killed six people, five of them students at the University of California, Santa Barbara, and wounded thirteen others. He had shown signs of a desire to commit violence, and his mother had once talked with mental health officials, who sent the police to his apartment. He seemed calm and rational and did not meet their criteria for someone who should be detained for investigation. Had they searched his apartment, they would have found three handguns, plenty of ammunition, and a manifesto expressing his desire for "retribution." The City College of Santa Barbara said they had a "strong crisis intervention response structure." But Roger had caused no problems in class and was therefore not on their radar either (Nagourney & Goode, 2014).

Campus shootings continue. At Umpqua Community College, seven were killed and two wounded. Sacramento Community College, Savanah State University, and Texas Southern University each lost one student in 2015. Kansas State University and Mississippi State were put on lockdown while an active shooter was pursued (Reed & Brennan, 2015).

These horrifying events raise a variety of policy issues. There were clear signs that Seung Cho was deeply troubled and there were a variety of points at which some action could have been taken to keep him from harming himself and others. The first problem was that those who had useful information hesitated or were forbidden by law from sharing it. In order to protect people from the stigma of mental illness, keeping treatment records private is generally a good idea. But this can also handicap future interventions. To avoid jeopardizing Cho's admission chances, Virginia Tech was not told about his high school problems. His parents were not told of his hospitalization. Because the hospitalization was not court ordered, his name was not placed on the FBI's Mental Defective List that gun dealers check before selling a gun. Thus, he got little help in college and had no problems in buying a deadly 9-mm Glock 19 and a 22-caliber Walther (Egan, 2007; Fisher, 2007; Schulte & Craig, 2007).

A second question is: Why was someone this disturbed not recognized as being dangerous and hospitalized? Jared Loughner had expressed violent intent to numerous teachers. Several called campus security, but the college's basic response was to suspend him until he could get a mental health examination. John Holmes had told a friend about wanting to kill people. Apparently, he had discussed violence with his psychiatrist. Adam Lanza had no history of mental health problems other than difficulty socializing in high school. He was believed to be autistic, which is not in itself any predictor of violence. John Zawahari had been in trouble with the police for violent threats and had been hospitalized for a psychiatric examination. So, four out of five were showing clear signs of problems. Some were getting help and some were not. But none of them was taken out of circulation (Hostege & Anglen, 2012).

Should standards of dangerousness be less exacting? Mental health professionals reply that it is not easy to determine who is dangerous and who is not. An alternative would be better monitoring of outpatients and creation of community crisis stabilization units that would provide brief psychiatric interventions. This raises a third question. Increasing the mental hospital population and providing new community services will be expensive. States with shrinking budgets are unlikely to commit to these expenses, even if it could prevent future tragedy (Jackman & Jenkins, 2007; Jenkins, 2007).

Fourth, how can we prevent people with unstable minds and murderous intentions from buying weapons? Many states provide no mental health information to the FBI, and the Supreme Court decided in 1995 that the federal government could not require this. A national database is expensive to maintain, and consulting may take time. In 2007, Congress passed a bill that had been hung up for years to provide funds to streamline the reporting process. However, the entire system can be evaded simply by buying online or at a gun show, where some dealers conduct checks and some don't (Editorial, 2009; Egan, 2007; Freskos, 2016).

Finally, should universities do more to identify and help students in trouble? A 2005 survey found that four out of ten college students were, at times, so depressed that they found it difficult to function, and one in ten had considered suicide. Counseling services are often poorly staffed and require advanced appointments. Walk-in clinics could help, but some kind of early warning system that actively seeks out those in serious trouble is needed. What is available on your campus (Lewin, 2011; McGinn, 2007)?

We'll conclude with two policy proposals from the National Rifle Association (NRA). Mental health is the real problem, it says, not guns. Let's have a national registry, not of gun owners, but of people with mental illness. They were not really serious about that. When Congress struck down an Obama administration rule that prevented people so seriously impaired that they could not handle money from buying guns, the NRA supported it, and so did President Trump (Editorial, 2017).

The other proposal from the NRA is to arm teachers, an idea that after Newtown some teachers were considering. College students in five states are allowed to carry guns; in some cases, even concealed weapons are allowed. Those familiar with the psychology of gunfights say that the experience involves "a kaleidoscope of sensory distortions including tunnel vision and a loss of hearing." Police officers are trained in gun use and in dealing with stressful situations. Yet New York police officers in shooting situations hit their targets only 30 percent of the time. If the target was shooting back, it was 11 percent (Paalazzolo & Eder, 2012; Ripley, 2013).

As many as twenty-three campuses now allow concealed weapons to be carried on campus. Seventeen ban guns outright. Some states allow individual campuses to decide. Rules vary. In Tennessee, faculty may carry guns, but students may not. In Wisconsin, guns can be banned from specific buildings if they have signs saying so. In Mississippi, gun carriers must have safety instruction, but most states do not require this (National Council of State Legislatures, 2017).

A teacher or student might have brought down Lanza or Choi before maximum killing was accomplished. But with multiple shooters in crowded classrooms, the collateral damage might have been just as bad. It might be that would-be mass killers would avoid schools where they knew there would be armed teachers and students. But the killers at Columbine knew that the high school had an armed guard. They even traded shots with him. And since most gun deaths are not classroom massacres but cases of accidental discharge, bar fights, road rage, or arguments getting out of hand, increasing the number of guns in college communities just increases those possibilities.

Opioid Epidemic

Opioids are a class of narcotics that includes cocaine and heroin. We commonly think of them as street drugs, but many other opioids are available by prescription as painkillers. Oxycontin, Vicodin, and Percocet are some of their proprietary names. They can be addictive; people using them as painkillers may feel a powerful urge to continue use for the euphoric state they induce.

And this is happening across the country and across all socioeconomic levels, afflicting young and old alike. The Rust Belt and Appalachia seem particularly hard hit, and the toll on middle-aged white men is noticeably high. More important, users are overdosing in large numbers. In 2015, opioids killed over 33.000 people ("Opioid Tide," 2017).

Middle-aged white men are not the first demographic category you think of as having high rates of addiction. But, taken in the context of areas of the country where good-paying jobs are disappearing and not being replaced by anything but minimum-wage positions, you might expect both a certain amount of depression and a certain number of people who have done hard manual work and been injured. If you are thinking, as does Golub et al. (2015), of a conjunction of external and structural forces combined with an internalized subculture of pessimism, distrust, and a willingness to blame people or forces outside yourself for your trouble, a chemical euphoria might be very attractive. This subculture and its substance abuse has been vividly described in J. D. Vance's (2016) *Hillbilly Elegy*. In 2016, drug overdoses are expected to exceed 59,000. This is now the leading cause of death among Americans over age 50 (Katz, 2017).

But other, very different sections of the socioeconomic landscape are showing effects. In wealthy New Rochelle, New York, school nurses stock a nalozone kit (nalozone is an antidote for opioid overdoses). The New York State Health Department is making it available throughout the state. New York City schools, interestingly, have so far not seen the need for it (Harris, 2017). Suboxone is a similar antidote. The doctor treating pop culture icon Prince was carrying it when he arrived, too late, on the day Prince overdosed on fentanyl (Eldren, 2017).

One response to this epidemic is legislation to control the inappropriate prescription of opioids. A number of states have databases that allow them to monitor pharmacies, pain clinics, and in some cases even physicians. This allows identification of patients at risk of overdose because their prescribed dosages are particularly high or of those who are obtaining opioids from several sources. An eight-year study conducted by the National Center for Injury Prevention and Control found that these laws reduced overdose death by 12 percent (Dowell, Zhang, Noonan, & Hockenberry, 2016).

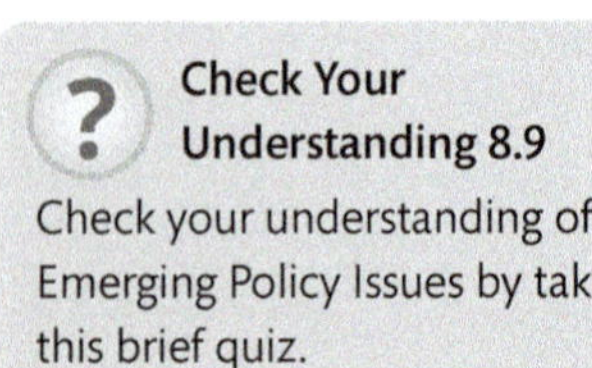
?
Check Your Understanding 8.9
Check your understanding of Emerging Policy Issues by taking this brief quiz.

CONCLUSION

Mental illness and substance abuse have been individual and social problems since the founding of the country. And debates over the degree of individual and social responsibility for them have continued for at least that long. The policy pendulum has swung back and forth as we weigh individual freedom versus collective obligation. The issues are complex, and morality as well as practicality are involved. Of the many substances that are abused, some are legal and some or not. Should we decriminalize some and/or make others harder to obtain? Should everyone be subjected to drug tests? Should people with a mental illness who might harm others be denied privacy and confidentiality? Should parents be allowed to refuse to vaccinate their children if this results in the deaths of others? Are our communities safer with more guns or fewer guns? Should cyberspace be more carefully regulated? How do we reintegrate our veterans into peacetime society? What roles can social workers play in all this?

The use and abuse of illegal substances are not just problems for specific groups in American society, as we used to think. We find these problems in all socioeconomic, racial, and religious groups. Different drugs are adopted and discarded by various groups at various times, in various places. The extent to which use is considered a problem and the extent to which abuse is prosecuted seems to depend a lot on who the users are. And in the pharmacological revolution, this issue can only get more complicated.

Recall what you learned from this chapter by completing the Chapter Review.

9

Health

LEARNING OUTCOMES

- Explain how insurance works, including the relationship between premiums and benefits, and the importance of the makeup of the risk pool.
- Discuss the benefits and risks of individual medical savings accounts.
- Explain the role of the individual mandate in the operation of the Affordable Care Act.
- Contrast the employer-based insurance system to the single-payer system.
- Describe how the "chargemaster" works in determining hospital bills.

CHAPTER OUTLINE

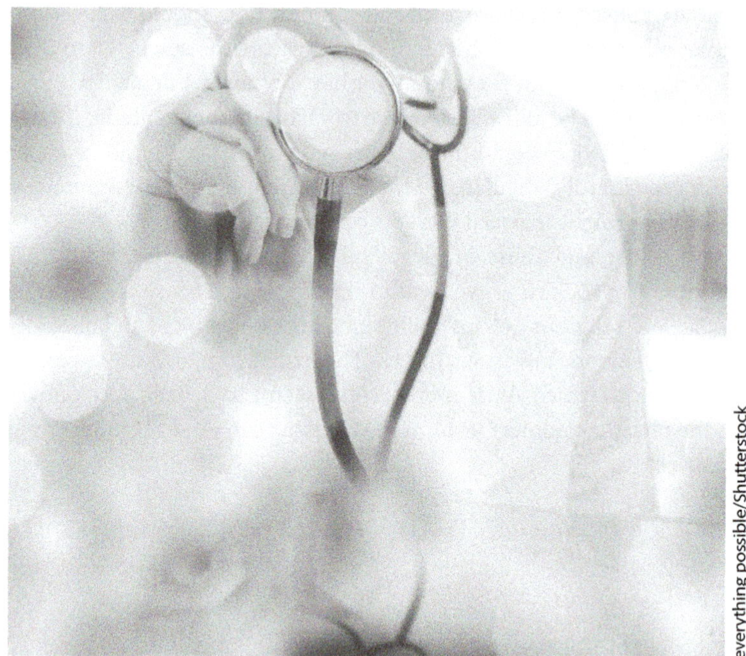

everything possible/Shutterstock

No one knew how complicated health care was.
—President Donald J. Trump

When Janice S. felt severe pain in her chest, she feared a heart attack. She was taken by ambulance to a nonprofit hospital four miles away. After three hours of tests, doctors decided it was only indigestion. She was very relieved until she got the bill. The ambulance ride was $995, her brief encounters with doctors totaled $3,000, and the hospital itself billed her $17,000. This included $199.50 each for three blood tests and $7,997.54 for a stress test involving X-ray-computed tomography, also known as a CT scan. The radioactive dye used in the test was an additional $872.44. Janice had been unemployed for a year and was uninsured. She was 64 years old, just shy of qualifying for Medicare, which would have covered most of this at a much lower cost (which we'll talk about later). She was devastated. She found online a medical-billing advocate who was able to negotiate the hospital and doctors' bills down to about $11,000. The ambulance company offered her a $25 a month payment plan. How will she pay it? And what will she do the next time she feels chest pains (Brill, 2013)?

Susan Patel has just graduated from college. She studied hard and earned good grades. Her starting salary as an elementary school teacher is reasonable and she hopes to increase it by earning a master's degree. Sharing an apartment with two former schoolmates keeps housing costs manageable. She has a car but takes public transportation to and from work. Television and the public library are her primary source of entertainment, and she splurges once and a while on a rock concert.

Susan thinks of herself as a responsible person. She would like to have health insurance, but she has student loans to pay off, which will take several years. After that, she will get insurance and start thinking about a 401(k) for retirement. Now, the new Affordable Care Act is going to force her to get insurance or pay a penalty. That will make a dent in her carefully planned budget. She is resentful. She recalls Justice Antonin Scalia asking during the Supreme Court challenge to the constitutionality of the ACA whether the government can force citizens to eat broccoli just because it's healthy (Stewart, 2012).

Susan has looked into insurance premiums. Mostly they are higher than the penalty. She is young and healthy. Why should she be penalized for being healthy? She thinks she will accept the penalty and put off buying health insurance until later.

Thoughts on Social Work Practice

If you or a client are uninsured and too young for Medicare, do you dare go to the emergency room? Is there a safety-net hospital in your area? What sort of national health policy will save you from bankruptcy if you face a medical catastrophe?

Thoughts on Social Work Practice

Do you know how insurance works? What are the responsibilities of the "young invincibles"? Should you be forced to buy broccoli?

THE PROBLEM THAT HEALTH POLICY WAS DEVELOPED TO SOLVE

It used to be said that the United States had "the best health care in the world." Unfortunately, this is not the case, if it ever was. Life expectancy is below many other industrialized countries. Infant mortality is higher than some third-world countries; we rank 50 in the world, nine spots below Cuba. We are bad at preventing deaths from treatable and preventable conditions. We are below average in vaccinating children. Canadians survive longer after renal dialysis and kidney transplants than Americans. Americans wait longer to see primary-care physicians than citizens in Great Britain, Germany, Australia, and New Zealand. And, of those four countries and the United States, the United States has the highest rate of deaths due to surgical mistakes (Brill, 2015a; Shea, Holmgren, Osborn, & Schoen, 2007).

If we were getting the world's best health care, it might be understandable that we pay far more for it than any other country. Since we're not, how do we explain the fact that we are paying over $9,024 per person every year, while Canada is paying half that? Britons pay only $3,487, and average care in Italy is $3,207. Given this, it's not surprising that individual procedures are also much more expensive. A coronary bypass will cost you $67,583 in the United States but only $40,954 in Canada (but you'll have to wait longer for it) and around $16,000 in Germany or France. A simple appendectomy is $13,003 in the United States but $5,606 in Canada and about $3,000 in Germany and France. The U.S. average is calculated over a tremendous range of charges, depending on what city you're in, but we'll discuss that later (Peter G. Peterson Foundation, 2017; Brill, 2015a; Emanuel, 2011; Rosenthal, 2013a; Zakaria, 2012).

Thus, there are two big problems with the U.S. health system: Many people are left out of it, including those who need it the most, and it is extremely expensive. The two problems are interrelated. Because people don't have insurance or cannot otherwise afford to go to doctors, they let problems get worse. When they do seek help, it is often in hospital emergency rooms, which are by far the most expensive treatment

mavoimage/123RF.com

Does this young, healthy woman need medical insurance? Maybe not now; most likely she will later. If she is not in the pool now, premiums will go up.

environments. Those who are not insured and who have low incomes are unlikely to be able to pay those bills, notwithstanding the best efforts of the bill collectors that hospitals will turn loose on them. Therefore, those costs will have to be shifted to the rest of us.

Before the Affordable Care Act, it was estimated that those without insurance received about $86 billion in health services and could pay about $30 billion. Medicare, Medicaid, other levels of government, and some charities stepped in to shoulder about $43 billion. Doctors take a hit too. Between 1.7 and 10 percent, depending on what sources you consult, was shifted to private insurance companies. Some argue that this was a big deal, while others say it didn't affect premiums much and that hospitals ate some of the difference. These calculations don't deal with the extent to which hospitals' estimates already had a factor built into them for predictable losses to the uninsured. Medicare and Medicaid are paid for by taxpayers, so whether we are paying through private insurance premiums or taxes, we are subsidizing those who don't or can't buy insurance (Families USA, 2005; Frakt, 2011; Hadley, Holahan, Coughlin, & Miller, 2008).

Another expensive inefficiency in the U.S. system is health insurance. Any insurance scheme, whether it is to protect against robbery, car theft, accident, disease, or death, works only if there is a broad mix of enrollees. The risk and cost must be shared as broadly as possible. The young and healthy must be enrolled as well as the old and sick. Those who don't need it now may need it later. Some may not need it at all, but they do not have to worry that a serious disease or accident will be a financial catastrophe. The more enrollees you have, the lower the cost is to everyone to keep the system running. If the insurance program is private, a profit will have to be built in. The main way to insure profit is to try to enroll as many of the young and healthy as possible and to keep out as many as possible of those who may need services. Companies whose clientele do not include enough of the young or who do not terminate clients who get too sick have to charge more. That can't work for an entire country. This is why many countries have adopted universal health care or "single-payer" systems, where everyone pays and everyone is included.

In single-payer systems, which exist in countries like Canada and the United Kingdom and almost all of what we consider the developed world, the government is usually the health care provider. But this needn't be so. Switzerland has a single-payer system with private providers. Some countries provide basic coverage and allow private insurers to offer supplemental coverage. Providers may be public, private, or both. The important thing is that the basic care is financed by everyone (Zakaria, 2012b).

This is a hard balance to strike, and it is absolutely a key to the success of the Affordable Care Act. If insurance companies overestimate the number of young, healthy members they enroll, they will set premiums too low. For its part, if the government sets the penalty for not having insurance too low, the same thing will happen. As we will see, both sides fell short.

Check Your Understanding 9.1
Check your understanding of The Problem That Health Policy Was Developed to Solve by taking this brief quiz.

THE PROPOSED SOLUTION: THE PATIENT PROTECTION AND AFFORDABLE CARE ACT OF 2010

As a comprehensive attack to both increase accessibility and reduced costs, this may be the most important piece of health policy legislation since the 1965 Medicare Act. But it was never accepted by the majority of the Republican Party. Republicans campaigned against it from the beginning. As *New York Times* columnist Gail Collins observed, "House Republicans vote to repeal it as often as they change their socks" (Collins, 2013). Their attempt to repeal and replace it has failed three times but is still underway.

Access

The ACA aimed to cover more people with health insurance, keep more people on it, and ease the burden on all who have it. To *get people insured,* all citizens were required to purchase insurance or pay a penalty. Those who couldn't afford it were given subsidies. Those who still couldn't afford it because it would cost 8 percent of their annual incomes could opt out. Each state was asked to set up an insurance exchange where companies could compete for the new enrollees. If states choose not to set up an exchange, the federal government did it for them. People cannot be denied insurance because they have a preexisting condition that may prove to be expensive.

Medicaid would be expanded to cover everyone with incomes up to 133 percent of the federal poverty level. For the first two years (2014–2016), costs for this was absorbed by the federal government. In 2017, federal financing was 95 percent and will gradually decrease to 90 percent in 2020 and thereafter. Because of the Supreme Court decision, to be discussed later, states can choose not to do this and many did not. Businesses that employ more than 50 workers were required to offer them health insurance and got tax credits to help them do so.

To *keep people covered,* insurance companies are no longer allowed to drop them if they developed expensive illnesses. Children can remain on their parents' policies until they turn 26 years old. There are no lifetime caps on the claims policyholders can make.

To *ease the burden of those covered,* preventive care is now encouraged by making some screening tests free and eliminating co-pays on others. The so-called doughnut hole that was built into senior drug programs, where after a certain point they bear full costs until they reach a level of coverage again, closed, saving $20.8 billion between 2010 and 2015 (Walsh, 2017).

Costs

The ACA contains a variety of measures to either increase revenues, cut costs, or redirect spending to avenues that produce better results. It claims to be the "biggest middle-class tax cut for health care in history" and promises to "reduce the deficit by more than $100 billion in ten years (Titles I and IX)."

Individuals with wages over $200,000 and couples with combined wages over $250,000 pay an additional 0.9 percent payroll tax on income that exceeds those income amounts. Investment incomes over those amounts are taxed at 3.8 percent. A cap of $2,500 has been set on Health Savings Accounts that allow setting aside tax-free money for medical expenses. A 2.3 percent tax on the sale of medical devices like implants to hospitals has been levied but will not be applied in retail stores, like those that sell eyeglasses. Employers are no longer subsidized for providing drug benefits (Dooren, 2012).

An indirect approach to lowering costs is encouraging health plans to include "wellness" features like support for quitting smoking, losing weight, eating healthier diets, and getting counseling for depression. Healthy workers, it is assumed, will not only make fewer claims for benefits but will be more productive, pay less out-of-pocket for drugs, earn more, and pay more taxes.

A major attempt to redirect medical expenses is embodied in accountable care organizations (ACOs). These are groups of health care providers who coordinate services, share information, and are held accountable for the outcomes of their services. They are compensated not for the number of tests they perform or the treatments they apply but by the resulting improvements in the health of their clients. They are penalized for high rates of readmission and iatrogenic diseases. The latter means catching a disease that leaves you sicker when you leave the hospital than when you went in. ACOs will share any profits that accrue to these results. This is not in itself a radical new idea but rather a growing realization by health professions that a lot of money is wasted by unnecessary procedures and insufficient coordination and follow-up. The ACA now rewards efforts to curtail this waste (U.S. Department of Health and Human Services, 2011).

For example, an enormous amount of money is spent on readmitting hospital patients, sometimes just weeks after their discharge, because no one is following up on whether they are taking their medications, participating in therapy, modifying their diets, and otherwise doing things that facilitate their recovery rather than making them sick again. Some of this can be as simple as calling people with serious heart impairments on the eve of a large snowstorm and reminding them not to go out and shovel (Lowrey, 2013a).

There are signs that this is working. A study of New York hospitals found that 30-day readmission rates fell for patients with heart attack, heart failure, and pneumonia. All were targets of the ACA's Hospital Readmissions Reduction Program (Carey & Lin, 2015). A Massachusetts ACO reduced hospitalizations, ER visits, and Medicaid spending by having physicians target high-risk patients who had behaviors they thought could be modified to reduce risk (Hsu et. al., 2017). A study in the *New England Journal of Medicine* reported a "small but meaningful reduction of spending with unchanged or improved quality of care" (McWilliams, Hatfield, Chernew, Landon, & Schwartz, 2016, p. 2366).

Social workers will be interested to know that ACOs that are trying to coordinate physical and mental health care are hiring more clinical and bachelor's-level social workers for their medical care coordination teams (Fullerton, Henke, Crable, Hohlbauch, & Cummings, 2016). Brill reports that ACA-inspired pilot programs have led to similar efforts among private insurers (Brill, 2015a, p. 432).

Another redirection of resources will be equalizing the fees-for-service that doctors receive for Medicare treatment versus Medicaid care. This should help low-income people who are finding it increasingly hard to find physicians who accept Medicaid clients. Primary-care doctors and gerontologists will also get better compensation. Hospitals that now receive special payments because they serve low-income areas (disproportionate share hospitals) will be reevaluated, reducing payments by 75 percent, and increasing them thereafter based on actual uncompensated care provided to the uninsured.

Significant funds are being directed to research; demonstration and pilot projects will experiment with ways to reduce costs and improve quality of care. A Patient-Centered Outcomes Research Institute will study the clinical effectiveness of medical treatments. Independence at Home demonstrations will explore ways to prevent hospitalization and rehospitalization by delivering primary care at home. Alternatives to tort litigation will be studied in order to reduce the high cost of malpractice insurance physicians must pay.

Consumer-operated and -oriented plans (CO-OPs) will be enabled with $4.8 billion. These will be governed by majority vote of members, and all profits will be used to lower premiums or improve benefits.

Insurers will have to report the percentage of their premiums that actually go to benefits. If it is less than 80 percent (85 percent for plans covering large employers), they will have to send rebates to customers. For employee plans, rebates will go to the employers, who may or may not pass them on to workers (Bernstein, 2012; Goodnough, 2012b). States will receive grants to set up reviews of premium increases charged by companies in the exchanges, possibly excluding those who cannot justify increases.

Check Your Understanding 9.2

Check your understanding of The Proposed Solution: The Patient Protection and Affordable Care Act of 2010 by taking this brief quiz.

HISTORY OF HEALTH CARE POLICIES

The rise of the germ theory of disease made health a public concern. The lives of rich people could be threatened by the unsanitary conditions that the poor were forced to live in. Diseases could be spread by germs in the water, in the air, and on human carriers. Some sort of collective response to this was necessary. Slum clearance became an issue. But concern shifted from the environment to individuals. "Dispensaries" were established in cities around 1790 where medicine could be given to those who couldn't afford it and where doctors volunteered their services and used the clinics to train their students. When training was transferred to hospital internships, dispensaries disappeared and were gradually replaced by public health departments created by cities and states. They proliferated after the Civil War. The federal government built a series of "marine hospitals" in port cities, so-called because they dealt with diseases brought by ship from exotic places. They were placed under the control of a Surgeon General in 1871 (Starr, 1982).

More sophisticated bacteriology led to what Paul Starr called "the modernization of dirt." Public health reformers had been concerned with water and air pollution and the poor sanitary conditions of slums. Now it was argued that dirt wasn't in itself the problem. A better understanding of how diseases were transmitted provided a narrower, and cheaper, response to curtailing disease. Washing your hands before eating became more important than cleaning up the environment. Also important was having physicians examine people who might have a disease. Thus, the "new public health" supported the power of the medical profession and directed it toward narrow clinical judgments rather than social reform. The stress on "checkups" also gave doctors a lot more to do (Starr, 1982, pp. 189–194).

The federal government entered briefly into health provision during Franklin Roosevelt's New Deal with the Resettlement Administration's medical cooperatives. Community members paid an annual fee to support a local clinic. This was a kind of proto health maintenance organization (HMO), about which we will hear more later. By 1942, they were providing affordable health care to over 600,000 people in forty-three states. Initially, medical societies cooperated, but a fear of so-called socialized medicine eventually forced the cooperatives out of business. The idea was then reinvented in the private sector and elicited less alarm. Industrialist Henry J. Kaiser established the Kaiser-Permanente plan in 1942. By the 1950s, the Kaiser plan had a growing network of its own physicians, hospitals, and clinics and an enrollment of half a million people. Twenty years later, an alternative type of HMO appeared, whereby health organizations contracted with private physicians to deliver services in their own offices rather than in company facilities (Clark, 1999; Starr, 1982).

Roosevelt considered including health insurance in his epochal Social Security Act, but he and his advisors feared that the opposition of the medical establishment would doom the whole effort. He returned to it in his last important speech in 1944 on what he called the "Second Bill of Rights" but died before he could go further. His successor, Harry Truman, not only supported the idea of universal health care but campaigned on it in 1948. He actually had some Republican support, and some compromise might have been possible; but opposition from both liberals and the American Medical Association could not be overcome (Starr, 1982).

With no "public option" under consideration, health insurance fell naturally into the private sector as a fringe benefit that employers could offer to workers in a period when wages were frozen. It became a way of competing for employees. Another major accomplishment of the New Deal, the right to collective bargaining under the Wagner Act, allowed workers to take better advantage of this opportunity. There were now many players. The Depression left hospitals with many unpaid bills. They needed to broaden the pool of potential users of hospital services to spread their risks. Prepaid programs to cover hospital costs like Blue Cross and Blue Shield emerged to meet this need. The unions subscribed in large numbers. Traditional indemnity insurance companies were also growing and entered the market of hospital insurance. Competition increased and brought a broader range of services but also led to the exclusion of older and more vulnerable workers and higher costs for those less healthy. By the mid-1950s, nearly two-thirds of the population had some kind of health coverage, though it varied greatly by occupation and region. Those who were retired, self-employed, unemployed, or forced to take a job without fringe benefits were losing out, setting the stage for the reentry of government participation (Starr, 1982).

By the 1960s, health practitioners and health infrastructure had grown considerably. Among other contributions was the Hill-Burton Act of 1946, which put $75 million a year for five years into hospital construction. Those left out of the employer-based health plans, particularly seniors, were increasingly vocal, and a new majority of Democratic legislators brought in by the Goldwater candidacy of 1964 were sympathetic to reform.

It was hard for opponents of government action, like the AMA, to ignore a constituency like seniors, plainly both "needy" and "deserving." And seniors were also likely to vote.

Both parties had put forth proposals and the resultant act combined them. The Democratic Party provided compulsory hospital insurance and the Republican contribution was government-subsidized insurance to cover physicians' bills. Medicaid, which expanded assistance to the states for medical care for the poor, was the third part. President Lyndon Johnson signed the law in 1965 (Starr, 1982).

A Democratic Congress pushed a Republican president, Richard Nixon, in the 1970s toward a national health system. His response was health maintenance organizations (HMOs): comprehensive, prepaid health care corporations similar to Henry Kaiser's, which would be self-regulating and, most important, private. The HMO Act of 1973 required businesses with more than 25 employees to join up. This represented an interesting change in the ideological landscape. As Paul Starr notes:

> Prepaid group practice was originally associated with the cooperative movement and dismissed as a utopian, slightly subversive idea. The conservative, cost-minded critics of medical care had now adopted it as a more efficient form of management. They had substituted the rhetoric of rationalization and competition for the older rhetoric of cooperation and mutual protection. The socialized medicine of one era had become the corporate reform of the next (Starr, 1982, p. 396).

Nixon actually moved much farther with a national insurance plan that would cover the entire population with more comprehensive benefits than had heretofore ever been offered. He said in 1974 it was "an idea whose time has come in America." For those not employed, a government-run program, something like the current insurance exchanges, would be created. States would regulate insurers, approving plans and rates, and auditing regularly. One current commentator says it was in some ways stronger than the Obama plan. Senator Ted Kennedy later regretted not taking Nixon's deal. Then Watergate swept Nixon out of office and the opportunity was lost (Krugman, 2009; Starr, 1982).

It was assumed that the prepaid, comprehensive nature of HMOs would naturally contain medical costs. Prevention was a lot cheaper than acute care. But this was not enough to counteract steadily rising hospital costs. This was because, initially, hospitals were reimbursed by Medicare for what they said their costs were. Private indemnity plans also increased premiums as a result. There was no check on these increases. As we will see, nobody knew what the real costs were. In 1983, the Reagan administration attempted to cope with this by standardizing payments based on a system of diagnosis-related groups (DRGs). The average cost of treating patients in each diagnostic group became the basis for reimbursements. Hospitals now had an incentive to keep costs down. They could pocket any difference between what the treatment cost and what the DRGs said they should cost. Congress could also take advantage of the cost reduction by transferring savings in Medicare into the general deficit reduction. Medicare became their "cash cow" (Frakt, 2011).

Still costs rose. Companies, including large corporations, began to complain about the bite employee health benefits were taking out of profits. Enter managed care. The prepaid nature of HMOs allowed them some control over access to care. They could decide what you needed and how much of it. The market power of HMOs had also increased enough in the 1990s so that they could bargain with hospitals for better rates with the threat of excluding them from their programs (Frakt, 2011).

As HMOs proliferated and competed, they began to feel squeezed. In turn, they squeezed their clients, restricting or eliminating certain services and increasing copayments. Clients resisted. Some HMOs responded by becoming preferred provider organizations (PPOs), which gave clients a greater choice of doctors. This, in turn, shifted power back toward hospitals. Medicare was similarly squeezed as Congress became more concerned about budget deficits. The Balanced Budget Act of 1997 hoped to save $115 billion by 2002 by cutting post-acute care and hospital outpatient departments (Frakt, 2011). This, as we have seen, only increased the problem down the line with expensive rehospitalizations.

President Bill Clinton tried to harness managed care in his massive health care reform plan introduced in 1993. The Clinton proposal called for the administration of health insurance through large purchasing alliances. These alliances would offer several insurance options to consumers, including managed care plans. The alliances would operate under state control, with a national health board setting pricing standards. The plan was very complicated and took a long time to develop, largely in secret, allowing opposition forces to gather. The insurance industry was particularly effective in television ads against the plan featuring an anxious couple named "Harry" and "Louise." The plan died in 1994 (Klein, 2009).

President George W. Bush added prescription drug coverage to Medicare. A monthly fee of $25 and a $250 deductible would cover 75 percent of prescription drugs up to $2500. Private insurers were given subsidies to help them offer managed care plans with similar benefits. Competition among insurers and drug companies was supposed to bring drug prices down, but there was no provision in the bill for limiting drug costs. The many new customers were a bonanza for drug companies. The program was enacted with no provision for paying for it other than deficit spending.

Check Your Understanding 9.3
Check your understanding of History of Health Care Policies by taking this brief quiz.

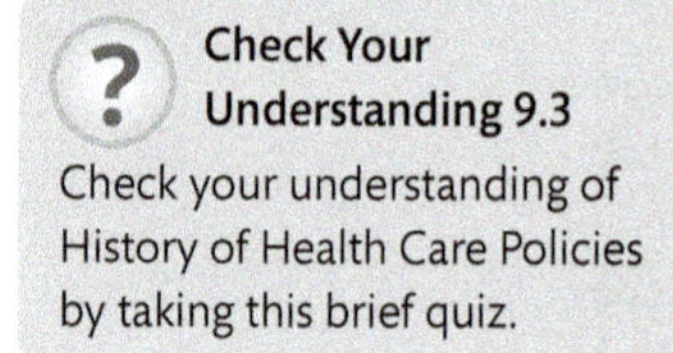

SOCIAL ANALYSIS OF HEALTH POLICY

Is adequate health care a basic human right? If so, is it the obligation of government to see that every citizen has it? If not, is it just another commodity in the marketplace? And what happens to those who are unable to secure it in the marketplace? These are basic value or moral questions that form the context of health policy.

Behind these values are assumptions about how governments and markets work or should work. If you believe that governments are usually inefficient and often corrupt, you don't want to trust anything as important as your health to government. Government, said Ronald Reagan, is the problem, not the solution. Markets, he believed, were far superior for solving the problems of the world. But some people have the same feeling about markets: They're usually inefficient and often corrupt. They are tools of the selfish. Trusting the market with your health could leave you sick or dead. And there are probably some of us that don't have a lot of faith in either governments or markets. What then?

Maybe we feel confident enough in our own abilities to navigate governments and markets that we don't worry much about our own fate. We'll make out just fine. But what about others? Do we assume that everyone else should be able to do the same, or are some weaker and less endowed than we are and might not come out so well as common citizens or players in the market? Should we worry about them? Do we have an obligation to help them or act in their behalf?

It doesn't take much looking around to see that there are indeed large groups of people who haven't made out very well. Is it their own fault? The Social Darwinists, proponents of a sociological theory popular beginning in the 1830s but still very much around today, believed that it *was* their fault. They were simply lazier, less intelligent, and/or less virtuous than those who were successful in life. Those who made out well were entitled to their goodies and should feel no guilt about those less well off. Their historical role models were mountain men and captains of industry who struck out on their own. Adam Smith, the theorist of laissez-faire capitalism, believed that individuals looking after their own interests in the marketplace would be guided by "the invisible hand" to ultimately contribute to the interests of all. The novelist Ayn Rand, the muse to a number of important politicians including Speaker of the House Paul Ryan and Senator Ron Paul, argued that it was your moral obligation to be selfish.

Others, perhaps inspired by religion or secular humanitarianism, see an obligation to be "their brothers' keepers" (however, Christians quote the Bible on both sides of this issue) (Collins, 2013). They believe markets work only in the context of a stable government and a system of law and justice. (It is interesting to note that Adam Smith, the apostle of free markets, agreed with this.) They see cooperation more than competition leading to the betterment of everyone. Their historical role models are those who formed wagon trains and built forts for the common defense and joined together for barn-raisings and quilting bees for the common prosperity. Oliver Wendell Holmes, Jr., a noted jurist, said, "[T]axation is the price we pay for a civilized society." President Franklin Roosevelt believed that "[t]he test of our progress is not whether we add more to the abundance of those who have much; it is whether we provide enough for those who have too little."

It also doesn't take much to notice that there are patterns to those who are doing well and those who are not. There are differences in gender, age, skin color, religion, and ethnic background. Why is that? Are some groups inferior to others? This is still widely believed. Or are there obstacles placed in their way? Is there discrimination in hiring, school admission, job promotion, and housing? Are differences in access to nutrition and health care important in this?

What should the goals of a good health policy be? Should it be universal coverage, coverage of as many people as is practical, or coverage of those who need it the most? Should there be a means test that screens out those who are well off and don't need government assistance? Should we strive to keep the private sector central to the system in order to keep the market healthy? Should the public sector predominate because health is a right of citizenship, or should we be totally pragmatic and let each sector do what it does best?

Bringing these cosmic questions down a more practical level, what kind of trade-offs should we be willing to make? To what extent should cost be the limiting factor on what we provide?

Check Your Understanding 9.4

Check your understanding of Social Analysis of Health Policy by taking this brief quiz.

ECONOMIC ANALYSIS OF HEALTH POLICY

The cost of health care does not seem to have been a concern in earlier health policy, perhaps because we did not evaluate it in normal market terms. For the vast majority of middle-class voters, it was something we or our insurance paid for; we didn't ask how much up front. If our children or our aging parents were sick, we wanted them to be taken care of. We didn't shop around for a bargain. I once heard a corporate health expert try to convince an audience that health consumers should act like he instructed his teenage daughter to behave when she needed new jeans. Compare costs; are the designer labels really worth it? No one asked him whether he would have told her to ask the price local hospitals charged for an appendectomy if she was feeling a sharp pain in her right side. I strongly suspect he would have been off to the Emergency Room and would not have worried about surgical bargains or speed limits.

We are not usually in a market frame of mind when facing health problems. But over the last few decades we have been forced to consider costs because they and the price of insurance to cover them have persistently grabbed us by the collar and demanded attention. Controlling health costs has been on the agendas of Presidents Nixon, Reagan, Clinton, and Obama. As the title of the legislation indicates, they are at the heart of the Affordable Care Act.

Hospitals

The major actors in the health care market have been hospitals, insurance companies, drug companies, governments, and doctors. Their relative strength in the market has changed over the years. Some of them have had more interest in controlling costs than others.

Access to health care is another central theme in health policy, and it also has important economic implications. If we want everyone to have access, how do we pay for it if they can't? Presidents Truman, Nixon, and Clinton all tried and failed to enact universal health care programs. They failed for a variety of reasons, but cost and how to share it was one of them. President Johnson succeeded in creating services that covered elders and some of the poor, but the programs were by no means universal. Part of the problem was that programs relying on a combination of private and public participants are more complicated and costly than one where a single payer, the government, covers everyone. But there is as yet insufficient political support for the single-payer format, although support appears to be growing. But for now, we are left with mash-ups. Will the current one work?

Let's begin with hospitals. Care in hospitals accounts for almost one-third of our health expenses, and that does not include the increasing number of cases treated in the emergency room but not admitted to the hospital. So an inquiry into why health care costs so much should start here. And here we make a truly astounding discovery: Hospitals do not know what things cost. They'll present you with a bill. It is based on something called a chargemaster. Every hospital has one but they don't want to talk about it. Steven Brill, an investigative reporter who tried hard to get to see one, says, "[O]fficials treat it like an eccentric uncle living in the attic." He could find "no process, no rationale, behind the core document that is the basis of hundreds of billions of dollars in health care bills" (Abelson, 2013; Brill, 2013, p. 22).

If you do get to see a breakdown of your bill, you will notice things like $24 for a niacin pill that costs a nickel at your local drugstore; $1.50 for an acetaminophen tablet that costs $1.49 for 100; or a box of gauze pads for $77, probably $3.98 at Walgreen's. A surgical gown costs $39; you can get 30 of them online for $180. A blanket costing $13 is billed at $32 and can be used again. A marking pen, also reusable, is $3, comparatively cheap but is probably good for scores of patients. If asked about this stupefying markup, you may be told that this is part of the overhead cost of your room. But you've already paid a room charge of probably several thousand dollars a day (Brill, 2013, pp. 37, 39; Brill, 2015a, pp. 6, 449, 250).

Tests, appliances, and implants are typically billed at astronomically inflated prices. A chest X-ray costs $283 at the same hospital where Medicare would reimburse at $20.44. Medicare would pay $13.94 for a troponin blood test that is billed as $199.50. A Medtronic simulator that cost the hospital perhaps $19,000 was charged to a patient for $49,237. A transfusion of the drug Flebogamma for the hospital cost $4,615, but for Medicare it was $2,123. Even staff charges can be orchestrated to the point of charging $800 an hour for a nurse (Brill, 2013).

We have seen how the same operations can cost vastly different amounts from country to country. The same is true of American cities. A colonoscopy in a Long Island surgical center cost one patient $6,385. Another in Keene, New Hampshire, paid $7,563.56. In Chappaqua, New York, a colonoscopy with a polyp removal was $9,142.84. Even more interesting is that the average U.S. cost for a colonoscopy was only $1,185. In Switzerland, it would cost $655. This is a routine procedure. So are deliveries of babies. When Renee Martin, a professional whose insurance did not cover pregnancy, called a local hospital to find out how much maternity care would cost, the finance office couldn't tell her. They then gave her a range of $4,000 to $45,000. In response to a $935 bill for an ultrasound, she pointed out that the machine was quite old, that the test only took twenty minutes, and she had already paid a radiologist $256 to read it. They reduced the charge to $655. "I feel like I'm in a used-car lot," she said (Rosenthal, 2013b).

One common justification for chargemaster prices is that it covers the overall cost of running the hospital; however, room and facilities charges are also levied, which you would think would be covered by overhead. Another is that it allows hospitals to cover the costs of the poor; some cost-shifting does occur, but as we have seen, it is a lot less than you'd expect. They also claim that it covers research, but most research is funded by drug companies or the federal government. But their main response, if pressed, is that they really don't expect anyone to pay that much. Medicare has its own cost list that is much lower, insurance companies try to bargain down toward Medicare rates, and the rest may find medical-billing advocates who will bargain for them. Most hospitals recover around 35 percent of the chargemaster rates. Hospitals with big names may get 50 percent. Starting at such a high level guarantees that even the hardest bargaining will still leave a tidy profit. In fact, the average profit margin for "nonprofit" hospitals is 11.7 percent. It is actually legal to claim a nonprofit status, thus paying no income taxes, and still make money. They can also afford to pay their CEOs multimillion-dollar salaries (Brill, 2015a).

In addition to the private and nonprofit hospitals is a third category of hospitals: They are publicly owned, usually by cities or counties. They are known as safety-net hospitals because they serve the poorest and sickest, and usually the uninsured members of the population. Medicaid has given such hospitals payments in recognition that they serve a "disproportionate share" of the neediest patients. The ACA has cut these payments based on the assumption that most people coming to these hospitals will now be insured. However, an early study suggests there will still be a gap. The units of government that support safety-nets have increasingly squeezed budgets; they often must rely on bond issues to keep them open. They are also partially funded by Emergency Medicaid, a program that would be cut by the first Trump budget. The expansion of Medicaid under the ACA was a lifesaver to many. But even with that, many are closing, leaving the neediest demographic without a safety net (Neuhausen, 2014; Colliver, 2015; Goodnough,

2012a; Nuila, 2017). Safety-net hospitals are important subsidies to private and nonprofit hospitals. By providing care for patients without insurance, they allow private, nonprofit hospitals to concentrate on paying customers. Said one administrator of a safety-net hospital: "If we go down, they go down" (Nuila, 2017).

How does Medicare come up with its own schedule of costs? Hospitals are required to file cost reports on everything they do. (So they do, in fact, know what things cost; it is just that they don't use this in billing.) Medicare pays the composite average cost, adjusted for things like cost-of-living. A panel of doctors provided by the American Medical Association reviews them every year, recommending updates. Hospitals don't have to treat Medicare patients, but they all do. They know that despite all their grumbling, the rates still allow them a reasonable profit. Some would say their profit margins would be the envy of any business, large or small. On top of that they will get more from the insurance companies and also from any unsuspecting, noninsured patients who don't know that they are in a used-car lot (Brill, 2015a).

Medicare doesn't always have the upper hand in dealing with hospitals. Hospital Corporation of America (HCA), controlling 163 hospitals across the country, showed soaring profits in late 2012. One factor that contributed to their prosperity was the hospital's decision in 2008 to change the coding of emergency room patients to higher levels of seriousness. Nearly overnight, HCA's patients appeared to be much, much sicker. Medicare reimbursements for the highest categories soared from $48,000 in 2006 to $949,000 in 2010. Earnings in 2009 were up by $100 million. HCA also started advertising its ER services on highway billboards. At the other end of the scale, they began turning away anyone who they felt might not need emergency care, particularly if they were unable to pay for it. This organization has a long history of fraud. In 2002, it paid a record-breaking $2 billion to settle a similar case. Its CEO, Rick Scott, said that he knew nothing about it; he went on to become governor of Florida (Creswell & Abelson, 2012).

Hospital Corporation of America is still at it. In 2015, *Health Affairs* published a report of the fifty hospitals with the highest markups. A quarter of them were owned by HCA. Another hospital giant, Community Hospital Systems, owned half of them. Both are private, for-profit hospital chains (Bai & Anderson, 2015; Potter, 2016).

This problem may be fueled by electronic recordkeeping methods. The use of electronic medical and billing systems was first encouraged by the Bush administration. The system received a boost of tens of billions of dollars in Obama's economic stimulus package in 2009. But the system makes it easy for an ER doctor to click a box indicating that a full examination had been performed when it hadn't and makes it possible to "clone" records by copying them from other cases. The system has the potential for better documentation of the care provided. Some argue that doctors were actually underbilling under the old system. But its advocates also admit that it makes it easier to commit fraud. This may be bad news for the success of the ACA, which presses for more electronic records. More federal oversight may be in order (Abelson, Creswell, & Palmer, 2012).

Drugs

Prescription drugs account for about 10 percent of the national health cost, not the major problem, but a good-sized chunk of it. We spent over $457 billion on prescription drugs in 2015. And drugs cost about 50 percent higher in the United States than in the rest of the world because other governments regulate profit margins. Brill (2015a) estimates that the

United States might save $94 billion if we paid the prices charged in other Western countries (p. 235). Our drug prices have been rising since 1957 when tracking began. Between 2008 and 2016, prices for the most popular brand-named drugs increased by 208 percent. They dropped in 2012 for the first time because a number of important drugs had become available as generics. However, that is expected to be a temporary trend because a number of expensive specialty drugs have been introduced recently, and their patents will not expire for a while. Drug companies sometimes conspire with competitors to keep generic drugs off the market, and courts have declared this to be legal. There are also now fewer competitors to buy off. In 2015, the value of mergers and acquisitions reached $300 billion, the largest number and value ever, and the number of drug giants is fewer, making cooperation easier.

Yet another contribution of drug cost inflation is the trend of physicians selling drugs out of their own offices. This practice can increase the price to patients and/or their insurers as much as tenfold (AARP, 2017; Bach, 2015; Leibowitz, 2008; Meier, 2012; Thomas, 2013).

Insurance

The role of insurance companies has become increasingly reactive. Classic indemnity insurance, where you pay a monthly premium and send your bills to the company after you receive treatment, has largely been replaced by prepaid, managed care plans where you must have your treatment approved in advance. As we've seen, insurance companies try to manipulate the pool of clients so that as many of them as possible are healthy and unlikely to need benefits, and as few as possible are sick or likely to get sick. Thus, their vigilance in looking for preexisting conditions increased—this means you can't get insurance if it looks like you might be expensive to cover. And even if you managed to get insurance and later develop a condition that is expensive, they stop covering it.

The market power of insurance has varied. In some places where there are multiple hospitals, they can negotiate lower prices in exchange for including the hospitals in their plans. In other places, a hospital may be large and famous enough to charge the companies what it wants to or at least keep them closer to the chargemaster rates than to the Medicare rates. Under the ACA, the landscape for insurance changed dramatically because the goal is universal coverage, or at least covering as many people as possible. The pool has greatly enlarged. Gate-keeping devices like excluding those with preexisting conditions were made illegal, but that was supposed to be balanced by bringing in many younger, healthier clients.

Despite enormous difficulties in the computer-based enrollment process, which we'll talk about later, the goals set by the program were eventually met. But the mix of healthy and ailing people was not accurately predicted by the insurance companies or the government. By 2016, the giant insurers—Aetna, Humana, Blue Cross Blue Shield—were losing money. They pulled out of many of the state insurance exchanges. Critics of the ACA predicted collapse.

The collapse didn't happen. There were smaller companies in many of the exchanges who took up some of the slack. But choices were narrowed. There was a risk-sharing provision in the ACA that would have allowed the government to mitigate the insurers' losses, but it was blocked by Republicans. Those covered by Medicare, Medicaid, or employer programs were not affected, nor were those with lower incomes, for example, $97,200 for a family of four. Still, several million people were caught in rate hikes, which was enough for critics to declare that the ACA was in a "death spiral" (Edwards, 2016; Krugman, 2016).

The penalties ($100 the first year, going up to $695 by 2016) for not participating were not large enough to discourage the young and the healthy from opting out. Many, it seems, do not understand the principle of the insurance pool: Pay when you don't need it so it will be there when you do. Instead they ask: Why should I be penalized for being healthy? A large public education effort called Enroll America is underway, bankrolled by insurers and hospitals. The Trump administration tried to cancel any government efforts to enroll new members but backed off after public outcry (Goodnough, 2012a; Goldstein, 2017).

The requirement that businesses with 50 or more full-time employees offer health benefits has prompted some to predict that employers will cut workers' hours, thus adding to the number of low-income workers and weakening the economy. Others say that employers know that doing so would risk losing the best workers and reduce the productivity of those who remain. Ron Nelsen, who runs Pioneer Overhead Door in Las Vegas, has five employees. When deciding to hire more workers, he doesn't think about the cost of health insurance. "I hire people when demand necessitates it" (Greenhouse & Abelson, 2012; Harwood, 2013).

Physicians

As millions more gain insurance, there will most likely be a shortage of physicians and other health care personnel to serve their needs. Though many of the new enrollees will be young and healthy, even young and healthy people may decide it is wise to seek a doctor's advice rather than tough out the pain and/or dose themselves with over-the-counter drugs. And that's a good thing because it may avoid more expensive conditions in the future. But it still means we need more doctors. The Association of American Medical Colleges estimates that, by 2055, we will have a shortfall of between 46,100 and 90,400 doctors. Increases in insured citizens alone will require 16,000 to 17,000. The problem cannot be remedied quickly; it takes a decade to train a physician. Specialties take longer, however; and one thing the ACA does is pay primary care physicians better, thus encouraging doctors already in school to get into practice earlier (Pear & Lowrey, 2012; Pear, 2013b; Caroll, 2017).

Doctors themselves, however, are part of the problem of health costs. An estimated 30 percent of what is spent on medical tests and procedures is unlikely to benefit the patients who receive it. That's a pretty large amount of waste. It stems from understandable impulses. Doctors want as much information on what they're dealing with as possible and want to do everything in their power to help their patients. Patients themselves and their loved ones want to do everything possible, and costs are the last things they are thinking about. Doctors also know that if they fail to cure a patient, a malpractice suit may soon follow; not doing all possible tests may be at the heart of it. It should be noted here that one of ACA's goals is to reduce medical litigation, and the primary opponents of tort reform come from members of the president's own party who receive campaign contributions from trial lawyers (Brill, 2015a; Brody, 2012).

Some of this excess care may be less noble. Medicare patients in hospitals and convalescent centers report getting almost daily visits from attending physicians who have no direct connection to the case but have the ability to pop in, look over the patient, and rack up a few dollars. The attempt by the ACA to reward hospitals and doctors based on the quality of outcomes and not on the quantity of tests and checkups may discourage this. It may already have. Private insurers are endorsing the reward system and signing up with ACOs. The growth in health care costs slowed sharply from 2009 to 2012, enough to predict a significant lowering of the federal deficit (Brill, 2015a; Lowrey, 2013b; Pear, 2012c).

Physicians are at the center of a component of the ACA that supports the idea of the "medical home." This "home" is the office of your primary care doctor who would have all your medical records, know all the drugs you are taking, and coordinate the care of any specialists you have been referred to and all the other services you might be receiving. This looks a bit like managed care and is indeed concerned about costs. In fact, *Business Week* estimated it might reduce the inefficiencies in the system by $67 billion a year. But its primary concern is its focus on patients, making sure that what's happening in one part of your medical care is supporting, and not subverting, what's happening in another (Arnst, 2009).

State Governments

The expansion of Medicaid to cover everyone with an income of 133 percent of the federal poverty level or lower is another key part of health care reforms. This was originally required so that states could continue to get federal Medicaid funds. But the Supreme Court's decision that declared the ACA to be constitutional also declared that this expansion could not be considered mandatory; it was an option. Some states embraced the expansion, some didn't. Because 100 percent of the costs in the first three years would be entirely covered and reimbursement would drop gradually, but only to 90 percent in 2020, this would seem to be a relatively painless decision. The current federal share averages 57 percent. But in the current topsy-turvy politics (to be discussed in the next section) nothing is easy. For some Republicans, the ACA must be blocked at all costs regardless of what benefits it may have to the states. For some, Medicaid beneficiaries are not worthy of public support and even an additional 10 percent is too much to spend in a time that calls for austerity (Goodnough & Pear, 2013; Pear, 2012a).

A RAND Corporation study of 16 states that were likely to refuse expansion found that they would lose $8.4 billion in federal transfer payments, spend $1 billion on uncompensated care, and still suffer the reductions in Medicare and "disproportionate share hospital" payments that Medicaid expansion was supposed to offset. They also estimate that this would lead to an additional 19,000 deaths. In Texas, whose governor refused expansion, there was strong lobbying by the Texas Medical Association, as might be expected, but also by the Chambers of Commerce of Dallas, Ft. Worth, San Antonio, and other cities; the City Councils of Austin and Waco; religious-based advocacy groups; and the state's former deputy comptroller, who said that Medicaid expansion would boost the state economy by $68 billion (Fernandez, 2012; Goodnough, 2013; Pear, 2013c; Price & Eibner, 2013; Rodnofsky & Weaver, 2012).

A computer simulation conducted by the Agency for Health Care Research and Quality predicted Medicaid expansion would cut in half the annual out-of-pocket expenses of those in the program compared with people in states which opted out. It would reduce the number of families who were paying 10 to 20 percent of their income on health (Hill, 2015).

It will take time to assess those predictions. What we do know so far is that Medicaid expansion has further increased access to health insurance and reduced stress from financial insecurity, particularly among low-income patients. The service capacity of community health centers has improved. It did not raise state spending. In one state, getting an appointment for primary care was easier. This may be because the ACA paid Medicaid doctors at the higher rate enjoyed by Medicare doctors (McMarrow, Gates, Long, & Kenney 2017; Cole, Galarraga, Wilson, Wright, & Trivedi, 2017; Decker, Lipton, & Sommers, 2017; Sommers & Gruber, 2017; Tipirneni et al., 2017).

Since immigration is currently being hotly debated, it is useful to look at the impact of immigration on Medicare. It is widely assumed that immigrants are a drain on public resources. In the case of Medicare, however, not only are they not draining resources but they are actually contributing enough that they may well be keeping the program viable for the future. A Harvard study found that from 2002 to 2009 immigrants put in $115 billion more than they took out, while American-born citizens took out $28 billion more than they put in. This should not be a total surprise because immigrants are younger and therefore healthier, and mostly too young to qualify for benefits. As they age, the difference will be less dramatic, but for now they are propping up the system. Many of these contributors are undocumented workers who did this through fake Social Security cards and who cannot claim any benefits now or later. The Social Security Administration estimates that they kicked in $12 billion in 2010 with no hope of getting it back. If paths to citizenship are eventually created, this disparity will also diminish. But it should be offset by increased productivity as they emerge from the shadow economy (Tavernise, 2013; Zallman, Woolhandler, Himmelstein, Bor, & McCormick, 2013).

In conclusion, the ACA already seems to be slowing the rise of health care costs and may do more as reimbursement shifts from amount of care to quality of outcome, and more ACOs are established. Better pay for primary care physicians, gerontologists, and Medicaid doctors should produce better care and save money. Increasing use of electronic records should curtail duplication of effort, offering better coordination and cost savings, although some warn that is may not be as effective as expected (Terhune, Epstein, & Arnst, 2009).

Between 2000 and 2009 immigrants put $115 billion more into Medicare than they took out while native-born Americans took out $28 billion more than they took in.

However, there is nothing in the ACA that addresses one of the greatest escalators of health costs, the hospital chargemaster. Hospitals have succeeded in keeping it locked in the attic while enjoying an 11 to 12 percent profit margin. There is no discussion of it in Congress and hardly any in the news media. In order for us to see real savings, this bizarre system of determining prices in a used-car-lot fashion will have to be exposed.

Steven Brill renders a harsher verdict. "The new law hasn't come close to making health insurance premiums and out-of-pocket costs low enough so that health care is truly affordable to everyone . . . as it is in every other developed nation. . . . Instead, it provided massive government subsidies so that more people could buy health care at the same inflated prices [charged by the private sector]" (Brill, 2015b, p. 39).

> **Check Your Understanding 9.5**
> Check your understanding of Economic Analysis of Health Policy by taking this brief quiz.

POLITICAL ANALYSIS OF HEALTH POLICY

Health policy is a deadly serious matter. This section will provide a bit of comic relief. It is only a slight exaggeration to say that the politics of the ACA has been hilarious. The act is closely modeled after a program introduced in 2006 in Massachusetts by its Republican governor with support from both parties. Conservatives as well as liberals praised it. Newt Gingrich called it the most important step forward in years. Edmund Haislmeier of the Heritage Foundation said it was "one of the most promising strategies out there." Stuart Altman, an adviser to Hillary Clinton, thought it would be a catalyst for other states. When that governor decided to run for president, he thought this accomplishment would allow him to steal a key Democratic issue. The greatest difference between his plan and Hillary's, he said, "was that mine got passed and hers didn't" (Zakaria, 2012).

But when the governor, Willard "Mitt" Romney, began to seek the Republican nomination for president, he had to disavow his primary achievement. Gingrich and Haislmeier denounced it. Republican primary voters searched frantically for someone other than Romney to nominate. What had changed? A plan modeled on Romney's had become the major achievement, after a great struggle, of President Barack Obama. Suddenly, the ideas couldn't be any good because they had been adopted by Barack Obama. Watching Romney explain why his program worked for Massachusetts but couldn't work for the country and why some parts of it were worth saving while repealing the context they depended on was like watching a series of *Saturday Night Live* skits (Pear & Goodnough, 2012).

Central to both programs was the "individual mandate," the requirement that everyone should have insurance. This idea not only had Republican support but came from the country's top conservative think tank, the Heritage Foundation. Conservatives have traditionally been concerned about "free riders," those who benefit from a public policy without paying for it. That describes precisely the people who don't have insurance and accept hospital care when they have an accident. Now Republicans see the mandate as an infringement on individual liberty. Either they have become bleeding-heart liberals generously paying the bills of the uninsured or they don't know who is really paying for them. In any case, the free riders are forgiven (Roy, 2011; Zakaria, 2012a).

Another amusing aspect of this lock-step partisan opposition to Obama is that it is strong enough to keep otherwise powerful corporate leaders from speaking up for their own interests. Heads of businesses, large and small, are not blind to the amount that health care costs take from their bottom line. The appeal of the work-based insurance system that we inherited from the post-war wage freeze has dimmed long ago.

The benefit package is not the recruitment tool it once was. *Business Week* found that "[S]ome CEOs are so fed up with the status quo that federal intervention is sounding OK." Managing health benefits takes time and resources away from what they should be doing, that is, running businesses. "[M]any CEOs would secretly love the federal government to take on the burden. . . . " "[M]any . . . would even pay a new tax if it got them out of the insurance business." Those who defend the old system, said the research director of a business-oriented think tank, are saying, "I've got the best stateroom on the *Titanic,* and I'm not moving." All these utterances would be hard to believe if they were not coming from *Business Week* (Arnst, 2009).

Conservative columnist Ross Douthat sees a bipartisan consensus among policy scholars that the employer-based system (and the ACA's mandate that they get deeper into it) must go. He also sees a bipartisan consensus among politicians not to talk about it. John McCain proposed in his 2008 presidential campaign that the tax incentives that promote employer coverage be eliminated. Obama attacked him for it, which in effect locked him into the same system if he wasn't locked in it already. Maintaining the status quo while trying to get everyone into it is what makes the ACA so cumbersome. It is in this sense deeply conservative, says liberal economist Paul Krugman. A single-payer system would be much simpler and cheaper, and CEOs might have discovered that they liked it. But it seemed too radical for Obama, and he chose to save the status quo. If the insurance exchanges don't work, Obama may also have chosen the best stateroom on the *Titanic* (Douthout, 2013; Krugman, 2013).

The politics of health policy prior to the ACA have been covered in the History section. Politics leading up to it were more ordinary. The president had for a long time (some say too long) hung back, leaving Congress to hash out the form of the act. He did unleash staffers and even cabinet members for earnest lobbying of wavering Democrats and potential Republican converts. In the end, not a single Republican in either chamber voted for the bill. More interesting were the lobbying efforts with interest groups. The Administration managed to convince the pharmaceutical industry to support the act and grant $80 million cuts in drug prices, arguing that increased insurance coverage and Medicaid expansion would produce many new customers. The *Wall Street Journal* disapproved of this but also noted that George W. Bush had courted them for his 2003 Prescription Drug Act. The administration made a similar pitch to the insurance industry. Both efforts paid off. Harry and Louise did not reappear (Obamacare's secret history, 2012; Stolberg, 2009).

A legal challenge to the act moved toward the Supreme Court and there was much speculation about how the politically divided Supremes would decide on its constitutionality. Proponents of the law defended it under the "commerce clause" of the Constitution, Article 1, Section B, Clause 3, giving the federal government power to regulate foreign and domestic commerce. It should, they believed, allow government to require the purchase of insurance. Opponents argued that people not engaged in commerce should not be forced to buy services they didn't want. The Court's decision shocked both conservatives and liberals by upholding the constitutionality of the law, not through the commerce clause but through the right of Congress to levy taxes. To pull this off, Chief Justice John Roberts joined with the four liberal justices, a surprise to many. Those not surprised noted that Roberts had worked hard on a number of decisions to find a consensus in the Court regardless of his deeply conservative principles. Some conservatives were outraged; more astute ones noted that by bypassing the commerce clause, Roberts had made it harder in the future for government to use this argument in defense of programs (Liptak, 2013a, 2013b).

The Court also decided that the federal government could not compel the states to expand Medicaid. It was up to them, and we have considered the results above (Pear, 2012b).

Since Obama chose to work within the established private insurance system, the ACA had to create a way to enroll them in the system. States were asked to set up their own insurance marketplace exchanges. The federal government would take over for those that chose not to, which would involve an enrollment website. It was a disaster.

On opening day, October 1, 2013, the website denied entry to many, kicked others out after a few steps, and generally froze for long periods. The failure of implementation will be a case study in future policymaking textbooks. No one was in charge. The head of operations for the Center for Medicare and Medicaid Services said, "[I have] twelve bosses, including three or four in the White House, and no one is making decisions" (Brill; 2015a, p. 274). The many agencies involved in implementation didn't talk to each other. One had commissioned an outside evaluation that predicted great problems. They didn't share it. Turf battles excluded from meetings people who might have given them a broader view of what was happening. The people with the most appropriate technological knowledge were consistently marginalized. There was no time for pilot testing, a result of the politically imposed October deadline. The president and cabinet officers were told that everything was under control.

Once it was clear that nobody had much of anything under control, an ad hoc team was quickly assembled to fix it. They did. That story would make a good film script. By December 23, they were enrolling in a single day five times the number logged in during all of October. By February, they had 3.3 million on board, though the initial goal was 4.4 million. By December 2016, the total had reached 6.4 million. It eventually reached 8 million (Brill, 2015a; Shear & Abelson, 2014; Pear, 2016).

An interesting shift in the political winds concerns attitudes toward a single-payer program. Obama deemed it a taboo and decided to work within the existing, employer-based system. Depending on how the questions are asked, however, many citizens now favor a Medicare-for-all approach. Vermont came close to implementing a single-payer plan. California is considering one. And as the Republican efforts to replace the ACA continue to undermine the private insurance part of the system; a government-run program may be all we are left with (Reich, 2016; Worthen, 2014; Rampell, 2017; Leonhardt, 2017; Ho, 2017).

? Check Your Understanding 9.6

Check your understanding of Political Analysis of Health Policy by taking this brief quiz.

PROGRAM/POLICY EVALUATION

It is clear that the ACA has succeeded in bringing insurance coverage to millions of citizens. Research has noted a few other accomplishments. It was feared that the large increase in newly insured patients would reduce access to health care for those already insured. This did not happen. Furthermore, thanks to ACA subsidies, it reduced the financial burden of those privately insured, particular those who were spending more than 10 percent of family income for insurance premiums and out-of-pocket medical expenses (Abdus & Hill, 2017; Boudreaux, Gonzales, & Saloner, 2017).

While we await a full evaluation of the ACA, it may be useful to look at how the inspiration for the ACA, Romney care, has fared. It was not an immediate success. Costs remained high in the first few years. But in 2011 the *Boston Globe* reported that the plan ". . . has, after five years, worked as well or better than expected" (Mooney, 2011). After ten years, the picture was even clearer. An analysis in *Health Affairs* concluded: "Massachusetts achieved near-universal health insurance coverage within two years of passage . . . and has sustained that high coverage, including during the Great Recession and its aftermath, while the U.S. uninsurance rate rose to 16 percent in 2010" (Long, Skoper, Shelto, Nordahl, & Walsh, 2016, p. 1634). Premiums did increase, but the private insurance market remained stable. There are also still gaps in coverage, particularly among those with less than a high school education, poor people, and minorities.

As this is being written, three attempts to repeal the ACA have failed. However, the administration can still undermine it and is trying hard to do so. First, it cut funds for outreach efforts to inform citizens of their insurance options and to encourage those who are young and healthy to enroll, thus maintaining a viable risk pool. Second, it will not pay the subsidies promised to low-income purchasers of insurance. Third, it is weakening the enforcement of the mandate for all citizens to buy insurance or pay a penalty. All of these factors make the task of insurance companies extremely difficult. They can't set premiums with any assurance of profit in such a climate of uncertainty. To protect themselves, they must increase the cost of the policies they sell or get out of the business. When the president said after the second attempt at ACA repeal dissolved that he would just let it fail on its own, he was doing more than that. He was actively promoting its failure. It is his right to do so, and is entirely consistent with his campaign promises. But it should be clear that, if he succeeds, the failure is not the fault of the legislation (Garthwaite & Bagley, 2017; Krugman, 2017).

As this political battle plays out, there are two things to keep an eye on. Despite seven years of firm resolution that the ACA must be repealed, the Republicans have had great difficulty finding a coherent replacement. But two ideas keep reappearing: high-risk insurance pools and individual health savings accounts.

High-risk pools are a way of dealing with two facts: (1) One of the most popular parts of the ACA is that it bans insurance companies from refusing coverage to those with preexisting conditions and (2) eliminating the mandate that everyone must have insurance reduces the size of private insurance pools to the point that insurance companies cannot possibly cover preexisting conditions. We have four decades of experience with high-risk pools. Many states have tried them. In general, their experience is that the premiums offered are much higher than normal insurance, the programs are expensive to administrate, and many people who might qualify are excluded. Most important, they are very, very expensive. The second repeal bill provides $8 billion over five years to fund the pool. The AARP estimates that it would take $178 billion a year (Hall, 2015; Politz; 2017; Flowers & Noel-Miller, 2017).

The individual health savings account is an idea that appeals to those of us who believe that everyone should take responsibility for their own health and make sensible provisions to handling the costs associated with this responsibility. The question is: What happens if we don't? Social Security was established based on the assumption that not enough of us would or could set aside retirement accounts. It was morally and practically easier to set up a system that ensured that everyone would have a basic income in retirement than to have to deal with a large number of impoverished elders.

Social Security is a pretty bare bones income. It makes sense to have a little more to ensure a comfortable old age. But how many people are doing that? One-third have saved nothing at all. Another 23 percent have less than $10,000. Only 25 percent have over $100,000 (Kirkham, 2016). And if that is the case, is it realistic to assume that most people would establish a health savings account? And if they could, how far would it go? A single medical emergency might easily cost more than $100,000.

Health savings accounts (HSAs) are attractive because they are untaxed. This makes them particularly attractive to people who worry about tax liability. People with low incomes have more pressing worries. As might be expected, those in the top quintile of income are most likely to have HSAs. Of those in the first three quintiles, less than 4 percent have HSAs. How are we going to persuade the rest of the population to sign up (Helmchen, Brown, Lurie, & Sasso, 2015; Lieber, 2017)?

If the ACA survives, what could improve it? The Urban Institute thinks it is underfunded. Better subsidies would bring more insurers. That would cost 0.2 percent of the gross domestic product, which is half as expensive as the tax cuts proposed in the Republican health plan. Paul Krugman suggests bringing back the public option, insurance provided by the government in areas where private companies don't want to serve (Krugman, 2017).

Brill has a more complicated proposal, another way to integrate public and private interests. He notes the trend of hospital consolidations and suggests we might as well embrace the emergent oligopolies but regulate them. Some already operate on flat rates. They act as their own insurance companies. You pay the monthly fee and you are covered for whatever happens to you. The doctors work for the hospital and have no incentive to inflate the cost of treatment with unnecessary tests, procedures, or drugs. Each market would have to have at least two fully integrated, provider-insurance company players. Operating profits and executive salaries would be capped. "Let the foxes run the henhouse," he says, "with conditions" (Brill 2015a, p. 431f).

More interesting is a conservative alternative to both the ACA and Republican replacement plans. This would provide universal catastrophic insurance but would leave other coverage to the individual. This would bother conservatives, on the one hand, because it would be a universal entitlement, but, on the other hand, it would place most of the responsibility back in the hands of individuals, upholding their commitment to individual liberty. It would bother liberals who don't believe individuals would provide for themselves adequately, but it would at least reassure them that a health crisis wouldn't wipe out people's finances completely (Domenech, 2017).

Check Your Understanding 9.7

Check your understanding of Program/Policy Evaluation by taking this brief quiz.

CONCLUSION

The Patient Protection and Affordable Care Act of 2010 is the most important piece of health legislation since Medicare. If it survives, we will still be facing the chargemaster and will still need to look hard for ways to bring down the costs of health care. And we will still be facing the moral and professional dilemma: Is health care a right that should be available to all or reserved for those who can afford to buy it in the marketplace?

Recall what you learned from this chapter by completing the Chapter Review.

10

Child Welfare: Family Preservation Policy

LEARNING OUTCOMES

- Examine the consequences, intended and unintended, of the passage of child abuse and neglect reporting laws.
- Discuss the research by Henry Maas and Richard Engler, reported in their book *Children in Need of Parents,* and its effect on child welfare policy and practice.
- Describe the basic principles/ideas of the child rescue approach, the permanency planning approach, and the family preservation approach to child welfare policy and practice.
- Discuss what is know about the outcomes of long-term foster care and what this knowledge means for the development/reform of child welfare policy.
- Discuss why family preservation as a child welfare policy appeals to both liberal and conservative factions in our society.
- Explore evaluations of family preservation programs and whether these provide enough evidence to continue, expand, or discontinue this approach to child welfare policy.

CHAPTER OUTLINE

Gloria Rosazza/123RF.com

With twenty years of experience, Rhonda Swenson is the senior worker in her local family and protective services office. When she was recently contacted by her alma mater and asked to complete a questionnaire giving her opinion about which classes had most influenced her career as a social worker, the answers she gave surprised even her. Upon reflection, she concluded that the classes in research and statistics had been most influential, even though she had hated these classes with a passion while enrolled in them. The explanation for her answer to this question was not that she had come to love research and statistics; she had not. The reason was a concept she had studied in these classes that had remained in the back of her mind ever since she began her job as a child welfare caseworker. This concept is type 1 and type 2 error. In research, type 1 error is the (false) detection of an effect that is not present, while type 2 error is the failure to detect an effect that is present. These are sometimes referred to as false positive and false negative. Very early in her career, Rhonda realized that type 1 and type 2 errors were the key threats to her work as a child abuse and neglect investigator. In her job, type 1 error meant concluding that a home is not dangerous for a child when it actually is. This type of error results in leaving a child in a home where he or she is likely to be harmed or even killed. Type 2 error means concluding that a home is unsafe for a child when it is actually safe. This results in breaking up a family, sometimes permanently, when the child could have been left at home and saved all sorts of trauma. For the entire 20 years that Rhonda had been a child welfare worker, she had constantly been reviewing every case she had ever had in her mind trying to determine if she had committed one of these errors. Because she had followed agency policy and erred on the side of caution, removing a child at any sign of danger, she was fairly sure that she had seldom, if ever, been guilty of type 1 error. However, she was sure that this same caution had resulted in type 2 error and at least a few children, perhaps more, who spent time in foster care unnecessarily. Five years ago, Rhonda's agency had put in place a new policy that considerably reduced her angst about committing type 1 or type 2 error. This policy is known as family preservation and was operationalized by establishing a family preservation unit in Rhonda's office. This unit is staffed by specially trained social workers to whom Rhonda can refer cases where she suspects a child may be in danger but thinks the situations may not be severe enough to justify removal of the child. The family preservation worker, who has a very small caseload, becomes involved with the family and provides many hours of treatment/supervision per week for a limited number of weeks. If the family preservation worker, based on her intense involvement with the family, concludes that removal is necessary, this will, of course, be done. However, the goal of the family preservation worker's efforts is to identify and work on any and all problems severe enough to put the child in danger, and then withdraw from the case, leaving the family with much stronger child-rearing and problem-solving skills. Since having this option, Rhonda now feels her type 2 error rate is almost zero.

Thoughts for Social Work Practice

Speculate on ways that child welfare policy might help a social worker reduce type 1 and type 2 errors.

Life for many children in the United States is far more difficult than it should be. The Children's Defense Fund has gathered data indicating that, each day in the United States, 4 children are killed by abuse or neglect, 187 children are arrested for violent crimes, 408 children are arrested for drug crimes, 847 babies are born to teen mothers, 1,392 babies are born into extreme poverty, 1,837 children are confirmed as abused or neglected, and 4,408 babies are born to single mothers (Children's Defense Fund, 2017). To these figures could be added the millions of children who are afflicted by severe mental or behavioral disorders. Our society's concern for these problems is expressed in a formal service delivery system known as child welfare. This system is composed of government and private agencies that are given the responsibility to

- Respond to the needs of children reported to public child protection agencies as being abused, neglected, or at risk of child maltreatment
- Provide children placed in out-of-home care with developmentally appropriate services
- Help children find a permanent home in the least restrictive living situation that is possible (Pecora, 2008)

Although child welfare has a broad mandate, as a field of social work and of social welfare policy, it has in recent decades focused more and more on the problems of child neglect and, even more so, abuse, providing what are known as child protective services. This narrowing of focus has been driven by two developments. The first is a rapidly increasing awareness among the general populace of the problem of child abuse, resulting in an ever-more efficient system for reporting abuse, and laws in every state mandating that professionals who deal with children report suspicions of abuse. The result of this is that maltreatment reports have increased from 9,563 in 1967 to more than 4 million in 2015 (McCurdy & Daro, 2000; U.S. Department of Health and Human Services, Administration for Children and Families, Children's Bureau, 2017). The other development contributing to the narrowing of focus is that funding for child welfare has not increased fast enough to allow agencies to deal with the massive increase in reports while still attending to broader child welfare concerns. Thus, broader concerns such as day care and child health have been pushed aside while agencies spend an ever-increasing proportion of their resources on child protection.

It is an old truism that every solution contains within it the seeds of a new problem. This has proven to be true in child protective services. One of the obvious ways to deal with a child in a substandard or dangerous home situation is to move the child from the home into substitute care. After the child is placed, the home can be assessed and, if there is hope for remediation, services can be delivered to strengthen the family and eventually return the child home. Predictably, as the number of reports of child abuse and neglect skyrocketed, the number of children in foster care kept pace. Unfortunately, as the number of children needing foster care has increased, the number of licensed foster homes has not kept pace. Between 1990 and 2003, the number of children in foster care increased by 27 percent, while the number of foster homes increased by only 16 percent (Kaye & Cook, 1993; Child Welfare League of America, National Data Analysis System, 2017). The number of children in foster care has declined, falling steadily from a high in 1999 of 567,000 to 397,000 in 2012. Unfortunately, the number is once again on the rise, reaching 428,000 in 2015. The general decline in the number of children in foster care since 1999 may be a result of successful efforts by states to reduce the length of time children spend in care, to locate more permanent homes for children and reduce the number of children entering care through family preservation policies. The reason for the more recent increases in entries to foster care are not completely understood but are suspected to be related to rising levels of parental substance abuse (Committee on Ways and Means, 2017, Table 11-3).

At the same time the child welfare system is being subjected to increasing pressure to protect abused and neglected children, it is also being severely criticized for breaking up families and then not providing services to rebuild them. The child welfare system has been criticized for being overzealous, not following due process, and trampling on the rights of parents accused of abuse and neglect of their children. A political action group, the National Coalition for Child Protection Reform, has been formed to champion the cause of parents involved in the child welfare system (Wexler, 1995). Although many of these critics greatly overstate their case, it is true that the system deserves criticism for not putting enough effort into helping families resolve problems once a child has been removed. Child welfare researchers have found that once a child is removed from the biological parents, the amount of clinical services provided to the child and parents actually declines (Fanshel & Shinn, 1978; Gambrill, 1990; Lindsey, 1994). The National Center for Resource Family Support (2003) found that reunification was a goal for only 42 percent of foster children in 2000.

The combination of these factors, as well as others that will be discussed later in this chapter, has led to great pressure on the child welfare system to reduce the number of children placed in foster care. One possible remedy, enthusiastically embraced by almost all stakeholders in the system, is an approach known as family preservation. This approach is based on the belief that in many cases in which placement appears to be imminent, it is possible to prevent placement by the provision of intense services delivered in the child's home over a brief, time-limited period. Tracy and Piccola (2013) state that family preservation programs, regardless of the specific model adopted, generally share an explicit value base that includes:

- Families should be maintained together whenever possible
- Children need continuity and stability in their lives
- Separation has detrimental effects on both adults and children

These values are operationalized in service delivery models that emphasize family strengths, mobilize formal and informal supports, and provide a variety of concrete and clinical services calculated to meet individual family needs (Tracy & Piccola, 2013).

Family preservation services begin, as do most child welfare interventions, with a child being referred to an agency as being in danger of serious harm. A social worker investigates the complaint and, if the complaint is confirmed, decides whether the family is a good candidate for family preservation services. For the family to be considered an appropriate case for family preservation services, the child must be at risk of placement, but the social worker must be convinced that the child can remain safely in his or her own home if intensive services are provided. Depending on the model of family preservation being applied, the family is given services for periods ranging from four to six weeks in the least intensive to three months or longer in the most intensive models. The social workers providing services have small caseloads and work with each family for many hours each week, sometimes twenty or more. After the provision of the brief, intensive services, the agency withdraws to a supervisory role and leaves the family to function—presumably with a greatly increased problem-solving capacity. Table 10.1 summarizes the differences between traditional child welfare social services and family preservation services.

Table 10.1 Service Delivery Contrasts

Traditional Social Services	Family Preservation Services
Services in office	Services in client's home
Waiting list	Immediate response
50-minute hour	As long as session is needed
Weekly or less	Frequent–often daily
Business-only hours	7 days a week, 24 hours a day
Selective intake	Accept almost all cases
Worker defines solutions	Family selects solutions
Indefinite duration	Predetermined length
Long-term, often years	Short-term, 4 to 6 weeks
Large caseloads, 12 to 50	Small caseloads, 2 to 3
Focus on individual	Focus on family system
Concentrate on immediate symptom	Concentrate on underlying skills and interactions
Soft services only	Blend of hard and soft services
No special use of crisis	Use crisis as teachable moment
Solve problem for client	Help client solve own problem

Source: Reprinted with permission, Edna McConnell Clark Foundation. From *For Children's Sake: The Promise of Family Preservation*, by Joan Barthel, 1992.

The several models of family preservation differ in length and intensity of service and also in psychosocial theory base. The original model, called Homebuilders, provides the shortest and most intense services. In this model, social workers carry only two cases at a time, spend as many as twenty hours a week with each case, are available twenty-four hours a day, and generally complete services within four to six weeks. This approach is based on cognitive-behavioral theory and relies heavily on devices such as behavioral checklists. The Homebuilders approach also focuses on concrete services. Another approach is based on structural family therapy, utilizes family systems theory, and emphasizes the relationship between the family and other systems. Special attention is given to improving the relations of the family with the community. In this model, social workers have somewhat larger caseloads and work with each family over a longer period of time, generally three to twelve months. Other variations of family preservation utilize psychodynamic and behavioral approaches and involve longer periods of contact with families (Schuerman, Rzepnicki, & Littell, 1994).

Since its inception in 1974 with the original Homebuilders program, family preservation has grown in popularity until it can now be said to be the policy of choice for dealing with child abuse and neglect. Some form of family preservation service is now in place in every state in the nation. The services are provided by both public and private agencies, generally in some form of partnership. The approach is specified in laws at both the federal and state levels and in the policies of public and private agencies. The approach is probably undergoing the most thorough evaluation of any social welfare innovation in history; it has become so popular that a backlash has developed against it. We now turn to a detailed discussion of the development of child protective services and the growth and current dominance of family preservation as the service of choice.

HISTORICAL ANALYSIS

If a time machine were to transport someone from the early nineteenth century into the present age, they would find child protective services almost as baffling as all of our technological marvels. Although few people during this earlier age would have approved of unnecessary cruelty or neglect toward children, the notion of children as a group with the right to protection, and of the government as having the right to provide such protection, was entirely foreign to the thinking of the era. By the end of the nineteenth century, thinking on this matter had undergone a remarkable transformation. Many people, particularly those in the middle and upper classes, had begun to believe firmly in the right of children to a certain level of care and the right of government to step in and enforce the provision of adequate care when parents were judged to be unable, or unwilling, to provide such care.

Two general developments during the nineteenth century account for the changing attitude toward the rights of children to protection and of government to provide it. The first is that the position of children in the economy changed radically, and along with this the method of valuing children. During the early years of the century, children had direct economic worth, and their rights and value were judged accordingly. Viviana Zelizer (1985), in her book *Pricing the Priceless Child,* documents how during the nineteenth century the concept of the "useful" child who made a valuable contribution to the family economy gradually evolved into the "useless" child of the twentieth century who is economically worthless, in fact, very costly, to the family but is considered to be emotionally priceless. The reasons for this transformation were many, including the decline in useful tasks that could be performed by children in a maturing industrial economy, the decline in birth and death rates, and the rise of the compassionate family. Because of this changed concept of the value of children, society began to view them as worthy of protection (Zelizer, 1985).

The second general factor that accounts for the emergence of child protection at the end on the nineteenth century is, in fact, a result of the first. Stemming from the changed conception of the value of children, the common law interpretation of children's and women's rights evolved. Before the nineteenth century, the relationship between parents and children in this country generally followed English common law. Under the law at that time, children's rights were considered to be relatively unimportant. Likewise, mothers were entitled to "no power but only reverence and respect." The father, in contrast, was given practically absolute control over all matters pertaining to his wife and children. Although fathers were expected to protect and care for their children, the duty was "merely a moral obligation creating no civil liability" (Tiffin, 1982, pp. 142–143). In other words, if a father was cruel or neglectful toward his children, society would not approve but was powerless to intervene. In the second half of the nineteenth century, the system of family law began to change. Two new legal principles emerged as dominant. One was the recognition of equal rights between mother and father, with the mother's rights, at least in regard to children, often being given preference. The second was the recognition by the legal system of children as being of paramount importance, vital to the future of society, and therefore as appropriate objects of the court's protection (Tiffin, 1982).

The Child Rescue Movement

By the second half of the nineteenth century, the stage was set for outside intervention into family life for the purpose of protecting children. An incident in New York City in 1873 served to ignite what has come to be called the child rescue movement. Henry Bergh was a prominent philanthropist who had directed his efforts toward the protection of animals and, for this purpose, had in 1866 founded the New York Society for the Prevention of Cruelty to Animals (SPCA). It was to Bergh and his society that charity worker Etta Wheeler turned with her concern about the treatment of Mary Ellen Wilson, an eight-year-old girl who was being abused and neglected by her stepparents. Bergh directed his attorney, Elbridge T. Gerry, to seek custody of the child and prosecution of the stepparents. Gerry did this and, amidst much publicity, was successful. Media coverage of the Mary Ellen Wilson case caused a flood of public opinion resulting in the passage in New York in 1875 of "an Act of the incorporation of societies for the prevention of cruelty to children" (Williams, 1980). The idea of organizing to protect children from cruel treatment caught on, and in a very few years there was an anticruelty society in every major city in the country. In a manner similar to the SPCA, agents of the new child protection societies were quasi law-enforcement officers with power to "prefer a complaint before any court or magistrate having jurisdiction for the violation of any law relating to or affecting children." In 1877, the American Humane Association (AHA) was incorporated to provide coordination among the local societies and to disseminate information and provide assistance. By 1900, its membership was comprised of 150 humane societies throughout the country, most dealing with both child and animal protection, but about twenty restricting their activities to protection of children (Bremner, 1971).

The Societies for the Prevention of Cruelty to Children (SPCC) did not view themselves as social welfare agencies. Rather, they viewed themselves as law enforcement agencies specializing in the investigation of charges of child abuse and neglect. When they received a complaint, they would conduct an investigation and, if the charge was substantiated, remove the child and prosecute the parents. The child would be turned over to a child placement agency or children's home, and the SPCC would close the case and have no further responsibility for the child. Only in cases of lost or kidnapped children did the society ever consider returning the child to its parents. In describing the work of the Massachusetts Society for the Prevention of Cruelty to Children, its board chairman, Grafton Cushing, said in 1906, "There is no attempt to discover the cause of the conditions which make action by the [society] necessary, and therefore no endeavor to prevent a recurrence of these conditions. In other words, there is no 'social' work done. It is all legal or police work" (Anderson, 1989).

Social Work Takes Over

From its onset, there were many problems with the child rescue approach. Among these problems were that it was not concerned with the prevention of child maltreatment; it gave no recognition to the possibility that a child might love his or her family despite its problems and prefer to remain in the family of origin; and it had no appreciation for the difficulties of establishing a viable life for the child once the child was removed. At the same time the child rescue movement was emerging, social work as a profession and as a scientific approach to social problems was also developing. It was not long before people both inside and outside the child rescue agencies began to advocate for a social work approach to the problem of child maltreatment.

The foremost advocate for a social work approach to child welfare was C. Carl Carstens, a trained social worker appointed in 1906 as director of the Massachusetts Society for the Prevention of Cruelty to Children. Carstens advanced a new approach to child maltreatment that came to be known as child protection, as opposed to child rescue. The child protection approach involved providing personal services to families with the goal of preventing the recurrence of maltreatment; seeking out the causes of abuse, neglect, exploitation, and delinquency; and preventing maltreatment through environmental reforms. When the 1912 annual meeting of the American Humane Association rejected Carstens's proposal that the child rescue approach be replaced by a child protection approach, he withdrew the Massachusetts society from membership in the AHA and founded the Bureau for the Exchange of Information among Child-Helping Agencies, which in 1921 became the Child Welfare League of America (CWLA) (Anderson, 1989).

Carstens became the first executive director of the CWLA and retained this position until his death in 1939. During his tenure, the CWLA and the AHA remained competitors around the issue of whether a child rescue or a child protection approach was the appropriate response to the problem of child maltreatment. However, gradually the AHA began to change and by the time of Carstens's death had adopted standards that referred to child protection and defined it as "a specialized service in the general field of child welfare" and recognized that the work involved "psychological factors" as well as "standards of physical care." The standards further called for member organizations to employ workers with college degrees and "special training in the social sciences and knowledge and experience in the social and legal phases of child protection work" (Anderson, 1989).

During the same period that social work was taking over the field of child welfare, forces were also at work moving the responsibility from private to public auspices. The American Humane Association, the societies for the prevention of cruelty to children, the Child Welfare League of America, and all of the loosely affiliated agencies were all privately funded and operated. This arrangement befitted an era when government was small and took little responsibility for anything beyond "protecting our shores and delivering the mail," as the expression went. As the twentieth century progressed, government showed an increasing willingness to be active in the area of social welfare in general and child welfare in particular.

The 1909 White House Conference on Children resulted in the establishment in 1912 of the U.S. Children's Bureau, located in the Department of Commerce and Labor. It was charged with investigation and reporting on "all matters pertaining to the welfare of children and child life among all classes of our people" (Trattner, 1999). In 1918, the Infancy and Maternity Health Bill (Sheppard-Towner Act) was passed, which set up infant and maternal health centers administered by state health departments. In 1935, child welfare services became a predominantly public function with the passage of the Social Security Act, which, under provisions of Title IV, Grants to States for Aid to Dependent Children, and of Title V, Grants to States for Maternal and Child Welfare, mandated that all states provide services for dependent children and provided funding for these services.

Thoughts for Social Work Practice

Child protective services was originally a law enforcement function and has gradually evolved into a nearly total social work function. Do you think that this change has perhaps gone too far and some aspects should be returned to law enforcement? Why or why not?

Child Abuse Becomes the Dominant Theme

During the earlier part of the twentieth century, when child welfare was becoming a social work function and a responsibility of the public sector, it was a relatively small and broad-based area of social welfare. In 1955, for example, there were only slightly more than 5,000 professional employees of public child welfare agencies nationally (Lindsey, 2003, p. 20). The eleven-page entry on child welfare in the 1949 *Social Work Yearbook* devotes only two paragraphs, less than one-third of a page, to "Protection from Neglect and Cruelty." The remainder of the entry deals with a wide range of child welfare concerns including poverty, health care, disabilities, and juvenile delinquency (Lundberg, 1949, pp. 98–109). A series of related events that began in the 1950s resulted in the child welfare system experiencing tremendous growth while at the same time narrowing to an almost exclusive focus on child abuse and neglect.

The event that triggered these changes in the child welfare system was the discovery of child abuse by the medical profession. Due to advances in radiological techniques, physicians began to identify traumatic injuries in children that did not fit any known explanation. Physicians were hesitant to blame these unexplained injuries on parents until 1955, when P. V. Woolley and W. A. Evans investigated the home situations of a sample of children displaying such injuries and found that the infants "came invariably from unstable households with a high incidence of neurotic or frankly psychotic behavior on the part of at least one adult" (Woolley & Evans, 1955, p. 20). The wide public attention given these findings virtually exploded into an anti-child abuse crusade six years later when pediatrician Henry Kempe published the results of his research on child abuse under the catchy name "battered child syndrome." Social policy expert Alvin Shore (2000) considers this to be a blow to child welfare . . . with the identification of child abuse as a specific family and social problem. The model of child abuse that was offered and was bought by

Table 10.2 Increase in Reports of Child Maltreatment

Year Maltreatment	Reports	Rate per 1,000 Children
1967	9,563	0.1
1975	294,796	4.5
1980	1,154,000	18.0
1985	1,919,000	30.0
1990	2,559,000	40.0
1994	3,110,000	46.0
1997	3,195,000	47.0
1999	3,244,000	46.0
2004	3,000,000	42.6
2006	3,600,000	47.6
2011	3,426,000	45.8

Source: Duncan Lindsey, *The Welfare of Children* (New York: Oxford University Press, 1994), p. 93; Karen McCurdy and Deborah Daro, *Current Trends in Child Abuse Reporting and Fatalities: The Results of the 1994 Annual Fifty State Survey* (Chicago: National Committee to Prevent Child Abuse, 1995), p. 5; Ching-Tung Wang and Deborah Daro, *Current Trends in Child Abuse Reporting and Fatalities: The Results of the 1997 Annual Fifty State Survey* (Chicago: National Committee to Prevent Child Abuse, 1998), Table 1; Nancy Peddle and Ching-Tung Wang, *Current Trends in Child Abuse Prevention, Reporting and Fatalities* (Chicago: National Center on Child Abuse Research, 2001), p. iv; U.S. Department of Health and Human Services, Administration on Children, Youth, and Families, *Child Maltreatment 2004*; *Child Maltreatment 2006*; and *Child Maltreatment, 2011* Available from http://www.acf.hhs.gov/programs/cb/research-data-technology/statistics-research/child-maltreatment

legislatures and the public was the so-called medical model: a distinguishable pathological agent attacking the individual or family that could be treated in a prescribed manner and would disappear. This model does not characterize child abuse accurately, but belief in it leads to public frustration, if not fury, that abuse persists. So identifying child abuse as a problem led to public dissatisfaction with child welfare agencies and an enormous number of children to care for.

As a result of the discovery of child abuse and the passage of reporting laws, child welfare caseloads increased dramatically (see Table 10.2). The result of the studies by Maas and Engler (1959) and others was dissatisfaction with the favorite tool in the social worker's toolkit: foster care. This resulted in a situation with which we are still struggling: recognition of a problem, commitment to do something about it, but no really good idea about what to do, plus a general unwillingness on the part of society to pay the massive cost of any solution. As Costin, Karger, and Stoez (1996) have noted, "Able to document abuse, health and human service professionals generated enough reports to indicate that non-accidental injury to children was epidemic. Remedying child abuse, however, was another matter" (p. 116).

In response to the rapidly emerging problem of child abuse, a section was included in Title XX of the Social Security Act, passed in 1972, which made protective services mandatory in all states and provided federal funding to pay for these services. Once funding was in place for services, however, it quickly became apparent that no one had much useful information on how to design action programs. This problem led to the passage in 1974 of the Child Abuse Prevention and Treatment Act (CAPTA). This act had two major components. First, it established within the Department of Health and Human Services the National Center for Child Abuse and Neglect, a research and data clearinghouse designed to help remedy the huge gaps in knowledge that were becoming apparent as attempts were made to remedy child protection problems. The second component was a model statute for state child protection programs, which was eventually adopted by all 50 states. The model statute specified the following provisions:

> (1) A standard definition of child abuse and neglect, (2) standard methods of reporting and investigating child abuse and neglect, (3) guarantees of immunity for those reporting suspected injuries to children, and neglect, and (4) development of prevention and public education efforts to reduce the incidence of child abuse and neglect. (quoted in Costin et al, 1996, p. 116)

CAPTA provided only a limited amount of funding to support these activities by the states (initially, only $22 million), but in spite of this, all 50 states were in compliance with the provisions of the bill by 1980.

The massive increase in child abuse referrals resulting from publicity and reporting laws created a major problem for child welfare agencies. The heightened public awareness of the problem led to large increases in staff, but these have not nearly kept pace with the increased demand for services. In 1967, around the time that child abuse and neglect became a national issue, state agencies employed approximately 14,000 staff with child protection responsibilities. In 2015, this number had increased to only 33,996 (Lindsey, 2004, p. 20; U.S. Department of Health and Human Services, 2015, Table 2-3). This trend has continued and has resulted in child welfare agencies assigning an ever-increasing proportion of staff to the function of protective services until this one service has virtually taken over public child welfare agencies. In their 1990 analysis of child welfare, Sheila Kamerman and Alfred Kahn (1990) confirmed this phenomenon, concluding,

> Child Protective Services (CPS) (covering physical abuse, sexual abuse, and neglect reports, investigations, assessments, and resultant actions) have emerged as the dominant public child and family service, in effect "driving" the public agency and often taking over child welfare entirely. . . . Child protective services today constitute the core public child and family service, the fulcrum and sometimes, in some places, the totality of the system. Depending on the terms used, public social service agency administrators state either that "Child protection is child welfare," or that "The increased demand for child protection has driven out all other child welfare services."

Foster Care—From Solution to Problem

The beginnings of foster care in the United States were characterized by the same child rescue approach that characterized the societies for the prevention of cruelty to children. The originator of the idea of foster care was the Reverend Charles Loring Brace, who founded the New York Children's Aid Society in 1853. Brace's idea was to take homeless children from the streets of New York, where they were beginning to be perceived as a serious threat to social order, and transport them to rural regions of the country to be placed with farm families. Brace perceived this to be a win-win proposition, as the result would be homes for homeless children and additional hands to help the farm families with their labor-intensive lifestyle.

The technique of the Children's Aid Society was to gather homeless children in shelters in New York City and, when a large enough group was gathered, to send them by train to towns in the Midwest. Agents of the Children's Aid Society would precede the train into each town, organize a local placement committee of prominent citizens, and advertise the location and the date the children would be available for placement. When the day arrived, local families would inspect the children, and families who were deemed suitable by both the society's agent and the local committee could select one or more children. No money was exchanged between the parents and the society. As Verlene McOllough reports, "Willing families would sign placing-out agreements guaranteeing the child the same food, lodging, and education children born to them would receive. In return, the child would become part of the family, which in the nineteenth century generally meant taking on a sizable share of the work" (McOllough, 1988, p. 146). The work of the Children's Aid Society grew quickly and eventually became extensive. By 1873, the society was placing more than 3,000 children a year. Its peak year was 1875, when 4,026 children were placed.

The policies and techniques of the Children's Aid Society were the target of some well-deserved criticism. A major concern was that, in true child rescue fashion, if a child had living parents the society made no attempt to work with them so the child could return home. Quite the opposite; "as the Children's Aid Society ferreted out neglected children from the poorer districts, they convinced many impoverished parents that a child's best chance lay in permitting the society to find the child a new home far beyond the urban slums and its miseries" (McOllough, 1988, p. 146). Another criticism was raised by Catholics, who felt that the Children's Aid Society, founded and run by Protestants, was snatching Catholic children off the streets and sending them to the West to be reared as Protestants. Many of the states receiving children soon lost their enthusiasm for the society's work. Many of the children—one study estimated nearly 60 percent—became sources of trouble and public expenditure when their placements failed to work (Trattner, 1999, p. 118). Finally, the most serious criticism was the lack of study, the generally casual nature of the placement process, and the almost total absence of follow-up supervision after a placement was made.

Although the Children's Aid Society's program had many flaws, the basic idea of placing dependent children in a family setting caught on and had a tremendous impact on child welfare practice. Toward the end of the nineteenth century, advocates for a social work child protection approach to child welfare, notably John Finley of the New York State Charities Aid Association, Charles Birtwell of the Boston Children's Aid Society, and Homer Folks of the Children's Aid Society of Pennsylvania, began to develop sound administrative procedures for child placement. These procedures included placement of the child in his or her home community, if possible; thorough study of the child and the prospective foster home; providing foster parents with some financial support for the child; and careful supervision of the placement. By the turn of the twentieth century, foster care had replaced institutional placement in a number of cities. In 1909, the report of the first White House Conference on Children gave support to the foster care movement with the recommendation that "it is desirable that [children] should be cared for in families whenever practicable. The carefully selected foster home is for the normal child the best substitute for the natural home" (Trattner, 1999, pp. 118, 215). The spread of foster care continued until, by midcentury, it was the placement of choice for normal children who, for one reason or another, were not able to remain with their natural families.

Foster care became a standard item in the child welfare worker's tool kit and existed with little question or examination until the late 1950s. At this time, two things happened that began to profoundly shake social workers' and public policymakers' confidence in the foster care system. The first development was the publication of several studies of foster care that found serious deficiencies in the system. The second was the explosion of child abuse referrals, which led to a consequent explosion in the number of children placed in foster care and hence a huge increase in cost.

The study that opened the floodgates for criticism of the foster care system, conducted by Henry Maas and Richard Engler, was entitled *Children in Need of Parents,* published in 1959. Maas and Engler (1959) chose nine counties that were thought to be representative of the United States in general. They sent a research team into each community. The team

> studied these nine counties and, simultaneously, the children in care in each of them. Information about the children and their families was gathered from all sixty agencies serving the communities at the time of our study. Key persons were interviewed in each of the communities which produced these dependent children and/or offered placement resources. The legal systems through which many of these children came into care, or which influenced their destinies in care, were studied. And the networks of agencies serving these children and families were also examined.

Because there was no central data-reporting mechanism for foster care, the Maas and Engler (1959) study provided the first valid look into the overall picture of foster care in the United States. What they discovered was not comforting. They found that the assumption that foster care was a temporary respite for children and families experiencing difficulty was not true—the average length of a foster placement was three years; many children were destined to grow up in foster care, and in fewer than 25 percent of the cases was it probable that the child would ever be returned home. Equally disturbing was the finding that the parents of foster children indicated, in most cases, that they either had no relationship or a negative relationship with the child placement agency and that in only one-third of the cases did a parent ever visit the child in care. In an afterword to the study, Child Welfare League of America Executive Director Joseph Reid referred to foster children as "orphans of the living" (Reid, 1959, p. 380).

Following the study by Maas and Engler (1959) was a series of research studies revealing deficiencies in the foster care system and in the whole concept of foster care as the plan of choice for dependent and neglected children. A 1962 Children's Bureau national survey of child welfare agencies conducted by Helen Jeter corroborated the findings of Maas and Engler, estimating that 31 percent of children in placement were "in danger of growing up in foster care." Jeter found that for 64 percent of the children in public foster care, the only plan the agency had was to continue them in placement. Little evidence was found of work being done to address the problems that led to children being placed in foster care (Jeter, 1963). In 1966, David Fanshel and Eugene Shinn examined data from 659 children entering the New York foster care system and followed these children for the next five years. They found that the system was not guided by any systematic scientific knowledge or principles. Although they concluded that foster care had little harmful effect on the children, they also found that those children who eventually went home were returned to home situations that were little, if any, better than when they left. As in the Maas and Engler and the Jeter studies, Fanshel and Shinn (1978) found that many children were in foster care for long periods of time with little probability of ever returning home and with virtually no contact with their natural parents.

These studies, along with a number of journalistic and legalistic treatises on foster care, such as Goldstein, Freud, and Solnit's (1973) influential *Beyond the Best Interests of the Child,* identified three major concerns regarding foster care. The first was that foster care was in many, if not most, cases not a temporary but rather a long-term situation. The second concern was with what came to be called "foster care drift." This referred to the finding that many children in foster care were not in one stable foster home but placed in a series of homes. The final problem was that agencies placing children in foster care rarely had any kind of long-term plan for the children other than for them to remain in care until such time as they could be returned home (often never). As a result of these concerns, a new approach to foster care was developed in the late 1970s and 1980s known as the permanency planning movement.

Permanency planning is based on several interrelated ideas:

1. The child's own home is the best place for him or her, and removal should occur only under extreme circumstances.
2. In instances in which a child is removed, a specific plan should be developed immediately, monitored closely, and revised as needed. The focus of the plan should be obtaining a permanent living arrangement for the child in as little time as possible.
3. The primary goal of the plan should be to return the child to his or her own home. If this is not possible, steps should be taken to legally free the child for a permanent placement at the earliest possible time.
4. The preferred plan for a child who cannot return to his or her biological home is adoption. No child is considered unadoptable.
5. If adoption is not an option, then a long-term foster care plan should be developed with the child, the agency, and the foster family all making a commitment to a permanent placement.

Permanency planning became a part of national social welfare policy with the passage of P.L. 96-272, the Adoption Assistance and Child Welfare Act of 1980. This act directs federal fiscal incentives toward permanency planning objectives—namely, the development of preventive and reunification services and adoption subsidies. For states to be eligible for increased federal funds, they must implement a service program designed either to reunite children with their families or to provide a permanent substitute home. They are required to take steps, such as the establishment of foster placement review committees and procedures for regular case review, that ensure that children enter foster care only when necessary, that they are placed appropriately, and that they are returned home or else moved on to permanent families in a timely fashion. The act also creates fiscal incentives for states to seek adoptive homes for hard-to-place children, including children who are disabled, older, or minority group members (Allen & Knitzer, 1983, pp. 120–123).

When the permanency planning approach was implemented in the 1970s and 1980s, it appeared, for a while, that the problem of foster care was under control. The number of children in foster care declined from 520,000 in 1977 to 275,000 in 1984. However, after 1984 a number of factors in the social environment kicked in and caused this trend to reverse. Among these factors were the crack cocaine epidemic, economic problems leading to increased poverty and unemployment, AIDS, and a sharp rise in births to single mothers, particularly teenagers. By 1999, the number of children in foster care had risen to 567,000, and the Children's Bureau reports that the foster home population is currently at 428,000, a decrease from the 1999 high. Although the number of children in foster care has recently declined, largely due to family preservation policies that aim to reduce the length of time in care, the annual number of children entering foster care has continued to increase, from 251,450 in 2011 to 269,509 in 2005 (U.S. Department of Health and Human Services, AFCARS Report, 2016). Compounding the problems caused by the large number of children needing foster placement has been the corresponding decrease in the number of foster families. Since 1998 the number of licensed foster homes has not kept pace with the number of children needing care, particularly in large cities. Among the factors generally thought to explain the insufficient number of foster homes are the increased employment of women outside the home, the low payments made to foster parents, inadequate support services for foster parents, and a lack of training opportunities for foster parents (Everett, 2013, p. 385).

The Emergence of Family Preservation

Selecting a beginning point for the history of a social policy is always somewhat arbitrary, but the date and event generally cited as the beginning of the family preservation movement is 1974, when the Homebuilders program was piloted in Washington State.* To hear the originators describe the program, it appears to have begun almost by accident. Three psychologists—Jill Kinney, David Haapala, and Charlotte Booth (1991)—submitted a grant application proposing to develop "super foster homes," which they conceptualized as foster placements backed up with lots of training and professional consultation.

> Our funding agent, however, insisted that before placement, we try "sticking a staff member in to live with a family." This idea sounded outlandish, but it also seemed interesting. We knew we would learn about families, and since we wanted the super foster home funding, we decided to try the in-home services, assuming they would fail, our funding agent would be convinced, and we could then continue with our super foster home approach. . . . We were wrong: The approach was surprisingly effective. (pp. 3–4)

Two factors caused the idea of family preservation to be widely and rapidly embraced by the child welfare community. The first is the "reasonable efforts" provision of P.L. 96-272, the Adoption Assistance and Child Welfare Act of 1980. This provision requires that child welfare agencies provide services to prevent the necessity for placement and that the courts determine whether the agency has made "reasonable efforts" to accomplish this end. The act does not specify what these reasonable efforts might be, but states have seized on family preservation services as a way to demonstrate that they are in compliance with the law. The second factor is the explosive increase in the number of children in foster care. Faced with a trend with no end in sight, and the accompanying increase in costs, states began to perceive foster care as a situation that was out of control. Family preservation offered a way to rein in the situation. In 1982, there were 20 family preservation programs nationwide; by 1988 this number had increased to 333 and by

* Laura Curran and Stefani Pfeiffer argue that the roots of family preservation go back well beyond the mid-1970s date usually cited. They say, "[W]ell before the policy reforms of the 1970s, developments in social scientific theory and in the social work literature combined with the experiences of foster care workers to produce a recommitment to and revisions in the family preservation paradigm." Laura Curran and Stefani Pfeiffer, "'You Can't Tie and Untie Love That Fast': Family Preservation and Reunification in Midcentury Philadelphia," *Social Service Review* (March 2008), p. 61.

1991 to more than 400, and this number has continued to increase (Pecora, Whittaker, Maluccio, Barth, & Plotnick, 2000; Tracy & Piccola, 2013). Most of these programs were initially funded by federal demonstration grants and by grants from private foundations, notably the Annie E. Casey Foundation and the Edna McConnell Clark Foundation.

In 1993, family preservation became an explicit part of federal policy with the passage of P.L. 103-66, the Family Preservation and Support Program, which was part of the Omnibus Budget Reconciliation Act. The provisions of this act had a federal cost of $1 billion over five years to provide states with funds for services to avoid foster care placement for children and to preserve and strengthen families. As this act included a 25 percent matching requirement from the states, the actual amount to be spent on family preservation services over five years was actually $1.25 billion. As reported by the Congressional Research Service,

> the legislation was developed in response to a widespread perception of crisis in the child welfare system, as indicated by dramatic growth in the numbers of child abuse and neglect reports and children entering foster care, beginning in the mid-1980s. As the caseload has grown, the child welfare system also has faced high staff turnover and low morale, a shrinking supply of foster parents and foster homes, and a shortage of related support services such as drug and alcohol treatment and mental health care. (Spar, 1994, p. i)

In 2003, the Child Abuse Prevention and Treatment Act (CAPTA) was again reauthorized (P.L. 108-36, the Keeping Children and Families Safe Act) through fiscal year 2008. The act was then maintained for two years under continuing resolutions until it was once again reauthorized in 2010 for an additional five years. Changes to CAPTA included in the 2010 reauthorization are not major ones. There are a number of administrative provisions designed to:

- Improve program operation and data collection
- Improve systems for supporting and training individuals who prevent, identify, and respond to reports of child maltreatment
- Strengthen coordination among the various agencies that respond to child maltreatment, as well as dating and domestic violence

The major provision related to social work practice in the reauthorization is the encouragement of a "differential response" approach to child protective services. This provision, heavily lobbied for by the American Humane Association as well as other child advocacy organizations, allows agencies to respond to maltreatment reports in different ways based on factors such as the type and severity of the alleged maltreatment, the number and sources of previous reports, and the willingness of the family to cooperate with the agency. The act is funded for $93.9 million for 2010 and at $1.039 billion over the five-year reauthorization period (11th Congress, 2010).

The combination of P.L. 96-272, with its requirement that agencies demonstrate "reasonable efforts" to prevent foster home placement of children, and P.L. 103-66 and 108-36, each providing massive federal financial incentives to provide family preservation services, made family preservation the policy of choice in the twenty-first century for dealing with child maltreatment. Although a backlash developed to family preservation programs, embodied in the passage in 1997 of the Adoption and Safe Families Act, this continues to be the policy of choice for dealing with the problem of child dependency. Virtually every state had developed some form of family preservation program by the end of the twentieth century.

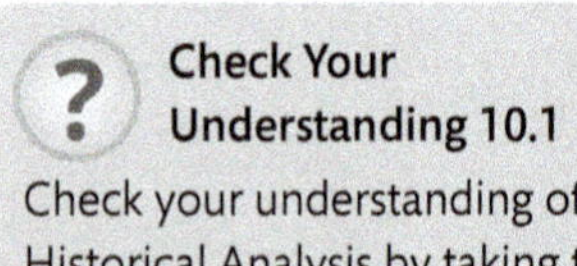
Check Your Understanding 10.1
Check your understanding of Historical Analysis by taking this brief quiz.

SOCIAL ANALYSIS

Problem Description

Family preservation is one aspect of society's response to the problem of child dependency. Child dependency as a problem has at least three levels. The primary level is the problem of child poverty. The secondary level, derived from the primary, is the problem of child maltreatment. Derived from the first two levels is the tertiary problem of the explosive growth of the foster care population.

Descriptive Data

A number of statistics regarding child welfare and family preservation were cited previously; a brief recap is provided here. Sources of data regarding child maltreatment have been getting better and better, but there are still problems related to different states using slightly different definitions and some states failing to report. From 1974 to 1986, the best source of data was the annual *National Study of Child Neglect and Abuse Reporting,* conducted by the American Humane Association and funded by the federal Children's Bureau. This was funded for a reduced study for 1987 and has not been funded since. The national study consisted of a nationwide compilation of data derived from official reports of child maltreatment documented by state child protective service agencies. This task has now been assumed by the Administration on Children and Families of the U.S. Department of Health and Human Services, under the name National Child Abuse and Neglect Data System (NCANDS). This system is providing ever better data, but is still plagued by the problem of missing data from states, making precise reports of national incidence difficult. Data regarding children in foster care were in the past even more limited than data pertaining to reports of maltreatment. A system has now been developed by the U.S. Department of Health and Human Services called the Adoption and Foster Care Analysis and Reporting System (AFCARS). This system is designed to collect uniform, reliable information on children in all forms of out-of-home care.

Four levels of data are important for understanding family preservation as a social welfare policy. The first level is data that estimate the actual incidence of child maltreatment ("estimate," because it is not possible actually to know the incidence of abuse and neglect due to the secret nature of the acts involved). The U.S. Department of Health and Human Services contracts for periodic National Incidence Studies of Child Abuse and Neglect (NIS). The most recent was NIS 4, released in 2010 and reporting on data collected in 2005 and 2006. The four national incidence studies employ a scientific sampling procedure to attempt to uncover incidences of child maltreatment that have escaped the formal reporting machinery. NIS 4 estimated that in the study year more than 1.25 million children in the United States experienced maltreatment. The report found that less than one-half of these cases were investigated by child protective services. NIS 4 contains both bad news and good news for children's advocates. The bad news in that, like the three earlier incidence studies, the data indicate that the actual incidence of abuse and neglect is far greater than indicated by official reporting statistics. The good news is that while NIS 1, 2, and 3 all found significant increases in the rate of child maltreatment, NIS 4 found a 19 percent decline in the number of children maltreated during the study year (Sedlak, Mettenburg, Basena, Petta, McPherson, Greene, & Li, 2010).

Table 10.3 Increase in Child Welfare Staff as Related to Child Abuse Referrals

Year	Child Welfare Professional Staff	Child Abuse Referrals
1967	14,000	9,563
2000	74,200	1,037,027
Percent increase	430%	10,744%

Source: Duncan Lindsey, *The Welfare of Children*, 2nd ed (New York Oxford University Press, 2004), p. 20; Child Welfare League of America, "The Child Welfare Workforce Challenge—Results from a Preliminary Study," paper presented at the Finding Better Ways, 2001 conference, Dallas, TX; U.S. Department of Health and Human Services, Administration on Children, Youth and Families, *Child Maltreatment 2000* (Washington, DC: U.S. Government Printing Office, 2002).

The second type of data that is important for understanding family preservation summarizes actual reports of child maltreatment. This information is presented in Table 10.3, which indicates that the number of reports has increased from 9,563 in 1967 to currently nearly 4 million. Most of this increase is undoubtedly a result of increased public awareness of the problem and more efficient reporting systems. However, there also is little doubt that a portion of the increase reflects an actual increase in incidence resulting from trends such as increased poverty, homelessness, drug use, and births to young single mothers.

The third type of data for understanding the family preservation policy is the number of confirmed reports. As the number of reports has increased, the proportion substantiated by protective services investigations has decreased. In 1975, approximately 60 percent of reports were substantiated; by 1987 this had fallen to 40 percent, and currently 17.3 percent are substantiated with an additional 0.7 percent classified as "indicated" (Peddle & Wang, 2001; U.S. Department of Health and Human Services, 2015).

The final figure—the one most directly relevant to family preservation policy—is the number of confirmed reports that lead to child placement. This was previously referred to when discussing the development and early success of permanency planning. To review, the number of children in out-of-home placements went from 567,000 in 1999 to a low of 397,000 in 2012, at which time the number began to once again increase, reaching 428,000 in 2015.

Relevant Research

There is a huge body of research relevant to child protective services. However, here we will address only the research most relevant to family preservation as a policy response to child placement. This research regards parent–child bonding, the effect of foster placement on child development, and the relation of poverty to child maltreatment. Research on program effectiveness will be described in the evaluation section.

Although Harry Harlow and his colleagues (1965) at the University of Wisconsin Primate Center had no specific interest in child welfare, their findings on infant–parent attachment were extremely interesting to social workers in the field. Duncan Lindsey (2003) describes the studies as follows:

> An experimental psychologist, Harlow wanted to understand the importance of a mother's nurturing on the growth and development of a child. He examined what happened to an infant monkey that was raised in a wire cage that provided

michaeljung/Shutterstock

Because American values consider the family unit to be almost sacred, government intervention requires strong justification.

> necessary physical nourishment but did not permit any emotional interaction or attachment with other monkeys. The monkey's cage allowed it to see and hear other monkeys but did not allow any physical contact. Harlow observed that the infant raised in an isolated cage suffered from intense neurotic behavior when compared to an infant monkey raised with a cloth surrogate mother. . . . Further, the effects of social isolation continued for the experimental monkey into adulthood. . . . Harlow's experiments provided dramatic evidence of the importance of parental affection and care to the developing child. The research emphasized the importance of providing children with parental nurturing. Children growing up in institutions or in a series of foster homes were deprived of the essential bonding and attachment that comes from a parent.

Research by John Bowlby (1985) on children who were separated from their parents at age two or three confirmed Harlow's primate studies. Bowlby found that these children tended to suffer from severe psychological distress and concluded that separation from parents has severe consequences for a child's development. A recent and thorough analysis of attachment theory research in relation to child welfare written by Mennen and O'Keefe (2005) concludes, "Research on maltreated children has supported many of the theoretical propositions of attachment theory."

Given the importance of the question, it is surprising that there are not more studies of the actual effects of foster placement on the development of children. The one major, but now somewhat dated, study of this question is the longitudinal study of children in foster care conducted by Fanshel and Shinn (1978). This study resulted in data contradictory to what would be expected based on the findings of Harlow and of Bowlby. Fanshel and Shinn employed a wide array of behavioral indicators and checklists to assess the adjustment of children returned home and of those still in foster care at the end of the five-year period covered by their study. They conclude, "From our involvement in these data and other investigations, we feel that children who enter foster care as infants and live stable lives in the same setting emerge as teenagers who are relatively free of problems." Children who entered care when they were older and those who did not have stable, long-term placements were found to have significant problems (Fanshel & Shinn, 1978). However, this can be at least partially explained by the findings of several studies that children entering foster care at an older age are more likely already to have severe behavioral and adjustment problems (Hochstady, Jaudes, Zimo, & Schachter, 1987; McIntyre & Kesler, 1986; Moffatt, Peddie, Stulginskas, Pless, & Steinmetz, 1985).

Recent research has demonstrated how harmful foster care is to the successful development of children. These studies confirmed the earlier findings of Maas that foster care is often not temporary care and that many children languish in foster care for five or more years. Each year 20,000 children "age out" of foster care—that is, reach their eighteenth birthdays and legally become adults without first returning to their own homes. Studies sponsored by the Pew Commission and the Chapin Hall Center for Children looked at the outcomes for those children who aged out of foster care and the findings can only be described as grim: They experience mental health problems at three times the rate of a comparable national sample; one-quarter have been tested or treated for sexually transmitted diseases, more than four times the rate of the national sample; two-thirds of the males and one-half of the females have been arrested, convicted of a crime, or sent to a correctional facility; nearly 40 percent fail to graduate from high school and over one-half read at or below the seventh-grade level; and nearly 40 percent end up on welfare (Courtney, Terao, & Bost, 2004; Pew Commission on Children in Foster Care, 2004). These findings have been validated by a 2010 review of research by Stott and Gustavsson who reported findings that among youth aging out of foster care: one-half do not have a high school diploma, 25 to 50 percent are unemployed, the majority have incomes below the poverty line and more than one-third receive need-based government assistance, the majority report housing instability, one-third to one-half have been arrested and jailed, significant numbers report health and mental health problems, about one-quarter report substance abuse problems, between 30 and 70 percent have either been pregnant or are the parent of a young child (Stott & Gustavsson, 2010). A 2017 study found that adverse experiences accumulate for foster children, with the result that those who age out have serious struggles, particularly in the areas of housing and homelessness, educational completion, employment and financial security, and mental health (Rebbe, Marius, Ahrens, & Courtney, 2017, p. 109). These studies make clear that attempting to divert children from foster care by working with their own families is a really good idea.

Unlike the question of the effects of foster placement on children, the effects of poverty are well researched and, consequently, well understood. One study concluded that the incidence of abuse and neglect is ten times higher among families with incomes below the poverty line than among those with middle-class incomes. In a 1969 survey of abusive families, Gil found that nearly 60 percent had been on public assistance at some time and that slightly more than 34 percent were receiving welfare at the time of the report. A journalist looking into abuse and neglect found that more than half the children removed from their homes as a result of abuse or neglect came from families receiving welfare. Leroy Pelton (1981) surveyed child protective service records in New Jersey and found that 79 percent of the families had incomes below the poverty line. Gelles conducted two nationwide surveys on family violence and found that "violence toward children, especially severe violence, is more likely to occur in households with annual incomes below the poverty line" (Gelles, 1992; Gil, 1970; National Center on Abuse and Neglect, 1982; Pelton, 1994; Vobejda, 1995). After two separate, thorough reviews of the research, Lindsey (2003) and Pelton (1994) conclude that poverty is at the root of nearly all child welfare problems. Making the situation worse are data indicating that the rate of child poverty has been steadily increasing—between 1967 and 2010 the poverty rate for young families with children soared from 14.1 percent to 37.3 percent (Lindsey, Sum, & Khatiwada, 2012). Data from the Third National Incidence Study of Child Abuse and Neglect indicate that children from families with annual incomes below $15,000 were more than 22 times more likely to experience maltreatment than children from families with incomes in excess of $30,000 (Houshyar, 2014, p. 1).

Is Family Preservation Policy in Accord with Research Findings?

One of the cornerstones of family preservation policy is the belief that foster care is bad for children. As reviewed in the preceding section, the research on this question is incomplete and results to date have been contradictory. However, when looked at more carefully, the results do not appear so contradictory. The study by Fanshel and Shinn (1978) concluded that children in foster care did not appear to suffer any serious consequences, with the caveat that the children they were talking about were those who entered foster care at a young age and who had stable placements. In *Beyond the Best Interests of the Child,* Goldstein, Freud, and Solnit (1973) argue that what is important to a child is a psychological parent, not necessarily a biological parent. A psychological parent is any caring adult who meets the child's day-to-day needs and does so over an extended period of time. It seems clear that the children studied by Fanshel and Shinn were fortunate enough to find psychological parents in their placements. Thus, it appears that the attachment and outcome research of foster care would lend support to either permanency planning (strive to provide a psychological parent to a child if the biological parent is unavailable) or to family preservation (support biological parents in their efforts to also be psychological parents). The Chapin Hall and Pew Commission studies, as well as the research review by Stott and Gustavsson, however, demonstrate that the outcomes of long-term foster care are highly detrimental to human development and in so doing lend strong support to a family preservation approach to child welfare.

Although family preservation policy may be consistent with the research and theory regarding attachment, it is hard to discount the arguments of scholars such as Lindsey, Pelton, and Gil that the real problem behind child maltreatment is poverty. It is ironic that just as our society is pouring money into family preservation programs in an attempt to hold families together, we are slashing financial assistance programs that provide many of these families their only hope for stability. Lindsey (2003) refers to child abuse as "the red herring of child welfare," arguing that it is a highly charged issue that draws attention away from the real and more difficult problem of child poverty (p. 27).

Major Social Values Related to Family Preservation

Family preservation policy occurs at the intersection of some of the most deeply held, and deeply dividing, of our society's values. These are children's rights, family rights, and the government's right to act in *parenspatriae,* the ultimate parental authority. As you saw in the historical analysis section, up until the nineteenth century children were considered to have few rights, and those they did have were clearly subservient to the rights of their parents, particularly the father. As time has passed, children have been given considerably more rights, and it now is quite clear that they have a right to a certain—albeit vague—level of care. Lagging only slightly behind the recognition of children as beings with certain rights was the recognition of the right of government to intervene in family life to safeguard the rights of children. Susan Downs, Ernestine Moore, Emily McFadden, and Susan Michaud (2004) observe that support for government intervention has increased in recent years due to a fear that U.S. society is experiencing breakdown in the family as a social institution and to "the realization that virtually all governmental actions directly or indirectly affect families." Nevertheless, Americans still have great ambivalence about this, being ever-fearful of government and believing that the government should be allowed in family life only in cases of the utmost urgency.

Family preservation policy represents a clever attempt to reconcile these seemingly contradictory rights. It recognizes the right of children to be protected but does it in such a way as to maximize the rights of parents to rear their own children. By its generally time-limited nature, family preservation seeks to make government intervention as short as possible and to get out of family life in the least possible time. This balancing of rights makes family preservation a very marketable policy to legislators and to the general public and, in part, explains its rapid spread.

Family Preservation Goals

Because family preservation policy includes an explicit and well-funded evaluation requirement, the manifest goals of the policy are clearer and more explicitly spelled out than is the case in most social welfare policies. This is because a basic requirement of program/policy evaluations is that goals be specified; if they are not, you have nothing to evaluate. The basic, stated goals of family preservation are as follows:

1. Prevent placement of children in families in crisis. This is the cornerstone of family preservation. The idea is to intervene in family situations that would normally be assessed as requiring placement of the children with intensive, time-limited services, which quickly improve family functioning to a degree that the children can remain in the home.
2. Protect children and prevent subsequent child maltreatment. Family preservation policy does not consider it enough simply to prevent placement. This must be done in a way that ensures that the children are protected from subsequent harm both in the short and in the long term.
3. Improve family functioning. Family preservation services seek to leave families with better daily-living and problem-solving skills than were present before intervention.
4. Prevent child abuse and neglect. This goal is sometimes categorized as family support, as opposed to family preservation; in any case, it is generally a component of family preservation policy. This goal is to improve the general social environment of families and to enable more families to care for their children adequately without the necessity of intervention of any kind. This may be viewed as an institutional approach to the problem of child maltreatment, as contrasted to the other services, which represent a clear residual approach.

Somewhere between a manifest and a latent goal of family preservation is the goal to decrease the cost of child protective services. One of the major motivating factors in the rapid spread of family preservation has been that it is perceived as a cost-efficient way to deal with child maltreatment. This goal lies between manifest and latent, because, although few people would deny it, it is generally not listed among the stated goals. We suspect that if within a few years the costs of child protective services do not decline or at least the growth shows signs of slowing, policymakers will lose considerable enthusiasm for family preservation, regardless of how well it achieves its stated goals.

We are not able to identify any purely latent goals of family preservation policy. A few scholars, for example, Ann Hartman (1995) and L. Diane Bernard (1992), have argued that a latent goal of all family policy is to preserve the existing patriarchal family structure and, along with it, existing power relationships in society. Bernard (1992) states,

> The oppression and exploitation of women in society is reflected and initiated in the family, which reinforces continued gender discrimination. The primary function of the family is to maintain the status quo. Preservation of the family and family stability are the primary goals of patriarchy, ensuring obedience and continuity. . . . The major purpose appears to be to restore stability and reestablish control by returning to traditional values.

We see little evidence that this is the case in family preservation policy. Nowhere in the policy is there a definition of the type of family that is to be preserved. In fact, many of the cases described in the literature appear to be female-headed, single-parent households, and changing these to traditional nuclear families is never mentioned.

Hypotheses

There appear to be two major hypotheses derived from family preservation goals. The first can be stated as, "If intensive, time-limited social work services are provided to families with children at risk of placement, and these services are provided in a timely fashion, then placement of the children can be permanently avoided." As we discuss in the evaluation section, we have serious doubts that this hypothesis will be upheld given the severity of the problems most of the target population is experiencing, the decline of supporting resources and services, and the relatively primitive state of social work intervention technology.

The second hypothesis appears to be, "If child placement is avoided via provision of intensive family preservation services, then reduction in foster home placement will save more money than the family preservation services cost." Once again, given the seriousness of the problems in the target population, we doubt that it will be possible, in most cases, to limit services to a brief period, and therefore services will cost more than anticipated. Also, as is discussed in the evaluation section, there is some evidence of a net-widening phenomenon in family preservation. This is a phenomenon first identified in probation and diversion services in criminal justice. What appears to happen in some instances is that, with the option of family preservation being available, social workers are referring cases to family preservation that would not even have been opened were these services not available.

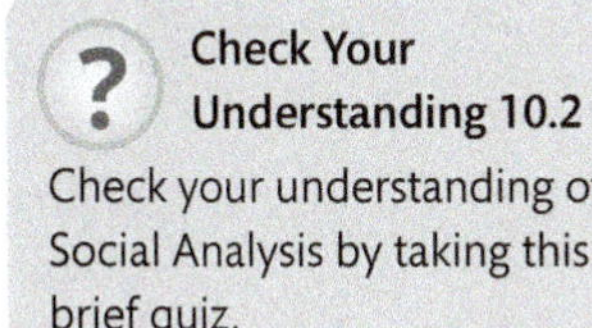
?
Check Your Understanding 10.2
Check your understanding of Social Analysis by taking this brief quiz.

POLITICAL ANALYSIS

Family preservation is one of those rare social policies that contain significant elements that appeal to stakeholders across the political spectrum. Liberals (a group that includes most social workers) favor family preservation because it operationalizes many of their most sacred values. Among the aspects of family preservation that appeal to this group are:

- It does not blame the victim.
- It proceeds from a strengths perspective.
- It emphasizes cultural sensitivity.
- It emphasizes a belief in people's capacity to change and desire to do so.
- It defines family in a flexible fashion and approaches each family as a unique system.
- It respects the dignity and privacy of family members.

Conservatives also find much to like about family preservation as a response to the problem of child maltreatment. Among the aspects of family preservation this group likes are:

- It shortens the time government is involved in people's lives.
- It emphasizes that people are ultimately responsible for solving their own problems.
- It emphasizes independence and seeks to wean people from the social service system.
- It resonates with the conservative emphasis on "family values."
- It is viewed as a potentially more cost-efficient way of protecting children.

Because family preservation policy exists at this intersection of liberal and conservative values, it has—up to this point—experienced little meaningful political opposition. At the Committee on Ways and Means hearing on the legislation that eventually led to P.L. 103-66, Family Preservation and Support Services, forty-three groups either testified or submitted testimony for the record. Not a single submission expressed any opposition to or even reservations about the act (Subcommittee on Human Resources of the Committee on Ways and Means, 1993).

There are, however, a few groups that oppose family preservation policy. One group consists of those very conservative ideologues that see in family preservation a continuation of trends that they believe are eroding the very foundations of our society. They believe that family preservation is another policy that removes accountability for responsible behavior from the individual and places it on society. Patrick Murphy (1993), the Cook County (Chicago) public guardian, for example, states, "The family preservation system is a continuation of sloppy thinking of the 1960s and 1970s that holds, as an unquestionable truth, that society should never blame a victim. But in most cases, giving services and money to parents who have abused their children does nothing but reward irresponsible and even criminal behavior" (p. 21). Murphy introduced a bill in the 1993 Illinois legislature that would require court approval for family preservation in cases of physical or sexual abuse. The bill passed, but in response to strong opposition by the Department of Children and Family Services and the American Civil Liberties Union, among others, Governor Jim Edgar vetoed it. Murphy and his allies persisted, however, and later in 1993, in response to the murder of a young girl whose family was receiving family preservation services, Illinois ended its Family First program. However, as Heather MacDonald (1994), another critic of family preservation, reported, "This decision does not mean, however, that Illinois is rejecting family preservation. It is now introducing the original Homebuilders model, which, though it has a vastly better safety record than the Family First program, embodies the identical philosophy" (p. 52).

Opposition to family preservation policy also comes from competing human service providers who see it as cutting into their "market." The National Council for Adoption, a group favoring policies that free more children for adoption, argues that family preservation programs often harm children who could be removed from hopeless parents and placed in good adoptive homes. The group's vice president, Mary Beth Seader, complains, "I know people who have been trying for two years to adopt these crack babies that have been abandoned in hospitals, but . . . the state is not terminating parental rights even if there is no contact with the biological mother" (MacDonald, 1994, p. 51). Residential treatment center personnel are another group who question family preservation. They argue that family preservation is being embraced so enthusiastically by policymakers because it offers an alternative much cheaper than residential treatment for children experiencing severe problems in their family setting. However, the argument goes, in many instances there is no substitute for the more expensive alternative. For example, David Coughlin of Boys Town says, "Family preservation? Who can be opposed to that? But some of these kids are going to be in trouble all their lives. These kids are always going to need help. You can't just blow across the top of a family for three months and expect their woes to go away" (Weisman, 1994, p. 62).

Perhaps the most important opposition to family preservation policy is currently coming from an increasingly influential segment of the social work profession that asserts that our emphasis on family preservation has been misguided and has put children at risk. The leader of this effort is Richard Gelles, former dean at the prestigious University of Pennsylvania School of Social Policy and Practice, who condemned family preservation in no uncertain terms in *The Book of David: How Preserving Families Can Cost Children's Lives*. In this book, Gelles (1996) uses the case of one child who was murdered by his parents while supposedly under the protection of the state child welfare division. Gelles argues that the agency's policies were so skewed toward the goal of preserving families that the social workers ignored all sorts of evidence that the home was unsafe, and the result was a child death that should have been prevented. Gelles (1996) states

> [T]he most compelling argument for abandoning the uniform policy of family reunification and family preservation comes from the data on children killed by their parents. Research clearly reveals the damage done by rigidly following the family preservation model. . . . 30 to 50 percent of the children killed by parents or caretakers are killed after they were identified by child welfare agencies, were involved in interventions, and were either left in their homes or returned home after a short-term placement. (pp. 148–149)

Gelles established a center at the University of Pennsylvania School of Social Policy and Practice dedicated to shifting policy away from family preservation and toward being child centered.

The 1997 reauthorization of the Child Abuse Prevention Act (CAPTA), titled the Adoption and Safe Families Act, made the safety of children a priority in all child welfare decision making. This act was viewed by some as representing a shift in federal policy away from family preservation and toward child-centered policy. The main aspect of the act that leads to this belief is its clarification of the requirement, contained in the original CAPTA, that agencies must demonstrate that they have made "reasonable efforts" to preserve a family before parental rights are terminated. Under this new law, reasonable efforts are not required when the court has found that

- the parent has subjected the child to "aggravated circumstances" as defined in state law (including but not limited to abandonment, torture, chronic abuse, and sexual abuse);
- the parent has committed murder or voluntary manslaughter or aided or abetted, attempted, conspired, or solicited to commit such a murder or manslaughter of another child of the parent;
- the parent has committed a felony assault that results in serious bodily injury to the child or another one of the parent's children; or
- the parental rights of the parent to a sibling have been involuntarily terminated.

In these specified cases, states are not required to make reasonable efforts to preserve or to reunify the family. They are required to hold a permanency hearing within thirty days and to make reasonable efforts to place the child for adoption, with a legal guardian, or in another permanent placement. In addition, the act mandates a permanency hearing by the end of every twelve-month period a child is in care.

The 1997 act was not as anti-family-preservation as family preservation advocates initially feared. Although agencies are relieved of the requirement of making family preservation efforts in the preceding specified instances, they continue to be required to make reasonable efforts to preserve and reunify families in all other cases. More important, the new law specifically continues and expands the Family Preservation and Support Services Program, renaming it the Promoting Safe and Stable Families Program. Funding lev-

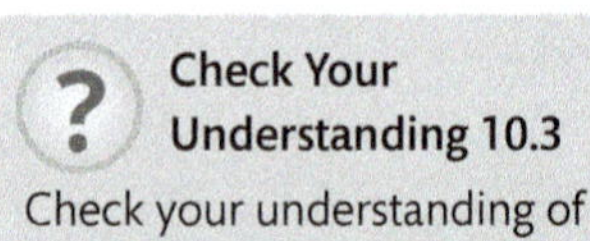
Check Your Understanding 10.3
Check your understanding of Political Analysis by taking this brief quiz.

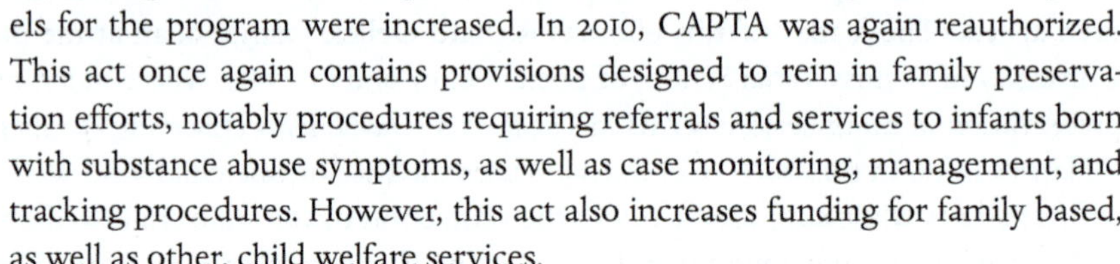
els for the program were increased. In 2010, CAPTA was again reauthorized. This act once again contains provisions designed to rein in family preservation efforts, notably procedures requiring referrals and services to infants born with substance abuse symptoms, as well as case monitoring, management, and tracking procedures. However, this act also increases funding for family based, as well as other, child welfare services.

ECONOMIC ANALYSIS

Although many good arguments have been made for the policy of family preservation, we think it is clear that economic considerations are the driving force behind its rapid growth. In the opening statement to the Committee on Ways and Means, Representative Fred Grandy said, "Principally, federal spending on foster care and adoption through Title IV-E of the Social Security Act has increased from $474 million to $2.5 billion, or roughly a 418 percent increase since 1981. And in the last five years, IV-E has increased by an average of $360 million a year" (Grandy, 1993). Policymakers and administrators are desperate to get control of what is perceived as a runaway increase in costs, and family preservation advocates have successfully used this as a way to sell the policy.

If family preservation can produce the results it promises—prevention of foster home or institutional placement through the provision of time-limited, intensive services—the potential cost savings are significant indeed. The Edna McConnell Clark Foundation has produced media kits stating that family preservation programs cost an estimated average of $3,000 per family per year, as compared to foster care at $10,000 per year per child, or institutional care, which costs $40,000 annually per child. Carolyn Brown and Susan Little (1990), writing about the Full Circle Program, a California family preservation program, assert, "Besides helping children and their families, this work has saved hundreds of thousands of tax dollars: Reunification services for a family cost an average of $2,600[,] . . . less than one month of residential care in California." Kinney, Haapala, and Booth (1991), founders of the original Homebuilders program in Washington State, report their costs as $2,700 per family. They report the costs of alternatives as $5,113 for foster care, $19,673 for group care, $25,978 for residential treatment, $42,300 for placement in an acute psychiatric hospital, and $100,200 for long-term psychiatric care. Marianne Berry (1992) evaluated a family preservation program in California and kept detailed per-hour cost records. She found that families in the program received an average of 67.35 hours of service at a cost of $41.22 per hour, for a per-case average cost of $2,776.17. Comparing this with foster care costs, she concluded that this "translates into a savings of $4,648 for every foster care placement this program prevented. . . . When placement is prevented for more than one child in a family, this savings is multiplied, resulting in an even greater economic benefit from this program."

The critical question on which the future of family preservation rests is whether the projected cost savings will actually materialize. To do so, the number of foster placements will have to begin to decrease or, at the very least, the rate of increase will have to slow and evaluation results will have to establish that family preservation is the reason. If this does not happen, policymakers will undoubtedly lose their initial enthusiasm for family preservation, critics such as Patrick Murphy will gain more credibility, and child welfare policy will turn to some other proposed solution. The results of evaluations of family preservation programs are continuing to come in and are being widely disseminated. It is to these results we now turn.

Check Your Understanding 10.4
Check your understanding of Economic Analysis by taking this brief quiz.

POLICY/PROGRAM EVALUATION

It is probably not stretching the truth to say that family preservation is one of the most carefully studied social welfare innovations in history. There are a number of reasons for this, principally that the program involves leaving children in potentially harmful situations, which calls for extremely vigilant monitoring. The increasing skepticism with which policymakers are now receiving claims of social policy advocates also has resulted in calls for close monitoring of innovations. The prototype family preservation program, the Homebuilders program, was originally funded under a National Institute of Mental Health research grant, which, of course, had knowledge development as a primary goal. When the Family Preservation and Support Program was passed in 1993, Congress included $2 million in fiscal 1994 and $6 million per year from 1995 through 1998 to fund research and evaluation as well as training and technical assistance. The act also requires states to develop new foster care and adoption information systems. The 2002 extension of the Promoting Safe and Stable Families Program includes $6 million per year for research, training, and evaluation out of the mandatory funding and dedicates 3.3 percent of discretionary funding for these purposes. The 2010 authorization of CAPTA specifies fifteen research and assistance activities and demonstrations as well as directing the Secretary of the Department of Health and Human Services (HHS) to conduct an in-depth study of the shaken baby syndrome.

When family preservation models were first implemented during the 1970s, they reported wildly positive outcomes. The Homebuilders program reported placement prevention rates varying from a low of 73 percent to a high of 91 percent of families served. Some of the more recent studies have reported success rates almost as high. An evaluation of a Connecticut program claimed that 82 percent of children at risk of placement were still in their own homes after one year of service. Berry's study of a family preservation program in California concludes, "A full 88 percent of the families receiving services in this program avoided otherwise imminent child removal for a year after being served" (Kinney, Haapala, & Booth, 1991; Berry, 1992).

These studies, sometimes referred to as "first-generation studies," have come under serious criticism for methodological problems. The major problem identified is that they lack any kind of control or comparison group. Thus, if a study finds that 90 percent of the children in the program were not placed, it cannot, without a control group, conclude that the services prevented placement, because there is no way of knowing whether the children really were at risk in the first place. It is possible to argue that, without the services, fewer than 10 percent of the children would have been placed, and therefore the program actually *increased* that rate of placement. This effect was in fact indicated in an analysis of data from the Illinois Family First program conducted by Littell (1997) in which she concludes, "Intensive FPS may have 'case finding' effects, resulting in increases in out-of-home placements and substantiated reports of maltreatment and decreases in case closings." In response to these criticisms, a number of more rigorous studies have been implemented. The results of these studies have been mixed. Some have found no significant differences in placement rates between experimental and control groups (Leeds, 1984; Willems & DeRubeis, 1990). An Oregon study found that significantly fewer children in less difficult cases were placed, but there was no significant difference in placement rates for children in families with more difficult problems (Szykula & Fleishman, 1985). In one study, the experimental group—the one receiving intensive family preservation services—actually experienced a *higher* rate of placement than the control group (Hennepin County Community Services Department, 1980; Stein, 1988).

Dagenais, Begin, Bouchard, and Fortin (2004) have conducted a useful meta-analysis of the net effect of intensive social service intervention on placement rates and the impact of these interventions on children and their families. They collected 156 reports of family preservation program evaluations and selected those that met criteria of good scientific methodology. The result was thirty-eight reports related to twenty-seven programs deemed scientifically worthy. The results of these evaluations were disappointing. The authors found that children who received the services evaluated in the studies were placed in substitute care almost as often as the children in the comparison groups. They did find, however, that the services had a positive impact on children and their families, but that it was slight: "only one variable—neglect, with reference to health care—from just one study indicated statistically lower rates of maltreatment subsequent to intervention" (Dagenais, Begin, Bouchard, & Fortin, 2004).

The most significant study of family preservation to date was conducted in Illinois by the University of Chicago's Chapin Hall Center for Children, under contract with that state's Department of Children and Family Services. The study began in 1989 after Illinois had implemented a version of the Family First program. The study ran for four years and involved three levels of data collection. The first level involved collecting descriptive data from all 6,522 cases involved in Families First in 1989. The second level was a randomized experiment, with a sample of 1,564 cases, to test program effects of subsequent placement and harm to children. The third level, involving a sample of 278 cases, was a series of interviews with parents in both the experimental and control groups to gather data on the effects of the program on child and family well-being over time and to assess clients' experiences and views on the services they received. The results of this study were that the Family First program in Illinois had no effect on either the frequency or the duration of placements (Schuerman, Rzepnicki, & Littell, 1994). A subsequent reanalysis of the data from this study, applying more powerful statistical techniques, confirmed the original conclusions finding that "it appears that the duration, intensity, and breadth of family preservation services have little impact on subsequent child maltreatment, out-of-home placement, or the closing of cases in child welfare" (Littell, 1997, p. 34). After a general review of family preservation programs, Pecora, Whittaker, Maluccio, Barth, DePanfilis, and Plotnick (2010) conclude:

> To date the field lacks conclusive evidence that FBS [family-based services] prevent child placement, and about which types of FBS programs are most effective with different client subpopulations including those involved in physical abuse, neglect, parent-child conflict, or other areas. We also need a better understanding of effectiveness with different age groups of children and of program components that contribute to success with different families (e.g., in-home services, active listening, client goal setting, concrete services). . . . Because the programs that have been evaluated varied significantly in target group, model consistency, program maturity, and services provided, it is premature to draw any conclusions about the effectiveness of any particular type of service for any particular clientele. (pp. 289, 301)

A number of scholars in child welfare have recently begun to criticize what they believe to be the overemphasis on placement prevention as the major criterion for effectiveness of family preservation services. They argue that there are a number of other, equally or more important, possible outcomes from services. Pecora and colleagues (2010, p. 295), for example, suggest the following additional types of outcomes:

- Improvements in child functioning (e.g., behavior, school attendance, school performance, self-esteem)
- Positive changes in parental functioning (e.g., depression, employment, substance abuse, anger management, self-esteem) or parenting skills such as the use of appropriate discipline techniques and child care
- Improvements in family functioning (e.g., family conflict, communication, cohesion, adaptability, or social support)
- Reunification of families after child placement

Berry (1992, p. 320) has argued that our focus on placement prevention has deflected attention from important questions regarding just which elements of intensive services contribute to family preservation and which do not. This knowledge would lead to an improvement in services rather than a simple judgment of whether the services were cost efficient.

As a result of this criticism of family preservation research, scholars have begun to take a more careful look at aspects of family preservation in addition to simple placement prevention and child safety. For example, Robert Lewis recently reported on a three-year study of the Families First model in helping families overcome serious problems in child behavior and child management. The study used a traditional experimental design, comparing outcomes for families receiving Families First services with a control group who did not receive the services. Lewis reports that the families who received the service reported significant improvements in child behavior, physical care and resources, parental effectiveness, and parent–child relationships as compared to families in the control group. In addition, Lewis (2005) found that these changes were retained after the program's conclusion, indicating "that the improved skills, behaviors, and relationship changes developed during the intervention may have become solidly implanted in parental and family functioning" (p. 508).

We agree that, as illustrated by the Lewis study, there are a number of dimensions of family preservation services that could profitably be examined for the purpose of increasing social worker effectiveness in designing programs and in responding to family needs. However, keep in mind that the family preservation policy has been touted and implemented based on the belief that it will eventually help manage the child welfare crisis by reducing the population in placement and (consequently) the huge and rapidly increasing cost of services. If family preservation does not live up to the cost-efficiency promise, regardless of how effective it is demonstrated to be as a social work practice approach, it will be de-emphasized, if not totally abandoned, by policymakers, who will then continue the search for cost containment in child protection.

Check Your Understanding 10.5

Check your understanding of Policy/Program Evaluation by taking this brief quiz.

CURRENT PROPOSALS FOR POLICY REFORM

The family preservation approach to child protective services continues to grow in popularity and influence as a service delivery strategy. Since 1999 when the number of children in and out of home care reached a high of 567,000, the number steadily declined until it was 397,000 in 2011. As we have previously noted, the number has increased slightly to 428,000, but this is still well below the 1999 level. No definitive research has been done to relate the decline specifically to the family-focused approach but some kind of link is hard to deny. One study, done by the state of Kentucky, compared cases assigned to the Family Preservation Program (FPP) (1,510 families and 3,229 children) to all cases served by other means. The study concluded that although "FPP-served families had high risks, young children, and repeated child welfare involvement . . . FPP was associated with fewer and shorter stays in OOHC [out of home care], higher reunification rates, and more placement stability." In response to this study the state doubled the funding allocated for family preservation services (Huebner, 2012).

A strong reform movement is afoot in the area of foster care and family preservation. There is a steady movement toward kinship care, described by the Child Welfare League of America as "one of the most stunning changes in the child welfare system." Kinship care is simply the practice of looking to a child's extended family for a placement resource before looking to foster care with an unrelated family. The Children's Defense Fund reports that over the past decade, the number of children living with grandparents, relatives, or close family friends without their parents present has grown to around 2.7 million children. We earlier reported on the Child Welfare League of America data that indicated a drop in licensed foster homes to less than 98,000 in 2004; however, in addition to this number, the CWLA also reported the licensing of nearly 10,000 kinship foster homes. Most children placed with relatives are members of racial and ethnic groups, mostly African American. One in five black children will spend time in kinship care prior to reaching adulthood. In other ways, the population placed in kinship care appears to be identical with the general foster care population (Child Welfare League of America, 2005; Everett, Hager, & Scannapieco, 1999).

The movement in foster care policy toward kinship care has been an interesting mix of macro- and micropolicy initiatives. On the macrolevel, there have been two significant events. The first is the Child Welfare League of America's National Commission on Family Foster Care, which convened in 1991 and developed *A Blueprint for Fostering Infants, Children, and Youth in the 1990s*. One of the major thrusts of this document was to support the significance of kinship care. The other significant macrolevel event was the 1979 Supreme Court ruling in *Miller v. Youakim,* in which the Court ruled that relatives not be excluded from the definition of foster parents eligible for federal foster care benefits.

Mark Courtney (1995) makes an interesting observation that the movement toward more kinship care may well be the result of microlevel as much as macrolevel policy change:

> Various states, localities, and individual social workers and judges have no doubt contributed to this trend in ways that cannot be easily observed, let alone described, given the decentralized nature of child welfare services. . . . Current permanency planning philosophy in child welfare places emphasis on keeping children "with family," even when they are removed from the home of their birth parents. . . . Common sense suggests that staying with relatives is likely to be less traumatic for a child removed from parental care than placement with unfamiliar foster parents or group care providers. . . . Paying kin to care for a child, as opposed to having to find an appropriate foster home, makes the difficult decision to remove a child from home easier for social workers and judges.

Early data indicate that kinship care is an effective tool for the goal of permanency but works to the detriment of family preservation/reunification if the family to be preserved is that of the biological parents. In a rigorous study of reunification of families with children placed in foster care in Chicago, Robert Goerge (1990) found that placement in the home of a relative was one of the strongest variables in reducing the probability of reunification. Courtney (1994) found that children in kinship care are more likely than children placed in family foster homes or group care to remain in the foster care system for long periods of time.

Kinship care is appealing to policymakers on two fronts. First, because it leaves children in the care of relatives, although not the parents, it appeals to profamily sentiments. Second, kinship care is cheaper than family foster care. Families are now eligible for licensure and payment as foster parents for related children, but under current policy in thirty-four states they can receive only the amount of the child's public assistance (Temporary Assistance for Needy Families [TANF]) payment. This amount is much lower than the prevailing foster care rate in most states, and it is even lower if more than one related child is placed in the same home. It appears that the inequity in this situation is becoming apparent, and pressure is mounting for states to provide the same level of support for children in kinship care as for those in family foster care. Thus, this foster care system reform, too, may eventually prove to be no cost-saver.

? Check Your Understanding 10.6

Check your understanding of Current Proposals for Policy Reform by taking this brief quiz.

CONCLUSION

By way of conclusion we wish to reemphasize that family preservation should not be interpreted to mean only one specific type of program or method. Family preservation is first and foremost a philosophy of practice with families in crisis. Robin Warsh, Barbara Pine, and Anthony Maluccio (1995) offer the following broader definition of family preservation:

> Family preservation is a philosophy that supports policies, programs and practices which recognize the central importance of the biological family to human beings. It underscores the value of individualized assessment and service delivery, with adequate system supports, in order to maximize each family's potential to stay, or again become, safely connected.

This general philosophy of family preservation can be expressed through any number of specific programs and techniques, including kinship care, shared foster care (in which the foster family and the biological family are in direct contact and share childrearing responsibilities), open adoption, family reunification programs, and a number of other profamily approaches, some of which undoubtedly have not even been thought of yet. Warsh, Pine, and Maluccio argue that defining family preservation in terms of one model, such as Homebuilders, confuses the concept. Thus, we conclude that although the specific family preservation models that have recently spread so quickly seem to be falling short of their goals, family preservation as a philosophy of child welfare policy is alive and well and has yet to demonstrate its full potential.

The second observation we wish to make is that true family preservation will, of necessity, involve a much wider range of interventions and benefits than just a direct response to incidents of child maltreatment. We have reviewed arguments concluding that poverty is actually the central child welfare problem. Lindsey (1991), for example, analyzed national survey data and demonstrated that family income is the best predictor of a child's removal from home. Courtney (2000) has analyzed cost data and concluded that it costs the federal government over eleven times as much per child to provide foster care as to provide welfare assistance to the child's family. Putting these findings together, we could argue that *if* poverty is the leading variable related to placement, and *if* placement is much more expensive than increased welfare payments, *then* we could save money and improve the lives of children and families by increasing welfare benefits to a level that enables people to live and care for their children decently. However, as with specific family preservation services, increased welfare supports are only a small part of the total response needed to deal adequately with the problem of child maltreatment. As Edith Fein and Anthony Maluccio (1992) have stated,

> No solutions to child welfare issues will be viable without supports to families. These include adequately compensated employment, availability of housing, accessible medical care, and decriminalization of substance abuse to remove the economic incentive for drug dealing. Other supports are also important, such as good day care, parenting education, and readily available mental health services. As we noted over a decade ago, "permanency planning [or family preservation programs] cannot substitute for preventive services and for increased investment in our children."

Thus, we conclude that it is unrealistic to expect any one specific approach to have a great impact on placement rates. Perhaps if family preservation programs were evaluated as one of a whole set of interventions to reduce placements, they would fare better.

Our final observation is derived from the first two: Although it is understandable to look for a "silver bullet"—a simple one-step remedy to a problem such as child maltreatment—it is highly unrealistic. Child maltreatment results from a huge number of variables, some relating to individual psychology and some to macrosocial and macroeconomic conditions, all interrelated along an almost infinite number of dimensions. As a society, we have a modest understanding of a few of the relevant variables and no knowledge of a number of others; as to how they are interrelated, our understanding is at an even more primitive level. To think that one program approach, such as family preservation, will be *the* solution is simplistic. The conclusion of Fein and Maluccio (1992) regarding permanency planning is also an appropriate conclusion for this policy analysis of family preservation:

> The complexity of human interactions precludes simple solutions, and the certainty of having solved a problem is destined to elude our grasp. These considerations, however, are not negative. They help define the dimensions of the problem and provide a challenge to those who choose to work seriously with children, society's most precious resource.

Recall what you learned from this chapter by completing the Chapter Review.

11

Immigration

LEARNING OUTCOMES

- Identify the contributions of the H1-B visa program to the American economy and its risks to individual workers.
- Discuss possible reasons why the crime rate among native-born citizens is higher than among immigrants.
- List the 12 steps in the vetting process that refugees must go through to enter the United States.
- Assess the overall impact of immigration on the American economy.
- Estimate where the greatest threat of terrorism originates.

CHAPTER OUTLINE

Igor Stevanovic/123RF.com

Indira Islas was six years old when her parents, both doctors, decided to escape the drug gangs in Guerrero, the most violent state in Mexico. Their clinic had been robbed of all its equipment and medicines and all their personal valuables. Relatives had been murdered or kidnapped. Her father had a visa for a trip they had planned to Disneyland. That got them in. They never went back.

Indira's father drives a truck; her mother cleans houses. Their professional careers are lost but they have hopes for their children. And Indira is determined to fulfill them. She became a top student and champion cross-country runner. She volunteered in the local hospital. As she researched her college prospects, she found that, because she was undocumented, she was ineligible for federal financial aid programs and would have to pay out-of-state tuition at her state university. A philanthropic organization called The Dream US offered full four-year scholarships and she won one of their 76 awards. Majoring in biomedical sciences at Delaware State University, she is determined to become a doctor like her parents were and will never be again. She thought that dream was really achievable. The recent presidential election has now cast a deep shadow on that. She is registered with the Deferred Action for Childhood Arrivals (DACA) program. DACA was created by President Obama by executive order in 2012. This got her a Social Security number and a driver's license. These will become useless if the new president decides to dissolve DACA. And if he decides to deport her, they know right where to look (Russakoff, 2017).

Don Mallard is in his forties and had worked for the Walt Disney Company for ten years. His annual performance review said he was doing outstanding work that had saved the company thousands of dollars. His supervisor recommended a raise for Don. Instead, Disney gave Don a pink slip and brought in an immigrant with a temporary visa under contract with HCL Technologies, an outsourcing company based in India. Don was asked to stay for 90 days to train his replacement. For the first 30 days he explained the requirements of the job, for the next 30 they worked side-by-side. During the last 30, the recruit took over the job with Don making sure that he performed it correctly. For this, he received an additional 10 percent of his severance pay. The process was called "knowledge-sharing." Don called it "humiliating."

At Disney, 250 employees were laid off. HCL and other companies like it have performed similar services for other American companies. Southern California Edison cut 450 technology workers. The watchmaker Fossil dispensed with 100, and the University of California, San Francisco, laid off 80. Each year, 85,000 foreign workers enter the United States using a special temporary visa for high-tech workers. They are not allowed to make over $60,000 a year and thus can save companies considerable money when they replace workers making twice that or more (Preston 2015).

Thoughts for Social Work Practice

Do you know anyone in the DACA program? What, if anything, is your university or your community doing to protect them from deportation? Do you know any undocumented workers? Are there groups in your community who have developed recommendations for how to behave if ICE agents come to your door, or who are providing legal aid afterward? Should you help them? Could you start your own organization? Immigrants who are documented are sometimes reluctant to report crimes or ask for services like emergency medical care or family counseling because they fear this will lead to questioning that could expose undocumented relatives, friends, or neighbors. How can we make sure that everyone receives services to which they are legally entitled?

THE PROBLEMS THAT IMMIGRATION POLICY IS ATTEMPTING TO SOLVE

There was no chapter on immigration in the last edition of this text. It was not a major issue in American public life. Suddenly it is. How this came to be is not altogether easy to explain. But we'll try.

There certainly has been no lack of concern about immigration and policy solutions crafted to deal with them, as we will see. But until recently policies have been debated and enacted or defeated without great fanfare. Legislation often was bipartisan. Republican presidents like Ronald Reagan and George W. Bush supported immigration and worked with Democrats to administer it sensibly. Then a variety of social, economic, and political issues came together under the umbrella of immigration in the context of an increasingly divided nation. Positions hardened. The contested ground moved far to the right. Policies endorsed by Reagan and Bush are considered abominations by current Republicans. Policies once considered un-American are now standard positions.

The new policy agenda seeks to do a number of things: secure our borders, protect us against crime and terrorism, reverse a loss of both unskilled and highly skilled jobs, and end the waste of public resources devoted to education and health. To what extent are these real or imagined problems? To what extent does immigration have anything to do with them? And if it does, what policies can solve them?

Thoughts for Social Work Practice

Job loss in mid-career can be devastating to individuals, and place great stress on families. Suicide, domestic violence and substance abuse are possible consequences. People to whom this happens may not be inclined to seek help from a social worker. Are there any places and means for preventive intervention in this situation, or do you just have to wait for the fallout?

Check Your Understanding 11.1

Check your understanding of The Problems That Immigration Policy Is Attempting to Solve by taking this brief quiz.

HISTORICAL ANALYSIS

We are a nation of immigrants. What, you've heard that before? Well, it's true. Even the people we call "native Americans" probably crossed the Bering Straits from Asia to get here. We have a long and proud history of welcoming newcomers and helping them become part of the "American Dream." Yes, another cliché but a useful one because it encapsulates what has drawn people to our shores over the centuries. Social work has its own proud tradition of helping newcomers keep in touch with the cultures they came from while at the same time struggling to assimilate.

We have a less proud tradition of exploiting newcomers through low wages and discrimination in education, housing, and other aspects of life. Those who came earlier try to trap more recent arrivals in a class hierarchy or even pull up the drawbridge to exclude any new arrivals. Seeing immigrants as threats to our jobs or even as sowers of terror, though particularly popular now, is also a tradition that goes back a long way.

Alongside this ongoing struggle of liberation and oppression is a much happier tradition that comes with immigration. We can leave it at one word: pizza, although we are sure you can think of dozens of foods, art forms, types of music, articles of clothing, medicines, and scientific discoveries that immigrants brought us. Question: Why do so many first-magnitude stars have Arabic names?

Immigration policy, as seen by political historian Aristide Zolberg (2006), may be divided into three doors that allow entrance to this country. The front door is where those seeking to be citizens arrive and are welcomed and started on their path to citizenship. The side door is for refugees who are seeking asylum from political persecution. Then there is the back door, a somewhat mysterious portal for workers who are needed to take jobs in sectors of the economy where there are insufficient domestic workers. These workers have traditionally been from Mexico and Central America (Zolberg, 2006).

Front Door

It's common to think of immigration policy as something that didn't exist before the nineteenth century. In fact, Americans were concerned from the beginning with those who should be part of their nation and who should not. Inclusion or exclusion by race, religion, and national origin was practiced at the state level. But for a long time, this was overshadowed by the migration policies of the British Empire. England established colonies to extract wealth from the New World and serve as markets for British goods. They also used them as place to export troublesome citizens. Felons or debtors were given a choice between prison or "transportation," that is, being shipped to the colonies. Between 1718 and 1775, 50,000 convicts were dumped on our shores (Zolberg, 2006; Dinnerstein & Reimers, 2009, chap. 1).

Many immigrants were artisans and skilled workers responding to reports of a labor shortage. They could pay for their passage. But those too poor to pay could also agree to work for from three to seven years for "owners" in the colonies in exchange for passage. Families were often split up and children whose parents died had to work until age 21. This was known as indenture, and in the seventeenth century more than half of the immigrants to the English colonies came as indentured servants (Dinnerstein & Reimers, 2009, chap. 1).

The English were not the only ones seeking empires in the New World. The Spanish in California and Florida, and in Louisiana along with the French, had a colonial presence here. Even the Russians had a fort and trading outpost in northern California. New Orleans became, and remains still, a savory gumbo of Spanish, French, African, and English cultures.

From the beginning, some who had arrived earlier feared and resisted those who arrived later. Benjamin Franklin warned that Pennsylvania would become a "colony of aliens" because of the numbers of Germans settling there. The Germans and Dutch remained insular. The French Huguenots and Jews assimilated more easily. Catholics were particularly despised, even by otherwise reasonable figures like John Adams (Dinnerstein & Reimers, 2009, chap. 1). Yet, somehow, they managed to create a unified society. It is a work still in progress.

The first national statement of what was required to be a citizen of the now–United States was the Naturalization Act of 1790. What was required was a two-year residency. In 1880, that requirement was changed to five years, and still is. Citizenship, however, was restricted to whites. Between 1790 and 1820, there were only about 500,000 new arrivals. They included French-speaking refugees from the slave revolt in Haiti who were educated and from the middle and upper classes; they assimilated quickly (Dinnerstein & Reimers, 2009, chap. 2).

In the 1840s, the potato famine in Ireland touched off a massive migration. During the rest of the century, 4 million Irish fled starvation. Agricultural disruption was not quite as bad in Germany, but it was bad enough to dislodge 5 million people from that country. Scandinavians followed though in fewer numbers. Dutch religious dissenters joined the migration. Some called them "refugees from tolerance" because, unlike the English dissenters, they were unhappy with church attitudes they found too liberal, not too restrictive.

The West coast was also drawing new immigration during this period. The discovery of gold in California in 1849 came to the attention of Chinese merchants in Toishan province. Many in this depressed agricultural area saw new opportunities across the ocean. Many more were recruited to build the Central Pacific Railroad. Unlike earlier groups, Chinese immigrants were mostly males, hoping to earn enough money to support their families at home and return to them some day. Also in the West and Southwest, a kind of "default immigration" took place. The Treaty of Guadalupe-Hidalgo, which ended the Mexican American War in 1948, took Texas, New Mexico, Arizona, and parts of California from Mexico. As with the earlier annexation of Florida in 1819, a large population became Americans whether they wanted to or not. They did not cross the border, the border crossed them (Dinnerstein & Reimers, 2009, chap. 2).

We usually picture immigrants as people ambitiously or desperately seeking a new life. Many, however, were recruited. As the economy of the new country grew, it needed more workers. States, territorial governments, immigrant-aid societies, and the railroads advertised in foreign newspapers, published brochures and maps, and sent agents to Europe. Steamship fares were cheap, and families who were already established could send prepaid tickets to relatives and friends. Estimates vary, but perhaps anywhere from 25 to 70 percent of immigrants in the late nineteenth and earlier twentieth centuries made the voyage with prepaid tickets (Dinnerstein & Reimers, 2009, chap. 2).

The federal government began requiring the collection of vital statistics in 1819, but otherwise placed no impediments to anyone who wanted to become an American. In 1855, New York set up a reception center, called Castle Garden, that centralized the flow of newcomers, collected information, provided some overnight accommodations,

Everett Historical/Shutterstock

This is how Italian, German, and Russian immigrants looked to some people. How would they see Syrians?

and protected the unsuspecting from con artists by directing them to licensed boarding houses and legitimate agents for railroad and canal boat tickets. These services were partially funded by a fifty-cent tax, levied by Congress in 1882, on the immigrants. In 1890, the federal government took over supervision of immigration and replaced Castle Garden with Ellis Island. For West coast immigrants, Angel Island in San Francisco Bay became their arrival point (Dinnerstein & Reimers, 2009, chap. 2).

Assimilation varied considerably. Some groups, particularly the Irish Catholics, Germans, and Scandinavians, worked hard to preserve their heritage. Some chose isolation. Germans built communities where the architecture echoed that of their homeland, the newspapers were in their native language and ". . . not only stores and saloons, but banks, hospitals, orchestra halls, and social clubs . . ." reflected a German counterculture called *Deutschtum*. A Norwegian whose grandparents had lived in America for over sixty years commented, "There's no evidence that they had more than glancing contact with anyone who was not Norwegian" (Dinnerstein & Reimers, 2009, pp. 43–45). Keep this in mind in the face of current efforts to promote instant assimilation, like state laws requiring all official transactions be in English and school boards forbidding dual-language instruction ("Mr. King's English-only bill," 2012). American civic life seemed to have functioned well enough when large numbers of our ancestors spoke only German or Norwegian.

Of course, assimilation is harder to accomplish when there is significant hostility expressed toward those trying to assimilate. And there was plenty of that in nineteenth-century America. Such hostility is known as nativism. Discrimination in jobs and education was common. Nativists even coalesced briefly in the 1850s as a political party. They were called the Know Nothings because they tried to keep their operation secret and responded to queries about their party by saying they knew nothing. Ironically, the label also describes the intellectual content of their ideology. They were held together mostly by their dislike of the Roman Catholic Church. But they won local elections and when in office tried to restrict voting, make naturalization a longer process, and conduct investigations of Catholic churches, which they believed held nuns as sexual prisoners and strangled babies fathered by priests (Dinnerstein & Reimers, 2009, chap. 2).

A second major wave of immigration hit American shores beginning in the 1890s and extending to the 1920s. This time, the source was Eastern and Southern Europe. These newcomers were more likely to be illiterate and poorer than the earlier wave. Italians were the largest group, followed by Jews (fleeing pogroms in Central Europe), and Poles. They, too, encountered hostility from the earlier immigrants. German Jews had assimilated to the point that they felt they had more in common with their Christian neighbors than the bearded, ragged, more religiously orthodox, and darker-complected Jews from Russia. However, feeling the rise of anti-Semitism in the country and fearing that their impoverished co-religionists would only increase it, they overcame their initial aversion and established health facilities and social services to keep the newcomers from becoming public burdens (Dinnerstein & Reimers, 2009, chap. 3).

During this period, a new development in social work was underway. Young, well-educated, middle-class women and men were forming so-called settlement houses in the urban slums to help poor immigrants adjust to the New World. They lived where they worked and tried to bring social reform to their communities as well as individual support to their neighbors. Earlier social workers, the "friendly visitors" of the Charity Organization Society, focused on doling out financial relief and moral education. Settlement workers went far beyond that, tackling miserable housing conditions, dangerous public health threats, and starvation wages. They also respected the cultural traditions of the varied immigrant groups, arranging art exhibitions, concerts, and poetry readings to keep these cultures alive. They taught the second generation of immigrants to be proud of their parents (Trattner, 1999).

The varied immigrant groups had very different attitudes toward education. Italians associated it with their oppressive landowners and preferred to have their children working to support their families than wasting time in schools. Poles, Slavs, and French Canadians felt the same way. On the other hand, Czechs, Japanese, Armenians, and Greeks valued education and encouraged their children to absorb as much as possible. These attitudes made assimilation easier. However, another force, growing consumerism, was also at work to pull the younger generation out of ethnic enclaves and into the mainstream. Movies, department stores, radio, and mass advertising all were contributing to a mass culture that was impossible to ignore (Dinnerstein & Reimers, 2009, chap. 3).

As the second great wave of immigration was sinking into American soil, concerns about restricting the flow grew. In 1875, Congress had excluded prostitutes and convicts. "Lunatics," "idiots," and those likely to become government dependents were added later. But in 1882, the focus changed from individual characteristics to nationality when the Chinese Exclusion Act was passed. (Ironically, the Statue of

BOX 11.1 The New Colassos

Not like the brazen giant of Greek fame,
With conquering limbs astride from land to land;
Here at our sea-washed, sunset gates shall stand
A mighty woman with a torch, whose flame
Is the imprisoned lightning, and her name
Mother of Exiles. From her beacon-hand
Glows world-wide welcome; her mild eyes command
The air-bridged harbor that twin cities frame.
"Keep ancient lands, your storied pomp!" cries she
With silent lips. ***"Give me your tired, your poor,***
Your huddled masses yearning to breathe free,
The wretched refuse of your teeming shore.
Send these, the homeless, tempest-tost to me,
I lift my lamp beside the golden door!"

—**Emma Lazarus** (bold, italics added)

Liberty, whose arm was on display in 1876, was finally assembled and dedicated in 1886.) Numerous acts of violence, including both arson and murder, preceded and followed this legislation. A quietly devastating film on the act was produced by Ric Burns Steeplechase Films (*The Chinese Exclusion Act*). The poem by Emma Lazarus inscribed at the base of the Statue of Liberty still echoes in any discussion of immigration. See Box 11.1.

Competition for jobs was behind this, but cultural prejudices were involved. Media pictures of opium dens and rampant prostitution in Chinese neighborhoods were common. The Japanese were also targets but for opposite reasons. Instead of stealing the jobs of common laborers, they were seen as being too successful in agriculture. Fear on the West Coast of being overwhelmed by Asians led to the popular slogan of "the yellow peril." An invasion by Japan was predicted by an Alabama congressman. William Randolph Hearst's newspapers declared that ". . . every one of these immigrants is a Japanese spy" (Dinnerstein & Reimers, 2009, p. 75).

As World War I approached, fear was redirected to the Germans. German books were removed from libraries; orchestras refused to play music by German composers; people, towns, and companies with German names changed them, and sauerkraut became "liberty cabbage." All this culminated in the Johnson-Reed Immigrant Act of 1924. It established national origin quotas based on the white population recorded in the 1920 Census. After this, immigration to America would never be open to all who wanted to come; it was now a numbers game. And for some, the number was zero. The Oriental Exclusion Act of 1924 was, as its name states, categorical (Dinnerstein & Reimers, 2009, chap. 4).

The McCarran-Walter Act of 1952 reaffirmed the national origins system but repealed the ban on Asians. In 1965, the quota system was abolished entirely and immigration policy became focused more on occupational skills, family reunification, and refugees. People displaced by World War II; survivors of the Armenian genocide; and Hungarian, Cuban, and Hong Kong Chinese opponents of communism received special attention (Dinnerstein & Reimers, 2009, chap. 5).

Side Door

What is the difference between an immigrant and a refugee? Sometimes not much. We usually think of an immigrant as someone who voluntarily leaves home to find a better life, and a refugee as someone forced to leave by war or civil violence. The victims of the Irish potato famine are generally thought of as immigrants, but did they have any choice but to leave? How about the Russian Jews running from the murderous pogroms? In the nineteenth century, the difference didn't matter. Now it does.

Before 1965, there were no formal procedures for admitting refugees into the country. It was a temporary, ad hoc response to particular historical crises like the Holocaust or the Cuban revolution. The Internal Security Act of 1950 recognized refugees as people who would be physically persecuted if sent back to their home countries. The Immigration and Nationality Act of 1952 gave the Attorney General the authority to stop deportation of such people. But they could not become citizens without special legislation. The 1965 Immigration Act began to devise rules for handling refugees and set aside 6 percent of visas for people fleeing communist or Middle Eastern countries. Finally, the Refugee Act of 1980 established a process for seeking asylum. It made a distinction between *refugees* and *asylees,* the former being folks who make it to the United States and asked for asylum as opposed to those who make it into an overseas refugee-processing program. The act made it possible for both categories to become citizens after one year (Dinnerstein & Reimers, 2009, chap. 5; Ramji, 2006).

The first refugees arrived in America while it was still a British colony. They were the Acadians (French Huguenots) expelled from Nova Scotia by the British in 1755. They settled in south-central Louisiana and made an enduring contribution to our food culture. The next were also French, driven out of Haiti by the slave revolts in 1791. Their numbers were small and they presented no problems that required social policy. The upheaval caused by the Nazi occupation of much of Europe in the 1930s was a different matter altogether. With millions of Jews being slaughtered and thousands seeking sanctuary in the United States, our government did not live up to the inscription on its Statue of Liberty. The State Department was in charge. It was a bastion of white, ivy-educated aristocrats and riddled with anti-Semitism. There, anti-Semitism was ". . . respectable, perhaps even mandatory" (Zolberg, 2006, p. 275). For the most part, the United States turned its back on the refugees, and many who might have escaped were left to die in Nazi concentration camps. Only one group of 981 was accepted, owing to the intercession of Secretary of the Interior Harold Ickes, and allowed to live in an old Army base in 1944. They were expected to return home after the war; but their American escort Ruth Gruber, recruited by Ickes, lobbied Congress and the president on their behalf with the support of religious groups. They were allowed to stay (Gruber, 2000; Watkins, 1990, pp. 800–804).

Americans were more receptive to refugees from the Hungarian Revolution of 1956. Congress allowed 29,000 to enter and added 31,000 Dutch Indonesians the next year. President Kennedy ordered the admission of thousands of refugees from the Cuban Revolution in 1959, along with Hong Kong Chinese. Cold War politics was clearly behind this new attitude toward refugees. All were escaping communism. Welcoming opponents of our enemies had limits, however. When Fidel Castro decided in 1980 to allow those not happy with his regime to leave, he included not only political prisoners but also common criminals. The so-called boatlift was facilitated by a fleet of Cuban American boats that sailed to Mariel Harbor to pick up relatives and fellow citizens. Most were quickly assimilated, but some with criminal connections found immediate employment in the drug trade. (Al Pacino played a *marielisto* who becomes a crime lord in the movie *Scarface*.) Floridians were not happy. Most were probably unaware that many of our early settlers were convicts who chose to be transported to the colonies rather than go to jail. Some of the boatlift criminals were recently returned to Cuba (Dinnerstein & Reimers, 2009, chap. 6; Robles, 2017).

Back Door

The back door of U.S. immigration was the one through which Mexican workers and their families passed. It swung open and closed according to the respective needs and problems of the American and Mexican economies. The robust American agricultural economy and the building of the railroads in the Southwest were important magnets for young Mexican men who could make wages as much as five times what they might find at home. The faltering agricultural economy of central Mexico pushed many farmers north, and a new domestic railway system gave them a means to go there. World War I increased demand in the United States, and growers pressed Congress to exempt Mexicans from the immigrant quota system. Workers could cross the border with relative ease even without official approval: There was no Border Patrol until 1924 (Dinnerstein & Reimers, 2009, chap. 6).

The Great Depression reversed the movement. Between 1929 and 1940, a third of the Mexican American population was deported. Those who remained suffered extreme poverty. Woody Guthrie's song "Deportees (Plane Wreck at Los Gatos)" captures the mood of despair and rejection of the time, although the song was written in 1948 and the crash was part of a labor contract and not an actual government deportation (Klein, 1999).

War-related factory jobs and agricultural recovery reversed the trend again during the World War II and led to a labor contract agreement between the governments of the United States and Mexico. Known as the bracero program, it lasted from 1942 until 1947. *Bracero* means "strong arm." Working and living conditions and wages were government-regulated. Temporary extensions were approved after that. The program was officially reinstated in 1951 because of the Korean War and continued until 1964. During that period approximately 5 million people were involved. An estimated $200 million was sent by workers back to families in Mexico. The braceros were better paid than local Mexican Americans, but working conditions were not well monitored. One grower reported: "We used to own slaves, but now we rent them from the government" (Posas, 2006; Dinnerstein & Reimers, 2009, p. 132).

The current debate on immigration includes discussion of a path to citizenship. Most Republicans loudly denounce this as amnesty, even though the idea had been endorsed by John McCain and George W. Bush. It is interesting to note that the 1986 Immigration Reform and Control Act, which outlawed employment of undocumented aliens, also provided amnesty to those already here. It was signed by Ronald Reagan (Dinnerstein & Reimers, 2009, chap. 6).

In the 1980s, Mexican economic policy changed from one tied to imports to one emphasizing exports by encouraging foreign investors to build factories in Mexico. This was aided by the 1994 North American Free Trade Agreement (NAFTA). As more manufacturing jobs are created in Mexico, fewer Mexican workers cross the border. This eased the problem of undocumented workers in America but increased the concern that investors who might otherwise be building factories in the United States were now building in Mexico and taking jobs away from American workers (Martin, 2006).

The DREAM Act

In 2001, a bipartisan bill, the Development, Relief, and Education for Alien Minors (DREAM) Act, was introduced to offer children who had been brought to the United States illegally conditional residency with the possibility of eventual citizenship. Applicants had to have arrived before the age of 16; have lived in the United States five years; have graduated high school, earned a GED or been admitted to college; be of "good moral character"; and have registered for Selective Service if male. They would be subjected to criminal background checks.

Despite support from both parties in the Senate and the House, there were not sufficient votes to defeat a Republican filibuster. The bill was reintroduced in 2007 and met the same fate. Various compromise amendments were added in 2009 to 2011, but nothing could get past the Republican filibuster. Nonetheless, ten states—California, Illinois, Kansas, Nebraska, New Mexico, New York, Texas, Utah, Washington, and Wisconsin—acted to allow undocumented students to pay in-state tuition at their universities.

In 2012, President Obama issued Deferred Action for Childhood Aliens (DACA), which provided a renewable, two-year deferment from deportation and a work permit. In 2016, 714,546 applicants were approved (American Immigration Council, 2010).

Current Immigration Process

Here's how the current system works under the Immigration and Naturalization Act of 1965. The United States allows 675,000 lawful permanent residents each year. These are people who can work here and stay indefinitely. The numbers have been adjusted several times since the original act, which was set at 290,000. Refugees are handled separately. There are four paths in:

1. Family unification. Immediate relatives of U.S. citizens—spouses, parents, children under 21—are given first priority. Other family members can qualify but it takes longer, often much longer. Family members are the largest group of immigrants, approximately 480,000 annually. The immigrant's sponsoring family member is financially responsible for him or her.
2. Employment. *Temporary* visas are issued for limited periods to people with special skills needed in the U.S. economy. There are 20 subcategories here. One of them is the B1-H, which we will discuss later. Then there is the possibility of gaining *permanent* employment status. You have to have special skills and/or advanced degrees. There are 40,000 opportunities for athletes, entertainers, researchers, and business executives. Religious workers have a place. Also, if you have $1 million to invest, we'll make room for you. In fact, 10,000 slots are available for high-rollers. Overall, there are 140,000 possible visas. If you are an unskilled worker, you still have a shot, but it maxes out at 5,000.
3. Refugees and asylees. The number admitted in these categories changes yearly and is up to the president and Congress. In 2016, there were regional limits for refugees, ranging from 3,000 to 34,000. The cap was 85,000. For asylees, there is no limit. In 2014, 24,533 individuals were granted asylum.
4. Diversity. This is a lottery intended to make sure that immigration is not dominated by some countries to the neglect of others. It allocated 55,000 visas randomly to countries with low immigrant totals in the last five years.

On top of this, there is a limit on how many people can enter from a particular country. You can't exceed 7 percent of the total amount of people from your country immigrating in a single year.

> **Check Your Understanding 11.2**
> Check your understanding of Historical Analysis by taking this brief quiz.

This is just a quick overview. The details are a lot more complicated. Undocumented workers are often asked: "Why didn't you come in the legal way? My ancestors did." If the present system had been in place a generation earlier, their ancestors might have remained in the old country (American Immigration Council, 2016; Thadani, 2017; Vargas, 2012). For a guide to social work practice on this issue, see Cleveland (2017).

SOCIAL ANALYSIS

Crime

Presidential candidate Donald Trump set the tone at the start of his campaign for the latest round of concerns about immigration as a cause of crime. Mexico, he said, isn't *sending* us their best people. They're sending people with problems. "They're bringing drugs. They're bringing crime. They're rapists." Trump's words conjure up a picture of a mysterious travel agency in Matamoros processing these people: "Rapist? Fine, here's your ticket. Get on the bus. Check forger? Even better. Take a lunch voucher. Bad hombres? Great, we have a group rate." But this is no cartoon to large portions of the electorate.

And such stereotypes go back to colonial times. And there was some reason for it: Many earlier colonists *were* criminals. They were given the choice of prison or "transportation." If you can trace your ancestry back to British immigration, you might find a pickpocket among them. But there are no records of crime waves in the colonies resulting from this British policy. Most likely most of them seized the opportunity for a new life and never looked back.

In the mid-nineteenth century, the Know-Nothings argued for restriction of immigration because they thought it increased crime. Immigrants for Southern and Eastern Europe, and later IndoChina, were poorer and entering with less human capital; therefore, they might resort to crime more easily to survive. Another layer of suspicion was added to those who arrived without documentation. They'd already broken the law, why not continue (Kposowa, 2006, pp. 58–59)?

Actual research on these assumptions has produced no confirmation. The 1931 Wickersham Commission looked at arrest, conviction, and imprisonment statistics and found that the native-born committed more crimes than immigrants. More recent looks at incarceration rates continue to find more natives than immigrants locked up. This is true even of the least educated. Attempts to correlate periods of high immigration with rises in the crime rate found the opposite: As immigration was increasing, crime was going down (Riley, 2008, pp. 184–197; Rumbaut & Irving, 2007).

One theory to explain the lower immigrant incarceration rate was deportation. After serving their time, some convicts were sent out of the country and could not commit further criminal acts. A 2007 investigation of this found no such links. Instead, the study argued that the immigration process selected for individuals less likely to commit crimes. So it may actually be that Mexico is sending us their *best* (Butcher & Piehl, 2007).

While immigration as a cause of crime may be mythical, efforts to restrict immigration and increase deportation may become a real cause of crime, or at least an obstruction of justice. Police forces across the country expect that fear of mass deportation will prevent victims of crime and witnesses to it from reporting the crime. Even native-born or naturalized citizens may believe that their cooperation may lead to the exposure of others who are without papers. Said the police commissioner of Suffolk County, New York, "We solve crimes based on people coming to us. It's that simple." The International Association of Police Chiefs "strongly oppose any initiative that would mandate that state and local law enforcement agencies play a role in the enforcement of federal immigration law" (Robbins, 2017).

Terrorism

The roots of fears of alien terrorists also go back a long way. President John Adams was given the authority to deport anyone with "dangerous" ideas. This isn't exactly terrorism, but that was the time of the French Revolution, a pretty bloody affair. The fledgling government felt that a violent overthrow might be possible. President Adams, however, declined to use the power (Dinnerstein & Reimers, 2009, chap. 1).

Later in the century, during the second great wave of immigration, anarchists became symbols of violent politics. The anarchist, someone who didn't believe in any organized government, was a popular figure in political cartoons. He usually had unruly hair and perhaps a bushy mustache. He was always carrying a black, spherical bomb. Its ropey fuse was always burning. A genuine anarchist, Leon Czolgosz, assassinated President William McKinley in 1901. He was not an immigrant, however; he was born in Detroit (Riley, 2007, p. 189).

Terrorism stopped being the subject of cartoons when 19 men, mostly Saudi Arabians, hijacked four domestic airlines. They crashed two of them into the World Trade Center in New York City and one into the Pentagon. The fourth was brought down in a Pennsylvania field by its passengers. None of the hijackers had snuck across the border. All had legal visas. The date in 2001, 9/11, became code for the terrorist threat. Surveillance legislation and a new cabinet-level department, the Department of Homeland Security, were created in response. It was now apparent how vulnerable the country was.

Although totally irrelevant to the 9/11 attack, another response was a heightened interest in strengthening our border with Mexico. A Brookings security specialist said: "I know of no evidence that there's been a terrorist threat from a Latino virtually ever." For terrorists in general, there are easier ways to get into the United States than crossing the Mexican border. The chances of getting intercepted are high. Drug dealers may accept the odds; if you're a terrorist, why take the risk (Grillo, 2017)?

Another way to stop alien terrorists is not to let anyone in, even through legal channels. This is, of course, ridiculous. So perhaps we can just be selective and forbid certain groups based on religion or country of origin who appear likely sources of threats. Both have been proposed and one has been attempted. On January 27, 2017, Present Trump ordered U.S. Customs officials to stop admitting anyone entering the United States from seven countries—Iran, Iraq, Syria, Somalia, Sudan, Libya, and Yemen—regardless of whether they were U.S. citizens, held green cards, or had visas. It caused chaos at airports and provoked demonstrations nationwide. The order was suspended, unanimously, by the Ninth Circuit Court of Appeals. Another, narrower order has been issued and promptly blocked by two other courts.

The president has said numerous times that refugees simply cross the border. We need to stop them "until we understand what in the Hell is going on." He wants them to be properly vetted. He is obviously unaware that the current refugee-vetting process

BOX 11.2 Steps in Vetting Refugees

1. Register with the United Nations.
2. Interview with the United Nations.
3. Refugee status granted by the United Nations.
4. Referral for resettlement in the United States (achieved by less than 1 percent of refugees worldwide).
5. Interview with U.S. State Department.
6. Background check.
7. Higher-level background check for some.
8. Another background check through law enforcement and terrorist databases.
9. Fingerprints and photos.
10. Second fingerprint screening.
11. Third fingerprint screening through FBI and Homeland Security databases.
12. For Syrians only: case review by U.S. immigration headquarters.
13. For Syrians only: additional review for some cases.
14. In-person interview with Homeland Security (usually done in Jordan or Turkey).
15. Homeland Security approval.
16. Screening for contagious diseases.
17. Cultural orientation class.
18. Match with a U.S. resettlement agency.
19. Multiagency security check before leaving for the United States.
20. Final security check at an American airport.

This process usually takes two years.

Source: Park & Buchanan, 2017. See also www.cbsnews.com/news/60-minutes-syrian-refugee-crisis-immigration.

involved ten steps with numerous interviews and background checks. Syrians must complete two additional steps. The process takes at least two years (Park & Buchanan, 2017). (See Box 11.2.)

A more extreme idea is creating internment camps. Kris Kobach, Kansas secretary of state and advisor to President Trump, in the process of defending a Trump campaign proposal for a database of all Muslims, cited the Supreme Court's 1944 upholding of President Roosevelt's executive order that created Japanese internment camps. Kobach denied that he was proposing such a thing, just that he was saying it could be considered constitutional. We should all revisit the horrors of the World War II for instruction on these matters. These camps, in generally forbidding interior landscapes, were where 120,000 West Coast residents of Japanese ancestry, most of whom were American citizens, were sent in the interests of preventing acts of sabotage on the coast without any evidence that this might be a real danger. They lost their homes, businesses, farms, and any possessions they could not carry (Bromwich, 2016; Rothstein, 2011; Ornstein, 2011).

And if we want a lesson in immigrant patriotism, 14,000 young Japanese men enlisted in the Army, despite this mistreatment of their families. They became the 442 Regimental Combat Team. Poorly led, they fought in Italy and Germany, took very heavy casualties, earned 9,486 Purple Hearts, 4,000 Bronze Stars, 500 Silver Stars, 52 Distinguished Service Crosses, and 21 Medals of Honor—the highest award in the U.S. military. They received eight Presidential Unit Citations. They were the most highly decorated unit in the history of American wars. Their motto was "Go for broke." There is also a 1951 Hollywood movie by that title starring Van Johnson.

Between 9/11 and the Trump bans and deportations, the United States has undergone a significant narrowing and restricting of its visa process. Edward Alden has provided a book full of examples of how a wide variety of foreign scientists, businesspeople, physicians, engineers, and others who have made important contributions to the United States in their respective fields and are now harassed and detained at every border crossing. Such people are increasingly reluctant to come here for any reason, however harmless. We are losing their talent and expertise. We are also losing young people with talent and skills who are looking for opportunity and finding it elsewhere. We are paying a high price for increased security. "[T]he United States," he says, "needs to become as serious about encouraging good people to come to this country as it has been about keeping bad people out" (Alden, 2008, p. 292).

Terrorism is real, and policies to protect us from it are warranted. But thought and resources should be focused on realistic measures. Our many airports and seaports, nuclear plants and gas pipelines, bridges and shopping malls might need better security. Closer attention to "watch lists" might keep better track of people most likely to cause trouble and prevent the apprehension of people who happen to have the same names as the suspects (Riley 2008).

As in the case of crime prevention, attempted crackdowns on immigrants in an effort to stop terrorism could have the opposite effect. Numerous Middle East experts have warned that the ban on Muslims is an excellent recruitment tool around the world for Al Qaeda and the Islamic State of Iraq and Syria (ISIS). It could also increase the number of domestic would-be terrorists (Nichols, 2017). Two psychologists who studied the radicalization of American Muslims concluded that those most vulnerable to jihadi recruitment were those who felt unwelcome in the United States and thought they could never become "real" Americans. They were looking for a cause that would give their lives a purpose. Thus, President Trump's ban may well promote the psychological conditions that fuel the radicalization he seeks to combat (Lyons-Padilla & Gelfand, 2015, 2017).

Cultural Insecurity

We have seen in reviewing the history of immigration that groups who arrived early were often afraid that later arrivals who were culturally different from them would engulf them and submerge their cultural identity. From Benjamin Franklin's worries about the Germans to Western and Northern Europeans' worries about the Eastern and Southern Europeans, to the "yellow peril," there were always groups on the horizon who might take over "our" country. Throughout the nineteenth and twentieth centuries, the political and cultural upper hand was held by Anglo Saxons and, to a lesser extent, the Northern and Western European part of the population. Old, white guys ran the Senate and the corporations nationally, and the school board and the police department locally.

But as the century turned, a demographic change had taken place that could no longer be ignored. We had a black president; female, black, Asian, and Hispanic CEOs; three women, a black, and a Hispanic man on the Supreme Court; and a swiftly rising minority population. In several states, whites will be the minority in a few decades or less. Skin color is no longer a guarantee of superiority and power. The sense of the deluge is now very real to some people. And a vigorous response is now growing. White nationalists have new respectability and are now advising the president. To call someone "politically correct" is now a good way to shut them up. If you have trouble getting your head around "cultural insecurity," congressional representative Steve King (R-Iowa) sums it up nicely for us: "You can't restore our civilization with someone else's babies" (Steinhauer, 2017).

One can see current policies like closing the border and banning some immigrant groups as aimed less at physical safely than as maintaining cultural superiority. They are unlikely to be successful. And it is hard to see what *could* accomplish this. What can be done about cultural insecurity? Perhaps it would help if people could be reminded that all these people who were seen as scary earlier in history have gradually become customers, then business partners, then neighbors, and finally family members. And the folks who managed to hang on to parts of their cultural heritage didn't prevent you from holding on to yours. Some of those formerly scary people are now pillars of the community like Juan Carlos Hernandez Pacheco of West Frankfort, Illinois. He has run a popular Mexican restaurant in town for ten years. He fed exhausted firefighters after a big fire and hosted a law enforcement appreciation dinner. He belongs to the Rotary Club and raises money for the high school sports team. But he never finished his application for citizenship. And, ten years ago, he had two DUI convictions. So federal agents arrested him. He is about to be deported (Davey, 2017a).

The citizens of West Frankfort (settled by some of those Germans who scared Ben Franklin) began to reconsider the immigration policy that they had previously supported. Said one business owner, "[P]eople should follow the rules and obey the laws, and I firmly believe in that. But in the case of Carlos, I think he may have done more for the people here than this place has ever given him. I think it's absolutely horrible that he could be taken away" (Davey, 2017a).

Others agreed. The mayor, the county prosecutor, the fire chief, the Rotary Club president, the high school athletic director, and a number of representatives of law enforcement came to his aid. The immigration judge released Pacheco on bail, and Pacheco rode home from the detention center in Missouri in a car lent by a local dealer. Some in town believe that, despite his activity in the community, he broke the law and should still be deported. His future is very much uncertain. But Pacheco doesn't blame those who voted for the man whose policy has put him in peril. He doesn't think the vote was about immigration. "[This] is a coal miner town," he said (Davey, 2017b).

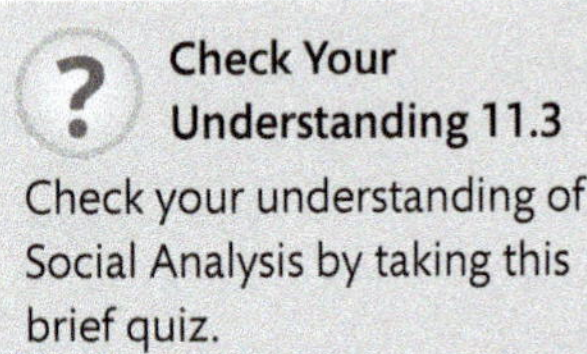
?
Check Your Understanding 11.3
Check your understanding of Social Analysis by taking this brief quiz.

ECONOMIC ANALYSIS

Jobs

Do immigrants take jobs badly needed by native-born workers and keep wages down by being willing to work for less pay? Or do they create jobs by bringing new ideas to existing companies and by starting new companies. Both could be true. For answers, we need to look at both ends of the job market—high income and low—and both at the national level and in specific localities.

When we think of immigrant workers, we usually think of farm laborers harvesting crops, construction workers building houses in the suburbs, restaurant employees clearing tables and washing dishes, and hotel housekeepers who bring us fresh towels. But let's begin by looking at the other end of the job spectrum: positions that command wages of $60,000 and up.

Immigration policy, historically, has favored applicants with particular skills. High-technology companies have complained for some time that there are not enough highly trained workers in fields like engineering and computing to meet their needs. This led to the creation of a special visa, called H1-B, in 1990. Each year 65,000 applicants are given temporary visas to enter the United States and work for high-tech companies. Twenty thousand more visas are available for those with master's degrees. This is only 0.05 percent of the U.S. workforce of 160 million, but many argue that the program is essential to keep the United States on the cutting edge of world technology (Lee, 2017).

Holders of the H1-B visa often move on to gain citizenship and found their own companies. Amar Awadallah came from Egypt to work for Yahoo! and then founded Cloudera, a software company that employs 1,100 workers. Eric Setton, a Frenchman hired by Hewlett-Packard, went on to start Tango, a mobile messaging app. Holders of H1-B visas now occupy 13 percent of U.S. technology jobs (900,000 people). According to one nonpartisan think tank, the National Foundation for American policy, more than half of the $87 billion startup companies they studied were founded by people from outside the United States. Well-established companies started by immigrants include E-Bay, Yahoo!, and Instagram. An immigrant from Russia helped found Google; its current CEO is from India. A child of immigrants created Apple (Lee, 2017; Manjoo, 2017).

This impact is seen not just in Silicon Valley giants. The Small Business Administration reported in 2012 that 10.5 percent of the immigrant workforce were business owners, compared with 9.3 of those born here. Immigrants may be more creative as well as more entrepreneurial than native-born citizens. In 2006, a quarter of international patent applications filed in the United States were written by foreign-born inventors (Rampell, 2013).

Some question whether there really is a scarcity of home-grown talent in the high-tech fields. The H1-B program may just be a way to broaden the field of applicants from which the companies can choose. They also point to frequent abuse of the program when foreign workers are brought in to replace people already holding the job and performing well just to save labor costs. H1-B visa holders are only allowed to make $60,000 a year. This gave Eversource Energy, a Connecticut utility company, a substantial savings when it replaced Craig Diangelo, who made $130,000, with an Indian visa holder. Diangelo even had to train the new worker to do his job. The company laid off 220 employees (Wakabuyshi & Schwartz, 2017).

Latinos are among the fastest growing immigrant populations in the United States and are often seen as having a negative impact on the American economy. Let's look at that impact. From 2007 to 2012, Latinos were starting small businesses at a rate 60 times that of non-Latinos. They also had a large impact as consumers. They bought 25 percent of all Toyota Corollas in 2015. And they bought luxury cars as well as economic compacts. Their purchase of high-ticket cars rose 16 percent from 2013 to 2015 compared with 5 percent for non-Hispanics. From seventeenth-century political philosopher John Locke, an important influence on our founding fathers, we inherited the conviction that ownership of property was a key to a stable society. For a while, it was a prerequisite for voting. Hispanics accounted for 40 percent of the growth in home ownership in 2014 (Berenson, 2016).

Undocumented workers also play a part in the growth of the economy. They are consumers who buy what others produce. They pay sales taxes in the process. Unless they are working "off the books," they pay payroll taxes, which puts money into Social Security, a benefit they will never receive. Legal immigrants, who will receive benefits, are currently putting millions more than they are taking out because they are younger and healthier. The same is true of Medicare. Thus, immigrants, documented or not, are now sustaining the Social Security program, which is being stretched by the retirees of the baby boom generation (Davidson, 2013; Tavernise, 2013).

The most severe problem when it comes to jobs occurs in the lower end of the socioeconomic spectrum. Low- and unskilled workers have the most to fear because many immigrants, particularly those from Eastern Europe and Latin America, come from economies where wages are miniscule, working conditions are brutal, and benefits are nonexistent. Their competition with native-born workers could be fierce enough to keep wages low or even depress them. The results of several attempts to measure this effect range from 9 percent reduction to no effect. The researcher who found the greatest harm, Harvard economist George Borjas, used a model that assumed that companies don't change and that unskilled domestic workers and immigrants are interchangeable; in other words, the market is a zero-sum game: For each worker hired, one must be fired (Riley, 2008, p. 77).

But other economists reject this interchangeability. They see hiring of unskilled workers as creating other jobs at a higher level. Having someone to lug materials around and clean up the job site frees other workers to use their skills more efficiently and produce more, creating other jobs. This goes back to Adam Smith, the father of laissez-faire economics and still a favorite of modern conservatives. The economy grows when labor is divided and people specialize. Workers are not competing for the same piece of the pie, they are making a larger pie. Even Borjas concludes that overall immigration increases the gross domestic product (GDP) by 2 percent (Riley, 2008, pp. 52–80; Davidson, 2013; Applebaum, 2017; Porter, 2017).

Unskilled workers, like farmhands, are usually thought to be the most threatened by undocumented immigrants. Blocking immigration could potentially open thousands of jobs in agriculture to native-born workers. And wages would have to increase in order to attract new workers. But that hasn't happened. Farmers instead have turned more to technology for harvesting, have switched to less labor-intensive drops, and even rented land in Mexico (Porter, 2017).

Looking at the economy as a whole, however, ignores the fact that the effects of immigration are not evenly distributed. The effects at the upper end of the economy are felt in Silicon Valley. The effects at the lower end are felt in Arizona and Texas. Some communities with dense immigrant populations may also be poorer, have more crime, and have a disproportionate effect on public resources like schools and hospitals. And there the competition may be of the zero-sum kind. Politicians representing these districts will be more concerned with job stealing. They are less likely to be looking at the GDP (Davidson, 2013). And they will serve as a source of horror stories for other politicians who can get political support in their districts for telling them, even if their constituents aren't feeling any such competition.

It is not just along the southern border that immigration has effects. Meat-packing plants in the Midwest and clothing mills in the South have attracted large numbers of Hispanic families. And in some places, this influx has revived small towns on the verge of extinction. The younger population has moved away and the newcomers are providing the labor to keep these industries going. Ulysses, Kansas, for example, is now half Hispanic. Homes, farms, and businesses have been restored and are now prospering. Children fill the schools again. This has been unsettling to what remains of the original residents, but they are slowly adjusting to their new neighbors (Sulzberger, 2011). Storm Lake, Iowa, has a similar story (Cohen, 2017). Dayton, Ohio, didn't wait for immigrants to bring new life to their city. They advertised. Dayton had a sizable Turkish community

The American welcome mat is still maintained by some.

already established. A Turkish community leader went to the mayor and proposed trying to attract more Turks. The city had 14,000 empty houses. They established a Welcome Dayton program. They held community meetings to discover if the residents were ready to welcome newcomers and found that the only opposition came from anti-immigrant groups from out of town. They coordinated the city services to help each deal with new immigrants as well as the ones they already had: Muslims, Chinese, Filipinos, and Latin Americans. Classes to teach English and offer instruction on how to open small businesses were organized. Red tape was cut so that immigrant doctors and engineers could be certified and do what they had been trained to do. The police chief gave full cooperation so that no one would be afraid to report crimes. New businesses, restaurants, shops, and even a trucking company have appeared. Similar projects are underway in Chicago, Cincinnati, Columbus, Cleveland, Indianapolis, St. Louis, and Lansing (Preston, 2013).

Public Resources

Fears that immigrants would become public charges were present from the beginning. Even before there was much in the way of public services, American colonists were concerned that the newcomers should be able to take care of themselves and do their part to help the nation grow. Massachusetts passed the first law in 1645 that attempted to exclude "rogues," "vagabonds," "the lame," "the infirm," and other "undesirables." Ship captains were required to report on passengers who might fall into these vague categories. Federal legislation that included public charge concerns began with the Immigration Act of 1891. More recently, the Illegal Immigration Reform and Immigrant Responsibility Act of 1996 made not only undocumented but also documented legal aliens ineligible for public services. Those with documents might qualify after five years of residency. In that same year the Personal Responsibility and Work Reconciliation Act made sure that even legal immigrants could not get welfare, food stamps, or health insurance (Edwards, 2006; Fix, 2009).

More recently, it was thought that "welfare's magnetic force" would draw immigrants to become public charges. It did not matter that 65 percent of immigrant families had two parents, compared with only 40 percent of the native born. Nor was it noticed that 80 percent were in the labor force as opposed to 70 percent of natives. Even before welfare reform, low-income immigrant families used Temporary Assistance for Needy Families (TANF) and food stamps less than low-income native-born families. Between 1996 and 2013, TANF families dropped from 4.6 million to 2 million. Most people who were eligible for TANF didn't use it. There were lots of reasons for not using it, but among Hispanic citizens there was now the added reason: the new immigration enforcement. Even if they are U.S.-born citizens and are legally entitled to benefits, which they may sorely need in the economic turnaround, they might have a personal connection to someone who is undocumented. Involvement in public social services might lead to the exposure of undocumented people (Fix, 2009, p. 30; Pedraza & Zhu, 2015).

If there were welfare magnets, however, they would not be in states like Arkansas and North Carolina, which have welfare benefits among the lowest in the country. Yet these states have seen unusually large increases in immigrants. Construction and manufacturing jobs are the magnets. Jason L. Riley, a member of the *Wall Street Journal*'s editorial board, concludes: "There appears to be no correlation between generous welfare benefits and growing immigrant populations." Even George Borjas, the economist most worried about the effect of illegal immigrants on domestic unskilled workers, states, "Although . . . the magnet effect . . . comes up most often in the immigration debate, it is also the one for which there is no empirical support." Borjas, by the way, is a Cuban immigrant (Riley, 2006, pp. 108, 103).

Overall, the impact that immigration has on the American economy seems quite positive. There are many more benefits than costs. But what about those specific localities that are bearing the costs? There is a solution, although it would probably not be politically popular at the moment. Military bases occupy large chunks of land. They are usually near small towns or cities that depend for much of their sustaining revenue on property taxes. Military bases don't pay those taxes. Therefore, the federal government pays compensation to those "federally impacted areas." The same logic could be applied to areas differentially affected by immigration. Military bases are a central part of national defense. The cost should be shared by the nation, not just the towns near the bases. Immigration benefits the American economy; those benefits should be shared with areas paying more than their share of the costs.

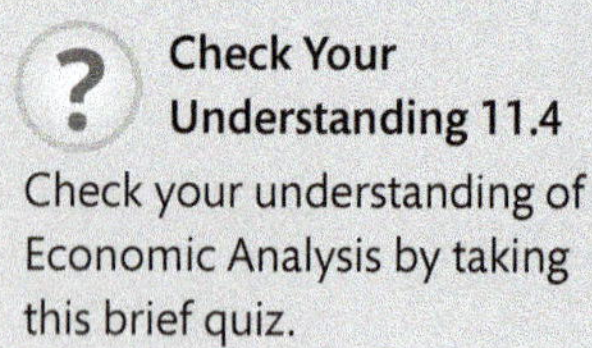
?
Check Your Understanding 11.4
Check your understanding of Economic Analysis by taking this brief quiz.

POLITICAL ANALYSIS

Why is immigration a major social policy concern now? It wasn't when the last edition of this text was published. The economic arguments are fairly minor. There is the slowly growing social factor in changing demographic patterns. But the force that rolled these into a case for radical social policy seems to be political.

Ronald Reagan was a champion of immigration. He believed the following: "All of the immigrants who came to us brought their own music, literature, customs, and ideas. And the marvelous thing, a thing of which we're proud, is they did not have to relinquish these things in order to fit in. In fact, what they brought to America became American.

And this diversity more than enriched us; it has literally shaped us" (Reagan 1984). Reagan signed the Immigration Reform and Control Act in 1986, which had a process for legalizing immigrants already here. In 1998, Bill Clinton and Congress approved citizenship for thousands of refugee Haitians. George W. Bush worked with Senator Ted Kennedy, a Democrat, and John McCain, a Republican, on a bill that included both strengthening of the borders and a path for citizenship for undocumented residents. It had broad bipartisan support. But right-wing talk show hosts opposed it. The "path to citizenship" became "amnesty," which became an easy-to-understand sound bite that emphasized illegality and brought discussion to an end.

Talk radio got considerable help from House Republicans. Dennis Hastert organized "field hearings" where members went back to their constituents to talk about immigration. They thought it was a convenient wedge issue that allowed them to change the subject from the many problems already facing the country. The Iraq War was not going well. Their attempt to privatize Social Security was widely rejected. House Speaker Tom DeLay was indicted for violation of campaign law. Conservative critics were upset with heavy Republican spending. The attempt to change the subject didn't work; they lost heavily. But it did make any consideration of immigration reform toxic (Riley, 2008; MacGillis, 2016).

In 2013, a bipartisan group in the House began working on a compromise bill. Optimism ran high in both parties after Obama's reelection that some kind of agreement could be reached. Even some talk-show luminaries like Charles Krauthammer and Sean Hannity were supportive. But forces in both parties combined to doom the operation. The White House froze out the Republicans, believing that a Senate bill, which it liked better, would pass and then be forced on the House. The Republicans were ultimately trapped because Speaker John Boehner, while claiming to want a deal, wouldn't endorse one unless he had a majority of his party on board. The compromise bill could have passed with less than a majority of Republicans, but Boehner was unwilling to violate the Hastert Rule by which no legislation would be allowed a vote on the floor without that majority (MacGillis, 2016). Politics, not fear of job loss, threat of terrorism, or cultural insecurity, paralyzed immigration reform.

Check Your Understanding 11.5
Check your understanding of Political Analysis by taking this brief quiz.

THE CURRENT POLICY ARENA

President Trump's immigration policies are evolving. At the moment, we have public discussion about the following topics.

The Wall

Although President Trump has stated again and again that Mexico will pay for an extended wall along the border, no funds from the South have been sighted. So the president has decreed by executive order that the wall will be built with U.S. funds to be reimbursed at some future time. No policy has been offered to deal with American landowners whose property the wall must cross and who are less than excited about having it.

The Ban

President Trump has ordered a halt to the entry of all immigrants from seven countries. People from Iraq, Iran, Sudan, and Syria were declared ineligible for a visa waiver by a 2015 law signed by President Obama. The other three countries—Libya, Somalia, and

Yemen—were added later. The State Department considers Iran, Syria, and Sudan sponsors of terrorism, and the other four as havens for terrorists, as well as eight other countries not included in Trump's ban. None of the 9/11 hijackers came from any of these seven countries. Fifteen came from Saudi Arabia, two from the United Arab Emirates, and one each from Egypt and Lebanon. Pakistan has been a sponsor of terrorists and is also not on the list. All of the 12 jihadist terrorists who killed other people in the United States since 9/11 were American citizens or permanent residents. None had ties to the seven banned countries (Qiu, 2017).

Two versions of the ban have now been stopped by court decisions. There may be further iterations. There may be appeals. There have been large demonstrations against the ban. The effects of the ban on businesses, universities, research projects, and families are yet to be determined. See the discussion above on closing borders.

Deportation

Many people have been picked up and scheduled for deportation in the weeks when this text was written. The Obama administration's deportation program, which transported, up to now, record numbers, claimed to prioritize perpetrators of serious crimes. It is not clear what the present priorities are, and some examples of offenses leading to deportation are quite minor. The case of Carlos, already discussed in this chapter, is based on decade-old DWI convictions.

? Check Your Understanding 11.6

Check your understanding of The Current Policy Arena by taking this brief quiz.

CONCLUSION

Immigration policy is still a work in progress. By the time you read this, much may have changed. Fear of immigrants may have intensified. New acts of terrorism may have increased calls for further restriction of immigration. The social, political, and economic impact of immigration restriction may have forced a reconsideration of restrictive policies. There may be a rediscovery of our long-standing commitment to the "lamp beside the golden door." Social workers with an interest in poverty, education, health, mental health, community organization, and advocacy in all these areas will have much to do.

Recall what you learned from this chapter by completing the Chapter Review.

Part Four

Taking Action

12

Politics and Social Welfare Policy

Sentavio/Shutterstock

After years of ignoring the issue, the Louisiana State Legislature passed six laws in a single session granting legal protections and redress to adult survivors of childhood sexual abuse. This package of legislation was enacted largely through the efforts of Carolyn Evans, a graduate student in social work at Louisiana State University and now in private practice. Evans's field internship experience in a recovery center for survivors of sexual abuse had helped convince her that current policies were inadequate for dealing with the problem. The legislation she helped create and pass is a comprehensive package that broadens the definition of criminal sexual activity with minors and extends the time limit for reporting the crime. Instead of a limit of three years past the age of majority, survivors can now initiate prosecution up until the time they reach age twenty-eight. The legislation also allows survivors to sue for damages (which can compensate for money spent on therapy and for earnings lost due to emotional problems) and requires those convicted of abuse to participate in a sex offender treatment program.

The journey toward enactment of the child sexual abuse legislation began with Evans's exploration of the topic in a social work Independent Readings course. As she studied what remedies were available for individuals like those at the recovery center, she realized that Louisiana law provided inadequate

LEARNING OUTCOMES

- Define *lobbying* and describe how it works in the legislative process.
- Contrast the pluralist and elitist models of community power structure.
- Identify the main weakness of the incrementalist model.
- Describe the process by which a policy becomes legitimized.
- Evaluate the claim that engineering a nondecision is the most powerful exercise of power.

CHAPTER OUTLINE

protection for sexually abused children and little recourse for people who did not fully recognize what had happened to them until they were adults. She also discovered that some states had developed legislation to fill these gaps. Perhaps Louisiana could adopt similar laws. On the advice of a law student acquaintance, she took her research and her recommendations to a state senator who had a record of concern about family and children's issues. When he expressed an interest in her project, she "gingerly handed him" her eight-inch-thick stack of research findings. At his request, she also summarized the major items she felt ought to be in a protective package. He turned her work over to a legislative aide, who set the recommendations into several bills to submit to the legislature. This package of bills was essentially the same as the final legislation, with one exception: In the bills initially proposed, no time limit was put on when survivors had to report the abuse.

What followed was a complex process of testimony, lobbying, negotiation, and collaboration with other state legislators. It began with Senate committee hearings on the bills. In consultation with the senator and his staff, Evans and several other supporters attended the hearings and provided written testimony. As the hearings were being held, she also had the chance to attend a "legislative luncheon" sponsored by the state chapter of the National Association of Social Workers. This is a yearly affair held at the state capital, attended by legislators sympathetic to social work issues. Evans presented her concerns and her legislative goals to the group and was later approached by several women legislators who promised their support if the bills were sent by the committee to the floor of the legislature.

The first bill to come before a Senate committee, and one that Evans regarded as key, was the bill abolishing the statute of limitations for reporting child sexual abuse; in other words, no matter how late in life people realized they had been abused, they could still initiate prosecution of the alleged abusers. This policy, Evans reasoned, would not only help adult survivors but would also deter people from committing abuse in the first place. The senator presented the bill to the committee in a calm and matter-of-fact manner. He had already secured the support of the committee chair. The only objection raised at the hearing was voiced by a representative of the insurance industry, who argued that insurance companies might have to bear the costs of successful suits for damages (because those sued might try to use their homeowner's policies to cover judgments against them). With no time limit on initiating suits, many more could be filed. However, this argument was not taken seriously enough to prevent the bill from being reported out to the legislature.

The bill was then introduced on the Senate floor. The senator's presentation was again calm and low-key, aimed in part at dispelling the concerns of the insurance industry and predictions of a rash of false accusations. The problem was defined as the need "to protect our women and children from sexual abuse"; this appeal, made by a male legislator to a mostly male Senate (often skittish about what they saw as "feminist issues"), was successful. The bill passed unanimously and proceeded to the House.

"Now," the senator told Evans, "your work really begins." The State House of Representatives presented a formidable challenge because it contained many powerful and philosophically divided factions. This often led to intense, even rowdy debates in committees and on the floor. Buoyed by the bill's success in the Senate but nervous about its fate in the House, Evans took advantage of the short period before the House committee hearings to "learn the lay of the land." She spent time observing proceedings on the House floor, determining state representatives' interests from their speeches. With this understanding, she was able to approach legislators individually to explain the importance of the child sexual abuse bills. In each encounter, she tried to tailor her talk to their particular legislative concerns (a tactic known as *partisan policy analysis,* which we discussed in Chapter 3). She found all but one willing to discuss the issues. She was "surprised and touched at their treatment of me. I had expected them to treat me like a nuisance. Instead, they were courteous and listened carefully to what I had to say." Legislators, she learned, appreciated the chance to hear directly from someone at the "grassroots level" who had observed a problem firsthand.

When the lead bill was introduced in the House committee by its Senate sponsor, it faced more opposition than in the Senate. One particularly adamant woman legislator opposed the bill on the grounds that giving adults the chance to prosecute for sexual abuse they thought they had suffered as children would lead to "a witch hunt" of innocent individuals. Another committee member seemed amused by the issue. This would not be the first time that legislators demonstrated skepticism about the seriousness of the problems faced by survivors of sexual abuse.

In the same hearings, however, one of the women legislators who had earlier promised support spoke favorably about the bill; she was backed by several male legislators. Evans and her supporters sat ready to present testimony, but the senator was able to handle the objections successfully and the bill received enough support to be reported out of the committee.

Evans and the senator then had to find a representative who could introduce and defend the bill effectively in the House. The senator originally asked a member of the influential legislative Black Caucus to present the bill. When it turned out that he was unable to do so, Evans was fortunate in locating a legislator from New Orleans who had already proposed legislation similar to hers. Like the senator, this was a man with strong interests in issues involving women and children. A close rapport quickly developed between Evans and the representative and his aides, and he agreed to introduce the bill.

By now, with Evans's help, a coalition was beginning to build around the legislation. The group included the women legislators who had heard her presentation at the National Association of Social Workers (NASW) luncheon. A human services lobbyist also offered her advice and support. Several social work students and faculty members sat with Evans in the House gallery, waiting for the bill to come up. As they waited, they wrote personal notes to each representative, asking him or her to support this important legislation.

The New Orleans representative presented the bill in a manner similar to that of the senator, stressing its importance as a protection against sexual abuse of children. This time, as in the House committee, debate was spirited. Representatives rose to proclaim the ridiculous nature of a bill that would allow "a sixty-year-old woman to sue her eighty-year-old father." The possibility of such lawsuits could "destroy the family." While some cried "witch hunt," others remained unconvinced of the seriousness of the issue or the need for legislation. Questions arose about the implications for the insurance industry. The representative fielded questions knowledgeably; other legislators argued in support; and Evans and her student/faculty companions wrote feverishly from the gallery, sending notes to lawmakers about the importance of the issue. In the end, the bill was defeated by one vote.

When the bill was defeated, arrangements were made immediately by the sponsoring representative to have it brought up again before the close of the legislative session. In the meantime, one of the supportive women legislators gave Evans a list of all the lawmakers who had voted no, with the directive "now you really have to work hard." Evans lobbied individually with each one, speaking with great conviction about the problems of child sexual abuse and its effects on survivors. As she did so, she discovered that the lack of a limit on reporting time was particularly troubling to lawmakers; most were amenable to a compromise of a ten-year time period for filing a suit. When the bill was reintroduced with this change, Evans found she had won over almost every negative vote. The bill passed 98 to 1.

Thoughts for Social Work Practice

Can a social worker, particularly a clinical social worker, become a policymaker? Carolyn Evans's work resulted in the passage of six laws in Louisiana. Is there an issue that you have encountered in your practice that should become the basis of a law? Can you imagine getting it done?

The other bills in the legislative package proceeded through a similar process, but this time with much less debate. With the major concern over an unlimited time period for prosecution of alleged abusers resolved, most legislators felt able to support a broadened definition of sexual abuse, the right to sue for damages, and court-mandated treatment for those convicted of abuse. Within six months of its development, this student-inspired package of policies became state law (Evans, 1993; Kuzenski, 1993; Martin, 1993).

We tell this story not only as a lesson that policy changes can indeed stem from the vision and work of one individual uniting with others, but primarily as an example of how policymaking takes place within a political context. Perhaps this seems obvious, because we are using an example of law making, which you would expect to involve politics and politicians. Yet politics permeates policymaking in all areas, including social work agency regulations, personnel policies of large organizations, court decisions, and urban planning projects. An important school of thought in political science and history holds that "politics—the facts of power, the relations of domination . . . insinuates itself in the [very] tissue of reality" (Chatelet, 1979). The argument is that power and politics are everywhere and cannot be isolated in the glass case of congressional or state legislative proceedings.

We use this particular case, however, because the development of child sexual abuse legislation in Louisiana nicely illustrates the role of politics in various stages of policy creation. It also demonstrates, in a particularly dramatic way, a social worker's involvement in the politics of policy. Although this example may be somewhat unusual, social workers are constantly involved in political life in more subtle ways, beginning with their relationships with clients and including their positions in organizations and communities.

The political context of policy is first seen in the politics of problem definition and agenda setting. If a problem such as sexual abuse cannot even get on the legislative agenda, nothing is going to be done about it. We have noted the inclination of a legislative body to define the sexual abuse survivor issue as part of a "feminist agenda," an agenda that some see as trivial, radical, or even vindictive. In this situation, both the student and supportive lawmakers were careful to frame the problem primarily in terms of children and the need to protect them from abuse and its potential effects. This is a good example of the way power is involved in language and in the structuring of arguments.

Politics is also critical to the second stage, the development of a proposed policy solution to the problem, in various ways. In this case, the student brought her initial research, including examples of laws in other states, to a legislator; he, in turn, had it translated into language appropriate for legislation. This was a situation in which existing legislation served as a guide for the policy. In other instances of policymaking, the choice and shape of the proposed policy is generally hammered out through debate and compromise.

A third stage in policy development is the enactment or legitimization of a policy; the current example suggests the importance of lobbying, compromise, and other political tools in achieving this goal. The power and interests of the various legislators and lobbies helped dictate what kind of legislation could be passed. Two other stages, which we did not touch on in this particular example, but which are nonetheless of great importance, consist of the implementation and the evaluation of policy. Policy evaluation has already been discussed in Chapter 3. We will see later how politics affects the implementation stage.

Finally, our example of child abuse legislation indicates that each step in policy development involves a number of political players. In this case, they included advocates (the student and her supporters), professionals (NASW members), and lawmakers who represented a variety of interests and constituencies (including insurance companies, parents, women concerned about issues of abuse and exploitation, attorneys, people worried about the strength of families, and the legislative Black Caucus). Political scientists call such people and groups *stakeholders*. Stakeholders are all the actors interested in and potentially affected by a policy, such as interest groups, public officials, individuals and their families, civil servants, businesses and corporations, professional organizations, and labor unions. Important stakeholders in social welfare policy include the beneficiaries of those policies, such as public welfare recipients or people receiving Social Security checks. Each group has particular assumptions and concerns regarding policies and the problems to which they are intended to respond. As we will see, stakeholders play a major role in each of the stages of policy development.

This chapter will introduce you to the politics of policymaking. It does this within a larger discussion of *process analysis* of policies (see Chapter 3). Process analysis looks at the development, enactment, and implementation of policies. All of these areas are influenced by politics in its broadest sense, that is, viewed as the play of power, not just the formal politics of the legislative process.

The chapter begins with an introduction to ideas about the political context of policymaking. It then describes and critiques various models of policy development and social change. Finally, it examines political factors as they come into play during the various stages of the policy process: problem definition and agenda setting, the framing of policy solutions, policy enactment, and policy implementation.

THE POLITICS OF POLICYMAKING

Politics is one of those words that is used often and with confidence, yet it is rarely defined in a concise manner. The *Random House Dictionary*, for example, gives a circular definition of *politics* as "the practice of conducting political affairs." Perhaps the best single statement for our purposes is the general one that "politics has to do with who gets what, when, and how." As Talcott Parsons elaborates, the polity (or government) of a society is the organization of different collectivities for the purpose of attaining their goals. The political process, Parsons (1986) notes, "is the process by which the necessary organization is built up and operated, the goals of action are determined and the resources requisite to it are mobilized" (p. 96). So politics is about how groups organize to try to get their needs met and to achieve their goals. Power is a central component of this activity.

The meaning of *power* has long been a subject of debate among philosophers, political theorists, and others. Many definitions have been offered. Robert Dahl (1986), a political scientist, calls power the control of behavior, in which *A* gets *B* to do something that *B* would not otherwise do. Power has also been described as the ability to influence people through physical force, rewards or punishments, or propaganda and similar ways of shaping opinions. Power has been seen as being an attribute of individuals, or of groups, or of economic classes—or of all three (Lukes, 1986).

Authority is an important dimension of politics. This is power that is regarded as legitimate by those upon whom it is exercised. We grant power to our elected officials because we had a hand in choosing them. Ideology may confer legitimacy; in earlier times, it was widely believed that kings had a divine right to exercise power. Officeholders may claim legitimacy even if you didn't choose them. Leaders try to promote their legitimacy because it's easier to exercise power through authority than coercion. Thus, power is interactive.

As philosopher Hannah Arendt explains, the person "in power" is put there, or empowered, by others (Arendt, 1986). Stated another way, the power of command does not exist unless others accept the commander's authority. College students, for example, generally concede to professors the power to give out grades—even when these might not be the grades they would like. When power is not accepted or is not accorded to the powerful, people may not obey the commands. In this case, coercion is always a handy backup (Russell, 1986).

The view of power as a relationship should make you think of the various ways in which those exercising power achieve their credibility or legitimacy, including position in an organization or government (CEO, chairperson, elected official), possession of specialized skills or knowledge (engineer, teacher, social worker, physician), or tradition ("kings have always been obeyed").

Most of these conceptions of power are fairly limited, focusing on powerful individuals or groups and their effects on those they dominate. Michel Foucault (1986) has developed a much broader view of power as something that circulates through society and is never in just one person's hands. Foucault was a French philosopher whose works on power and the nature of knowledge have had a strong influence on political science, history, and other disciplines over the past thirty years. Foucault faulted modern political theorists for their reliance on an idea of power stemming from the development of an absolute monarchy in Europe from the Middle Ages through the sixteenth century. Power, Foucault reasoned, is no longer constituted in the relationship between a king and his subjects, a relationship that stressed laws, limits, and obedience. Although the modern state has assumed some of the power of the king, modern relations of power extend beyond the limits of the state. The state lacks total control and instead operates on the basis of already existing power relations. These power relations go beyond laws and are embodied in families, institutions, organizations, and bureaucracy. It is built into the language we use in everyday life, to the extent that we don't even think about it.

Foucault (1986) uses the term *discourse* to describe this permeation of language, mores, and values by power relationships. This is a word social workers throw around a lot. It is used instead of *argument, conversation, policy,* or other small-scale political positions. For Foucault, a discourse is a big deal, a cultural whole.

In his examination of institutions such as the prison and the insane asylum, Foucault focused on the mechanics of power—the small-scale, immediate points at which power is carried out ("Truth and power," 1979; Taylor, 1986). He came to think of power in terms of a universal surveillance, in which people are kept under constant scrutiny. In the prison and the mental institution, for example, doctors, wardens, chaplains, psychiatrists, and social workers possess the power to discipline, supervise, and socialize people into meeting "normal" expectations of behavior. This new kind of power, Foucault concluded, is everywhere.

The preceding paragraph presents only a few generalizations from a vast and complex body of work. But it points to at least two themes that are useful to think about: the universality of power and the shape it takes in the bureaucracies and institutions in which social workers are often employed. And though the lesson may seem depressing, Foucault points out that "there is . . . always something which in some way escapes the relations of power; something in the social body [and] in the individuals themselves which is not . . . reactive raw material . . . which responds to every advance of power by a movement to disengage itself" ("Power and Strategies," 1979). Furthermore, Foucault saw a role to be played by intellectuals or professionals who join in the "everyday struggles" of those with little power at "the precise point where their own conditions of life or work situate them (housing, the hospital, the asylum, the laboratory, the university . . .)." Foucault's list of intellectuals included social workers ("Truth and Power," 1979).

Other writers have also spoken about the positive aspects of power and particularly about the possibility that power is not a finite substance but one that can be multiplied. For example, when public officials create democratic institutions, they may fear losing power, but, in fact, by widening the circle of decision making they are increasing the power that circulates throughout the community. The discussion of social change and empowerment later in this chapter gives insight into the potential of sharing power rather than being bound up in a system with the powerful on one side and the powerless on the other. (We are indebted to Matt Leighninger for his contribution to this discussion.)

Check Your Understanding 12.1
Check your understanding of The Politics of Policymaking by taking this brief quiz.

MODELS OF POLICYMAKING

Although there is universal agreement that policymaking is a political process, there is a lively debate as to how this process works. The debate centers on the interrelated questions of who makes policy and how policies are made. If we do not understand how the policy process works and who is central to the process, we have little chance of influencing policy outcomes.

Who Makes Policy?

In light of the preceding discussion, this question concerns which individuals and groups have the power to get *their* policy goals, rather than the policy goals of others, adopted. The most important theories regarding this question are referred to as *pluralism, public choice, elitism, and neo-elitism.*

Pluralism

Traditionally, political scientists have depicted policy as the output of government institutions. The study of policy therefore consisted of the study of governments and what they do. More recently, political scientists have developed other models of policy or decision making that introduce additional actors to the scene. One of the major models, established by Robert Dahl, Nelson Polsby, and others in the 1950s and 1960s, is the pluralist approach. Still a major approach to policy study in the United States, pluralism assumes a sort of "marketplace of ideas," in which numerous groups and interests compete for power and influence in making policy. Individuals are able to participate in decision making through membership in organized groups. These groups have relatively equal power. Some groups may have more power over particular issues than others, but the essential assumption in pluralism is that all voices will be heard. Power is widely diffused rather than centralized. A pluralist description of the development of health care reform would visualize physicians, allied health professionals, hospitals, insurance companies, businesses, labor unions, health reform advocates, and consumers joining in the debate over health care and each having some say in its resolution (Dye, 2013; Peters, 1986). Pluralism is the model of decision making that most of us hope exists; it is the model that tends to be taught in high school civics classes.

The pluralist model has been subjected to important critiques. One of the most potent is the argument that not every voice manages to make it to the debate. Certain powerful persons and groups can prevent those with threatening or opposing ideas from reaching an audience and presenting their ideas in public. Those in power may manipulate existing values or use institutional procedures to stifle demands before they get to the relevant decision-making arena. Not so long ago, branding a policy proposal as "socialistic" was an effective way to discredit the proposal and prevent any serious discussion. With the rise to prominence of Bernie Sanders, who describes himself as a "democratic socialist," you don't hear that much anymore. Organizational rules can also be manipulated to suppress challenges to the interests of powerful decision makers (Bachrach & Baratz, 1970). In a case study of the difficulties faced by poor coal miners in Appalachia, John Gaventa tells how a group of miners and their families appealed to a state regulatory agency to deny a permit to a strip mine operator who planned to work close to their homes. To thwart their efforts, a state official mailed them information on the appeals process *after* the permit had been granted (Gaventa, 1980).

Political scientist Robert Salisbury offers another example of the uneven playing field for political voices. In describing the attempts of various groups to influence public policy in Washington, Salisbury differentiates between interest-based groups with *personal* membership, such as consumer organizations that advocate for health care reform, and *institutions,* such as hospitals and insurance companies, that also seek to influence the reform process. Salisbury observes that institutions have long-time concerns, often with a variety of policies; these concerns tend to be represented by lobbyists. Institutions generally have more resources than interest groups to devote to policymaking. They also have less obligation to consult with people other than top management in making decisions about policy issues. Membership groups, however, must stay in close touch with their members in order to keep their legitimacy. Because of these factors, Salisbury (1984) notes, large institutions have come to dominate interest representation in the federal government.

This critique of pluralism focuses both on who gets what—and how—and who gets left out—and how (Bachrach & Baratz, 1970). Powerful people are said to control the agenda of public discussion and to limit such discussion to relatively unimportant topics. Truly important topics are reserved for private negotiations among only those groups with the required power and influence. One might see this in a private psychiatric hospital for adolescents in which staff members try to raise the question of why patients get discharged when their private insurance runs out and get firmly redirected to what they "ought to be concerned with"—perfecting their therapeutic techniques.

Public Choice Theory

A somewhat different version of the pluralist model is public choice theory, which brings an economic dimension to the discussion. The traditional economist's view of marketplace behavior stresses individuals pursuing their own private interests. Public choice theorists apply this notion to the political arena and assume that all political actors—voters, taxpayers, candidates, legislators, bureaucrats, interest groups, parties, bureaucracies, and governments—seek to maximize their personal benefits. Public choice theorists offer a useful discussion of the separate interests of voters, politicians, and bureaucrats, explaining that the interests of politicians and bureaucrats are to win elections and to expand their power. Voters, in turn, are usually concerned with how policies will affect them (Dye, 2017). This understanding of the difference in goals between public officials and voters will be helpful when we talk about policy development and implementation.

Elitist Model

The elitist model of policy development and social change contrasts with the pluralist approach. Rather than conceptualizing policy as the product of a multitude of groups and interests, this model sees it as reflecting the goals of a select group of individuals—or what C. Wright Mills called the "power elite." The power elite represents the interests of wealthy citizens and the leaders of corporations and military institutions. It may also include the leaders of well-financed interest groups. Sometimes, the division between the powerful and the powerless is depicted as a class struggle between capitalists and workers. In the elite model, people on the lower rungs of society are viewed as powerless and therefore apathetic; even if they had strong opinions, they would rarely have the resources to organize as interest groups. As Thomas Dye (2017) notes, "Policies flow downward from elites to masses; they do not arise from mass demands."

In his study of Appalachian coal miners, Gaventa (1980) offers a vivid picture of the control exercised by a large mining company over a several-county area. Company men held offices in local government, miners lived in company houses and had to buy supplies at company stores, and the company hired the people who taught in the schools. Control was so thorough and far-reaching that miners in that area rarely protested low wages or dangerous working conditions. As Gaventa (1980) observes, the elite used their power to keep the non-elite quiet. Although the pluralist and elitist models seem at opposite ends of the spectrum, it is possible that both can be useful in analysis of policies. Perhaps each side is correct, depending on the situation. In the case of certain foreign policies, for example, some interests and groups—the leaders of the armed forces, the defense industry, and certain government officials and business interests, such as large

XiXinXing/Shutterstock

Those who control agendas can define or eliminate debate.

oil companies—have between them enough power to make the crucial decisions. Yet in other cases, such as policies to protect the rights of those with disabilities, many different and opposing groups can enter fairly equally into the debate (Jansson, 1999).

Neo-Elitist Model

This is a merging of pluralism, public choice, and elitist theory. This approach is based on Schattschneider's (1960) famous book *The Semisovereign People* and was further developed in Bachrach and Baratz's (1970) study of race relations in Baltimore. This approach agrees with pluralism that everyone potentially has a voice in the political decision-making process, but argues that the deck is so stacked in favor of powerful elites that low-status, low-power groups are effectively excluded. The system is seen as having a strong permanent bias in favor of some groups over others and the political agenda is nearly always shaped by "insiders." Schattschneider argued that "whosoever decides what the game is about will also decide who gets in the game."

Bachrach and Baratz (1970) coined the term *nondecision* to explain how low-power groups are excluded from the policy process. They define nondecision as "a means by which demands for change in the existing allocation of benefits and privileges in the community can be suffocated before they are even voiced." The needs and desires of low-power groups never get on the policymaking agenda and are thus never debated and never acted upon. In their study of race relations in Baltimore during the early years of the Civil Rights Movement, Bachrach and Baratz showed how powerful business and political leaders, working in concert, operated systematically to screen out the interests of the minority black community. They found that many types of tactics were used, including co-opting black leaders, state violence against others, labeling prominent black leaders as communists and troublemakers, and using the media to publicize scares of the potential of racial violence. This "mobilization of bias," they argued, involved the ability of powerful groups to manipulate the political agenda against weaker groups, even to the point of the systematic exclusion of whole sectors of society (Bachrach & Baratz, 1970).

Heffernan (1979) asserts that the critical first postulate of the neo-elitist model is that powerful groups effectively conspire to keep low-power groups out of the political game. The reason, for example, that welfare recipients do not have any effective input into financial assistance policy (even though they are the people directly affected by this policy) is that powerful groups such as employers needing low-wage workers, tax payers wanting their tax rates lowered, and state governments wanting to reduce welfare costs, work together to keep welfare recipients from having any political voice. "In the elitist model the few control the choice for the many. In the neoelitist model, the majority conspire to keep the few from having any influence in public choices . . . this conspiracy takes place *effectively* but not necessarily *deliberately*" (Heffernan, 1979).

How Are Policies Made?

The models described in the previous section focus on *who* makes policy or influences social change. In this section, we address the closely related issue of *how* change comes about. Major theories include rational decision making, incrementalism, and conflict theory. Rationale decision making and incrementalism are closely related to pluralism and public choice theory, while conflict theory undergirds elitist and neo-elitist perspectives.

Rational Decision Making

The rational decision-making approach presents this process in a nice, neat package: Concern over an unmet need or social problem leads to development of first informal and then formal groups of concerned persons, who gather information about the problem. These organized groups develop general policy solutions and lobby for change. Decision makers review the range of existing and proposed policies, identify all the relevant social goals and values, and study the consequences of each policy alternative. On the basis of all this information, an operational policy is then formulated, enacted, and, finally, carried out (Dye, 2017; Huttman, 1981). The rational decision-making model views the policy process as occurring in a manner similar to the problem-solving approach used in social work practice.

Incrementalism

Many observers of policy development have questioned the seeming logic of the rational decision-making version of how policies come about. In the real world, they argue, policymaking is messy. It is not just a simple matter of the problem driving forward the political process. Generally a problem becomes politically significant only when it is attached to a "politically imaginable solution" (Rodgers, 1998). For example, in the Middle Ages, poverty seemed an unchangeable fact of life. It was only when governments and economies were more organized, and more capable of tackling the problem, that antipoverty policies began to develop.

One of the best-known alternatives to the rational decision-making model is presented by political scientist Charles Lindblom (1980). Lindblom describes policy change as "an untidy process" rather than a neat series of steps. It is rarely possible for decision makers to review all policy alternatives and research their costs, benefits, and "fit" with social goals. In addition, the rational model does not take into account people's reluctance to undertake major change. Lindblom proposes an alternative model, the incremental approach, which views change as occurring in small steps, based on a series of compromises. Because rapid change can upset the status quo and shift the balance of power, policymakers tend to do the politically feasible—they propose incremental modifications and variations of existing policies and programs. Lindblom (1980) concludes: "Many policymakers . . . see policy making as a never-ending process in which continual nibbling substitutes for the good bite that may never be offered." This model fits with the colloquial definition of politics as the "art of the possible" (pp. 4–5, 38). What is possible is generally a very small change from current policy, even if all rational logic and data indicate that a much larger change is called for. Rather than depicting policy development as rational decision making, Lindblom describes it as "muddling through." We can see the challenges to major change in the criticisms, generally by Republicans, regarding President Obama's health care reform, which began with proposals for major changes in the health care system and by the time of its passage had been reduced to comparatively small (although still significant) changes. Although Lindblom's formulation makes a lot of sense, it fails to explain why sudden and major change does occasionally occur. To explain this, it is necessary to turn to conflict theory.

Conflict Theory

Policy historians have noted that incremental change is the norm, but occasionally rapid and fundamental change will occur. For example, for more than a half a century the Aid to Families with Dependent Children (AFDC) reigned as the major financial

Betto Rodrigues/Shutterstock

Mass demonstrations can influence policy, but earlier involvement in decision making is more effective.

assistance program in the United States. Despite long-running and widespread dissatisfaction with this program, it was changed only in incremental ways. Then, in what seemed like a sudden turn of events, in 1996 it was replaced by a totally new program that took a radically different approach to providing financial assistance to very poor families with children—the Temporary Assistance for Needy Families (TANF) program. This phenomenon of long periods of stability followed by sudden and sometimes dramatic change is referred to as punctuated equilibrium. True, Jones, and Baumgartner (2007) say, "Punctuated-equilibrium theory seeks to explain a simple observation: Political processes are generally characterized by stability and incrementalism, but occasionally they produce large-scale departures from the past" (p. 155). Conflict theorists attempt to deal with this difficult issue of how and why major change sometimes takes place. They stress the existence of conflicts and contradictions that are built into society, even though the tendency is toward maintenance of the status quo. When conflicts erupt, the result can be major changes in the system. Marxist social theorists describe these conflicts as occurring along class lines, between an oppressed working class and a dominant elite. When conflict builds, and its sources are recognized by those who are exploited, violent revolution can occur, as in Russia in 1917. However, change may also come through nonviolent means, as in Mahatma Gandhi's movement for independence in India.

Some conflict theorists use a political economy perspective. This perspective focuses on political policies and economic processes, on the relations between the two, and on their mutual influence on social institutions such as the family and social welfare. The political economy approach is essentially an offshoot of Marxism, adding a political and social dimension to Marx's stress on class struggle. Feminist writers have used a political economy perspective to describe what they see as the oppression of working women. They assert that under a capitalist system, men have the power to control women's labor both in the home and in the labor market, where women face occupational sex segregation in the form of less prestigious and lower-paying jobs. They also argue that welfare policy has been used to reinforce a whole social system of women's subordinance (Abramovitz, 1988; Gordon, 1994; Martin & Chernesky, 1989; Nelson, 1990).

Policy analysts don't often talk about revolution (there are relatively few references to oppression, conflict theory, or political class struggle in standard policy texts) (Heffernan, 1992; Piven & Cloward, 1971; Skocpol, 1988). However, U.S. history yields a few examples of policy changes that were influenced, at least to some degree, by antagonism between oppressed and dominant groups. Franklin Roosevelt's New Deal programs after 1935 were justified in part by a rhetoric focusing on political conflict—the people against elite economic groups. The Community Action initiative of Lyndon Johnson's Great Society included a clause mandating the "maximum feasible participation of the poor" in program development, which had the potential of giving people at the bottom rung of the economic ladder some power in making policies. An understanding of conflict theory is helpful in examining these policy developments as well as responses to the student uprisings and the revolts in the African American ghetto in the 1960s.

As in the relationship between pluralism and elite theory, the incremental and conflict models of policy development, although often contradictory, might each be seen as useful in explaining particular instances of social change. Conflict theory helps us to understand periodic occurrences of large-scale structural change, whereas incrementalism sheds light on a society's ongoing policy shifts.

During the 1960s, social workers talked much more about broad-scale social change than they do today. Awareness of the problems of oppression and powerlessness took a different shape starting in the 1990s, emerging in a stress on empowerment. This can be defined as "a process of increasing personal, interpersonal, or political power so that individuals can take action to improve their life situation" (Gutierrez, 1990; Segal, Silverman, & Temkin, 1993). It can include a union organizer's attempt to bring people together in groups to push for better working conditions and a school social worker's commitment to helping parents gain more say in school policies. There has been a tendency lately to turn *empowerment* into a buzzword and to use it so widely that the original strength of the concept has been lost. Social workers and others have equated empowerment variously with peer counseling, a focus on client strengths, and enhancing people's self-concepts—all worthwhile endeavors, but none capturing the significant power gains implied by the concept. The ultimate in misleading and superficial uses of the term is a billboard (seen by one of the authors) in which a large hospital advertised itself as "The Place Where Empowerment Begins." A complex and powerful hospital setting is one of the last places one would expect people to develop control over their lives.

Nevertheless, empowerment can be an important goal for social workers as they seek to gain more control over their own lives and to assist clients in doing the same. Once people who feel powerless achieve some success in this attempt, they tend to increase their activity in political and other areas. They become involved in an active, self-creative process in which "they are able to do things collectively that they could not have done alone" (Ferguson, 1984; Goodwyn, 1976; Piven & Cloward, 1979).

Phases in the Policy Process

Having discussed broad ways of thinking about policy development, we now move to a more concrete description of how policies come about. At the risk of sounding like the rational decision-making school of policy development (whose sense of precision does not seem to us to accurately reflect the policy process), we have organized the following discussion in terms of separate phases. This is simpler and easier to follow than a portrayal of several steps in policymaking going on at the same time. However, in reading this section you should bear in mind that these different parts of the policy process frequently overlap.

Problem Definition and Agenda Setting

All policies relate to some sort of perceived problem or issue. How does this issue or problem get defined? For whom does it represent a difficulty? In Chapter 5, we discussed some of the social aspects of problem definition. Here, we need to look at the political dimension by explaining the role of stakeholders in problem definition and discussing the ways in which definitions get publicized and accepted by a broad audience.

Heffernan (1979) describes problem definition as arousing the passion of stakeholders. "From a political perspective," he notes, "a problem is one that touches a significant number of people or a number of significant people and about which a case has been made that a change by the government [or a nongovernmental organization] will improve things." Social problems are defined by particular individuals and groups, and acceptance of these definitions by society is based largely on the power of the definers. For example, the rapid rise of Mexican immigration to the United States has become an increasingly contentious issue among politicians and elected officials at the local, state, and national levels, as well as among employers, immigrant rights organizations, anti-immigrant groups, social agencies, law enforcement personnel, and the general public. Each of these groups, along with the newcomers themselves, has played a role in defining the problems and issues of today's immigration. However, as in the example at the beginning of this chapter, some stakeholder groups have had more influence and power than others in that definition and in developing responses and "solutions" related to the latest wave of immigrants. As we saw in Chapter 11, it was the force of partisan politics that brought this issue to a boiling point.

It is hard to overemphasize the importance of problem definition and agenda setting for efforts to influence policy. As Dye (2017) has said, "The power to decide what will be a policy issue is crucial to the policymaking process. Deciding what will be the problems is even more important than deciding what will be the solutions."

Theories about how policy problems are defined and agendas set follow the pluralist and elitist perspectives we have been discussing. The pluralist perspective believes in what Dye refers to as agenda setting from the bottom up. He explains that "this 'democratic-pluralist' model assumes that in an open society any problem can be identified by individuals or groups, by candidates seeking election, by political leaders seeking to enhance their reputation and prospects for reelection, by political parties seeking to define their principles and/or create favorable popular images of themselves, by the mass media seeking to 'create' news, and even by protest groups deliberately seeking to call attention to their problems" (Dye, 2017). Important questions about the policy process from this perspective include whether public opinion should set the policy agenda, or if we would be better off leaving this task to experts; whether public opinion shapes policy or if policy shapes public opinion (evidence indicates that the latter is most often the case); whether the news media accurately reflects public opinion; whether public opinion polls are accurate and what their effect is on policy decisions; and, finally, whether the opinions received by policymakers are in fact those of the majority of the public or if they have an elite bias.

The elitist perspective on problem definition and agenda setting is referred to by Dye as agenda setting from the top down. This model focuses on the role of leaders in business, finance, and the media, as well as in government. Policy agendas from this perspective are a result of these leaders reacting to societal developments that they perceive as threatening to their interests, or to opportunities that they think may advance their interests. The initial impetus for policy change and resources for research, planning, and formulation of policy are derived from corporate and personal wealth. Research indicates that the overwhelming majority of Americans believe in the elitist explanation of problem definition and policy response, believing that the government is "run by a few big interests looking out for themselves" instead of "for the benefit of all the people" (Dye, 2017).

Legitimation

In this phase, a generally formalized policy solution or set of solutions is formally enacted or legitimized. In the process, the proposed policy receives further refinement and definition, largely through negotiation and compromise. Individuals and groups seek to influence the decision makers in the final shaping of policy. This often occurs through the formation of coalitions, as in the child sexual abuse legislation. As public choice theory suggests, the personal agendas of policymakers, including reelection or reappointment considerations, come into play along with concern for other stakeholders and for the public interest. After the final details of the policy are decided—for example, how much will be budgeted for a particular program or initiative and which organizations or departments will carry it out—the policy is enacted through the legislative process or other legitimizing procedure.

Ironically, although one would expect this last phase of policymaking to stress the practical aspects of how the policy will be implemented, frequently these details are not given the attention they deserve. The need to respond quickly to demands to "deal with the problem" often takes precedence over figuring out whether the proposed solution can be successfully carried out.

The policy legitimation process is essentially the same for agency policies as it is for federal or state legislation. Suppose that in a family and children's counseling center, for example, the issue of providing evening hours to accommodate the schedules of working parents is raised. A group of newer staff members has proposed the change, based on feedback from clients. They suggest the agency curtail some of its daytime hours in order to accommodate the new system. Some of the senior staff, long accustomed to daytime work, oppose the idea. Each group has developed its position and presented it in staff meetings. The agency administrator is highly sensitive to public perceptions of her organization, which affect both funding and also her reputation as an agency head. She appears to be leaning toward establishing evening hours in order to show the agency's sensitivity to client needs. The opposing staff members, seeing the writing on the wall, start talking to the other workers about limiting these hours to two nights a week and rotating them among all agency personnel. Because neither the newer staff nor the administrator relish the idea of a disgruntled group of senior workers, the compromise seems reasonable. After consulting with workers at the agency's weekly staff meeting, the administrator proposes a policy of Monday and Wednesday night hours to the board of directors. They concur and the policy is made official.

Policy Implementation

The final stage of policymaking is called implementation. Many people think that once a policy is enacted, the process of alleviating a problem is well under way and implementation is simply a matter of carrying out a clearly specified program or initiative. This is far from the truth. Sometimes, if there is sufficient lack of leadership and staff coordination, implementation can be a complete disaster. Aaron Wildavsky, who coauthored the classic book on implementation, would be writing another were he alive today (Pressman & Wildavsky, 1984).

Policies on both the governmental and private levels are often broadly stated—long on mission and short on detail. The implementation phase is generally a time of filling in the detail through regulations, personnel procedures, program guidelines, and other specifications, all of which further shape the policy. This administrative process is often referred to as "secondary legislation." Heffernan describes it as a phase in which people "strive to translate abstract objectives and complex procedural rules to the street-level reality where the problems are encountered." Flynn observes that in both the government department and private agency, the details of implementation constitute the closest part of the policy world for social work practitioners. Here are the memos, manuals, rules, and verbal directives to which workers must respond. It is also an important area for worker discretion and influence (Flynn, 1992; Pruger, 1973).

There are political as well as organizational aspects to the implementation of the programs or actions called for in a policy. Sometimes the politicians or officials who enacted a policy do not really want it carried out; their activity was intended to convey attention to a problem, and they may care less that the proposed solution is actually implemented. Often the proposed approach is impractical, complicated, or capable of creating hardships that could eventually lead to negative publicity. For example, in the past, state legislators have created the appearance of cracking down on "welfare loafers" by passing legislation imposing stiff regulations that limited eligibility for benefits. Yet these same legislators sometimes looked the other way when state officials interpreted the regulations to allow for a number of exceptions. Even the strict federal welfare reform act of 1996 included certain exceptions. For example, although the legislation instituted a five-year lifetime limit on cash assistance, states are allowed to exempt 20 percent of their caseload from this limit.

Factors such as agency capabilities, which could include worker skills and computer capacity, and agency resources, such as budget and staff size, also affect policy implementation. In addition, an agency's ideology may color the way in which a program or approach is set up and administered. Martha Derthick, who has written extensively on the administration of government programs, argues that a major problem in implementation is the lack of policymakers' attention to such agency characteristics. She contends that legislators, and even presidents, tend to attach low priority to administration and are often unable to foresee the administrative consequences of their policy choices. Presidents, particularly early in their terms of office, are often eager to bring about dramatic transformations in domestic policy. As they pursue the "big fix," they do not want to hear that the solution will take time and necessitate changes in organizational mission or structure. Members of Congress must also play to their constituencies and often have little time to attend to the details of administration. In our federal system of government, both the executive and legislative branches of government are supposed to give guidance to administrative agencies; this guidance is sometimes contradictory. Consequently, government agencies must work in an unpredictable environment, often with little concrete direction and with demands for immediate results (Derthick, 1990).

Check Your Understanding 12.2
Check your understanding of Models of Policymaking by taking this brief quiz.

CONCLUSION

This chapter has indicated the importance of political elements in all stages of the policymaking process, including problem definition, the proposal of a policy solution, and legitimatization of the policy. Even in the implementation phase, in which it appears that the major task is the technical one of transforming agreed-upon goals into action, political considerations come into play. Stakeholders such as elected officials, advocacy groups, social agencies, individuals and groups opposing the policy, members of the public, and the people to be affected by the policy all help to shape the implementation process and, ultimately, the policy itself. Successful policy creation, implementation, and revision thus demand an understanding of what's at stake, for whom, and why.

Recall what you learned from this chapter by completing the Chapter Review.

13

Taking Action: Policy Practice for Social Workers

Daniel Ernst/Shutterstock

LEARNING OUTCOMES

- Explore the nature of policy practice skills, including analytic skills, interactional skills, and political skills.
- Describe the basic components of the program evaluation process, including identifying the goals of the program, describing the characteristics of the organization delivering the program, examining the way services are being carried out in the program, defining measurable outcomes, measuring the outcomes of the program, and reporting and disseminating the findings of the evaluation.
- Describe and discuss the subprocesses on negotiation, the stages of negotiation, and negotiation strategies and tactics.
- Explore the major political skills needed by a social worker engaging in policy practice, including coalition building, information dissemination, and lobbying.
- Speculate about why information and testimony by a social work practitioner with no direct policy skills and/or experience might be invaluable in the policy process.

CHAPTER OUTLINE

The focus of this book, quite intentionally, has been on the development of a set of largely passive skills, those of the policy analyst. Social work, however, is an action-oriented profession, and social workers are action-oriented people. In this chapter, we present a brief discussion of what we consider to be the most important skills that social workers can develop to take the results of policy analysis, results that almost always reveal that policies are deficient in a number of ways, and translate them into action strategies to improve policies to better fit our vision of a just and equitable society. We wish to note, however, that although policy analysis is a passive activity, it is a necessary prerequisite to any type of action strategy, and thus a necessary policy practice skill. For an action strategy to be effective, it is imperative that the people taking the action have a firm grasp on the problem they are dealing with and on achievable goals. You must do your homework before taking action, and that

Thoughts for Social Work Practice

Do you think that every social worker, even those in the purest form of direct practice (for example, a psychotherapist), has a professional responsibility to engage in policy practice? Why or why not?

homework is policy analysis. The skills discussed in this chapter are all built on solid policy analysis.

There is no one universally accepted definition of *policy practice* and the differentiation of policy practice, as taught in the policy curriculum, and the term *macro practice,* taught in the practice curriculum, is blurry. Some scholars view policy practice as political social work with effort focused on the development of policies and legislation that promotes social and economic justice, improves the well-being of social service users, and provides opportunities for self-determination (Colby, 2008; Haynes & Mickelson, 2009; Hoefer, 2013). Others view policy practice as closer to macro social work practice aimed at the development, implementation, modification, or preservation of social welfare policies at the organizational, local, national, and international levels (Jansson, 2008). We tend to agree with the latter approach and view policy practice as overlapping with general macro practice.

As we begin this discussion, we must first refer back to the previous chapter's discussion of who makes policy. Obviously, if pluralist theory is true and everyone has a voice in the policy process, then grassroots strategies of organizing as many people and groups as possible to support a policy proposal is the best strategy. However, if elitist theory is correct and the policy process is controlled by a small number of wealthy and powerful individuals and groups, then the only way to influence the process is to cater to the interests of this group. The authors tend to think that neo-elitist theory is probably the best reflection of reality. This is the theory that holds that many groups have influence in the policy process, but the degree of influence is greatly varied, with some groups having little to no power, and a few having a greatly disproportionate amount of power and influence. So, grassroots strategies are important and useful, but we must remember that there are powerful elites who must be convinced that our action plans will benefit, or at least will not hurt, them.

Policy practice skills can be divided into three groups, and we will discuss one major skill from each. The first group is analytical skills. These skills include policy analysis, needs assessment, and program evaluation. We have devoted this entire book to policy analysis, so in this section we will discuss program evaluation in a bit more detail. The second group of skills is interactional skills. At one time, a popular position among social work theorists was that social work administration was just the application of casework (*direct practice* in twenty-first-century terminology) skills to another setting. Although very few people would make that argument today, it is true that general social work practice skills provide the basis for all other practice specialties, including policy practice. A good policy practitioner needs to understand and be skilled at problem solving, relationship building, communication, interviewing, and all of the other basic interactional skills. Beyond this, however, there are some specific interactional skills necessary for policy practice. In this chapter, we will discuss those we believe to be the most important—persuasion and negotiation. The third group of skills is political skills. The political skills discussed in this chapter are building coalitions, information dissemination, lobbying, candidate support, and running for office.

It is probably obvious to the careful reader that the skills we are discussing overlap. For example, lobbying (a political skill) depends on policy analysis (an analytical skill), and the lobbyist needs to be skilled at bargaining, negotiation, and persuasion (interactional skills). We divide the skills into these groups not because of conceptual precision, but rather because this division is convenient and effective for educational purposes.

ANALYTICAL SKILL: PROGRAM EVALUATION

Lucian Coman/Shutterstock

Is a financial assistance such as SSI or TANF successful because it in some way improves the lives of recipients, or is it successful only if it makes recipients more self-sufficient (i.e., gets them off welfare)? This is the kind of question addressed by defining outcomes.

Policies are translated into programs, and these programs cost large, sometimes staggering, sums of money. One of the first questions asked of policymakers and those who implement programs is "What are we getting for our money?" To answer this question, policy professionals turn to the policy practice skill of program evaluation.

Consider the following scenario: You've been working at the Greenville Family Services Center for about a year. This agency, funded by the United Way, as well as several small state contracts and client fees, provides counseling, parent education, and a variety of other services to children and their families. The agency's clientele ranges from middle-class to lower-income families. Six months ago, the center began to implement a pilot community outreach project in which it delivers its services directly in schools and several neighborhood community centers.

Today, the center's director stopped you in the hall. "I've been thinking," she said, "about a new project for you. You're pretty fresh out of school, and so your knowledge about research and policy issues is probably more up-to-date than that of a lot of the other staff. And you've been here long enough to have a feel for our philosophy and how we operate. I'd really like you to take on an interim program evaluation of how this new community project is going."

"Wow," you answer, both flattered and inwardly terrified. "I know we've talked about these things in class, but I've never actually done an evaluation. But I guess I can try."

"Good!" she exclaims, "Then that's settled. Come into my office on Monday and we'll talk about how you'll proceed."

Saturday rolls around and you are sitting in your favorite coffeehouse wondering what you've gotten yourself into. But then again, how hard can it be? You've saved texts and notes from your classes. There are probably some straightforward steps in the books on how to conduct an evaluation.

Actually, a text will only get you so far in this process. It can describe some techniques to use. More important, it can orient you toward the sorts of questions you need to ask as you plan your evaluation. Even policy analysis texts like this one—although they don't aim to teach you specific macropractice or research skills—can still offer a frame of reference for approaching your new task. (Note that Chapter 3 describes several types of policy and program evaluation.) Box 13.1 outlines the basic components in the program evaluation process and the questions that can guide them.

1. Most important, you need to find out the *goals* of the program, because achievement of these goals is what you'll be evaluating. Was the agency trying to reach out to new clients? To make services convenient for existing clients? Or perhaps to make services more successful by locating them in the actual environment where clients may be experiencing their difficulties so that the

BOX 13.1 An Outcome Evaluation Instrument for Residential Programs

The person who developed the following outcome evaluation instrument is a staff member in a state Office of Children's Services. At the time that she devised this set of outcome measures, she was also a social work student enrolled in a required course in Program and Practice Evaluation. She decided to meet the class assignment of presenting a sample program evaluation by creating an instrument that could actually be used by her agency.

Problem: To develop an outcome instrument that would allow the state office to monitor and evaluate the work of a large variety of residential programs for troubled youth that contract with the state to provide services.

Solution: The following outcome data will be provided annually to the Office of Children's Services by the residential program:

How many youths are served in the facility, by age and sex?

What is the average length of stay per child by each level of care (i.e., mild, moderate, or controlled)?

What is the number of children in this placement at least six months whose level of care at the end of the review period was (1) less severe than at placement, (2) more severe than at placement, (3) the same as at placement?

What is the number of behavioral incidents reported, documented, or investigated internally by the program? (Behaviors to count include running away, abusing substances, becoming pregnant, committing a crime, contracting an STD, and initiating sexual perpetration.)

How many children have exhibited (1) good or markedly improved school attendance, (2) good or markedly improved grades, (3) good or markedly improved school behavior?

How many children have learned an art, sport, or other skill not normally obtained from daily living experiences?

How many children have been discharged (1) because they successfully completed their treatment plan; (2) because of difficulty with their behaviors or emotional states and the provider did not feel they were appropriate for the facility; (3) because they were admitted to a psychiatric hospital, ran away, or were incarcerated; (4) because of other reasons beyond the control of the provider (e.g., court decision to return child to family)?

How many children have been discharged (1) to a less restrictive environment, such as a family setting; (2) to a more restrictive environment, such as a boot camp, psychiatric hospital, or other institution?

This response to the class assignment became the first draft of an outcome evaluation instrument that was adopted by the state office. It has been in operation for one year, and the student is helping to evaluate and refine it for further use.

Source: Adapted from an evaluation instrument developed by Sybil Willis. Used with her permission.

worker can observe some of their daily problems firsthand, watch their interactions with the environment, and help them to practice new behaviors? Are some goals manifest, or direct, and others latent, or not openly communicated? Perhaps the director wants staff to see and more fully understand the actual challenges—such as low incomes, crowded schools, and inadequate recreation facilities—that some clients face.

This could be pretty easy, you think. And it may not be hard to find out all the formal and some informal goals by talking with the director, board members, and key staff persons and by reading the official description of the project. You may find different goal expectations on the part of supervisors and direct-service staff, and you should take this into consideration as you think about how to structure your evaluation. Another factor may further complicate your life: Human "experiments," especially program experiments, are "messy" ones. You can't put a glass dome over the project to shield it from outside occurrences and from staff and administrative reactions. One evaluator, who titled his study

"The Family Preservation Evaluation from Hell," reported that when the administrator of the project being evaluated read the rather tepid preliminary findings, she "informed the principal investigator that the results could be explained by the fact that throughout the project she did not conform to the case assignment protocol of the overflow design. Instead, she claimed, she had been assigning the tougher cases, with poorer prognoses, into [the experimental group] and assigning the remaining cases, with better prognoses, to [the control] group, thus putting her project at a disadvantage in respect to the outcome findings" (Rubin, 1997). Thus, some compromises in your evaluation design will become inevitable as you try to accommodate changes in goals and services.

2. You will want to describe the *characteristics of the organization* in order to set the context for the new approach and to help you determine what changes have occurred. This includes a description of the *types of clients* involved in the new program. The backgrounds and practice techniques and interventions of *staff* are also important pieces of information related to the services that are being carried out to meet project goals. The *organizational structure* of the agency and of the new project will also be helpful in understanding how the new services are delivered and what constraints might hinder full execution of the goals.
3. You will probably find it helpful to do some *process evaluation,* which involves examining the way services are being carried out in the new program. For example, one program goal may be to treat clients with respect. You will need to devise ways to find out if direct workers, the receptionist, and other members of the staff are "doing this right"—for example, by observing whether they address clients by Mr., Mrs., or Ms., or in an overly familiar way, such as using their first names, and responding to them in a timely way when they come in for appointments or meetings.

   In both the process evaluation and the outcome evaluation we describe later, it is crucial that you understand the demands that a program evaluation generally makes on the direct-service workers, secretaries, financial officers, and similar staff members. These are the people who will be supplying you with various kinds of information, such as client statistics, financial reports, and responses to questionnaires about counseling outcomes. This means additional work for them; each interview with the evaluator, for example, cuts into time that a direct-service worker might be spending with a client. It will be important, therefore, to bring staff members on board and to help them see that the evaluation not only will be useful to the agency but also could help them carry out their jobs. One good way of doing this is to find out what the direct service and other staff members would like to learn from this evaluation. What additional information would they like you to seek that would assist them in their work? This gives you new questions to add to the study.
4. Next, you will want to define *outcomes* that can be measured to determine whether the project's goals are being met. Defining outcomes is a basic step in finding out whether a program achieved what it wanted to. In other words, you need a fairly concrete way to think about the program's goals, which will give you something to observe and measure. Usually, you will involve the agency director, key program staff, and anyone else who played a major role in setting the project's goals in this endeavor. Together, you can decide how the goals

could be operationalized into outcomes, such as an increase in clients served by the agency, a change in types of clients being seen (maybe more lower-income families or youth, or more people from a particular neighborhood), and differences in the "presenting problems" or perhaps psychiatric diagnoses of the people being worked with. You may be thinking, "But this isn't finding out about changes in clients' satisfaction with the agency's services or about whether people's problems are alleviated more quickly or effectively since the program began to be offered outside the agency." And you would be right. In order to find out about the success of many of the agency's efforts, you would really need a *baseline,* or knowledge of what clients were experiencing before the change was enacted. For example, what was the level of client satisfaction with services, and how quickly and effectively were problems handled in the past? This kind of information is necessary for before-and-after comparisons. The outcome goals we've described are the sorts of things your agency has probably kept records on, such as number of clients and families served in a given month. You will therefore be able to measure changes in these particular outcomes. It may well turn out that your interim evaluation will include a design for a fuller evaluation and specify what baseline data—such as client satisfaction information—the agency should now begin to gather.

5. You will need to *measure* the outcomes of the program. Here's where things get complex; there are many different kinds of measurement to use, some simple and some sophisticated (consultation with a research methodologist; for example, a social work faculty member who teaches program evaluation might be helpful here). The two major types of measurement are qualitative and quantitative. Studies can use one or combine both. One example of a qualitative approach would be to interview clients about their level of satisfaction with the new way of receiving services: What do they like or not like about it and why? You could also ask about the usefulness of the community-based intervention and, if a client was served by the agency before the project was implemented, you could explore which of the two approaches seemed most helpful and why. You could also observe client–worker interactions in both settings and look for differences in such measures as levels of relaxation and rapport. Finally, you could develop a set of interview questions to use with the agency workers.

   The quantitative approach means producing data that can be statistically manipulated. We have already discussed some simple versions of this approach, such as noting the number of clients using agency services under the new program in comparison to the number using services under the old one. You might also use a written survey of client satisfaction and analyze the responses in a variety of ways, such as looking at the different ways in which particular variables (age, ethnicity, income level) seem to affect specific responses.

6. At the end of all of this, you will need to write a *report* or otherwise *disseminate* your findings. This might include suggestions for change. The report or other presentation of the study should be as clear and concise as possible. In the practical world of program evaluation, one hopes that one's findings, both positive and negative, will help organizations further refine their programs. This could involve expanding them, adding new elements, and abandoning approaches that

don't seem to be meeting program goals. The report stage can be a delicate one. Your interpersonal skills and your awareness of the political elements in policymaking will be called on, especially when you need to explain what parts of the program aren't working without arousing defensiveness among administrators and staff. Most important, you need to work to make sure that your evaluation doesn't end up on the shelf but instead continues to help the agency as it moves forward.

Check Your Understanding 13.1

Check your understanding of Analytical Skill: Program Evaluation by taking this brief quiz.

INTERACTIONAL SKILLS: NEGOTIATION AND PERSUASION

The analytical skills of policy analysis, needs assessment, and program evaluation often result in findings that significant needs are not being met. They also often reveal steps to be taken to meet these needs. However, typically, all of the stakeholders do not agree that these steps should be taken or some may have an alternate set of steps in mind. When these questions arise, negotiation and persuasion are called for. Negotiation is not typically listed as a social work practice skill. However, Lens (2004) has argued that it should be considered a social work practice skill because the long-accepted social work skills of brokering and cause advocacy usually are called upon as a result of some kind of dispute. She explains that "One party, such as a caseworker from a government agency, exercises her discretion to deny a client a resource or service. Or a law or systemwide policy offends or hurts a vulnerable population. What occurs next is often negotiation, a dance of conversation between two opposing parties that may involve trade-offs, pressure, and accommodation. . . Social workers spend much of their time negotiating to resolve disputes between clients and their environment" (Lens, 2004).

Thoughts for Social Work Practice

Because negotiation sometimes involves secrecy and misrepresentation, can it be considered a tool of ethical social work practice?

Let's imagine another scenario: You have been working for several years as a social worker for the West Side Community Center (WSCC). The WSCC is an agency that grew out of a settlement house established prior to World War I. Over its century of operation, the center's staff has witnessed the neighborhood change from Jewish to Irish to Italian and to African American to its current mix of African American, Hispanic, Asian, and non-Hispanic Caucasian. Throughout all of these changes, the common denominator of the population is that it has been hardworking and poor. Often first-generation immigrant, generally poorly educated, community residents have been vulnerable to both neglect and exploitation by those with more privilege and power. Because of this, the WSCC has devoted much time and many resources to analyzing and intervening in policies that affect the lives of the residents. Since beginning work at the WSCC, you have been involved in efforts to increase public transportation services to the neighborhood, to establish a new public health clinic, and to provide on-site day care for the children of neighborhood high school students.

Your supervisor calls you into her office and really peaks your interest with her opening words, "I've got a sticky one for you." She reminds you of the housing study you did last year in which you concluded that, due to an increase in population density in the neighborhood, combined with a reduction in affordable housing stock largely due to gentrification slowly creeping west from downtown and exacerbated by the housing authority's decision to demolish three large public housing complexes, a shortage of rental property was imminent. The housing authority was using the revenue from the property sale to provide rental subsidies for low-income renters but, regardless of how well intentioned this move was, the reduction in housing stock has resulted in people having to leave the neighborhood to find housing.

Community residents have approached the WSCC requesting help with a problem related to the shortage in rental housing. One of the community's largest landlords, a man who owns four apartment complexes with a total of over 300 rental units, has begun to raise rents by 15 percent each time a lease comes up for renewal. A fiery young resident of one of the complexes has organized a rent strike that nearly a third of the residents have joined. The strike has been going on for over a month, and the landlord is threatening eviction, further legal action, and is withholding all maintenance services. The tenants are resolved to fight the rent increases (many really have little choice), but are frightened by what the landlord will probably do if the strike continues and they are anxious for some resolution. Many of the residents know the landlord and believe that he is not a bad person and will be amenable to negotiation if they are represented by someone the landlord views as reasonable. Because of its longstanding history in the community, and its reputation as a positive force for change and as an advocate for community residents, they believe that the West Side Community Center should fill this role. The following section summarizes the basic concepts of negotiation that you will need to be familiar with in order to negotiate effectively with the landlord (Popple, 1984).

Subprocesses of Negotiation

Walton and McKersie (1965) conducted research that revealed four sets of activities that they assert account for almost all behavior in negotiations (Kochan & Lipsky, 2003). These activities, or subprocesses, are distributive bargaining, integrative bargaining, attitudinal structuring, and intraorganizational bargaining.

Distributive Bargaining

Distributive bargaining is what most people think of when they refer to negotiation. It is the part of the negotiation process that involves the division of resources. As such, distributive bargaining is competitive and zero-sum. Each party in a distributive bargaining situation has a subjective point beyond which they are unwilling to go in order to reach agreement. This is referred to as their *resistance point*.

Let us apply this to the situation of the rent strikers. The tenants, and you as their negotiator, have looked at the rental market and have found that there is an affordable rental housing shortage that is driving rents up. They realize that they will probably have to pay more rent, and that if they have to move, they will only be able to find properties that are either less desirable or more expensive. The analysis of the rental housing market indicates that for about 8 percent more rent than the tenants are currently paying they will be able to find equal or better housing. Therefore, an 8 percent rent increase is the tenants' resistance point, because if rents are increased at a greater rate than this, they will break off negotiations and pack up and move elsewhere.

The landlord is frightened by the rent strike and the prospect that a large number of his tenants might move out en masse. However, his expenses have increased and he knows that rental property is in short supply, so he feels he needs and deserves at least some increase in his revenue. He has analyzed the situation and believes that he must increase rents by at least 6 percent for his business to remain viable. If the tenants will not agree to at least a 6 percent increase, he will proceed with evictions and look for new tenants. Thus, a 6 percent increase is his resistance point.

The resistance points set the boundaries within which an agreement can be reached and are referred to as the *bargaining range,* in this case between 6 and 8 percent. If an agreement is not reached, the parties return to their *status quo point,* that is, where they were before the negotiation began.

In addition to their resistance point, each party to a negotiation will have what Walton and McKersie refer to as their "realistic level of aspiration." This is the agreement that the party hopes to reach. In our example, the rent strikers hope that they can get the landlord to agree to a 4 percent rent increase. Because he has only raised rents an average of 3 percent a year for the past five years, and inflation has not increased, they feel that he might be happy with 1 percent more than past increases. The landlord, for his part, thinks that the residents will realize that his maintenance costs have increased as the buildings have aged, and that rental property in the neighborhood has become scarcer and therefore more in demand, and he hopes that based on these points the tenants may be amenable to a 9 percent increase. The closer each party to a negotiation comes to his or her realistic level of aspiration, the more satisfied they will be with the agreement.

The status quo point, resistance point, and realistic level of aspiration make up each party's *utility schedule.* Generally, negotiators attempt to discover their opponent's utility schedule without revealing their own.

Integrative Bargaining

The second subprocess of negotiation is integrative bargaining. In any negotiation, the potential exists for the development of solutions that result in a gain for both parties. Walton and McKersie refer to this as "integrative bargaining" and describe it as basically following the problem-solving model so familiar to social workers. In integrative bargaining, problems are defined, alternate solutions developed and analyzed, and one solution is implemented. This subprocess has been referred to as a "win-win" approach to negotiation (Fisher, Ury, & Patton, 1991).

In our example of negotiating the rent increase with the landlord, there are probably some opportunities for integrative bargaining. Perhaps the landlord would agree to provide flowers and gardening tools and supplies to tenants who wish to improve their building's appearance; maybe he could donate a couple of extra office computers for a homework center in the apartment clubhouse. Or, perhaps the tenants would agree to form a neighborhood watch program in cooperation with the local police department, which would not only increase the tenants' security, but might reduce the landlord's insurance cost. The key is that integrative bargaining in not zero-sum. The solutions developed result in a gain for one or both parties and in a loss to neither.

Attitudinal Structuring

The third subprocess of negotiation is attitudinal structuring. In negotiation, as in any interpersonal interaction, the attitudes held by the parties toward one another significantly affect the process and the outcome. Therefore, one of the subprocesses of negotiation involves attempting to manipulate the opponent's attitudes. In certain instances, a cooperative attitude may be desired, because this leads to more integrative bargaining and to more expeditious handling of problems. In other cases, particularly involving groups, a more competitive attitude may be fostered because this contributes to internal cohesion of the group.

Attitudinal structuring interacts with distributive bargaining when the parties involved attempt to influence the other's attitude toward the object of the bargaining. One type of attitudinal structuring involves attempts to build up the perceived value of the commodity being offered. In our example, the landlord may try to build up the value of his apartments by talking about how the neighborhood has improved, attracting a more affluent population, therefore making higher rents obtainable. This technique is referred to as *demand creation*. The opposite occurs when a party to a negotiation attempts to convince the other that he or she has less interest than originally thought. In our example, the tenants might try to convince the landlord that, after contemplating having to move, they are finding that there are numerous apartments available in more desirable complexes for lower rents. This technique is referred to a *motivational withdrawal* (Tedeschi & Rosenfeld, 1980).

Intraorganizational Bargaining

The final subprocess of negotiation is intraorganizational bargaining. It is rare for there to be total and immediate agreement within collectivities being represented at a negotiation. Thus, it is necessary to engage in bargaining within the organization in order to resolve conflict so that a unified front can be presented at the bargaining table. In our example, the landlord has probably had to resolve a number of issues with employees of his firm, with his lawyer, and with his accountant. The tenants group probably has had even more areas to be resolved: Did they want to do the rent strike to begin with? Will non-rent-strikers provide some other form of support? How far are they willing to push the situation (i.e., are they ready to be evicted if the landlord is uncooperative)?

Stages of Negotiation

Another important dimension of negotiation is that of time. Karrass (1992) divides negotiations into three broad stages: the preconference stage, the conference stage, and the postconference stage. Douglas (1962) has further divided the conference stage into three stages: establishing the negotiating range, reconnoitering the negotiating range, and precipitating the decision making crisis. Each of the stages tends to be dominated by one or two of the subprocesses described by Walton and McKersie, although any of the subprocesses may occur during any of the stages.

The Preconference Stage

The preconference stage includes all of the activities that occur prior to actually sitting down at the negotiating table. It is high in integrative bargaining, attitudinal structuring, and intraorganizational bargaining. It is also high in integrative bargaining, because there are a number of problems to be resolved prior to a negotiation that, if resolved successfully, will result in some gain to each side. The first issue to resolve is whether the negotiation should occur at all.

As the rent strikers' representative, the first thing you will need to do is to persuade the landlord that it is in his best interest to negotiate rather than simply having his attorney file eviction orders. After this, a number of details will need to be worked out, such as where the negotiation will take place, the number of negotiators, who will provide supplies, and so forth.

Attitudinal structuring is high in the preconference stage because it is important for participants to set the correct tone. The tenant group you represent may want the landlord to see them as tough, or irreplaceable, or as a potential public relations nightmare as the papers report on mothers of infants and elderly people being put out on the street by a greedy businessman.

Intraorganizational bargaining is at its highest during the preconference stage. It is generally agreed that it is disastrous for a group to begin bargaining without presenting a unified front. If the landlord perceives that only a few of the tenants are willing to go all the way with the rent strike, he might well decide to take a hard line and wait for the rent strike to collapse. However, if he thinks the rent strikers will all hold out to the end, and that other tenants may well join them, he will be much more likely to be willing to make concessions.

The Conference Stage

The next stage is the conference stage. The conference stage is the heart of the negotiation; it is when the parties actually meet and hammer out an agreement. Based on an analysis of a number of actual negotiations, Douglas (1962) identified three phases that successful negotiations must go through during the conference stage. The first phase is establishing the negotiating range, "the stretch of territory within which the parties propose to move around while they reach for consensus on a single settlement point" (Douglas, 1962). During this phase, the parties make long speeches, stating impossible demands and emphasizing the intractability of their position. To the untrained observer it appears at this point that settlement is impossible. In reality, however, the negotiators realize that all they are doing is setting the outer limits of the range within which they will reach an agreement. Douglas (1962) explains, "Strength and vigor in a party and a ring of conviction in its presentation can help spell out an impression of intractability, which becomes part of the accounting data of party A as it goes about determining how long it dares continue to press party B for concessions, in lieu of modifying its own position." This phase involves intraorganizational bargaining, whereby the parties reach internal consensus on their utility schedule, and attitudinal structuring, whereby they attempt to impress the opposition with their resolve.

In the second phase, reconnoitering the negotiating range, attitudinal structuring and intraorganizational bargaining continue, but distributive bargaining occupies center stage. In this phase, the parties look for areas that hold some promise of agreement. The parties probe each other, attempting to ascertain the other's resistance point while at the same time giving hints as to their own aspiration level. During this phase, the focus shifts from promoting one's own position to attacking the opponent's. Through a long, circuitous process, the parties attempt to gain some idea of what the other party will agree to, without publicly altering the position taken during the first phase.

In the third and final phase of the conference stage, precipitating the decision-making crisis, the crisis is reached. The crisis either concludes with a formal agreement or with the parties going on record as having reached an impasse. In our example, the crisis may be precipitated by the eviction date being reached, by the landlord facing bankruptcy unless he receives the withheld rent, or simply by one of the parties reaching their resistance point and issuing a final ultimatum. Intraorganizational bargaining reaches a peak during this phase, as the negotiators clear the final offers with those to whom they are responsible.

The Postconference Stage

The final stage is the postconference stage. This stage is dominated by distributive bargaining, which, because of its competitive nature, is not conducive to problem solving. Thus, in the postconference stage integrative bargaining dominates as the problems in formalizing and implementing the agreement are worked out. The postconference stage consists of four activities: agreement elaboration, agreement approval, contract administration, and final contract closure (Karrass, 1992).

Strategy and Tactics in Negotiation

Strategy refers to the overall plan for a negotiation, whereas *tactics* refer to the maneuvers, techniques, and gambits used to implement the strategy. Some elements of strategy and tactics, such as concession behavior, have been studied empirically; some, for example preparation of goals, are common sense; the majority have been developed by trial and error and would be classified as practice wisdom. In the following discussion, strategy and tactics are divided according to the negotiation stage in which they are most likely to be found.

Preconference Strategies

The preconference stage is a time for planning. During this stage, the overall negotiation strategy is developed. The first step is to list the issues to be dealt with. An *issue* is defined as any information upon which there is disagreement. It is important that issues be stated as problems rather than as demands, because demands involve only one solution. As a problem is discussed, other solutions may become apparent (Nierenberg, 1986). In our example, rather than stating a demand that the rent increases be rolled back, you would be better advised to start with the problem that many, if not most, of the tenants will not be able to afford a large rent increase and will have to move out unless some other plan is offered.

The next step is to study the opposition. In order to negotiate effectively, it is necessary to have as much information as possible about the opposition. By studying the landlord's business, you might find that he is having cash flow problems. If he is not able to settle the rent strike quickly and begin to collect money, he is at risk of going into bankruptcy. Thus, you can infer that he will be very anxious to settle the rent strike. The importance of studying the opposition is illustrated by a popular "how to" book on labor negotiation that devotes almost one-half of the content to a detailed description of procedures for collecting and analyzing data prior to entering a negotiation (Morse, 1979).

The third step in preparing for a negotiation is to objectively assess the strengths and weaknesses of your own position. As the representative of the rent strikers, you would want to have data about the availability of rental housing in the area, what alternative housing would cost, what laws and regulations exist regarding tenant–landlord relations, and so forth.

Based on the issues listed, the analysis of the opponent's position, and the analysis of your group's strengths and weaknesses, the next step is the preparation of goals. Goals should be grouped into categories of essential, desirable, and tradable, and alternative goals should be prepared in case one of the essential goals cannot be achieved

(Hermone, 1974). Goals should be quantified, if possible, to allow for rapid and accurate analysis of trade-offs. For example, the landlord may have computed that being able to be paid directly from tenants' bank accounts each month would be worth 1 percent of the rent increase. So, if you offer him a 7 percent increase (remember, his resistance point is 6 percent and his realistic level of aspiration is 9 percent), he might come back with an offer of 7 percent to any tenant who agrees to pay by automatic withdrawal. The tenants group may have computed that cable TV is worth 1 percent of the rent increase, so they might counter that they will settle for 7 percent increase and payment by automatic deduction, but the landlord will have to negotiate a group rate with the cable company and provide free cable as part of the lease agreement.

Another essential preconference strategy is to develop an agenda. Negotiators prepare specific agendas for their own use that list the issues to be dealt with and the order of their presentation. They may or may not prepare a general agenda to be given to the opposition. Presenting the other side with an agenda has the advantage of putting them on the defensive, defining issues in your own way based on your assumptions, and allowing you to decide when various issues will be raised. It has the disadvantages of revealing your position in advance and giving the opposition an opportunity to prepare a reaction to the issues on the agenda.

The final issue for preconference strategy is to decide on a negotiation site. There are advantages to negotiating at your headquarters, and there are advantages to going to your competitor's site. When on your own home territory, you are quickly able to obtain approval and consultation when needed; you can arrange for meeting interruptions for strategic purposes; and you have the psychological advantage that being at home provides. Going to your opponent's location has the advantages of allowing you to devote your full attention to the negotiation without interruption, of enabling you to stall if necessary by pleading that information needed or group approval is not available, and of placing the burden and distraction of hosting the meeting on your opponent. The general consensus among negotiators, however, seems to be that being on home turf is best (Karrass, 1992).

Conference Strategies

The conference stage is the heart of the negotiation. It is heavily weighted toward distributive bargaining and is the stage where strategy and tactics become most evident. A long list of "dirty tricks" is available that can be used by negotiators during the conference stage, for example putting an "out of order" sign on the restroom and serving large amounts of coffee. These are more talked about than actually used. Most negotiations, and certainly those in which social workers are involved, are carried on in a spirit of honesty and cooperation. This type of "above the board" negotiation has been referred to as "principled negotiation" (Fisher, Ury, & Patton, 2004).

The list of legitimate strategies and tactics for use in the conference stage is also long. Karrass (1992) discusses seventy. Many of the techniques are familiar to social workers, such as the use of silence and the art of questioning. Some of the major strategies are discussed below.

An obvious question that must be addressed before the conference stage can begin is where people should sit. Although this may at first seem silly, the perceived importance of seating arrangements in negotiations is illustrated by the familiar news reports of international negotiations that go on for weeks before the shape of the table is agreed upon. Social workers are familiar with the importance of seating arrangements in clinical practice. It is generally conceded that sitting at the head of the table during negotiations puts one at an advantage, because we tend to impute authority to the person in this seat.

How the conference is opened is another important strategy decision. The practice wisdom suggests several options. Generally, it is felt to be advantageous to take the lead, because this allows you to control discussion and to introduce issues in a manner and at a time beneficial to you. As to how to open the meeting, one way is to relate a humorous story to relieve tension. Another is to begin by stating the ground rules to prevent misunderstandings later. Still another option is to attempt to set a cooperative attitude by stressing the gains to be had by both sides if the negotiation is brought to a successful conclusion.

Research on negotiation indicates that most conferences begin in a somewhat different manner than suggested by the practice wisdom. Douglas (1962) found that negotiators often begin by making long-winded speeches in which they state impossible demands, emphasize the conflict between the two parties, and "strive for a convincing demonstration that they are impossibly at loggerheads." In their review of negotiation research from a communication theory perspective, Tedeschi and Rosenfeld (1980) found the same behavior in the laboratory that Douglas found in the field.

The key to successful negotiation is tactical concession behavior. The general pattern is for the two sides to make unrealistic initial offers and then each to scale back demands in a stepwise fashion until an agreement is reached. The timing and presentation of these concessions is vitally important. Because of its centrality, concession behavior has been more thoroughly studied than other aspects of the negotiation process. Karrass (1992) has conducted extensive laboratory studies of negotiation and found that successful negotiators "avoided making first concessions, conceded slowly and avoided making as many large concessions as did their opponents" (p. 198). Walton and McKersie (1965) have identified what they call the "concession dilemma." If a negotiator makes a concession, he or she suffers "position loss." This means that they have lowered their demands and potential payoff. But if they refuse to make a concession, they suffer "image loss" and are seen as rigid and not bargaining in good faith. This dilemma gives rise to the general principle of "never give anything away; always receive some concession in return" (Hermone, 1974).

One of the items in the negotiator's utility schedule is his or her level of aspiration, that is, what is the settlement realistically hoped for. Research by Karrass indicates a strong correlation between aspiration level and final outcome. Negotiators with a high aspiration level obtained better settlements than those with a low level. However, the higher the aspiration level, the greater the likelihood of an unsuccessful end to the negotiation (the tenants being evicted; the landlord filing for bankruptcy). Findings on aspiration level give rise to another general principle of negotiating: Develop your aspiration level based on the cost to you of negotiations breaking down (leaving you at your status quo point) (Karrass, 1992).

Common sense, as well as most of the practice wisdom on negotiation, says not to reveal your utility schedule. There are two basic reasons for this. The first is that if your opposition knows your resistance point, they will settle for nothing else, and thus you eliminate any chance of reaching your aspiration level. The other reason is that if you reveal your resistance point, the opposition probably will not believe you and will attempt to go below this point. Douglas (1962) asserts that revealing your resistance point will be heard by the opposition as "We offer this now, and you may legitimately figure that there is more to be had where this came from."

Good negotiation technique involves knowing when to reveal your true position. If you reveal too early, your opposition may not take you seriously and will press for additional concessions that cannot be made. This may cause the negotiation to break down. If you wait too long to reveal your position, you risk being viewed as inflexible and unreasonable, and your opponent may break off negotiations feeling an agreement is not possible. Knowing when to reveal your position is something that can only be learned by experience.

Another area of tactics in the conference stage involves authority. A frequent negotiation tactic is to wait until a deal appears to be concluded and then reveal that final approval must be obtained from a superior or supervisory committee of some sort. The superior indicates that the deal is almost acceptable, but one final concession must be made. For example, you might reach an agreement with the landlord that he will settle for a 7 percent rent increase and will provide free cable TV. You might then tell him that you need to run the offer by the tenants' council. You then come back and say that they like the deal, and will sign it, but only if he agrees to waive all late fees for the rent strikers and to not make any reports to the credit bureau. A general principle of negotiating is to always be clear at the outset what authority the person you are dealing with has. If the person does not have the final authority, you can plan your strategy accordingly.

A final conference stage tactic is referred to as *final offer and threat of withdrawal.* When attempting to extract a concession that an opponent is reluctant to make, one tactic is to restate your last offer, pick up your papers, and indicate that unless a concession is made there is no point in continuing. This places the burden of whether to continue on your opponents, and you hope they will make a concession. This is obviously a risky tactic. It leaves the committed bargainer in an inflexible position. If the opponent does not make a concession, the committed bargainer then has a choice of letting the negotiation break down or of losing creditability by withdrawing the threat.

Postconference Strategies

Because the negotiating process in the conference stage is imperfect and ends with a general agreement with many details remaining, the postconference stage is necessary. This stage is high in integrative bargaining and is straightforward, calling for a minimum of strategy and tactics.

Skill at problem solving is imperative during this stage. Relationship skills are especially important, because during this phase not only is cooperation crucial, but the smart negotiator is already laying the groundwork for the next series of negotiations. In our example, during the postconference stage issues will need to be resolved such as how the new leases will be prepared and signed, how long tenants will have to get their rent payments up-to-date, how maintenance that the landlord deferred due to the strike will be brought up-to-date, and other such details.

Check Your Understanding 13.2

Check your understanding of Interactional Skills: Negotiation and Persuasion by taking this brief quiz.

POLITICAL SKILLS

As has been emphasized throughout this book, policies are nearly always the result of political processes. Therefore, it should come as no surprise that the most important policy practice skills are political skills. Below we discuss what we see as being the essential political skills for a social worker to possess. These are building coalitions, information dissemination, lobbying, political action for candidate election, and running for office.

Building Coalitions

Most social work students know something about the value of coalitions. The notion of joining with others to make a change is probably a familiar one. You may have heard more about this in courses covering community organizing or social action, however, than in policy courses. Although coalitions can serve a variety of purposes, including large-scale political reform, we will talk here only about those that focus specifically on formulating, promoting, changing, or opposing a policy (Wyers, 1991). Such coalitions could focus on agency policies, court cases and legal decisions, city and county ordinances, legislative rules and regulations, rulings by government administrators, and state or federal legislation.

The typical coalition draws together representatives of a variety of groups that have some interest or concern regarding the policy in question (the notion of stakeholder, which we discussed in Chapter 6, is useful here). Members agree to work together on a particular policy issue, and the coalition gains its power from the combined efforts of its member organizations. These organizations represent different constituencies with a variety of sources of influence and power; when the coalition speaks, it is not the number of coalition members that matters, but the number and influence of people and interests it represents. As Bruce Jansson (2014) notes, this is particularly important in dealing with issues related to those with less power in our society, such as low-income families, homeless people, and those who are institutionalized.

Coalitions take shape in various ways. The Mental Health Reform Coalition in Louisiana had its informal beginnings in the cooperation between lobbyists and directors of several advocacy groups that occupied the same office building. Because organizations advocating with and for those with mental illness and their families are relatively few in number in Louisiana, it was not difficult to identify and bring in other groups. Because these organizations had somewhat different agendas, however, a certain amount of negotiating and reaching consensus on common goals had to take place before all agreed to join. In other situations, it might take more effort to find potential coalition members. Sometimes, in doing preliminary research on a policy issue for your organization, you will come up with the names of other local, state, or national organizations that are working on the same issues. These can be contacted with the idea of making a common cause. It's important to remember, also, that fairly different groups may share an interest in one particular issue, as we will see in the example at the end of this section (Richan, 2006).

Once the representatives of different organizations have come together, they typically engage in negotiating goals and an agenda and devising strategies for their work (intraorganizational bargaining). In the case of the Mental Health Reform Coalition, all the organizations represented were interested in having a greater impact on the funding and service delivery decisions of the state Office of Mental Health and in promoting a mental health parity law in Louisiana. However, the groups had to agree on goals and priorities in these two areas. Negotiations regarding an agenda to promote with the state office called for some compromise between those groups valuing community-based mental health services and those lamenting the closing down of such institutional programs as a children's mental health facility in New Orleans. Similarly, in planning a lobbying campaign for a mental health parity law, an agreement had to be reached that both children's mental health services and adult services would be covered in the legislation.

The following scenario further illustrates the process of developing a coalition. Suppose a large development corporation has proposed a major development project at the edge of a university campus. The current area is home to several student bars, a bookstore, a branch of the Gap, a comfortable coffeehouse, several fast-food restaurants, a great Vietnamese restaurant, an old-time diner, a popular sandwich shop, and a middle-sized grocery store convenient for those families living in university housing. The area targeted by the developers also includes several blocks of a low-income, mostly African American neighborhood. The development proposal includes plans for a major conference center hotel, individual office buildings, and a large mall with spaces for upscale stores and restaurants. The design is intended to convey a sophisticated city atmosphere, but it will include old-fashioned touches such as gas street lights and balconies on many of the buildings. Some of the existing restaurants and stores may relocate into the new mall, but not all will be able to afford the rent. In addition, the several blocks of the low-income neighborhood on the project site would be razed, with compensation paid to homeowners and landlords. The woman who heads the development corporation has been quoted as saying that tearing down this area would be "no great loss."

The proposed project is attractive to some groups, including the city government and the Chamber of Commerce, which visualize business expansion and additional tax revenues. But an unusual collection of opposing bodies is beginning to emerge. The first, interestingly, is a faction within the student government, which worries that such a "glitzy" project will change the funky, comfortable atmosphere of the existing commercial area and that the new stores and restaurants will be too expensive for most students. Married students in university housing, many of whom are international students with no cars, are concerned that their closest grocery store will disappear. Most faculty are not yet sure what to make of the development proposal, although some echo student concerns about the loss of at least part of the existing campus restaurant and shopping area, and others worry about increased parking problems. Those business owners who suspect they won't be able to relocate into the new project are clearer in their opposition to it.

A community economic development group in the African American neighborhood, made up largely of local businesspeople and clergy, has also raised concerns about the effects of the development on their neighborhood, especially the loss of three or four blocks of housing. Interestingly, several departments in the university have created a university–community partnership program through which university faculty and students and the economic development group work together on community improvement projects in the neighborhood. The program is carried out with the blessing of university administrators.

The university–community partnership program hired a recent social work graduate several years ago to staff the program. This person has become the catalyst in bringing the various interest groups together in opposition to the new project, at least in its present form. She has spoken individually with the community development group members, business owners, leaders of the informal faction in student government, members of the international student association, and members of the faculty senate. As she proceeds, she is identifying common goals and possible actions, including questioning the zoning regulations that allow construction of such a large development close to campus as well as the destruction of several blocks of homes. There is also some question whether the city should be issuing building permits for structures that might strain existing roads and utilities.

As you can see, this is a promising scenario for the creation of a unique and potentially strong coalition of a variety of groups opposed to the development project. Its success will depend in part on the groups' ability to work together on a common agenda, to gain support from presently uncommitted bodies such as the university administration, and to fashion successful strategies aimed at influencing policies on commercial development.

Information Dissemination

As Haynes and Mickelson (2010) point out, data on social problems or needs are absolutely essential to any type of policy change strategy:

> No matter what form of intervention a social worker may undertake—community organization, casework, administration, or political activity—the resource most needed and used is information. Before any diagnosis can be reached or community organization strategy developed, information about the client's background and presenting problem or the community's problem and demographics must first be obtained. Intervention in the political arena has the same basic requirement because the same processes are used by the social worker in the political arena as in case or community work.

The first step in information dissemination is documentation. As social workers, we keep copious records and notes on all our cases, so we are already in possession of a great deal of documentation. Policymakers have a great deal of macrolevel data available to them to help in their decision-making process, and social workers are perfectly capable of adding to this data. Our professional organizations, such as the National Association of Social Workers (NASW) and the Child Welfare League of America, keep massive databases, which are available to policymakers. However, this information is available from a number of sources and is not the most valuable contribution social workers can make. What social workers are in a unique position to provide is a human face to go with the statistics. As Weiss-Gal (2013) notes social workers "close and frequent contact with clients provides them with firsthand knowledge about the causes, manifestations, and impacts of social problems and the populations that experience them, as well as with an understanding of the details and limitations of existing policies under consideration" (p. 304).

One of the authors once served on the budget committee of a large social service funding organization. One of the agencies that received much of its funding from this group provided rehabilitation services to people who were alcohol or drug dependent. The executive director of the agency was a brilliant, Ivy League–trained public administrator who came to the budget committee year after year with beautifully detailed and presented materials on needs, services, trends, outcomes, and the historic decline in funding to the agency. When he began his presentation, the budget committee would listen attentively, albeit with a somewhat glazed-over look, and would, in the end, cut the agency's appropriation. One year, however, he did something different. He began his presentation by handing out copies of all the charts, graphs, and tables on which he usually based his presentation. He then said that he was going to do something different that year, and he introduced a woman who was the agency's senior clinical social worker. She took over the presentation and spent twenty minutes describing a case she had worked with for many years. She described the client, a woman who came to the agency alone, crack addicted, and asked the agency to find a home for her two grade-school-age children because she could not take care of them and, in any case, felt she would not live much longer. The social worker described how she convinced the mother to try getting off drugs one more time; she placed the woman and the children in the agency's shelter and got the mother into drug treatment, job training, and intensive counseling. The children were enrolled in a tutoring program, support groups for children of addicted persons, and recreation groups. A team was formed between the agency, the state department of social services, the county mental health agency, and the children's schools. Eventually, housing was found in a safe neighborhood, the mother got her drug habit under control, and she found a job. At the conclusion of the presentation, the social worker passed around pictures (with permission, of course) of the two children who were now young adults. One was working as a certified auto mechanic and the other was a college student preparing to be a grade school teacher. Following the presentation, the budget committee voted to give the agency the largest budget increase in its history. The reason was clearly that the social worker had provided a type of documentation that made the executive director's charts, graphs, and statistics come alive and have real meaning and import for the decision-making committee.

There are a number of ways in which social workers can provide documentation to influence the policy-making process. One is giving testimony. Whenever legislative bodies consider a policy change, they hold a public hearing in which anyone can address the body. Social workers can provide documentation based on their practice experience, which can lead to particularly persuasive testimony. The National Association of Social Workers and several other professional social work and social work education organizations work through Action Network for Social Work Education and Research (ANSWER) to promote legislation that supports the profession and the people and communities with which it works. Advocacy work by ANSWER and individual social workers in Spring 2006 helped defeat the Health Insurance Marketplace Modernization and Affordability Act, which would have rolled back state provider mandate laws and repealed state mental health parity laws as well as other mental health coverage mandates. Social workers have also fought for a fair, equitable, and comprehensive plan regarding the latest wave of immigration across the country's border with Mexico. NASW's position is that "immigration is the foundation and essence of American society. . . . Any proposal that diminishes the well-being of immigrant citizens and denies immigrant workers basic protections is detrimental to the ideals of this great nation." NASW (www.socialworkers.org/advocacy) has lobbied against bills that discriminate against immigrants and which criminalize those who would assist undocumented immigrants in need (NASW Arizona Chapter, 2010). More recently, social workers, through ANSWER, have lobbied extensively for responsible health care reform, federal student loans and loan forgiveness programs, social work workforce issues, support for evidence-based practice in social work, and the Social Work Reinvestment Act (NASW, 2017).

Social workers can also act as expert witnesses when legislative committees or administrative bodies request testimony about an issue. For example, a school board considering establishing a program of after-school activities may request that a social worker from one of the communities targeted provide testimony on the activities of gangs in the area and proved strategies for deflecting children from gang membership. Unlike providing testimony, which anyone can do simply by signing up, serving as an expert witness requires an invitation. In order to be invited to serve in this role, one must be able to demonstrate that by some combination of education and experience one is indeed an "expert."

The most accessible and practical means of providing documentation is written communication. Social workers should regularly communicate with their elected representatives regarding pending legislation relevant to social welfare. Contrary to popular opinion, legislators do pay attention to their mail, and a communication from someone who can establish professional expertise regarding an issue can have a real effect. A letter to the editor of a newspaper or newsmagazine or, even better, an op-ed piece can help sway public and decision-maker opinion. Letters should be neat and professional appearing. You should start by stating the subject and your credentials for discussing it, clearly state and back up your opinion, recommend specific action, and sign your name, address, and phone number.

Lobbying

Supplying documentation, testifying, acting as an expert witness, and engaging in written communication can be identified as individual components of the larger process of lobbying. Lobbying is simply the purposive, goal-directed, planned process of attempting to influence the position of a decision maker, usually an elected one. In the past, many social workers have tended to shy away from formal lobbying, believing that it is a self-serving activity that has no place in an altruistic profession, that it requires a lot of money, and that it requires formal training in politics and the political process.

Although it is true that much of lobbying is self-serving, not all is. Many decisions regarding the welfare of oppressed and disadvantaged groups are made in the policy arena of Washington, DC, state capitals, and city and county courthouses. If, as social workers, we are serious about improving the lives of these groups, we need to actively attempt to influence decisions that affect their lives. We should also realize that being self-serving is not always a bad thing. Many of the lobbying activities of professional social work are in regard to issues such as licensing and Medicare reimbursement rates for social workers. These issues could be seen as self-serving, but they have wider implications.

It is also true that money plays a part in lobbying. However, great deals of money are not essential. The activities we have described cost very little and can be very effective.

Finally, social workers are already trained in most of the skills essential for effective lobbying. Lobbying is mostly a process of developing relationships and effective communication, both skills central to social work training. The specific knowledge needed for lobbying, such as familiarity with the legislative process, correct forms of address for various officials, and understanding the various roles of officials, are easily obtainable from literature available from groups such as the League of Women Voters.

The specifics of lobbying are beyond the scope of this book, but we do want to make one essential point. A social worker considering lobbying should realize that lobbyists, rather than being perceived as a nuisance, are an essential source of information, and even a personnel resource, for legislators. Elected officials are required to deal with an incredible range of complex, technical issues, most of them in areas in which they have little or no expertise. These officials rely on lobbyists who have—either as individuals or as representatives of groups—the needed technical knowledge. A legislator who is trained as an engineer and is on a committee dealing with a piece of child abuse legislation will welcome input from a group of social workers trained and experienced in child welfare. Moreover, much of the legislation lawmakers introduce is written for them by lobbyists or by professionals acting as lobbyists. The vignette on childhood sexual abuse legislation at the beginning of Chapter 6 is a good example of a professional's involvement in this process.

Social workers have been involved in lobbying in many ways for many years. In the early years of the twentieth century, social worker C. C. Carstens, General Secretary of the Massachusetts Society for the Prevention of Cruelty to Children, had the Speaker of the Massachusetts House of Representatives on his board of directors. Each year, Carstens would prepare an agenda of children's issues, which the speaker would proceed to introduce to the House. During the New Deal, President Roosevelt's chief of staff was social worker Harry Hopkins, and social workers had substantial influence on the development of the Social Security Act. In the 1950s, the profession became formally involved in the legislative process through the establishment of a legislative office in Washington by the National Association of Social Workers. Most NASW state chapters now have a government relations director (a title that means, essentially, "lobbyist").

The NASW lobbies regarding a variety of social policy issues. For example, in 2009, its lobbying included statements about the need to address the issue of inequities that women face in such areas as employment, health, mental health, and education. The Association's stand on racism stresses its concern about racism in all aspects of American society, including education, employment, and housing. NASW has taken a strong stand regarding lesbian, gay, and bisexual issues, stressing that people of same-sex gender orientation "should be afforded the same respect and rights as other-gender sexual orientation." NASW also addresses the contentious topic of immigration by noting that in "various times throughout its history, immigration policy in the United States has expressed protectionist, exclusionary, and humanitarian impulses. Policies have been liberalized, only to turn again toward exclusion. The profession of social work is concerned with immigration policies because they affect the lives of clients and the well-being of people within and beyond our borders. NASW supports immigration and refugee policies that uphold and support equity and human rights, while protecting national security; . . . . immigration policies must promote social justice and avoid racism and discrimination or profiling on the basis of race, religion, country of origin, gender, or other grounds" (NASW, 2010).

Political Action for Candidate Election

Another important social policy action strategy for social workers is working to put people in elected office who reflect values and goals consistent with those of social work. Social workers can, of course, work individually for political candidates. Campaigns for political office rely heavily on volunteers to do everything from answering the phone, to stuffing envelopes, to going door-to-door to promote the candidate, to helping raise money, to developing issue papers and campaign strategy. The political process is, for better or worse, one of quid pro quo (you scratch my back and I'll scratch yours), so one of the best ways of gaining influence with an elected official is to have a record of campaign participation. Those involved in the early stages of a campaign, particularly one waging an uphill battle, will earn particular gratitude from the candidate.

Another strategy is to work through a political action committee (PAC). PACs are organizations set up to collect and disburse voluntary contributions from members of special-interest groups for the purpose of furthering the political goals of the groups. In 1976, the National Association of Social Workers established a PAC called Political Action for Candidate Election. This was initially established to support candidates for national-level offices. Since 1976, all but four NASW chapters have set up state-level PACs. Haynes and Mickelson (2010) observe, "Poor people, sick people, the elderly, and children do not make political campaign contributions, and indeed often don't or can't vote. Thus, a social workers' PAC is a necessary advocacy group, not for professional self-interest and protection, but for the disadvantaged and disenfranchised as well" (pp. 82, 153).

Running for Office

Calls for social workers to become involved in electoral politics are as old as the profession itself. In 1896, James B. Reynolds, speaking at the most prestigious professional conference of the era, urged social workers to go into politics. Jeffrey Brackett, founding director of the Boston School for Social Workers, was elected to the Baltimore city council in 1900; Zebulon Brockway, a progressive prison administrator and reformer, was elected mayor of Elmira, New York, in 1905; Thomas Osborn, another penologist, was elected to the Auburn, New York, Board of Education in 1885, was nominated for lieutenant governor in 1888, and was elected mayor in 1903. The first woman elected to the U.S. House of Representatives was Jeanette Rankin, a social worker and Republican from Montana, in 1916. More recently, Ronald Dellums, a psychiatric social worker, was elected to Congress in 1970 and as the Oakland, California mayor in 2006. Dellums was followed in Congress by Barbara Lee, another social worker who was the only member of Congress to vote to deny President Bush war powers following the September 11 attacks. Barbara Mikulski, another social worker, was elected to the House and subsequently the Senate; Debbie Stabenow, a Michigan social worker, has served in the Senate since 2010. Along with Barbara Lee, social workers Susan Davis from California and Kirsten Sinema from Arizona currently serve in the House of Representatives (NASW, 2017).

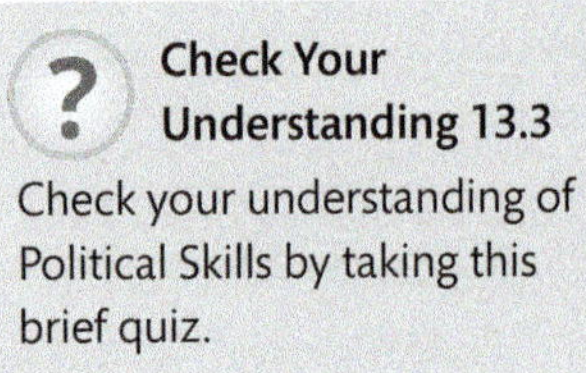

?
Check Your Understanding 13.3
Check your understanding of Political Skills by taking this brief quiz.

With the vast number of elected offices on the national, state, and local level, it is hard to fix the exact number of social workers currently holding office. However, it is clear that it is rapidly increasing. NASW currently lists 196 social workers holding elected offices on the state and local level (NASW, 2017). Apparently, the interest that NASW has focused on electoral politics is trickling down to the members, who are becoming involved on an individual level.

CONCLUSION

The famous social caseworker Mary Richmond once spoke of social work as retail and wholesale. *Retail* meant one-on-one social work with individual clients to solve individual problems. *Wholesale* meant social action social work attempting to find collective solutions to problems affecting thousands of people. We hope that the policy analysis skills and the policy practice examples that we have presented in this book have, at the very least, sensitized you to the absolute necessity for wholesale approaches to the problems we as social workers address. All social workers learn conventional macropractice skills for intervention in large systems. Less commonly taught is what we consider to be the ultimate macropractice approach: that of becoming involved in the electoral process and, ideally, becoming an elected official.

? Recall what you learned from this chapter by completing the Chapter Review.

14

Conclusion

elwynn/Shutterstock

At the end of a sentence, you expect a punctuation mark; at the end of a road, you expect a destination; at the end of a book, you expect a conclusion. After writing three hundred and some odd pages about social welfare policy, we think we have learned several lessons from the process of developing our policy analysis framework and applying it to the six areas in the previous chapters.

LEARNING OUTCOMES

- Explore the relation of economic policy and social welfare policy, including which one is dominant and why.
- Using one of the areas of social welfare policy discussed earlier in this text, examine the degree to which this policy is motivated by compassion and the degree to which it is motivated by protection.
- Examine your own beliefs (ideology) about one of the areas of social welfare policy discussed earlier in this text and compare these beliefs to data presented regarding the policy. If they are different, have the data caused you to modify your beliefs?
- Discuss your thoughts regarding the degree to which policymakers actually know the plight of most people who have left the Temporary Assistance for Needy Families (TANF) rolls.
- Discuss our society's expectations of social welfare policies and what might be some effects of lowering these expectations.

CHAPTER OUTLINE

LESSONS FROM POLICY ANALYSIS

Thoughts for Social Work Practice

Social workers are often asked to address groups of influential citizens, such as Rotary Clubs, on issues of social welfare policy. Realizing that policies such as financial assistance to the poor are not popular, how might a social worker giving an address to a civic group use the concept of partisan policy analysis to present financial assistance policy in a manner that might result in increased support?

When in graduate school, one of the authors had a favorite economics professor who was fond of saying that the key to understanding economics is the realization that everything is related to everything else—in at least two ways. This is also a useful observation for social welfare policy. All parts of policy are infinitely complex and interrelated in a seemingly endless variety of ways. This same professor also used to say that if you took all the economists in the world and laid them end to end, they would never reach a conclusion. Although a cynic might also say this about social welfare policy analysts, we do not want to end this book on such a note. We think several broad, general conclusions can be drawn from the analyses we have presented, and we will identify these in the following sections.

The Bottom Line Is the Bottom Line

The primary issue in practically every area of social welfare policy is *cost*. Put another way, social welfare policy is always subservient to economic policy. Every policy reform we have discussed has as its driving goal the reduction of expenditures, or else a fear that costs will get out of control. The 1996 welfare reform legislation has as its centerpiece requirements that recipients become employed, with time limits for this to happen. The argument is that we are spending too much and that work requirements will reduce costs. The main argument for family preservation is that by intervening in a family quickly and intensively, we can avoid foster care and thus reduce total long-range cost. Most proposals for reform of Social Security are based on assumptions that the system will go broke at some future date unless costs are reined in. The current debate about reform of the Affordable Care Act is largely about cost. Issues of humanitarianism, quality of life, promoting a good society, and mutual responsibility are all secondary to doing it cheaper.

As social workers, we have often been pulled into the cost game and we have sold policies we wished to pursue based on promised cost reductions. Lindblom's notion of partisan policy analysis is why we do this. (If you will remember from Chapter 3, Lindblom is the political scientist who argues that people perform policy analyses directed toward the goals of those they wish to influence.) Realizing that policymakers are greatly concerned with cost, social workers try to sell policies based on cost reduction. Social workers did this in 1962 when we convinced Congress that providing social services to welfare recipients would help them solve the problems leading to their dependency, get them off welfare, and thus save costs. We did this again in 1993 with arguments advocating for the Family Preservation and Support Program. Legislators quickly soured on the 1962 Social Service Amendments when they did not produce the expected cost savings. Now that family preservation is firmly in place and foster care placement rates—hence costs—are continuing to rise, it is highly likely that Congress will also sour on this, even if it can be demonstrated that by other criteria the concept is a success.

Compassion and Protection: Dual Motivations for Social Welfare Policy

Our review of current social welfare policies has confirmed Ralph Pumphrey's (1959) historical review of social welfare in the United States. He argued that all social welfare is driven by two more or less compatible motives. On the one side is the desire of people to make the lives of others better. "This aspect of philanthropy may be designated as *compassion*: the effort to alleviate present suffering, deprivation, or other undesirable conditions to which a segment of the population, but not the benefactor, is exposed." On the other side are aspects of policies that are designed for the benefit of their promoters and of the community at large. Pumphrey (1959) called this motivation *protection* and stated, "It may result either from fear of change or from fear of what may happen if existing conditions are not changed." Pumphrey (1959) concludes by offering the hypothesis that social welfare policies that have proved effective have been characterized by a balance between compassion and protection.

Aspects of compassion and protection have been evident in all the policies we have analyzed. Public welfare policy is concerned with helping poor people (actually the children of poor people) but is also concerned with protecting society against the threat of dependent adults; family preservation policy seeks to help keep families together but also seeks to protect society from the excessive costs of an escalating foster care population; Social Security is designed to assure that the elderly are afforded a reasonably comfortable retirement, but it also protects families from having to assume responsibility for the care and support of aging relatives.

val lawless/Shutterstock

A policy that seeks to keep mental patients on their medications, but only results in extending their compliance time by a few weeks will be judged by many people to be a failure. However, perhaps an average of few weeks of extra compliance is actually a very significant accomplishment.

Ideology Drives Out Data in Social Welfare Policymaking

Social welfare policies are influenced much more by social values than they are by data from empirical research. It causes policy analysts no end of frustration to see situations such as the welfare reform debate. Even though masses of data have been presented to Congress demonstrating that many poor people can't work and that there are not jobs for a majority of those who can, Congress continues to pass reform packages that feature time limits on assistance ("Testimony of Sheldon Danziger," 1996). These time limits are based on the work ethic and confidence that America is the land of opportunity, which often results in the belief that work can be found by anyone who tries hard enough. As empiricists and social scientists, we express outrage, sometimes amusement, at what we view as antiscientific, anti-intellectual behavior.

Is this tendency to promote values over data really so difficult to understand? We don't think that it is. Even social workers and allied social scientists find it hard to accept data that contradict deeply held values. For example, we are finding the research that casts doubt on the effectiveness of family preservation programs difficult to deal with because these programs are embodiments of some of our most cherished values. When Richard Herrnstein and Charles Murray (1996) published *The Bell Curve: Intelligence and Class Structure in American Life,* social workers immediately rejected the book's main theses, in most cases never having bothered to read the book. We have read the book and found ample grounds on which to reject Herrnstein and Murray's assertions empirically. However, and this is our point, many of our colleagues rejected it without objectively assessing the arguments because these were so out of line with social work values.

Although we understand the tendency for ideology to drive out data in policy-making, we do not excuse it. One of the ongoing challenges to policymakers will always be to make the process more rational and data based. This is the only way we will ever bring about meaningful social change and a more just society.

Policymakers Are Generally More Sophisticated Than They Appear

Political scientists Theodore Marmor, Jerry Mashaw, and Philip Harvey (1990) argue that the central feature of social welfare policy is misinformation. They say,

> A quite remarkable proportion of what is written and spoken about social welfare policy in the United States is, to put it charitably, mistaken. These mistakes are repeated by popular media addicted to the current and the quotable. Misconceptions thus insinuate themselves into the national consciousness; they can easily become the conventional wisdom.

However, policymakers themselves generally know better. With the legion of consultants, expert staff members, and social scientists providing testimony before committees and all of the data and expertise available from government bureaus and private think tanks, all at the beck and call of legislators, they usually have a pretty good grasp on the reality of social welfare problems. Also, some policymakers, for example, the late Daniel Patrick Moynihan, were experts in social welfare-related areas before they were elected to office. Others specialize in one or two areas of policy after election and quickly become quite expert.

With popular misconceptions about social welfare so strongly entrenched, how can legislators make policy in this area and hope to remain in office? Marmor, Mashaw, and Harvey present three options. They can try to correct the conventional wisdom, they can act as if the conventional wisdom is true, "or they can speak in terms that reflect popular understanding but attempt to govern on the basis of their quite different conception of the facts." The first option is a sure road to political death; the second is generally too cynical even for career politicians. So most see "dissembling as the only path available to policy reform combined with political success" (Marmor, Mashaw, & Harvey, 1990). Marmor, Mashaw, and Harvey were writing in 1990, perhaps a more reasonable time. We fear that, in 2017, acting as if the conventional wisdom is true (for example, the belief that the coal industry can be revived in West Virginia) is no longer too cynical for many career politicians.

These observations explain why reforms of social welfare policy have such a high failure rate. If reforms are marketed in terms of dominant misconceptions, they are destined to fail. As we saw in the chapter on welfare reform, nearly every politician is currently on the bandwagon supporting the five-year time limit on welfare benefits. However, all except for perhaps the most dense have seen the data that, having now passed five years, there are large numbers of welfare recipients for whom there simply is no work, or who, for various reasons, are unable to work. They further realize that taking the steps necessary to guarantee work will result in a more, rather than a less, expensive welfare program. Thus, because social welfare policies are designed and marketed in a way that virtually assures eventual failure, reform will always be a key feature, perhaps even focus, of the system.

Our Expectations for Social Welfare Policy Are Unrealistic

The common denominator of all the policies we have analyzed, with perhaps the exception of Social Security, is that, for some of the reasons already mentioned, they have had disappointing outcomes. In an interesting analytical twist, the prominent sociologist Amitai Etzioni (1994) argues that the problem may well be not that the policies are failures, but rather that people expect too much from them. He argues that human behavior is extremely difficult to change and that the very act of attempting to do so is a tremendous challenge. He says, "We all know how difficult changing human behavior is, but this knowledge has not changed our basic optimistic predisposition. Once we truly accept that human behavior is surprisingly resistant to improvement, however, some rather positive, constructive lessons follow." These lessons are summarized below.

Lower Your Expectations—Expect Change to Cost Much More than Predicted

Because behavior change is so difficult to accomplish, we should be happy with any positive results at all. Viewed from this perspective, we should celebrate the fact that family preservation programs are successful in reaching and helping a few families, that a welfare-to-work program places 10 or 15 percent of participants in jobs, that boot camps for young offenders have a 50 percent graduation rate. Regarding this last example, Etzioni (1994) observes, "We must acknowledge that hoping to assimilate people raised for twenty years in one subculture (say, the inner city, as a gang member) into a different subculture (of work and social responsibility) in only a few months is laughably ambitious" (p. 16).

Creaming Is Okay

Social programs are often criticized for concentrating on the part of the target population with the fewest problems. For example, welfare-to-work programs often admit recipients with a comparatively high level of education, few problems, and recent work experience because they are easy to place in jobs and make the program look effective. As we saw in the review of family preservation, that policy is currently under criticism because the clients selected for services are not the most serious cases. Researchers have concluded that most of family preservation's clients were never in danger of having the children removed in the first place. Critics say that the practice of creaming is undesirable because it directs services to people who may not even need them and it avoids dealing with the really tough problems. Etzioni disagrees, arguing that we never have enough money to help everyone and so it only makes sense to concentrate our efforts on those most likely to benefit. "The resources saved this way can then be applied to some of the more difficult cases. Policymakers should, though, recognize the fact that the going will get tougher and tougher" (Etzioni, 1994, p. 16).

Thoughts for Social Work Practice

The sociologist Amitai Etzioni argues that we should consider the practice of creaming to be okay. Do you think that you, as a professional social worker, can do this within the strictures of the National Association of Social Workers (NASW) Code of Ethics?

Don't Expect to Scrape the Bottom of the Barrel

We must recognize that even with concentrated and persistent effort, no social welfare policy will ever be able to reach everyone and every social problem. In a situation analogous to a medical patient with an illness too severe to cure, there are some people who will never be adequate parents, some welfare recipients who will never be able to get a job, some criminals who will never be "rehabilitated," and some social problems, such as poverty, that will never be completely eradicated.

Don't Allow the Best to Defeat the Good

We generally tend to evaluate social welfare policies relative to the original promises of their sponsors rather than to some reasonable level of achievement. Because of the nature of the political process, policies are almost always oversold initially in order to get enough support to be enacted. Because, as we have noted again and again, social welfare policies rarely exhibit spectacular success, they should be measured against other policies rather than against some ideal standard. For example, a welfare-to-work program that increases the level of paid employment by nine hours a month will be considered a failure if measured against the standard that all participants should find full-time jobs. However, if compared with other programs that increased work by only five hours per month, this program could look very good. "As long as the social goal at hand must be served, we must settle for the comparative best (which is often not so hot), rather than chase elusive perfection" (Etzioni, 1994, p. 16).

Be Multifaceted but Not Holistic

In social work school, we teach students to utilize a systems approach. This approach illustrates how the various aspects of a person's life and problems are related and that anything affecting one aspect of a system will reverberate throughout the whole system. This approach also illustrates that policies must address a number of facets of a person's life to be truly effective. Probably the best example in this book is child welfare policy. It is now quite fashionable to point out that it is impossible to address child abuse and neglect effectively without at the same time addressing poverty. Etzioni accepts this but argues that a holistic approach would cost so much and be so complex that it would never be practical for the large number of people who need help. We must search for policies that recognize the systems aspect of problems but are less exacting than a holistic approach. Thus, while we recognize that poverty is the major factor leading to child neglect, we can still provide therapeutic day care programs that address only a few targeted aspects of the neglect and by doing so make some children's lives better. As Etzioni (1994) concludes,

> It's no use pretending that poverty or welfare will be abolished, AIDS or cancer cured in this century, drug abuse or teen pregnancy sharply reduced. Let's instead dedicate our efforts to effective but clearly delineated projects in each of these areas. This humbler approach is likely to have a very attractive side effect: it may enhance public willingness to pay for such projects and may also restore public trust in our leaders and institutions. (p. 16)

There are slight indications that Etzioni's advice about lowering expectations is beginning to sink in, for program evaluators at least. In their meta-analysis of scientifically adequate evaluations of family support programs, Dagenais, Begin, Bouchard, and Fortin (2004) found evidence of only very slight effects by the twenty-seven programs evaluated. After discussing the disappointing data, they surprisingly conclude, "Investigators would, therefore be wise to give up on obtaining spectacular results and content themselves with more modest program gains. Not even a small change in a family should be taken lightly, however."

Check Your Understanding 14.1
Check your understanding of Lessons from Policy Analysis by taking this brief quiz.

Recall what you learned from this chapter by completing the Chapter Review.

References

CHAPTER 1

Atherton, C. (1969, May). The social assignment of social work. *Social Service Review, 43,* 421–429.

Austin, D. M. (1983, September). The Flexner myth and the history of social work. *Social Service Review, 57,* 367, 369.

Bruno, F. J. (1928, June). The project of training for social work. *Adult Education Bulletin, 3,* 4.

Colby, I. C. (1989). *Social welfare policy: Perspectives, patterns, insights.* Chicago, IL: Dorsey Press.

Council on Social Work Education. (2015). *Educational policy and accreditation standards,* rev. ed. March 27, 2010. Alexandria, VA: CSWE.

Dingwall, R. (1976, June). Accomplishing profession. *Sociological Review, 24,* 331–349.

Flexner, A. (1915). Is social work a profession? *Proceedings of the National Conference of Charities and Correction, 1915.* Chicago, IL: Hildmann Printing Co.

Freidson, E. (1984). The changing nature of professional control. *Annual Review of Sociology, 10,* 3, 10–12.

Greenwood, E. (1957, July). Attributes of a profession. *Social Work,* 2, 46.

Jansson, B. (1990). *Social welfare policy: From theory to practice.* Belmont, CA: Wadsworth.

Lee, P. R. (1915). Committee report: The professional basis of social work. *Proceedings of the National Conference of Charities and Correction, 1915.* Chicago, IL: Hildmann Printing Co.

Lee, P. R. (1937). *Social work as cause and function, and other papers.* New York: New York School of Social Work.

Lubove, R. (1965). *The professional altruist: The emergence of social work as a career, 1880–1930.* Cambridge, MA: Harvard University Press.

Mangold, G. B. (1914). The new profession of social service. In J. E. McCullock (ed.), *Battling for social betterment.* Nashville, TN: Southern Sociological Congress.

Mendes, P. (2003, September). Teaching social policy to social work students: A critical reflection. *Australian Social Work, 56.*

Petracchi, H. E., & Zastrow, C. (2010). Suggestions for utilizing the 2008 EPAS in CSWE-accredited baccalaureate and masters curriculums—reflections from the field, part 1: The explicit curriculum. *Journal of Teaching in Social Work, 30*(2), 125–146.

Pittman-Munke, P. (1999, June). Bridging the divide: The casework policy link. *Journal of Sociology and Social Welfare, 26,* 210.

Popple, P. R. (1985, December). The social work profession: A reconceptualization. *Social Service Review,* 560–577.

Popple, P. R., & Leighninger, L. (2011). *Social work, social welfare, and American society* (8th ed.). Boston, MA: Allyn and Bacon.

Richmond, Mary E. (1930). The retail method of reform. In Joanna Colcord and Ruth Mann (eds.), *The Long View, Papers and Addresses by Mary E. Richmond.* New York: Russell Sage Foundation, 214–221.

Ritzer, G. (1975, June). Professionalization, bureaucratization, and rationalization: The views of Max Weber. *Social Forces, 53,* 628.

Schorr, A. L. (1985, June). Professional practice as policy. *Social Service Review, 59,* 185–186, 193–194.

Spencer, S. (1959). *The administration method in social work education,* Vol. III, Social work curriculum study. New York: Council on Social Work Education.

Starr, P. (1982). *The social transformation of American medicine.* New York: Basic Books.

Stuart, P. H. (1999, July). Linking clients and policy: Social work's distinctive contributions. *Social Work, 44,* 335.

Wilensky, H., & Lebeaux, C. (1965). *Industrial society and social welfare* (2nd ed.). New York: Russell Sage Foundation.

CHAPTER 2

Anderson, J. E. (2011). *Public policy-making* (7th ed.). Stanford, CT: Cengage Learning.

Blakemore, K. (1998). *Social policy—An introduction.* Philadelphia: Open University Press.

Council on Social Work Education. (2015). *Educational policy and accreditation standards.* Alexandria, VA: Council on Social Work Education.

Dean, H. (2012). *Social policy* (2nd ed.). Malden, MA: Polity Press.

Dear, R. B. (1995). Social welfare policy. In Richard L. Edwards (Ed.), *Encyclopedia of social work* (19th ed.). Washington, DC: NASW Press.

DiNitto, Diana M. (2016). *Social welfare: Politics and public policy* (5th ed.). Boston: Allyn and Bacon.

Dye, T. R. (2006). *Understanding public policy* (6th ed.). Upper Saddle River, NJ: Prentice-Hall.

Eulau, H., & Prewitt, K. (1973). *Labyrinths of democracy.* Indianapolis: Bobbs-Merrill.

Frohock, F. M. (1979). *Public policy: Scope and logic.* Englewood Cliffs, NJ: Prentice-Hall.

Gerston, L. N. (2004). *Public policy making: Process and principles* (2nd ed.). Armonk, NY: M. E. Sharpe.

Gil, D. (1992). *Unravelling social policy* (5th ed.). Rochester, VT: Schenkman Books.

Jansson, B. S. (1994). *Social welfare policy: From theory to practice* (2nd ed.). Belmont, CA: Wadsworth.

Lipsky, M. (2010). *Street-level bureaucracy: Dilemmas of the individual in public services, revised edition.* New York: Russell Sage Foundation.

Marshall, T. H. (1950). *Citizenship and social class.* New York: University Press.

Office of the General Assembly of the Presbyterian Church (U.S.A.). (1988). *Life abundant: Values, choices, and health care: The responsibility and role of the Presbyterian Church (U.S.A.).* Louisville, KY: Author.

Organization for Economic Cooperation and Development. (2011). *OECD factbook, 2011.* Paris, France: OECD.

Pal, L. (2006). *Beyond policy analysis: Public issue management in turbulent times* (3rd ed.). Toronto, Canada: Thompson/Nelson.

Pal, L. (2009). *Beyond policy analysis* (4th ed.). Toronto, Canada: Nelson Thompson Learning.

Popple, P. (2019). *Social work practice and social welfare policy in the United States—A history.* New York: Oxford University Press.

Popple, P., & Leighninger, L. (2011). *Social work, social welfare, and American society* (8th ed.). Boston, MA: Allyn & Bacon.

Rein, M. (1970). *Social policy: Issues of choice and change.* New York: Random House.

Ryan, W. P. (1999, January-February). The new landscape for nonprofits. *Harvard Business Review 7*(1), 127–136.

Sharkansky, I. (1970). The political scientist and policy analysis. In Ira Sharkansky (Ed.), *Policy analysis in political science.* Chicago: Markham, 1–27.

Simeon, R. (1976, December). Studying public policy. *Canadian Journal of Political Science, 9*, 548.

Titmuss, R. (1950). *Problems of social policy.* London: H.M. Stationary Office.

CHAPTER 3

Bendix, A. (2017, March 22). Do private school vouchers promote segregation. *Atlantic.*

Bobrow, D. B., & Dryzek, J. S. (1987). *Policy analysis by design.* Pittsburgh, PA: University of Pittsburgh Press.

Brown, E., & McClaren, M. (2016, December 26). How Indiana's school voucher program soared, and what it says about education in the Trump era. *Washington Post.*

Bruni, F., & Goodstein, L. (2001, January 26). Bush to focus on a favorite project: Helping religious groups to help the needy. *New York Times*, p. 17.

Chambers, D., & Wedel, K. (2016). *Social policy and social programs: A method for the practical policy analyst* (6th ed.). Boston, MA: Allyn and Bacon.

Chen, H. (2005). *Practical program evaluation: Assessing and improving planning, implementation, and effectiveness.* Thousand Oaks, CA: Sage.

Colorado school voucher ruling appealed. (2013, April 12). *Denver Post*, p. B1. Retrieved from http://denverpost.com

Crenson, M. A. (1998). *Building the invisible orphanage: A prehistory of the American welfare system.* Cambridge, MA: Harvard University Press.

Dillon, S. (2002, January 6). Florida supreme court blocks school vouchers. *New York Times*, p. 14.

Ettenborough, K., & West, M. (2001, January 30). Valley organizations view plan as godsend or intrusion. *Arizona Republic, 1*, 4.

Faith-based by fiat. (2003, December 23-February 5). *Washington Post Weekly Edition*, p. 25.

Follick, J. (2005, June 8). Florida supreme court takes up vouchers. *New York Times*, p. 13.

Gilbert, N., & Terrell, P. (2013). *Dimensions of social welfare policy* (8th ed.). Boston: Pearson.

Giving and volunteering in the United States. (1988). Washington, DC: Independent Sector.

Green, E. L. (2017, April 20). D.C. school vouchers are found to bring lower scores but higher safety. *New York Times*, p. A16.

Greenwood, D. (2014, March). *Decision to contract out: Understanding the full economic and social impacts.* Colorado Springs, CO: Colorado Center for Policy Studies.

Grinnell, R., Gabor, P. A., & Unru, Y. (2015). *Program evaluation for social workers.* New York: Oxford University Press.

Harrington, M. (1962). *The other America: Poverty in the United States.* New York: Penguin Books.

Hill, M., & Bramley, G. (1986). *Analyzing social policy.* New York: Basil Blackwell.

House Committee on Ways and Means. (2016). *Green book, 2016: Background material and data on programs within the jurisdiction of the Committee on Ways and Means.* Retrieved from http://greenbook.waysandmeans.house.gov/2012-green-book

Hudson, J., Lowe, S., & Horsfall, D. (2016). *Understanding the policy process: Analyzing welfare policy & practice.* Chicago: University of Chicago Press.

Huttman, E. (1981). *Introduction to social policy.* New York: McGraw-Hill.

Independent Sector. (1968). *Giving and volunteering in the United States.* Washington, D.C.: Author.

Irwin, L. G. (2003). *The policy analyst's handbook: Rational problem solving in a political world.* Armonk, NY: M. E. Sharp.

Jimenez, M. A. (1993, March). Historical evolution and future challenges of the human services professions. *Social Service Review, 67*, 3–12.

Kahn, A. J., & Kamerman, S. B. (1987). *Child care: Facing the hard choices.* Dover, MA: Auburn House.

Kamerman, S. B., & Kahn, A. J. (1981). *Child care, family benefits, and working parents: A study in comparative policy.* New York: Columbia University Press.

Keister, J. (2001, August 20). Faith based initiative, red flags right, left, and center. *Social Work Today I*, 10–14.

Lindblom, C. E. (1980). *The policy-making process* (2nd ed.). Englewood Cliffs, NJ: Prentice-Hall.

Love, J., Kisker, E., Ross, C., & Schochet, P. (2005). *Making a difference in the lives of infants and toddlers and their families: The impacts of Early Head Start.* Washington, DC: Department of

Health and Human Services. Retrieved from www.acf.dhhs .gov/programs/core/ongoing_research/ehs/ehs_intro.html

McDonald, D. (1963, January 19). Our invisible poor. *New Yorker Magazine, 38,* 82–132.

Meckler, L. (2003, January 29). Faith-based treatment for addicts draws fire. *Arizona Republic,* p. 13.

Murray, C. (1994). *Losing ground: American social policy 1950–1980* (2nd ed.). New York: Basic Books.

National Conference of Catholic Bishops. (1986). *Economic justice for all: Pastoral letter on Catholic social teaching and the U.S. economy.* Washington, DC: Office of Publishing and Promotion Service, United States Catholic Conference.

Pal, L. A. (1987). *Public policy analysis: An introduction.* Toronto, Canada: Methuen.

Pal, L. A. (2006). *Beyond policy analysis: Public issue management in turbulent times* (3rd ed.). Toronto, Canada: Thomson/Nelson.

Pierre, R. E. (2002, August 5–11). Skeptical about vouchers. *Washington Post National Weekly Edition,* p. 29.

Reality of vouchers gets mixed reactions, poll says. (2002, August 7). *Arizona Republic,* p. 3.

Royse, D., Thyer, B., & Padgett, D. (2010). *Program evaluation: An introduction* (5th ed.). Belmont, CA: Wadsworth.

Ryan, W. P. (1999 January-February). The new landscape for nonprofits. *Harvard Business Review,* 127–136.

Schalock, R. L. (2001). *Outcome-based evaluation.* New York: Plenum.

Schemo, D. J. (2001, December 9). Voucher study indicates no steady gains in learning. *New York Times,* p. 33.

Shilts, R. (1987). *And the band played on: Politics, people, and the AIDS epidemic.* New York: St. Martin's Press.

Silk, M. (2001, February 26-March 4). New rules for an old alliance. *Washington Post Weekly,* p. 22.

Sosin, M. (1986). *Private benefits: Material assistance in the private sector.* Orlando, FL: Academic Press.

Steinberg, J. (2002, February 10). Cleveland case poses new test for vouchers. *New York Times,* p. 1.

Steiner, G. Y. (1981). *The futility of family policy.* Washington, DC: The Brookings Institution.

Stiglitz, J. E. (2012). *The price of inequality.* New York: W.W. Norton & Company.

Surgey, N., & Lorenzo, K. (2014, October 8). *Profiting from the poor: Outsourcing social services puts most vulnerable at risk.* Madison, WI: Center for Media and Democracy.

Trattner, W. I. (1999): *From poor law to welfare state: A history of social welfare in America* (6th ed.). New York: Free Press.

Vance, J. D. (2016). *Hillbilly elegy.* New York: Harper.

Westinghouse Learning Corporation and Ohio University. (1999). *The impact of Head Start: An evaluation of the effects of Head Start on children's cognitive and affective development.* Washington, DC: Office of Economic Opportunity.

Wildavsky, A. (1979). *Speaking truth to power: The art and craft of policy analysis.* Boston, MA: Little, Brown.

Woodward, K. (2001, February 12). Of God and mammon. *Newsweek,* 24–25.

Zernike, K. (2002, June 30). Vouchers: A shift, but just how big? *New York Times,* p. 3.

CHAPTER 4

Abramovitz, M. (1988). *Regulating the lives of women: Social welfare policy from colonial times to the present.* Boston, MA: South End Press.

Achenbaum, W. A. (1983, Spring). The making of an applied historian: Stage two. *The Public Historian, 5,* 21–23, 30–41.

Achenbaum, W. I., & Trattner, W. A. (Eds.). (1983). *Social welfare in America: An annotated bibliography.* Westport, CT: Greenwood Press.

Alexander, J. K. (1983). The functions of public welfare in late-eighteenth-century Philadelphia: Regulating the poor? In Walter I. Trattner (Ed.), *Social welfare or social control.* Knoxville, TN: The University of Tennessee Press, 68–81.

Allen, B., & Montrell, W. L. (1981). *From memory to history: Using oral sources in local historical research.* Nashville, TN: American Association for State and Local History.

Allison, G., & Ferguson, N. (2016, September). Why the U.S. president needs a council of historical advisors. *The Atlantic,* pp. 16–22.

Barzun, J., & Graff, H. F. (1985). *The modern researcher* (4th ed.). San Diego, CA: Harcourt Brace Jovanovich.

Berkowitz, E. D. (1989). *Disabled policy: America's programs for the handicapped.* Cambridge, England: Cambridge University Press.

Burwell, N. Y. (1994, March). North Carolina public welfare institutes for Negroes, 1926–1940. *Journal of Sociology and Social Welfare, 21,* 67–82.

Carlton-LaNey, I. (1994, June). The career of Birdye Henrietta Haynes, a pioneer settlement house worker. *Social Service Review, 68,* 254–271.

Chambers, C. A. (1990, March 3). Doctoral research and dissertations on the history of social welfare and social work. Faculty Development Institute, Council on Social Work Education Annual Program Meeting, Chicago, IL.

Chambers, C. A. (1986, September). Toward a redefinition of welfare history. *Journal of American History, 73,* 407–433.

Chandler, S. K. (1994, March). Almost a partnership: African Americans, segregation, and the Young Mens' Christian Association. *Journal of Sociology and Social Welfare, 21,* 97–111.

Crenson, M. A. (2001). *Building the invisible orphanage: A prehistory of the American welfare system.* Cambridge, MA: Harvard University Press.

Diner, S. J. (1970, December). Chicago social workers and blacks in the Progressive Era. *Social Service Review, 44,* pp. 393–410.

Elwood, D., & Summers, L. (1986). Poverty in America: Is welfare the answer or the problem? In Sheldon H. Danziger & Daniel H. Weinberg (Eds.), *Fighting poverty: What works and what doesn't.* Cambridge, MA: Harvard University Press.

Fisher, R. (1999, September). Speaking for the contribution of history: Context and origins of the social welfare history group. *Social Service Review, 73,* 191–217.

Gordon, L. (1991, September). Black and white visions of welfare: Women's welfare activism, 1890–1945. *The Journal of American History, 78,* 559–590.

Gordon, L. (1988). *Heroes of their own lives: The politics and history of family violence.* New York: Penguin Books.

Gordon, L. (1994). *Pitied but not entitled: Single mothers and the history of welfare.* New York: Free Press.

Guest, G. (1989, March). The boarding of the dependent poor in colonial America. *Social Service Review, 63, 93, 95.*

Heineman, M. B. (1981, September). The obsolete scientific imperative in social work research. *Social Service Review, 55,* 371–397.

Herrick, J., & Stuart, P. (2005). *Encyclopedia of social welfare history in North America.* Thousand Oaks, CA: Sage.

Holden, G., Barker, K., Covert-Vail, L., Rosenberg, G., & Cohen, S. (2009, November). Social work abstracts fail again. *Research on Social Work Practice,* 19.

Hudson, W. W. (1982, June). Scientific imperatives in social work research and practice. *Social Service Review, 56,* 246–258.

Jencks, C. (1985, May 9). How poor are the poor? Book review of Charles Murray's *Losing Ground. New York Review of Books.*

Katz, M. (1990). *The undeserving poor.* New York: Pantheon Books.

Leashore, B. R., & Cates, J. R. (1984, Summer). Use of historical methods in social work research. *Social Work Research and Abstracts, 21,* 24–25.

Leighninger, L. (1995). Historiography. In Richard L. Edwards and June Gary Hopps (Eds.), *Encyclopedia of social work* (19th ed., Vol II). Washington, DC: NASW Press.

Leighninger, L., Barrett, N. J., Debie, M. A., Halleck N., Krol, L., Maodush-Pitzer, C., Richardson, J., Smith, K., Vanderwel, L., Vanderwoude, R., & Wilson, M. (1987, June). Sexual harassment policies in social service agencies. Field Studies in Research and Practice, School of Social Work, Western Michigan University.

Lerner, G. (1974). Community work of black club women. *Journal of Negro History, 59,* 158–167.

McKensie, R. (1999). *Rethinking orphanages for the 21st century.* Thousand Oaks, CA: Sage.

Mohl, R. A. (1963). The abolition of public outdoor relief, 1870–1900: A critique of the Piven and Cloward thesis. In Trattner, W. (Ed.), *Social welfare or social control.* Knoxville, TN: University of Tennessee Press.

Muncy, R. (1991). *Creating a female dominion in American reform, 1890–1930.* New York: Oxford University Press.

Murray, C. (1994). *Losing ground.* New York: Basic Books.

Patterson, J. T. (2000). *America's struggle against poverty, 1900–1994.* Cambridge, MA: Harvard University Press.

Peebles-Wilkins, W. (1989, Spring). Black women and American social welfare: The life of Fredericka Douglass Sprague Perry. *Affilia, 4,* 33–44.

Piven, F., & Cloward, R. A. (1993). *Regulating the poor: The functions of public welfare.* New York: Vintage Books.

Reid, W. (1974, September). Developments in the use of organized data. *Social Work, 19,* 585–593.

Reisch, M. (1988). The uses of history in teaching social work. *Journal of Teaching in Social Work, 2,* 3.

Rochefort, D. A. (1981, December). Progressive and social control perspectives on social welfare. *Social Service Review, 55,* 581–582, 586.

Rouse, J. A. (1989). *Lugenia Burns Hope: Black southern reformer.* Athens, GA: University of Georgia Press.

Schwarz, J. E. (1983). *America's hidden success.* New York: W. W. Norton.

Scott, A. F. (1992). *Natural allies: Women's associations in American history.* Urbana, IL: University of Illinois Press.

Shafer, R. J. (1980). *A guide to historical method* (3rd ed.). Homewood, IL: Dorsey Press.

Smith, E. P. (1990). The care of children of single parents: The use of "orphan asylums" through the 1930's. Presented at the Annual Program Meeting of the Council on Social Work Education, Chicago, IL, p. 1.

Smith, E. P. (1995, January/February). Bring back the orphanages? What policymakers of today can learn from the past. *Child Welfare, 74,* 115–142.

Smith, S. L. (1995). *Sick and tired of being sick and tired: Black women's health activism in America, 1890–1950.* Philadelphia, PA: University of Pennsylvania Press, 1995.

Stadum, B. (1992). *Poor women and their families: Hardworking charity cases.* Albany, NY: State University of New York Press.

Trattner, W. I. (1986). *Biographical dictionary of social welfare in America.* Westport, CT: Greenwood Press.

Tyson, K. B. (1992, November). A new approach to relevant scientific research for practitioners: The heuristic paradigm. *Social Work, 37,* 541–556.

Wilson, W. J., & Neckerman, K. M. (1987). Poverty and family structure: The widening gap between evidence and public policy issues. In Sheldon H. Danziger & Daniel H. Weinberg (Eds.), *Fighting poverty: What works and what doesn't.* Cambridge, MA: Harvard University Press.

CHAPTER 5

Alabama Department of Human Resources. (1991, March). *Task force on staffing for child welfare services, final report.* Montgomery, AL: Alabama Department of Human Resources.

Anderson, M. (1978). *Welfare: The political economy of welfare reform in the United States.* Stanford, CA: Hoover Institution Press.

Blakemore, K. (1998). *Social policy: An introduction.* Philadelphia, PA: Open University Press.

Brewer, G. D., & deLeon, P. (1983). *The foundations of policy analysis.* Homewood, IL: Dorsey Press.

Carroll, L., & Gray, D. J. (Ed.). (1971). *Alice in wonderland—Authoritative texts of Alice's adventures in wonderland.* New York: Norton Critical Editions.

Commager, H. S. (Ed.). (1947). *America in perspective.* New York: Random House.

Coven, M. (2003, October). *An introduction to TANF.* Washington, DC: Center on Budget and Policy Priorities, p. 1.

Easton, D. (1956–1957). Political systems. *World Politics, 9,* 381.

Etzioni, A. (1964). *Modern organizations.* Englewood Cliffs, NJ: Prentice Hall.

Georgiou, P. (1973, September). The goal paradigm and notes toward a counter paradigm. *Administrative Science Quarterly, 18,* 291–310.

Gilder, G. (1981). *Wealth and poverty.* New York: Basic Books.

Gupta, D. K. (2001). *Analyzing public policy: Concepts, tools, and techniques* (pp. 74–78). Washington, DC: CQ Press.

Higgins, M. (1983, September 3). Tent City: Struggling for shelter in Phoenix. *Commonweal,* 494–496.

Hutchison, E. D. (2015). *Dimensions of human behavior—person and environment* (5th ed.). Thousand Oaks, CA: Sage Publications.

Levitt, S. D., & Dubner, S. J. (2005). *Freakonomics: A rogue economist explores the hidden side of everything.* New York: William Morrow.

Mead, L. (1986). *Beyond entitlement: The social obligations of citizenship.* New York: Free Press.

Methvin, E. H. (1985, April). How Uncle Sam robbed America's poor. Editorial review of Charles Murray. *Losing Ground, Reader's Digest,* 6–11.

Murray, C. (1984). *Losing ground.* New York: Basic Books.

Pal, L. (2006). *Beyond policy analysis: Public management in turbulent times* (3rd ed.). Toronto, Canada: Thomson/ Nelson.

Perrow, C. (1961, December). The analysis of goals in complex organization. *American Sociological Review, 26,* 856–866.

Piven, F. F., & Cloward, R. A. (1971). *Regulating the poor: The functions of public welfare.* New York: Vintage.

Schiff, L. (1990, March 5). Would they be better off in a home? *National Review,* 33–35.

Spector, M., & Kutsuse, J. (1987). *Constructing social problems* (2nd ed.). New York: Aldine de Gruyter.

Tavris, C. (2003, February 28). Mind games: Psychological warfare between therapists and scientists. *The Chronicle Review, The Chronicle of Higher Education,* pp. B7–B9.

Thibaut, J., & Kelley, H. (1959). *The social psychology of groups.* New York: Wiley.

Tropman, J. E. (1989). *American values and social welfare: Cultural contradictions in the welfare state.* Englewood Cliffs, NJ: Prentice Hall.

Tullock, G. (1972). Economic imperialism. In J. Buchanan & R. Tollison (Eds.), *Theory of public choice: Political applications of economics.* Ann Arbor, MI: University of Michigan Press.

Turner, J. (1991). *The structure of sociological theory.* Homewood, IL: Dorsey Press.

van den Berghe, Pierre L. (1975, Summer). How problematic are social problems? *Social Problems Theory Division Newsletter, The Society for the Study of Social Problems,* 4, 17.

Wacquant, L., & Wilson, J. (1989). Poverty, joblessness, and the social transformation of the inner city. In P. H. Cottingham & D. T. Ellwood (Eds.), *Welfare policy for the 1990s.* Cambridge, MA: Harvard University Press.

Williams, R. M., Jr. (1979). Change and stability in values and value systems: A sociological perspective. In Milton Rokeach (Ed.), *Understanding human values: Individual and societal.* New York: Free Press.

Williams, R. (1970). *American society: A sociological interpretation* (3rd ed.). New York: Alfred A. Knopf.

CHAPTER 6

Administration for Children and Families, U.S. Department of Health and Human Services. (2005). *Healthy marriage initiative: Activities and accomplishments 2002–2004.* Washington, DC: U.S. Government Printing Office.

Amott, T. (1992). Reforming welfare or reforming the labor market: Lessons from the Massachusetts Employment Training Experience. *Social Justice, 21,* 33–37.

Banfield, E. C. (1970). *The unheavenly city: The nature and future of our urban crisis.* Boston, MA: Little, Brown.

Blank, R. (1997). *It takes a nation: A new agenda for fighting poverty.* Princeton, NJ: Princeton University Press.

Bopp, S., & Falk, G. (2012, October 2). *Temporary Assistance to Needy Families (TANF): Welfare-to-work revisited.* Congressional Research Service Report to Congress. Retrieved from http://greenbook.waysandmeans.house.gov/2012-greenbook

Brauner, S., & Loprest, P. (1999). Where are they now? What state studies of people who left welfare tell us. *New Federalism: Issues and Options for the States.* Washington, DC: Urban Institute.

Burt, M. R. (2002). The "hard to serve": Definitions and implications. In A. Weil & K. Finegold (Eds.), *Welfare reform: The next act* (pp. 163–178). Washington, DC: Urban Institute Press.

Center on Budget and Policy Priorities. (2012, August 22). *Chart book: TANF at 16.* Retrieved from http://www.cbpp.org/cms/?fa=view&id=3566

Clinton signs controversial welfare bill. (1996, August 23). *Dallas Morning News,* sec. A, p. 32.

Coe, N. B., Acs, G., Lerman, R. I., & Watson, K. (1998). Does work pay? A summary of the work incentives under TANF. *New Federalism: Issues and Options for the States.* Washington, DC: Urban Institute.

Committee on Ways and Means, U.S. House of Representatives. (1995). *1995 Green book.* Washington, DC: U.S. Government Printing Office.

Corbett, T. (1993, Spring). Child poverty and welfare reform: Progress or paralysis? *Focus, 15.*

Cyert, R. M., & Marsh, J. G. (1963). *A behavioral theory of the firm.* Englewood Cliffs, NJ: Prentice Hall.

Danziger, S. (1966, February 29). Testimony before the Senate Finance Committee.

Duncan, G. V., & Hoffman, S. D. (1988, June). The use and effects of welfare: A survey of recent evidence. *Social Service Review, 83,* 38–257.

Edin, K. (1991, November). Surviving the welfare system: How AFDC recipients make ends meet in Chicago. *Social Problems, 38,* 462–474.

Edin, K., & Lein, L. (1997, April). Work, welfare, and single mothers' economic survival strategies. *American Sociological Review, 62,* 253–266.

Ellwood, D. (1988). *Poor support: Poverty in the American family.* New York: Basic Books.

Free, L. A., & Cantril, H. (1967). *The political beliefs of Americans: A study of public opinion.* New York: Simon & Schuster.

Funiciello, T. (1990, November-December). The poverty industry: Do government and charities create the poor? *Ms., 33–40.*

Gordon, L. (1994). *Pitied but not entitled: Single mothers and the history of welfare, 1890–1935.* New York: Free Press.

Gordon, L. (1995). How we got "Welfare": A history of the mistakes of the past. *Social Justice, 21,* 13–16.

Greenberg, D., Donna L., & Mandell, M. (2003). *Social experimentation and public policymaking.* Washington, DC: The Urban Institute.

Gueron, J. M. (1994, Summer). The route to welfare reform. *Brookings Review, 12,* 14–15.

Halbert, L. A. (1918). Boards of public welfare: A system of government social work. *Proceedings of the National Conference of Social Work, 1918.* New York: Hildeman Publishing Company, 20–21.

Handler, J. F., & Hasenfeld, Y. (1991). *The moral construction of poverty: Welfare reform in America.* Newbury Park, CA: Sage.

Hauan, S., & Douglas, S. (2004, October). *Potential employment liabilities among TANF recipients: A synthesis of data from six state TANF caseload studies.* Washington, DC: U.S. Department of Health and Human Services, Office of the Assistant Secretary for Planning and Evaluation.

Hill, M. S., & Ponza, M. (1984). Does welfare dependency beget dependency? Videograph. Ann Arbor, MI: Institute for Social Research.

Institute for Research on Poverty. (2017, March). "TANF turns 20," *Fast Focus,* 26. Madison, WI: University of Wisconsin.

Jencks, C. (1974, April). What's wrong with welfare reform. *Harper's, 288,* 19–22.

Jost, K. (1992, April 10). Welfare reform. *CQ Researcher, 2,* 316.

Katz, S. (2012). TANF's 15th anniversary and the great recession: Are low-income mothers celebrating upward economic mobility? *Sociology Compass, 6*(8), 657–670.

Kim, J., & Joo, M. (2009, December). Work-related activities of single mothers before and after welfare reform. *Monthly Labor Review,* 3–17.

Kim, J. (2010). Welfare-to-work programs and the dynamics of TANF use. *Journal of Family Economics, 31,* 198–211.

Kirp, D. L. (1986, Spring). The California work/welfare scheme. *Public Interest.*

Krugman, P. (2012). *End this depression now.* New York: W.W. Norton.

Lens, V. (2002, July). TANF: What went wrong and what to do next. *Social Work, 47,* 280–281, 284, 285.

Lerman, R. I., Loprest, P., & Ratcliffe, C. (1999). How well can urban labor markets absorb welfare recipients? *New Federalism: Issues and Options for the States.* Washington, DC: Urban Institute.

Lerman, R. (2002). Family structure and childbearing before and after welfare reform. In Alan Weil & Kenneth Finegold (Eds.), *Welfare reform: The next act.* Washington, DC: Urban Institute Press.

Levitan, S., & Gallo, F. (1993, March). Jobs for JOBS: Toward a work-based welfare system. *Occasional Paper 1993–1.* Washington, DC: Center for Policy Studies, The George Washington University, 1993.

Levy, F. S., & Michel, R. C. (1986, May). Work for welfare: How much good will it do? *American Economic Review, 76,* 399–404.

Lopoo, L. M., & DeLeire, T. (2006). Did welfare reform influence the fertility of young teens? *Journal of Policy Analysis and Management, 2.*

Loprest, P. (2001, September). How are families who left welfare doing over time? A comparison of two cohorts of welfare leavers. *Economic Policy Review* (Federal Reserve Bank of New York), *7,* 9–11.

Loprest, P. J. (2012, March). *How have the TANF caseload changed over time?* Washington, DC: The Urban Institute. Retrieved from http://www.urban.org

Loprest, P. J., & Zedlewski, S. R. (2002). *Making TANF work for the hard to serve,* No. 2 in series, *Short takes on welfare policy.* Washington, DC: Urban Institute, 2002. Retrieved from www.urban.org/publications/310474.html

Lowell, J. S. (1890). The economic and moral effects of public outdoor relief. In *Proceedings of the National Conference of Charities and Correction, 1890.* Boston, 1890, pp. 81–82.

Lubove, R. (1986). *The struggle for Social Security, 1900–1935.* Pittsburgh, PA: University of Pittsburgh Press.

Mizrahi, T. (1996, Spring). The new "right" agenda decimates social programs, devalues social work and devastates clients and communities. *HCSSW Update* (School of Social Work, Hunter College of the City University of New York), 1.

Moffitt, R. (1990, March). *Incentive effects of the U.S. welfare system: A review.* Madison, WI: Institute for Research on Poverty, University of Wisconsin.

Newman, K. S. (1996, Summer). Job availability. *National Forum: The Phi Kappa Phi Journal, 76,* 20–24.

Nightingale, D. S. (2002). Work opportunities for people leaving welfare. In Alan Weil & Kenneth Finegold (Eds.), *Welfare reform: The next act.* Washington, DC: Urban Institute Press.

Norris, D. F., & Thompson, L. (Eds.). (1995). *The politics of welfare reform.* Thousand Oaks, CA: Sage.

Patterson, J. T. (1994). *America's struggle against poverty, 1900–1994.* Cambridge, MA: Harvard University Press.

Perlis, L. (1962). "Statement," Community Services Activities Papers, folder 78, Social Welfare History Archives, University of Minnesota—Twin Cities, quoted in Patterson, J. (1994). *America's Struggle Against Poverty, 1900–1994.* Cambridge, MA: Harvard University Press, 133.

Popple, P. R., & Leighninger, L. (2011). *Social work, social welfare, and American society* (8th ed.). Boston, MA: Allyn and Bacon.

Poverty across generations: Is welfare dependency a pathology passed from one generation to the next? (1983, March). Paper presented at the Population Association of America Meeting, Pittsburgh, PA.

Reilly, G. D. (1983). Madame secretary. In K. Louchheim (Ed.), *The making of the New Deal: The insiders speak.* Cambridge, MA: Harvard University Press.

Sutch, Richard. Has social spending grown out of control? *Challenge* (May-June 1996), p. 12.

Taylor, M. J., & Vogel-Ferguson, M. B. (2011). Attitudes toward traditional marriage: A comparison of TANF recipients and a general population of adults. *Families in Society, 92*(1), 225–229.

U.S. Department of Health and Human Services. (1995). *Characteristics and financial circumstances of AFDC recipients, FY 1993.* Washington, DC: U.S. Government Printing Office, p. 1.

U.S. Department of Health and Human Services, Administration for Children and Families. (2012, June 1). *TANF: Ninth Report to Congress.* Retrieved from http://www.acf.hhs.gov/programs/ofa/resource/ninth-report-to-congress

U.S. House of Representatives. (1996, July 31). The conference report on the Personal Responsibility and Work Opportunity Reconciliation Act of 1996.

Walt, C., Proctor, B., & Smith, J. (2012). U.S. Census Bureau, Current Population Reports, P60–243, *Income, poverty, and health insurance coverage in the United States: 2011.* Washington, DC: U.S. Government Printing Office.

Weil, A., & Finegold, K. (2002). *Welfare reform: The next act.* Washington, DC: Urban Institute Press.

Wood, R. G., Moore, Q., & Rangarajan, A. (2008, March). Two steps forward, one step back: The uneven economic progress of TANF recipients. *Social Service Review,* 10.

Zedlewski, S., & Alderson, D. (2001). Do families on welfare in the post-TANF era differ from their pre-TANF counterparts? *Assessing the New Federalism,* Discussion Paper 01–03. Washington, DC: Urban Institute.

CHAPTER 7

Achenbaum, W. A. (1983). *Shades of grey: Old age, American values and federal policies since 1920.* Boston: Little, Brown.

Achenbaum, W. A. (1986). *Social Security: Visions and revisions.* New York: Cambridge University Press.

Altmeyer, A. J. (1968). *The formative years of Social Security.* Madison, WI: University of Wisconsin Press.

Bacon, P., Jr. (2008, July 8). Candidates diverge on how to save Social Security. *The Washington Post,* p. A1.

Badger, A. (1989). *The New Deal: The depression years 1933–40.* New York: Hill and Wang, 102–104, 231–234.

Bailey, J. (2006, March 24). Northwest muscle may leave deep bruises. *New York Times,* p. C3.

Baker, R. L. (1987). *Social work dictionary.* Silver Spring, MD: NASW, 49.

Basler, B. (2005, February). What do Americans think about taking money out of Social Security for private accounts? *AARP Bulletin, 46,* 10, 13.

Beck, R. (2004, September). Corporate pension troubles show signs of worsening. *Arizona Republic,* p. D2.

Beck, R. (2005, July-August). Corporate pension troubles, Tim Gray, "Pension Roulette," *AARP Bulletin, 46,* 14.

Bennett, A. (2012, June 3, 11). The cost of hope. *Newsweek,* 52–55.

Berkowitz, E. D. (1991). *America's welfare state: From Roosevelt to Reagan.* Baltimore, MD: Johns Hopkins University Press.

Berkowitz, E. D., & McQuaid, K. (1992). *Creating the welfare state: The political economy of 20th century reform,* rev. ed. Lawrence, KS: University Press of Kansas.

Bethell, T. N. (2008, December 3). The gender gap. *AARP Bulletin, 46,* p. 11.

Blueprints for recovery of Big 3. (2008, December 3). *Arizona Republic,* p. 6.

Brigham, J. (1990). *Property and the politics of entitlement.* Philadelphia, PA: Temple University Press.

Brooks, D. (2005, March 18). Here's the obituary, a bit early, for Social Security reform. *Arizona Republic,* p. B11.

Burns, E. (1936). *Toward Social Security.* New York: Whittlesey House.

Carroll, A. (2017 March 18). Cost can be debated, but Meals on Wheels gets results. *New York Times,* p. A10.

Cates, J. R. (2005). Social Security: United States. In J. M. Herrick & P. H. Stuart (Eds.), *Encyclopedia of social welfare history in America.* Thousand Oaks, CA: Sage.

Cates, J. R. (1983). *Insuring inequality: Administrative leadership in Social Security 1935–54.* Ann Arbor, MI: University of Michigan Press.

Cauchon, D. (2006, January 17). Pension funds fall short of guarantees. *USA Today,* p. 7A.

Christman, J. (1994). *The myth of property: Toward an egalitarian theory of ownership.* New York: Oxford University Press.

Cohen, W. J. (1983, June). *Social Security: The compromise and beyond.* Washington, DC: SOS Education Fund.

Coll, B. (1988). Public assistance: Reviving the original comprehensive concept of Social Security. In G. D. Nash, N. H. Pugach, & R. F. Tomasson (Eds.), *Social Security: The first half century.* Albuquerque, NM: University of New Mexico Press.

Crawley, E. J. (2012, November 29). AMR pension default would set record, if sought. Reuters.com. Retrieved from www.reuters.com/assets/print?aid=USTRE7AS2A02011129

Crenshaw, A. B. (2004, October 18–24). All this talk about pensions. *Washington Post Weekly Edition,* p. 21.

Crenshaw, A. (2005, January 24–30). Upping the ante on retirement: In Bush's "ownership society," you've got to play to win. *The Washington Post National Weekly Edition,* p. 18.

Dao, J. (2005, May 4). "55 and out" comes home to roost. *New York Times,* sec. 4, pp. 1, 4.

Department of Health and Human Services. (2008). *A profile of older Americans: 2008.* Retrieved from www.mowaa.org/document.doc?id=69

DeSilver, D. (2015, October 20). What is the House Freedom Caucus and who's in it? Pew Research Center. Retrieved from www.pewresearch.org/fact-tank/2915/10/20

Dionne, E. J. (2005, February 8). Sheer Social Security nonsense. *Arizona Republic,* p. B7.

Downey, K. (2009). *The woman behind the New Deal: The life of Frances Perkins, FDR's secretary of labor and his moral conscience.* New York: Doubleday.

Dugas, C. (2004, November 11). Pension cutbacks to expand in U.S. *USA Today,* p. D1.

Ferguson, W. R., Jr. (2009, February 1). President of TIAA-CREF, letter to the editor. *New York Times,* p. 8.

Fetterman, M. (2006, January 13). Facing cash woes in retirement? *USA Today,* p. B3.

Fineman, H. (2005, February 14). Special report. *Newsweek,* 38.

Fox-Grage, W., & Ujvari, K. (2014). The Older Americans Act. Washington, DC: AARP Policy Institute.

Gordon, L. (1994). *Pitied but not entitled: Single mothers and the history of welfare.* New York: Free Press.

Government Relations and Policy. (2016). Older Americans Act: Viewpoint. Washington, DC: National Committee to Preserve Social Security and Medicare.

Greenhouse, S., & Chan, S. (2005, December 23). 60-hour transit strike ends, and New York cheers. *New York Times,* pp. 1, 24.

The growing need for Social Security. (June 2005). *AARP Bulletin 46,* p. 23.

Hacker, J. (2006). *The great risk shift: The new economic insecurity and the decline of the American dream.* New York: Oxford University Press.

Jackson, K. K. (2005, July/August). Culturally competent end-of-life care. *Social Work Today,* 28–31.

Jansson, B. (1997). *The reluctant welfare state: A history of American social welfare policies* (3rd ed.). Pacific Grove, CA: Brooks/Cole.

King, N., Jr., & Greenberg, S. Poll shows budget cut dilemma. *Wall Street Journal* (March 3, 2011). *New York Times* (January 9, 2005), p. 18.

Klein, J. (2011, June 11). The long goodbye. *Time,* 19–25.

Kornblut, A. E. (2005, April 6). Bush renews focus on his plan for revamping Social Security. *New York Times,* p. 16.

Krugman, P. (2004, December 20). Inventing a crisis. *Liberal Opinion Weekly,* 5.

Krugman, P. (2006, February 3). State of delusion. *New York Times,* p. 27.

Krugman, P. (2006, April 21). The great revulsion. *New York Times,* p. 23.

Lacey, M. (2000, January 28). Clinton claims bragging rights to nation's prosperity: Asks tax relief for struggling families. *New York Times,* p. A1.

Leff, M. H. (1987). Historical perspectives on old-age insurance: The state of the art on the art of the state. In Edward D. Berkowitz (Ed.), *Social Security after fifty: Successes and failures.* Westport, CT: Greenwood Press.

Maeng, D. R., Graf, T. R., Davis, D. E., Tomcavage, J., & Bloom, F. J., Jr. (2012, May/June). Can a patient-centered medical home lead to better outcomes? *American Journal of Medical Quality,* 210–216.

Marsh, M. W. (2012, March 7). At airline, a pensions compromise. *New York Times,* p. B1.

Maynard, M. (2005, May 11). United Air wins right to default on its pensions. *New York Times,* p. 1.

McSherry, M. (2006, January 17). Alcoa eliminates pension for new salaried workers. *US News Today,* p. 20.

Meckler, L., & King, N., Jr. (2009, January 20). Deficits restrict Obama as his promises come due. *The Wall Street Journal,* p. 3.

Morin, R., & Russakof, D. (2005, February 14–20). Is Social Security in crisis? *The Washington Post Weekly Edition,* pp. 19–20.

Moynihan, D. P. (1994, November-December). The case against entitlement cuts. *Modern Maturity, 37,* 14.

Obama, B. (2009, January 21). The address: All this we will do. *New York Times,* pp. 2–3.

Orloff, A. S. (1993). *The politics of pensions: A comparative analysis of Britain, Canada, and the United States 1880–1940.* Madison, WI: University of Wisconsin Press.

Ornstein, N. (1994, March 7–13). Escaping the entitlement straitjacket. *Washington Post Weekly Edition,* p. 25.

Passell, P. (1996, February 18). Can retirees' safety net be saved? *New York Times,* sec. 3, p. 1.

PBS Newshour. (2015, May 5). Hospice and African American seniors. Retrieved from www.pbs.org/newshour/bb/african-american-senour-less-likely-to-use-hospice

Pension Benefit Guaranty Corporation. (2012). *Annual Report,* Retrieved from www.pbgc.gov/res/reports/ar2012.html

Pension Rights Center. (n.d.). Companies that have changed their defined benefit pension. Retrieved from www.pensionrights.org

Perkins, F. (1963). Foreword. E. D. Witte, *The development of the Social Security act.* Madison, WI: University of Wisconsin Press.

Perkins, F. (1946). *The Roosevelt I knew.* New York: Penguin.

Peterson, K., & Timiraos, N. (2016, December 15). GOP's Freedom Caucus wants quick action on Social Security & Medicare. *Wall St. Journal.*

Porter, E. (2005, October 22). Reinventing the mill: Can steel workers provide a road map for other ailing industry giants? *New York Times,* p. B1.

Privatization fought. (2005, May 6). *NASW News, 50,* p. 1.

Quadagno, J. (1988). *The transformation of Old Age Security.* Chicago: University of Chicago Press.

Quinn, J. B. (2004, March 9). Social Security isn't doomed. *Newsweek,* 47.

Quinn, J. B. (2005, May 23). Fresh worries on pensions. *Newsweek,* 51.

Raum, T. (2005, March 31). Despite long odds, Bush touts private retirement accounts. *Arizona Republic,* p. 6.

Reed, C. (2016, December 7). Loyalton's pension default is a wake up call. *San Diego Union Leader.*

Reich, C. (1978). The new property. In G. B. Macpherson (Ed.), *Property: Mainstream and critical positions.* Toronto, Canada: University of Toronto Press.

Rosenbaum, D. E. (2005, March 8). At heart of Social Security debate, a misunderstanding. *New York Times,* p. 16.

Rosenbaum, D. E. (2005, March 1). Public view on Social Security needs to swing soon, senator says. *New York Times,* p. 14.

Samuelson, R. J. (2011, March 11). Why Social Security is welfare. *Washington Post.*

Samuelson, R. (1996, January 8). Great expectations. *Newsweek,* 24–27.

Savage, T. (2017, January 3). Coming pension defaults. *Huffington Post.*

Shear, M. D. (2009, January 16). Obama hints at Social Security, Medicare changes. *Arizona Republic,* p. 6.

Singletary, M. (20 March 2017). "In his first budget, Trump to struggling seniors: You'll be on your own," *Washington Post.*

Skocpol, T. (1995). *Protecting soldiers and mothers: The political origins of social policy in the United States.* Cambridge, MA: The Belknap Press of Harvard University Press.

Sloan, A. (2012, April 26) Fixing Social Security, *Washington Post.* Retrieved from washingtonpost.com/business/economy/fixing-social-security—the-right-way/2

Sloan, A. (1998, February 2). Books, cooked D.C. style. *Newsweek,* 42.

Social Security. (2005, January 24–30). *Washington Post National Weekly Edition,* p. 24.

Social Security: Where we stand. (2005, February 20). *New York Times,* p. 18.

Stevenson, R. W. (1998, November 29). Squaring off, at last, on Social Security. *New York Times,* p. 5.

Stevenson, R. W. (2005, February 4). Bus, on road, pushes warning on retirement. *New York Times,* pp. 1, 15.

Stoesz, D. (1996). *Small change: Domestic policy under the Clinton presidency.* White Plains, NY: Longman.

Stranahan, S. (2005, December 4). The big fix. *AARP Bulletin, 45,* 1.

Survey detects pessimism on Social Security payouts. (2005, June 19). *New York Times,* p. 7.

The growing need for Social Security. (2005, June). *AARP Bulletin, 46,* 23.

The Terminator takes aim at state pensions. (2005, April). *AARP Bulletin, 46,* 6.

The text of the president's State of the Union address to Congress. (1999, January 20). *New York Times,* p. A22.

Thomas, H. E. (2009, September 21). The case for killing Granny. *Newsweek,* 35–40.

Toner, R., & Connelly, M. (2005a, June 17). Bush's support on major issues tumbles in poll. *New York Times,* p. 1.

Toner, R., & Connelly, M. (2005b, June 19). Poll finds broad pessimism on Social Security payments. *New York Times,* p. 18.

Toner, R., & Rosenbaum, D. E. (2005, May 12). Lawmaker may hold key to Bush Social Security plan. *New York Times,* p. 19.

Tropman, J. E. (1987). *Public policy opinion and the elderly, 1952–1978.* Westport, CT: Greenwood Press.

United's pension debacle. (2005, May 12). *New York Times,* p. 26.

U.S. Department of Health & Human Services, Administration on Aging. (2015). *A profile of older Americans,* p. 10.

U.S. Social Security Administration. (1998, March). *Basic facts.* Washington, DC: Author.

U.S. Social Security Administration. (January 2009). Monthly statistical snapshot. *A profile of older Americans: 2008.* Retrieved from www.ssa.gov/policy/docs/quickfacts/stat_snapshost

U.S. Social Security Administration. (2009). *Beneficiary data.* Retrieved from ssa.gov/gact/ProgData/icp.html

U.S. Social Security Administration. (June 2010). *Social Security is important to women.* Retrieved from ssa.gov/pressoffice/factsheets/women.htm

U.S. Social Security Administration. (2015). *Annual statistical supplement.* Retrieved from www.ssa.gov/policy/docs/statcomps/supplement/2015/3e/html

U.S. Social Security Administration. (2017). *Quick facts.* Retrieved from www.ssa.gov/policy/quickfacts/stat-snapshop

War clouds: Bush's poll numbers drop as Americans lose patience with Iraq and Social Security. (2005, June 13–19). *Washington Post National Edition,* p. 11.

Walsh, M. W. (2004, June 13). Healthier and wiser? Sure, but not wealthier: As pensions slip away, retirees may take a fall. *New York Times,* sec. 3, pp. 1, 9.

Walsh, M. W. (2005, January 30). Taking the wheel before a pension runs into trouble. *New York Times,* sec. 3, p. 8.

Walsh, M. W. (2008, April 17). Market turmoil leaves big pension funds falling short. *New York Times,* p. C3.

Weber, H. (2006, April 8). Unions gain influence in bankruptcies. *Arizona Republic,* p. D6.

Weisman, J. (2005, February 14–20). The White House explains further. *Washington Post Weekly Edition,* p. 17.

Wild, R. (2005, November). Now you see it, now you don't. *AARP Bulletin, 46,* pp. 12–14.

Wiles, R. (2005, February 2). Social Security: Bush to make case. *Arizona Republic,* p. 1.

Wiles, R. (2005, March 27). Traditional pensions vanishing. *Arizona Republic,* p. D1.

Will Donald Trump cave on Social Security? (2016, December 12). Editorial. *New York Times.*

Witte, E. D. (1963). *The development of the Social Security Act.* Madison: University of Wisconsin Press.

Zhang, B., Baohui, A. A., Wright, A. A., Huskamp, H. A., Nilsson, M. E., Maciejewski, M. L., Earle, C. C., Block, S. D., Maciejewski, P. K., & Prigerson, H. G. (2009, March). Health care costs in the last week of life. *Archives of Internal Medicine,* pp. 480–488.

CHAPTER 8

Abele, R. (2016, September). *Audrie and Daisey.* [Review]. *Los Angeles Times,* p. z921.

Action for Mental Health. (1961). *Final report of the Joint Commission on Mental Health and Illness.* New York: Wiley.

Alcindor, Y. (2014, April 7). Killer diseases creeping back. *USA Today.*

Alcoholics Anonymous, General Services Office. (2016). Retrieved from www.aa.org/assets/en_us/smf_132_en_pdk

Alcoholic beverages and tobacco. (2008, November). *Standard and Poor's industry surveys.* Retrieved from www.netadvantage.standardandpoors.com

Allday, E. (2013, May 7). Whooping cough warning—shots advised. *San Francisco Chronicle,* p. A1.

Allowing concealed weapons on college campuses is a silly, and dangerous, idea. [Editorial]. *Los Angeles Times.*

Alter, J. (1999, September 6). The buzz on drugs. *Newsweek,* p. 26.

Alvarez, L., & Eckholm, E. (2008, January 8). Purple Heart is ruled out for traumatic stress. *New York Times,* p. A19.

Alvarez, L. (2012, April 27). State worker drug test struck down in Florida. *New York Times,* p. A16.

American Academy of Pediatrics. (2013, April). Vaccine safety: Examine the evidence. Retrieved from https://www.aap.org/en-us/documents/immunization_vaccine_studies.pdf

Anderson, E. (1998, July 23). Drug testing begins for welfare recipients. *New Orleans Times-Picayune,* sec. A, pp. 1, 12.

Alcoholics Anonymous. (1999, April). *AA at a glance.* Retrieved from www.alcoholics-anonymous.org

AA as a Resource for the Health Care Professional. (April 1999).

Azar, B. (1997, December). Researchers debunk the myth of the "crack baby." *APA Monitor.* Retrieved from www.apa.org/dec97

Begley, S. (2009, March 2). Anatomy of a scare. *Newsweek*, pp. 43–47.

Bennett, A., & Golub, A. (2101). Sociological factors and addiction. In H. J. Shaffer (Ed.), *APA addiction syndrome handbook, Vol. 1, Foundations, influences, and expressions of addiction* (pp. 195–210). Washington, DC: American Psychological Association.

Booth, W. (1996 September 17). "Florida county sets drug tests for welfare clients." *Washington Post*, p. A2.

Braddock, D. (1987). *Federal policy toward mental retardation and developmental disability.* Baltimore, MD: Paul H. Brooks.

Bride, B. E., & Nackerud, L. (2002, June 29). The disease model of alcoholism: A Kuhnian paradigm. *Journal of Sociology and Social Welfare*, 125–141.

Burke, A. C. (1992, December). Between entitlement and control: Dimensions of U.S. drug policy. *Social Service Review, 66*, 572–573.

Budget does in child welfare drug testing. (2008, December 1). Retrieved from chicagobreakingnews.com/2008/12/ao-dcfs-suspends-jobseekers

Campbell, J. (1998). Consumerism, outcomes, and satisfaction: A review of the literature. In R. W. Manderscheid & M. J. Henderson (Eds.), *Mental health United States, 1998.* U.S. Department of Health and Human Services. Washington DC: U.S. Government Printing Office.

Carson, E. A., & Sabol, W. J. (2011, December). Prisoners in 2011. U.S. Department of Justice Bureau of Justice Statistics.

Castellani, P. J. (2005). *From snake pits to cash cows.* Albany, NY: SUNY Press.

Center for Disease Control and Prevention, Children's Mental Health. (2017, March 23). Retrieved from www.cdc.gov/childrensmentalhealth/basics.html

Ciolino, C. (1991). Substance abuse and mood disorders. In M. S. Gold & A. E. Slaby (Eds.), *Dual diagnosis in substance abuse.* New York: Marcel Dekker.

Coates, G. (1999, August 1). Welfare drug screening off to shaky start. *New Orleans Times-Picayune*, sec. A, p. 4.

Cocores, J. A. (1991). Treatment of the dually diagnosed adult drug user. In Gold and Slaby (Eds.), *Dual diagnosis in substance Abuse* (pp. 237–251). New York: Marcel Dekker.

Cohen, J., & Levy, S. J. (1992). *The mentally ill chemical abuser: Whose client?* New York: Lexington Books, 18–21, 85, 86–90.

The Community Mental Health Center. (1964). Washington, DC: American Psychiatric Association.

Congress says, let the mentally ill buy guns. [Editorial]. (2017, February 15). *New York Times.*

Covert, B., & Israel, J. (2015, February 26). What 7 states discovered after spending more than $1 million drug testing welfare recipients. *Think Progress.*

Cox, J. (2007, March 7). Workplace drug use hits lowest on record. Retrieved from money.cnn.com/2007/03/07/news/drug_test/intex.htm

Crawford, M. B. (2016 May 27). No place for warriors. *New York Times.*

Crosson-Tower, C. (1998). *Exploring child welfare.* Boston, MA: Allyn and Bacon.

D. Meyers & C. Redmond. (1998, August 6). Stiffer tests urged. *Baton Rouge Advocate*, sec. A, pp. 1, 4.

Cunha, D. (2015, August 15). Why drug testing welfare recipients is a waste of taxpayers' money. *Time.*

Dain, N. (1980). *Clifford W. Beers: Advocate for the insane.* Pittsburgh, PA: University of Pittsburgh Press, 112–121.

Dao, J. (2013, February 7). Study seeks biomarkers for invisible war scars. *New York Times*, p. A17.

Davis, N. J., & Stasz, C. (1990). *Social control of deviance: A critical perspective.* New York: McGraw-Hill.

Dokoupil, T. (2012, November 12). A return to the battlefield. *Time, 25.*

Dowell, D., Zhang, K, Noonan, R. K., & Hockenberry, J. M. (2016 October). Mandatory provider review and pain clinic laws reduce the amounts of opioids prescribed and overdose death rates. *Health Affairs, 35*, 10, 1876–1883.

Duara, N. (2016, October 5). Long wait times and schedule manipulation persist at Phoenix VA Hospital, watchdog says. *Los Angeles Times.*

Egan, T. (1999, September 19). A drug ran its course, then hid with its users. *New York Times*, p. 1.

Eldren, S. M., Kovaleski, S. F., & Sisario, B. (2017, April 10). Unsolved mystery in purple. *NewYork Times*, p. C1.

Facts on the alcoholic beverage industry. (2016). *Statista.* Retrieved from www.statista.com/topics/1709/alcoholic-beverages/

Fisher, M. (2007, September 2). When privacy laws do more harm than good. *Washington Post*, p. C1.

Flaherty, D. K. (2011, October). The vaccination-autism connection: A public health crisis caused by unethical medical practice and fraudulent science. *Annals of Pharmacology, 45*(10), 1302–1304.

Fox, M. (2011, October 17). CDC: Alcohol addiction costs U.S. $224 billion a year. *National Journal.*

Frank, R. G., Koyanagi, C., & McGuire, T. G. (1997, July/August). The politics and economics of mental health "parity" laws. *Health Affairs, 16*, 109, 112–114.

Friedman, R. A. (2013, May 21). The book stops here. *New York Times*, p. D3.

Friedman, R. A. (2012, July 10). Good news for mental illness in health law. *New York Times*, p. D6.

Freskos, B. (2016, November 11). Nearly half of Americans are now covered by universal background checks, but giant loopholes remain. *The Trace.*

Gamwell, L., & Tomes, N. (1995). *Madness in civilization: Cultural and medical perceptions of mental illness before 1914.* Ithaca, NY: Cornell University Press.

Gold, M. S. & Slaby, A. E., (1991). *Dual diagnosis in substance abuse.* New York: Marcel Dekker.

Goode, E. (2013, February 22). Incarceration rates for blacks have fallen sharply, report shows. *New York Times.*

Golub, A., Bennett, A. S. & Elliott, L. (2015, March 30). Beyond American's war on drugs: Developing public policy to navigate the prevailing pharmacological revolution. *AIMS Public Health, Vol. 2*, pp. 142–160.

Grossman, M., Chaloupka, F. J., & Shin, K. (2002, March/April). Illegal drug use and public policy. *Health Affairs, 21*, 135.

Grube, J. W., & Wallack, L. (1994, February). Television beer advertising and drinking knowledge, beliefs, and intentions among schoolchildren. *American Journal of Public Health, 84*, 254–258.

Hagland, M. (1999, September). Physician unionization: A threat to integration? *Healthcare Leadership Review*, 4.

Harrell, A. (1995). Drug abuse. In G. Galister (Ed.), *Reality and research: Social science and U.S. urban policy since 1960* (pp. 156–179). Washington, DC: Urban Institute Press.

Harris, E. A. (2017, April 1). In school nurse's room: Tylenol, bandages, and an antidote for heroin. *New York Times*, p. A18.

Harris, G. (2008, March 8). Deal in an autism case fuels debate on vaccine. *New York Times*, p. 8.

Hilzenrath, D. S. (1997, July 14). Finding something left to squeeze. *Washington Post Weekly Edition*, p. 20.

Hoetz, P. J. (2017, February 8). How the anti-vaxxers are winning. *New York Times*, p. A25.

Hofstadter, R. (1994 [1992]). *Social Darwinism in American thought*. Philadelphia, PA: University of Pennsylvania Press.

Hostege, S., & Anglen, R. (2012, January 12). Suspect fueled early concerns at college. *Arizona Republic*, p. A1.

Human Rights Watch. (2000, June 7). United States: Stark race disparities in drug incarceration. Retrieved from www.hrw.org./en/news/2000/06/07

Husak, D. N. (1992). *Drugs and rights*. New York: Cambridge University Press.

Inciardi, J. A., McBride, D. C., & Rivers, J. E. (1996). *Drug control and the courts*. Thousand Oaks, CA: Sage.

Jackman, T., & Jenkins, C. L. (2007, December 14). Kaine plans overhaul of system criticized after Va. Tech killings. *Washington Post*, p. 6.

Jenkins, C. L. (2007, September 2). Va. Tech report may signal tough choices on reforms. *Washington Post*, p. C1.

Jeter, J. (1996, December 4). Maryland may tie drug testing, welfare cash. *Washington Post*, sec. A, pp. 1, 16.

Jeter, J. (1996, December 5). Drug testing plan could balloon Maryland welfare costs. *Washington Post*, sec. E, pp. 1–5.

Jeter, J. (1997, January 30). Welfare panel in Maryland alters drug strategy. *Washington Post*, sec. C, pp. 1, 5.

Johnson, A. (2009, February 13). U.S. court rejects vaccine connection to autism. *Wall Street Journal*, p. 3.

Jolly, N. (2016, October 1). Meet Ellie: The robot therapist treating soldiers with PTSD. Retrieved from *News.com*.

Junker, S. (2016). *Tribe: On homecoming and belonging*. New York: Twelve.

Kalb, C. (2008, March 24). Mysteries and complications. *Newsweek, 64–65*.

Katz, J. (2017 June 6). U.S, drug deaths climbing faster than ever. *New York Times*.

Kershaw, S. (2008, November 13). Sharing their demons on the Web. *New York Times*, p. E1.

Kessler, R. C., Heeringa, S., Lakoma, M. D., Petukhova, M., Rupp, A. E., Schoenbaum, M., Wang, P. S., & Zaslavsky, A. M. (1997). The individual-level and societal-level effects of mental disorders on earnings in the United States: Results from the National Comorbidity Survey Replication. *American Journal of Psychiatry*. Published online ahead of print May 7, 2008.

Kirk, S., & Kutchins, H. (1997). *Making us crazy*. New York: Free Press.

Klein, J. (2013, July 1). Can service save us? *Time*, pp. 24–34.

Kluger, J. (2014, October 6). Who's afraid of a little vaccine? *Time*, 40–43.

Lamothe, D. (2015, February 3). Clay Hunt Veterans Suicide Prevention Act passes Senate, will head to White House. *Washington Post*.

Lee, R. (2015, March 12). Experts identify genetic biomarkers linked to PTSD. *Tech Times*.

Levine, M. (1981). *The history and politics of community mental health*. New York: Oxford University Press.

Lewin, T. (2011, January 21). Record level of stress found in college freshmen. *New York Times*, p. A1.

Lewis, D. (1998, June 30). The Center for Alcohol and Addictions Studies, Brown University. Pregnant substance abusers need our help. Retrieved from www.jointogether.org

Lieby, J. (1978). *A social history of social welfare and social work in the United States*. New York: Columbia University Press.

Mather, K. (2013, April 13). The whole school knows. *Los Angeles Times*, p. A1.

Martin, M. (2010, May 3). Crack babies: Twenty years on. National Public Radio. Retrieved from www.npr.org/templates/story/story:php?storyld=126478643

Medlineplus. (2017). Fetal alcohol spectrum disorders. U.S. National Library of Science. Retrieved from http://medlineplus.gov/fetalalcoholspectrumdisorders.html

McCloy, M. (2001, January 16). Eleven counties seek $9 million for drug courts. *The Arizona Republic*, p. B5.

McGinn, D. (2007, August 20–27). After Virginia Tech. *Newsweek*, 70.

McGuire, R. T. Frank and Thomas G. (1994). Health care reform and financing of mental health services: Distributional consequences. In R. W. Manderscheid & M. A. Sonnenschein (Eds.), *Mental health, United States, 1994*. Center for Mental Health Services. Washington, DC: U.S. Government Printing Office.

McHugh, P. (2013, May 18–19). A manual run amok. *Wall Street Journal*.

McNeil, D. G., Jr. (2009, January 13). Book is rallying resistance to the antivaccine crusade. *New York Times*, p. D1.

Minaya, M. (2007, October 29). Providing the structure the autistic need for college life. *Washington Post*, B2.

Michigan appeals court decision strikes down welfare drug testing law. (2003, April 9). Retrieved from www.drugpolicy.org//news/04_09_03

Mnookin, S. (2011, January, 10, 17). Autism and the affluent. *Newsweek*, 11.

MSW@USCSTAFF. (2016, March 2). Five most popular social work careers. University of Southern California.

Nagournay, A., & Goodnough, A. (2015, January 22). Measles cases linked to Disneyland ride, and debate over vaccinations intensifies. *New York Times,* p. A13.

Narcotics Anonymous. (2000, March 26). Networking with professionals. Retrieved from www.na.org/networking.htm

National Alliance for the Mentally Ill. (2015). Mental illness by the numbers. Retrieved from www.nami.org/learn-more/mental-health-by-the-numbers

NASW. (2017). Mental health. Retrieved from wwwsocialworkers.org/pressroom/features/issue/mental.asp

National Council of State Legislatures. (2017, March 31). Guns on campus: Overview.

National Health Care Quality Report. Retrieved from www.nhqrnet.ahrq.gov

National Institute on Alcohol Abuse and Alcoholism. (1993, April). Alcohol research and public health policy. *Alcohol Alert,* 20, 330. Retrieved from http://silk.nih.gov/silk/niaaa1/publication/aa20htm

National Institute on Alcohol Abuse and Alcoholism. (1995, July). The genetics of alcoholism. *Alcohol Alert,* 18, 357. Retrieved from http://silk.nih.gov/silk/niaaa1/publication/aa18htm

National Institute on Alcohol Abuse and Alcoholism. (2017, February). Alcohol facts and figures. National Institutes of Health. Retrieved from www.niaaa.nih.gov/alcohol-health/overview-alcohol-consumption/alcohol-facts-and-statistics

National Institute on Drug Abuse. (1999, December). *Community drug alert bulletin.* Washington, DC: U.S. Department of Health and Human Services, p. 42.

Nelson, S. (2017, February 14). House GOP reopens push to drug test the unemployed. *US News.*

Oh so close to mental health parity. (2008, October 1). [Editorial]. *New York Times,* p. A30.

O'Neill, J. V. (2001, January). Expertise in addictions said crucial. *NASW News, 46,* 10.

Offit, P. A. (2008). *Autism's false prophets.* New York: Columbia University Press.

Okie, S. (2009, January). The epidemic that wasn't. *New York Times,* p. D1.

Opioid tide: From coast to coast. (2017, January 8). *New York Times,* pp. 11, 18.

Paalazzolo, J., & Eder, S. (2012, September 22–23). Push to let college students carry guns picks up steam. *Wall Street Journal,* A3.

Pace, P. R. (2009, January). Victory for mental health parity. *NASW News, 54*(1), 6.

Pagliaro, A. M., & Pagliaro, L. A. (1996). *Substance use among children and adolescents: Its nature, extent, and effects from conception to adulthood.* New York: Wiley.

Pardeck, J. T. (1998). *Social work after the Americans with Disabilities Act.* Westport, CT: Auburn House.

Pear, R. (2008, March 6). House approves bill on mental health parity. *New York Times,* p. 14.

Phillips, D. (2015, September 20). A unit stalked by suicide, trying to save itself. *New York Times,* pp. A1, A20–A22.

Poland, G. A., & Jacobson, R. M. (2011, January 13). The age-old struggle against the antivaccinationist. *New England Journal of Medicine, 364*(2), 97–99.

Reed, M., & Brennan, C. (2015, October 3). Recent campus shootings raise safety concerns. *USA Today.*

Ruelas, R. (2008, September 21). Soldiers reluctant to seek help for stress disorder. *Arizona Republic,* p. A17.

Ripley, A. (2013, January 28). Your brain under fire. *Time,* pp. 34–41.

Roehrig, C. (2016, June). Mental disorders top the list of the most costly conditions in the United States: $201 billion. *Health Affairs, 34*(6), 1130–1135.

Rothman, D. (1971). *The Discovery of the asylum.* Boston, MA: Little, Brown.

SAMSHA. (2015, October 27). Substance use disorder. U.S. Department of Health & Human Services. Retrieved from www.samsha.gov/disorders/substance-use

SAMSHA. (2016, September). 2015 national survey of drug use and health. U.S. Department of Health & Human Services, Tables 2.42B, 2.43B, and 2.46B. Retrieved from www.samhsa.gov/data/sites/default/files/NSDUH-DetTabs–2015/pdf

Schemo, D. J., & Medina, J. (2007, October 27). Disabilities fight grows as taxes pay for tuition. *New York Times,* p. A1.

Schulte, B., and Craig, T. (2007, August 31). Unknown to Va. Tech; Brigid Schulte, Killer's parents describe attempts over the years to help isolated son, *Washington Post,* p. A1.

Schwarz, A. (2012, June 10). Risky rise of the good-grade pill. *New York Times.* Retrieved from www.nimh.nih.gov/statistics/index.shtml; cdc.gov/features/childrensmentalhealth/www.nimh.nih.gov/statistics/index.shtml

Senior, J. (2016, May 19) Disbanded brothers: Back in a divided nation. *New York Times,* p. C1.

Shanker, T. (2008, April 6). Army is worried by rising stress of return tours. *New York Times,* p. 1.

Singer, S. (2011, March 30). Gov. Rick Scott's drug testing policy stirs suspicion. *Palm Beach Post.*

Spiegel, P. (2008, September 21). VA doctors tell Mullen that vets need mental health screenings. *Los Angeles Times.*

Specialist credentials are readied. (1999, September) *NASW News, 44,* 1, 10.

Steinhauer, J. (1999, January 10). Rebellion in white: Doctors pulling out of H.M.O. systems. *New York Times,* pp. 1, 20.

Steinhauer, J. (2008, November 27). Women guilty in Web fraud tied to suicide. *New York Times,* p. A1.

Stoesz, D. (1996). *Small change: Domestic policy under the Clinton presidency.* New York: Longman.

Sulzburger, A. G. (2010, November 11). States adding drug test as hurdle for welfare. *New York Times,* A1.

Szasz, T. (1974 [1961]). *The myth of mental illness.* New York: Harper & Row.

Tavis, C. (2017). How psychiatry went crazy. *Wall Street Journal,* p. C5.

Team Rubicon. (2017). Retrieved from https://teamrubiconusa.org/?gclid=CNWUkceYr9MCFYphfgodtUUI4A

Tessler, R. C., & Goldman, H. H. (1982). *The chronically mentally ill.* Cambridge, MA: Ballinger.

Thompson, D. (2016 May 5). 6 years later, Obamacare still divides America: Poll, *Harris Poll.*

Torrey, E. F. (1997, June 13). The release of the mentally ill from institutions: A well-intentioned disaster. *Chronicle of Higher Education, 43,* B4–B5.

Trull, T., Solhan, M., Tragesser, S., Jahng, S., Wood, P., Piasecki, T., & Watson, D. (2008, August). Affective instability: Measuring a core feature of borderline personality disorder with ecological momentary assessment. *Journal of Abnormal Psychology, 117*(3), 647–661.

Tyson, A. S. (2008, April 18). Combat stress may cost U.S. up to $6 billion. *Washington Post,* p. 15.

U.S. Department of Health and Human Services. (2007). *2007 National Survey on Drug Abuse and Health.*

U.S. Department of Health and Human Services. (2000). *Highlights, 1998 National Household Survey on Drug Abuse,* Table 11.

U.S. Department of Health and Human Services, Substance Abuse and Mental Health Services Administration. (2016). *2015 National Survey on Drug Abuse and Health.* Retrieved from www.samsha.gov/data/nsduh/2k11results/nsduhresults2015

U.S. Department of Health and Human Services, Substance Abuse and Mental Health Services Administration. (2011). *2011 National Survey on Drug Abuse and Health.*

U.S. Equal Employment Opportunities Commission. (2002, May). *Americans With Disabilities Act: Questions and answers.*

Vance, J. D. (2016). *Hillbilly elegy.* New York: Harper.

The Virginia Tech betrayal. [Editorial]. (2009, February 8). *New York Times,* p. WK9.

Waldman, M., Nicholson, M. S., Adilov, N., & Williams, J. (2008). Autism prevalence and precipitation rates in California, Oregon, and Washington counties. *Journal of Pediatrics and Adolescent Medicine, 162*(11), 1026–1034.

Weir, K. (2015). RoboTherapy: A new class of robots providing social and cognitive support. *Monitor on Psychology.* Washington, DC: American Psychological Association.

Whitaker, T., & Arrington, P. (2008). *Social workers at work.* NASW Membership Workforce Study. Washington, DC: National Association of Social Workers.

Winsten, J., & Serazin, E. (2013, February 7). Rolling back the war on vaccines. *Wall Street Journal,* p. A15.

Woodiwiss, M. (1998). Reform, racism, and rackets: Alcohol and drug prohibition in the United States. In R. Coomber (Ed.), *The control of drugs and drug abusers.* Amsterdam, Netherlands: Harwood Academic.

Young, A. M. (1994, Fall). Addictive drugs and the brain. *Phi Kappa Phi National Forum, 79,* 15–18, 23.

Zimberg, S. (1993). Introduction and general concepts of dual diagnosis. In Solomon, J., Zimberg, S., & Scollar, E., (eds.), *Dual diagnosis: Evaluation, treatment, training, and program development.* New York: Plenum, 5–6.

Zoroya, G. (2008, March 7). A fifth of soldiers at PTSD risk. *USA Today,* p. 11A.

CHAPTER 9

AARP. (2017, April). Our nation's health care bill: $3.2 trillion annually. *AARP Bulletin,* 8.

Abelson, R. (2013, May 20). E.R.'s account for half of hospital admissions, study says. *New York Times.*

Abdus, S., & Hill, S. C. (2017, May). Growing insurance coverage did not reduce access to care for the continuously insured. *Health Affairs, 36,* 781–796.

Abelson, Reed. (2013, May 20). E.R.'s account for half of hospital admissions, study says. *New York Times.*

Abelson, R., Creswell, J., & Palmer, G. (2012, September 21). Medicare bills rise as records turn electronic. *New York Times.*

Arnst, C. (2009, May 18). A secret wish for health reform. *Business Week,* 23.

Arnst, C. (2009, July 6). The family doctor: A remedy for health-care costs? *Business Week,* 34–37.

Associated Press. Young people may choose to pay penalty. *San Francisco Chronicle,* p. C4.

Bach, P. B. (2015, January, 15). Why drugs cost so much. *New York Times,* p. A25.

Bai, G., & Anderson, G. F. (2016, June). Extreme markups: The fifty US hospitals with the highest charge-to-cost rations. *Health Affairs, 34,* 922–928.

Bernstein, N. (2012, August 10). Health insurer rebates may stall in employers' hands. *New York Times,* p. A14.

Boudreaux, M. H., Gonzales, G., & Saloner, B. (2017, May). Medical financial burden declined for consumers in the nongroup market. *Health Affairs, 36,* 833–837.

Brill, S. (2015a). *America's bitter pill.* New York: Random House.

Brill, S. (2015b, January 19). What I learned from my $190,000 surgery. *Time.*

Brill, S. (2013, March 4). Bitter pill: How outrageous pricing and egregious profits are destroying our health care. *Time,* 22–23, 26–27, 30–49.

Brody, J. E. (2012, May 29). Trimming a bloated health care system. *New York Times,* p. D7.

Carey, K., & Lin, M-Y. (2015, June). Readmission to New York hospitals fell for three target conditions from 2008 to 2012 consistent with Medicaid goals. *Health Affairs, 34,* 978–985.

Caroll, A. (2017, November 7). A doctor shortage? Let's take a closer look. *New York Times.*

Clark, T. R. (1999). The limits of state autonomy: The medical cooperatives of the Farm Security Administration, 1935–1946. *Journal of Policy History, 11*(3), 258.

Cole, M. B., Galarraga, O., Wilson, I. B., Wright, B., & Trivedi, A. N. (2017, January). At federally funded health centers, Medicaid expansion was associated with improved quality of care. *Health Affairs, 36,* 41–48.

Collins, G. (2013, July 13). The house just wants to snack. *New York Times,* A17.

Colliver, V. (2015, March 3). Strapped public hospital needs "miracle" to survive. *San Francisco Chronicle,* pp. A1, A9.

Creswell, J., & Abelson, R. (2012, August 14). A giant hospital chain is blazing a profit trail. *New York Times*.

Decker, S. L., Lipton, B., & Sommers. (2017, May). Medicaid expansion coverage effects grew in 2015 with continued improvements in coverage quality. *Health Affairs, 36*, 819–825.

Department of Health and Human Services, Center for Medicare & Medicaid Services. (2011, November 2). *Medicare shared savings program: Accountable care organizations, proposed rules 76. Fed. Reg. 67.*

Domenech, B. (2017, March 21). How Trump can fix health care. *New York Times*, A25.

Dooren, J. C. (2012, December 26). New year brings health-overhaul changes. *Wall Street Journal*, p. A5.

Douthout, R. (2013, July 7). A hidden consensus on health care. *New York Times*.

Obama Care's secret history. (2012, June 12). [Editorial]. *Wall Street Journal*, p. A12.

Editors of AARP. (2017, May). Why drugs cost so much. *AARP Bulletin*, 16–24.

Edwards, H. S. (2016, August 29). Cracks in the Obamacare crystal ball. *Time*, 14.

Emanuel, E. J. (2011, October 30). How much does health cost? *New York Times*, p. BW6.

Families USA. (2005). *Paying a premium: The added cost of the care for the uninsured.* Washington, DC: Families USA.

Fernandez, M. (2012, March 5). Texans rebut governor on expansion of Medicaid. *New York Times*, p. A13.

Flowers, L., & Noel-Miller, C. (2017). State high-risk pools failed consumers in the past and would again. AARP.

Focus on Health Reform. (2013, April 23). Summary of the Affordable Care Act. Retrieved from kaiserfamilyfoundation .files.wordpress.com/2011/04/8061-021

Frakt, A. B. (2011, March). How much do hospitals shift costs? A review of the evidence. *Milbank Quarterly, 89*(1), 90–130.

Fullerton, C. A., Henke, R. M., Crable, E., Hohlbauch, A., & Cummings, N. (2016, January). The impact of Medicare ACOs on improving integration and coordination of physical and behavioral health care. *Health Affairs, 35*, 1257–1265.

Garthwaite, C., & Bagley, N. (2017 June 6). The uncertain strategy. *New York Times*, p. A21.

Goldstein, A. (2017, January 17). Trump administration backtracks partway on ACA enrollment outreach. Washington, DC: Washington Post.

Goodnough, A. (2013, July 13). Lines are drawn over opting out of Medicaid plan. *New York Times*, p. A1.

Goodnough, A. (2012, December 20). Next challenge for the health law: Getting people to buy in. *New York Times*, p. A16.

Goodnough, A. (2012, July 31). Rebates on health insurance could play as a selling point. *New York Times*, p. A10.

Goodnough, A. (2016, December 28). Safety-net hospitals fear cuts as health law's repeal looms. *New York Times*, pp. A1, A14.

Goodnough, A., & Pear, R. (2013, February 22). "G.O.P. governors providing a lift for health law. *New York Times*, p. A1.

Greenhouse, S., & Abelson, R., (2012, December 1). The cost of change. *New York Times*, p. B1.

Hadley, J., Holahan, J., Coughlin, T., & Miller, D. (2008, September-October). Covering the uninsured in 2008: Current costs, sources of payment, and incremental costs. *Health Affairs, 27*(5), 399–415.

Hall, J. P. (2015, February 13). Why high-risk pools won't work. The Commonwealth Fund.

Harwood, J. (2013, April 30). The next big challenge for Obama's health care law: Carrying it out. *New York Times*, p. A10.

Helmchen, L., Brown, C. W., Lurie, I. Z., & Sasso, A.T. (2015 September). Health savings account: Growth concentrated among high-income households and large employers. *Health Affairs*, 34, 9, 1594–1598.

Hill, S. C. (2015, February). Medicaid expansion in opt-out states would produce consumer savings and less financial burden than exchange coverage. *Health Affairs*, 34, 340–349.

Ho, C. (2017, June 3). Health system reform in play. *San Francisco Chronicle*, pp. A1, A9.

Hsu, J., Price, M., Vogeli, M., Brand, R., Chernew, M. E., Chaguturu, S. K., Weil, E., & Ferris, T. G. (2017, May). Bending the spending curve by altering care delivery patterns: The role of care management within a Pioneer ACO. *Health Affairs, 36*, 877–833.

Kirkham, E. (2016 March 4). 1 in 3 Americans have saved for retirement. *Time.*

Klein, E. (2009, August 3–9). The ghosts of battles past. *Washington Post Weekly Edition*, pp. 25–26.

Krugman, P. (2017, March 27). How to build on Obamacare. *New York Times*, p. A29.

Krugman, P. (2009, August 31). Missing Richard Nixon. *New York Times*, p. A17.

Krugman, P. (2013, May 27). The Obamacare shock," *New York Times*, p. A17.

Krugman, P. (2013, June 7). The spite club. *New York Times*, p. A23.

Krugman, P. (2016, October 28). Obamacare hits a pothole. *New York Times*, p. A25.

Leibowitz, J. (2008, February 25). This pill not to be taken with competition. *Washington Post*, p. A15.

Leonhardt, D. (2017, March 3). Republicans for singer-payer health care. *New York Times*, p. A25.

Lieber, R. (2017, February 25). Health savings accounts may cut costs, not headaches. *New York Times*, pp. B1, B4.

Liptak, A. (2013a, June 29). Congress's taxing powers cited-Medicaid growth limited. *New York Times*, p. A1.

Litpak, A. (2013, June 29). Roberts' delicate twist. *New York Times*, p. A1.

Long, S. K., Skopec, L., Shelto, A., Nordahl, K., & Walsh, K. K. (2016, September). Massachusetts health reform at ten years: Great progress, but coverage gaps remain. *Health Affairs, 35*, 1633–1637.

Lowrey, A. (2013, April 23). A health provider strives to keep hospital beds empty. *New York Times*.

Lowrey, A. (2013, February 12). Slower growth of health costs eases U.S. deficit. *New York Times*, p. A1.

Lowrey, R., & Pear, A. (2012, July 29). Doctor shortage likely to worsen with health law. *New York Times*, p. 1.

McMorrow, S., Gates, J. A., Long, S., K. & Kenney, G. M. (2017, May). Medicaid expansion increased coverage, improved affordability, and reduced psychological stress for low-income patients. *Health Affairs, 36*, 808–819.

McWilliams, J. M., Hatfield, L. A., Chernew, M. E., Landon, B. E., & Schwartz, A. L. (2016, June 16). Early performance of accountable care organizations in medicine. *New England Journal of Medicine, 374*, 2357–2366.

Meier, B. (2012, July 12). Drugs dispensed by doctors cost insurers dearly. *New York Times*, p. A1.

Mooney, B. C. (2012, June 26). RomneyCare: A revolution that basically worked. *Boston Globe.*

Neuhausen, K., Davis, A. C., Needleman, J., Brook, R. H., Zingmond, D., & Roby, D. H. (2015, June). Disproportionate-share hospital payment reductions may threaten the financial stability of safety-net hospitals. *Health Affairs, 33*, 988–995.

Nuila, R. (2017, May 28). Medical misfits. *New York Times*, SR1, p. 6.

Pear, R., & Goodnough, A. (2012, September 11). It will be tricky for Romney to keep the best of health law while repealing it. *New York Times*, p. A11.

Pear, R. (2012, October 2). Administration advises states to expand Medicaid or risk losing federal money. *New York Times*, p. A19.

Pear, R. (2012, July 25). Court's ruling may blunt reach of health law. *New York Times*, p. A16.

Pear, R. (2012, May 23). Gains in health system seen as lasting by some. *New York Times*, p. A12.

Pear, R. (2013, March 22). Expanding Medicaid with private insurance. *New York Times*, p. A14.

Pear, R. (2013, May 31). Health law is fostering competition, U.S. study says. *New York Times.*

Pear, R. (2013, February 25). Panel on health care work force, lacking a budget, is left waiting. *New York Times*, p. A9.

Pear, R, (2016, December 22). 2017 sign-ups to health plan hit 6.4 million. *New York Times*, pp. A1, A18.

Pfeffer, J. (2016, May 17). To fix high drug prices, stop the merger madness. Fortune.com. Retrieved from http://fortune.com/2016/05/17/high-drug-prices-mergers-pharma-competition

Politz, K. (2017, February 22). High-risk pools for uninsurable individuals. Menlo Park, CA: Henry J. Keiser Family Foundation.

Potter, W. (2016, June 15). Here's what happens when Wall Street runs hospitals. Huffington Post.

Price, C. C., & Eibner, C. (2013, June). For states that opt out of Medicaid expansion: 3.6 million fewer insured and $8.4 billion less in federal payments. *Health Affairs, 32*(2), 1030–1036.

Rabin, R. C., & Abelson, R. (2013, July 17). Under exchanges, many New Yorkers will see big savings on health plans. *New York Times*, p. A1.

Rampell, C. (2017, April 19). Public health coverage for all gains favor. *San Francisco Chronicle*, p. A10.

Reich, R. (2016, August 28). Why a single-payer system is inevitable. *San Francisco Chronicle*, p. E8.

Rodnofsky, L., & Weaver, C. (2012, September 18). States seek a middle ground on Medicaid. *Wall Street Journal*, p. A6.

Rosenthal, E. (2017). An American sickness: How healthcare became bigness and how you can take it back. New York: Penguin Press.

Rosenthal, E. (2013, July 1). American way of birth: Costliest in the world. *New York Times*, p. A1.

Rosenthal, E. (2013, June 2). The $2.7 trillion medical bill: Colonoscopies explain why U.S. leads the world in health expenditures. *New York Times*, p. 1.

Roy, A. (2011, October 20). How the Heritage Foundation, a conservative think tank, promoted the individual mandate. *Forbes.* Retrieved from forbes.com/sites/roy/2011/10/20

Shea, K. K., Holmgren, A. L., Osborn, R., & Schoen, C. (2007, May). Health system performance in selected nations: A ChartPack. *Commonwealth Fund*, 28, 56, 129.

Shear, D., & Abelson, R. (2014, February 13). Over 1 million added to rolls of health plan. *New York Times*, pp. A1, A16.

Sommers, B. D., & Gruber, J. (2017, May). Federal funding insulated state budgets from increased spending related to Medicaid expansion. *Health Affairs, 36*, 939–944.

Starr, P. (1982). *The social transformation of American medicine.* New York: Basic Books.

Stewart, J. B. (2012 June 13). How broccoli landed on the Supreme Court menu. *New York Times.*

Stolberg, S. G. (2009, September 27). Taking health care courtship up another notch. *New York Times*, p. 20.

Tanner, M. D. (2008, January/February). Lessons from the fall of RomneyCare. *Cato Policy Brief.* Washington, DC: Cato Institution.

Tavernise, S. (2013, May 30). For Medicare, immigrants offer surplus, study finds. *New York Times*, p. A12.

Terhune, C., Epstein, K., & Arnst, C. (2009, May 4). The dubious promise of digital medicine. *Business Week*, 31–37.

Thomas, K. (2013, March 19). U.S. drug costs dropped in 2012 but rises loom. *New York Times*, p. A1.

Tipirneni, R., Rhodes, K. V., Hayward, R. A., Lichtenstein, R. L., Reamer, E. N., & Davis, M. N. (2015, August). Primary care appointment availability for new Medicaid patients increased after Medicaid expansion in Michigan. *Health Affairs, 34*, 1399–1405.

U.S. Department of Health & Human Services, *Patient Protection and Affordable Care Act.* Retrieved from hhs.gov/healthcare/rights/law/index

Walsh, B. (2017, January/February). A battle looms. *AARP Bulletin*, 33–35.

World's best health care. *New York Times*, p. A20.

Worthen, M. (2014, April 6). As Vermont goes, so goes the nation? *New York Times*, p. SR5.

Zakaria, F. (2012). Health insurance is for everyone: List of countries with universal healthcare. Retrieved from truecostblog .com

Zakaria, F. (2012, March 26). Health insurance is for everyone. *Time*, 22–23.

Zallman, L., Woolhandler, S., Himmelstein, D., Bor, D., & McCormick, D. (2013, June). Immigrants contributed an estimated $115.2 billion more to the Medicare trust fund than they took out in 2001–2009. *Health Affairs, 32*(6), 152–1159.

CHAPTER 10

Allen, M. L., & Knitzer, J. (1983). Child welfare: Examining the policy framework. In B, G. McGowan & W. Meezan (Eds.), *Child welfare: Current dilemmas—future directions.* Itasca, IL: Peacock.

Annual Report of the MSPCC 26 (December 31, 1906), p. 4. Quoted in P. G. Anderson, The origin, emergence, and professional recognition of child protection. *Social Service Review* (1989, June), 223–227.

Bernard, L. D. (1992, Summer). The dark side of family preservation. *Affilia: Journal of Women and Social Work, 7*(2), 156–159.

Berry, M. (1992, July). An evaluation of family preservation services: Fitting agency services to family needs. *Social Work, 37,* 320.

Bowlby, J. (1958, March). The nature of the child's ties to his mother. *International Journal of Psychoanalysis, 39,* 350–373.

Bremner, R. H. (Ed.). (1971). *Children and youth in America—a documentary history,* Vol. II: 1886–1932. Cambridge, MA: Harvard University Press.

Brown, C. L., & Little, S. (1990, November-December). Family reunification. *Children Today, 23.*

CAPTA Reauthorization Act of 2010, 111th Congress, 2nd Session, December 18, 2010.

Casey Family Programs, National Center for Resource Family Support. (2003, February 18). General foster care statistics. Retrieved from www.casey.org

Child Welfare League of America. (2005, October). Kinship care fact sheet. Retrieved from https://www.cwla/wp-content/uploads/2015/05/National-Fact-Sheet-2015-Final.pdf

Child Welfare League of America. (1994). *Kinship care: A natural bridge.* Washington, DC: Author.

Child Welfare League of America, National Data Analysis System. Out-of-home care homes and facilities, 2003. Retrieved from http://ndas.cwla.org

Children's Defense Fund. (2015). *The state of America's children handbook, 2015.* Washington, DC: Author.

Courtney, M. E. (1994, March). Factors associated with the reunification of foster children with their families. *Social Service Review, 68,* 81–108.

Courtney, M. E. (1995, Summer). The foster care crisis and welfare reform: How might reform efforts affect the foster care system? *Public Welfare,* 31.

Courtney, M. (2000, February). Managed care and child welfare services: What are the issues? *Children and Youth Services Review, 22,* 87–91.

Courtney, M., Terao, S., & Bost, N. (2004). *Midwest evaluation of the adult functioning of former foster youth: Conditions of youth preparing to leave care.* Chicago: Chapin Hall Center for Children.

Dagenais, C., Begin, J., Bouchard, C., & Fortin, D. (2004). Impact of intensive family support programs: A synthesis of evaluation studies. *Children and Youth Services Review, 26,* 249–263.

Downs, S., Moore, E., McFadden, J., & Costin, L. (2012). *Child Welfare and Family Services: Policy and Practice,* 8th ed. Boston: Allyn & Bacon, 15.

Everett, J. E. (2013). Foster care. In Franklin, C. (Ed.), *Encyclopedia of social work.* New York: Oxford.

Fanshel, D., & Shinn, E. B. (1978). *Children in foster care: A longitudinal investigation.* New York: Columbia University Press.

Fein, E., & Maluccio, A. N. (1992, September). Permanency planning: Another remedy in jeopardy. *Social Service Review, 37,* 344–345.

Gambrill, E. (1990). *Critical thinking in clinical practice: Improving the accuracy of judgments and decisions about clients.* San Francisco, CA: Jossey-Bass.

Gelles, R. J. (1992). Poverty and violence toward children. *American Behavioral Scientist, 35,* 258–274.

Gelles, R. J. (1996). *The Book of David: How preserving families can cost children's lives.* New York: Basic Books.

Gil, D. (1970). *Violence against children: Physical abuse in the United States.* Cambridge, MA: Harvard University Press.

Goerge, R. M. (1990, September). The reunification process in substitute care. *Social Service Review,* 436.

Goldstein, J., Freud, A., & Solnit, A. J. (1973). *Beyond the best interests of the child.* New York: Free Press.

Grandy, F. (1993, April 21). Opening statement, Subcommittee on Human Resources of the Committee on Ways and Means, House of Representatives, 103rd Congress, First Session, Hearings on President Clinton's budget proposal for new funding for child welfare services targeted for family support and preservation services, 3.

Hager, R. L., & Scannapieco, M. (1999). *Kinship foster care: Policy, practice, and research.* New York: Oxford University Press.

Hartman, A. (1995, March). Ideological themes in family policy. *Families in Society: The Journal of Contemporary Human Services,* 182–192.

Hennepin County Community Services Department. (1980). *Family study project: Demonstration and research in intensive services to families.* Minneapolis, MN: Hennepin County.

Hochstady, N. J., Jaudes, P. K., Zimo, D. A., & Schachter, J. (1987, January). The medical and psychosocial needs of children entering foster care. *Child Abuse and Neglect, 11,* 53–62.

Huebner, R. A. (2012). Family preservation: Cost avoidance and child and family service review outcomes. *Journal of Public Child Welfare, 6,* 206–224.

Jeter, H. (1963). *Children, problems and services in child welfare programs.* Washington, DC: U.S. Children's Bureau.

Kamerman, S. B., & Kahn, A. J. (1990, December). Social services for children, youth and families in the United States. Special issue of *Children and Youth Services Review, 12,* 7–8.

Kaye, E., & Cook, R. (1993). *National survey of current and former foster parents.* Washington, DC: U.S. Department of Health and Human Services, Administration on Children, Youth and Families.

Kinney, J., Haapala, D., & Booth, C. (1991). *Keeping families together: The homebuilders model.* New York: Aldine De Gruyter.

Leeds, S. J. (1984). Evaluation of Nebraska's intensive services project. Iowa City, IA: National Resource Center on Family Based Services. Reviewed in Schuerman et al., *Putting Families First,* 34–35.

Lewis, R. E. (2005). The effectiveness of families first services: An experimental study. *Children and Youth Services Review, 27,* 499–509.

Lindsey, D. (1991, Spring). Factors affecting the foster care placement decision: An analysis of national survey data. *American Journal of Orthopsychiatry, 6,* 272–281.

Lindsey, D. (1994). *The welfare of children.* New York: Oxford University Press, 90–96.

Littell, J. H. (1997). Effects of the duration, intensity, and breadth of family preservation services: A new analysis of data from the Illinois Family First Experiment. *Children and Youth Services Review, 19,* 34.

Lundberg, E. O. (1949). Child welfare. In M. B. Hodges (Ed.), *Social Work Yearbook, 1949.* New York: Russell Sage Foundation, pp. 98–109.

Maas, H. S., & Engler, R. E., Jr. (1959). *Children in need of parents.* New York: Columbia University Press.

MacDonald, H. (1994, Spring). The ideology of "family preservation." *The Public Interest, 51,* 52.

McCurdy, K., & Daro, D. (2000). *Current trends in child abuse prevention, reporting, and fatalities: The 1999 fifty state survey.* Working Paper Number 808. Chicago, IL: National Center on Child Abuse Prevention Research, iv.

McIntyre, A., & Kesler, T. Y. (1986, Winter). Psychological disorders among foster children. *Journal of Clinical Child Psychiatry, 15,* 297–303.

McOllough, V. (1988, Fall). The orphan train comes to Clarion. *The Palimpsest,* 146.

Mennen, F. E., & O'Keefe, M. (2005). Informed decisions in child welfare: The use of attachment theory. *Children and Youth Services Review, 27,* 557–593.

Moffatt, M. E. K., Peddie, M., Stulginskas, J. L., Pless, I. B., & Steinmetz, N. (1985, May). Health care delivery to foster children: A study. *Health and Social Work, 10,* 129–137.

Murphy, P. (1993, June 19). Family preservation and its victims. *New York Times,* p. 21.

National Center on Abuse and Neglect. (1982). *Study findings: National study of incidence and severity of child abuse and neglect.* Washington, DC: Department of Health, Education, and Welfare.

Pecora, P. J. (2008). Child welfare—overview. In T. Mizrahi & L. E. Davis (Eds.), *Encyclopedia of social work* (20th ed.). Washington, DC: NASW Press, New York: Oxford University Press.

Pecora, P., Whittaker, J. K., Maluccio, A. N., & Barth, R., with Plotnick, R. D. (2000). *The child welfare challenge* (2nd ed.). New York: Aldine De Gruyter.

Pecora, P. K., Whittaker, J., & Maluccio, A., with Barth, R. P., & Plotnick, R. D. (2000). *The child welfare challenge: Policy, practice, and research* (2nd ed.). New York: Aldine De Gruyter.

Peddle, N., & Wang, C-T. (2001). *Current trends in child abuse prevention, reporting, and fatalities: The 1999 fifty state survey.* Chicago, IL: National Center on Child Abuse Prevention Research.

Pelton, L. (1981). Child abuse and neglect: The myth of classlessness. In L. Pelton (Ed.), *The social context of child abuse and neglect.* New York: Human Sciences Press.

Pelton, L. (1989). *For reasons of poverty: A critical analysis of the public child welfare system in the United States.* New York: Praeger.

Pew Commission on Children in Foster Care. (2004). *Fostering the future: Safety, permanence and well-being for children in foster care.* Washington, DC: Author.

Reid, J. H. (1959). Action called for—recommendations. In Maas and Engler (Eds.), *Children in need of parents.* New York: Columbia University Press, 380.

Schuerman, J. R., Rzepnicki, T. L., & Littell, J. H. (1994). *Putting families first: An experiment in family preservation.* New York: Aldine De Gruyter.

Sedlak, A. J. Mettenburg, J., Basena, J., Petta, I., McPherson, K., Greene, A., & Li, S. (2010). *Fourth national incidence study of child abuse and neglect (NIS-4).* Washington, DC: U.S. Department of Health and Human Services.

Shore, A. L. (2000, March). The bleak prospect for public child welfare. *Social Service Review,* 126.

Spar, K. (1994). The family preservation and support program: Background and description. *CRS Report for Congress.* Washington, DC: Congressional Research Service—Library of Congress.

Stein, T. J. (1988, Fall). Projects to prevent out-of-home placement. *Children and Youth Services Review, 7,* 109–121.

Stott, T., & Gustavsson, N. (2010). Balancing permanency and stability for youth in foster care. *Children and Youth Services Review, 32,* 619–625.

Subcommittee on Human Resources of the Committee on Ways and Means. (1993, April 21). House of Representatives, 103rd Congress, First Session, Hearings on president Clinton's budget proposal for new funding for child welfare services targeted for family support and preservation services.

Szykula, S. A., & Fleishman, M. J. (1985, March). Reducing out-of-home placements of abused children: Two controlled field studies. *Child Abuse and Neglect, 9.*

Tiffin, S. (1982). *In whose best interest? Child welfare reform in the Progressive Era.* Westport, CT: Greenwood Press.

Tracy, E. M., & Piccola, T. D. (2015). Family preservation and home-based services. In C. Franklin (Ed.), *Encyclopedia of social work* (20th ed.). New York: Oxford University Press.

Trattner, W. I. (1999). *From poor law to welfare state—a history of social welfare in America* (6th ed.). New York: Free Press, 118, 215, 218.

U.S. Department of Health and Human Services, Administration on Children, Youth and Families, Children's Bureau. (2015). *Trends in foster care and adoption—FY 2002–2011.* Based on data submitted by states as of July 12, 2012. Retrieved from http://www.acf.hhs.gov/programs/cb

Vobejda, B. (1995, October 26–November 1). Are there no orphanages? *Washington Post Weekly Edition,* p. 32.

Warsh, R., Pine, B. A., & Maluccio, A. (1995, December). The meaning of family preservation: Shared mission, diverse methods. *Families in Society: The Journal of Contemporary Human Services, 76,* 625.

Weisman, M.-L. (1994, July). When parents are not in the best interests of the child. *Atlantic Monthly,* 62.

Wexler, R. (1995). *Wounded innocents: The real victims of the war against child abuse* (rev. ed.). Buffalo, NY: Prometheus Books.

Wheeler, C. E., Grietje Reuter, Struckman-Johnson, D., & Ying-Ying T. Yuan. (2016). Evaluation of State of Connecticut intensive family preservation services: Phase V annual report. Sacramento, CA: Walter R. McDonald & Associates.

Willems, D. N., & DeRubeis, R. (1990). The effectiveness of intensive preventive services for families with abused, neglected, or disturbed children: Hudson County Project final report. Trenton, NJ: Bureau of Research, New Jersey Division of Youth and Family Services.

Williams, G. (1980). Protection of children against abuse and neglect: Historical background. In G. J. Williams & J. Money (Eds.), *Traumatic abuse and neglect of children at home.* Baltimore, MD: The Johns Hopkins University Press.

Woolley, P. V., & Evans, W. A. (1955, September). Significance of skeletal lesions in infants resembling those of traumatic origin. *Journal of the American Medical Association, 181,* 17–24.

Zelizer, V. A. (1985). *Pricing the priceless child: The changing social value of children.* New York: Basic Books.

CHAPTER 11

Alden, E. (2008). *The closing of the American border: Terrorism, immigration, and security.* New York: Harper-Collins.

American Immigration Council. (2010, July 13). The DREAM act. Washington, DC: Author.

American Immigration Council. (2016, August 12). How the United Sates immigration works. Washington, DC: Author.

Applebaum, S. (2017, August 4). With fewer immigrants, more jobs? Not so, economists say. *New York Times,* pp. A1, 14.

Berenson, T. (2016, September 16). How Latinos drive America's economic growth. *Time,* 32–35.

Bromwich, J. E. (2016, November 18). Muslims denounce talk of Japanese internment as "precedent" for registry. *New York Times,* p. A18.

Butcher, K. F., & Piehl, A. M. (2007, July). *Why are immigrants' incarceration rates so low? Evidence on selective immigration, deterrence, and deportation.* Cambridge, MA: National Bureau of Economic Research.

The Chinese Exclusion Act. (2017). Retrieved from caamedia.org/blog/2017/03/13/chinese-exclusion-act-a-new-film-about-a-19th-century-law-with-21st-century-lessons/

Cleveland, C. (2017, December). How the immigration and deportation systems work: A social worker's guide. *Journal of Sociology & Social Welfare,* pp. 55–73.

Cohen, P. (2017, May 30). In rural Iowa, a future rests on immigrants. *New York Times,* pp. A1, 12.

Davey, M. (2017a, February 27). He's a local pillar. Now he could be deported. *New York Times,* pp. A1, 10.

Davey, M. (2017b, March 3). Immigrant lacking papers is free, with help of many. *New York Times,* p. A16.

Davidson, A. (2013, February 17). Coming to America: Are illegal immigrants actually detrimental to the U.S. economy? *Time,* 19.

Dinnerstein, L., & Reimers, D. (2009). *Ethnic Americans: A history of immigration* (5th ed.). New York: Columbia University Press.

Edwards, J. R., Jr. (2006). Public charge. In J. Loucky, J. Armstrong, & L. J. Estrada (Eds.), *Immigration in America today: An encyclopedia* (pp. 265–268). Westport, CT: Greenwood Press.

Fix, M. (2009). *Immigrants and welfare: The impact of welfare reform on America's newcomers.* New York: Russel Sage.

Grillo, J. (2017, May 7). Bring on the wall. *New York Times,* SR 1, p. 6.

Gruber, R. (2000). *Haven: The dramatic story of 1,000 World War II refugees and how they came to America.* New York: Three Rivers Press.

Klein, J. (1999). *Woody Guthrie: A life.* New York: Random House.

Kposowa, A. J. (2006). Crime. In Loucky, J., Armstrong, J., & Estrada, L. J. (Eds.). *Immigration in America today: An encyclopedia* (pp. 58–59). Westport, CT: Greenwood Press.

Lee, T. (2017, February 17). Using H1-B visas to block immigration. *San Francisco Chronicle,* C1.

Lyons-Padilla, S., Gelfand, M., Moraniadi, H., Farood, M., & Edmond, M. (2015, December). Belonging nowhere: Marginalization and radicalization among Muslim immigrants. *Behavioral Science & Policy, 1*(2), 1–12.

Lyons-Padilla, S., & Gelfand, M. (2017, February 19). A Muslim ban is unscientific. *New York Times,* SR12.

MacGillis, A. (2016, September 18). The gang that failed. *New York Times Sunday Magazine,* pp. 52–57, 80.

Manjoo, F. (2017, February 9). Why Silicon Valley booed Trump's immigration ban. *New York Times,* p. B1.

Martin, P. (2006). Mexico-U.S. Migration. In Loucky, J., Armstrong, J., & Estrada, L. J. (Eds.). *Immigration in America today: An encyclopedia* (pp. 222–232). Westport, CT: Greenwood Press.

Mr. King's English-only bill. (2012, August 10). Editorial. *New York Times.*

Nichols, M. (2017, January 29). Experts: Refugee ban could be used as ISIL recruiting tool. *U.S.A. Today,* p. 929.

Orenstein, P. (2011, September 25). Did I know you at camp? *New York Times,* p. 18.

Park, H., & Buchanan, L. (2017 January 31). Refugees already face strict vetting. *New York Times,* p. A10.

Pedrara, F. I., & Lhu, Z. (2015 Spring). The "chilling effect" of America's new immigration policy. *Pathways* (pp 13–17). Stanford, CA: Stanford Center on Poverty and Inequality.

Porter, E. (2017a October 25). A policy as good for farms as locusts. *New York Times,* pp. B1–2.

Porter, E. (2017b, February 8). Make America great: Allow more immigration. *New York Times,* pp. B1–2.

Posas, L. A. (2006). Guestworkers. In Loucky, J., Armstrong, J., & Estrada, L. J. (Eds.). *Immigration in America today: An encyclopedia* (p. 162). Westwood, CT: Greenwood Press.

Preston, J. (2013, October 7). Ailing cities extend hand to immigrants. *New York Times,* pp. A1, 17.

Qiu, L. (2017, February 24). Fact-checking assertions about the president's travel ban. *New York Times,* A19.

Ramji, J. (2006). Refugee law and policy. In Loucky, J., Armstrong, J., & Estrada, L. J. (Eds.). *Immigration in America today: An encyclopedia* (p. 274). Westport, CT: Greenwood Press.

Rampell, C. (2013, July 2). Immigrants rank higher as entrepreneurs. *New York Times*, p. B20.

Reagan, R. (1984, April 30). Remarks at Fudan University, Shanghai, China. In Riley, J. L. (Ed.). *Let them in*. New York: Gotham.

Riley, J. L. (2008). *Let them in*. New York: Gotham.

Robbins, L. (2017, February 23). Police fear Trump's order may handcuff their efforts to fight gangs. *New York Times*, p. A14.

Robles, F. (2017, January 15). For Cubans, an expulsion long delayed. *New York Times*, p. A1.

Rothstein, E. (2011, October 10). The how of an internment, but not all the whys. *New York Times*, pp. C1, 5.

Rumbaut, R. G., & Irving, W. (2007, February 21). The myth of immigrant criminality and the paradox of assimilation: Incarceration rates among native and foreign-born men. Washington, DC: American Immigration Council.

Russakoff, D. (2017, January 29). The one way we can fight back is to excel. *New York Times*, pp. 34–43, 51.

Steinhauer, J. (2017, March 14). Hurling insults, then rebuked by own party. *New York Times*, p. A1.

Sulzberger, A. G. (2011, November 14). Hispanics reviving faded towns on the plains. *New York Times*, p. A1.

Tavernise, S. (2013, May 30). For Medicare, immigrants offer surplus, study finds. *New York Times*, p. A13.

Thadani, T. (2017, March 2). Will immigration plan favor tech over families? *San Francisco Chronicle*, pp. A1, 8.

Trattner, W. I. (1999). *From poor law to welfare state*. New York: Free Press, 163–191.

Vargas, J. A. (2012, June 25). Not legal. *Time*, 35–43.

Wakabayashi, D., & Schwartz, N. D. (2017, January 6). Some tech workers see visas as threat. *New York Times*, p. B1.

Watkins, T. H. (1990). *Righteous pilgrim: The life and times of Harold L. Ickes, 1874–1952*. New York: Henry Holt, 1990, 800–804.

Zolberg, A. (2006). *A nation by design: Immigration policy in the fashioning of America*. New York: Russell Sage Foundation, 10.

CHAPTER 12

Abramovitz, M. (1988). *Regulating the lives of women: Social welfare policy from colonial times to the present*. Boston, MA: South End Press.

Arendt, H. (1986). Communicative power. In S. Lukes (Ed.), *Power*. New York: New York University Press.

Bachrach, P., & Baratz, M. S. (1970). *Power and poverty: Theory and practice*. New York: Oxford University Press.

Chatelet, C. (1979). Recit. In M. Morris & P. Patton (Eds.), *Michel Foucault: Power, truth, strategy*. Sydney, Australia: Feral Publications.

Dahl, R. (1986). Power as the control of behavior. In S. Lukes (Ed.), *Power*. New York: New York University Press.

Derthick, M. (1990). *Agency under stress: The Social Security Administration in American government*. Washington, DC: Brookings Institution.

Dye, T. R. (2017). *Understanding public policy* (15th ed.). Upper Saddle River, NJ: Pearson.

Evan, C. (1993, December 9). Personal interview.

Ferguson, K. (1984). *The feminist case against bureaucracy*. Philadelphia, PA: Temple University Press, 1984, p. 103.

Flynn, J. P. (1992). *Social agency policy: Analysis and presentation for community practice* (2nd ed.). Chicago, IL: Nelson-Hall.

Foucault, M. (1986). Disciplinary power and subjection. In S. Lukes (Ed.), *Power*. New York: New York University Press.

Gaventa, J. (1980). *Power and powerlessness: Quiescence and rebellion in an Appalachian valley*. Urbana, IL: University of Illinois Press.

Goodwyn, L. (1976). *Democratic promise: The populist movement in America*. New York: Oxford University Press.

Gordon, L. (1994). *Pitied but not entitled: Single mothers and the history of welfare*. New York: Free Press.

Gutierrez, L. (1990). Working with women of color: An empowerment perspective. *Social Work, 35*, 149–153.

Heffernan, W. J. (1979). *Introduction to social welfare policy: Power, scarcity and common human needs*. Itasca, IL: F. E. Peacock.

Heffernan, W. J. (1992). *Social welfare policy: A research and action strategy*. New York: Longman.

Huttman, B. (1981). *Introduction to social policy*. New York: McGraw-Hill.

Jansson, B. S. (1999). *Becoming an effective policy advocate: From policy practice to social justice* (3rd ed.). Pacific Groves, CA: Brooks/Cole.

Kuzenski, S. T. (1993, July 30). Social work student guides six bills through legislative session. *LSU Today* (Louisiana State University News Service), pp. 1, 7.

Lindblom, C. E. (1980). *The policy-making process* (2nd ed.). Englewood Cliffs, NJ: Prentice-Hall.

Lukes, S. (1986). Introduction. In S. Lukes (Ed.), *Power*. New York: New York University Press.

Martin, K. (1993, July 11). La. can thank woman for strides against child sexual abuse. *Baton Rouge Sunday Advocate*, p. 3.

Martin, P. Y., & Chernesky, R. H. (1989). Women's prospects for leadership in social welfare: A political economy perspective. *Administration in Social Work, 13*, 118–119.

Mills, C. W. (1956 [1970]). *The power elite*. Oxford University Press.

Morris, M., & Patton, P. (Eds). (1979). *Power, truth, and strategy: Michel Foucault*. Sydney: Feral Publications.

Nelson, B. (1990). The origins of the two-channel welfare state: Workman's compensation and mothers' aid. In L. Gordon (Ed.), *Women, the state, and welfare*. Madison, WI: University of Wisconsin Press.

Parsons, T. (1986). Power and the social system. In S. Lukes (Ed.), *Power*. New York: New York University Press.

Peters, B. G. (1986). *American public policy: Promise and performance* (2nd ed.). Chatham, NJ: Chatham House.

Piven, F. F., & Cloward, R. A. (1979). *Poor people's movements: Why they succeed, how they fail.* New York: Vintage.

Piven, F. F., & Cloward, R. A. (1971). *Regulating the poor: The functions of public welfare.* New York: Vintage.

Power and strategies. (1976). Interview with Foucault by the Revoltes Logiques Collective. In Morris and Patton (Eds.), *Michel Foucault*, p. 52.

Pressman, J. L., & Wildavsky, A. (1984). Implementation. Berkeley, CA: University of California Press.

Pruger, R. (1973, July). The good bureaucrat. *Social Work, 18,* 26–40.

Rodgers, D. T. (1998). *Atlantic crossings: Social politics in a progressive age.* Cambridge, MA: Belknap Press of Harvard University Press.

Russell, B. (1986). The forms of power. In S. Lukes (Ed.), *Power.* New York: New York University Press.

Salisbury, R. H. (1984, March). Interest representation: The dominance of institutions. *American Political Science Review, 78,* 64–76.

Schattschneider, E. E. (1960). *The semisovereign people.* New York: Holt, Rinehart, and Winston.

Segal, S. P., Silverman, C., & Temkin, T. (1993). Empowerment and self-help agency practice for people with mental disabilities. *Social Work, 38,* 707–712.

Skocpol, T. (1988). Introduction. In M. Weir, A. S. Orloff, & T. Skocpol (Eds.), *The politics of social policy in the United States.* Princeton, NJ: Princeton University Press.

Taylor, C. (1986). Foucault on freedom and truth. In D. C. Hoy (Ed.), *Foucault: A critical reader.* Oxford, England: Basil Blackwell.

True, J. L., Jones, B. D., & Baumgartner, F. R. (2007). Punctuated-equilibrium theory—explaining stability and change in public policymaking. In P. A. Sabatier (Ed.), *Theories of the policy process.* Boulder, CO: Westview Press, 155.

Truth and power. (1979). Interview with Michel Foucault by Alessandro Fontano and Pasquale Pasquino. In Morris & Patton, *Michel Foucault*, 38–39, 41–47.

CHAPTER 13

Douglas, A. (1962). *Industrial peacemaking.* New York: Columbia University Press, 18–21, 36, 73.

Fisher, R., Ury, W., & Patton, B. (1991). *Getting to yes: Negotiating agreement without giving in* (2nd ed.). New York: Penguin Books.

Haynes, K., & Mickelson, J. S. (2010). *Affecting change: Social workers in the political arena* (7th ed.). Boston, MA: Allyn and Bacon.

Hermone, R. H. (1974). How to negotiate and come out the winner. *Management Review,* 1.

Jansson, B. (2014). *Becoming an effective policy advocate* (7th ed.). Belmont, CA: Brooks/Cole.

Karrass, C. L. (1992). *The negotiating game: How to get what you want.* New York: Harper Business.

Kochan, T. A., & Lipsky, D. B. (Eds.). (2003). *Negotiations and change: From workplace to society.* Ithaca, NY: Cornell University Press.

Lens, V. (2004, July). Principled negotiation: A new tool for case advocacy. *Social Work,* 24.

Morse, B. (1979). *How to negotiate the labor agreement: An outline summary of tested bargaining practice expanded from earlier editions.* Southfield, MI: Trends Publishing Co.

Myers, R., & Granstaff, C. (2008). Political social work. In T. Mizrahi & L. E. Davis (Eds.), *Encyclopedia of social work* (20th ed.). Washington, DC: NASW Press and Oxford University Press.

NASW. (2012). Social workers in elected office 2012. Retrieved from www.socialworkers.org/pace/state.asp

NASW, Arizona Chapter. (2010). Government relations updates Retrieved from www.socialworkers.org/advocacy; NASW Arizona Chapter. Social workers, immigration policies and state benefits. Washington, DC: NASW, 2010. Retrieved from www.naswaz.com

Nierenberg, G. (1986). *The complete negotiator.* New York: Nierenberg and Zeif Publishers.

Popple, P. (1984, Summer). Negotiation: A critical skill for social work administrators. *Administration in Social Work, 8,* 1–11.

Reynolds, J. B. (1896). The settlement and municipal reform. In A. O. Wright (Ed.), *Proceedings of the national conference of charities and correction.* Boston, MA: George H. Ellis.

Richan, W. C. (2006). *Lobbying for social change* (3rd ed.). New York: Haworth Press.

Rubin, A. (1997). The family evaluation from hell: Implications for program evaluation fidelity. *Children and Youth Services Review, 19*(1 & 2), 85.

Tedeschi, J. T., & Rosenfeld, P. (1980). Communication in bargaining and negotiation. In M. Roloff & G. Miller (Eds.), *Persuasion: New directions in theory and research.* Beverly Hills, CA: Sage.

Walton, R. E., & McKersie, R. B. (1965). *A behavioral theory of labor negotiations: An analysis of a social interaction system.* New York: McGraw-Hill.

Wyers, N. L. (1991, Fall). Policy-practice in social work: Models and issues. *Journal of Social Work Education, 27,* 242.

Index

Q

R

S

T